THE LIFE OF LOUIS XVI

John Hardman is one of the world's leading experts on the French Revolution and the author of several distinguished books on the subject, including *Marie-Antoinette: The Making of a French Queen* and *Barnave: The Revolutionary Who Lost His Head for Marie-Antoinette*.

Further praise for *The Life of Louis XVI*:

'The definitive contribution to our understanding of Louis XVI as a man and a monarch.'
P.M. Jones, *English Historical Review*

'Monumental ... Scholars probing the mysteries of the late Old Regime and French Revolution will be working in its shadow for many years to come.'
Thomas E. Kaiser, *Journal of Modern History*

'A highly readable, well-paced biography ... Hardman shows sensitivity and sympathy for a monarch who was not blind to what was happening around him but who felt increasingly trapped by forces he could not control.'
Alan Forrest, author of *Napoleon: Life, Legacy, and Image*

'Simply the most authoritative biography of Louis XVI ever written ... Tells all the good stories with considerable verve, and offers insightful analyses of the politics of this tragic life.'
Peter Campbell, former Professor of French History, University of Versailles Saint-Quentin

The Life of
LOUIS XVI

JOHN HARDMAN

YALE UNIVERSITY PRESS
NEW HAVEN AND LONDON

To Alan Peachment

For information about this and other Yale University Press publications, please contact:
U.S. Office: sales.press@yale.edu   yalebooks.com
Europe Office: sales@yaleup.co.uk   yalebooks.co.uk

Typeset in Minion Pro by IDSUK (DataConnection) Ltd
Printed in Great Britain by Clays Ltd, Elcograf S.p.A

Library of Congress Control Number: 2023935505

ISBN 978-0-300-22042-1 (hbk)
ISBN 978-0-300-27364-9 (pbk)

A catalogue record for this book is available from the British Library.

10 9 8 7 6 5 4 3 2 1

CONTENTS

ILLUSTRATIONS AND MAPS

Plates

Maps

France and its historic provinces.

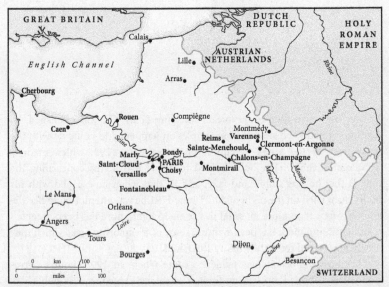

Sites in France visited by Louis XVI, shown in bold. Bondy, Sainte-Menehould, Châlons and Clermont are points on the king's ill-fated journey to Varennes.

PREFACE

IT IS NOW MORE than twenty years since my *Louis XVI* was published. Its gestation had been slow but its completion happened to coincide with the bicentenary of the king's execution on 21 January 1793, which made a re-evaluation timely. The book helped to dispel two myths concerning the king: i) that he was stupid and lazy; and ii) that when he escaped with his family from Paris on the night of 20/21 June 1791 he was attempting to flee the country. Since then more material has come to light, more has been accepted as authentic and more has been written, some of it exploring areas which may have been covered too lightly in my 1993 book.

The most important new evidence came when, in 1998, Louis's correspondence with his long-serving foreign secretary Vergennes was published, quadrupling the number of authentic and available letters Louis wrote before the Revolution.[1] These have contributed to a more complete understanding of contemporary foreign policy, Louis's primary field of expertise, and one which was central to his métier as king. In particular we now have a better understanding of France's role in the American War of Independence. Vergennes was also, for some years, Louis's chief minister, and the letters also shed light on important matters of home policy, notably finance and the disastrous Diamond Necklace Affair.

The publication of this correspondence, combined with the work of such scholars as Peter Campbell and Munro Price, has helped to establish the authenticity of most of the material published in two collections that I treated with considerable caution in 1993: those of Soulavie and Feuillet de Conches.[2] Soulavie was given privileged access to Louis's papers immediately after the fall of the monarchy in August 1792 and hastily transcribed what he could in the limited time available, publishing the material in six volumes once the revolutionary dust had settled on Bonaparte. An English edition of Soulavie came out a year later, in 1802, and where the translation is good I have used this version. Many of the king's letters Soulavie transcribes conform to those published in the Louis XVI–Vergennes correspondence. The same can be said of the material published in the 1860s by Feuillet de Conches, *conservateur* of the National Archives, who has often been treated as a gamekeeper-turned-poacher.

As regards secondary works published in the intervening period, the greatest input into the present volume has been from the work of Price, Caiani, Shapiro and Petitfils, and my own study of the 1787 Assembly of Notables, the turning point of Louis's reign – all of which are works of archivally based empirical history.[3] Price's work sheds light on the necessarily secret diplomacy centring on the flight to Varennes. Caiani opens up a hitherto neglected area of the reign: Louis's court during the Revolution, the one place in which he had some freedom of action. This helps to resolve the problem of discovering what the king actually thought when he was under virtual house arrest in the Tuileries and could not freely express himself. The only area left to explore is, precisely, Louis's ostensibly overt policy – his relations with those ministers who operated under the constitution. Most were not privy to his innermost thoughts and so his dealings with them have been neglected and remain so in the present book, perhaps justly, though they are a hill, if not a mountain, worth some future researcher's while climbing. Shapiro's book takes further a theme I explored in the 1993 book: the shock, or 'trauma' as he puts it, caused by Louis's *volte-face* from supporting the third estate in its claims against the nobility and clergy in 1787–88 to apparently deserting them in 1789. Petitfils's excellent work of synthesis provides not new information but personal details of Louis's life which were neglected in the 1993 book and help the new one to present a more rounded picture of the king.

I have to thank my brother-in-law, Professor Harry Procter, for his pains-taking help in preparing a very long text for submission to the publisher and also for helping me cope with the joys of electronic copy-editing. My thanks also go to my godson, Tom Dunn, for his photography. Thanks are also due to the Victoria and Albert Museum for allowing free use of images from their collection. Their remit of objects over paintings coinciding with my own predelictions is reflected in my choice of illustrations.

CHAPTER ONE

A DARK AND DIFFICULT CHILDHOOD

FROM CHILDHOOD ON, HISTORY was the favourite reading of Louis-Auguste, known successively as duc de Berry, dauphin and king of France as Louis XVI. The work he returned to most was David Hume's *History of England*: on the occasion of Hume's visit to France in 1763, the nine-year-old Berry made him a pretty speech and had his younger brothers, the comte de Provence and the comte d'Artois, do the same. Artois, who was only six, forgot his lines. Berry had inherited his penchant for history from his mother, Maria-Josepha, daughter of Augustus III, elector of Saxony and king of Poland, but Hume's *History* was also a favourite with his father, Louis-Ferdinand, the dauphin, born in 1729, the only son of the king, Louis XV. The dauphin particularly liked the section in Hume's work relating to the death of Charles I, which pampered his extreme morbidity. The life of the martyr-king was, in turn, to feed his son's *amor fati*.

The dauphin, Louis-Ferdinand, had been a vivacious, indeed a boisterous boy, but he soon had the stuffing knocked out of him by an invasively religious or *dévot* education. Exactly the same fate was to befall his eldest surviving son, the future Louis XVI, who had a temper as a little boy. *Dévot* means more than just 'devout', it implies bigotry. Louis-Ferdinand became a monumental bigot; his son, though just as repressed, was merely devout. Indeed he was to chide his justice minister for dragging his feet on emancipating the Protestants and Jews.[1]

Louis XV was no *dévot*, though he lived in perpetual fear of eternal damnation because of his string of extra-marital liaisons. His queen, Maria Leszczyńska, however, was a *dévot*, partly as consolation for these same liaisons. The supervision of the dauphin's education fell to her and she chose as his governor and tutors men of the *dévot* persuasion. He was fed on a strict metaphorical diet of religious exercises – his literal diet was broader and, since he eschewed all physical exertion, his waistline became broad as well. Indeed he gluttonized to such an extent that he was described as a 'monster of grease'. Despite his dread of exercise, his overdeveloped sense of duty prompted him to participate in the dynastic sport of hunting; but when he accidentally killed one of his grooms, he welcomed the excuse to give up even this pursuit.

Though the spirit of Louis-Ferdinand's education was narrowly religious, its content was wide. Apart from works by the Bourbon in-house bishops, Bossuet and Fénélon, and the customary Latin authors, he not only read Montesquieu's *De l'esprit des lois*, published in 1748, but met the great man several times in his private apartments. He also taught himself English and read Locke, and Bolingbroke's *The Idea of a Patriot King* as well as David Hume. His mind, however, was not contaminated by these Enlightenment thinkers. Naturally, he rejected Hume's materialism; but he also roundly rejected Montesquieu's view that the *parlements*,* the appeal courts which registered royal legislation, were 'intermediary powers' that protected the people from the king as well as the king from the people. He read the works of the Enlightenment without being enlightened by them. He read Rousseau's *Émile* for guidance on the education of his children but thought the book was literally 'infernal', rejecting as it did 'any kind of revelation, the divinity of Jesus Christ, the evidence of miracles' and putting in their place 'a vague communication between the soul and the All-Powerful'.[2] He saw *philosophes* such as Voltaire and Diderot as 'corrupt libertines . . . haughty spirits vain enough to think they could work out everything from scratch'.[3] So Maria Leszczyńska was able to rejoice that, 'although I have only one son, Heaven has been pleased to make him wise, virtuous and beneficent'. Whether she would have welcomed his extravagant piety, such as crossing himself whenever he passed a place of public entertainment, is another matter.

Despite his aversion to any form of exercise, the dauphin saw himself as a general – not an armchair general but an active participant on the battlefield. He also, despite his embonpoint, thought he cut a dashing figure in his red uniform. But the king could not afford to lose his only son to war. He did, however, relent on one occasion, allowing the dauphin to be present at the battle of Fontenoy in 1745, which ended in a great French victory, though it had hung in the balance for some time (a street in Liverpool is actually called Fontenoy Street, as if the English had 'won'). Riding over the field and contemplating the dead and wounded, the king addressed to his son words which may be interpreted as an attempt to put him off the pursuit of arms but were probably just an expression of his humanity: 'See my son the pain a sensitive man feels in winning victories! The blood of our enemies is still the blood of men. True glory, my son,

---

* In the following, '*parlement*' will refer to the parlement of Paris, and '*parlements*' to Paris and the thirteen provincial institutions collectively.

lies in sparing it!' One is reminded of Wellington's lament that 'nothing except a battle lost can be half so melancholy as a battle won'.

The king may also have felt an incipient rivalry with his son. This was in the nature of things – in Hanoverian England rivalry between the king and the prince of Wales was almost institutionalized and given a name: the 'reversionary interest' of the prince. The year before Fontenoy an incident occurred which seemed to bear this out and was the start of bad relations between king and dauphin. The king fell ill at Metz in August 1744 and was thought likely to die. In that event the dauphin would not only have been king but, technically of age, would not even have needed a regent. Instead of waiting for the apple to drop, the *dévot* party, which guided the dauphin, headed by his ambitious governor, the duc de Châtillon, sought to exploit the king's fear of damnation by making him send away his current mistress, the duchesse de Châteauroux, and express a public apology to God and the nation, before taking communion. Getting rid of the duchesse, they also hoped, would return the king to the bosom of his long-suffering wife and thus cement the ascendancy of the *parti dévot* whatever the issue of the king's illness. The king quickly recovered and never forgave his son's party for his public humiliation.

The battlefield, and his son's presence on it, reminded the king how fragile the continuance of the dynasty was: He and his son were the only legitimate male descendants of Louis XIV, except for the Spanish Bourbons, who were barred from the succession by international treaty. The dauphin had married a Spanish Bourbon, Marie-Raphaelle, but she died after giving birth to a daughter in 1746. Women were barred from the throne by the Salic Law – one of the few constitutional or fundamental laws on which everyone was agreed – and in any case she died in infancy. So Louis XV quickly married his son to Maria-Josepha, daughter of the elector of Saxony, who was also king of Poland. She gallicized her name to Marie-Josèphe. One result of this union was that the Bourbons ceased to be inbred. Hitherto, brides had been selected from a small number of Catholic ruling houses, but Maria Leszczyńska was not of royal blood and the House of Saxony, the Wettins, had only recently converted to Catholicism in order to qualify for the Polish throne.

Marie-Josèphe was a petite blonde with intense blue eyes, which she transmitted to Louis XVI. She was naturally vivacious but curbed her high spirits to conform to her husband's gloomy disposition, which had been intensified by the death of his first wife, whom he adored despite her long Bourbon nose and unfashionable red hair. Marie-Josèphe had the mortification of reading a letter, handed to her by mistake, in which the dauphin said his new wife would never replace the old in his affections. The new dauphine cultivated piety and austerity to win over her husband, even playing the macabre game of entering her predecessor's chamber with funerary candles chanting, 'We are dead! We are dead!' In the end she won Louis-Ferdinand round, but at the cost of her true nature and personal happiness. She signed her letters to a favourite brother, 'Marie-Josèphe la triste'.

Despite the friction between father and son, when in 1750 the dauphin turned twenty, the customary age for the heir to the throne to start attending the council, Louis XV did not block the move. That would have been to cut off his nose to spite his face, for attending council was the principal way for the dauphin to learn the craft of kingship, the *métier des rois*.

Though he hated the *Encyclopédie*, the dauphin had an encyclopaedic knowledge. So, to a lesser extent, would his son Louis XVI, who actually bought the *Encyclopédie* out of his pocket money. The *Encyclopédie*, published between 1751 and 1772 and edited by Denis Diderot, bore the subtitle, *Systematic Dictionary of the Arts, Sciences and Crafts*. Its relationship to a modern encyclopaedia is similar to the relationship Dr Johnson's dictionary has to a modern one; that is to say, each contains short articles on the headings of available knowledge, but each has an agenda, or slant behind it. But whereas Johnson's slant is obviously individual, that of the *Encyclopédie* is collective. Moreover, the titles of some of the entries were themselves loaded, such as *lettres de cachet* or 'feudal rights'. Nearly all the contributors subscribed to the intellectual currents endorsed by the *philosophes*, who made up the majority of contributors; published in instalments, it was in effect their in-house magazine. The *philosophes* were not philosophers in the narrow, modern, or even classical sense but rather men who sought above all to propagate in France many of the intellectual currents of seventeenth-century England – Newtonian physics, the political philosophy of John Locke *et al.* – and apply them to French social and political questions.

The dauphin's erudition was, however, no substitute for a political apprenticeship, something to which we will return when considering the education of Louis XVI, who inherited the throne a year before *he* was due to enter the council. The minister of war, the comte d'Argenson, recorded his impressions of the youth he saw across the magnificent council table, which was veneered in exotic woods and mounted with fire-gilded ormolu. The dauphin had 'an extremely large paunch, [was] inimical to any form of exercise or even movement, [and] was totally without passions, or even preferences'. The dying fire of youth, d'Argenson concluded, was being 'extinguished by corpulence and religious devotion'.[4]

The dauphin entered the *Conseil des Dépêches*, which dealt with home policy, at a critical time in the relations between the crown and the *parlement*, the court of appeal which gave what Louis XVI would call 'simulated consent' to royal legislation. Real consent would have come from the only elected national representative institution, the Estates-General, but these did not meet between 1614 and 1789, a period which may be defined as the classical period of the ancien régime, itself a relatively new political structure that was superimposed on France's medieval feudal society. France, however, was a sophisticated political community – not, like Prussia for example, a military despotism – so unpopular measures such as taxation had to be sold to the public; and here the *parlement* came in.

There were actually thirteen *parlements* covering the vast area of France, but the most important – 'the *parlement*' – was that of Paris, whose jurisdiction in fact covered half the country. The kings had given the *parlements* the additional role of registering royal legislation, though there was a difference of opinion as to what that involved. Crown lawyers argued that registration was necessary only to show that the king was speaking *ex cathedra*, a formal promulgation rather than just an off-with-his-head whim. *Parlementaires* argued that registration involved 'verifying' whether the proposed legislation conformed to natural justice and the fundamental laws, or unwritten constitution, of the kingdom. If they saw a conflict they could 'remonstrate', but since the *parlementaires* were technically the king's delegates, he could enforce registration by appearing in person or sending a personal representative in what was called a *lit de justice*. But this created a bad impression – Voltaire quipped that a *lit de justice* was a bed where justice slept – and undermined the unstated propaganda aim of the whole exercise. It was in the interests of both crown and *parlement* to make a go of simulated consent since the ancien régime's political system gave them both a heightened existence. Until the 1750s both halves of the system appreciated this but from that date relations steadily deteriorated, until, in 1788, the *parlementaire* Samsons pulled the temple of the ancien régime crashing down about both them and the king.

Under Louis XV there were two disputes: the first, religious, ended in total victory for the *parlement*; the second, over increased taxation, continued until it brought the temple down and led to the Estates-General whose very summoning by definition ended the ancien régime. It was the religious dispute which most exercised the dauphin, and though it seems remote to us, and in any case was settled by the 1760s, we must touch on it because it enabled the *parlementaires* to develop an ideology of resistance to the king in a seemingly loyal way, to be *plus royaliste que le roi*.

The Jansenists were a Catholic sect that believed in predestination and had many adherents in the *parlement*. In 1713 Louis XIV, in pursuance of his policy of religious uniformity – the confessional state – had induced the pope to condemn Jansenism as heretical in the Bull *Unigenitus*, with the Jesuits spearheading the assault on the Jansenists in France. However, the *parlementaires* condemned ultramontane papal interference in the Gallican Church, and in 1764 the *parlement* was able to force a reluctant Louis XV to dissolve the Society of Jesus in France.

The surrender was a blow to the king's pride but did not interfere with his running of the country. Losing control of the level of taxation obviously would. The nobility had been exempt from direct taxation because they provided military service in lieu, but in 1696 Louis XIV had summoned the feudal levy for the last time – it was so antiquated that he sent it straight back home. The logical consequence was that the nobility should pay taxation to support national defence. At first this was expected only in times of war, but in 1749 the *vingtième*, or twentieth tax, was introduced, provocatively at the conclusion of a war, to underline that it was a permanent tax. The central aim of government for the next forty years – that is as long as the regime lasted – was to make every social grouping and every French province pay its fair share of this tax.

The *parlementaires* did not like paying the tax. They were not soldiers: theirs was a nobility of the 'robe' (the lawyers' gown) rather than of the sword, but they enjoyed the privileges of nobility. However, they would have accepted the tax if the king had stuck to his original intention of also taxing the clergy – the *parlementaires*' bêtes noires. But Louis XV, in arguably the biggest single blunder of his reign, capitulated to clerical pressure and to specious arguments such as the 'donation of Constantine', whereby the first Christian emperor had given land to the church unencumbered and in perpetuity. The problem did not go away: clerical resistance to taxation was to defeat Louis XVI's major reforming initiative too.

Taxation forms the sinews of war – to get it Louis XV had to sacrifice the Jesuits. The increasing cost of warfare around the middle of the century meant financial matters became controversial. Montesquieu, a president in the *parlement* of Bordeaux, wrote in the section of *De l'esprit des lois* dealing with taxation: 'A new distemper has spread itself over Europe, infecting our princes and inducing them to maintain an exorbitant number of troops.' There was competition for empire between France and England – a second Hundred Years War had begun in 1689 – and land-grabbing by the new continental powers, Russia and Prussia. The pressure was worse for France because, with a coastline longer than her land frontiers, she needed a navy as well as an army.

The duc de Choiseul, war and/or foreign secretary between 1758 and 1770, thought that entente with (or in the dauphin's view capitulation to) the *parlement* was essential in order to raise the money needed to restore the navy and seek revanche against England for the humiliations suffered at the Peace of Paris in 1763, when France lost Canada and (much more importantly) her influence in India. The humiliations of the Seven Years War and the assertiveness of the *parlement* were obverse and reverse of the same coin. Louis XV lost prestige because the conduct of foreign policy was the essential component of kingship: if he couldn't get that right what was his point? Instead of skulking in his harem, the Deer Park (*parc aux cerfs*), he should have died at the head of his troops at Rossbach in 1757, the most crushing French defeat since Agincourt. Instead he daren't even show his face in Paris. Needless to say the dauphin, despite his now enormous bulk, thought his presence at the front would have saved the day.

His prestige shot to pieces like his army, the king was no match for the resurgent and rancorous *parlementaires*, whom he dubbed 'the republicans'. Pressing their advantage more than was perhaps wise, they forced the king not only to dissolve the Society of Jesus but to expel the individual Jesuits from the country. This was the final straw for the dauphin, for the Jesuits were at the heart of the *parti dévot* and provided, he believed, ideological underpinning for the monarchy. He told his friend, the bishop of Nancy, that he had seriously considered ceasing to attend the council lest he seem 'to condone the iniquity'. His quarrel with Choiseul was fierce and open. Choiseul even had the effrontery to tell the dauphin to his face that 'though he would have the misfortune to be his subject he would never have that of serving him' – a missile so explosive it shot around the court. Yet so brazen was Choiseul's neck that he seriously expected to 'serve' the dauphin's son, Louis XVI, as a minister!

The dauphin naturally blamed his father for supporting Choiseul, with however bad a grace and with whatever misgivings. He is reported to have told the king that 'one could dispense with *parlements* but not bishops' and to have received the stinging rejoinder, 'My son, you should wish me a long life for you don't yet know how to behave'. The dauphin sent the king a strong memorandum on the subject of the *parlements*, accusing them of claiming that the king, 'insensible to the people's misery, was needlessly squandering their blood and treasure'; the dauphin was too delicate to allude to the popular belief that the king was not just squandering his subjects' blood but drinking that of their children to fortify his passions. The *parlement* was also putting it about that the king was in the process of 'establishing an extreme despotism limited only by his whims' and that the *parlementaires*, 'braving exile and prison', were all that stood between France and calamity. They also claimed to be the only 'true citizens' and 'patriots' – here the dauphin himself uses the new terminology which would flower in the Revolution and which the *parlements* played a major role in spreading.[5]

Another source of friction between dauphin and king was the new *maîtresse en titre*, Madame de Pompadour, whose reign lasted from 1745 until her death from tuberculosis in 1764. Pompadour was much more of a threat to the dauphin than the earlier mistresses, because, although of bourgeois extraction with a maiden name (Poisson) meaning fish, she was intelligent and cultivated, and in some ways acted as a prime minister. Moreover, her policies were opposed to those of the *dévots*. *Philosophes* were among her society and she promoted the 1756 'diplomatic revolution' whereby the hereditary enemies, France and Austria, became allies. It was a logical move, given that both countries each now had a new enemy more dangerous than the old: France being threatened overseas by England; and Austria by Prussia, to whom she had been forced to cede Silesia. Austria, however, gained more out of the alliance than France, and France fared disastrously in the war, as the dauphin never tired of reminding his father. The bond between Louis XV and Madame de Pompadour was more than physical and indeed it was only when it became purely platonic around 1750 that she achieved her maximum power. There was no question of dislodging the favourite, and the dauphin therefore had to at least be polite to her. But somewhere deep inside him a glass tube clanked.

The dauphin also took a long time to accept his second wife, who went through a miserable few years. The kindly king did his best to cheer her up, making coffee for her with his own fair hands (an accomplishment of which he was immensely proud) and serving it from a little gold three-legged coffee pot. He also called her by her childhood pet name of Pépa. Familiar names were more common among the German ruling families than in the French one, and we don't really know what members of the Bourbon dynasty called each other in private, though the evidence suggests they were usually formal. Louis XVI's aunt Adélaïde called him 'Berry', and his cousin the duc d'Orléans called his children 'Chartres', 'Beaujolais' and 'Montpensier', after their ducal titles, continuing even when he was put under revolutionary pressure to rename himself Philippe Égalité. Louis XVI seems to have called Marie-Antoinette 'Madame' – at least when he was angry with her. An exception was Louis XV, who had pet names for his children.

Given the dauphin's resentment at his second wife's very existence it is perhaps not surprising that there were no children from the union for several years. This was worrying as lack of issue would have opened the door either to the ambitious Orléans branch, the descendants of Louis XIV's younger brother, or to a counter-claim from the Spanish Bourbons. The Orléans had long coveted the throne – an ambition which haunted Louis XVI and which they finally achieved in 1830. The regent Orléans had not poisoned Louis XV's immediate family in 1711–12, as was suspected, but by engaging him to a six-year-old Spanish princess he had given the sickly boy every opportunity to die without issue. Hence, when the regent died in 1723 the engagement was cancelled and the adolescent king married to Maria Leszczyńska. If the dauphin and Marie-Josèphe still produced no heir and the Spanish Bourbons had asserted their claim (as descendants of Louis XIV), the consequence would have been even more disastrous: civil war and/or intervention from the great powers to prevent the union of France and Spain.

Fortunately the couple became closer after the death of the only child of his first marriage and, on 26 August 1750, she gave birth, albeit to a daughter, who could not inherit the throne. In 1751 she bore a son, the duc de Bourgogne, in 1753 another, the duc d'Aquitaine, who died the following year, and, on 23 August 1754, the duc de Berry, the subject of this biography. Berry was followed by the comte de Provence and the comte d'Artois, by another sister, Clothilde, and finally, in 1764, by his sister Élisabeth, the constant companion of Louis XVI's last years. Of the boys, the dauphin made the curiously prophetic remark, 'some day they will rule'. And so they did: Berry became Louis XVI; and, after the Revolution, Provence became Louis XVIII, and Artois, Charles X. The boys were mostly named after members of their mother's Saxon family; Berry was named Louis-Auguste after her father, the elector of Saxony. But Louis-Auguste was also the name of Louis IX (1214–70) who had been canonized as St Louis; and it was through descent from him that the Bourbons, in the person of Henri IV, claimed the throne on the assassination of his very distant cousin Henri III in 1589, no direct ancestor having reigned in the intervening centuries. Though the association with the saint's name was fortuitous, the choice of his Christian names, as with Tristram Shandy, whose Christian name was an error, was to condition the character of their recipient: the king-saint was held up to his namesake as a model from the cradle to the scaffold when, according to tradition, his confessor speeded him from this world with: 'Fils de Saint Louis, ascendez au ciel.'

Elder brother

The first-born son, the duc de Bourgogne, was the favourite of his parents; not just because he was the heir for which they had hoped for four years, but because of his resemblance to the dauphin. Not only did he have the dauphin's jet-black hair and piercing dark eyes, he also shared – and cultivated – other of his father's characteristics: hard work superimposed on a foundation of laziness and an exaggerated piety which seems, at least to the modern eye, impious. He lived, therefore, in an atmosphere of adulation. In 1755 *Le Mercure de France* informed its readers that the four-year-old displayed 'a decided taste for arms' and in 1758 that he showed 'firmness for one of such tender years'.

After the death of the duc d'Aquitaine in infancy, the duc de Berry was the next brother and the two played together. Bourgogne bullied Berry a little and dreamed up sins for him to confess, though, to be fair, he dreamed up more for himself. He also cheated him at cards, which Berry particularly resented as he had no liking for them in any case. When he was sixteen his confessor attempted to overcome this dislike, suggesting playing cards would be social cement for the royal family, but Berry never played more than the occasional game of whist. (In this at least he resembled his father, the dauphin.)

In eighteenth-century France royal children saw very little of their parents and that mostly on ceremonial occasions. The same applied to children of court families; one thinks of poor Talleyrand, whose hurt foot developed into a permanent limp because no one noticed it, thus disqualifying him from military service and forcing him into a career in the church for which he had no calling. With parents so distant, the supervision of the royal children fell to the *gouvernantes des enfants de France*. The current *gouvernante* was the comtesse de Marsan, of the princely House of Rohan. Marsan encouraged her charges to call her 'the dear little friend', but whether Louis-Auguste thought that way about her is disputed. With an eye to the main chance, Marsan, who had to look to the interests of a family declining from great heights through debt, lavished her attention on Bourgogne as the heir and her affection on Provence as the most immediately engaging if (as it would turn out) the most false. Nevertheless Berry was quite a pretty child, with blond hair, deep blue eyes, dimples and a rose mouth. He was also sickly, suffering a series of illnesses. He lost weight when teething in 1756 and he and his brothers were sent to Meudon for the air for four months; thirty years later he would try the same cure for his own eldest son, but with less success.

On 1 May 1758, just short of his seventh birthday, Bourgogne was 'passed over to men', which meant exchanging his governess for a governor, the atrabilious duc de La Vauguyon, who would supervise his education. La Vauguyon was the friend and former *menin*, or official playfellow, of the dauphin. Shortly afterwards Bourgogne had a bad fall from a rocking horse and hurt his leg. He promised the attendant who was meant to be looking after him that he would say nothing but, untreated, he developed a limp – like Talleyrand. A tumour formed and was operated on by infected instruments, which scraped the bone. Tuberculosis passed from the bone to the lungs and, on 21 March 1761, he died.

For the last months of Bourgogne's long agony Berry kept his brother company. On 8 September 1760 his own 'passage to the men' was advanced by a year (he was only six) and he joined Bourgogne, La Vauguyon and a string of preceptors. At this time Berry was given the diamond shoe-buckles his brother had outgrown and went straight from the strange, babyish, long fur-lined blue robes that princes wore to the dress of an adult. His educational diet was moral texts and the classics. Bourgogne disliked the latter, having a particular aversion to Latin, which was to become a favourite with his younger brother. Bourgogne liked the texts, however. One which La Vauguyon made them transcribe ran: 'Son [actually thirteenth great-grandson] of Saint-Louis be like your father: imitate his faith, his zeal for religion. Be saintly, just and good like him.'

Berry did not attend his brother on his deathbed because he was ill himself. Quite likely he had also contracted tuberculosis. Although people were well aware that smallpox was infectious and instituted strict quarantine regimes, strangely, there seems to have been no awareness that tuberculosis was passed on. We are left to imagine what effect Bourgogne's death had on his brother. The only hard fact we have is that he gave his own eldest son the same Christian names, Louis-Joseph-Xavier, though the last two had no other relevance – Pépa had called Bourgogne after her ancestor, the Emperor Joseph, and Xavier after her favourite and sorely missed brother. What should be noticed is that Berry was made to worship a boy who does not seem especially lovable, even through the rose-tinted lens of his hagiographers. What is also clear is that Berry's devastated parents would have preferred him to have died instead, or at the least did not think he could replace his brother. Replace him, however, he did, for he was now the ultimate heir to the throne of St Louis.

The education of a king

How do you educate a future monarch? The problem is no nearer solution today than it was in the 1760s, or in Richelieu's time or Machiavelli's. The perfect educator would have been a second Richelieu: skilled alike in home and foreign affairs, he would have been himself not a humble tutor but 'the great minister of whom France had need'.[6] The dauphin, who had been given carte blanche by the king over the education of his children, turned to his grandfather, Stanislas, the ex-king of Poland, but was a king who had lost his own throne the best man to advise a future one how to keep his? There was no immediate threat, but Louis XV for one thought his successor would have his work cut out in 'facing the republican multitude'.[7] Less dramatically, the king was wont to say, 'I see clearly how the machinery of state works, but I don't know what will happen to it after me and how Berry will cope with it'[8] – this is the probable origin of the apocryphal 'après moi le déluge'. In the absence of a Richelieu, Louis XV himself would have been the best man to instruct a future king in his métier, but to initiate a successor is to be reminded of your own mortality, something of which Louis was all too conscious; he was wont to say, when a companion died, 'he was exactly my age'.

With the king washing his hands of his grandchildren's education, the dauphin asked their governor, La Vauguyon to suggest preceptors and do a little teaching himself. It is said that La Vauguyon got the job by bribing a valet to find out what the dauphin was currently reading so that he could casually drop references to it. La Vauguyon's contribution consisted mostly of nauseous pieties. He wrote an 'abbreviated summary of the virtues' of the duc de Bourgogne, skipping over his faults and placing in his mouth words that surely even that hypocritical little boy could never have had the effrontery to utter on his deathbed: 'Here I am like a second paschal lamb ready to be immolated for The Lord.' Berry was meant to meditate on his brother's said virtues. In 1763 La Vauguyon drew up a general plan for Berry's education but it was so stuffed with pieties and flatteries that it proved too much even for the dauphin, who, to his credit, opted for a more practical education. In some ways it was quite up to date, with due attention to the sciences at which Berry excelled.

Thirty years ago this would have been a controversial statement. How could Louis XVI have 'excelled' at anything except hunting and ironwork? He was a dullard – how else could he have thrown away his throne when George III of England rose to an equal challenge. However, a reassessment of Louis XVI's general abilities was initiated when Madame Girault de Coursac performed an imaginative reconstruction of the boy's homework. Her conclusion was that, in contrast to the traditional view of Louis-Auguste as a dull and lazy boy, he was a precocious child and was particularly adept at 'science' subjects such as mathematics, physics and geography. Her claims are based on her attempt to recreate his lessons using the publications of his tutors. In 1768, when Louis-Auguste was fourteen, Le Blonde dedicated his *Éléments d'Algèbre* to his royal pupil, writing in the preface: '. . . the pleasure you found in the solution of the majority of the problems it contains and the ease with which you grasped the key to their solution are new proofs of your intelligence and the excellence of your judgement . . .' The *Éléments d'Algèbre* contains linear simultaneous equations, quadratic equations, the concept of real and imaginary numbers, and progressions and series. The Abbé Nollet, in the preface to *L'Art des expériences* of 1770, the basis of his university course of experimental physics, claims a similar degree of comprehension for the royal dedicatee. Unfortunately, Madame de

Coursac does not discount the degree of flattery necessarily involved in such dedications, though, to be credible, flattery must bear some relationship to truth – it would have been an impressive thing for the boy to have been set the problems, regardless of whether he had solved them. We are, though, able to control and modify Coursac's verdict using other evidence. The dauphin was not one to overrate his son's abilities. Indeed he felt it necessary to obtain reassurance from a Jesuit proto-psychologist that his son's apparent backwardness resulted from shyness and deliberate reserve. Watching the three boys, Berry, Provence and Artois, playing, the priest observed that, though Berry lacked the vivacity and gracious manners of his siblings, he was in no wise inferior 'as to the solidity of his judgement and his good heart'.[9] The dauphin's relief betrayed his lack of faith in his son, but he revised his opinion when he wrote to his friend, the bishop of Nancy, 'Berry is making great progress in Latin and astonishing progress in history which he learns through facts and chronologies which is the best way for him, given his admirable memory. Provence's progress is even greater given his natural talent and you would never believe how many Latin words he had crammed into his skull in a month!'[10] (The dauphin personally examined the boys in Latin and history every week.)

Some objective confirmation of Berry's mathematical abilities comes from his skill in cartography, which has always been generally acknowledged. His tutor in geography was Philippe Buache, the leading cartographer of the day, who specialized in oceanic exploration. Louis was an adept and enthusiastic pupil and would always have a map-in-progress on his table throughout his reign. As dauphin he made a splendid map of the environs of Versailles, which is now in the Bibliothèque Nationale.[11] To make this Louis would have had to understand the mathematics behind scale and projection. Likewise, some of the problems Le Blonde claimed Louis solved involved compound interest on loans. Louis understood this matter as king, as well as the effects of inflation[12] and market forces.[13]

Thus far Louis-Auguste's education was similar to that to be had by anyone whose parents were able to employ the best private tutors; but it was considered necessary to train a future king more specifically in his métier. Louis-Auguste's training in the theory of kingship is summarized in *Les Réflexions sur mes entretiens avec M. de La Vauguyon*, on which he started work when he was thirteen. Following a suggestion of the dauphin's, La Vauguyon asked Jacob-Nicolas Moreau, and the Jesuit Berthier to draw up some maxims concerning kingship. Moreau, who can be called the philosopher of the *dévots*, if that is not a contradiction in terms, would have the post of historiographer royal created for him in 1774 by his pupil, then the new king. La Vauguyon next discussed the maxims thoroughly with his royal pupil, who, between 1767 and 1769, condensed them into thirty-three 'reflections'. These have been in the public domain since their publication in 1851.[14] While far too much has been made of them, both as an assessment of Louis-Auguste's abilities or as pointers to the policies he would pursue as king, the lad did a competent job of mastering and summarising the texts, albeit without the sparkle or verbal felicity of his brother, Provence. It has rightly been said that Louis-Auguste's 'reflections' are 'banal', though the banality lies as much in the original as the commentary on these hopelessly outdated 'pastorals on paternal monarchy'.[15] One of the reflections, however – that entitled 'On my faults' – is significant: 'My greatest fault is a sluggishness of mind which renders mental efforts wearisome and painful. I want absolutely to conquer this defect and after I have done so, as I hope to . . . I shall cultivate the good things which are said to be in me'.[16]

This shows self-knowledge – much of the erudition Louis-Auguste was to achieve derived from a sense of duty rather than one of pleasure – but also self-deprecation, for there were subjects for which he showed natural aptitude and from which he derived considerable pleasure. These were practical ones: not the amateur blacksmithing for which he was and is pilloried and for which he showed no particular talent, rather the natural sciences, geography, history and languages.

In any case, the material on which the boy had to reflect was hardly calculated to stimulate a thirst for abstract reasoning. However, another work of Moreau's did have an immense influence on the future king. Indeed, *Les Devoirs du prince* has been called (with some exaggeration) 'a blueprint for the reign of Louis XVI'.[17]

Moreau's *Les Devoirs du prince* certainly has its fair share of rhapsodizing about paternal monarchy and has little purchase on the modern mind – and, most likely, neither did it capture that of Louis-Auguste. For example, the king's legislative role is compared with that of Moses, and the ten commandments are given almost *in extenso*. However, halfway through the book Moreau forgets that he is a half-baked *publiciste* and remembers that he has worked with the dauphin in the struggle to take the propaganda fight to the *parlementaires* (he would assist the chancellor Maupeou in implementing his reforms in 1771). In short, like the dauphin, Moreau thought that Louis XV, by letting his position go undefended, was selling the pass.[18] In 1766 Louis XV did, briefly, reassert his authority in what has become known as the *séance de flagellation*, letting the *parlement* feel the edge of his tongue for encroaching on his sovereign authority. The heart of that speech had been written by Charles-Alexandre de Calonne, a brilliant classical scholar at the time beginning his career in the royal administration as a *maître des requêtes*, presenting reports to the royal council. Moreau, who had lent Calonne archival material for his report, considered it to be 'the strongest one that has ever been written against the *parlements*'.[19] The closeness of Moreau's and Calonne's views and their cumulative impact on Louis XVI would be manifested in the programme Calonne as finance minister presented to the Assembly of Notables in 1787.

Moreau defined sovereignty in a way that was relevant to present conflicts. The idea of royal sovereignty went back to Bodin in the sixteenth century, if not before, and had been echoed in the old texts, but Moreau defined it in relation to disputes with the *parlement*. He emphasized that the essence of sovereignty was legislative self-sufficiency. Power was not shared, because French kings were 'clothed in an absolute power for which they are responsible only to God'.[20] In the Moreau-inspired *séance de flagellation*, Louis XV had declared, 'legislative power belongs to me unfettered and undivided'. Legislative power therefore remained the bedrock of Louis XVI's beliefs: in June 1791, in the episode known as the flight to Varennes, he fled Paris to raise his standard in defence of his legislative powers.

So far, so conventional – anyone in the *dévot* circle would have held similar beliefs. But Moreau was not a typical member of the parti *dévot* and he carried the implications of legislative supremacy to regions which would have made them quake: state law could override both customary laws and fiscal privilege, however time-honoured. This was the essence of Calonne's 1787 programme, which Louis XVI embraced wholeheartedly.

So Moreau provides the key to one of the enigmas concerning Louis XVI: why did this conservative, *dévot*-reared monarch embark on the royal revolution of 1787 which both trailed and led to the larger Revolution of 1789? In *Les Devoirs du prince* can be found, in embryo, much of the 1787 programme. In particular, Moreau eloquently expounds the central tenet that all classes of society should pay a strict proportion of their wealth regardless of social privilege. This was a question not only of natural justice, which the kings were traditionally meant to uphold, but also of simple economics: if the peasants paid so much tax that they had literally to eat their seed corn, there would be no crop to tax next year and the economy would stagnate. This idea made central the importance of agriculture, a centrality which was exaggerated by the eponymous *Économistes*, otherwise known as the Physiocrats.

Neither Moreau nor Calonne was a fully fledged Physiocrat, but they did believe in their central tenet that land is the basis of all wealth. Moreau thought that the best form of direct tax was one 'levied on landed properties which is itself a fixed percentage of their product'. He added that taxation of individuals rather than their property was nearly always unjust.[21] Some of the elements of physiocracy can actually be derived from the pastorals on paternal monarchy of Fénélon and Bossuet; St Louis, dispensing justice under an oak tree, would have wanted fair assessments had general taxation existed in his time. So would Moses. But Moreau was able to translate this into a modern programme and make the application of justice less abstract; thus Louis-Auguste was able to find in the *Devoirs* a relevance which in the old texts had eluded him. If there had not been this dynamic paradox within Louis XVI, the *dévot-philosophe*, the years of his reign would have been as placid as his external demeanour.

Just as paradoxical as his political thinking was Louis-Auguste's attitude towards England, which can be described most succinctly using the hackneyed phrase 'a love-hate relationship'. It was a relationship that had as an obvious consequence the war against England which resulted in American independence and the near-bankrupting of France; but it also resulted in the harder to demonstrate influence of English political institutions on France. In any effort to explore this influence, a good starting point is Jean-Frédéric Phélypeaux, comte de Maurepas, who was appointed naval minister in 1723 but had been dismissed and exiled to his estates in 1749 for circulating scurrilous verses about Madame de Pompadour. Despite, or rather because of this, Maurepas continued to enjoy the confidence of the young court centred on the dauphin. Maurepas was also a personal friend of La Vauguyon, who turned to him to provide tutors for his charges. This was a stroke of fortune for Maurepas, who, by placing his protégés about the future king, was able to mitigate the loss of influence and contacts which were the purpose of internal exile. This is the simplest explanation of why Louis XVI made him his chief minister.

It was Maurepas's choice of tutors that developed Louis-Auguste's scientific, and in particular his nautical bent, as was to be expected from a long-serving naval minister. Maurepas had appointed Buache hydrographer in his newly formed map bureau at the naval ministry, so it was natural for him to foster in his pupil an interest in oceanography. The fruit of his interest in things naval and of Maurepas's return to power in 1774 was to be naval rearmament and a resumption of war with England, which Louis XV had eschewed.

Maurepas also supplied as tutor the abbé de Radonvilliers, of the Académie française, who instilled in Louis-Auguste an abiding love of Latin, which he learned so he could study Roman history. Poetry left him cold: when his mother showed him a book of verse, he said, 'what's the point of that?' A favourite Latin author was Tacitus, whom he claimed to 'love and admire'. In his own letters, he was to display a Tacitean brevity, if not a Tacitean wit. Radonvilliers, a philologist, was also interested in the common features of languages. Thus Louis-

Auguste ended up proficient in Latin, Italian and Spanish and had a smattering of German, his mother's tongue. These were fairly conventional accomplishments in a man of education. What was more unusual was his mastery of English. The dauphin had learned English, but Louis-Auguste's mother disapproved of 'a language full of dangers'. So Louis-Auguste taught himself English – at least he later claimed that the impetus to learn languages came from himself, not La Vauguyon. He told his defence counsel, Malesherbes, 'I felt at the end of my formal education that I was still a long way from having completed it. I formed the plan of acquiring the instruction I lacked. I wanted to learn English, Italian and Spanish. I taught myself.'[22] In doing this he adopted Radonvilliers's preferred method of translating passages from English (and presumably the other languages) into French without bothering with the grammar. This required the heavy use of a dictionary. The journalist Mercier, on a visit to Louis's library, noticed a well-thumbed book, which was 'Boyer's English dictionary and was dog-eared like a student's textbook, which shows that it was consulted daily'.[23] Louis translated passages from David Hume's *History of England*, from the *Spectator* (to which he took out a subscription) and from Gibbon's *Decline and Fall of the Roman Empire*; but he translated the whole of Horace Walpole's *Historic Doubts on the Life and Reign of King Richard III*.

This book had been published in 1768 when Louis-Auguste was fourteen. Curiously, he returned to the task in prison in the Temple in 1792 and his work was published posthumously in 1800.[24] Madame Girault de Coursac considers that the translation was done by Louis-Auguste's brother, Provence. She found the importation of such Anglicisms as 'improbable' and 'unquestionable' as uncharacteristic of her Gallic hero, and, indeed, as Colin Duckworth puts it, 'he appears to have entered so thoroughly into the English mind that his turns of phrase have been severely criticized by French purists'. But Duckworth knew the work was by Louis-Auguste because in 1949 the manuscript, entirely in Louis's hand, turned up at Sotheby's and Duckworth was able to compare it with the printed text.[25] An interesting statistic: Louis XVI's library contained 7,833 books, of which 586 were in English; whereas Voltaire, the author of *Lettres anglaises* and a great Anglophile, possessed only 287 in a library of similar size.[26]

Whatever he said to Malesherbes, Louis's English was not entirely self-taught. He had a tutor called Le Clerc de Sept-Chênes, who translated and published sections of Gibbon's *Decline and Fall*. Louis may have helped him with this, but equally Sept-Chênes may have helped him with his *Richard III*. When Louis was about twelve, Sept-Chênes read to him Hume's account of the English Civil War (which he was to read on his own, obsessively, for the rest of his life). When Sept-Chênes closed the book, Louis-Auguste said, 'as for me, in

the place of Charles I, I should never have drawn my sword against my people'
– a promise which, for better or worse, he was to keep.[27]

Louis XVI, then, was fascinated by England and all things English: language,
literature, history and its parliamentary system. For example, he wrote to an
English correspondent for information as to the identity of the political satirist
who wrote under the pseudonym 'Junius'. Junius wrote letters to the *Public
Advertiser* attacking the early governments of George III between 1769 and
1772. Louis's informant identified Junius as a Mr Fitzherbert, but the author is
now considered more likely to have been Sir Philip Francis. It is remarkable
that a teenage boy – Louis-Auguste was seventeen in 1772 – should have taken
such an interest in English politics; and not a passive interest – he went to the
trouble of seeking inside information from English contacts. This suggests that
his 'sluggishness of mind' was induced only by the soporific and sterile plati-
tudes peddled by La Vauguyon; when something awakened his interest he was
capable of taking the initiative.

But why this interest in England? And did this fascination have any implications? As we shall see, his knowledge of the English political system (he
subscribed to *Hansard*) was valuable for the formulation of foreign policy, the
conduct of which was the main task of a French king, and he had a much better
understanding of English politics than did his foreign secretary, Vergennes.
This is not surprising since, as Vergennes confessed, the king read the reports
of parliamentary debates 'in their entirety' whereas the minister only had time
to skim through them.[28]

Louis had, however, a deeper fascination with the whole of English culture;
though, as said, this fascination was also a revulsion. His love of the sea naturally attracted him to the world's principal maritime power. Captain Cook was
an early hero and Louis based the instructions he personally wrote for La
Pérouse's ill-fated voyage around the world (1785–88) on Cook's remit. Not
surprisingly, *Robinson Crusoe* was one of his favourite books. But this admiration of England's naval prowess, like Kaiser Wilhelm II's, led Louis to embark
on an arms race which was almost certain to lead to war. And for all his love of
English culture, he told his uncle, Charles III of Spain, that England was an
'inveterate' enemy and that the time had come to 'humiliate this power which is
the natural enemy and rival of our House'.[29]

At an even deeper level it may be (indeed it must be, given his knowledge of
both) that he realized that French and English institutions were converging like
railway tracks seen through a train's rear window (though they were to diverge
again during the Revolution). And this leads to Louis's final and most important
ambivalence: after the collapse of the absolute monarchy, might he have accepted

an English-style political system? His finance minister, Necker, who 'made no secret' of his preference for such a system, thought that the king would, 'but only when it was too late' – too late because by then the rails had diverged too far.

The new dauphin

The dauphin Louis-Ferdinand only lived long enough to lay the foundations of his sons' education. In 1762 he became even more languid than usual and was soon coughing blood. He had contracted that perennial Bourbon disease, tuberculosis; in the dauphin's case he probably caught it from his eldest son, the duc de Bourgogne. Louis-Ferdinand lost the weight for which he was so well known – a portrait of him as colonel of his regiment shows his green uniform hanging off him.

He husbanded his remaining resources for the education of his children. There was an incident which is seen as emblematic of his relations with Louis-Auguste. Hearing that the boy had not learned his lesson properly, the dauphin stopped him attending the ceremonial hunt held on the feast day of St Hubert, the patron saint of hunting, on 3 November 1765. It was a public event, attended by ambassadors and members of the royal family, so Berry's was a public humiliation. Several members of the royal family pleaded with the dauphin on his deathbed to show mercy. But he refused, saying that he would forgive anyone else, but, given his future role, his son could not afford to be negligent. The dauphin even ignored his father the king's protest, 'when you stop your children from following my hunt, you are punishing me as much as them'.[30] These details are taken from a hagiography of the dauphin by the abbé Proyart, who went on to write one of Louis XVI and a good synography of Robespierre. They are meant to garner admiration for the deceased but have the opposite effect. And this is the curious thing about the dauphin's reputation: most of the information which damns him in our eyes is derived from people who venerated him at the time.

There followed a sequel to this episode which is intended as a happy ending but is in fact so nauseous that one hopes it is fabricated, as in the lives of *official* saints. Very near to death, the dauphin summoned his children to repeat their lessons to him. Horace Walpole, then visiting Versailles and maybe working on his Richard III book, noticed that the boy looked that day 'sickly and poor sighted'. Berry approached the deathbed and told his father that 'the part of the day which passed most quickly was that spent in study'. The dauphin responded: 'Ah! My boy, what pleasure you give me! Because since time spent in study passes so quickly it proves that you are applying yourself.'[31] Either Berry, at

the age of eleven, had become a consummate hypocrite, or the episode is apocryphal. One hopes the latter but fears that, either way, it symbolizes the relationship between father and son.

The dauphin died on 20 December 1765, leaving Berry as the new dauphin
and heir to the throne. Louis XV was doubly devastated in that he and his son
had never been properly reconciled. He wrote to his grandson, the duke of
Parma, 'I can't get used to no longer having a son and when my little grandson
is summoned, I feel the difference, above all when I see him come in'. It is not
quite clear what Louis XV means by the last clause – probably that the pretty
boy that Berry had been was turning into a gangling, clumsy youth. 'Poor
France,' the king sighed. 'A king who is fifty-six and a dauphin who is eleven.'
But did he hear his son's deathbed pronouncement that 'it would require two
successive good reigns, one to extirpate the abuses in the realm and the other
to keep them from recurring'?[32]

On 1 March 1766 a memorial mass was held at Notre-Dame for the late
dauphin. Kings never attended funerals and deathbeds, so Louis XV was represented by the new dauphin, Louis-Auguste. When he got back from the ceremony, La Vauguyon stood the boy in front of a portrait of his father and
exhorted him to return to it every day to 'meditate before his image' and
'propose one of his virtues to imitate'.[33] The number of these is not given. Still
less that of his vices, which included marital infidelity (for which he castigated
his father) and, *ergo*, hypocrisy. The dauphin has been described as 'easy to
caricature'[34] – but is that a defence?

Marie-Josèphe went into exaggerated mourning for her husband, cutting
off her blonde hair and commissioning a mausoleum for the late dauphin in
Sens Cathedral, where his body was placed under the high altar; his heart was
interred at Saint-Denis, now a socialist suburb of Paris but then the burial place
of the kings. The chief ornament in Marie-Josèphe's apartments was a scale
model of the tomb.

She obtained the king's permission to take over the education of her sons
from her husband, giving them more freedom to play outside and to learn to
ride, though she did stop the English lessons. Marie-Josèphe was the one who
first exploited the coincidence between the new dauphin's Christian names and
that of St Louis. For she saw herself in the role of Queen Blanche, the saint's
mother, who had brought him up from the age of twelve, after the death of his
father. So St Louis became yet another role model for his namesake Louis-
Auguste to add to Bourgogne and Louis-Ferdinand. 'What a king Louis IX was,'
Marie-Josèphe told her son. 'He was the arbiter of the world. What a saint! He
is the patron of your august family and the protector of the monarchy. May you

follow in his footsteps.³⁵ This was echoed in the *Réflexions* in which Louis-Auguste wrote that a king of France, provided he is just, will be the natural arbiter of Europe;³⁶ for a few years after the end of the War of American Independence in 1783 Louis XVI actually achieved this aim. Marie-Josèphe's supervisory role did not last long, however: she duly contracted tuberculosis from her husband. The symptoms were recognized in April 1766 and on 13 March 1767 she died. Among her bequests to her eldest son were her husband's papers, a jewel-encrusted reliquary containing a piece of the true cross and a silver-gilt one containing an unspecified relic of St Louis.

The diary

For Louis-Auguste, the almost simultaneous deaths of both his parents marked the end of childhood. But it was not just a personal matter. He was now heir to the throne and it can be no coincidence that his father's death prompted him, twelve days later, on New Year's Day 1766, to begin the celebrated diary, which has become one of the stoutest sticks with which historians have beaten his memory.

Louis XV now had to take a direct interest in the training of his heir. The new dauphin was too young to attend council – the best, indeed the only apprenticeship – but he could at least be instructed in the central role of a king: the conduct of foreign policy.

These two things – the diary and his letters on foreign policy – form the largest bodies of Louis XVI's writings in the period before the Revolution,³⁷ after which his words can seldom be taken at face value because of the constraints upon him. What a contrast there is between the two areas! The diary must be one of the dullest ever published; the letters to his foreign secretary are full of wisdom and insights. The diary was published in 1873; the letters as recently as 1998, which may go some way to explaining the king's poor reputation.³⁸ The diary entry of 'Rien' for 14 July 1789, the day of the storming of the Bastille, ranks with the apocryphal 'let them eat cake' and 'après moi le déluge' in the annals of Bourbon insouciance. But Louis really did write it. So how does a revisionist navigate round the rock that is Louis's diary?

In format, the diary is a cross between an engagement diary and the traditional hunting record of the kings. Louis decided – and this takes some explaining – that it was worthwhile making a retrospective fair copy of the engagement section. Since the storming of the Bastille was not an official engagement, 14 July was left blank in the original, which is what 'Rien' in the fair copy signifies. Begun as a youthful exercise, Louis kept the diary until he was dethroned and imprisoned in August 1792: his hunt had been disbanded and a prisoner has few official engagements except his trial, which might have deserved a mention.

The diary's hunting/engagement format partly explains the banality of some of the entries in this numbing catalogue of trivial achievement, but it was Louis himself who chose the format, or rather didn't have the initiative to depart from the tradition. The purely factual tone set by the entry for his mother's death – '13 [March 1767] death of my mother at eight in the evening' – is continued over a period of twenty years, with only one display of feeling, or rather pique, which occurs in the entry for 9 July 1786: 'the queen gave birth to my second daughter . . . there were no congratulations, no firework display and no Te Deum'. In a crowded field perhaps the prize for banality goes to the entry for 23 December 1780, after the death of his mother-in-law, the Empress Maria-Theresa: 'respects of three hundred and nineteen men in the morning and two hundred and fifty-six women at six o'clock'. Moreover there is absolutely no intellectual development: the entries when he is eleven are of the same order as those when he was thirty-eight, when his world was collapsing around him.

More than half the space is devoted to the achievements of his hunt, a minute record not only of every deer or boar but of every swallow killed. It is when Louis actually departs from the hunt/engagement format that one really does begin to wonder what is going on in the king's mind. There is, for example, a complete record of personal details, such as taking a bath or yogurt for constipation; as well as nine colds, four fevers and one attack of piles. At times of stress the tone becomes pedantic. Coming back to Paris a prisoner after the flight to Varennes, he spent a night at Dormans and notes that there was no *coucher* – the formal handing to the king of his nightshirt before he retired to bed. He feels that, even if there had been a courtier to hand him his shirt, it would be inaccurate to say there was a *coucher* because there was no bed – he slept in an armchair. Trotsky rightly talks of the 'depressing spiritual emptiness' of the diary.[39] Whatever Louis's reflections on the events of his times, he does not choose to confide them to his diary.

The abbé Proyart claims, however, to have had sight of another 'repertory' 'started at the very beginning of . . . [Louis's] reign' in which he recorded 'his observations on its principal events'. This 'record of his conscience, his opinions, his projects and his motive in everything he had done' would form a counterpart to the banality of the known diary. Proyart believed that the revolutionary authorities, who assiduously published everything to the king's discredit, deliberately suppressed the reflective diary which, Proyart believed, 'would have restored the monarch to the love of his subjects and the veneration of the world'.[40]

* * *

On Marie-Josèphe's death La Vauguyon once more assumed responsibility for the new dauphin's education, but in 1770 he informed his charge that he was now old enough to receive his instruction direct from the king.[41] In listing the king's qualifications for this task, La Vauguyon concentrates exclusively on his successes in foreign policy – acquiring Lorraine and Corsica, containing Austria, etc. However, not only does he omit any mention of the king's notorious failures – losing India and Canada – he also makes no reference to home policy beyond the anodyne seeking 'the happiness of his peoples'. This is because kings regarded the conduct of foreign policy as their main task – it was the thing to which Louis XV devoted the most time, to the extent that he even had a covert foreign policy – *le secret du roi* – served by its own agents, who were kept secret from the official ministers.

But home and foreign affairs were always linked, and never more closely than in the crucial year, 1770. The chief minister, Choiseul, was pursuing his policy of entente with the *parlement*, so he could raise sufficient funds for naval rearmament and a war of revanche against England. He saw his opportunity when war threatened between England and Spain, France's ally, over possession of the Falkland Islands. Louis XV, however, wrote to the king of Spain, asking to be excused from supporting his claim because he wanted to sort out his problems with the *parlement,* which had tried his 'patience' to the limit and had to be dealt with 'by every means available'. One of these means was the dismissal of Choiseul.[42]

In the long interval between Choiseul's dismissal and the appointment of a new foreign secretary, the foreign office was run by its *premier commis* – the equivalent of a permanent secretary in the modern British civil service. This man was the abbé Jean-Ignace de la Ville, of the Académie française, and a former minister plenipotentiary to the Dutch Republic. Louis XV would have discussed foreign policy with the new dauphin, but in 1771 La Ville was seconded to give him regular instruction. The dauphin displayed remarkable aptitude for his subject; one does not have to draw this conclusion from anything his tutor said about his ability in printed dedications: rather, from the outset, when he was aged just nineteen, his correspondence with his foreign secretary, Vergennes, shows a complete mastery of his brief, a sureness of touch and often penetrating insights.

Bridging the worlds of the diary and of foreign policy is a description of the forest of Compiègne that Louis-Auguste wrote and published as a fifty-eight page booklet in 1766.[43] On the one hand it is a tour de force for an eleven-year-old, even if he had help: it has been said that if he had not become king 'he might perhaps have become a geographer respectable enough to win a seat in the Academy'.[44] On the other hand, there is no personal judgement, no pleasure in the vistas, no colour. It would be too much to expect a Wainwright but there is something chilling in such mechanical compilations as: 'This forest has thirty-two thousand acres of which five thousand are clearings. It contains avenues, large paths, large roads, squares, pits, bridges, rounds, wards, fences, patches, hills, pools, fish ponds, moats and boats. It is surrounded by villages and hamlets.' His mind was that of an accountant.

Louis-Auguste's character

The intellectual discrepancies between Louis's diary and his correspondence with Vergennes represent the polar oposites of Louis's mind and even suggest that 'there were in him two men', in the words of Soulavie, who had privileged access to Louis's papers after the fall of the monarchy. Soulavie, however, is making a different distinction; for the two Louis Soulavie distinguishes are 'a man who *knows* and a man who *wills*. The first of these qualities is very extensive and varied. But in great matters of state, the man who wills and commands is almost never to be seen.' Soulavie is referring to Louis XVI's fabled indecision. Louis could make out an excellent case against a course of action – for example entering the American war – and then give way to pressure to do the opposite. Louis 'was endowed with an understanding methodical and analytical'. Furthermore, 'he was endowed with a spirit of foresight' and 'alone beheld from a distance the destiny and ruin of France' so that he became 'the Cassandra of the Nation' – the Trojan princess who was fated to prophesy accurately but never be believed.[45]

Soulavie explained this duality in terms of Louis-Auguste's childhood: the repressive upbringing intensified by the premature deaths of so many of his immediate family. There is much truth in this. Imagine the effect on a sensitive boy of being forced to feel respect, and ending up actually feeling it, for a string of people who, even using the evidence of their hagiographers, were far from deserving of it. First there was Bourgogne, the elder brother who was the spitting image of the dauphin, in feature and in character, dark in both. Then Marie-Josèphe, the self-styled 'la triste', who suppressed her natural vivacity to appeal to her morbid husband and felt everyone else should do the same. The chameleon La Vauguyon took on their colours to preserve his influence, but the range of the palette was not great.

What did Berry actually feel for these people? He never spoke against his parents' memory and, as said, gave his own son Bourgogne's Christian names. Accounts of his bearing at the time of his mother's death are ambiguous, suggesting illness as much as sadness. His diary entry with its horological precision – 'death of my mother at 8.0 in the evening' – would be considered unfeeling in a normal journal. What did Berry feel when La Vauguyon stood him in front of the dauphin's portrait? When he told his dying father that the hours of study flew by, was he humouring a dying man or was this early evidence of the duplicity his enemies accused him of in the Revolution – *le Roi Janus*, the two-faced king? Did he in the first case, as he undoubtedly did in the second, feel that one did not need to tell the truth when under duress? For the time studying could not have flown by. And in a way he suffered as much duress in childhood as he did during the Revolution.

Louis-Auguste's aunt Adélaïde, 'who loved him dearly', knew what was being done to the boy. 'With a view to dissipating his timidity', she told him, 'speak at your ease, Berry; exclaim, bawl out, make a noise like your brother Artois; dash my china to pieces and make yourself talked about.'[46] Berry was naturally diffident but this quality was reinforced by his strict upbringing and education. Nor was it just a casual by-product of the system. His tutors stressed the need for *retenue* – a key word throughout his life – meaning sometimes 'reserve' and sometimes 'restraint'. Louis-Auguste's timidity was shared to a lesser extent by Louis XV, Louis XIII and even Louis XIV, and may be said to have been a Bourbon characteristic. Thus Louis XIV was informed, in connection with the education of his son: 'though timidity, common with children who possess good judgement, prevents them from speaking, this silence stems from *retenue* not stupidity'. Louis-Auguste's tutor, Berthier, even developed a theory that such timidity is a necessary royal characteristic, and though his pupil did not incorporate this section in his *Réflexions* he clearly took it to heart.

These tendencies were reinforced by the injunction in 1770 of Louis-Auguste's confessor, the abbé Soldini: 'Never let people read your mind' ('Ne vous laissez jamais pénétrer'), which finds an echo in two despatches from the Austrian ambassador that year: 'His sombre and reserved character have so far rendered him impenetrable' (14 July); and, on 17 December: 'one cannot predict the impressions that are made on a prince so taciturn and evasive'. This evasiveness (his brother Provence was to remark that pinning him down was like trying to hold oiled billiard balls together) combined with the qualities of embarrassment and *retenue* to produce a fourth, special kind of silence.

This was not just the silence that can be mistaken for stupidity, though it often was; rather it was silence when the situation, or very often a direct question, required an answer, and he found it more convenient to hold his peace. His confessor set before him 'the example of Jesus who warned his apostles that there were many things he could not say to them', but a more exact comparison, if one be sought, is with Jesus's silences to the direct questions of Pilate (who was only trying to help) and the High Priest (who wasn't). This technique was occasionally used by Louis XV, as when, towards the close of the Seven Years War, the foreign minister asked him whether a particular avenue for peace should be explored, hoping thereby to evade responsibility for either concluding an inglorious peace or prolonging a disastrous war. Refusing to fall into the trap, the king gave no reply, though in an absolute monarchy the decision was his ultimate responsibility.[47] Louis-Auguste acknowledged this in a youthful exercise: 'a king who expects his ministers to decide for him is asking more from them than he has a right to expect since they only owe him advice'[48] – though whether that represents more than the parroting of a platitude is open to question. As we shall see, Maurepas would not let Louis XVI evade responsibility for entering the American war.

Thus Louis turned a natural tendency, reinforced by education, into a tool of government. But his timidity also had severe drawbacks. It is said today that fear of public speaking is the most common phobia. This would not be a problem in a private citizen – it would be like a man with a fear of camels simply not going to Egypt. But for a king it was a different matter. He could find no rousing words to inspire his troops before his palace was attacked on 10 August 1792, for, as Marie-Antoinette said, 'he fears above everything else speaking to assembled men'. His fear was almost as bad, though, when speaking to individuals. In 1782 his valet-de-chambre told the naval minister:

> I am sure that when you ask him to speak to naval officers, to those you want him to praise, he does nothing of the sort . . . he is seized by timidity and when he wants to say something obliging, the words stick in his throat and with the best will in the world nothing comes out. Try to give him a ready-made phrase, he won't be offended and he'll use it.[49]

Vergennes, the foreign secretary, didn't need to be told how to handle the king. When the commercial treaty with England was about to be signed in September 1786, Vergennes asked the king,

> to be so good as to treat Mr Eden with consideration and to let him know that he lends himself with pleasure and interest to everything which can

establish friendly links with and good relations between himself and the king of England and between their respective peoples.[50]

This is not just a ready-made phrase but a whole speech, written by a man who knew possibly less about the subject than the king, which Louis would have used verbatim.

The bent of Louis-Auguste's education was repressive, but this has to be put in context. Everything concerned with the role of kingship, religion, family relations, in short the world of Versailles where conventions were drained of meaning, was stultifying. But there was a world of the imagination beyond Versailles and even France. And Louis entered it with joy. Physics, for example, and the natural sciences – the world itself. It is significant that Provence gave up physics as soon as he could, whereas Louis-Auguste kept it up even after his formal education ended with his marriage in 1770. Geography also allowed him to travel the world in his mind's eye, as did everything nautical. It was said of him that he knew as much as it was possible to know about the navy without having gone to sea. Sadly he only saw the sea once; his entire life was bounded by Versailles and the smaller palaces which ringed it. He compensated for this by planning and funding La Pérouse's ill-fated voyage of exploration. Like physics and geography, history took him out of his immediate world, though he drew gloomy parallels from it, and languages took him not only to other places but to other times. For example, the Italian authors he read were the classics, Tasso and Dante – escapism perhaps, but who wouldn't have wanted to escape the gilded mausoleum of Louis's youth? In all the fields that he actually enjoyed be basically taught himself or relied on experts, mostly recommended by Maurepas, sometimes on Louis's own initiative. What he actually thought of La Vauguyon was revealed much later. When the education of his own son was being discussed, Louis was asked by La Vauguyon's son whether he could be the dauphin's governor, but the king replied: 'I am sorry to have to refuse you, but you know that neither of us could have had a worse upbringing.'[51]

Papa roi

The death of Louis-Ferdinand brought Louis XV and his grandson together; they wept in each other's arms. It also removed the impediment to what was to become a great shared pleasure: hunting. Since the late dauphin had given up hunting he saw no reason why his son should learn. This meant that Louis-Auguste did not have his first riding lesson until he was thirteen and did not ride to the hunt – as opposed to following in a *calèche* – until he was fourteen. This event he notes in his diary: 'Tuesday 18 [July 1769]: First stag hunt on horseback.' Soon he was hunting up to five times a week. Hunting was a life-line for the young prince; a sickly, gangling youth who was outgrowing his health, he remained subject to bouts of illness throughout his teens, but these diminished as the fresh air and exercise helped him grow in strength.

Louis-Auguste did not adopt his father's censorious tone regarding the private life of the king, and, whatever he thought of Madame du Barry, who became the official mistress after her presentation at court in 1769, he took the initiative of asking La Vauguyon to have him invited to the hunting suppers over which she presided. The king appreciated the gesture and, shortly after-wards, wrote to the duke of Parma: 'Destiny has given me another son who seems sure to be the happiness of my remaining days; and I love him with all my heart because he returns my love.'[52]

Louis XV associated his grandson in the attack on the *parlement* for which the dismissal of Choiseul paved the way. Moving beyond its traditional points of friction with the king, the *parlement* had had the effrontery to strip the royal governor of Brittany, the duc d'Aiguillon, of his peerage. The king, through his chancellor, René Augustin de Maupeou, responded with the disciplinary edict of 3 December 1770 which reaffirmed the legislative self-sufficiency of the king and forbade the *parlement* from using the weapons of mass resignation or judicial strikes – the equivalent, say, in such a litigious society, of a modern transport strike. Louis-Auguste accompanied his grandfather to the *lit de justice* and wrote on his copy of the disciplinary edict, 'that is the correct public law, I am absolutely delighted with M. le Chancelier'.[53]

The *parlement* responded precisely with a mass resignation – but both sides manoeuvred. Then on the night of 19/20 January, following the exile of Choiseul on Christmas Eve 1770, musketeers roused each *parlementaire* and asked him to state in writing whether he would resume dispensing justice on the morrow. Those who consented soon retracted and the *parlementaires* were exiled, not, as heretofore, to some agreeable town such as Pontoise but, often singly, in the dead of winter, to mountainous snow-bound regions or to isolated and desolate places, some of which even Louis-Auguste would not have been able to find on the map. Unable to gain any defectors from the *parlement*, Maupeou replaced it with the rival conciliar body, the *Grand Conseil*, and reduced the *parlement*'s vast jurisdiction by creating six less prestigious *conseils supérieurs*. The refractory *parlement* of Rouen was abolished, as were those of Douai and Metz, and replaced by *conseils supérieurs*; the remaining *parlements* were remodelled. In April 1771 Maupeou suggested replacing all the *parle-ments* with *conseils supérieurs*, but Louis XV refused on the grounds that it would foster an impression of despotism.

Among recent Anglo-Saxon historians,[54] there is a belief that despotism is precisely what Maupeou intended to establish, and in this they follow an opinion widespread in the 1770s. Maupeou had shown that the king's power was not subject to restraint either in theory or in practice. The fact that the coup was bloodless, carried out in the provinces by a 'councillor of state without a military escort', served only to emphasize the point.[55] The king was above the law, of which he was the sole interpreter. The vindictiveness of Maupeou's actions further demonstrated their arbitrary nature. These Anglo-Saxon historians make the further point that the coup permanently altered people's perception of the monarchy and led to the demand for constitutional safeguards. This view was earlier expressed by de Tocqueville: 'The disappearance of the French *parlement*, an institution almost coeval with the monarchy, made the nation vaguely aware of standing on the threshold of an age of violence and instability, when anything might happen.'[56]

Many contemporaries undoubtedly shared this view. De Tocqueville's great-grandfather, Malesherbes, in a private letter, talked not just of 'ministerial despotism' but of the personal despotism of the king: 'In fact, the king has no particular liking for this man [Maupeou] but he is greatly attached to his despotism.'[57] Malesherbes believed that Maupeou had raised an issue that might one day change the constitution and even the dynasty. The head of the *parlement*, its *premier président*, when faced with the disciplinary edict, should have privately told the king that the *parlement* was only a court of law and that in future he must 'address himself directly to his subjects in the most suitable way suggested by his wisdom'.[58] What he meant by this was that, by the coup, Louis XV had unilaterally destroyed the gentlemen's agreement to govern France without reference to the Estates-General and that henceforth the king must take the risk of summoning that genuinely representative body. In other words, the *premier président* should have called the king's bluff by admitting that the *parlement* did not have any legitimate grounds for resisting his absolute authority. The king wanted to have his cake and eat it, or, as the tax-farmer Augeard wrote, 'it is necessary that the king must be master of the *parlement* but that no one should realize it'.[59] But the coup, Diderot thought, had destroyed this fiction and rent the 'spider's web' which hid the face of despotism.

Not everyone shared such a view or shares it now. Modern French historians tend to qualify the 'despotism' of the Maupeou coup as 'enlightened', emphasizing its positive, enabling aspects and linking it to a movement affecting other European monarchies at the time.[60] They also adduce the support of Voltaire, who wrote an *Éloge de Maupeou*, and point to the abolition of venality of office and the tips, or *épices*, which litigants had to give to the judges, and above all, cite the plans that were being drawn up to abolish seigneurial courts and redeem feudal dues. Maupeou and his secretary, Lebrun, were working on a codification of French laws which, after the Revolution, when Lebrun was third consul, became the basis for the *Code Napoléon*.

The coup is best seen, however, as a return to the traditional royal policy of seeking centralization and uniformity in alliance with the third estate (the commoners) at the expense of the first estate (the clergy) and the second (the nobility), whether the nobility was represented by feudal barons or, in the eighteenth century, by the *parlementaires*. Maupeou was innately conservative, and at his installation he wore three different robes, one of which had not been seen within living memory. Educated by the Jesuits, he remained their ardent supporter and attempted to have the Order recalled, although he failed to carry this in the council. He believed the exiled *parlement* to be infected with the spirit of the free-thinking *philosophes* and was particularly worried by distortions of the French language in *parlementaire* remonstrances, such as novel uses of the words *liberté*, *citoyen* and *patriote*, which 'he portrayed [to the police minister] as harbingers of an approaching revolution.'[61]

Such divergent views on the Maupeou coup d'état, or 'revolution' as it was called at the time, suggest that there was no agreed constitution – no one could say, like those who offered Cromwell the crown, 'for we know what a king can do'. After the violence and assassinations of the sixteenth and early seventeenth centuries, culminating in the civil war known as the *Fronde* (1648–53), Louis XIV had managed by force of personality to restore a semblance of order to a weary country, and under Louis XV prosperity returned, a superb network of roads was built (today's *routes nationales*) and the country was well administered. Indeed this is sometimes described as the 'administrative monarchy': a country ruled by numerically able technocrats with sophisticated data at their disposal, complex financial instruments such as a futures market (still illegal in England), and armed with the mathematics behind state annuities, though these created the millstone of debt round Louis XVI's neck which he was too honourable to remove.

But for all this success, basic questions remained unanswered, or rather *the* basic question: that of consent to acts of government and in particular to taxation. This was not democratic consent (that was some way off) but the consent of those asked to contribute to financing the state; those in a position to refuse either by tax evasion, overawing the king's local agents, and/or concerting opposition through the *parlements*, which became a surrogate democracy for the disenfranchised – that is, all Frenchmen save the king, who claimed to be their sole representative. This was the dilemma which would haunt Louis XVI from the day of his accession to the meeting of the Estates-General in 1789 when the power of the *parlements* by definition collapsed, like a mummified corpse exposed to the air.

The growing closeness, in public and private, between the old king and his grandson gives the last four years of the reign a special quality. One might almost give it the name applied to the fine furniture of the Louis XV/XVI period, 'transitional': something between curly rococo and the severe classicism that seems designed for a Revolution inspired by republican Rome. The association of Louis-Ferdinand's son in these events may almost be said to represent the late dauphin's benediction on them, and surely that embittered prince would have rejoiced to see the essence of his policies being implemented by his protégés, who were now in the ministry. What might have qualified his delight at Choiseul's discomfiture, however, would have been his son's Austrian marriage – Louis-Ferdinand had favoured a Saxon match – which Choiseul had engineered shortly before his precipitate fall and which was to cast some doubt upon the finality of that event.

Marriage

An arranged marriage is the ultimate form of repression; and although it was the lot of royals until very recent times, marriage to a scion of the hereditary enemy of France compounded the pressures on Louis-Auguste. Marie-Antoinette was fully aware of this, telling her favourite brother, Joseph, the Holy Roman Emperor, 'the king's natural distrust was confirmed in the first place by his governor before my marriage. M. de La Vauguyon had frightened him about the empire his wife would want to exercise over him and his black mind took a pleasure in frightening his pupil with all the bogies invented about the House of Austria.'[62]

The marriage between the dauphin and Marie-Antoinette was meant to consolidate the 'diplomatic revolution'. Maria Antonia Josepha Johanna was the fifteenth of the sixteen children of Maria-Theresa, queen of Bohemia and Hungary, the last of the Habsburgs, and of the late Francis, duke of Lorraine, who had been elected Holy Roman Emperor but had had to cede his patrimony of Lorraine to Stanislas Leszczyński prior to its incorporation into France. That would have made for friction between Maria Leszczyńska and Marie-Antoinette had not the former, Louis XV's queen, died in 1768, before the marriage took place – whereupon the indefatigable Austrians floated the idea of a marriage between the old king and Marie-Antoinette's twenty-five-year-old sister Elisabeth. There was also opposition to Louis-Auguste's marriage to Marie-Antoinette from Marie-Josèphe, who, like her husband, preferred a Saxon match. Marie-Josèphe was also aware that her family had a better dynastic claim to the Habsburg dominions than Maria-Theresa, who was descended from Emperor Charles VI, whereas they were descended from his elder brother, Emperor Joseph I, after whom Marie-Josèphe was named. These female oppositions, while they delayed Louis-Auguste's marriage, also emphasized the fact that the Austrian alliance was deeply unpopular in France, as it was associated with humiliation. The *dévot* party, headed by Louis-Ferdinand, led the opposition; after his death La Vauguyon carried on the good work.

Maria-Theresa, fully aware that her daughter was virtually illiterate, asked Choiseul to recommend a tutor who would improve her French and instruct her in the ways of Versailles. Choiseul recommended the abbé Vermond, who had been the *grand vicaire*, or assistant, to Loménie de Brienne, archbishop of Toulouse. This association was to culminate in 1787 in Brienne's appointment as prime minister, through Marie-Antoinette's influence. Before the marriage, however, what worried La Vauguyon was Choiseul's continuing to exert his influence through the abbé. La Vauguyon and a *dévot* bishop warned Maria-Theresa that Vermond was 'one of the most notorious *Encyclopédistes* in the whole of Paris' and that 'M. le Dauphin, brought up on diametrically opposite lines, detested them and appeared to have made up his mind on that subject'.[63]

La Vauguyon was speaking out of turn and the empress ignored his warning. Vermond arrived in Vienna and was told to devote one hour of the day to teaching her daughter 'religion, the history of France, a knowledge of the great families and especially those who occupy positions at court . . . and the French language and spelling'. After a year's tuition, however, she still wrote 'inexpressibly slowly'[64] and when signing her marriage contract she made two spelling mistakes in writing her own Christian names. Her writing was the despair of Vermond. After a year he confessed to Mercy-Argenteau, the newly appointed Austrian ambassador to France, who was to become her unofficial guardian, that 'this was the field where he had made the least impression'. (It is hard to imagine that twenty years later she would be spending hours writing coded letters in invisible ink!) Vermond added that 'a little laziness and much flightiness have made it more difficult to teach her . . . I can't get her to go deeply into a subject though I suspect she can'.[65]

At the same time, Vermond gave Mercy a pen-portrait of the dauphin: thin, pale, slightly bow-legged, blond hair, high forehead, large but not disproportionate nose. Like everyone else, he commented on the dauphin's eyes – not their colour, which was a fine, deep blue, but that they lacked 'fire', they 'blinked'; people speculated that he was short-sighted, though from their extreme convexity in the portraits the fault would rather seem to lie in the other direction. Vermond commented, perceptively, that the dauphin's smile suggested 'kindnesses' rather than 'gaiety' and that this, coupled with the lack of anima-tion in the eyes and a certain nonchalance, gave an appearance of stupidity. This portrait does not resemble the familiar ones of him as king, plump and kindly, but it was the face that was to appear on his coinage, unchanged until 1791, and thus the one that was known by the millions of his subjects who never saw him in the flesh. The dauphin, according to Vermond, 'had no liking for the arts and a special loathing of music', despite or perhaps because of harpsichord lessons; and because of his clumsiness, his dancing and fencing lessons were similarly counterproductive. 'The navy', Vermond continued, 'is his favourite study and on this subject he possesses as much knowledge as can be acquired without having gone to sea.' He had no 'love of luxury even that associated with his station in life'. Finally, he was possessed of 'firmness or, if you prefer, stubborn-ness' – all in all a very perceptive portrait.[66]

Two years later, on 16 May 1770, the couple were married. They had met for the first time two days before, at the edge of the Forest of Compiègne, where the Austrian envoys had handed the archduchess over to Louis XV; Louis-Auguste wrote in his diary, 'Entrevue avec Madame la dauphine'. Louis was sixteen; Marie-Antoinette a year younger. They were an ill-matched couple: he would become possibly the most widely read of all the French kings; she was extremely ignorant. The Habsburg court was deeply philistine – for example, Maria-Theresa completely failed to appreciate Mozart's genius; whereas the Saxon court was highly cultured – Marie-Josèphe's father had founded the Meissen porcelain factory. Sadly the one cultural field in which Marie-Antoinette took an interest – music and opera – Louis-Auguste detested, though to accommodate his wife he did attend six operas with her in Paris in 1773. She loved dancing and Louis, the gangling bear, took the dancing lessons which had been deliberately omitted from his education; the result was merely a dancing bear. Nevertheless, he attended twenty-four balls in 1773. He was taciturn and withdrawn, she vivacious and company-loving. She was also much better looking.

For seven years, their marriage was not consummated. Several explanations have been offered, but two jostle for the lead, both agreeing that something happened in the summer of 1777. The traditional explanation is that Louis suffered from phimosis – a tight foreskin – which made erections painful. This, however, was rectified in 1777 with surgery to loosen the skin. Against this theory is the fact that the numerous medical examinations ordered by a Louis XV anxious about the continuance of his dynasty revealed nothing abnormal.

The second theory that seems to have gained acceptance puts the couple's problems down to a combination of Marie-Antoinette's coldness towards her husband, amounting almost to frigidity, and Louis's staggering lack of technical knowledge. This needed a marriage counsellor, who arrived opportunely in 1777 in the shape of Marie-Antoinette's favourite big brother, Emperor Joseph II. Accounts of his intervention generally stress his advice to his brother-in-law – which has become celebrated; but his catechizing of his sister may have played an equal part:

> Are you ... tender when you are together? ... Are you not cold, distracted when he caresses and talks to you? Do you appear bored, even disgusted? In that case how do you expect a man who is himself cold to come close and finally love you? ... Don't lose heart and throughout your life sustain him in the hope that he may still have children.[67]

Joseph gave his brother Leopold his analysis of Louis's problems.

> Here is the mystery of the conjugal bed. There are strong erections ... he introduces his penis, leaves it there for maybe two minutes without agitating it, takes it out, still hard, without ever ejaculating, and says goodnight. This is incomprehensible since he has spontaneous emissions alone. ... He says frankly that he is satisfied and that he only does it out of duty and takes no pleasure in it. Ah! If I could have been present just once I could have sorted it out. He should be whipped like a donkey to make him ejaculate out of anger![68]

Other theories abound. Louis's penis was so big that Marie-Antoinette found his attentions painful. The onset of adolescence was late with him – as his brother Provence suggested. Or, as his doctor suggested, he outgrew his strength which, in his opinion, produced humours. He may simply have been ill, possibly, as I have suggested, with a mild form of tuberculosis. Or, more prosaically, they never found time to see each other: he occupied with hunting (from which he returned 'trembling' with fatigue) and she with dancing.

But overriding all these considerations was the simple pressure of expectation – one more pressure superimposed on all the others: pressure to construe his Latin, pressure to produce a male heir. And on top of this he had to sustain all the ribald jokes over the long years. An anecdote about the wedding banquet sums this up. Louis XV is said to have told his grandson not to eat too much before the wedding night and the dauphin to have replied, 'Why not? I always sleep better when I have dined well.' Not only is this apocryphal, like 'après moi le déluge', it doesn't even approximate the truth. In fact an eyewitness noted that the dauphin was nervous and preoccupied throughout the meal; he ate little and spent his time 'staring at his plate and playing with his knife'. It had been the same during the wedding ceremony, when he shook with nerves and blushed when placing the ring on Marie-Antoinette's finger. At midnight there was the formal *coucher*, where the king himself ceremonially handed the dauphin his nightshirt, doubtless with some heavy joke, and the archbishop of Rheims blessed the bridal bed. Then the curtains were drawn, no doubt to the usual sniggers. A bad start.

But seven years later something must have clicked for, on 20 December 1777, Marie-Antoinette was able to write to Joseph: 'I had great hopes, my dear brother, of telling you this time that I was pregnant. My hopes have once again receded but I have great confidence that it will not be long, since the king is living with me in the fullest sense, especially since our return from Fontainebleau when he has hunted less.' She had not long to wait. On 19 June Louis was able to tell his cousin, Charles III of Spain, that the queen was pregnant, 'which fills me with joy'.[69] Instead, however, of the hoped for son and heir she gave birth to a daughter, who could not succeed to the throne. Marie-Antoinette then suffered a miscarriage and she did not finally produce a dauphin until 1781, eleven years into the marriage; the duc de Normandie followed in 1785, and the following year a girl who died in infancy.

In time, Louis was to grow to love Marie-Antoinette, and the fact that he never took a mistress enhanced her potential influence; but because from the start her relatives leaned heavily on her to intercede for them, and because of the feeling that Austria had exploited France in the late war, Louis determined to exclude her from all major decisions.

The death of a king

On Wednesday, 27 April 1774, the dauphin breakfasted with the king and Madame du Barry in the Petit Trianon, the charming villa in the grounds of Versailles designed by Gabriel and completed in 1768. This was the last occasion on which the dauphin saw his grandfather, alive or dead; his diary notes: 'Thursday 28: King's illness. Friday 29: In the morning smallpox is diagnosed. 7 [May]: Last rites of the king at six in the morning. 10 [May]: Death of the king at two in the afternoon and departure for Choisy.' A bland account of a dramatic fortnight.

The king felt indisposed on the 27th, had a headache and hunted from a *calèche*. Madame du Barry had wanted to keep him at the Peitit Trianon so she could control events, but the senior doctor told Louis sententiously, 'Sire, Versailles is the place to be ill.' As the nature of the king's illness became apparent the factions circled like vultures around his rotting carcass.

Madame du Barry was well aware of the position – if the king was deemed to need the last sacraments no priest would administer them unless she was banished. As du Barry was the somewhat incongruous linchpin of the *parti dévot*, which was headed by the duc d'Aiguillon, who held both the war and foreign affairs portfolios, and by his rival Maupeou, the concern of this faction was to persuade the king that he was not seriously ill. (They were aided in this by Louis's belief that he had already had smallpox in 1728.) So there was the further incongruity of the *dévot* party keeping the priests – including the archbishop of Paris, who travelled the twelve miles from the capital – away from the king on the specious pretext that if he knew his true condition the shock would release the poison and kill him. Bleeding was the only remedy offered by the doctors and three bleedings were considered necessary. Since, however, a third bleeding was usually accompanied by the last rites, d'Aiguillon persuaded the doctors to make do with a copious second bleeding.

The adherents of the duc de Choiseul – still exiled to his estates at Chanteloup – rejoiced indecently and said the king should make his confession so he could get to heaven quickly. One of their number, the duc de Liancourt, even mocked the king's daughters for selflessly attending the king's deathbed well knowing the risk of contracting the disease, which they did, albeit in a mild form. The main reason, Liancourt said, why three-quarters of people were not touched by their devotion 'was the object of their sacrifice. The king was so degraded, so despised, above all despised, that nothing that anyone did for him had any claim on public sympathy.'[70] A canon of Notre-Dame relates that when the king fell ill at Metz in 1744, 6,000 candles had been lit for his recovery; by the time Damiens attempted to assassinate him in 1757, the number had been reduced to 600, while during his last illness it was only three. Such was the public indifference at Paris and Versailles; even inside the palace, a diarist noted that 'a foreigner would not have been able to tell that they were losing their king.'

This was written by the duc de Croÿ, who was sympathetic to Louis XV, as he would be to his successor. Croÿ, with his son and son-in-law, was one of a group of friends who risked contagion in order to show their attachment and comfort the king: these included two Rohan princes, one of whom was the prince de Soubise, the vanquished of Rossbach, whom Louis had made a minister without portfolio to make up for his humiliation. Out of respect for Louis XV's memory and to reward Soubise's brave returning of the king's favour, Louis XVI was to allow Soubise to linger on in the council, contributing nothing, until his cousin, the cardinal de Rohan, brought disgrace to his family and to Marie-Antoinette in the Diamond Necklace Affair. Another attendant at the deathbed was the maréchal de Broglie, who was to be Louis XVI's generalissimo at the time of the storming of the Bastille.

Croÿ gives a graphic description of the king's face as the pustules coalesced to form a solid mass. He beheld, illuminated by the priests' white candles, 'a bronze mask enlarged by the crusts . . . the mouth open without however any disfigurement of his face . . . in short it looked like a Moor's face, a negro's, coppered and inflated'[71] - or perhaps, since the king's face still retained its handsome features, a Renaissance bronze. The windows had to be kept open and the stench from the king's putrid body polluted the Cour de Marbre below. By this time the king knew his condition and made his confession; du Barry was sent away and the grand almoner announced to the courtiers: 'Messieurs, the king has asked me to tell you that he asks God's forgiveness for having offended him and for the scandalous example he has given his people. That if God restores him to health, he will devote himself to penitence, the support of religion and lightening the taxation [*soulagement*] of his people.'

The dauphin was in tears - after all the king was the only member of his family he liked, for the simple reason that he was the only one who was likeable. The dauphin told the finance minister to distribute 200,000 *livres* to the poor to pray for the king's recovery but if he thought the sum 'was too much, given the needs of the state', the rest should come from the dauphin's private purse.[72] He and his brothers were not allowed near the king for fear of contagion - the nearest he could get was the first step of the staircase leading to the king's chamber. The inability to give his heir advice on running the country was, Louis XV's biographer Michel Antoine considers, 'an extra trial in his illness'. 'But why', he adds, 'had he not begun several years ago to prepare this good and timid boy to exercise the métier of a king?'[73] This was not entirely fair: the king had supplied his heir with the best teacher of foreign policy, and the dauphin had accompanied him on his visits to discipline the *parlement*. He had also read Maupeou's edicts and the pamphlets against the coup d'état for which La Vauguyon had rebuked him. Antoine speculates that the heart of this final meeting, 'which God did not permit', would have been the king's injunction to his heir to preserve the new arrangements for the *parlements* despite the undoubted opposition.

Precise as always, Louis-Auguste's diary notes: '10 [May]: Death of the king at two in the afternoon and departure for Choisy.' The king had retained full consciousness to the last. At a pause in the death rattle, his confessor asked him whether he was in much pain. 'Ah! Ah! Ah! Beaucoup!' Louis replied. 'As long as I live,' the abbé recalled, 'those three Ahs! will stick in my memory.' A valet snuffed out a candle that had been placed in a window to signal the king's passing. Immediately there was a mighty roar, like a thunder roll, or the crashing of a series of mighty waves. It was the stamp of courtiers' feet as they rushed headlong from the king's ante-chamber to those of Louis-Auguste – the sound of power escaping from a vacuum as the great chamberlain announced in the salon of the Oeil-de-Boeuf, 'Messieurs, le roi est mort! Vive le roi!'

As so often with key moments in the life of Louis XVI, accounts of his reception of the news are at total variance. The most celebrated has Louis and Marie-Antoinette falling to their knees, saying 'May God guide and protect us for we are too young to reign.' Louis's brother Provence has the new king throwing himself into the arms of Marie-Antoinette and saying 'what a burden but you will help me to bear it'.[74] Neither is plausible. All Louis's Bourbon predecessors, save Henri IV, who had fought his way to the throne as a mature man, had been younger: Louis XIII had been ten, Louis XIV and Louis XV five. Louis XVI was nineteen. As for relying on Marie-Antoinette, he rigidly excluded her from all important acts of government until the regime began to collapse. Louis may, however, have uttered the words recorded by the English ambassador, 'it seems as if the universe is about to fall on me' – prefiguring the words he used when his flight was stopped at Varennes in 1791.

The prescribed autopsy was omitted for fear of contagion. The king's body was encased in a lead coffin into which was poured a mixture of lime, vinegar and camphor. But no one at court would shroud the gangrenous body and solder it into its lead casing. Labourers were paid extra to do the job, and one was said to have died from retching. Then, for good measure, the coffin was placed in a hermetically sealed oak casket filled to the brim with earth. It spent the night in the Feuillants monastery near the Tuileries, which, after it had been deconsecrated during the Revolution, would become the home of the club of that name which tried to save the monarchy.

Next day the cortège set off for the basilica of Saint-Denis – the prototype for Gothic cathedrals and the resting place of kings. The cortège consisted of only three carriages: the first two contained officiating priests and household officers on duty that day – there were no volunteers, no mourners – the last carried the coffin, draped in a blue velvet mantle strewn with the lilies of France and topped with the crown. The new king 'regretted that the usage in place for princes who die of smallpox stipulated that the coffin should be transported to Saint-Denis without ceremony'.[75] This is an extraordinary statement: no king had died of smallpox, certainly not since the Middle Ages – Louis was sheltering behind an etiquette of his own devising. It was a mournful journey and when the cortège reached the Bois de Boulogne some wretches parodying the rich velvet voice of the defunct, called out 'tally-ho, tally-ho' as the outriders carrying their torches went by. There was a fine drizzle, and the light was fading as they arrived at the basilica. The service was perfunctory, and, as an extra precaution, Louis XV was bricked up in his mausoleum. It was a solitary end to what had always been a solitary life. An age not noted for its prudery neverthe-less judged Louis XV's vices harshly while scarcely comprehending his gentler virtues, such as his hatred of warfare.

The hatred felt for Louis XV by people of all classes is important to note. The great romantic French historian Jules Michelet thought that the damage done by him to the monarchy was such that it was beyond the strength of any successor, let alone Louis XVI, to restore it. He was referring to the king's moral degrada-tion. Of course, he did not accept the stories about the king bathing in children's blood to renew his jaded appetites, but he did think that the king's only contact with the common people was through its daughters, whom he bought for his harem and from whom he learned the vernacular. Others, at the time, and among historians, have come to the same conclusion without needing to dwell on the king's morals. Following de Tocqueville they argue that Maupeou's coup d'état demonstrated that the *Louis quatorzième* system did not offer sufficient safeguards and the king could tax and imprison at will. Therefore recourse must be had to the Estates-General which, as said, had not met since 1614.

These two verdicts on Louis XV – moral degradation and despotism – are synthesized by Barnave, the early radical who came to think that 'it was neces-sary to stop the Revolution' and that he could do a deal with Marie-Antoinette to accomplish this. Writing of the earlier 'revolution' – for contemporaries so qualified Maupeou's coup – Barnave said: 'Frenchmen combined such submis-siveness with such contempt for their master that they seemed ready to suffer everything.'[76] Despite opposition from the chattering classes of the day, however, these policies were bedding in – litigants, no longer afraid that the old *parlement* would come back and reverse their verdicts, were appearing before the new courts. But 'time was refused'.[77]

CHAPTER TWO

YOUTH ON THE THRONE

'L E ROI EST MORT! Vive le roi!' The old formula symbolized the continuity of the state. Half an hour later theory was followed by practice when a messenger fought his way through the throng of courtiers in Louis-Auguste's apartments with an urgent note from the minister of the interior, the duc de la Vrillière.[1] His official title was minister for the *Maison du Roi*, but since his duties extended beyond the king's household and court to include responsibility for Paris and general matters in many provinces, he was effectively the minister for the interior, the name he was given in the Revolution. He was therefore the man to pose the questions of immediate concern.

La Vrillière had been in his post since 1725. In 1770 Louis XV had made him a duke, to underline his loyalty to the *noblesse d'état*, or service nobility – royal administrators of fairly recent nobility who, rather than the feudal court nobility, were the bulwark of the Bourbon regime, with which they were coeval. La Vrillière was now seventy, a great age at the time; indeed it is remarkable how many of Louis XVI's advisers before the Revolution were old men – only one was of similar age and he lasted only nine months. In the Revolution most of the leading politicians were Louis's age or younger. This could explain a lot.

La Vrillière had to write to the king because he could not see him in person: like all the ministers he was in quarantine, having attended Louis XV on his deathbed. According to standard procedure, La Vrillière put his questions on the right-hand half of the page, leaving the left for the king's answers. The king replied that he would be known as Louis rather than Louis-Auguste; he would be Louis XVI; he would retain his grandfather's ministers and communicate with them by letter until the ten days of quarantine had elapsed. In the interim, La Vrillière asked, should the ministers form committees to deal with foreign and home affairs? No, Louis replied, 'if anything important crops up, the matter should be sent to me'. He did not want the ministers forming a cabinet in his absence. The bishops, military commandants of the provinces and their civilian counterparts, the thirty intendants, should be kept at Versailles until he had seen them. How long they hung around Versailles is not known, but the king left for Choisy, a château nine kilometres to the south of Paris, at four o'clock the same day and was not to return to Versailles for three months. Pestilence hung about the palace. Louis XV had had the virulent 'black' strain of smallpox and there was no question of his lying in state or of the new king's paying his last respects, much as he would have liked to.

The throng which had stampeded out of the dead king's ante-chamber was now seated in hundreds of carriages locked wheel to wheel on their way to scramble-accommodation at Choisy. Louis XVI travelled in the same coach as his brothers, Provence and Artois, and their wives – the ugly daughters of Emmanuel, king of Sardinia and duke of Savoy, from the oldest reigning dynasty in Europe, which was to provide the kings of a united Italy in the nineteenth century. Now that Louis was king, his relations with his brothers changed. Marie-Antoinette had already chided him as dauphin for retrieving a hat he had forgotten rather than sending Provence to fetch it; now Louis himself told his foreign secretary, 'I am not happy with the way in which . . . [the duke of Parma] has been writing to me since I became king. He has not asked my permission to write informally.'[2] But for the moment, in the carriage, they were just brothers in a strange new world, and soon Louis dropped the requirement for his brothers to address him as 'Your Majesty'. Midway, Artois's wife made some pleasantry which broke the ice and they all started giggling nervously. After all, they were young and it was a beautiful spring day. When they arrived at Choisy the lilacs on the terraces scented the evening air.

La Vrillière's letter had asked what the new king wanted to do with his existing ministers, including himself. Was he trying to bounce Louis into making a premature decision as to their fate? It was not a straightforward one: 'talented but disreputable' would summarize Louis XVI's view of his grandfather's ministry, the latter quality being epitomized by their association with Madame du Barry, the incongruous conduit from the *dévot* faction to the king. He had been polite to her for the sake of his grandfather, and 'out of consideration for the memory of the king' he now granted her a pension – but she had to spend it in a convent. Later she would be guillotined. The main reason for du Barry's exile was neither her unsavoury reputation nor the glacial relations between her and Marie-Antoinette: the mistress was wont to call the dauphine 'the little red-head', though not to her face because Marie-Antoinette refused to speak to her. The new king gave the real reason for du Barry's exile to La

Vrillière: 'since she knows too much she must be confined sooner rather than later. Send her a *lettre de cachet* to enter a provincial convent and command her to see nobody.'[3]

A *lettre de cachet* was an executive order under the king's signet seal, or *cachet*, to imprison or exile an individual. It had no other control than the counter-signature of a secretary of state, usually for the *Maison du Roi*, unless he himself was being exiled. La Vrillière, notorious as the comte de Saint-Florentin before his elevation to a dukedom, holds the all-time record for the number of *lettres de cachet* issued; but this was the first of the new reign – issued just one day into it. All the characteristics of the instrument were present: distance from Versailles – the greater the distance from the sun the longer the shadow of disgrace; and incommunicado – again varying with the disgrace from total, through immediate family, to friends with individual permission. *Lettres de cachet* were held to symbolize all that was arbitrary about the regime because they put private individuals outside the law, but what is unusual is that the *nomenklatura* themselves were victims and in proportionately larger numbers: Maurepas had been exiled by a *lettre de cachet* and the king's cousin, the duc d'Orléans, would shortly follow Madame du Barry. A minister receiving an unexpected visit from the minister for the *Maison* feared the worst; and if the minister for the *Maison* was himself to be served with a *lettre de cachet*, someone else had to deliver it. Only the king was free of this fear, and Maurepas would plead in vain for Louis XVI to end the barbarous practice of exiling ministers. But it would be an exaggeration to draw parallels with Beria's Russia.

The fate of the ministry was bound up less with that of Madame du Barry than with that of the *parlement* of Maupeou. Louis was inclined to keep both the ministers (or most of them) and the *parlement* (or most of it). But there was no need for an immediate decision. What he felt he needed was what his three predecessors had all had: an adviser. But because they had all been minors and he had achieved his majority, and also because he had been inculcated with the notion that he must be a 'firm' ruler, he did not want to have a prime minister, as they had, but rather an informal adviser. So he wrote the following letter:

Monsieur, overwhelmed as I am by the proper grief which I share with the kingdom I nevertheless have duties to perform. I am king. The word implies a multitude of obligations but I am only twenty. I do not think I have acquired all the necessary knowledge. Moreover I cannot see any of the ministers, since they were all interned with the king in his illness. I have always heard you well spoken of for your probity; and your reputation for a deep understanding of affairs of state is well deserved. This is why I am asking you to be so good as come to assist me with your advice and understanding. I would be obliged, Monsieur, if you would come to Choisy as quickly possible where I will be delighted to see you.[4]

This letter was still signed Louis-Auguste. Louis XVI's letters never mention the recipient's name, except on the envelope – he always used simply 'Monsieur'. And this has given rise to the legend – if it be a legend – that the man who received this letter, Jean Frédéric de Phélypeaux, comte de Maurepas, was not the man to whom Louis originally addressed it. The intended recipient was Machault, the finance minister who had introduced the *vingtième* tax and of whom Louis XV said: '[the *parlements*] have forced me to dismiss Machault, the man after my own heart. I will never get over it.'[5] An austere man, with a face like Manchester, Machault nevertheless accumulated a sumptuous collection of contemporary artefacts, pieces of which dazzle when they come on to the market today. According to the story, Louis's aunt Adélaïde – she who had told him to smash her china – got wind of what was afoot, didn't like Machault for trying to tax the clergy, and persuaded Louis to send for Maurepas instead. Providentially, the courier had been delayed while a broken spur was replaced, so all that was needed was for La Vrillière to place the letter in a new envelope addressed to Pontchartrain, Maurepas's estate, instead of Thoiry, Machault's. It may be no accident that both men had been in their time minister of the marine – Louis was determined to rebuild the navy. Louis instructed La Vrillière to send the letter 'with permission to return to court', thereby ending Maurepas's long exile. There was no need to alter the letter, since 'Monsieur' and the compliments could be applied to or at least accepted by either. This episode prompted a biographer of Turgot to ask, 'was the incident of the spur fatal to the monarchy?'[6]

But even if one wanted to stray down the by-ways of counterfactual history, this one would prove to be a cul-de-sac: from what we have seen of Maurepas's formative influence on Louis's intellectual development, it was likely he would turn to him. And if Adélaïde further influenced him she was herself probably swayed by the abbé de Radonvilliers, Maurepas's protégé and Louis's language teacher. It was always going to be Maurepas. He had been living in exile on his estates at Pontchartrain for the past twenty-five years. Internal exile, often coupled with a severe restriction as to visitors, was the invariable lot of ex-ministers, a measure designed to prevent them from maintaining the threads of a political faction and staging a comeback. 'It seemed', wrote one of Maurepas's colleagues, 'that fortune had wished to mature him by experience and above all by disgrace.'[7] Another colleague added that, despite his cold cynicism and frivolous wit – he was one of the most refined products of the ancien régime – 'deep down he believed that he was eternally damned and only accorded his confidence and what he called his friendship to those whose souls he believed to be in the same case'.[8]

Soulavie thought that Maurepas was too like Louis XVI to be a good adviser. They both had prodigious memories, were both stuffed full of information but both lacked 'character'. The same could be said of another influential minister, Jacques Necker, finance minister 1776–81 and 1788–90, whose ability to see both sides of a question in all its ramification made him, like his king, indecisive. But it was difficult to predict what Maurepas would advise or what motivated him, beyond a desire to die in harness – he was seventy-four, having been born with the century – and a burning hatred of Louis XV for having deprived him of the best years of his ministerial life and cloistered him in gilded house arrest. He must have smiled bitterly on reading the new king's encomium on the late king and wondered if the former could be so naïve as to believe that his grief was shared by the nation.

Pontchartrain was nearby (all the *noblesse d'état*, whatever the provincial origins of their bourgeois ancestors, had estates in the Île-de-France), and Maurepas obeyed the king's instruction to get there as soon as possible so that he could closet the king before the quarantine of his existing ministers expired.

Maurepas was right to be worried. One of Louis's first letters – still using Louis-Auguste – had been to Maupeou and it had suggested continued confidence in the chancellor:

Monsieur, in the great misfortune which overwhelms me I have the further one of not being able to see anyone. I have always taken the greatest plea-sure in the zeal and loyalty that you have displayed for the interests of the king and of the monarchy; I do not doubt that you will be as loyal to me. If any matter arises before I can see you, write and I will reply on the spot.[9]

Adélaïde lamented to Radonvilliers that her nephew could not see any of the ministers and it is certainly possible that if he could have, Maupeou and not Maurepas may have become his mentor, particularly as he already knew him from his time as dauphin.

So Maurepas lost no time, and in the early morning of 13 May his carriage carved its way through those of the stragglers from the Versailles exodus arriving at Choisy. However, his first meeting with the king did not go as Maurepas had planned.

At this first meeting Maurepas began with generalities: 'I will be nothing in the eyes of the public. I will be for you alone: your ministers will work with you; I will never speak to them in your name and I will never undertake to speak to you on their behalf. Just defer decisions that are not of a routine nature. We will have a chat once or twice a week and if you have gone too quickly, I will tell you.' Duty compelled him, however, to observe that the reign of Louis XV had been happiest when Cardinal Fleury had been prime minister (1726–43), as it was essential for there to be a 'centre', a prime minister: 'If you will not or cannot be such a man, you must necessarily choose one.' Maurepas hinted that he, Maurepas, should be that man but received for an answer one of the silences for which Louis became celebrated.[10] Advisers to former young kings, such as Cardinals Mazarin and Fleury, had effectively run the country, and this was what Maurepas was hoping to be offered. That, however, was not what Louis XVI had in mind. What he intended is not exactly clear, since he never defined Maurepas's role; his status was to remain ambiguous until his death in 1781, and many of the ills of the reign of Louis XVI before the Revolution stemmed from the fact that he failed to take the old man's advice.

It was also in the logic of the situation that whatever he thought of their policies, Maurepas would want to winkle out the existing ministers. Their quarantine ended, Louis held his first council – that for home affairs, the *Conseil des Dépêches*[11] – on 19 May. The court had had to leave Choisy on the 16th because the king's aunts were diagnosed with smallpox, so the council was held at La Muette near the Bois de Boulogne. So there they were, Louis XV's formidable ministers, feared and hated in equal measure, just like their master. Unlike the late king, they were neither nice nor nice to look at, but like him they had been prepared to endure unpopularity for power and to exercise that power for something they thought worthwhile. There was Maupeou, who, as chancellor, took precedence after the king, and stood as his proxy in his absence, and as such did not wear mourning for Louis XV, though he was one of the few who would voluntarily have donned it. Louis XV had been fond of his minister, calling him his 'little Seville orange' because of his sallow skin. To the impartial eye he was small, ugly, with bushy black eyebrows and a sagging mouth. The second member of the 'triumvirate' who had dominated Louis XV's last years was the duc d'Aiguillon, who held two portfolios: foreign affairs and war. He too had a harsh face and a yellow complexion. His close association with Madame du Barry was notorious, but he was a man of financial integrity; one of the richest men in France as the descendant of Cardinal Richelieu's sister, he was above financial temptation.

The yellow complexion of his colleagues contrasted with the green tints of the controller-general of finance, the abbé Joseph-Marie Terray. His minor orders signified nothing to anyone – or to himself for that matter, apart from the fact that he enjoyed two fat livings: the abbeys of Saint-Martin de Troarn and Notre-Dame des Molesmes. A tall, proud man, he was nevertheless prepared to stoop to keep his job, and contemporary cartoons depict him bowing so low that his large, aquiline nose and clerical bands are seen from behind, between his legs; withal he was a brilliant if ruthless finance minister, whose measures probably prolonged the life of the regime by a generation. Lesser lights in the ministry were La Vrillière and Bourgeois de Boynes, the minister of marine, who had so run down the navy that on Louis XVI's accession there was only one ship-of-the-line in service.

After the king, who sat in a *fauteuil*, and the chancellor, Maupeou, the next in precedence at the council table was Maurepas. He had been made a *ministre d'état* in 1738. Technically; *ministres d'état* were the only true ministers. There were no letters of provision; the king simply asked a man, often casually, if he would come to council. Having attended once, he was a minister for life. This could be embarrassing, so if he fell from favour, as Maurepas did, he was generally exiled. When Louis XVI asked Maurepas to come to Choisy, that *ipso facto* ended his exile and restored him to his seat on the council, where precedence depended on date of first attendance.

At their first meeting at Choisy, Maurepas had said, loftily, to the king: 'Concerning your present ministers, I shall say nothing: some are my close relatives [his Phélypeaux cousin, La Vrillière, and d'Aiguillon], the others are known only to me by public repute.'[12] But what did he really think as he resumed his seat in the council, blinking across the table at those 'close relatives' and strangers as though he had woken from a sleep of thirty years? For in that body, where it was the convention that the king should abide by majority decisions, Maurepas could be expected to be outvoted by Louis XV's old ministers, who retained their portfolios, Maurepas having none, and continued to run the country. If he wanted a meaningful position he would have to winkle the existing ministers out. This he was bound to do, whether he agreed with the policies pursued by Louis XV after 1770 or not; otherwise, as his friend the abbé de Véri put it, 'he would cut a ridiculous figure'.

As it happened, Maurepas did not agree with the policies of the sitting ministers. At first he played his cards close to his chest – 'concerning your present ministers I shall say nothing' – but as the summer wore on it became clear to the young king that his special adviser was tendering unpalatable advice: to dismiss the existing ministers and recall the old *parlement*. Maurepas was, moreover, aware that such a decision would be, as he himself put it, 'against the principles of the king's education'.[13] Most people in the ministerial milieu took the view, on constitutional as well as moral grounds, that a king's (especially a young king's) deepest convictions should not be violated; that, in the jargon, a *simple prévention* (prejudice) could be overcome, but not a *décision précise*. Maurepas was acting out of turn.

Maurepas's advice came as a shock both to the king and to Adélaïde, who quickly regretted recommending him. It would also have made Louis's father turn in his hallowed grave. That prince, or so we are told, had made a list of ministers his son might employ, and on his death Marie-Josèphe had placed them in a casket to be opened by Louis-Auguste on his accession. It included Maurepas (but also Machault) and several who subsequently were to hold office. Equally, Adélaïde could have forged the list and placed it in the casket she gave her nephew. Either way, how could they have made such a colossal mistake in choosing Maurepas? Just because Maurepas's enemy Madame de Pompadour supported the *parlements* it did not follow that Maurepas would oppose them.

To understand Maurepas's position we have to go back to his days as a young minister in the 1730s and 1740s. In 1737, as well as the naval portfolio he had been given responsibility for Paris; this in recognition of his skill in handling the *parlement* of that city for Louis XV. In this he was aided by secret reports from key *parlementaires* which told him what was actually going on – the official reports gave little inside information. He was wont to quote a maxim of his grandfather, the Chancellor Pontchartrain: 'Point de parlement, point de monarchie'; and he spelled this out to Louis XV in 1732 when advising him not to take drastic disciplinary action against the *parlement* on the grounds that it was inadvisable to 'throw down a precipice a body from which the king has received and may still receive great services'. With his dismissal in 1749, 'the government lost a capable minister whose legal knowledge, foresight and skill as negotiator were indispensable in its dealings with the *parlement*'.[14]

There followed the bitter disputes of the 1750s, but Maurepas and the coterie that formed round him – the abbé de Véri, Maurepas's confidant, the companion of his exile and chronicler of his second ministry; and Miromesnil, *premier président* of the suppressed *parlement* of Rouen – believed that the *parlement* posed no serious threat to the regime because, as Véri put it, 'it had never had the slightest intention of gaining control of the troops which are the basis of real power'.[15] Miromesnil thought Louis XV's fears had been 'puerile', adding, 'How can one fear three or four thousand unarmed men in black robes?'[16] Maurepas told the *lieutenant général de police*, Lenoir, that the *parlement* would be restored but that if 'disputes arose they were not to be treated as matters of state but as police matters' and, as a general principle, Lenoir was instructed that in order to prevent tension, 'it is necessary for the police to act often'.[17] Thus Maurepas was led to the paradoxical conclusion that by using force you could avoid the imputation of despotism – the despotism which Louis XV had invited by suppressing the *parlements* without resorting to force. The first-resort use of what was believed to be the ultimate basis of power was to be a disturbing feature of the reign.

The storms of the 1750s had been followed in the 1760s by royal capitulation, but even in the Choiseul period of entente with the *parlement*, Maurepas thought mistakes had been made. The ministry had been divided, and each faction had its own *parlementaires* in its pay, so that it was a moot point whether divisions in the *parlement* caused or reflected those in the ministry. These divisions had not existed in Fleury's time and, under Louis XVI, Maurepas sought to replicate these conditions by creating a 'ministère harmonieux'. This would also have the effect – indeed this was his primary purpose – of making Maurepas a de facto prime minister, with the other ministers dependent on and coordinated by himself. Since Louis XVI would not make him an official prime minister, his aim would be to do precisely the opposite of what he had stated in his first meeting with the new king: 'I will be for you alone: your ministers will work with you; I will never speak to them in your name and I will never undertake to speak to you on their behalf.'

The replacement of the ministry

On 2 June the duc d'Aiguillon resigned, in anticipation of being dismissed, from his two ministries (foreign affairs and war), an event neither hastened nor retarded by Maurepas, who told the king: 'I will only act as his relation in seeking to obtain from you some relaxation in the *traitements de rigueur*' (i.e., to moderate the depth and duration of his exile).[18] Maurepas, himself a prominent casualty of the system, thought that loss of office was sufficient punishment for a disgraced minister without his having to endure exile; however, his hopes of persuading the new king to surrender this instrument of control were short-lived, despite exile undermining trust between the monarch and his chief agents of execution. The fall of d'Aiguillon resulted not from a change of policy but from the personal intervention of Marie-Antoinette, who detested him for his links with Madame du Barry and his haughty manner towards herself, whom he had called a 'coquette'. Maria-Theresa and the Austrian ambassador, Mercy-Argenteau, were, however, appalled by her intervention (d'Aiguillon had deplored but permitted the partition of France's traditional ally Poland between Prussia, Austria and Russia in 1772). Louis also received unsolicited advice, expressed without the proper diplomatic protocol, from his late mother's favourite brother, Xavier, urging him to keep d'Aiguillon. Louis replied that 'though he was still young he knew perfectly well what opinion he should form of each of his ministers'.[19] Maria-Theresa was also shocked that her daughter only cared about revenge and took no interest in influencing the appointment of d'Aiguillon's replacements. Marie-Antoinette should have tried harder, since the successful candidate, Vergennes, was to prove an implacable obstacle to her brother Joseph's territorial ambitions, and she was to find herself bawling at the minister like a fishwife.

Public opinion designated the duc de Nivernais, who had married Maurepas's sister, for the foreign office, but he had been one of the twelve peers who had protested against the suppression of the old *parlement*. Maurepas did not dare put forward the name of a man so compromised but waited for the king to raise the subject – in vain, it turned out, for the king operated his silent veto. Finally, the comte de Vergennes was appointed, a fifty-seven-year-old career diplomat of modest origins within the administrative *robe* and a 'worka-holic' who managed on four hours' sleep. It is not clear whether the dominant influence in his appointment was the king personally – he had figured on the old dauphin's list of men to employ, and was described as 'methodical, wise and capable' – or Maupeou, whose protection Vergennes had sought after Choiseul had recalled him from the embassy at Constantinople for contracting an unsuitable marriage. Maupeou had probably already assisted his appointment as ambassador to Stockholm where, in 1772, Vergennes had advised Gustavus III on carrying out a coup analogous to Maupeou's own.[20] Whether or not he owed his appointment to him, Vergennes certainly defended Maupeou's work in the council.

The other appointment, as minister for war, was the comte du Muy. An old soldier and a *dévot*, he was a former *menin* and lifelong friend of Louis's father, and chose to be buried near Louis-Ferdinand's mausoleum at Sens. He had declined office under Louis XV because, possessing only one estate, which he detested, he dreaded exile. Now, 'counting on the coming moral reformation',[21] he accepted office under the son of his revered friend.

The appointments of Vergennes and du Muy seemed to strengthen the position of Maupeou, who had already benefited from the resignation of his rival d'Aiguillon – d'Aiguillon had lately been gaining at Maupeou's expense through his appointment to the war ministry in January and had contemplated a partial restoration of the old *parlement*. The duc de Croÿ was able therefore to write of 'le début où le Chancelier domina'. At the beginning of July Véri thought that Maurepas should retire from the ministry, 'unless he becomes its soul; having no portfolio, he cuts a ridiculous figure there'.[22] D'Aiguillon told Moreau that the king 'paid no more heed to M. de Maurepas than to the other' ministers. But it was not just to the ministers that Louis listened – he worked secretly with unofficial advisers and took what Véri called 'transversal' decisions independently of the official ones. Fairly early on in his reign it became clear that, whether from a natural suspicion, the way he had been brought up or simply from opening and resealing private correspondence, Louis tended to judge people by their defects rather than their qualities.

However, despite his lack of progress with the king, Maurepas had no intention of returning to Pontchartrain, developing instead a three-pronged assault on the centres of power. The first prong was to emphasize the distinction which the king already made between the undeniable achievements of his grandfather's ministry, particularly in the fields of the judiciary and finance, and their manner and agency, which he found distasteful (a moral, even austere, tone being the main tangible difference between late-Louis XV policies and those which his grandson intended to pursue). Maurepas's second prong concerned the king's residence; and the third the decision-making role of the *Conseil d'État*.

In terms of the first prong, nothing had caused the new king to revise his opinion of 1770 that the chancellor had 'put the crown back on the king's head', but whereas Louis XV had been fond of Maupeou, his 'little Seville orange', the new king found him uncongenial.[23] Not only was Louis's sense of justice affronted by the fact that the exiled *parlementaires* had not been given financial compensation for the loss of offices, which were regarded as incorporeal property, Maupeou had used the coup to settle old scores with his personal enemies in the *parlement*. Maurepas was aided by the fact that Maupeou did not bother to defend his work before the king: Maurepas asked the king whether Maupeou had discussed the question of the *parlement* with him: 'Not a word,' the king replied, smiling, 'he scarcely does me the honour of . . . noticing me, let alone speaking to me'.[24] Terray, the controller-general of finance, presented a contrast to the chancellor both in physique and in manner. Whereas Maupeou suggested the finality of his achievement by his very aloofness, Terray, by contrast, 'multiplied his contacts with the king in order to creep into his confidence'.[25] His progress with the king was aided by the fact that Louis's boyhood interest in mathematics had developed into one for public finance, 'a field', Louis was later to tell the nation, 'which the King understands'.[26] Terray plied the king with memoranda on the economy, working out the production and consumption of each province, and on the need for a government budget. 'I hand him reports on all branches of my administration,' Terray reported, 'he reads them with me, summarizes them, asks me questions. If he follows my advice in three months he will know as much about finance as I do.'[27] Nor was it easy to deny Terray's talents: since his appointment in 1768 he had increased annual revenue by about 80 million *livres* and reduced the deficit to 25 million. He instituted a minute, parish-by-parish investigation, or *vérification*, into evasion of the *vingtième* by the nobility. It was slow work and over the next ten years only a quarter of the parishes had been covered, but revenue in these had been raised by 50 per cent. His measures were, however, harsh: notably the 'bankruptcy' or forcible reduction of the rate of interest on government stock, or *rentes*, of 1770; and in 1771 new taxes – one-tenth on life annuities and one-fifteenth on *rentes*.

In terms of the the king's residence, Maurepas's second prong, Versailles, which the king preferred to any of his other palaces, worked to Maurepas's disadvantage because of its formality: here official ministers had the advantage over unofficial, and the king, surrounded by ceremonial, was hard to closet. However, in the heat of the summer, when Versailles, with its rudimentary sanitation, became unpleasant, it was customary for the kings to spend a month or two in the smaller royal châteaux, such as Compiègne or Marly; and in the autumn they went to Fontainebleau, thirty-eight miles to the south-east, for the hunting. In 1775, for example, Louis spent fifty-seven nights away from Versailles. In 1774 it was necessary for the royal family to decamp to Choisy to avoid infection and they remained there from 10 to 17 May, with Aunts Adélaide and Victoire, who had been in contact with their father, living in a separate building. Then, however, instead of returning to Versailles, Louis proceeded to travel round his palaces until 1 September. We learn from his diary that his summer was spent as follows: Choisy, 10–17 May; La Muette, 17 May–16 June; Marly, 16 June–1 August; Compiègne, 1 August–1 September. September was spent at Versailles. Then the travelling resumes: Choisy (again), 5–10 October; Fontainebleau, 10 October–10 November; La Muette, 11–12 November.

It is hard to resist the conclusion that Maurepas arranged this itinerary for his royal charge to suit his own political purposes. Away from Versailles, ministers did not have automatic access to the king, apparently having to write for permission to see him.[28] Not surprisingly, most of the major decisions of the reign of Louis XVI were taken in one of the smaller palaces, which also meant that most of them were taken in the summer or autumn. It must have seemed to Louis like an over-prolonged holiday, as when a child whose parents have been overtaken by calamity is whisked off by a caring relation on a long trip which soon breeds anxiety instead of excitement. No wonder Croÿ talks of 'this curious excursion [to Compiègne] so striking in events'.[29]

Maurepas's third stratagem was an institutional change: the transference of decision-making from the *Conseil d'État* to ad hoc *comités*, from which ministers who were hostile to Maurepas's policy as it unfolded could be excluded when it was a matter of general policy, or surrounded when it concerned their department. Under Louis XV, committees had prepared work for the council but decisions had usually been taken, in the council.[30] The rationale Maurepas gave for the change was that it would be easier for the king to learn his craft in informal committees, as he explained in a circular designed to still the complaints of excluded ministers:

> The function which I have come here to perform has as its sole aim to teach the king to carry out his vocation. Nothing would give me greater delight than to be able to please all the ministers and still carry out this duty. But I do not see how I can teach a young man his craft of kingship in councils of eight to ten people where everyone speaks in order of rank and often extempore. Committees are lost conversations . . . and it does not matter whether they lead to a conclusion or not. The king must be able to speak his mind without making law. . . . I do not claim that the committees decide everything. Their conclusions are often sent either to the *Conseil d'État* or the *Conseil des Dépêches* for their definitive form because I have no wish to deprive any member of the ministry of the consideration which is his due.[31]

Maurepas was aided in his plans for a new committee system by the fact that Louis was finding the tensions in full council intolerable: a divided council preserved his independence but made government more difficult. On one occasion the strain got to him and he stormed out of the *Conseil des Dépêches* without saying a word. An astounded Maurepas had to fetch him back so that he could at least fix a time for the next meeting.

Meanwhile, on 18 June, at Marly, the king had himself vaccinated against smallpox. Vaccination (as opposed to the inoculation developed by Edward Jenner in England in 1796) was risky, but Louis (who never experienced physical fear) decided to set an example to his subjects. Smallpox pustules erupted on the king's nose, fingers and stomach, but by 30 June he was clear and the procedure pronounced a success. 'The whole nation', Voltaire commented from the comfort and safety of his *fauteuil* on the Swiss border, 'is touched and instructed'. At the same time Provence and Artois were also vaccinated. The duc de Croÿ thought it was insane to risk wiping out the entire dynasty at one fell swoop, thereby opening the succession to the Orléans branch, who had coveted the throne since the time when all that stood in their way was the sickly boy-king, Louis XV. As it was, the current duc d'Orléans and his son, the duc de Chartres (the Philippe Égalité of the Revolution), were stirring up trouble by presenting the king with a petition in favour of the exiled *parlement* and were letting it be known that they had done so. Louis exiled them to their estate at Villers-Cotterêts for their pains.

The system of committees had taken shape by the beginning of August and from July Maurepas began to take a stronger line with the king: on 20 July Turgot, the intendant of Limoges, replaced Bourgeois de Boynes at the ministry of marine, which administered the colonies as well as the navy. Boynes was a soft target because he had run down the navy. Faced with Terray's demands for economy he had not been able to stand up for funding, and he had also been maladroit, giving the navy a similar organization to the army, replacing cadet training on board with a naval college at Le Havre, running down naval supplies and ship maintenance. All this must have distressed Louis-Auguste.

Next, Maurepas began to criticize Maupeou and Terray more openly. Terray continued to hold his ground with the king, to the extent that Véri thought they would have to buy him off by giving him Maupeou's job, to which Maurepas replied: 'But how can we place a man who has forfeited his honour at the head of the judiciary?'[32] In order to restrain Terray, Maurepas made a cynical exception to the move towards more informal government by resurrecting the *Conseil royal des finances*; it met for the first time in years on 19 July.[33] Rumour also came to Maurepas's aid; in July the king received an anonymous letter accusing him of personally profiting from Terray's grain monopoly, the *régie des grains*. On 30 July he wrote to Maurepas: 'Whilst you are in Paris, try to get to the bottom of the so-called grain treaty – and find me a *contrôleur-général*. Adieu and good-night till we meet at Compiègne.'[34]

Still the king deferred a final decision. During the court's stay at Compiègne, Louis used the pretext that it was the custom for the chancellor to preside over the privy council to review the judicial decisions which had been taken by the *parlement* over the past year. So Maupeou would have to be kept on until the backlog had been cleared. Eventually, however, at ten on the morning of 23 August, his patience exhausted, Maurepas went empty-handed for his usual tête-à-tête working-session, or *travail royal*,[35] with the king:

'You don't have your portfolio,' said the king, 'do I conclude there is not much business?' 'I beg your pardon, Sire, but the matter about which I must talk to you has no need of papers. It is a question of your honour . . . if you

do not want to keep your ministers, say so . . . and appoint their successors.'
'Yes, I have decided to change them,' said the king, 'it will be on Saturday,
after the *Conseil des Dépêches*.' 'No, Sire,' the minister replied with some
petulance, 'that is not how to govern a state! I repeat: time is not a commodity
with which you can dispose at pleasure. You have already lost too much for
the good of affairs and I am not leaving until you have decided . . .' 'But what
do you expect me to do,' replied the king; 'I am overwhelmed by business
and I am only twenty. It's all getting me down.' 'You have always said you
want an honourable ministry. Is yours so? If not change it. That's what you
are there for. These last days the abbé Terray has given you an opportunity
by asking you after his *travail* whether you were satisfied with his
administration.' 'You are right,' said the king, 'but I was scared. It's only four
months since I've been accustomed to being frightened when I spoke to a
minister.'[36]

Louis would have treated what he regarded as Terray's unfair question with
silence; and his embarrassment at the minister's importunity – for that is what
it was – became a template for ministerial dismissals that lasted for the rest of
the reign: the king simply refused to see a doomed minister.

So, with a heavy heart and against his better judgement, Louis dismissed
Maupeou and Terray. Apart from Maurepas's arguments, Louis was influenced
by public opinion, which required that the new king take an active decision on
the question of the *parlement*. In his youthful *Réflexions,* he had written: 'I
must always consult public opinion, it is never wrong.' But while public opinion
seemed unanimous,[37] it was often illusory since it could be invoked selectively.
An existential decision, a decision not to decide, would have suited Louis's
temperament and his political beliefs more; and it would have been a decision
in favour of the Maupeou settlement. As he deferred his decision, however, the
immense popularity which had greeted the start of his reign began to cool.
Coming back from the memorial service for Louis XV at Saint-Denis on 25
July Louis had been greeted by glacial silence which, as would smugly be said
by his opponents during the Revolution, was 'the lesson of kings': his own
weapon was turned against him. At length, when the *dévot* faction stressed the
perils of cancelling his grandfather's achievements, he replied: 'That may be
true. It may be considered politically unwise, but it seems to me to be the
general wish and I want to be loved.'[38]

Maupeou's carriage was stoned as he left Compiègne, and his effigy was
burnt on the Place Dauphine. He would not resign the office of chancellor –
even, it was said, for the promise of a dukedom – and by convention a

chancellor, as the last of the great medieval officers of state, could not be dismissed without being put on trial. Since Maupeou lived until 1792, he was the last chancellor of France; he even made a point of leaving his effects behind in the chancery, which in 1789 he was anxious to retrieve.[39] His verdict: 'I have won the king a lawsuit which has been dragging on for three hundred years. If he wants to throw it all away that's his look-out; he is f----d.'

Terray was dismissed on the same day. Louis was sorry to see him go, lamenting to Maurepas, 'I'm sorry; I would really like to have been able to keep him, but he is too great a knave. It's a pity, a pity!'[40] Maurepas chose the replacements for the fallen ministers. Maupeou's replacement as justice minister – with the title keeper of the seals, since Maupeou retained that of chancellor – was Armand-Thomas Hue de Miromesnil, who had the reputation of being a 'cunning Norman'. He had been head or *premier président* of the rebellious *parlement* of Rouen, capital of Normandy, and had incurred the displeasure of Louis XV. Unlike the other presidents and councillors in the *parlements*, the *premier président* had not bought or inherited his office but had been appointed directly by the king. As such he was expected to try to run his *parlement* in the king's interests. Miromesnil, however, saw his role as that of mediator between crown and *parlement*, speaking in the king's name to the *parlement* and in the *parlement*'s to the king. This was not Louis XV's conception of the job description and in 1760 he had summoned Miromesnil to Versailles for a rebuke: 'M. *le premier président* I am very displeased with you – personally displeased; you have not carried out my orders; do not let this happen again.'[41] The force of 'personally' is that Miromesnil not only incurred an official dressing down for handling a situation badly but that Louis XV himself experienced displeasure. Likewise, Louis XVI would come to feel that Miromesnil had betrayed him in his hour of need.

The main political function of the chancellor/keeper of the seals was to manage the *parlements* in the king's interests. It would simply not be good enough, if the *parlement* were restored, for Miromesnil to revert to the equidistant stance for which Louis XV had rebuked him; divided loyalties undermined the regime. So Miromesnil devised a plan, which he had shown Maurepas, his 'lifelong friend', to restore the old *parlement* but impose such conditions on it that it would not cause any trouble. But would it work?

Louis also had grave misgivings about Maurepas's other recommendation: that Anne-Robert-Jacques Turgot move from the marine to the finance ministry. His official title and that of most of his successors in the job was *contrôleur-général des finances* but for ease of reference we shall use 'finance minister', the title two of the successors[42] adopted. It should be borne in mind, however, that all of them, whatever their title, also had a general responsibility for home affairs. As such their functions overlapped with those of the minister for the *Maison du Roi*, and this led to damaging jurisdictional conflicts between the two. Louis's misgivings about Turgot did not concern his professional competence: he was a brilliant economist, almost the equal of Adam Smith, whose *Wealth of Nations* was published in 1776. Turgot's administration as intendant of Limoges, one of the poorest districts, had likewise been exemplary. Rather, Louis complained that 'he is deeply ideological [*systématique*] and hand in glove with the Encyclopédistes'.[43] In other words, it was once more a question of loyalty to the king's conception of the monarchy, but this time from a different angle, with the king caught in a pincer movement between the traditional opponents of the Bourbon monarchy, the *parlements* as represented by Miromesnil, and the new rationalist opposition as represented by Turgot. And these two were his principal agents of execution. Also disturbing in a man with Turgot's reputation for fearless integrity was the fact that he swallowed his doubts about the wisdom of restoring the *parlement*, presumably out of gratitude to Maurepas for his appointment. The king could have done with the fearless candour Turgot was to employ when his own job was on the line. Vergennes, it is true, represented traditional Bourbon kingship, but at this stage his influence on home affairs was limited.

There was no logical reason why the fall of Maupeou should have entailed that of his creation, the *parlement Maupeou* – unless you believe that genesis is constitutive of essence. Indeed getting rid of Maupeou might have cleansed its original sin. The country was divided, or rather its elite was – the vast majority of the population was indifferent or perhaps inclined to support the Maupeou experiment, which conferred cheaper and more accessible justice; and no one had greater recourse to the law courts than the litigious French peasant. The elite, what would today be called the *bien pensant* or left-liberal establishment, opposed Louis XV's policies. They included, apart from the exiled *parlementaires*, the lower legal fry (the *basoche*) who had pleaded before them, the pamphleteers, most of the princes of the blood, most of the dukes and most of the *philosophes* (but not Voltaire). They called themselves the patriot party, which Louis XVI considered presumptuous, calling them 'soi-disant patriots'.[44] They also, in the main, were to oppose the king in the run-up to Revolution.

Ranged against them – again among the elite – was a smaller but determined grouping including the *dévots* and the adherents of a strong administrative, or what Soulavie called 'military', monarchy. There were two princes of the blood, Aunt Adélaïde, who now regarded Maurepas as a traitor, plus

Provence who, on his brother's accession, was styled 'Monsieur' and was, until the birth of the dauphin in 1781, heir to the throne. Moreau, who had helped with his education as well as his brother's, now headed Monsieur's council, where he continued his influence; and on 25 August the king revived the post of historiographer royal in his favour.[45] Among the ministers, Vergennes, bravely stepping outside his brief, asked a series of rhetorical questions in full council: 'Did the former *parlement* deserve the late king's punishment? Was it permissible for the king to suppress the *parlements* by virtue of his authority? In both cases, would it not be more dangerous to recall the exiled *parlement* than to let the new one remain, even with the faults it contains?'[46]

The buffeted king was, in Soulavie's words,

a silent spectator during the debates which tore to pieces the royal authority and analysed it before the eyes of the people. In the progress of this transaction, the king was not destitute either of information or advice; he carefully collected the opinions and memoirs on the subject; he classed them in his cabinet with particular attention, and he wrote on the covers of the memoirs of the two parties the words: 'opinions favourable to the return of the old *parlements*'; 'opinions favourable to the existing *parlements*'; and he embraced that which was to him the most fatal.

However, he accepted the advice tendered by Maurepas – the man he had summoned to advise him. But it was not as simple as that. In a monarchy which was still partly personal as well as bureaucratic it was considered necessary to re-educate the king on *parlementaire* affairs and to make him think that the recall of the *parlement* had been his own decision because it would be more difficult to restrain the restored *parlement* if the king's spirit had been broken. The process would involve hours of discussion and the council was deemed unsuitable for this, both because of the publicity and because Vergennes and du Muy were unsound on the *parlementaire* question: the presence at the Quai d'Orsay of memoranda advocating the retention of Maupeou's settlement even after the fall of the chancellor suggests discreet activity on the part of the foreign secretary.[47] So government by committee was not abandoned once the fall of Maupeou and Terray had removed its original raison d'être. Accordingly, a select cabinet of four ministers – Maurepas, Miromesnil, Turgot and Sartine (who had succeeded Turgot as naval minister) – met in complete secrecy to discuss the question of the *parlement*. Véri has left a detailed account of its aims and methods:

The *comité* of four ministers has had frequent discussions before the king. The aim is to persuade this prince that the result will be his own doing in order that he may bring to bear the degree of warmth and involvement necessary in all large-scale operations of this kind. The will of the master, known and reputed as constant, is the true means of ending internal troubles. It is essential to give him this in reality and not be content with the appearance.

The method that has been adopted has been to place before his eyes all that has been said, written, thought and circulated, for and against, on this subject. The ministers wanted to know his opinion on everything and establish the most detailed discussion with him. . . . This method has had the desired effect which was to make him regard the plan which has been determined as his own – and to be able to circulate this opinion among the public.

Because, whatever the decision, the capital point is that it should come from his mind and not from the council of his ministers. As this decision is different from the ideas he had before ascending the throne, he has himself confessed his astonishment: 'Who would have said, a few years back when I went to the *lit de justice* with my grandfather that I would be holding the one I am about to hold?'[48]

Brainwashing is a twentieth-century concept with twentieth-century techniques, and perhaps 're-education' would more aptly describe what was done to the young king by his ministers, who were aware that they were violating the 'principles of his education'. Véri's uninhibited account of the process tells us something of the dilemma facing the ministers of a king who was expected to rule personally. It would have been convenient if the ministers could simply have told themselves that they were forcing the king's hand in his own best interests, the conventional device employed in an explicitly constitutional monarchy, such as England's. But the king's active co-operation was needed because the programme outlined in the *lit de justice* of 12 November (Louis had finally returned to Versailles that very day) was not a crude capitulation to the old *parlement*, but a complicated system of checks and balances which would depend for its success on the spirit in which it was operated, which depended in turn on the king's spirit being left intact.

The *parlement* was divided into several chambers: the *Grand' Chambre* and several *chambres des enquêtes* (investigation) and *requêtes* (pleas), which did the preliminary work. The *Grand' Chambre* tended to be staffed by more senior, establishment figures, the *enquêtes* with younger hotheads who wanted to make a name for themselves. One of the key points of the 1774 settlement was to increase the powers of the *Grand' Chambre*, whose key figures could be bought with royal patronage, at the expense of those of the *enquêtes*. And provision was made for a 'plenary court' – consisting of the princes and great dignitaries of state – to pronounce forfeiture against the *parlement* if it broke certain conditions. For example, if it went on judicial strike it would automatically be replaced by the *Grand Conseil* – a parallel prerogative court within the royal council which had formed the nucleus of the *parlement Maupeou*. Only one further remonstrance was to be permitted after the enforced registration of an edict. These were only paper rules, but the king's demeanour at the *lit de justice* seemed to the ministers of the committee to offer hope that the rules would be obeyed: 'We were astonished at the tone of firmness and personal volition which the king brought to his speech. The ministers of the committee did not expect it . . . [to achieve this firmness] he learned his speech by heart. As he repeated it to his ministers, one of them would mark time with his hand. "Too fast", he would tell him, "we didn't hear you properly!"'[49]

As the king left the Palais de Justice after the *lit* he was greeted by thunderous applause and as he crossed the Pont Neuf he noticed that someone had scribbled at the base of the statue of Henri IV, the first and most popular of the Bourbon kings, 'Resurrexit' – 'he is reborn'. Louis would not have been human if he had not been flattered. He also liked the concision of the concept: 'What a splendid conceit,' he said, modestly adding, 'if it's true. Even Tacitus could not have written anything so laconic or so fine.'[50]

On 23 October, a fortnight before the *lit de justice* restoring the old *parlement*, the new *parlement*, hearing talk of the impending change, sent a deputation to the king at Fontainebleau to seek reassurance. It had already passed a decree in a vain attempt to scotch the rumours. But instead of reassurance, the *parlement* received the crushing reply from the king 'that he was surprised that . . . [it] should make any remonstrances to him upon mere public reports'.[51] Louis had been at Fontainebleau since 10 October and would leave on 10 November in time for the *lit de justice*. Kings went to Fontainebleau for the autumn hunting but it was also the château where important decisions were often made, such as setting the annual budget. It is inconceivable that Louis had not already made the decision to recall the old *parlement* when he dismissed the new one's concerns as gossip. So here we have a second example of Louis's duplicity (the first was pretending to like study to please his father). Too much should not be made of this – he had to conceal 'market-sensitive information', just as today a finance minister necessarily denies rumours of a currency realignment. But it was a straw in the wind.

An important but neglected aspect of the recall of the *parlement* – and one that was more damaging – is the ingratitude displayed by the new king to those who had seconded his grandfather in his struggle against the *parlements*. As Soulavie says, 'Louis XVI, indulgent towards the exiled *parlement*, appeared unjust, severe and scornful to that which was submissive'. This was put most forcefully at the time by Monsieur, comte de Provence, in a memorandum presented to his brother the king: 'Will the king confiscate the places of an obedient *parlement*, which has re-established the crown on the king's head, only to give them to a *parlement* which had attempted to dethrone him? Will he abandon the members of a faithful *parlement* to public scorn, to the outrages of a *parlement* vindictive and flushed with victory on its return?'[52]

Another example of Louis's ingratitude is provided by his treatment of Bourgeois de Boynes. Boynes, 'one of the finest minds in the council',[53] had been made minister of the marine not for his nautical skills but as a reward for past services and loyalty. He had combined the posts of intendant of Franche-Comté with *premier président* of its *parlement*, which had caused a storm, fanned by the *parlement* of Paris. In this struggle he had been supported by Moreau. Then he had advised Maupeou on his judicial reforms. He didn't expect to keep his job under a king who was a naval fanatic but he did at least expect a decent lump-sum pension, the case for which he outlined in a memorandum which Turgot showed the king. 'But the king', as Turgot informed Boynes, 'has decided to restrict your pension to twenty thousand *livres*' (£833). Ministers were not well paid and had heavy expenses, such as entertaining as many as fifty people to dinner, which was taken in the mid-afternoon. Boynes had lost money on the exercise. More shocking than this, however, was Turgot's tactless comment: 'at least I have the satisfaction of telling you that I did not detect, in the way the king spoke of you, any traces of the *mécontentement* [personal displeasure] which I had been led to expect'.[54] Even if the king buttoned his lip on this occasion, restricting his expression of 'displeasure' to limiting the pension, was this any way to reward the sacrifice of one of the most loyal and intelligent servitors of the crown?

Nor was it just a question of ingratitude (to which Louis himself was abnormally sensitive when he perceived that he was its object). In his moving conclusion to his study of the conflicts between Louis XV and his *parlements*, Julian Swann has eloquently depicted the psychological damage done to the loyalists by the recall of the *parlements*. Of these loyalists, known as 'the king's good servants', Swann writes: 'Whilst undoubtedly a minority ... [they] were still sufficiently numerous to provide a functioning judicial system between 1771 and 1774. Had Louis XVI given them the opportunity they would have continued to do so.'[55]

But the new king broke their heart, or at least their spirit, and they were thus unavailable to help him when he was fighting for his life and that of the regime in 1787–89. And it was not just the members of the *parlement Maupeou* who were spurned, but the ministers, military commandants and intendants who had helped the late king to recover his authority. When there was talk of Terray's recall to office in 1777, he told a confidant, 'do you seriously believe that having been insulted by the people, having been forced to rely on the protection of soldiers, I would return [to office] again?'[56] Similarly, d'Aiguillon's son, in whose family loyalty to the absolute monarchy was seemingly absolute, was the man whose speech led to the dismantling of the society of the ancien régime in the National Assembly on the night of 4/5 August 1789.

Aunt Adélaïde also reproached Louis for his decision (though if she did substitute Maurepas's address for Machault's she bore an equal responsibility) and, as Soulavie comments,

> The king, who had sound judgement, acknowledged that the side which she had taken in these debates was the safest and that it would have been more prudent to suffer things to remain in the state in which his grandfather had left them; but he owed it that the love of his people, who seemed to desire the re-establishment of the old magistracy, had prevailed on him more than the love of power, and that he had resolved to recall the *parlements* chiefly for the purpose of restraining the abuses of the royal authority . . . a revolution is imminent and the government turned out of its natural course when the state calls exclusively into its administration jansenistical opinions and parties. . . . We shall see the king, in many circumstances of his reign, support this revolution, which he had begun in 1774, and favour incessantly the popular interests of dawning liberty, in preference to the interests of power.[57]

It was a stark choice: power or popularity. A love of power tends to corrupt, a love of popularity to enslave, as Louis was to discover. A recognition of the dangers of power seems inherent in Soulavie's analysis: 'he had resolved to recall the *parlements* chiefly for the purpose of restraining the abuses of the royal authority'. Even Moreau, who advocated absolute monarchy, saw the need to temper and restrain it, but there seemed to be no institutional checks on Louis XV. Louis XV seemed like an Ottoman sultan – Turkey being considered the archetype of despotic monarchy; indeed, the organized nature of the Parc aux Cerfs resembled the sultan's seraglio. Vergennes, the new foreign secretary, the client of Maupeou, had married a subject of the sultan, and, when his turn came, would be accused of acting like a vizier. So was the other minister to whom Louis XVI most gave his trust: the finance minister Calonne.[58] Things Turkish were *à la mode* – Mozart wrote a Turkish rondo – but not in government, and Louis XV's reforms seemed to be tainted at the source. Symbolically, the measures against the *parlement* coincided with the introduction in 1771 of a new head of the king on the coinage, the handsome young man being replaced by a grim old tyrant, the Tiberius of the Trianon. Thus, Maurepas was able to exploit the new king's dilemma: power or popularity; heart or head.

He and Véri accused the king of indecisiveness because it took him so long to decide the fate of Maupeou and Terray and that of the *parlement Maupeou*. Véri thought that if this 'spirit of indecision really took hold M. de Maurepas would be forced to usurp, so to speak, the function of prime minister for decisions'.[59] However, not only did Louis have to make the most important decision of his reign at its very outset, he also faced a structural dilemma: the man whom he had summoned to advise him was tendering advice with which he disagreed, while his official advisers, the ministers, were tendering advice which contradicted that of his personal adviser. Moreover, his initial reaction – to maintain the Maupeou settlement – seems to us correct, and his subsequent concession to an ill-defined and fleeting public opinion appears to us as weakness rather than realism.

The evil Louis XV did lived after him; the good was bricked up at Saint-Denis. The harm done by the Maupeou coup in 'underlining the need for . . . a reconstitution of the body politic'[60] was permanent; the benefits achieved by reversing it were transient: the disposition to criticize the government continued, but the government could no longer afford to disregard it. If the slavish maintenance of the status quo had been the objective, as it was for both Maurepas and Miromesnil, the restoration of the *parlement* was probably necessary. Louis, however, in contrast with both men, was to show himself to be accessible to plans for reform, and in the long run the ancien régime could only be reformed over the dead bodies of the *parlements*.

Equally important was the effect of the process of re-education on the impressionable king. Véri, through Maurepas's eyes, saw a distrustful, suspicious king emerging – unsurprisingly. In 1777 Beaumarchais, trying to persuade Maurepas to put more pressure on Louis to help England's American colonists, reminded him of the pressure he had exerted on him to recall the old *parlement*:

You are too forgetful of the fact that this fresh but strong-willed ['*ferme*'] young soul [the king] has been turned round and brought back even from afar on several occasions; you forget that as dauphin Louis XVI had an invincible dislike for the former magistrates and that their recall honoured the first six months of his reign.[61]

No wonder Louis took unofficial advice when the official was uncongenial. He not only opened private mail, he also received it. The result was that he only ever gave his full trust to two ministers – Vergennes, foreign secretary until his death in 1787; and Calonne, finance minister 1783–87. Both ministers led the king into decisions which were, to say the least, controversial.

CHAPTER THREE

THE BRIGHT BEGINNING

1774–76

THIS CHAPTER IS ABOUT rival centres of power. Indeed 'centre' was a word often used within the governmental milieu. The king was the natural centre but if, as Maurepas said, 'he could not or would not be his own prime minister he must necessarily choose one'. And though Louis did neither, Maurepas became at least in his own words 'the shadow of a centre of union'. The role of prime minister was, however, in the words of Marie-Antoinette's guardian, the Austrian ambassador, 'necessarily' – again that word – 'exercised at the expense of the queen'.[1] This was particularly so in the case of Maurepas, for his style of informal premiership depended on physical access to the king, a sphere which obviously overlapped with the queen's. But nothing could be done without money; so a fourth centre was the finance minister; but was he, in Véri's words, 'a mere money gatherer' or 'the man without whom the ministries could not operate'?[2]

With the finance minister there was a further distinction to be made: whether France was at peace or at war. Maurepas explained this in a passage in which he assigns each sphere its place in the governmental firmament:

> Mistrust of M. Turgot could not enter into his mind even if he were certain that he wanted to have the principal credit . . . [because] in time of peace he believed that a controller-general should have the principal influence because his department required this; he had seen that the state was badly governed when controllers-general were too subjected or too opposed to other ministers . . . for less important matters his advice was to allow the queen the disposition of a mass of domestic matters and court favours which fall within a queen's proper sphere of influence.[3]

If France was at war, however, it was the duty of the finance minister – and none questioned this – to provide the money for whatever military campaigns the king thought necessary; even if that meant financing them with unorthodox and detrimental measures, such as borrowing money at ruinous rates of interest. France in the period under consideration, 1774–76, was at peace, but there was the growing possibility of intervention in England's quarrel with her North American colonies – the Boston Tea Party occurred on 13 December 1773. Though at peace, France was re-arming.

So, in the first two years of the new reign there were potentially four centres of power, represented by four people: Louis XVI, Maurepas, Marie-Antoinette and Turgot. In the first part of this chapter we look at the strained relations between Louis, Maurepas and Marie-Antoinette and in the second at the intense relationship between Louis XVI and Turgot, at once the most distinguished and most disinterested minister he ever employed. Great hopes were invested in the partnership, and its ending on 12 May 1776, with mutual recrimination, has been called one of the 'thirty days which made France'. But Turgot did not operate within a vacuum – otherwise his reforms, given the king's support, could have been instantly applied or would not have been needed in the first place. Instead, he operated within a court system that was at the apex of one of entrenched privilege – social and (just as important) regional.

Louis's apartments

When he finally returned to Versailles, Louis set about making himself comfortable in his private apartments, though the system created by the Sun King was so formal that the term 'private' is relative.

Much of the suite of rooms known as *l'intérieur du roi* overlook the Cour de Marbre, and at the time was fairly public. Its most famous room was called the *Oeil-de-Boeuf* because it was shaped like the eye of an ox. Here the courtiers had gathered to wait for the dénouement of Louis XV's last illness. Two rooms further on was the *cabinet du conseil*. Curiously – and maybe as a result of the stressful meetings of the council in 1774 – Louis installed a bathroom with two baths next to the council chamber. Several rooms along, in what had been Adélaïde's gilded study, Louis had his working library with his travel and science books and periodicals including the *English Review*, the *Annual Register* and French-language journals produced in the Low Countries and half-heartedly banned by his own censors and foreign secretary, Vergennes. These included the *Gazette de Leyde*. There was also the official *Gazette de France*, which served as a court circular, whose entries Louis monitored and sometimes wrote. Louis did most of his work here, seated at a small bureau made of acajou, a tropical wood favoured by the court *ébénistes* such as Riesner, who made this desk in the classical *Louis Seize* style.

The truly private apartments were arranged on several floors above the *intérieur du roi*. These had also been occupied by Louis XV: the rococo furniture and decor were left untouched – an action of piety, perhaps, or economy, or simply inertia. The staircase leading to the apartments was hung with Louis's hunting trophies as dauphin. On the first floor was the drawing room, hung with engravings of the French canals; above was the geography room, equipped with maps, globes and instruments. On the third floor, Louis housed his grandfather's collection of fine wood-working tools, with rose-wood and silver mounts, to which he added his own, more extensive, collection of scientific instruments, barometers, chronometers, telescopes and a rose lathe for decorative engine turning, such as those used to create the superlative gold snuff boxes that Fabergé would strive in vain to emulate. On the fourth floor – Louis XV's games-room – Louis installed his main library, which was to contain everything published in France during his reign plus the 586 English books he owned.

On the fifth floor was a smithy where Louis indulged his passion for locksmithing. An interest in the mechanical arts was quite usual for the period and was made fashionable by Rousseau's educational treatise, *Émile*, in accordance with which, for example, Louis's young cousin, Louis-Philippe of Orléans, had dutifully to learn how to use a plane.[4] Nevertheless, Louis was made to feel ashamed of his 'mechanical pursuits', as Marie-Antoinette described them, and either practised them in secret or abandoned them for months on end. His *valet-de-chambre* credited himself with a *bon mot* which is too neat and too insulting for him ever to have uttered to the king: 'Sire, when a king does the work of the people, the people will seize the functions of the king.'[5]

Right at the top of his wing of the palace was a small turret, or belvedere, just large enough to contain an armchair and a telescope, through which Louis liked to watch arrivals and departures at Versailles. Sometimes the king clambered over the roofs and chimneys of the château to watch the tilers and chimney sweeps at work. Then at night he would chase away stray cats. On one occasion, though, he shot the pet Angora cat belonging to Madame de Maurepas, herself a somewhat feline, manipulative individual, who used the wiles of the species to get her way with her husband. Fortunately Louis was able to source an identical replacement for the animal.[6]

Louis spent much of his time in the private apartments, and these periods are generally signified in his diary by the word *rien*. He had 'nothing' to do in the way of hunting or public engagements, but was reading or seeing ministers or engaged in metalwork. A man of simple tastes, he attached little importance to representation or public display. Louis XIV, acting on the medieval notion that when a man was not at court he was in rebellion, had enforced attendance. Louis XVI did not, even stipulating that court service was to be 'reduced to what is absolutely necessary'. The ceremonies of the *lever* and the *coucher* remained the focal points of the court's day, but there was no life to them. The *lever* was at eleven o'clock, but the king had already risen at seven, been shaved, put on a simple grey coat, possibly slipped in to the queen's apartments, and had also done three hours' work. Then he took off his coat, put on his night shirt and was formally handed his day shirt, in the presence of the select few who had the *grandes entrées*, and then, before a larger gathering, his brown coat and silver-hilted sword. (On ceremonial occasions he would wear blue velvet and crown jewels, such as the large diamond known as the Regent, in his hat and another attaching the *cordon bleu* of the Saint-Esprit, the highest order of chivalry.) Then the king passed into a small room to have his natural ash-blond hair powdered (he wore no wig). For the *coucher* at night the ceremony was performed in reverse order, ending with the night shirt.

It was the same with the meals: there were the formal and the real. The formal *dîner* took place in public, after mass in the chapel; but the king scarcely touched the food. He would retire to the billiard room where a plank was placed across the table. From it he picked up a pâté and a cutlet or two with his fingers and washed them down with water. (Breakfast had been even simpler: dry bread softened with citrus water.) His main meal was supper and he served excellent ones in the private apartments to invited members of the *noblesse présentée*;[7] there were also hunting suppers and sometimes he dined *en famille*. He tended to content himself with soup, a roast and a sweet biscuit for dessert, maybe dipped in Malaga wine. No one seems to know how much he drank. Most witnesses say he was abstemious, but hostile ones, among whom one must count Véri and Mercy-Argenteau, think he could hit the bottle. Véri even considered him to have been a solitary drinker, though he also recounts an incident out hunting in 1775 when 'he was surprised by drink ... [and] the officer in attendance had the quick wits to bundle him into his carriage without anyone noticing or at least daring to speak of it'.[8] Perhaps the clue to the discrepancy lies in the word 'surprised'. He was a moderate drinker but alcohol went to his head.

Many ceased going to court, because with the king either inaccessible or uncommunicative they could get nothing out of it. When Louis made the duc de Croÿ a marshal of France, he remained totally silent 'as ceremonies bore the king';[9] but what could the king say on the occasion of making a marshal out of a man whose fighting days were long over?[10] Croÿ was one of the few courtiers who liked Louis and respected his abilities. He was one of the few, moreover, with whom the king could have a natural conversation – most often based on their common interest in geography. So Croÿ tried another tack. In 1777 he presented the king, at his *lever*, with the latest map of the newly-charted Antarctica. The king, he noted, 'had just taken pleasure in reading Mr. Cook's journals and was an amazing expert in geography. He examined the map for a long time as a true connoisseur; he even placed his finger exactly on all the most remarkable locations and spoke to me for a long time in the most flattering way, so that my trouble was well rewarded.' In 1779, Croÿ notes, 'the king talked to me for a long time about geography and he spoke well'.[11] Louis similarly astonished a man of letters when he made a comparison between one of Horace's poems and a Latin hymn by the seventeenth-century poet Jean de Santeuil. 'You know he wasn't trying to impress you,' Louis's valet told the man of letters, 'but you are a littérateur, so he talked literature to you.'[12] What Louis lacked was small-talk – a rather admirable quality in a private individual but a disaster in a king.

Apart from family, ministers and senior bureaucrats, Louis's companions were mostly menials – out hunting, he talked to the hunt servitors rather than his nobles. It is often said that he couldn't cope with the Revolution because he had never left his gilded cage, but in fact he had an easy familiarity with the lower orders, dropping in on peasants and chatting to workmen around his châteaux. He also had a rather crude sense of humour and a love of practical jokes, which he played on his pages and courtiers, to the distress of Croÿ who 'would have desired a better tone from him'. Let it not be forgotten that it was the nobility he alienated first, not the people.

Above the king's apartments, crammed into the eaves of Versailles, had been the cramped quarters of Madame du Barry, which were connected to the king's by a 'secret' communicating passage. In an act which seemed symbolic of the 'coming moral regeneration', Louis replaced Madame du Barry with Maurepas and his wife, whom an enchanted public christened 'Baucis and Philemon'. These cramped quarters, to which he was often further confined by gout, were to be the centre of Maurepas's power for the next seven years. Necker, the finance minister from 1776 to 1781, has left a graphic description of them: 'I can still remember that dark, long staircase of M. de Maurepas which I ascended in trepidation and heaviness of heart. . . . I can still remember that *entresol* apartment, placed under the eaves of Versailles but above the king's apartments which in its smallness and situation seemed the very essence, the refined essence of all human vanity and ambition.'[13]

The key to Maurepas's power was his physical access to the king – hence the importance of the communicating passage. It seems, though, such was the king's thoughtlessness that Maurepas, despite his gout, did not use this secret passage until 1775, when he was granted the *grandes entrées*; previously he had to hobble the long way round to see the king. Dozens of people had the *grandes entrées*, but Maurepas, to whom they really would have given the chance of casually dropping in on the king, was denied them. And this formal approach to informality mattered because Louis denied Maurepas both the formal title of *premier ministre*, which was available under the ancien régime, and the delegation of authority which, for example, the young Louis XV had given Cardinal Fleury in the following instruction: 'We order [such and such a minister] to work with and despatch all affairs under the direction of [Fleury] and to carry out his instructions as if they were our own.'[14]

Maurepas, in short, was never a viceroy, and, in particular, the king always retained the power of final decision: every decision of any importance had to be thrashed out with him, a process which could take weeks or months or end inconclusively. Instead, just as his quarters, squeezed under the eaves, had been an afterthought in the construction of Versailles, so Maurepas's power had to be squeezed into the interstices of the existing political edifice. This meant that in the period 1774–76 Maurepas developed a complicated system that exploited his physical access to the king – the only concrete advantage Louis had given him – to regulate or filter all Louis's political encounters: the king would consult Maurepas before taking important decisions and the other ministers would consult Maurepas before bringing up important matters with the king.

In practice this meant that Maurepas would descend his long staircase to sit in on a minister's weekly *travail* with the king or, as Maurepas's favour and gout increased, the minister and the king would venture up to Maurepas's apartments. The system quickly became institutionalized: in 1774 Louis XV's old ministers resented and contested it; by 1780 it had become routine. For example, on one occasion when Maurepas was indisposed, he caused both Louis and Necker embarrassment by asking the latter to have his *travail* alone with the king.[15] The new arrangement of government by *comité* continued and was easily grafted onto this scheme: thus, for example, a war cabinet might consist of Maurepas sitting in on the foreign secretary's *travail* with the king, while the relevant service minister was in attendance.

Maurepas, however, was under no illusions that this arrangement, with himself as 'at least the shadow of a focal point', compensated for Louis's failure to take his initial advice that if he could not be his own prime minister he must 'necessarily choose one'. It was a failure that led to many of the ills of the reign:

ministers constantly engaged in demarcation disputes, undermining each other's policies and spending money regardless of the total amount available, since there was no one to enforce a global budget and a *ministre ordonnateur* needed only the king's signature to spend any amount. The absence of a clearly defined prime minister also encouraged the political pretensions of the queen or at least magnified the ministers' fears of danger from that quarter.

Maurepas and Marie-Antoinette

Mercy-Argenteau's point about the influence of a prime minister in France being necessarily exercised at the expense of that of the queen had a special relevance to Maurepas's position. Though he was not a full-blooded prime minister, Maurepas's influence was based on physical access to the king and this was reinforced by the very layout of the royal apartments: Maurepas's apartments communicated directly with the king's, but to get there from her own apartments the queen had to pass either through a crowded room or the apartments of the king's hostile aunts, Adélaïde and Victoire, 'Mesdames Tantes' as they were known. In 1775 Mercy arranged for the construction of a secret passage connecting the king's apartments to the queen's, though he complained that she did not make sufficient use of it.[16] This passage was later to save her life.

In the struggle between Maurepas and Marie-Antoinette for the king's ear, the advantage lay almost entirely with Maurepas. Such, however, was his fear of her influence – a fear that 'bordered on the puerile'[17] – that he believed it was the queen's ultimate intention to replace him with the duc de Choiseul, and the other ministers with a 'shadow' ministry of Choiseulistes. He was wrong in this assumption. The queen wished to display gratitude to the man who had arranged her marriage and to bait Maurepas, who rose to it. But the advice coming to her from Austria was summed up in the words of its chancellor, Kaunitz: 'Choiseul is the man least suited to our purposes.'[18]

The reality was that there was a group of ministerial aspirants who knew that Maurepas would block their careers – men such as the marquis de Castries, a mildly successful general in the Seven Years War who believed that soldiers rather than lawyers should hold the service ministries; the baron de Breteuil, the well-connected ambassador to Vienna, who wanted to be foreign secretary; and the comte de Guînes, an accomplished flautist (he commissioned a concerto from Mozart without paying for it) who was ambassador to London. They had been associated with Choiseul when he had patronage at his disposal, but now, as Véri put it, 'if any of them became a minister, assuredly he would not work for Choiseul's return'.[19] Increasingly they looked for protection not to

Choiseul but to the queen herself, and in the course of the reign they were transformed into what could be called a 'queen's party'. But in 1775 that was a long way off.

The chief reason why Maurepas's fears were groundless was that Louis had resolved that Choiseul should not return to power and that, whilst the queen could have a say in the disposal of court patronage – military promotions became her forte – she should have none in the conduct of major affairs. Louis had come to accept the recall of the *parlement* as a pacifying synthesis of the warring creeds that had rent his grandfather's kingdom, but to reappoint one of the protagonists, Choiseul, would upset the balance completely and represent a denial of everything that he and his father had stood for. Nor would Choiseul's aristocratic ridicule of Louis's new *noblesse de robe* or *robin* ministry, which made an impression on Marie-Antoinette,[20] have found favour. The 1760s had not just been a time of dependence on the *parlement*, it had also been a period in which three of the six ministries had been occupied by *grands seigneurs*, who had quickly shed their old notions that such bureaucratic functions were degrading and who now believed that they alone were competent to run at least the service ministries. They had a different conception of the monarchy from that of the kings, who had always relied on *hommes de robe*, men with a legal background trained up in the royal administration, and from Maurepas, who, for all his pride in his aristocratic connections with the Richelieu and La Rochefoucauld families, gloried in the continuous ministerial traditions of his family, which went back to 1610, and 'on whom *homme de robe* was a title which always had claims.'[21] Maurepas's ministry, with only one soldier, du Muy, and five lawyers in the principal departments, represented a temporary reversal of the trend for aristocratic incursion.

Marie-Antoinette's fatuous frivolity was on full display in summer of 1775. She laid great stress on 'character', believing she had it in equal measure to her feisty mother, the Empress Maria-Theresa, who had held together the sprawling Austrian possessions on the death of her, the empress's, father, Charles VI; and in superior measure to Louis XVI, whom the queen called at this time 'the poor man'. She would display this 'character' by making a show of support for Choiseul, who had put her in the way of being queen of 'the finest realm in Europe'.[22] She decided to make this gesture by giving Choiseul a long audience at the time of the king's coronation at Rheims in June 1775. Knowing the king's dislike of Choiseul she thought it necessary and possible to trick him into giving permission for the audience by employing a device regularly used by parents today to get their offspring to do something against their will. Afterwards she boasted to a childhood friend in the following terms:

You will never guess the artifice I employed in seeming to ask for the [king's] permission. I told . . . [him] that I wanted to see M. de Choiseul and that the only problem was finding the right day. I succeeded so well that the poor man himself arranged the time which suited me best to see him. I think that I have made a suitable use of a woman's prerogative on this occasion – I bet old Maurepas can't sleep in his bed tonight.[23]

Her friend showed this letter to Maria-Theresa who wrote a stinging letter to her daughter, accusing her of behaving like a Pompadour or a du Barry rather than a Habsburg. And, she continued, having shown such frivolity, 'you dare to busy yourself with matters of state, with the choice of ministers'.

For this was precisely what Marie-Antoinette was, with embarrassing clumsiness, trying to do. She had secured the dismissal of the duc d'Aiguillon the previous year but now, convinced that he was behind a spate of scurrilous pamphlets against her, she insisted that he be exiled to his remotest possession, Aiguillon itself, which, as she pointed out to her correspondent, 'is in Gascony'. Maurepas had been trying to dissuade Louis from exiling ministers and, though he failed on this occasion, even for his own relative, at his estate at Pontchartrain he ostentatiously feted d'Aiguillon on his way to exile – the dumbest insolence available to him.

Maurepas had skipped the coronation, pleading his age, and relaxed at Pontchartrain. Marie-Antoinette came back from Rheims full of herself and fatuously told Maurepas that 'after the coronation the king will devote himself entirely to his royal calling, the economy and public order'.[24] When La Vrillière retired, 'half pushed, half jumping', having orchestrated the coronation, Marie-Antoinette informed Maurepas that if he wanted good relations with her, Sartine must be moved to be minister for the *Maison du Roi* and a Choiseuliste called d'Ennery must replace Sartine at the marine. In September Marie-Antoinette demanded that another Choiseuliste, Castries, replace the war minister du Muy, who had died following surgery to remove a gall stone – the operation was a success but the prolonged pain endured with military stoicism killed the patient.

Where did all this bluster lead? Marie-Antoinette got her meeting with Choiseul, but when, after the coronation, Choiseul's turn came to kiss the king's hand, he withdrew it and averted his gaze, not bothering to control 'a terrifying grimace'. Seeing no point in remaining at court, Choiseul departed for his estate at Chanteloup, turning an involuntary exile into a voluntary one. He died an embittered bankrupt in 1785. As for Sartine, Marie-Antoinette had not taken the elementary precaution of asking him if he actually wanted to swap ministries. He didn't: with a naval war on the horizon and a navy-mad king who gave him an extra 40 million *livres* – a tenth of the royal budget – to rebuild the navy, he was looking forward to becoming 'the important man in the ministry'.

The vacancy at the *Maison du Roi* still had to be filled: 'The capital point', Maurepas told Véri, 'is not to allow the queen to choose ministers or direct major affairs.'[25] But so misplaced were his fears that he managed to install his candidate, Malesherbes, the *premier président* of the *Cour des Aides*,[26] even though the unwillingness of the king to appoint Malesherbes was matched only by Malesherbes's unwillingness to be appointed. Only a month before, on 6 May, the *Cour des Aides* had promulgated its *grande remontrance*, which castigated ministerial despotism, particularly that of the finance minister, and argued that the only protection available to the citizen was the convocation of the Estates-General. Louis also frowned on Malesherbes's conduct as royal censor when he had allowed the publication of radical literature: Louis told Maurepas, 'he [Malesherbes] is too dangerous an *Encyclopédiste* – don't mention him for anything.'[27] And when Maurepas returned to the charge, Louis reminded him that he had already said no.

For his part, Malesherbes regarded his appointment as 'next to a fatal illness the worst thing that could befall me' and only accepted office on the singular condition that he could raise the question of his resignation from time to time. Malesherbes's reluctance did not only stem from the fact that he had no administrative ability. It was that he shared the king's view that he was too closely identified with the *parlementaire* opposition, though he did in fact have very ambivalent views on the political role of the *parlement*, as we shall see when considering the prelude to the Revolution. In a nutshell, he believed that the Estates-General should take over the political role of the *parlementaires* who should be confined to their original role as appellate judges.

Malesherbes was the archetypal absent-minded professor (his family had to persuade him to sleep fully clothed because of his tendency to get up in the middle of the night to jot down an idea and subsequently catch cold). It was therefore unfortunate that he was appointed to a department needing a grasp of administrative detail simply because that was where the hole in Maurepas's defences happened to have appeared. For, in the long run, Louis's grasp of detail would have complemented Malesherbes's breadth of vision but lack of focus, something Maurepas perhaps realized when he said to the king: 'He is a man I am giving you to replace me and you will do well to place your confidence in him . . . he will provide the link between policies and ministers. I must soon retire because of my age and, even more, because of the queen's opposition.'[28]

Despite the reluctance of the one to appoint and the other to be appointed, Louis and Malesherbes got on well, each respecting the other's simplicity and basic integrity. On several occasions Louis gently tried to convert his minister: 'My dear Malesherbes, without religion there is no true happiness either for societies or individuals.'[29] To please the king, Malesherbes started attending mass, but crossed his fingers. Malesherbes also took time off from his thankless task of reforming the *Maison du Roi* and *lettres de cachet* to talk with his customary insight to the king about the more general aspects of government. In a letter to Maurepas he summarizes two memoranda he sent the king: 'One concerns the establishment of provincial assemblies which would present the king and the people with the advantages, without the disadvantages, of provincial estates and which would rid the king of the pressure which is beginning to be brought to bear upon him – and will, I foresee, for the rest of his reign – for estates, be they provincial or general.'[30]

The rise of the Polignacs

The rise of the queen's favourite, the comtesse Jules de Polignac, is best explained by the supposition that her uncle, Maurepas, 'planted' her at Versailles in the hope that she would give Marie-Antoinette the companionship she was not getting from Louis and would neutralize the queen's political influence, which was difficult within the conventions to deny.

Madame de Polignac was a country-cousin of Maurepas, beautiful and suggestible but of a family which, though good, 'had never had a place at court and whose connections were not sufficient for it to shine at Versailles'.[31] In 1775 Maurepas brought her to court and launched her in the salon of the princesse de Rohan-Guéménée. The princess was the daughter of the maréchal-duc de Soubise, whom the king, out of respect for the memory of the duke's personal friend Louis XV, had allowed to continue attending the *Conseil d'État*. Maurepas permitted this touching eccentricity to pass: he had reduced the *conseil* to a largely ceremonial status and he prided himself on his alliance with the Rohan family. The princess had become *gouvernante des enfants de France* in succession to her aunt, Madame de Marsan, Louis's former governess. Her only official duties concerned Louis's eleven-year-old sister, Madame Élisabeth, but her salon was one of the most brilliant and the queen a frequent visitor. There she encountered Madame de Polignac and a deep and lasting attachment formed between them. Around them grew the queen's *société intime*, a tight-knit group which included Artois (who became the lover of Madame de Polignac's sister, Madame de Polastron), the marquis de Vaudreuil and the comte d'Adhémar.

Much has been made of the baleful influence of this group. Marie-Antoinette is blamed for ceasing to hold court in her state apartments and retreating with the Polignacs to the privacy of the Petit Trianon. At the same time, following the dismissal of her *dame d'honneur*, the comtesse de Noailles, 'Madame Etiquette', she is blamed for becoming *too* accessible. Much also is made of the Polignacs' so-called monopolization of pensions and the resentment of those excluded. This, for example, has been presented as the d'Aiguillon faction's motive for circulating damaging pamphlets depicting Louis as a cuckold and Marie-Antoinette as a harpy,[32] even though the queen's treatment of d'Aiguillon in 1774 should be sufficient explanation.

In any case, before 1780 the Polignacs only enjoyed two court offices.[33] In that year things improved: Madame de Polignac was made *gouvernante des enfants de France* – in fact there was only one 'child', Louis's daughter Madame Royale, born in 1778; M. de Polignac was made a duc and *directeur-général des postes*; and their daughter received a dowry of 800,000 *livres*. This was, however, as nothing compared with the 1.8 million *livres* a year which the entirely parasitic Noailles were said to have enjoyed under Louis XV. Moreover, their expenses were considerable because 'the queen and a part of the royal family had contracted the habit of eating and living with them every day'. The words are those of the austere d'Ormesson, controller-general in 1783, who was asked by the duc de Polignac for a pension of 380,000 *livres* a year. Embarrassed, because he was much richer than the duc and because 'ministers needed three hundred thousand a year to entertain less exalted members of the court', d'Ormesson proposed to the king that the duc be given 400,000.[34] Much misunderstanding concerning the level of expenditure on the court (only 6 per cent of the total) can be dispelled by reminding oneself that at the time there were twenty-four *livres* to the pound sterling.

What is completely ignored is that the Polignacs fulfilled the political purpose of their institution in a way which Maurepas could never have dared to expect. In 1776 Madame de Polignac told the queen 'that it would be in her interest to persuade the king to nominate M. de Maurepas prime minister', which prompted Mercy to say that she was 'manifestly . . . conducted by the comte de Maurepas'.[35] In that year also, she persuaded the queen to end the exile of Maurepas's nephew d'Aiguillon.[36] With a solitary exception,[37] the queen's *société* sided with Maurepas in all his disputes with her. Nor were these services merely personal to Maurepas: he was, after all, the king's chief minister and the two men were in total agreement about the need to restrict the political influence of the queen. After Maurepas's death, the Polignacs supported those ministers who continued this tradition, notably Vergennes and Calonne. In this way they held the ring and let the king and his ministers get on with governing. Initially the Polignacs may have regarded their sojourn at court as little more than a smash-and-grab raid; increasingly, though, they identified themselves with the interests they were paid to serve and, by the middle 1780s, had acquired a set of political views similar to the king's. Louis in turn, always a shy man who did not participate in the social life of the court, found it increasingly pleasant to relax in their company, forming, with a few servants, the audience of their amateur theatricals. They became his *société intime* as well as the queen's, and the only time he visited a private house in Paris it was that of Madame de Polignac.

* * *

Objectively, then, the queen's political position was weak; and she was aware of it, telling her brother, the Emperor Joseph II: 'I let the public think I have more influence [with the king] than I really have because otherwise I would have even less.'[38] But Véri believed the king feared her and she may have exploited the non-consummation of her marriage. Some of this comes over in another, desolating, confidence to her childhood friend: 'My tastes are not the same as the king's, who is only interested in hunting and the mechanical arts. You will agree that I would cut a poor figure in front of a forge; I would not play the part of Vulcan there and that of Venus would displease him much more than my tastes [for music and balls] of which he does not disapprove.'[39] The king probably did 'disapprove' of the queen's expenditure on balls. Certainly the intendant of *menus plaisirs* did, noting on 25 March 1775, 'I have been going over the accounts of the queen's balls. I am much grieved at the expenditure [for the month] which exceeds one hundred thousand *livres*, because of the quantity of gold embroidery which was used for the gowns and quadrilles'.[40] The only time, in these early years, that Marie-Antoinette showed any public emotion towards the king was during the coronation ceremony when she was seen to weep, but that was probably because she saw her husband bathed in the aura of majesty. Notwithstanding any or all of this, the king had a steely determination to keep his queen out of politics – both home and especially foreign affairs.

Unfortunately he did not make this sufficiently clear. Though he now had a ministry of his choosing if not exactly of his choice, one with which he was comfortable, far from giving them open support, he even 'set the example of showing contempt for his ministers'.[41] This may be explained by resentment at the way he had been manoeuvred over the recall of the *parlement*, by his natural *brusquerie* – courtiers called him 'the butcher' – his impenetrability or that

natural distrust of ministers and tendency to distance himself from their operations that he had inherited from his grandfather. Whatever its cause, Louis's
failure to make explicit his basic support for his ministers fed Maurepas's
neurosis and gave his enemies unwarranted hopes. It was in this unnecessarily
charged atmosphere that Turgot introduced his celebrated reform programme.

Louis XVI and Turgot

The appointment of Anne-Robert-Jacques Turgot to the finance ministry on
24 August 1774 and his dismissal on 12 May 1776 were regarded as turning
points in Louis's reign – both at the time and thereafter. Véri characterized the
period 1774–76 as 'les deux belles années de Louis XVI' – a sort of *quinquen-
nium Neronis*. Edgar Faure in 1961 wrote *La Disgrâce de Turgot* as a volume in a
series 'Thirty days which made France'; another in the series was the fall of the
Bastille and a third the fall of the monarchy on 10 August 1792. And yet when
one looks at what Turgot actually achieved – he deregulated the grain trade,
replaced the *corvée* (forced peasant labour on the royal highways) with a tax
payable by everyone but the clergy, and removed the monopoly of the craft
guilds – these seem exaggerated claims. But Turgot was important because, for
a while, he had the king's full backing, and because the measures he actually
introduced represented only the tip of the iceberg of his proposals. Indeed, there
is a direct link between the reforms he planned to introduce and the programme
that Calonne, with the full backing of his king, put before the Assembly of
Notables in 1787, thus launching France on her revolutionary path.

On a personal level, Louis opened himself up to no other minister in the
way he did to Turgot; he confessed to him that he could not cope with one-
to-one relationships, being 'more embarrassed dealing with one man than
fifty', and that he was well aware that people thought he was 'feeble'. Turgot in
turn gushed, 'the affecting kindness with which your majesty condescended to
press my hand between your own . . . will never be effaced from my memory'.
How does one explain this affinity? Turgot could be best described as a deist,
Louis a fairly conventional Catholic. But Turgot had attended theological
college, been tonsured and received into minor orders and a certain spiritual
aura remained with him. While at the Sorbonne he had encountered several
clerics who figure in our story: the abbé de Véri, Boisgelin, who became archbishop of Aix and would play a major part in defeating Louis's reform
programme of 1787, and Loménie de Brienne, who would try to pick up the
pieces. Turgot, still a bachelor when he was appointed to the ministry at forty-
seven, like Louis, was awkward with women; he had proposed in vain to the

woman who became the wife of the *philosophe* Helvétius and blushed whenever women were mentioned. Turgot, like Louis, became tongue-tied and preferred to express himself through memoranda. Both men were physically awkward, shy, gauche and unintentionally rude. Turgot had an encyclopaedic knowledge – he actually contributed five articles to the *Encyclopédie*; and though his forte was economics he was, like Louis, interested in geography and history – he had published a *Discours sur l'histoire universelle* – and, again like Louis, had translated passages from David Hume.

At the ideological level, we have noted Louis's initial doubts about appointing Turgot – 'he is very doctrinaire [*systématique*] and hand in glove with the Encyclopédistes'[42] – but we have also noted the two sides to Louis's political philosophy, captured by the phrase *dévot philosophe*. Indeed Soulavie, intending it as a criticism, claimed that 'in ... [Louis XVI's] reign philosophy was seated on the throne'. An exaggeration, perhaps, but if one strips Turgot's measures of ideological colouring they fall squarely within the reforming tradition of the administrative monarchy, as modernized and theorized in turn by Louis's mentor Moreau, whose links with Calonne we have examined.

In 1787 Calonne disinterred a memorandum written by Turgot's disciple, Pierre-Samuel Dupont, which envisaged a three-tier system of assemblies in those provinces which had not retained their local estates. These would assess a new land tax – the *subvention territoriale* – to replace the *vingtième*, which was marred by tax evasion on the part of powerful interests and regions. Some sources state that only the grain riots in the summer of 1775, derisively known as the 'Flour War', derailed Turgot's plan to introduce provincial assemblies. But the truth seems to lie in a remark Turgot made to his friend Véri. He explained that he had not introduced provincial assemblies because they would diminish the king's authority, adding, 'as a citizen I would have been very happy to; but acting as a minister of the king I made a scruple of abusing his confidence to diminish the extent of his authority. I intended to do it but I wanted to wait until the king was older and had more experience and maturity so that he could judge for himself and not through the eyes of another.'[43]

In 1788 a version of the Dupont–Turgot memorandum came into Louis's hands and he made extensive marginal comments on it. Turgot promised that 'at the end of a few years Your Majesty would have a new people and the first people' in Europe. Louis mused with prophetic cynicism:

Indeed! a new France regenerated and assembled in no time at all. But whilst it is coming into being the old France – that is to say the great men of the kingdom, the *parlements*, the assemblies of the *pays d'états* ... [and the old municipal officers] will continue to hold their own parallel assemblies and will perhaps revolt, asking to know what crimes they had committed to justify their forfeiture.[44]

So the big question is: how fast did Turgot plan to proceed? He distinguished between the desirable and the possible. An ambivalent passage in a memorandum he sent the king runs, 'One of the greatest benefits Your Majesty could give to his peoples would be to convert the *gabelle* [the obligation to buy a fixed quantity of salt, often at an exorbitant price] into another less vexatory form of tax [i.e., commutation into a money payment] but the clergy which pays the tax on the salt it consumes will resist paying the same sum if it is asked for it directly.' So should they be asked?

Turgot exhibited a similar caution in dealing with tax farming. The product of the indirect taxes was sold to the general farm, a syndicate of tax farmers on a six-yearly contract. One of Turgot's successors, d'Ormesson, planned to abolish tax farming, but Turgot limited himself to phasing out the abuse known as 'croupes'. The coveted position of farmer-general, of which there were sixty, was often secured by favour, which was returned by being given a cut or 'croupe' of the farmer's profit, expressed as a fraction of one of the sixty shares or a pension drawn on one. The list of *croupiers*, derived from Terray's own list, reads like a roll call of the great and corrupt of the ancien régime. It is headed by Louis XV himself, whose whole share, or four quarters, passed to Louis XVI, who gave it to his *valet de chambre*. No, an embarrassed king annotated Turgot's memorandum, 'I only disposed of two quarters'. Louis XV's daughters, Adélaïde, Victoire and Sophie, had pensions of sixty *livres* a piece, whilst Louise, a Carmelite prioress, secured pensions for her 'protégés'. 'Mme Giambone, the wife of a banker who [the wife] had been in the Parc aux Cerfs', had an eighth share, while 'Mme de Caveynac, formerly Mlle de Romans, mistress of Louis XV' had a third share. 'The family of Pompadour' enjoyed a pension of 12,000 *livres*, whilst the 'intendant of Mme du Barry' had 120,000 *livres*. Louis XV's ministers didn't do too badly either. A lieutenant-general had a pension of 3,000 *livres*, his only qualification being that he was 'a friend of the duc d'Aiguillon', whilst d'Aiguillon's son-in-law had a quarter share. Two separate quarter shares went 'to the family of the controller-general [Terray]', whilst his 'notary' had an eighth share. Finally a 'pension of three thousand *livres* went to Mme d'Amerval, daughter of the abbé Terray'. In addition there were shares or pensions for Provence's wife, the *premier commis* of the marine and foreign affairs departments, the banker Magon de la Balue, the wife of another banker, Le Normand, the family of Sénac de Meilhan, the high-flying intendant of Provence, the great chemist and future farmer-general Lavoisier, who would be guillotined in a batch with the other farmers-general, and finally the wife of Hérault de Séchelles, the sybarite attorney-general in the *parlement* and framer of the Jacobin constitution of 1793, guillotined along with Danton in 1794.

Turgot's objection to the *croupes* was twofold: it meant that farmers-general secured their position through favour, not merit or financial stability, and also that the financial position itself of such farmers was weakened by having to pay out to a host of parasites. The farmers-general played a key role in financing the state: though they made huge profits they advanced money to the always needy royal treasury against future receipts (*anticipations*). So Turgot moved cautiously: existing *croupes* would be honoured but no new ones would be allowed. In addition, the government would vet the suitability of future farmers-general. Even so there was resentment from potential *croupiers* and the farmers themselves, whom Turgot was trying to help.[45]

At this time there appeared a pamphlet entitled *Inconvénients des droits féodaux*, written by Turgot's secretary, Boncerf. It was Turgot's practice to 'fly a kite' by patronizing works relating to impending legislation, but when the pamphlet was denounced in the *parlement* Turgot had it withdrawn, as he had Condorcet's pamphlet on the *corvée*.[46] If, however, Turgot had gone ahead, he would have had Louis's full backing, for, as Turgot's associate Dupont said, 'the king desired the suppression of feudal rights'. Dupont was using the term 'feudal rights' loosely, as we do, implying that the *seigneur* had some ownership over his peasants, caricatured by the mythical *droit de seigneur* or right to a serf's maidenhead on her wedding night, as featured in Beaumarchais's *Barber of Seville* in which, despite Louis's misgivings, Marie-Antoinette played the role of Rosine before a select audience at Versailles in 1785. Such rights really amounted to *servitude personnelle* or serfdom. Louis was to abolish this on his crown lands in 1779, together with *mainmorte*, which prevented the serf from transmitting his land to any but his children. Louis hoped that his example would inspire other landowners to follow suit, but few did, though, ironically, one of these was Barentin, the reactionary keeper of the seals at the time of the fall of the Bastille.[47] 'Feudal rights', however, which properly were the equivalent of rent were a different matter, and Louis, as we shall see in 1789, had reservations about abolishing these.

Turgot's plans to introduce the new land tax, the *subvention territoriale*, however, must have been far advanced, because there is a document in the papers of Henri d'Ormesson, who administered the *vingtièmes*, entitled 'Memoranda and draft edict on the establishment of a *subvention territoriale* drawn up in 1775 by M. d'Ormesson at the request of M. Turgot'. All that is missing is the preamble, because Turgot liked to draft his own to explain his measures to the public.[48] This project also could have been derailed by the Flour War.

So we are left to consider the measures which Turgot actually introduced: deregulation of the grain trade and its aftermath, the Flour War, and the six edicts registered in the *parlement* by *lit de justice* on 12 March 1776.

The Flour War

Whether or not you were a Physiocrat – and Turgot sympathized with some of their views – all sides were agreed about the primacy of agriculture in general and grain in particular, which in France was the staple diet of some 26 million out of a population of about 28 million. The question was whether the grain trade should be treated as a matter of economic or of social policy. Do you aim to increase the yield and value of the crop, in which case free trade, including freedom to export – the 'laissez-faire, laissez-passer' of the Physiocrats – would seem to be appropriate? Or is your principal objective to prevent the people from starving or rioting, in which case you subordinate market forces to regulation? We have seen that, through Moreau, Louis had imbibed ideas that bore a kinship with those of the Physiocrats.[49]

Physiocracy, literally 'rule of nature', implied free trade, especially of agricultural produce, which Physiocrats regarded as the basis of all wealth – commerce and industry being derivative of it.[50] Accordingly, in September 1774, within a fortnight of becoming controller-general, Turgot abolished the elaborate regulations that governed the grain trade in France. These reflected the traditional view of the kings of France that the grain trade was rather a matter of policing than of economics. The farmer had not been allowed to sell his grain directly from his granary but was obliged to sell it all openly at market, where he had to serve private individuals before grain merchants and bakers. If he failed to sell his crop at three successive markets, he had to take whatever price he could get. Limited free trade in grain had been introduced by legislation passed in 1763–64, which had been supported by Louis's father, the dauphin, but Terray had re-imposed state controls and his contract to stock the markets had led to the allegations of a *pacte de famine*, a play on the *pacte de famille*, the family alliance with Bourbon Spain. The new king had set up a commission of inquiry to investigate the allegations that he personally profited from the *pacte* and, though this allayed his fears, it was discovered that two of the merchants working with Terray were siphoning off funds for extraneous speculations. Louis was sufficiently shaken to be receptive to Turgot's proposals.[51]

Unfortunately, free trade in grain was only workable in eighteenth-century France when the harvests were bountiful, as they had been in the 1760s, because until the completion of the *départemental* railway network in the 1870s, there were insuperable distribution problems and a national market could not therefore exist. The peasantry had an almost superstitious dread of allowing grain to leave their district, even if they had a glut, and the grain was being sent to an area where there was a dearth. The harvest of 1774 was poor, the price of bread almost doubled and in April–May 1775 the king had to face riots. These, known as the Flour War, were more serious than any for half a century, causing Louis temporarily to lose control of the Île-de-France and four adjacent provinces. The contemptuous phrase, *guerre de farines*, implies that the riots were a storm in a teacup and the police minister for one thought that Louis and Turgot had overreacted, but the episode offers in some ways a microcosm of Louis's reign.

The first serious trouble occurred at Dijon on 12 April, where the house of a judge in the local *parlement* was pillaged by rioters, including peasants and vagabonds. Turgot instructed the military commandant to take decisive action and Louis added, 'I have read this letter and approve its contents: I want my people to be happy but by the same token I am angered when they are carried away to totally irrational excesses.'[52] The rioters reached Versailles on the morning of 2 May. Most of the ministers were in Paris, where they usually had their main offices, maintaining a smaller establishment at Versailles, to which they returned for meetings of the council. A similar situation obtained in the days leading up to the storming of the Bastille on 14 July 1789, and it is interesting to compare the king's response in these two rare situations when he was without ministerial advice. There was, however, an important difference. When Turgot liberated the grain trade in 1774, he made an exception of Paris which then, as now, was heavily 'policed' in the French acceptance of the term. So, whereas in 1789 the Parisians stormed the Bastille, in 1775 they were mere spectators as bands from the surrounding countryside pillaged the markets and bakeries. 'They barred their doors, but leaned out of their windows to watch the riot going by as it if had been a procession', but did not fraternize with the rioters.[53] Another difference was that in 1789 the king was demoralized and he was not sure he was right; but in 1775 he had no doubts: 'We have a clear conscience on our side,' he told Turgot, 'and with that we are invincible.'[54] Arguably, though, there was a better case for using force in 1789 than in 1775, for Louis and Turgot's belief that the Flour War was driven by conspiracy rather than hunger was, as we shall see, completely wrong.

So, wearing the armour of righteousness, and in the absence of Turgot and of Maurepas, who was in Paris at the opera, Louis took control of the situation, giving detailed orders to the troops. He describes his actions in a series of letters to Turgot, the first of which is dated 2 May at 11 a.m.:

> I have just received your letter ... Versailles is under attack and it is the same men from Saint-Germain; I am going to liaise with ... [the war minister and the colonel of the Swiss Guard] to see what is to be done. You may count on my firmness. I have just sent troops to guard the market. I am pleased with the precautions you have taken for Paris: that was my main concern. You may tell M. Berthier[55] that I am satisfied with his conduct. You would do well to arrest the people you mention, but when you have them remember: no haste and lots of questions. I have just given orders here concerning the markets and mills in the surrounding area.[56]

In this, his first crisis, as he and Turgot plan operations by courier across the twelve miles separating Versailles from the capital, Louis recalls the heavy emphasis which his education had placed on the need for firmness. A second letter to Turgot, written at two that afternoon, displays another aspect of his education. Unlike the peripatetic kings, his forebears, Louis had seen nothing of France beyond the royal châteaux ringing Versailles, but his love of geography enabled him to see the whole country vividly in his imagination and make the necessary military dispositions:

> I have just seen ... [the intendant of Paris]; I am very satisfied with all the arrangements he has made for Paris and the Lower Seine; he had reported to me on what happened at Gonesse and on the support he has given the large farmers and grain merchants to keep trade open. I have ordered the Noailles Company[57] at Beauvais to concert action with him if he needs help; he has just left for Mantes where he will find the light cavalry and gendarmes at Meulan, with orders to liaise with him. He will find additional infantry in these two towns. The musketeers have orders to stand ready at Paris in case you have need of them: the Black [musketeers] in the Faubourg Saint-Antoine can send detachments along the Marne and the Grey [musketeers] in the Faubourg Saint-Germain along the Lower Seine. M. l'Intendant told me that he had no fears for the Upper Seine and the Marne where grain is not sent; all the same, we will guard them. The colonel-general [cavalry regiment] will proceed to Montereau and Melun and the Lorraine [regiment of dragoons] to Meaux. ... I have stationed troops along the road to Chartres and for the mills along the Orsay and Chevreuse valleys, with special precautions for the markets at Neauple and

Rambouillet. I hope that all communications will be kept open and that trade will not be interrupted.

It was a vast military operation, with some 25,000 troops deployed. But there were mistakes. Louis informed Turgot of a 'stupid manoeuvre' on the part of the governor of the town and château of Versailles, which was to let the rioters buy bread at two sous for a pound loaf, 'on the grounds that there was no middle way between letting them have it at this price and forcing them to buy it at its real value [eight sous] at the point of the bayonet'. His letter explicitly refutes the claim made in some memoirs that Louis harangued a crowd of 8,000 from the balcony of Versailles and ordered bread to be sold at two sous, and that Turgot had to rush over from Paris to get him to withdraw the concession. One source even claims that the military household refused to serve and that the captain of the bodyguard advised the king to flee secretly to Choisy or Fontainebleau.[58] In fact Louis told Turgot: 'you would be well advised to tell . . . [the duc de Biron, colonel of the French Guards] to give explicit orders to all the troops to prevent grain and bread being sold at a discount'.[59]

When the rioters reached Paris next day, Biron was closeted with Maurepas at 9 a.m. A ceremony to bless the colours of his regiment at Notre-Dame was scheduled and, despite Maurepas's pleas, he insisted on going ahead with it before dealing with the rioters. The ceremony was just a pretext: the general position of Biron, who remained in his post until his death in 1788, was that he would not take politically sensitive measures without both direct authorization from the king and a knowledge of the king's personal view of a situation;[60] and the king was at Versailles.

Nevertheless, Véri blamed Maurepas: 'You should have ordered him in the name of the king, and taken the event on your head until the return of the courier you should have sent to obtain the king's orders.' Maurepas should have co-ordinated operations with the military chiefs and made himself 'the centre, as if he had been the king'. 'But,' Maurepas replied, 'the king had written to M. Turgot; M. Turgot had gone out to take his orders and we were expecting them at any moment. As soon as he returned at midday, I went to liaise with him but seeing him give orders to everyone I withdrew.' That Véri was alive to all the implications of the triangular relationship between king, de facto prime minister and finance minister is clear from his riposte:

Eh bien . . . [Turgot] was possibly wrong to have played the role you should have played yourself – a role in which he was blamed but you would have been praised. The urgency of the matter required you to take overall control before he returned from Versailles since there was no central command and if M. Turgot had seen you playing the role appropriate to your position, he would not have assumed a role inappropriate to his.[61]

Turgot was himself aware of the invidious position in which he found himself. He later told the king that 'the kind of de facto preponderance I necessarily assumed because it was I who was being attacked deeply wounded . . . [Maurepas]. . . . From that moment it was put about that I wanted to run all the ministries and become prime minister.'[62]

Even when Biron at last deployed his troops, they had orders not to intervene unless there was danger to life. And Lenoir, the lieutenant-general of police, guarded only the central market, Les Halles. Paris was out of control. During the night the king convened a crisis meeting of the council. Lenoir was dismissed in a letter delivered by La Vrillière. Turgot wrote him a long letter at seven a.m. in which he did not hide the fact that he had asked the king to dismiss him. He could not risk another day of looting, which could jeopardize 'the repose and happiness of the king and his subjects for the rest of his reign'. Lenoir's peaceable disposition did not match the current situation, though the king had indicated he would soon find him other employment.[63] Maurepas, who was furious that Turgot should have intervened with the king saw to this.

Somewhat surprisingly, Louis was 'satisfied' with Biron's performance 'in pacifying the riots in Paris and its environs, without violence and solely by the wise measures you took and your . . . firmness in execution'. 'In his capacity of marshal of France', the king made him 'commander-in-chief [of all 25,000 troops] in Paris and its environs' – like Broglie in July 1789. But, unlike Broglie, he was given precise orders to put down the riot at all costs.

Once the king and Turgot had taken control, the Flour War was put down firmly, even brutally. There was a massive concentration of troops; they fired on the crowd and the rebels were cleared from the markets and towns. In all, 162 men were arrested. La Vrillière sent thirty men to the Bastille by *lettre de cachet*; they included a wide cross-section of society: a senior judge, a mayor, a postmaster, notaries, clerics, a retired professor of philosophy, etc. Hattot, an apprentice wig maker, was arrested for 'having spoken about a pretended plot to assassinate the king', and Jolivet, 'the queen's music seller for having told the *lieutenant de police* that the king ought to be assassinated'. Rouen's town trumpeter was arrested for peddling a bogus decree saying that bread was to be sold at two sous the pound loaf.[64] The rest were sent before a special military tribunal without appeal.[65] Even so, La Vrillière reproached the head of this tribunal with being dilatory. The judges wept when they condemned two men to death. The two, a wig maker and a gas worker, were hanged from an eighteen-foot-high gallows in Paris, as an example.

In the normal course of events the *Tournelle*, the criminal chamber of the *parlement*, would have dealt with the suspects. Louis, however, distrusted the *parlement* and thought the prince de Conti, a prince of the blood who patronized the *parlement*'s theorist Le Paige, was behind the riots. So, on 2 May, as the rioters were swirling around Versailles, he sent a letter to its *premier président* telling the *parlement* not to get involved since he was himself taking personal control.[66] The *parlement*, however, ignored his message and not only claimed jurisdiction for the *Tournelle* but issued a decree urging the king to reduce the price of bread 'to a level appropriate to the people's pockets'. Turgot woke Louis in the middle of the night of 4/5 May with the news, and Louis ordered the printer's blocks to be broken before the *parlement*'s decree could be placarded on the walls of Paris. Then he summoned the *parlement* to Versailles on the 5th. He treated them well, giving them the mid-afternoon *dîner* – the main meal of the day for the upper classes. Then he addressed them at the *lit de justice* and 'though ... [he] did not have an agreeable and sonorous voice, he deployed a tone of nobility and firmness which made up for this defect. He did not give the impression of being angry with the *parlement* but rather affected by the crushing news he was hearing'.[67] He told them that in the circumstances the normal judicial procedures were not appropriate. The king had also intended to strike the offending decree out of the *parlement*'s records but changed his mind at the last minute. As in 1774, he had memorized his speech but this time he forgot his lines, though, as he told Turgot, he managed to extemporize. Although the *parlementaires* were mortified they were also, Louis thought, somewhat subdued, which he put down to Conti's getting cold feet.[68]

Louis's letters to Turgot reveal a young man who felt compelled to prove himself. On 2 May he had needed to tell the minister 'you may count on my firmness' and on the 6th he opened himself up to Turgot, giving a rare glimpse of what he was feeling: 'Sometimes good can come out of evil and people will have seen from all this that I am not as feeble as they supposed and that I will know how to carry through what I have resolved to do. This knowledge will make it easier for you to do what has to be done. The truth is that I am more embarrassed dealing with one man than fifty'.[69] Very few of Louis's letters to his ministers have survived but it is unlikely that he ever opened himself up to this extent again.

When it was all over Louis wrote to Gustavus III of Sweden thanking him for sending grain to France:

The bad harvest and the wicked intentions of a few people whose manoeuvres had [sic] been uncovered led some scoundrels to come and pillage the markets. The peasants, led on by them and by the false report – sedulously circulated – that the price of bread had been lowered, joined them and they had the insolence to pillage the markets of Versailles and Paris, which forced me to order in troops who restored perfect order without difficulty. After the extreme displeasure I felt at seeing what the people had done, I had the consolation of seeing that as soon as they had been undeceived, they restored what they had taken and were truly sorry for what they had done.[70]

On 11 May Louis wrote to Turgot on a variety of topics. He excused him from attending the council on the 12th. He returned a fake decree ordering a reduction in the price of bread with the comment that it was clearly not written by a lawyer but came from the same stable as some of the others and that he wished they could have caught the pedlar. La Vrillière had just informed him of the two public hangings that evening but he 'wished they could have discovered the ringleaders of this odious machination' – we have seen that he suspected Conti. He concludes: 'I think that at the moment you should not hasten the arrival of [more] troops but without actually countermanding their orders and that we no longer need to guard every baker's shop though we should keep up the patrols on the streets.' Louis, having acted decisively was possibly coming round to Lenoir's view that he had been heavy-handed. Lenoir drew a telling contrast between Louis XV and Maupeou, who had carried out 'a major operation of state' without troops, and Louis XVI and Turgot, who blunted the impact of this ultimate deterrent by its massive deployment to quell a bread riot. And Louis admitted to Turgot, 'It is certainly true that at present we have too many troops in the environs of Paris but at first we couldn't know how things were going to turn out.'

There was also, as Véri said, the risk that 'troops in permanent garrison in capital cities would become Janissaries, Streltsy, or praetorian guards unless the military were restrained by the civil power and legal forms. The ministry is aware of the danger; so is the parlement. The decision has already be taken to end this general command.'[71] (What they did not envisage was that the guards would fraternize with the Parisians, as happened in 1789.) Biron would have liked to perpetuate his general command, but Louis told him that 'it would end after an agreed period', though it seems to have lasted until the autumn when Louis told him 'that he thought Paris was no longer agitated'. 'However', he continued, 'it is always necessary to keep the people under surveillance for

some time after there has been trouble, particularly when it had been occasioned by the price of bread'. And, knowing Biron's reluctance to take personal
responsibility, Louis made it plain that 'if circumstances require you to come
promptly to the aid [of the constituted authorities] and it is feared that my
orders will arrive too late, then . . . without waiting for them, I count on you to
deploy my regiment of guards wherever it may be needed and to repel force
by force'.[72]

The Flour War introduces us to the man who would prove to be Louis XVI's
nemesis: Jacques Necker. Necker, the son of a law professor of German extraction, teaching at Geneva, had come to Paris in 1748, aged sixteen, 'poor as Job',
and started as a humble bank clerk. He made a fortune out of privileged information, buying English stock just before the signing of the Peace of Paris in
1763. Fabulously rich and pushed by his wife, a literary social climber and
salon hostess, he now set his sights on entering the French government despite
two apparently insuperable handicaps: his Protestant religion and his total
ignorance of French institutions. Short, stocky, with an enormous up-turned,
self-satisfied face, Necker, with exquisite timing, brought out an attack on free
trade in corn – his *Mémoire sur les grains* – and just as the Flour War was
getting under way 'plonked it down outside my [Turgot's] door'.

This was how Turgot described the arrival of the weighty tome in a letter of
cold fury to its proud author. He continued: 'If I had occasion to write on this
topic and if I had felt the need to defend the opinion you have embraced, I
would at least have waited for a calmer period when the matter would only
have interested those in a position to judge without passion. But on this point
as on others each has his own way of thinking'. Privately, Turgot referred to
Necker as 'that joker' (*ce drôle-là*). Necker replied that his book had been
cleared by the censor on 12 March, when 'there was not the slightest scarcity of
grain anywhere'.[73] Necker was being disingenuous: he had produced his tome
precisely because it was topical. Moreover he was already in correspondence
with Maurepas and soon would be with the king.

The coronation

A month after the Flour War, the king was crowned. He and Turgot disagreed
on where the ceremony should take place, what vows the king should make
and how much the whole thing should cost, bearing in mind the expenses
incurred during the Flour War. Turgot wanted the king to be crowned in Paris
rather than Rheims, as was the custom. The tax farmers had promised 2 million
livres and the Paris merchants a further million in expectation of the trade the

event would generate for the capital. Turgot also wanted to drop the king's pledge to extirpate heretics. This had been inserted into the coronation service in the thirteenth century to deal with the Albigensian (Cathar) heresy, but was now seen as relating to Protestants.

Louis rejected Turgot's advice in a letter which is worth quoting for its rare delicacy of sentiment:

> I haven't summoned you to give you my reply to your letter of yesterday because I preferred to leave you a letter as a token of my way of thinking about you on this occasion. I think that the overture you made to me was that of a very honourable man who is entirely devoted to my service. I owe you the utmost gratitude and will always be grateful if you speak to me with the same frankness. I do not, however, at the present moment intend to follow your advice. I have thoroughly examined the matter subsequently. I have discussed it with several persons and I think there are fewer drawbacks in leaving things as they are. But I am none the less grateful for your opinion and you may rest assured that it will remain a secret as I trust this letter will so remain.[74]

The 'person' who persuaded Louis to maintain the oath to root out heresy was Maurepas; he was still smarting from Turgot's leading role in the Flour War and boasted to clerics that he had defended Holy Church against such atheists as Turgot and Malesherbes. And Louis was being slightly disingenuous in explaining why he had communicated by letter. Fearing that, in a tête-à-tête, Turgot would win him round, he sent his letter from Rheims, Turgot having remained at Versailles to run the government whilst Maurepas relaxed on his estate at Pontchartrain. Nevertheless, Louis heeded Turgot's advice more than he admitted. When he was asked to swear to crack down on heretics and duelling – an obsession with seventeenth-century kings – he simply mumbled the French equivalent of 'rhubarb, rhubarb'. And though he insisted on being crowned at Rheims (the only king of France to have been crowned at Paris was Henry VI of England), he told La Vrillière that though they couldn't compensate everyone fully for the 'pillaging of grains', 'all this will cost a lot' and that 'they must if possible cut down on the expenditure for my coronation'. Celebrations in Paris for the coronation, the marriage of his sister Clothilde and the childbirth of the comtesse d'Artois would be cancelled.[75]

The day before the crowning ceremony, Louis attended vespers conducted by Boisgelin, archbishop of Aix. This singularly unattractive man was even now playing both sides against the middle. A craven courtier avid for honours, he still felt it necessary officiously to tell the king to reduce taxation and remind him that he was beneath the law.

The coronation ceremony itself was spectacular. The king entered through the great west door of Rheims's gothic cathedral, with its maroon peeling paint and furniture of medieval iron work. He was greeted by the cardinal-archbishop of Rheims who escorted him down the nave to thunderous applause. He was wearing high-heeled red boots, a violet cloak strewn with fleurs-de-lys, and underneath that a satin dalmatic on top of a satin camisole – all this in stifling heat. Then a perspiring king knelt before the cardinal to be invested with the gold sword of Charlemagne and a golden sceptre that was nearly six foot long. He was anointed with the oil from the Holy Ampulla, which was believed to have been used at the baptism of the first king of France, Clovis, on Christmas Day 496 and to miraculously replenish itself. When, finally, the crown of Charlemagne was placed on his head, Louis is said to have remarked, 'it hurts me'.

After the ceremony, the king touched 2,400 people for scrofula, making the sign of the cross on their scabby faces. Four were cured. Louis XV had not touched for 'the king's evil' because he was denied the sacraments. Louis XVI resumed the practice but it was not mentioned in any of the official organs, being considered an obsolete superstition.

Turgot's six edicts

The celebrated 'six edicts' sent before the *parlement* in February 1776 were Turgot's swansong, narrow in scope but wide in implication. The most important was the commutation of the *corvée* into a money tax. The *corvée*, which had been introduced circa 1730 by simple executive decrees not registered in the *parlement*, required non-noble country dwellers to provide their 'arms or horses' for several days a year to make the superb network of roads France still enjoys. Nobles, clerics and town dwellers were exempt. They would not, however, have been exempt from the new tax that would replace the *corvée*. Another measure was the abolition of the craft guilds, which Turgot considered to be monopolies in restraint of trade. The other four edicts, relating to the grain trade, were less controversial.

The commutation of the *corvée*, however, symbolized a further incursion into noble privileges. True, the nobility were already subject to the *vingtième*, but that had from its inception been a universal tax: the labour on the roads had only ever been performed by those subject to the *taille* (the poll tax paid by the peasantry, the staple tax of the monarchy since the Middle Ages). So the nobility felt degraded by the association, hurt in their pride as well as in their pockets. And the clergy, who had got out of paying the *vingtième*, were also to pay the new tax. Similarly, the abolition of the guilds struck at the heart of the corporate organization of the ancien régime, that is, a system in which the government has dealings not with individuals but with 'corps' such as a guild, a municipality, a village or a province.

The commutation of the *corvée* confronted Louis with a moral dilemma, as it had for his father the dauphin, and one which was to become more acute as his reign progressed. On the one hand Louis's father believed that the nobility should be preserved in their property and status; on the other he believed that fiscal privilege 'makes the whole burden fall on the poor people'. Louis attempted to square the circle on this occasion by telling the *parlement*: 'I have no intention of blurring the distinctions between the Estates nor of depriving the nobility of my kingdom of the distinctions it has acquired by its services . . . which I shall always maintain. It is not a question here of a humiliating tax but of a simple contribution which everyone should take a pride in sharing, since I am myself setting the example by contributing in virtue of my domains.' Miromesnil, the keeper of the seals, thought this argument was specious since the king's station was so far above everyone else's as to remove any taint by association.

Louis had asked Miromesnil for written comments on Turgot's proposals. He knew they would be hostile but was playing by the Bourbon rule book, which said that decisions should be arrived at adversarially; he also wanted to bind the justice minister into the decision, because he would be responsible for guiding the measures through the *parlement*.

Something more must be said about Armand Thomas Hue de Miromesnil, as he bulks large in our story. It will be remembered that he had spent fourteen years as *premier président* of the troublesome *parlement* of Rouen and had been rebuked by Louis XV for putting its interests before those of the crown. Many considered that he was of insufficient calibre for the job of keeper of the seals, which his friend Maurepas obtained for him. In particular they thought that Malesherbes should have been preferred (incidentally, his father, the chancellor, had started Miromesnil on his career), though Malesherbes himself wrote a memorandum 'demonstrating that the office of chancellor should neither be given to himself nor to any of his class'.[76] Such candidates would lack the necessary objectivity in dealing with the *parlement*, either fawning before it, as Miromesnil was to do, or biting the hand that had fed him, as Maupeou had.

Véri considered that Miromesnil, a short man, only five foot four inches, with mousy hair, 'possessed a bourgeois figure, not at all that of the head of the judiciary'. But Miromesnil, 'normand et rusé', was one of the subtlest players in the game, and whilst he may not have had Malesherbes's breadth of intellect, his political skills were of a higher order, as were his political apophthegms, such as 'Time is my first secretary' and 'Consider [this to a *premier président*] that when you seek to harm a minister of the king it is to the king that you render that minister harmful'.[77] Asked in 1775 whether he would be embarrassed by Malesherbes's presence in the ministry, Miromesnil replied that he would be only too delighted to give him the chance to demonstrate his incapacity for administration.

Miromesnil was dangerous not because he lacked ability but because he possessed it. His was one of the most disastrous appointments Louis ever made and he was the biggest single obstacle to reform; the architect of the 1774 settlement, he was ultimately destined to wreck it. His need to curry favour with *parlementaires* who despised him increased his natural tendency of complaisance towards them, first manifested when he 'conspired in the degradation of the *Grand Conseil*',[78] allowing the *parlement* to contest its status as the supreme appellate court. The *Grand Conseil* had formed the nucleus of the *parlement Maupeou* and, according to the provisions of the 1774 settlement, was automatically to assume the *parlement*'s functions if the latter resorted to a judicial strike. It was essential therefore to maintain the council's prestige as a threat and a resource.

In the spirit of adversarial decision-making, Louis invited Turgot to reply by annotating Miromesnil's objections to his measures. This he did, according to Véri, in more than 'twenty pages . . . as an historian, a politician and a philosopher'. These 'objections and replies', which have survived,[79] amount to an in-depth discussion of privilege within the ancien régime, which was to be the rock on which it would founder. Of Miromesnil's objections it has justly been observed that 'he brought out more than anyone else the full implications of Turgot's reforming work . . . in them Miromesnil appears as dry, meticulous and full of anxiety for the future'.[80]

Miromesnil does not argue that the nobility should be exempt from the *vingtième*, since that had been a tax on all orders from its inception in 1749. Nor, interestingly, does he claim exemption for those who have bought offices conferring nobility (such as those in the *parlement*); only the old military nobility should not have to pay – the *noblesse d'épée*; perhaps he was thinking of his father, an army captain, or recollecting that he had contemplated a military career himself. For his part, Turgot concedes that 'the nobility's exemption from the *taille*' should continue but 'as a fait accompli', not something 'just in itself'.

Miromesnil deploys his favourite trope, the 'thin end of the wedge' argument:

It will perhaps be objected that a modest tax, levied on nobles and roturiers in the same proportion as the *vingtième*, is not sufficient to destroy noble privilege. To which I reply that it is nevertheless a first breach which will be taken as a certain foretaste of a greater destruction of this privilege, especially when it is a question of replacing with this tax on the nobility work which was only done by those subject to the *taille*.

He then broadens his argument out to a general defence of the social order:

There are three orders in France, the clergy, the nobility and the third estate. Each order has its rights, its privileges, perhaps its prejudices, but ultimately it is necessary to preserve them as they are. To infringe them would be to risk weakening that feeling of solicitude and love which all the king's subjects have for him. That sentiment would necessarily be weakened if he seemed to be desirous of depriving any order of the rights and privileges which it has enjoyed from time immemorial.

'Enjoyed from time immemorial': that is the clue to the conservative position. Long continuance establishes legitimacy even if, as Miromesnil readily concedes, it is based on 'prejudice'. It is answered by the reformers, who say, with Calonne, 'time only seems to hallow', or with Turgot, when he calls noble privileges 'superannuated pretensions'. This phrase comes in a passage which totally rejects Miromesnil's position:

The keeper of the seals seems here to be adopting the principle that according to the constitution of the state the nobility should be exempt from all taxation. He even seems to believe that it is a universal assumption which it would be dangerous to oppose. If this assumption is universal I must have been strangely deceived during my whole life as to what all well-informed men think because I cannot recall any society where this idea has been regarded as anything but a superannuated pretension and one abandoned by all enlightened men even in the order of the nobility. On the contrary, this notion must seem paradoxical to the greater part of the nation whose interests are grievously harmed by it and we no longer live at a time when their voice can be ignored.

Never have the origins of the French Revolution been put more succinctly.

Louis was given these observations as he was going in for supper on Sunday, 4 February; he read them through the night and had absorbed them by 10 a.m.

when Maurepas entered his cabinet. The king's time was not wasted, for here, presented cogently by two adversaries of exceptional intelligence, was all he needed to know about the central issue of home policy confronting him. The actual issue – the commutation of the *corvée* – was relatively minor, at least in money terms, but from that sliver of DNA it was possible to recover the entire body of arguments for reform and for conservatism.

Realizing its symbolic importance, Maurepas told the king: 'You personally are at stake here and consequently the outcome of the rest of your reign. Therefore it is your volition which must be displayed and not that of your ministers. Now in order to display it you must have it in the first place. Make yourself a master of every side of the question, make the decision truly your own and that will be all we need to deploy.'

The 'decision' was whether to enforce the registration of the edicts by a *lit de justice*. However embroidered his language, Maurepas is passing the buck to the king. Turgot told the king that 'he had seen M. de Maurepas change his mind ten times on whether to advise a *lit de justice*, depending on whether he had seen ... [Miromesnil], M. Albert or myself'. Albert was Lenoir's replacement as lieutenant-general of police, and by consulting him Maurepas underlined his belief that the *parlement* was capable of instigating riots. Malesherbes had no doubt that Miromesnil had 'hidden contacts among the *parlementaires* to undermine Turgot's operations' by informing the *parlement* 'with a hundred turns of phrase' of divisions within the ministry. He couldn't furnish 'legal proof' except to 'men within the legal fraternity' who know how to 'convey a message of what was required ... whilst preserving deniability'. Maurepas 'could have detected this if he had wanted to'. But 'the king had neither the experience nor the natural talent to discern such manoeuvres'.[81]

So Turgot sought to open Louis's eyes by warning him of 'the dangers from the *parlements* and all the cabals encouraged by the little tricks of ... [Miromesnil] and others'. 'When Louis XV was forty', Turgot warned, 'he still possessed the plenitude of his authority: ... no organization had chanced its arm. And you, Sire, are twenty-two and the *parlements* are already more animated, more audacious, more allied to court cabals than they were in 1770 after twenty years of successful encroachments.'

Miromesnil and Turgot were each full of anxiety for the king's future should his rival's policy be followed. The same scene would be played out eleven years later when Calonne tried to implement Turgot's full programme. On that occasion Miromesnil warned the king that he 'foresaw alarming consequences for your happiness and the rest of your reign' if he supported Calonne. Notice how both Miromesnil and Maurepas use the phrase 'rest of your reign', as if a single act could have endless repercussions. These were all men of integrity. Calonne said he would have been happy to sacrifice his place if that price was necessary for the success of his programme; Turgot said much the same. Miromesnil offered to act at Louis's counsel at his trial: if his offer had been accepted, as Malesherbes's was, it would have amounted to a death sentence. What was a twenty-one-year-old king, who was supposed to act on ministerial advice, to do?

Turgot's advice, which he proffered in the first of the many memoranda with which he plied the king, was that financial privilege, be it that of an order in society or that of a region, must be eliminated both as a matter of justice and to improve the country's financial position, which was too weak to support the war with England that threatened. But it was a circular dilemma: the king had to make himself financially strong through economies that challenged vested interests in order to have a chance of tackling other vested interests. Turgot hoped to achieve this primarily by buying out the court officials who had purchased their positions; for this purpose he was negotiating a loan from the Dutch at the comparatively reasonable rate of 4 per cent.

Miromesnil was no fool and realized all the implications of the Turgot–Malesherbes ticket, the direction in which they were travelling if not the speed. In 1782, whilst still denying that he had plotted with the *parlementaires* to bring Turgot down, he conceded, 'Yes I opposed him because our ideas differed. ... The privileges of the nobility and clergy are unjust in origin: agreed. The privileges of certain towns and corporations are in the same category. Agreed again. *Eh bien!* I believe we must respect them because they are linked to all the rest.'[82] In this classic statement of the conservative position, Miromesnil perceives that from Turgot's modest proposals to the destruction of the whole social order is but a short step. Reformist agendas had been circulating in the bureaux of the finance ministry for decades: abolition of internal customs barriers and tax farming; the *cadastre*, or Domesday survey of all landed wealth; and, more recently, the provincial assemblies. Miromesnil, who was well aware of the imperfections of the regime, was feeling his way towards what de Tocqueville would posit in his great general thesis: that the point of maximum danger to a repressive regime is when it starts to reform itself – a truth that is as axiomatic as a law of physics. If Turgot and Miromesnil were both right then the king was, to use Maupeou's word, well and truly 'f----d'.

Meanwhile Louis had to decide what to do about Turgot's six edicts. It was a big decision – with everyone telling him that the rest of his reign depended on it – and Maurepas insisted no one could make it for him. So he had the edicts read out a final time in a cabinet committee that evening. Excusing himself for making them go over it all again, he told the assembled ministers, 'I want to be able to reassure myself that I have arrived at my decision after due reflection and in the light of my inner conviction'. Thus fortified, Louis then took personal charge of sending the edicts through the *parlement*, adopting a tougher procedure: instead of circulating paper copies privately among leading *parlementaires* for discussion (the usual practice), he presented the edicts straight away in their final form on parchment.[83] And he further decided that 'after allowing a reasonable time for remonstrances' he would register the edicts by *lit de justice*, which he did a week later on 12 March.

The fall of Turgot

Louis XVI dismissed Turgot on 12 May, two months to the day after the *lit de justice*. This long interval suggests that it was not the queen's personal hostility[84] nor Miromesnil's ideological objections, nor even *parlementaire* opposition that brought it about. The main political issue during this interval was Malesherbes's resignation and replacement at the *Maison du Roi*. Malesherbes had only accepted office on the understanding that he could raise the question of his resignation from time to time, nor did he find the taste of power addictive, which may partly explain why, when the time came, the king was as reluctant to let Malesherbes go as he had been to appoint him in the first place. Louis made it a rule never to see anyone who was about to leave the ministry, in order to avoid embarrassment, perhaps, or the effects of persuasion; for usually the king had dismissed a minister. Resignations were rare and Louis treated them as cases of 'ingratitude'. In either case, the royal response was the same, inaccessibility, and poor Malesherbes was reduced to drafting the following letter to the king:

> I communicated to M. de Maurepas my intention to resign two months ago, so that he might notify Your Majesty and have the time to reflect on the choice [of a successor] he would propose to you. Your Majesty knows that for the last two months I have not been able to talk to you alone. Your Majesty has only allowed me to have one *travail* with you when you gave me to understand that you would find it disagreeable if I mentioned the subject [of my resignation]. The same prohibition on Your Majesty's part has been reiterated since and I have been told that my retirement is to be deferred from Easter to Pentecost. It is this impossibility of speaking which has forced me to write. . . . What affects me most painfully is being forbidden to speak to Your Majesty in person. Allow me to observe that I do not believe

that this has ever happened to any of your ministers. If I am unworthy to be heard by Your Majesty about my retirement and the department with which I have been honoured, am I worthy to remain a single day in your council? Nothing is more humiliating for me than to be reduced to this silence and I do not think, Sire, that I have deserved these humiliations.[85]

When Malesherbes was finally allowed to go, he kept in touch with the king. He resumed his seat on the council in 1787, plying the king with insightful analyses of the unfolding political crisis; but when he wanted to cease attending council in 1788 he was confronted with exactly the same response from the king.

Maurepas proposed as Malesherbes's successor Jean Antoine Amelot de Chaillou, the undistinguished scion of a ministerial dynasty. Turgot disagreed with the choice and bombarded the king with a remarkable series of letters, one of which was transcribed by Véri. In it Turgot accused Amelot of being sold to Miromesnil, who in turn was sold to the *parlement*. Instead Turgot proposed Véri, both to supplement Maurepas's weakness and to implement his own memorandum on economic reform of the royal household. He accused the king of avoiding him 'to hide the fact that Your Majesty has decided to choose [Amelot]'. But Louis was avoiding Turgot because he was also about to dismiss him, the reasons being supplied by Véri:

The personal inclinations of the king, which M. de Maurepas has reinforced but not produced, were the real cause of this event. ... M. de Maurepas and M. de Malesherbes had sized up the young man better ... they had taken his silence not as evidence of conviction but of embarrassment. If one adds to this the tenacity of this minister in wanting the assistance of his equals for the goal he saw clearly ahead, the advice he gave the king when his colleagues opposed him, and his desire to have colleagues who were of his opinion [all classic hallmarks of a prime minister], it is easy to see that the young man was bound to feel importuned in the end; which made him say: 'M. Turgot wants to be me and I don't want him to be me.'[86]

If Maurepas, the preponderant minister, felt that Turgot was usurping his role, how much more would the king feel this? In the vacuum resulting from the king's inability to appoint or be his own prime minister, Turgot was instinctively driven to make claims which would have effectively made him one – hence Louis's remark: 'M. Turgot wants to be me.'

Turgot was aware of this when he reminded the king of 'the de facto preponderance that he naturally assumed' during the Flour War. Then 'it was bruited that I wanted to run all the departments and become prime minister'. 'Thousands of people' told Maurepas that Turgot wanted to supplant him and 'he may sometimes have believed it'. And he would have had good cause because Turgot was seeking to 'run all the departments', telling the minister of war what he could spend, having to disclaim that he wanted to fix the size of the army, having himself proposed that minister, Saint-Germain, as a replacement for du Muy; and then the present controversy: seeking to place his man, Véri, at the *Maison du Roi* so he could reduce the pensions of courtiers, and rejecting Maurepas's candidate, Amelot. And Turgot agreed with Véri that if Maurepas had read the letter he sent the king he would have been justified in asking the king to dismiss him. For, as Véri told Turgot, he left the king with no options but to dismiss him or dismiss the rest of the ministry. So Turgot was effectively 'dismissing himself'. Turgot asked the king to keep his letters a secret, which technically he did but Louis told Maurepas, 'don't think that M. Turgot is a friend of yours for I have the proof to the contrary'.[87]

But Maurepas's conduct was not above reproach either. Turgot had prepared a budget estimate for 1776 which gave a deficit of 24 million *livres* on revenue of about 400 million. Maurepas showed this to Necker, with whom he was already in relations. Necker estimated the deficit at 37 million by allowing for a contingency fund. Maurepas then put it about that 'if he had kept the abbé Terray revenue would have matched expenditure'. 'That might be true', Turgot told the king, 'if the abbé Terray had slapped on twenty million of taxes or defaulted on twenty million of debt a year. I do hope for your sake, Sire, that M. de Maurepas has not communicated this way of thinking to Your Majesty'.[88]

This last was unfair of Turgot: of the three guidelines Turgot had set out at the start of his administration – no new taxes, no loans and no bankruptcy – no bankruptcy was the one Louis adhered to, with disastrous consequences, for the rest of his reign. Louis must have been annoyed by the tone as well as the content of Turgot's missives. For Turgot did not pull his punches: 'People think you are weak, Sire, and there have been occasions when I feared that your character had this defect. However in other, more delicate situations [e.g., the Flour War] I have seen you display true courage.' 'You have acknowledged', he continues, 'that you lack experience and that you have need of a guiding hand; but this guiding hand needs both intelligence and force of character'. Maurepas had the first but not the second quality and the role of Véri would be to keep Maurepas on course. Maurepas was ruled by his wife, 'a woman of infinitely less intelligence but infinitely more character', but Véri had influence over her. 'And so, Sire', Turgot continued, 'this is where you are: a weak and disunited ministry . . . the *parlements* in league with all the court cabals, emboldened by a notorious weakness in government . . . no ensemble, no fixed plans, no secrecy in the resolutions of your councils.'

Louis was also tired of Turgot's self-righteousness. As early as the summer of 1775, when Turgot was at the height of his power and 'believed the king was totally behind him', Louis had told Maurepas, 'You heard him [recommending a protégé] . . . it's only his friends who have merit and it's only his ideas which are any good'.[89] Turgot's intensity too must have embarrassed the king. 'Sire,' he wrote, 'there are people attached to their places for honours and profit. They can support the indifference with which Your Majesty has crushed me. A minister who loves his master needs to be loved in return. Well, Sire, . . . a sovereign also needs to be loved by those who serve him.' And again, 'when an honourable and sensitive soul finds as the only reward for his sacrifices cold indifference, it wilts and shrivels up'. Nor did the king need reminding 'that it was weakness that put Charles I's head on the block'!

Turgot wanted to resign, not to be dismissed. On 10 May he wrote to Véri: 'I won't need many days to put before the king the planned reform in his household. It will surely not be adopted and I will ask for my freedom.'[90] But that was not Louis's style. People didn't resign. Instead Louis adopted the stance he had with Malesherbes and all subsequent ministers in this situation: he simply refused to see them. On the 12th, Bertin, the secretary of state for agriculture, a ministerial survivor from the previous reign and an enemy of Turgot's, gave Turgot a *lettre de cachet* dismissing him and telling him to leave Versailles. He took up residence in Véri's town house – the abbé was visiting his benefice at Avignon – and then went off to the Midi himself. He departed, he told his host, 'without shame or remorse', which was more than could be said of Maurepas who 'by his weakness and courtier tricks had destroyed the best founded hopes for its happiness that a nation has ever conceived of a young king who wanted the best and whom your friend [Maurepas] delivered up to the flux and reflux of all the cabals'.[91]

How had it happened? Why had two honourable men who sincerely wanted the best for the country quarrelled? The root cause was that Louis distrusted his ministers. Neither of the protagonists, Miromesnil and Turgot, shared his conception of an absolute reforming monarchy. This is clearly so in the case of Miromesnil, who identified himself with the *parlement*'s obstinate defence of entrenched privilege, but, in his conscience-stricken way, it was no less true of Turgot, orthodox though the measures themselves were. The founding fathers of Physiocracy, Quesnay and the elder Mirabeau, had suppressed their *Treatise on Monarchy* because they had realized that the rule of nature was fundamentally incompatible with rule by an absolute monarch. Similarly, we have noted Turgot's recognition that provincial assemblies would 'diminish the king's authority'.

The conflict between a minister's sense of duty and his private inclinations was to be a powerful solvent of the regime. Louis must have seen the double irony of Turgot's observation, 'on a thousand occasions the interests . . . of your ministers are diametrically opposed to your own' in the context of Turgot's other observation that the *parlement*, whose recall Turgot had supported, was stronger in 1776 than before Maupeou's coup. As for Véri – whose lack of respect, let alone veneration, for the king comes across in his frequent use of the expression 'the young man' – he believed that France would be a republic within fifty years and he did not seem to mind, and yet Turgot seriously proposed to the king that he should be made a minister. His second choice was Boisgelin.[92]

Turgot's preferred successor would have been the *conseiller d'état* Bouvard de Fourqueux; of his other collaborators, d'Ormesson was too young and Dupont, the son of a watchmaker, too humble.[93] D'Ormesson became finance minister in 1783 and Fourqueux in 1787 with Dupont as his right-hand man. They, rather than his legislation, which was quickly reversed, would be Turgot's legacy, resuming his reforming work after the interruption of the American war.

CHAPTER FOUR

DRIFT TOWARDS WAR

1776–78

Louis XVI and Vergennes

THE MÉTIER OF A king of France was pre-eminently to conduct foreign policy. In a theoretically absolute monarchy internal politics was deemed not to exist – the foreign secretary, Vergennes, always apologizes to Louis for mentioning it – and *la politique* is translated as 'foreign policy'. Louis reckoned to understand foreign policy; unlike Louis XV, he read the intercepted correspondence between the foreign powers first before passing it on to Vergennes and he worked hard, though not as hard as Vergennes, who worked a twelve-hour day. Since, together with Miromesnil, Vergennes was Louis's longest-serving minister and one of only four to die in office, and since their correspondence was the most extensive of the king's to have survived, and almost certainly ever to have existed, it is worth making some remarks about the minister and his relationship with his king.

Charles Gravier, chevalier, then comte de Vergennes, was the second son of a councillor in a third-tier provincial tribunal,[1] whose father had been ennobled. His undistinguished birth raised obstacles, which his marriage had seemed to render insuperable, to his advancement to the higher reaches of the diplomatic service. As ambassador to Constantinople he had made what his colleague Castries called 'an indecent marriage to a woman of the people'[2] and had been recalled in disgrace by Choiseul in 1768, thereby creating an enmity between the two men which would endure until Choiseul's death in 1785 and was continued by his protégés, notably Breteuil and Castries. When, with the protection of Maupeou and at the insistence of the comte de Broglie, head of the *secret du roi*, Louis XV had recalled him from disgrace and appointed him to the prestigious Stockholm embassy, it was under protest: 'I disapprove of the choice of M. de Vergennes; it is you who are forcing me; but I forbid him to take his base wife [*vilaine femme*] with him.'[3] Marie-Antoinette was, in turn, to make difficulties about receiving Madame de Vergennes at court, though the lowliness of her birth was exaggerated: she was the daughter of minor Savoyard gentry and widow of an Istanbul doctor called Testa. Men are vulnerable through their wives.

Vergennes also had a numerous family to advance and none to support him. For Louis XVI, however, this very freedom from family alliances and from the socio-political assumptions of the high aristocracy, with whom Vergennes had to 'wage a continual battle',[4] made him attractive as a loyal servant of the crown. Louis let him promote his relatives, his cousin Le Clerc de Juigné becoming archbishop of Paris, while embassies and intendancies came the way of the family also. He scandalized the courtiers and his colleague, the finance minister d'Ormesson,[5] by obtaining the post of captain-colonel of the French Guards for his eldest son, a post to which the powerful Colbert family possessed the *survivance* or reversion. The king, however, distinguished between greed for office, which was understandable, and greed for money, which was not. As early as September 1775 Véri notes 'a few instances of petty greed for money', adding: 'The king has noticed them and the esteem which his work has won for him suffers from these peccadilloes. A man is always coloured by his beginnings.'[6] In 1783 this attitude would seriously damage him in the king's esteem (see below, pp. 188–9).

Relations between Louis XVI and his ministers were never easy and all who have left a record of their personal dealings with him – in particular Turgot, Maurepas, Malesherbes, Sartine, Castries and d'Ormesson – were constantly hurt. Vergennes was no exception and there were several occasions when even he, with such *consistance*, thought, however mistakenly, that he was in danger of losing the king's favour. In 1775 Vergennes and Turgot persuaded Louis to recall the queen's favourite, Guînes, from the London embassy on grounds of incompetence.[7] The king and Vergennes exchanged several letters that are characterized by nervous tension on both sides. Those of Vergennes in particular are punctuated with such expressions as 'It might seem that the minister was seeking to hide [from the queen] behind his master'.[8] The barely concealed hatred between Marie-Antoinette and Vergennes dates from this period. Vergennes was also on tenter-hooks in 1781 and 1785. In 1785 he tells Louis that rumours of a change in the ministry are damaging France's effectiveness abroad and in 1781 that similar rumours are undermining his ability to concentrate on his work:

Sire, when the heart is grievously afflicted, the mind cannot retain the freedom and activity necessary to sustain unremitting labour. My heart,

Sire, is a prey to profound melancholy. Various indications make me only too aware that Your Majesty's kindness towards me is no longer the same. I seek in vain to know what can have deprived me of it; I have nothing with which to reproach my conscience and I cannot imagine that Your Majesty accepts the sinister bias that the Choiseul faction is seeking to spread around.[9]

The neurasthenic quality of these letters is reminiscent of the similar relationship between Louis XIII and Richelieu (whose policies Vergennes sought to emulate) and raises the question whether it was a Bourbon characteristic to exploit the constructive tensions within a ministerial relationship.[10]

At the same time, Louis's letters to Vergennes can exhibit genuine kindness, solicitude for his health and even a desire to manage his susceptibilities, as when in May 1776, knowing Vergennes's paranoid fear of being supplanted by the ambassador to Vienna, Breteuil, Louis explains that a personal letter he has written to Breteuil contains nothing more sinister than the travel arrangements for Maria-Theresa's projected visit to Brussels. 'I tell you this', Louis concludes, 'to dissipate your fears (if you ever could have had any) and to demonstrate my confidence in you'.[11] Elsewhere, he shows gentle concern: 'Having worked so hard, it is right that you should rest and I gladly grant your request to be excused from seeing the ambassadors on Tuesday, whether I go hunting or not.' On 30 November 1784, Vergennes received one of the most unaffected letters Louis ever wrote: 'If you are not tired today and would like to come and talk to me this evening, come at half past six, if not tomorrow at the same hour'.[12] There is no standing on ceremony here, just the utter simplicity of a man enjoying his relations with a colleague. The king, alone at his desk, forgot ceremony, shyness and awkwardness – he even made a rough joke about 'Mme Potemkin' (Catherine the Great) being, at 'forty-five, a fine old age to be having a baby'. Once, on 5 January 1785, he does not bother to conceal from Vergennes that he had been unable to concentrate (this was possibly a foretaste of the bouts of depression that were from 1787 to afflict him): 'You did well to remind me of the courier; I had not forgotten it but for two days now I have not been in a fit state to apply myself.'[13]

Thus the two men quickly established a working pattern which was to last until Vergennes's death. Each would send the other the diplomatic despatches he had received first with comments. Vergennes would generally draft Louis's letters to foreign rulers, the king making modifications which he designated as either essential or optional. They would sometimes discuss the general situation by letter, but this was generally saved for their chats in the early evening.

Finally they would decide when to use the *Conseil d'État*, the supreme council for the elaboration of foreign policy, and what to show it and, during the American war, make arrangements for the war cabinet with the service ministers. From the growing understanding between these two men was born a successful foreign policy, a brilliant if insubstantial edifice, curious product of two sound rather than brilliant minds.

Vergennes's enemies at the time, and his recent biographer, have accused him of manipulating the king. He certainly flattered him. D'Ormesson, finance minister in 1783, who hated Vergennes, was only exaggerating when he wrote that Vergennes 'had persuaded the king that it was from the king himself that he had learned how to run the foreign office' and 'enthused about the superior intelligence of His Majesty which had alone provided him with the shaft of light to solve the problem whose solution he had been seeking for so long'. And Vergennes does actually use the phrase 'as Your Majesty has observed in such a *superior* way'.[14] But even Vergennes saw the dangers of over-egging the pudding. One of Louis's unofficial correspondents praised Vergennes so extravagantly that the minister, who received copies of the letters, told him to back off.[15] In 1784 there was a cringe-making moment when a despatch from the ambassador to London, obviously inspired by Vergennes, who had got him the job, said that the English court was worried that Vergennes had lost credit. Its reading in the council was followed by embarrassed silence all round.[16]

The main point, however, is not whether Vergennes employed flattery – all courtiers did (Castries, who was downright rude to the king, is an exception) – but whether Vergennes used this instrument to shape the king's policy. To do this effectively it would be necessary to persuade the king that he had reached a particular decision himself. Vergennes had watched, and watched in horror, as Maurepas had achieved this feat in persuading Louis that the recall of the *parlement* was his own doing, even though it 'violated the principles of his education'. Did Vergennes learn from this? D'Ormesson, who watched him at work, indicates that he may have done: 'M. de Vergennes prepared his reports for the king in such a manner that, having indicated several times in the course of his report, the nub of the decision, he concluded by posing the most simple and straightforward question as one that presented major doubts which could only be resolved by the superior intelligence of the king'.[17] Again this may be an exaggeration but it has to be said that the interminable, somnolent memoranda which Vergennes sent Louis to persuade him to enter the American War of Independence on the side of the colonists contain an element of flattery. Frederick the Great dubbed these productions 'the narcotics of Versailles'.

One source, however, the Swedish ambassador, Necker's son-in-law, suggests the opposite: that Vergennes, like all true courtiers, tried to anticipate the king's opinion and that on one occasion Louis had to trick him into revealing his opinion before showing his own hand.[18] Maybe the two men just bounced ideas off each other. When Vergennes says 'as Your Majesty has so superiorly observed', it doesn't necessarily mean that it was Vergennes's idea. And similarly, Louis's best analysis of the impact of the American war on English politics – something he knew more about than did Vergennes – begins with 'I am absolutely of your opinion . . .' or 'as you put it so well' – reverse flattery of which Louis, normally ungracious, was on occasion capable.[19]

The international situation

The bridge between the foreign policy of Louis XV and that of his grandson was Louis XV's personal diplomacy, *le secret du roi*. On 9 June 1774, the head of the *secret*, the comte de Broglie, wrote to the new king to explain its purpose:

> It consisted in preserving in Europe the equilibrium established by the Treaties of Westphalia [which in 1648 established the diplomatic framework of Europe for the next 150 years]; in protecting the liberties of the Germanic Federation, of which France was the guarantor in terms of those treaties; in binding together, by another perpetual treaty, Turkey, Poland, Sweden and Prussia, through the mediation and ultimately the accession of France; and finally in thus separating the House of Austria from Russia, confining the latter to her vast deserts.[20]

The *secret* was designed to counterbalance the new Austrian alliance, about which Louis XV, like many of his compatriots, had substantial reservations. Broglie claimed in a memorandum to Vergennes that 'it was not dictated by a spirit of antipathy towards the established system of alliances [with Austria] but solely by the desire of conforming to the principles and intentions of the late king relative to that great object'.[21]

This distinction may seem sophistical, but it was just such a delicate balancing act that Louis XVI and Vergennes were destined to perform: to prevent Austria from either exploiting France or reverting to her traditional, perhaps natural, alliance with England. As the king put it in a letter to Vergennes in 1778, which inhabits the same thought-world as the *secret*: 'We have an alliance which unites us very closely with Austria, but it does not oblige us to enter into their ambitious and unjust schemes. Yet again, we have to maintain the

reputation of France in Germany which has been only too considerably undermined for some time and, as you put it so well, the guarantee of the Peace of
Westphalia is inherent in the crown.'[22]

The king had to prevent the mistakes of the last reign from being repeated
in his own – sinking French resources into a continental struggle where France's
main interest lay in the overseas struggle with England. And there was an additional factor: Louis XVI was married to an Austrian, and her mother, Maria-
Theresa, and brother, Joseph II, tirelessly pressurized her to support Austrian
territorial ambitions. Austria, having lost the rich industrial province of Silesia
to Prussia, felt she needed to gain an equivalent (Bavaria) to survive as a major
Germanic power. In America, there was little chance of France's regaining
Canada, but England was facing growing unrest from her colonies as she tried
to make them contribute to the cost of defending them in the recent war.
The thirteen states were to declare their independence in 1776 and there was a
chance for France to regain the prestige to which she was entitled by her
resources and vast population of 28 million (though contemporary estimates
put it at 26 million). There was no logical connection between the American
and German conflicts, but since the other powers could not afford to fight each
other unless they obtained a subsidy from France or England – the point of
Frederick II of Prussia's observation that they were the only great powers – they
tried to entangle them in Europe. It was in the interests of neither France nor
England to be so entangled unless the one could ensure that the other would
be entangled much more deeply, as France had been in the Seven Years War.
Louis's analysis of the situation is given in a letter of 19 June 1776 to his Bourbon
cousin and ally, Charles III of Spain, in which he says he is eschewing continental entanglements so that he can 'concentrate exclusively' on 'humiliating'
England.[23]

In their discussions together in the saddle, Louis XV had never mentioned
the *secret* to his grandson, so that it came as a complete surprise when Broglie,
hoping for a dukedom, told an incredulous Louis XVI of 'the enormous volume
of papers . . . dispersed in several depots in the well-founded fear that the duc
d'Aiguillon [the official foreign secretary] would trick the late king into letting
him get hold of [the papers] from M. Dubois-Martin, their custodian'.[24] Louis
told Broglie to burn the lot,[25] though he relented to the extent that he accepted
Broglie's request that the new foreign secretary, Vergennes, who happened to
have been the second-in-command of the *secret*, and the minister for war, du
Muy, examine the matter. Vergennes's report was naturally favourable; nevertheless, Louis repeated his order to burn the papers, Vergennes managing to
salvage only a plan for an invasion of England which was to be resurrected in

1779 under Broglie's direction. But, as Vergennes dutifully fed the ministerial grate with his life's work, the firelight glinting on his magnificent ormolu *chenets*, he must have smiled at the thought that from the ashes of that conflagration would arise the phoenix of the young king's foreign policy. The man had been saved, indeed promoted; what did it matter now if the book was burned? And at least there would be no betrayal of the young king's basic beliefs (something he could not guarantee as, simultaneously, he began his rear-guard defence of Maupeou's work).

Louis XVI also sought to introduce a new element: the 'coming moral reformation', to which du Muy had referred when taking office, should also extend to foreign policy. As dauphin, Louis had received not only technical instruction in diplomacy from his *lecteur*, the veteran diplomatist the abbé de la Ville, who was also Vergennes's mentor, but instruction on international morality from Moreau, who, in 1773, published with the imprimatur of the foreign office a summation of his work, *Leçons de morale, de politique et de droit public, tirées de l'histoire de France et redigées par l'ordre et d'après les vues de feu M. Le Dauphin pour l'éducation des princes ses enfants* ('Lessons of morality, foreign policy and public law drawn from the history of France etc.'). When the abbé de la Ville died that year during a banquet to celebrate his elevation to the episcopacy, Moreau sought his job of *lecteur* to the dauphin, but Louis decided not to fill the vacancy.[26]

In a policy statement at the start of his reign, Louis told Vergennes that 'honesty and restraint must be our watchwords';[27] by 'restraint' he meant restraint in annexing territory. He believed that the emperor should learn to exploit his own territories fully before annexing new ones. Thus, in 1775, he told Vergennes that instead of annexing Moldavia from the Turks, Joseph should have supported Louis's own efforts to secure freedom of commerce in the Black Sea from the Ottomans.[28] By 'honesty' he meant, primarily, observance of international treaties. He told a diplomatic envoy: 'the first duty of sovereigns is the observance of treaties; I will set an example and justice will always be the basis of my conduct'.[29] The principal treaty was that of Westphalia which had constituted France the protector of the Holy Roman German Empire. Louis took this to be the protection of the smaller German states against incursions by the Austrian emperor. So when his brother-in-law, Emperor Joseph II, tried to get his hands on Bavaria in 1778 and 1785, Louis offered no help, despite the nominal continuation of the Austrian alliance, because the latter was overridden by an international treaty. Louis even scrupled to give the Young Pretender a pension because he 'believed that the Treaty of Aix-la-Chapelle [1748] forbids our having any dealings with him'.[30]

Louis believed that there had been a breakdown of international morality in the previous generation. It had begun with Frederick II's 'rape of Silesia' in 1740, but Louis considered that Joseph II shared Frederick's belief 'in the law of the strongest'.[31] Above all, there had been the partition of Poland between Austria, Prussia and Russia in 1772 – 'the tragedy of the North', as Broglie characterized it – negating as it did the original purpose of the *secret*: to place a French prince on the elective Polish throne. Louis XV, in the midst of Maupeou's reforms, had been unable to restrain his Austrian ally. Louis XVI despised the three former enemies for shelving their quarrels to conclude a shabby deal, as he wrote to Vergennes in 1775: 'I have absolutely no faith in the new accord of the co-partitioners; I believe them to be rather observing each other with mutual distrust.'[32]

The concept of an 'ethical' foreign policy has been largely discredited by the 2003 invasion of Iraq. But one should perhaps in any case view with suspicion any self-proclaimed act of morality. Did a good man ever proclaim his goodness? I mention this because, after proclaiming a new moral order at the start of his reign, we shall see Louis indulging in some highly underhand dealings against England, with which France was at peace, in the years preceding France's entry into the American War of Independence, the main subject of the next two chapters. Moreover, despite public protestations to the contrary, Louis was well aware that his actions were questionable.

The road to war

The two events which, more than any others, shaped the modern world occurred in the last quarter of the eighteenth century: American independence, achieved with French help, followed six years later by the French Revolution. Was the link merely temporal? Louis XVI, with the benefit of hindsight, thought there was a causative link. In 1792 Tippoo, the Sultan of Mysore, made the secret proposal that if Louis XVI sent him 6,000 French troops he would pay for them and guarantee to expel the British from India. But when the minister for the marine presented the proposal to Louis with his endorsement, Louis rejected it without hesitation: 'this bears too close a resemblance to the American adventure, which I never think about without regret. At that time they [his ministers] somewhat took advantage of my youth; we are suffering from it today. The lesson is too harsh to forget.'[33]

The question of whether Louis was bamboozled by his ministers who 'took advantage of his youth' can best be answered by disentangling the three strands to France's path to war: secret subsidy for the colonists; naval rearmament; and diplomacy. But first we should look at the background to England's quarrel with her colonists.

England and her colonies

Turgot wrote a position paper in 1776 saying, presciently, that the independence of all colonies, French, Spanish or whoever's, was in any case inevitable. In the case of England's colonies conflicts of interest were beginning to outweigh ties of kinship. Its colonial system, whereby the colonies could only trade with the motherland, buying her manufactured products and supplying her with raw materials, was manifestly one-sided and could not subsist as the colonies, despite these restraints, grew in power and in population. The American colonies' population numbered 200,000 in 1690, grew to 1.5 million by 1760, before taking off in the period under consideration until it reached 3.8 million in 1790. England's population of some 10 million was growing fast too, but not as fast. The population of the colonies was dispersed along the eastern coast of North America, which made it difficult to control. If the colonists had had their wish and expanded westwards the task would have been impossible – hence England's refusal to let the colonists move out beyond the Allegheny Mountains, an additional source of conflict.

The immediate cause of the quarrel between England and her American colonies is encapsulated in their cry: 'no taxation without representation'. England thought it right that the colonies should pay some of the cost of defending them in the recent war. The idea of the colonies' sending representatives to Westminster was not pursued as seriously as it should have been. The implications for the French polity, in which the taxpayer also had no direct voice, were not at first realized. In the 1760s a series of taxes, such as the Sugar Act of 1763, the Stamp Act of 1765, and the 1767 Townsend duties on glass, lead and tea, were imposed but most were as quickly withdrawn under pressure from English traders faced with a colonial boycott of these products. All that remained was the three-pence-in-the-pound tax on tea. It was retained to help the struggling East India Company, which was indebted to the British government; but also as a symbol – keeping alive the right of that government to tax the colonies. The last burden was in fact the lightest but felt like lead. As such it was resented, just as the symbolic remnants of feudalism were in France. For this was an age of symbols and slogans, 'self-evident' banner headlines such as 'give me liberty or give me death', 'no taxation without representation', Phrygian caps and trees of liberty – symbolism, whether of concepts or artefacts.

On 16 December 1773, fifty Bostonians dressed as Mohawks attacked three East India Company ships in the harbour and dumped 342 cases of tea into the sea. There had been previous, isolated attacks on British interests – a ship charged with preventing smuggling from the French sugar islands had been set on fire in harbour – but the Boston Tea Party was so flagrantly symbolic that the government of George III felt compelled to respond. Boston port was closed and the town put under military rule. The charter of Massachusetts was modified and a governor appointed with absolute power, civil and military. The colonists responded by forming armed militias, and on 5 September 1774, as Maupeou reached the destination of his Norman exile, the first Continental Congress opened. Here, in the presence of such future luminaries as George Washington and John Adams, a blanket boycott of British goods was decided, together with the raising of armed volunteers and, what immediately concerned Louis XVI, the purchase of arms in Europe, because there were no local munitions factories.

The reaction of George III and his prime minister Lord North – rumoured to be his illegitimate brother, they certainly looked alike – was swift: military reinforcements and a trade blockade, which again concerned France. On 19 April 1775, as the Flour War was getting under way in France, the real war in America began at Lexington, twenty miles from Boston, where a local militia drove off the regular troops of General Gage. It was only a skirmish but is regarded as the start of the War of Independence. A month later the second Continental Congress asked George Washington to form an army. On 4 July 1776 Congress declared American independence and shortly afterwards George III declared the colonists rebels to his crown. With long-term causes overlaid by short-term miscalculations and escalations over a two-year period, the revolutionary situations in America in 1773–75 and France in 1787–89 have points of comparison.

Secret aid to the Americans

In March 1776 Vergennes circulated a document known as the *Considérations* to his ministerial colleagues for their comments. Like most of Vergennes's productions of this kind, it was prolix, but its two conclusions were straightforward: France should supply clandestine aid to the Americans and should rearm her navy and put her own colonies in a state of defence against an English attack. At this stage American independence was not a French concern, certainly not one of Louis's, who respected George III as a person and as a fellow monarch. Kissinger said of the Iran–Iraq war 'it's a pity they can't both lose', but there was a real possibility that England and her colonies would, as Vergennes put it, 'work for their mutual destruction',[34] particularly if the struggle was prolonged by secret French aid. French policy was to prolong the dispute rather than end it in the colonists' favour.

In any case, pressure for action against England, at this stage, came from France's Bourbon ally, Spain. She was involved in a dispute with Portugal over the border between Brazil and Spanish America along the River Plate. Spain believed, wrongly – and staggeringly bad Spanish and French intelligence played a major part in the drift to war – that England was secretly egging on her oldest ally, Portugal, to resist Spanish claims. Spain favoured a Franco-Spanish invasion of England or at least Ireland or Jamaica, which could be swapped for Gibraltar, which had been ceded to England in 1713. Spanish demands were, as Vergennes said, 'gigantic'.[35] They were also unrealistic: Spain's army was of no account and while her navy of forty battleships looked impressive on paper they were, with their elaborate figureheads and vivid colours, as over-decorated and lumbering as their superannuated and superfluous commanders. Their main purpose was to guard the treasure ships bearing silver back to Spain from the mines of Peru; and military strategy and much else depended on the timing of their arrival; for Spain, like modern Russia, had become a resource economy.

France, however, had unusual treaty obligations towards Spain and it was these which led her to suggest arming the American colonists as a substitute for her ally's impossible demands. The 'family compact' between the two branches of the Bourbon dynasty was different in kind from France's other alliances because it was both offensive and defensive.

The only one of Vergennes's colleagues to oppose his proposals was Turgot; as his principal opposition was to rearmament and prophylactic defence, we will consider his arguments when we come to consider the implications of rearmament. An interesting if unsigned response to Vergennes's position paper is entitled 'Reflections on the necessity of helping the Americans *and preparing for war with England*'. Its interest lies in the fact that this, the most hawkish of the responses, is in the hand of one of Maurepas's secretaries, and the response has plausibly been attributed to the Mentor.[36]

When all the position papers had been gathered in, Louis presided over a ministerial committee in which the decision was taken to subsidize the Americans and rearm. Turgot was excluded because Louis always avoided ministers he was about to dismiss. On 2 May 1776 Vergennes 'had the honour of placing at the feet of Your Majesty the paper authorizing me to furnish a million *livres* for the service of the English colonists, providing Your Majesty deigns to affix his *approuvé*.' The sum was trivial – less than Marie-Antoinette had spent on balls the previous year – but Louis also facilitated the 'laundering' of a further million from Spain and allowed the Americans to trade in French ports and purchase arms and munitions. Such was the cloak-and-dagger secrecy that Vergennes used his fifteen-year-old son, Constantin, rather than his secretaries, to write the order, because 'It was essential that this operation cannot leak out or at least not be imputed to the government'.[37]

But how was it to be done? Luckily Louis was addicted to secrecy – his suspicious nature had been reinforced by his upbringing. His grandfather had his full-blown *secret du roi*, and he had the same during the Revolution. Knowing that Marie-Antoinette despised his 'mechanical arts', he knew it would be safe to keep the family archive relating to the House of Austria under the anvil of his forge, where it was found and partially transcribed by Soulavie in 1792. For the secret American business, he chose Pierre-Augustin Caron de Beaumarchais. The author of *The Barber of Seville* was a quintessential figure of the late ancien régime: financier, subversive playwright, polemicist, forger, and habitué of the ministerial ante-chamber and inner sanctums. The informal procedures of the regime enabled him to slip between the cogs of the political machine, whilst his protean activities enabled him to play a significant part in the early stages of France's involvement in the American war.

In April 1776 Vergennes wrote to Beaumarchais:

> It is necessary that in the eyes of the English government and of the Americans the operation should have essentially the aspect of an individual speculation to which we [France] are strangers. . . . We will secretly give you one million. . . . We will try to obtain a similar sum from Spain . . . with these two million you will establish a big commercial house, and at your risk and your peril will supply the Americans with arms, munitions, equipment and all other things that they will need to maintain the war. Our arsenal will deliver to you arms and munitions, but you will either replace them or pay for them. You will not demand money from the Americans, since they do not have any, but you will ask in return the produce of their soil which we will help you to sell in this country . . .[38]

Beaumarchais's involvement with the French government dated from the last years of the previous reign, when he had been commissioned to buy up two editions of pamphlets attacking Madame du Barry. He succeeded in this but when he returned (as he thought in triumph) in May 1774 it was only to find that Louis XV's death removed the reputation of his mistress from the list of the government's priorities. Nothing daunted, Beaumarchais offered his services to buy up another edition, this time attacking the reputation of Marie-Antoinette and reviving the contingent rights of the Spanish Bourbons to the French throne, on the grounds that any children of the queen's would not be sired by the king.

His 'contact' for these operations had been the police minister Sartine, and when Sartine became naval minister he used Beaumarchais for naval procurement. Both men, for patriotic and departmental reasons, considered naval war with England inevitable and endeavoured to make it so – and both were to pay a price, the one being out of pocket and the other out of office. Through Sartine, Beaumarchais made contact with the king, sending him a letter about his work for Louis XV and on 20 June another about the pamphlets attacking Marie-Antoinette. He thought it would aid his task if he had a written 'mission' from the king and on 5 July he sent the king a pro-forma 'model' for this. Knowing it would have no legal status, on 10 July Louis obliged by signing an order in exactly this form. Full of gratitude, Beaumarchais wrote back saying that he had commissioned a large, flat, gold locket in the shape of a lentil to house the precious document, which he wore round his neck. He regarded the locket as a talisman and claimed that it saved his life after one of his numerous travelling accidents.[39]

Beaumarchais's next assignment was to recover the correspondence of the transvestite chevalier d'Éon, a former agent of the *secret du roi* living in London. The papers were sensitive because they included the plans for an invasion of England (mentioned above) and because d'Éon required a high price for surrendering such a bargaining chip. Beaumarchais's task was complicated by the chevalier's adoption of female dress and his insistence that he was a woman, though his autopsy would show he was a man. For this assignment Louis gave Beaumarchais authentic instructions, countersigned by Vergennes, authorizing him to 'take what steps he considered necessary' to recover the papers.[40]

In December Beaumarchais sent the king a series of questions to answer. Could d'Éon wear the cross of his military order, the Croix de Saint-Louis, when wearing female garb? Since Louis was able to recall 'one example of a woman wearing the cross of Saint-Louis'[41] and reflecting perhaps that Joan of Arc had worn male armour, Louis replied 'only in the provinces', though one would have expected opinion to be more enlightened in the metropolis. Could d'Éon have 2,000 *livres* for the trousseau? 'Yes'. And what about d'Éon's existing male clothes? 'She must sell them.' When he had concluded the business and received a receipt from Vergennes for the return of the papers, could the king add 'in his own hand a few words expressing his satisfaction at the way I have fulfilled my mission'. 'Bon'.[42] Beaumarchais was friendly with an embittered ex-minister, Lord Rochford, and asked Louis whether, if Rochford arranged an audience with George III, he should accept. 'Cela se peut.' And if Rochford sought to involve him in English politics? 'C'est inutile.' And if so, could Vergennes supply him with a secret code? No reply.

In a series of memoranda, Beaumarchais advanced an analysis of English politics which, whilst totally erroneous, was bought by Vergennes with disastrous consequences. The American colonists, Beaumarchais argued, were bound to win their independence quickly and this would entail the fall of the North administration (which was friendly towards France); it would be replaced by one with Rockingham as its figurehead but with William Pitt, Earl of Chatham, as its driving force. The appointment of Pitt, the organizer of victory in the previous war and determined enemy of France, would be accompanied by an attack on the colonies of the French and Spanish Bourbons, using the massive armed forces England had built up in the American hemisphere.

Given that the preservation of the North administration was in France's best interests, it was illogical for Beaumarchais to work for its downfall. But this is what he was suggesting: 'I think he is hinting at his contacts with members of the Opposition', Louis mused to Vergennes, 'and he will be more explicit when he arrives back here.'[43] Beaumarchais's contacts with members of the Opposition, such as Wilkes and Rochford, made him exaggerate their chances of success, which he thought could be enhanced by the discreet use of French subsidies. Vergennes fell in with the Beaumarchais line, writing to the king on 22 January 1776: 'England is on the verge of despair. I can well believe with Beaumarchais that a revolution in the ministry cannot be long deferred. Desperate measures are perhaps all that will keep the ministry from the storm for a while and keep the sword of Damocles from falling on the heads of its individual members.'[44]

But if, as Beaumarchais argued, it was the Opposition which would attack the French sugar islands, why assist them to power with secret subsidies? Louis, with his intimate knowledge of English politics and his shrewd common sense, read the picture much better. 'The majority of the [North] administration is very considerable and as long as it lasts it will be able to lay down the law.'[45] In other words, the North administration, with the backing of George III, would not collapse through disintegrating morale but only when its majority was eroded by defections – which took six years and military defeat to bring about.

A further consideration which caused Louis to reject Beaumarchais's plan was that such underhand subsidies to the opponents of a government France was at peace with were dishonourable; on 25 November 1775 Louis wrote, 'as regards the reply Beaumarchais requests, you will tell him that we cannot do what he asks, that it is not just'.[46] Two years later he elaborated: to support factions opposed to government was a violation of the law of nations and would set a precedent for English intrigues with the *parlements* or the independent-minded province of Brittany. In an attempt to overcome the king's scruples, Beaumarchais wheeled out the old argument used by Machiavelli and Richelieu: 'But, Sire, the same morality does not apply to states as it does to private citizens'. Louis repudiated this notion at the time, but Soulavie, who maintained that Louis was and remained an honourable man, transcribed some private reflections of Louis's on authorizing 'certain [unspecified] unjust measures against the tranquillity of England' possibly in connection with the planned Franco-Spanish invasion of England in 1779: 'What a situation is mine! Why should I be obliged, by reasons of state, and the pretext of a great military operation already entered upon, to sign orders which my heart condemns, and to which my opinions are adverse?'

Louis's guilty conscience and his honesty are expressed in the marginal comments he made on the 1778 French manifesto which sought to justify French entry into the American war. Soulavie, who published these comments, concludes: 'It appears ... that Louis XVI was secretly ashamed of the part he was playing and that he wished, in his manifestos, to reduce the number of opportunities for reproach, which England might find in replying to his memorials.'[47] The manifesto proclaimed that Louis had 'remained a tranquil spectator' in the dispute between England and her colonies, avoiding 'the slightest suspicion' of 'entering into correspondences of any sort with the insurgents'. Louis noted that it would be 'difficult to persuade' the French, let alone the English, that France had remained aloof; 'it would therefore be better not to utter a syllable on this subject since true or false our asseveration will not be believed'. Nor, Louis argued, was it fair to argue that a section of English opinion favoured the colonists, since this section formed the opposition.

The manifesto skated on thin ice for a monarchist, arguing as it did that revolts of provinces or whole nations against their rulers were a fact of life which international relations should recognize, the examples of Charles I and Mary Queen of Scots being adduced. Louis, embarrassed by Louis XIV's alliance with Cromwell, wanted to omit these references and also to tone down references to Elizabeth I's helping the Low Countries shake off the Spanish yoke: 'The conduct of Elizabeth is neither a rule nor a precedent in the code of the law of nations'. Yet it would be difficult to find a closer precedent.

The French manifesto argued that England had clearly been unable to hold down her colonies, so that they had achieved a de facto independence which should be recognized (a guideline applied in British diplomacy to this day). Louis XVI, however, countered: 'What if England should reply to this that she would have been able to suppress the rebellion if France had not lent her aid to the insurgents?' Louis also vetoed any hostile references to George III in the French manifesto on the grounds that, under the English constitution, the king acted only on advice from his ministers. (The English manifesto adopted a similar stance: 'It is sad that the ministers of His Most Christian Majesty have surprised the religion of their sovereign to cover their baseless assertions with so respectable a name.'[48])

Louis would have preferred to avoid references to America altogether in the French manifesto since it was no good pretending that France had not given material assistance to the Americans. Instead since 'it is perfectly obvious that we have not been neutral . . . we must concentrate on the serious harm to public safety in allowing England to adopt the haughty tone it adopts with all the maritime and continental powers. We must show that she has abused her power.' However, Louis wrote these comments for himself; he didn't send them to Vergennes since he refers to the minister in the third person – 'M. de Vergennes' employs disparaging remarks about George III etc. He annotates Turgot's and Necker's memoranda on provincial assemblies in the same way. The French manifesto went out uncorrected.

It may be that the ideological confusion of a monarch supporting the rebellious subjects of a fellow monarch sapped Louis's morale. He comes near to acknowledging this in the reference to Tippoo Sahib which we quoted earlier. Louis's words are, however, quoted out of context, as they usually are. But the context makes it clear that Louis considered the secret subsidy to the Americans as morally wrong rather than impolitic. Bertrand de Molleville had explained that England could be told that the 6,000 troops needed by Tippoo Sahib to expel the English from India were being sent not to the subcontinent but to suppress the 'Negro rebellion' on Saint-Domingue. But, Bertrand continues: 'the king's *honest soul* did not hesitate for a moment in rejecting this proposal. "This," he said, "bears too close a resemblance to the American business which I can't think of without feeling regret."' He rejected the proposal because it was dishonourable and in this respect it resembled 'the American affair'. Quoted out of context Louis's words are taken to mean that the war created the deficit which led to the Revolution and this is still the primary meaning of his words. But the full context carries an implication of a sin being punished, or of Louis's will being sapped: I've encouraged rebellion so it serves me right if I have one on my doorstep. Vergennes and Maurepas had a burning hatred of England, but Louis loved the country, though, like Kaiser Wilhelm II, he showed it in odd ways.

It is also possible that Louis exaggerated the role of the ministers – Vergennes, Sartine, Maurepas – in initiating the secret subsidy. Véri even claims that the king had asked Beaumarchais to negotiate with the Americans without consulting his ministers at all and this evidence from Maurepas's confidant would be conclusive but for his qualification, 'or if he did consult them, they are denying it now'.[49] As we will see, buck-passing occurred at all stages of the 'American affair'.

At the end of 1776, Louis dispensed with Beaumarchais's services. On 28 October he told Vergennes that he'd 'like to wind up the affairs of that man who will play us a few tricks before long'.[50] Official secrecy meant that Beaumarchais could not present his receipt for the million *livres* to the Americans until the collapse of the ancien régime, in fact until 1794. His claim was not settled in his lifetime and his descendants had to wait until 1835 for repayment.[51] Nor was the secret kept for long: Lord Stormont, the English ambassador, protested to Vergennes: 'In the history of the world there is no example of aid given to the rebels of a country one professes to be friendly with.' When Vergennes blustered, 'We cannot stop smugglers', Stormont retorted, 'Do smugglers go in fleets, Sir?'[52]

The king was in control, taking from Beaumarchais what he needed and rejecting what, even then, he considered immoral or a waste of time. It was legitimate to subsidize the Americans but not the English opposition. What about rearmament, which could only be aimed against England?

Rearmament

There were parallels between the situation of the French navy in 1723, when Maurepas, at Louis's age, had become minister of the marine, and in 1774. At both dates the navy had been run down after a major war; run down in fact by Maurepas's father and grandfather, who had relied on a *guerre de corse*, privateering, rather than Colbert's magnificent navy. France had lost her naval superiority over England at the battle of La Hogue in 1692, and by 1723 even parity was only a dream. Maurepas, however, embarked on a programme of naval expansion the significance of which was not lost on the English press, even though the two countries were at that time allies. Nor did Maurepas abandon the *guerre de corse*, which operated out of Dunkirk. One of the chief French grievances in 1774 was the presence of an English commissioner resident at Dunkirk to ensure that the French did not repair the sluices of Mardyke which prevented the harbour from silting up. This humiliating clause in the 1763 Peace of Paris stemmed from the fact that the French could not be trusted to disable this hotbed of privateering against England: when, for instance, Fleury had promised his English ally in 1730 that the sluices would not be repaired, Maurepas managed to find a way round this promise. Louis XVI resented the presence of this commissioner as keenly as the loss of Canada.

We said that at the accession of Louis XVI France had only one battleship at sea. This was not as bad as it sounds. The rest were simply laid up in dock because it was expensive to run them: after just one year at sea they had to be completely overhauled, which was a costly business, and was one reason why everyone in government was gambling on a short, preferably one-campaign war. (The new English practice of copper-bottoming, which the French were slowly adopting, reduced the frequency of services.) Nevertheless, even after four years of rearmament, when France and England went to war in 1778 France had only sixty battleships to England's ninety – hence the importance of Spain's forty ships, which would give a theoretical parity. As said, the Spanish ships were no match for the English and French ones, but at least they could tie up the former.

The big debate in government, however, during these years of phoney peace, was not so much rearmament – on which both king and Mentor were determined – as naval manoeuvres and steps to protect French colonies from a surprise English attack. In August 1775 a squadron had left Brest for naval manoeuvres which Louis, personally, decided to prolong, giving Vergennes a letter for Sartine to that effect.[53] He also required a detailed and costed list of guns, provisions and so on from the naval intendant at Brest.[54] On 20 April 1776 a squadron under the command of the vicomte du Chaffault left Brest for six months' manoeuvres off the African coast; the ships were to be 'armed as for war and their crew to be slightly smaller than in time of war but much larger than in peace time'.[55] Another expedition, again under Chaffault and planned for the end of 1776, was blatantly provocative. Sent to the Caribbean, it was designed to gather intelligence about English military dispositions and to defend Saint-Domingue from an English invasion. But its primary purpose was to protect American traders from interception by English vessels when they were trading with French and Spanish colonies (which the old colonial system prohibited) or with the English sugar islands, from which they had been banned after George III declared them rebels. The squadron was also to protect neutral vessels wanting to trade with the colonies, even if they were shown to be supplying arms. 'Freedom of the seas' – from the English assertion of their perceived right to stop and search for what they termed contraband – was the great rallying cry of Louis XVI and was to culminate in the League of

Armed Neutrality of 1780, involving such non-combatants as Russia and the Dutch Republic.

Chaffault's instructions are not only signed with the king's *approuvé* but are written entirely in his hand.[56] They are extremely detailed, including steps for the preservation of the sailors' lives (having them spend the minimum time in the torrid conditions ashore), and decisions about which ships newly arrived in the West Indies should relieve which long-serving vessels. There are also detailed instructions on how to deal firmly but tactfully with English vessels pursuing American ones:

> In the eventuality of a ship from New England belonging to the insurgents being pursued by an English vessel and asking for protection from the French flag, le Sieur Chaffault will grant it; and if ... the English vessel persists in pursing the insurgent one and tries to capture it, le Sieur Chaffault will resist with all the forces that His Majesty has confided to him; but he will only come to this extremity after loud hailing the English vessel and telling its captain audibly that the king's orders are that his flag should provide protection to all ships which ask for it and to oppose by force any violence being done to that flag.

If the Admiralty had read these instructions they must have thought that Louis's injunction to treat English vessels 'in accordance with the good relations which subsist between the two crowns' was tipped with bitter irony. It was the sort of expedition 'where cannons go off of their own accord' and, for that reason, perhaps, it was never actually sent.

All this was expensive: sending troop reinforcements to the American hemisphere had cost 4 million *livres* in 1775 and would cost double that in 1776. The armed squadrons which Louis was keen to send out cost even more. Sartine was proposing naval estimates of 62 million for 1776, against the usual peacetime allocation of 30 million. But there was little any finance minister could do, once king and naval minister were agreed. In Turgot's opinion, given in a memorandum dated 6 April 1776, the money was wasted. Turgot thought, rightly, that the money could better be employed in secretly building up the stock of warships and *matériel*. For, he argued, French colonies could not be defended from an English surprise attack since no one knew which target they would select. Moreover, defensive measures could actually provoke an English attack. And all to placate Spain, a tetchy ally which, overestimating her own strength, would provoke England to war not over England's own colonial dispute but over her (imaginary) support for Portugal. For England was not picking a war with France; but if Spain attempted to annex Portugal or France Brazil, she would have immediately settled her differences with her colonies in order to resist, and resist successfully, this new threat to her vital interests.

Turgot was right to say that the measures taken were angled towards Spain. We have mentioned the secret subsidies to the Americans, which can be seen in this light, but on top of this on 22 April 1776, in a 'committee held in the king's apartments', probably consisting of Maurepas, Vergennes, Sartine and Saint-Germain but not Turgot, the king issued an executive order embodying 'the wise reflections of the king his uncle [Charles III]' providing: i) continuing the presence in American waters of four well-armed frigates and three corvettes with the same instructions as had been given to the Spanish vessels; ii) keeping twelve ships-of-the-line at Brest, ready to be armed at short notice; iii) 'Since it is to be presumed that the English, if they have hostile intentions, will start by blockading the port of Brest', eight battleships were to be held ready at Toulon to come to their assistance; iv) Sartine to continue refitting the laid up ships and assemble 'all that is lacking ... for construction, equipping and arming' others. On 26 April a further committee was held in Maurepas's apartments at which Aranda, the Spanish ambassador, himself was present.

Louis paid close attention to naval rearmament and manoeuvres. Sartine, a highly competent bureaucrat, had no military, let alone naval, training. To emphasize the importance he attached to the navy, Louis made him a *ministre*, giving him the right to sit in the council, but he constantly kept him on his toes. When Sartine told him that the *Renommée* had turned turtle on her first outing, Louis was *mécontent* and reminded him that there had been a spate of such episodes, 'that of the *Licorne*, the *Indien*, the *Moucheron*, and several other mishaps to several other ships leaving our ports, maybe of lesser consequence but annoying all the same.' In view of this we cannot accept the argument of the American historian Jonathan Dull, who, in his account of the navy under Louis XVI, argued that 'hawks' such as Sartine and Vergennes bamboozled the inexperienced and pacific Louis XVI into a rearmament which, as naval races usually do, carried with it its own momentum towards war. The two ministers, Dull argues, were determined on war from the outset and the delay in entering the war (until 1778) was precisely the time it took for rearmament to be completed. In persuading the king, they deployed an argument in which they did not believe, namely that once England's struggle with its colonies was over, whether they had won or lost, the English troops then present in the American hemisphere would be turned on the French sugar islands and the Spanish

Main. France, then, should waste no time in entering the war whilst she could have the colonists as an ally.

It is more likely, however, that Louis thought he could have his cake and eat it: he could indulge in naval rearmament without the risk of war, bringing off this usually impossible feat of gastronomic legerdemain because Lord North, the English premier, was prepared to suffer any humiliation to prevent France from going to war. But Maurepas, who, as an ex-naval minister, had been as keen as the king to build up the navy, was beginning to think that, since France was spending so much on rearmament, she might as well go to war, which would justify additional taxation. On 11 January 1777 he wrote to Noailles, ambassador to England: 'It is undeniable that both of us [France and England] are wearing ourselves out with compliments and assurances of good will and pacific intentions and all the while we are ruining ourselves with preparations for war.'[57]

But both Maurepas and Turgot were wrong. There was a big financial difference between rearmament and war if only because of the destruction of ships in battle. Naval expenditure in 1776 was some 47 million *livres* and 59 million in 1777, the last year of peace, by which time France had some sixty capital ships. Naval expenditure in 1778 and 1779, however, reached 150 million and 155 million *livres*, respectively. If Maurepas was in error, however, he was in the good company of Turgot, who had argued that rearmament would cause a *greater* deficit than war because rearmament was not a justification for new taxation. In the memorandum Turgot sent the king on his appointment, he had argued that there should be no new taxation in time of peace; it could be that the prolonged rearmament in the period 1776–78 accustomed Necker (and the country) to dispensing with new taxation and prepared them for doing what Turgot would never have contemplated: fighting a war on credit alone.

Spanish red herring

With the benefit of hindsight one can be misled into the impression that the decision to enter the war on the side of the American colonists in 1778 was the inevitable consequence of a series of steps going back to 1775, when Vergennes sent a secret agent called Achard de Bonvouloir on a fact-finding mission to America. Posing as an Antwerp merchant, de Bonvouloir was to give the Americans unofficial assurances that they could use French ports to obtain munitions and that France had no desire to reconquer Canada. Above all, he had to report on the resolve and capacity of the colonists for resistance. Notable landmarks on the road to war were the twin decisions taken in the spring of 1776 to rearm the navy and to give the Americans a secret subsidy. Then, on 31 August 1776, Vergennes presented his *Considérations* to the cabinet. His conclusion was seemingly unequivocal: 'If it were a question of weighing the advantages and disadvantages of undertaking a war against England, it would be easy to demonstrate that the former trump the latter so decisively that there is no room for comparison.' Of this document the American historian E. S. Corwin wrote: 'In the summer of 1776, when he thought that France could count on the active assistance of Spain, Vergennes definitely proposed war with England and the proposition was tentatively ratified by the king and council [*comité*].' Vergennes notes that Maurepas, Sartine, Saint-Germain and Clugny, Turgot's replacement, were present; but we simply do not know whether they endorsed Vergennes's conclusion – a point made by the Spanish foreign minister, Grimaldi:

> Although it appears that ... [Vergennes] submitted [the memorandum] to the council [*comité*] of His Most Christian Majesty and with its knowledge communicated it to us, we are given absolutely no indication of what the said council decided or even what it thought about the memorandum, information which we would have found extremely useful to enlighten us on the thinking of the French court.

Moreover it is likely that Vergennes and Spain were merely testing each other's resolve; for at the same time Vergennes wrote to d'Ossun, French ambassador to Madrid, 'nothing at the moment could justify war ... what could we desire more than that England should fight against herself. She is generous enough to spare us the trouble and expense of destroying her.'[58] Her bluff called, on 8 October Spain sent a less than bellicose response to Vergennes's memorandum on which Louis commented:

> It appears from M. de Grimaldi's letter that Spain is in no hurry to go to war, which suits me fine.... [The Spaniards] are right to fear for their [American] continental possessions because they are so poorly protected and of such an extent that it is difficult to guard them all; but if the English had really wanted to, they could easily have seized them without a declaration of war. ... [Spain's] intention to annex Portugal is abundantly clear ... but it is absolutely not in our interests. If we are forced to make war on Portugal it must be ... [to defend Spain's] claims in Brazil not to aggrandize this ally with possessions to which it has no claim and which would augment

its power too much. If we are forced to make war on England, it must be for the defence of our possessions and the abasement of its power, not with any idea of territorial aggrandizement on our part, but solely with the aim of trying to ruin her commerce and undermining her strength by supporting the revolt and separation of her colonies, despite the axiom of M. de Grimaldi that the sole point of going to war is to annex territory.[59]

Grimaldi's despatch ended what may be termed the Spanish phase of French rearmament – a phase in which Spain was the moving force in the alliance and was only interested in England and her colonies *qua* the ally of Portugal. In 1777 Spain settled her differences with Portugal, where a new queen – a child, whose mother, Charles III's sister, was regent – ascended the throne and a completely different scenario took shape. This makes it misleading to talk of the period 1775 to 1778 as a unity and to regard measures such as the subsidy treaty as steps on the inevitable road to a particular war. War could have broken out in 1776 if Louis had not stood up to his uncle Charles III of Spain (as Louis XV had in 1770 over the Falklands dispute), but it would have been a different war, aimed primarily at Portugal and fought on the Tagus rather than the Delaware. And the fact that France went to war with England in 1778 without Spanish support (that came a year later and was far from a foregone conclusion) throws doubt on the inevitability of France's intervention in the American war.

Louis ends his letter about the Spanish climb-down with an analysis of the news that had just come in that an English army under General Howe had occupied Long Island, evacuated by George Washington during the night of 28/29 August, and was set to walk into New York unopposed:

The [English] advantage is not considerable in itself and will only serve to draw them deeper and deeper into the war, and the more they fight the greater their mutual destruction. Even if they finally succeeded in repossessing [the colonies], they would only be the more weakened by it, finding their colonies wrecked and having used up their forces against them. Another benefit accruing from the advantage which they have just gained is the stability it will give to the present administration, with which we have reason to be satisfied, not only for its friendly behaviour towards us but also for the passion and pig-headedness with which they prosecute a war which, one way or another, can only do them harm. All these reasons combined make me think that we won't have war, at least for some time. But as you

rightly say that should not stop us from building up the navy, which would
be a great benefit both in itself and to convey a better idea of our forces than
is held at present.

Louis realizes that the friendly North administration has turned a blind eye
to French rearmament which had now passed from being a provocation to
being a deterrent. By now England would have been happy to end the naval
arms race with France and actually proposed this in March 1777.[60] So why,
having made this lucid and correct analysis, did Louis not stick to it instead of
entering the war some eighteen months later? The common sense answer is:
Saratoga. On 4 December 1777 news arrived that a British army of 5,000 men
had capitulated to American irregulars at Saratoga Springs on 17 October
1777; this convinced the French government that the Americans (who had
previously suffered a series of defeats) were a serious fighting force. Why not
jump on their bandwagon? The very next day after the arrival of the news,
French and American representatives started treaty negotiations. *Post hoc,
propter hoc*? Probably. But there are other interpretations.

On 23 July 1777 (six months before Saratoga), Vergennes submitted to the
king a memorandum which, in the opinion of Jonathan Dull, marked the
moment when France decided to enter the American war. Vergennes annotates
it as follows: 'Memoir communicated to the king on 23 July 1777 and approved
by his Majesty the same day'. But it is not clear whether Louis writes his
approuvé on the document in order to authorize a particular course of action
or whether he was being complimentary to the minister: he 'approved' of him
rather than his measures? This memoir is mainly a disquisition on Vergennes's
fallacious argument that 'there is no doubt that England desires to end the civil
war in order to commence a new one against the two crowns'. But it ends with
a very specific proposal: that France must sign up with the Americans 'by
January or February 1778'. Since France did sign the treaties with the Americans
in February 1778, Dull has concluded that it was on 23 July 1777 that this decision was taken; news of the American victory at Saratoga was an irrelevance;
the main consideration was the completion of French rearmament (although
Vergennes scarcely alludes to this in the memoir). Louis, then, according to
Dull, would be giving his *approuvé* to signing up with the Americans by
February 1778 at the latest and, since Louis tended to procrastinate, February
1778 it was.[61]

Then came Saratoga. Vergennes claimed that this dismayed him because it
ushered in the endgame, after which England would pounce on French colonies in the region. He may have been panicked by Benjamin Franklin who,

through an intermediary, sought to give the impression that England was prepared to settle her differences with her colonies. Franklin, the most cele- brated of the American delegates over in France to negotiate a treaty of alliance, was the ultimate *faux naïf*: he affected a fur cap like Rousseau and, also like him, abused the hospitality he received. For all his homespun airs and trapper's cap, Franklin was as smooth, wily and treacherous as any red-heeled courtier. He charmed Marie-Antoinette and ran rings round Vergennes.

While the assumptions of the decision-making parties may remain obscure, we are able to get closer to the actual mechanics of the conclusion of the two treaties (one commercial, one of alliance) signed with the Americans on 6 February 1778 – to the 'how' if not to the 'why'; and the former may shed some light on the latter. Precise information on the decision about how to treat with American delegates Benjamin Franklin, Silas Deane and Arthur Lee is contained in a retrospective memorandum drafted by Vergennes, probably in January 1780. The war had so far achieved little, and Vergennes was under attack. He reminded the king:

> This question [of treating with the American delegates] was the subject of long discussions and in-depth analysis in the various memoranda which were presented to Your Majesty at the time; you examined them by yourself; you caused them to be discussed by those of your ministers you were pleased to consult on this important decision and I would with the greatest respect remind you that when the time came to pronounce on whether to treat with the Americans, M. de Maurepas, challenged by Your Majesty to disclose his opinion, begged to be excused on the grounds that since the matter had been carefully weighed and pondered in the memoranda and discussions, it was for Your Majesty in his wisdom to pronounce and all his ministers could do was to await and execute his orders. It was in pursuance of your orders that I opened negotiations with the American delegates and concluded two treaties [with them] in February 1778.[62]

For the entire reign, this is the most detailed and precise description we possess of the making of a decision. Nevertheless, it requires careful reading and itself raises several questions. What was Maurepas refusing to do? Vergennes's use of the word 'challenged' (*provoqué*) suggests that Maurepas thought that Louis was making an unusual and unacceptable demand; Maurepas must already have given the king his private advice (that was his job) but now he was being asked either to opine strongly on a subject and therefore unduly influence the deliberations, or to 'take the sense of the meeting', responsibility for which (and Vergennes's letter is all about responsibility) lay with the king.

Another possibility is that Maurepas would not pronounce because he himself had doubts. Despite his flippant comment about rearmament being as expensive as war, it will be remembered that Beaumarchais had entreated him to stop sitting on the fence and bring pressure to bear on Louis, as Maurepas had concerning the recall of the *parlement*, Beaumarchais reminding him, 'You are too forgetful of the fact that this new and untouched ['*ferme*'] soul [meaning, the king] has been turned round and brought back even from afar on several occasions'. If Vergennes had been in Maurepas's position, which he would be as *chef du Conseil royal des finances* five years later, we may be sure he would have had no such qualms.

A further indication that Louis was brought to a decision is afforded by a rather cryptic note from Sartine to Vergennes, dated 5 December: 'I am curious to have an extract of yesterday's news [the report sent by Congress to the American legation about Saratoga]. M. de Maurepas and I chatted about it for a long time last night. It [the news] will determine victory [*décident la victoire*] but our response [*le parti que nous avons à prendre*] merits the most serious reflections. M. d'Aranda will be worth listening to. It seems to me that his last conversation made an impression.'[63] Aranda, unlike the Spanish government, was a 'hawk' and the 'impression' he made must be taken to be that upon Louis XVI. Sartine seems to be telling Vergennes that Aranda will be useful in bringing the king round.

Forced to take the plunge, on 11 December Louis authorized Vergennes to begin negotiations with the American representatives with a view to concluding a treaty of alliance. The authorization has the immediacy of the king's touch, being 'dictated' to Vergennes, who wrote it on Louis's personal pale-blue quartered notepaper. Louis recorded the moment in a personal way, adding in his own hand not just his *approuvé* but the date in full, 'approuvé le 6 Décembre 1777' – a rare usage: he generally omits the year and sometimes the month as well. It has been considered that the moment here preserved for posterity marked the renaissance of French foreign policy.[64] In fact Louis's instructions are very restrictive, insisting on maximum secrecy – only the 'president of the Congress' was to be kept informed – and above all stipulating that nothing be decided until the views of Charles III had been obtained: 'His Majesty expressly reserves the right not to conclude anything except in conjunction with the king his uncle', who was to set the timetable.[65] In sum, the American delegates were told that France would assist the colonists provided Spain also entered the war with the forty ships necessary to assure parity with the English navy. Louis wrote to his uncle Charles asking for his support.

A key date was 6 January 1778, when three pieces of intelligence reached the king. The first was Montmorin's despatch dated 29 December, detailing the Spanish response. The second was that the English spy, Paul Wentworth, had enjoyed a lengthy dinner at Benjamin Franklin's lodgings. And the third was that the elector of Bavaria had died without an immediate heir. Louis's brother-in-law Joseph was likely to claim the territory as a lapsed imperial fief and it would be easier to resist his request for support if France was already fully engaged in an overseas war; that might just tip the balance.

Montmorin said that the Spanish government was furious at France's moves, which it felt could lead to an English attack on the treasure fleets returning from South America, and it rejected Vergennes's arguments.[66] Although the Spanish government had itself used the argument of an English attack on French and Spanish colonies in 1775 and 1776, they now treated it 'with conspicuous levity'.[67] The reception of Montmorin's despatch on 6 January threw the French government into consternation.

Franklin had nothing to say to Wentworth but he knew that Vergennes's spies would report on the extended dinner and that he would be panicked into thinking a reconciliation between motherland and colonies was in the offing. Vergennes, informed the next morning, took the bait: 'I am frightened', he wrote to Montmorin, 'the American negotiators seem to have withdrawn their confidence; they have told us absolutely nothing either of the arrival of this emissary [Wentworth] nor of the frequent conferences they have had and continue to have with him'.[68] Judging by a private letter Maurepas wrote to Noailles on 1 January 1778,[69] he was also worried that Lord North would announce peace feelers in the new session of parliament which was about to open. Maurepas also gained this impression from a Doctor Forth, an agent of Lord North's with whom he was in correspondence. He learned this just as the ship carrying the treaties was about to sail for America and asked Louis whether it should be recalled. Louis, however, was not taken in: 'It is perhaps a lie on Dr Forth's part to embarrass us. Besides, such a proceeding, which will get out sooner or later, will give the impression that we are frightened'.[70] In view of this, Louis was probably lying himself when he told Charles III on 9 March, 'what I predicted has come to pass. England has outlined proposals for a reconciliation with America; the nation applauds the move and all that is missing is the consent of the latter for a reunion which whatever form it takes can only be harmful to us. I hope that the measures I have taken will thwart those of England'.[71] The curious fact is that Louis, who had dithered over whether to open negotiations with the Americans and had inserted the condition of Spanish consent, now that the refusal of that consent had occurred, thereby withdrawing his moral obligation to conclude the negotiations, instead drove them forward.

On 6 January 1778 Louis wrote to Vergennes that, though he did not want to add to Maurepas's burdens – he had been confined to his bed with gout for three weeks[72] – 'since the matter is urgent, come to my apartments tomorrow morning at nine thirty and if M. de Maurepas is fit we'll ponder the matter there'. Further crisis meetings were held in Maurepas's apartments and it was decided that the king should write directly to Charles III, enclosing a memorandum of Vergennes's, minuted with the king's *approuvé*, answering the Spanish arguments and formally asking Spain to enter the war. Louis rehearsed the argument that France was only pre-empting an English attack, with the additional variation: 'England has taken offence at this assistance [to the Americans] and has left us in no doubt that she will take her vengeance sooner or later.' It is unlikely that he believed a word of this. In his covering letter to Montmorin, Vergennes makes great play of the leading part taken by the king in these events:

> Believe me it was no mean sacrifice on the king's part to determine the path we are proposing. It was not the influence of his ministers that decided him: the factual evidence, the moral certainty of the danger and his own conviction alone compelled him. I could even say without exaggeration that His Majesty has given courage to us all because there was not one of those to whom he deigned to give his personal confidence who, whilst acknowledging the utility of our course of action, did not feel a real repugnance in adopting this course before obtaining Spain's adherence.
>
> M. le marquis d'Ossun, who arrived back [from Spain] with perfect timing, can vouch for how carefully this matter has been weighed and discussed.[73]

E.S. Corwin treats this despatch of Vergennes's differently, characterizing it as depicting 'the reaction of the king to ministerial alarmism'. He also says that Vergennes's 'manipulation of this evidence [from English parliamentary debates] is palpably disingenuous', but Louis's superior understanding of English politics surely rendered him proof against this.[74] Naturally, it was in Vergennes's interest to stress the king's role – and that of Charles's friend d'Ossun – both for Spanish consumption and to lessen his own responsibility should the war turn out badly, but it seems that, with Maurepas desperately ill,

Louis had finally to take the decision he had deferred for so long. This is borne out by Louis's letter to Vergennes of 4 February 1778.[75] They had just received Montmorin's despatch of 28 January which made it clear that when Charles III's reply finally came it would be a refusal: 'weakness and pride', Louis complains, 'that's what Spanish policy turns on, but right now we have nothing more to say to them; we have sent them our decision. It is for them to make up their minds.' In other words, the letters of 7 and 8 January to Spain represented Louis's 'decision' to enter the war. This squares with Dull's conclusion that 'serious negotiations [with the American commissioners] began only on 8 January'.[76]

The articles of the commercial and secret defensive treaties between Louis XVI and the Americans were drafted between 27 January and 4 February 1778 by Conrad Gérard, soon to be the first ambassador to the new republic, and the American envoys. The commercial treaty gave the participants 'most favoured nation status' and offered armed protection to all nations trading with the signatories in anything but armaments. The main provision of the second treaty was that neither signatory would sign a separate peace with England.

Signing was due to take place on 5 February, but on that day Gérard asked for a postponement until the 6th because he had come down with a cold.[77] This was a case of 'diplomatic 'flu' brought on by Vergennes's mistaken belief that the arrival of Montmorin's despatch on 4 February had given Louis cold feet. Louis's first letter to Vergennes of the 4th betrays no evidence of this – the French had already sent Spain their 'decision'; nor does the second, but it does read ambiguously: Louis meant to say that he expected 'a bit of bad temper' from Spain over French accession to the recent commercial treaty between Spain and Portugal sealing the restoration of good relations and wanted to discuss this matter with Vergennes and Maurepas. Vergennes, however, assumed that Louis's reference to the Spaniards' bit of temper referred to the French negotiations with the Americans – a surprising reading since by no stretch of the imagination could the deep Spanish resentment over these negotiations be laughed off so lightly. To clear up the misunderstanding Louis wrote a third note, received by Vergennes on 5 January: 'I left out "Portugal"; it was M. de Montmorin's letter concerning it that I wanted clarified and not the business of the insurgents which must be wrapped up.' As a result of this letter the business with the American 'insurgents' was indeed 'wrapped up' the next day when the two treaties were duly signed with the American commissioners.

The treaties with the Americans stipulated that public recognition of American independence should be deferred until Spain's further reaction had been obtained. Louis, however, did not wait for this. On 13 March Noailles informed George III that his king had recognized American independence and signed a commercial treaty; making no mention of the secret defensive alliance, he expressed – optimistically – the hope that France and England would continue to enjoy good relations: on 16 March the English ambassador, Lord Stormont, announced that he had been recalled (France affected surprise), and on 19 March Noailles was told to pack his bags. Charles III was simultaneously informed of this public recognition. Vergennes said that Charles's letter of 22 March in reply to Louis's of 9 March 'could not be more glacial'; Louis annotated Charles's response: '. . . [Montmorin] is right; Spain is not yet on the right track; it is very dilatory.'[78]

On 20 March Louis formally greeted the American delegates and, taking Benjamin Franklin by the hand, gave a formal and obviously prepared speech: 'Gentlemen, I hope that this will be for the good of the two nations. I would like you to assure the Congress of my friendship; I beg you also to convey to it that I am very satisfied with your conduct during your stay in my kingdom.' This, however, according to one of the envoys, Arthur Lee, was the only preparation Louis brought to the occasion: 'The king has his hair undressed, hanging down on his shoulders; no appearance of preparation to receive us, nor any ceremony in doing it.'[79] Croÿ, who recorded the king's words, prophesied that ahead lay 'an implacable war and perhaps the creation of a country larger than our own which could one day subjugate Europe.'[80] Afterwards Marie-Antoinette invited the Americans to her game of cards, and Franklin, now dressed in velvet with silk stockings, was honoured by being asked to stand behind her chair.

Louis was solicitous not to be the technical aggressor, so that technically he could ask for the support of his allies, Spain and Austria, and technically blame them when it was not forthcoming. (This pedantic and dishonest legalism was an unattractive and unappealing character trait he would display throughout the French Revolution.) So the first shot was fired by the English frigate the *Arethusa* after it had summoned the French frigate *Belle Poule* to surrender off the Breton coast at Roscoff. Badly mauled, the *Belle Poule* limped back to Brest; its captain received a hero's welcome and the command of a seventy-four-cannon battleship. 'War, war!' echoed through Versailles and the country was swept up by patriotic fervour. Louis gave the grand admiral, the duc de Penthièvre, stirring guidelines. English insults to the French flag and the law of nations had 'forced me to put an end to the moderation I prescribed for myself and did not permit me longer to delay the effects of my resentment. The dignity of my crown and the protection I owe to my subjects require that I take reprisals, that I take hostile action towards England.'[81]

In the previous war, French ships had avoided battle where possible. This time it was to be different. Sartine's instructions to the commander of a fleet of thirty-two battleships and sixteen frigates leaving Brest seem to have the king's personal touch, exuding as they do pride in his new navy: 'His Majesty has given you a commission of the highest importance . . . to make the French flag shine in all its splendour, to draw a line over past misfortunes and errors. Whatever circumstances in which the king's navy finds itself, the orders that His Majesty has expressly commanded me to convey to you and to all the ships' commanders is that his vessels will attack with the greatest vigour and on every occasion defend themselves to the last man.'[82]

The first Bavarian crisis, 1777–78

It was curious that Louis should have precipitated war precisely when the prospect of Spanish assistance seemed most remote; and here news of the death of the Bavarian ruler may have played a part. On 12 April Véri noted, 'I suspect (without having tried to find out) that our ministry accelerated its moves against England so that being involved in one war might serve as an excuse not to get involved in the one in Germany'.[83] Some support for this view is lent by an underlined passage in Louis's letter of 19 June 1778 to Charles III: 'I am all the more free to devote myself exclusively to this matter [war with England] in that I have adopted the course (of which Your Majesty will surely approve) of not intervening, except by my good offices, in the war which has broken out in Germany.'[84]

When the elector of Bavaria died, Louis knew what would happen next. Emperor Joseph would try to annex the country; Frederick the Great of Prussia would try to stop him and Marie-Antoinette would be prevailed upon to persuade Louis to support his Austrian ally. There was a structural imbalance in the Franco-Austrian alliance, between a satisfied power and a hungry one, and between a unified one with extensive overseas interests and a multinational land empire held together only by personal, dynastic links. These tensions had been present from the inception of the alliance in 1755; but since then two new factors had been added to the equation: the 'ambitious and despotic' (Louis's words) emperor, Joseph II, and an Austrian queen of France, his sister, Marie-Antoinette.

Joseph's pressure on Marie-Antoinette focused on his overriding ambition to acquire Bavaria as an equivalent for Silesia. The Bavarian branch of the Wittelsbachs became extinct in 1777; the Palatine branch was likely to follow suit, leaving the Duke of Zweibrucken as ultimate heir. Joseph exploited this situation to make two attempts to gain Bavaria: in 1777–78 on the basis of medieval titles which Louis, in common with most other rulers, considered spurious; and in 1784–85 by trying to persuade the Wittelsbachs to renounce their claim in return for being put in sovereign possession of most of the Austrian Netherlands (modern Belgium).

In the first Bavarian crisis Joseph mobilized, as did Frederick the Great, who was not prepared to countenance an increase in Austrian strength, and there was a standoff between the two German powers. Joseph asked for support from his ally, France, even promising a portion of the Austrian Netherlands in return for armed assistance. Louis declined the offer (since the acquisition of Belgium had been the central objective of French foreign policy for 300 years, to renounce Belgium was in effect to renounce all annexation) and made it clear to Vergennes that he did not regard Joseph's claims as constituting a *casus foederis*.[85] At the same time he praised Vergennes's handling of the Prussian ambassador, 'dispelling the notion of our detaching ourselves from the alliance with Vienna whilst not seeming to approve its usurpation.'

Louis and Joseph despised and detested each other. While giving his brother-in-law sex counselling during his visit to France in 1777, behind his back Joseph described Louis as 'sluggish in body and mind' and said that if Louis had been a donkey his problems could be solved by smacking him on the backside. For his part, Louis considered that his brother-in-law shared Frederick's belief 'in the law of the strongest'. He thought that when Joseph II, characterized by Louis as 'ambitious and despotic', took over the running of Austria, first as emperor and co-ruler from 1765 and as sole ruler on Maria-Theresa's death in 1780, the alliance had degenerated from its original principles: 'He must have positively hypnotized his mother', Louis told Vergennes, 'because all these usurpations are positively not to her taste.' Louis also despised Joseph for his crude annexationism. Instead of seizing what did not belong to him, he should develop his own backward territories. Joseph in his visit to France noted with envy how homogeneous and compact Louis's dominions were. That was why he wanted Bavaria, which would round off his territories. Louis, however, did not want Austria to be once more the dominant force in Germany: as guarantor of the Peace of Westphalia he wanted a balance of which he would be the arbiter.

Joseph was aided by the fact that, in 1777, Marie-Antoinette at last became pregnant – if she should give birth to a dauphin her position would be immeasurably strengthened. She duly began to throw her weight around, summoning Maurepas and Vergennes to her presence and, as she told her mother, Maria-Theresa, addressing them 'quite strongly'. But Maurepas was adamant. The urbane old man was worked up to fever pitch. He distrusted all standing alliances, such as those with Austria or Spain; France should be 'everyone's friend, no one's ally', he was fond of saying, and be 'self-sufficient, limiting herself to what she can achieve on her own'.[86] He stated quite simply that if Louis yielded to his wife's pressure to intervene in Germany he would resign. He was ultimately driven to a final elaboration of his system of regulating the king's contacts. He could hardly insist that the queen only talk to the king in his presence but he did insist that the queen only talk to him, Maurepas, in the king's presence, which, apart from being humiliating was also insulting to the queen because its sole purpose was to prevent her from pretending to Louis that Maurepas had made her concessions.[87] The king confided to Vergennes – 'this is for you alone' – that the queen had just had a letter from her mother saying that she had been 'abandoned by her allies' and that 'having had glory all her life it had been reserved for her old age to know humiliation'.[88] Even the queen's *accoucheur* weighed in, telling Louis how dangerous it would be to quarrel with a pregnant woman. 'I hear you', Louis replied, 'but the queen must not ask me for what I cannot give her.'[89]

In view of her condition, and because he was becoming genuinely fond of his wife as they came together physically, Louis generally treated her gently if firmly and silently. 'I could not hide from the king', Marie-Antoinette told her mother, 'the pain his silence caused me . . . over a matter of such importance to me . . . [but] I was disarmed by the tone he adopted. He told me, "You see that I have so many faults that I don't have a word to say in reply" ' – an elegant evasion.[90] On one occasion, however, he couldn't control his exasperation with his wife's meddling. Frederick had mobilized his forces on the border of the Habsburg kingdom of Bohemia and Joseph allowed him to enter there so he could activate his defensive treaty with France. Marie-Antoinette cornered her husband and asked him to support his ally with 30,000 troops. She blamed Vergennes, who bore the brunt of her wrath, for not stopping the conflict between the two Germanic powers. But Louis rounded on her: 'It is the ambition of your relatives which is going to upset everything. They began with [the partition of] Poland. Now Bavaria is the second volume. I am sorry for your sake.' 'But you can't deny, Monsieur,' Marie-Antoinette responded, 'that you were fully informed and in agreement on this Bavarian matter.' Louis replied brutally: 'So far was I from agreement that I have just ordered all the French diplomats to make known to the courts where they are resident that this dismemberment is done against our wishes and that we disapprove of it.'[91]

It is possible, then, that the French government, rather than clearing the European decks so that they could concentrate on an overseas war (the conventional view), involved themselves instead in an overseas war as a pretext not to support their Austrian ally in Germany. This concern, quite as much as hopes of activating the 'family compact', could also explain why the French government was so keen to present the *Belle Poule* incident as the English aggression which started the war. In other words, it was the Treaty of Versailles with Austria rather than that of El Pardo with Spain that was in view, especially as, on any interpretation, the latter did not require the element of aggression as a *casus foederis*. While it would be too much of a *jeu d'esprit* to suggest that France seriously expected Austria to provide Uhlans to fight in America, it is a fact that during the sessions of mutual recrimination which increasingly characterized the Franco-Austrian alliance, the Austrian reproach of lack of help over Bavaria and (later) Holland was matched with the French reproach of lack of assistance against England.

CHAPTER FIVE

AMERICAN LIBERTY AND ROYAL DEBT

1778–82

ALTHOUGH IT IS GENERALLY accepted that Vergennes and Sartine were the 'hawks', and Turgot and the war secretary, Montbarey, the 'doves', with Maurepas and the king somewhere in between, the spectrum of views within the government was not wide. Even Turgot could contemplate a short war, while Vergennes gambled on one. As for Maurepas, he was not interested in much beyond his lifetime, which came to the same thing – or so the cynics said. The government gambled on a one-campaign war. In the event there were five: in 1778, 1779, 1780, 1781 and 1782. They were lucky to escape a sixth, which would have been catastrophic. With luck and determination the one-year campaign plan could have succeeded. Its failure had two consequences: i) the need to bribe Spain into entering the war with her forty battleships; and ii) the need to consider wartime finance, which led to the rise of Jacques Necker, the necromancer who claimed to be able to square the circle by financing the war without raising taxes.

In breaking with England without having first secured Spanish participation, France had taken a calculated risk. In 1778, with her fifty-two capital ships and with the element of surprise, she would have near parity with and possibly local superiority over England. For France could recruit quickly from a system of naval reserves (*classes*) whereas England had to wait for returning merchantmen to crew all the ships in the Royal Navy. Vergennes hoped to capitalize on these factors to knock England out of the war in one campaign.

On 23 July a British fleet of twenty-nine battleships under Admiral Keppel attacked the French fleet 100 miles to the west of Ushant (Ouessant to the French). The battle was a draw, with a slight advantage to the French, who lost 127 men to England's 407, no ships being lost. The duc de Chartres, son of the duc d'Orléans, the next in line to the throne after the king and his two brothers and Artois's sons, had, as a naval lieutenant-general, commanded the vanguard, the blue squadron. He carried the news to Versailles, where for twenty minutes he and the 'victory' were celebrated. Then a clearer picture emerged. Orvilliers, whilst praising Chartres's 'admirable bravery', nevertheless asserted that if the blue squadron had not ignored or misinterpreted his orders to attack, 'the French flag would have gained the greatest glory'. Chartres was only a figure-head and La Motte-Picquet, who was effectively in command of the blue squadron, admitted that he himself had not seen Orvilliers's signal: two yellow flares, a blue and a red. Nevertheless, the king relieved Chartres of his command and transferred him to the army.

This was a blow not just to his pride but to his ambition as he had hoped to succeed to the post of grand admiral of France held by his father-in-law, the duc de Penthièvre. There was more than a suspicion that Louis was using Chartres's supposed misconduct as a pretext to prevent the Orléans branch, which he suspected of coveting the throne, from acquiring this prestigious position. Chartres, whose wife was the only child of Penthièvre, would in any case, with her inheritance coupled with the Orléans wealth, become the richest private individual in France. Whatever Louis's motives, his action permanently alienated Orléans, who would play a role – though its extent is contested – in bringing down the regime. Chartres's father, the old duc d'Orléans, had already annoyed Louis by refusing to salute the *parlement Maupeou* and had been exiled for his pains. Chartres in turn would suffer a similar fate for supporting the restored *parlement* in its battle to the death with Louis XVI.

The outcome of the war, however, would not be determined by a battle in the English Channel. Decisive victory could only be achieved in America. On 13 April the comte d'Estaing sailed from Toulon with twelve ships-of-the-line and five frigates. His ultimate destination was the West Indies, but first he was instructed to 'attack the English in the Delaware not only as far as New York but anywhere else in North America. . . . [He was] expressly ordered to perform some striking action which would be advantageous to the Americans and glorious for the king's arms.'[1] D'Estaing featured on Louis's father's list of men to employ; however, he had made his reputation as a soldier not a sailor, having transferred late to the navy. The winds were against him, but he was also dila-tory, taking time off to execute manoeuvres and capture prizes. The passage to the mouth of the Delaware, where the plan had been to defeat Lord Howe's squadron, therefore took eighty-five days. Howe had time to evacuate Philadelphia and enter the safe haven of New York, the main British base since its recapture in 1776. D'Estaing sailed in pursuit and arrived at Sandy Hook where he could see the English fleet in the bay. There was a chance of defeating

Howe here before Admiral Byron (uncle of the poet) arrived with reinforcements, but the waters were shallow and no pilot would guide the French vessels into the bay despite the offer of 150,000 *livres*.

D'Estaing now sailed on to Rhode Island, hoping to capture the English garrison of 6,000 men. Washington was to stop the English garrison at New York from coming to their relief whilst General Sullivan, with an army estimated at 10,000 men, and in conjunction with the French fleet, was to operate a pincer movement on the English garrison at Newport. It was a similar manoeuvre to the one which would succeed at Yorktown three years and half a billion *livres* later. If it had come off, so might Vergennes's gamble. The plan was for Sullivan to land on Rhode Island under the protection of the French fleet, but he took so long assembling his militia men that Howe was sighted off Newport with thirteen battleships. D'Estaing left the harbour to give chase with good hopes of success, but a violent gale wreaked havoc on his fleet, disabling his flagship, the *Languedoc*. The assault on Newport was abandoned and the fleet took refuge at Boston, where repairs were carried out. There was much recrimination on both sides, d'Estaing blaming Sullivan for squandering 'the most favourable opportunity, the precious moment of arrival when there is the element of surprise and often the least resistance'.[2]

D'Estaing then sailed to the West Indies where, the following year, he captured Grenada and St Vincent. He defeated the English fleet under Lord Byron, but failed to follow up his advantage and take Jamaica, an inestimable prize, as will be seen. In the autumn he was back in the United States, where Congress had asked him to halt the alarming English progress in the south. But, despite massive forces – a fleet of forty ships assembled in the West Indies and 4,000 troops – he failed in his objective of taking Savannah either by siege or by storm. The Americans retreated to Charleston and on 28 October the French fleet sailed away. It was the end of d'Estaing's war. We will, however, meet him again as the most outspoken defender of the royal programme of any member of the 1787 Assembly of Notables. Vergennes summed up the results of d'Estaing's campaign as 'des plus fâcheuses' (extremely trying).[3]

The Spanish alliance

The one-campaign plan having failed, Vergennes warned the king on 5 December 1778 'that it is a fact that Your Majesty cannot fight the English on equal terms for long and that a prolonged war which would not be exempt from disadvantages could entail the ruin of your navy and even of your finances'.[4] This alarming communication – its 'exempt from disadvantages' redolent of Hirohito's broadcast after Hiroshima – was conditional: unless Spain entered the war. In 1778 France had enjoyed near parity with England but for the 1779 campaign she would have about seventy ships to England's ninety. For Vergennes, the need for the Spanish alliance came down to a simple mathematical calculation based on the number of ships-of-the-line in service: Spain's forty ships, Vergennes argued, would be necessary to avert disaster.

Bringing Spain on board, however, was a difficult matter. Spain rightly feared a successful American rebellion would set an example to its own American colonies; Spain in any case shared the British desire to confine the nascent state behind the Alleghenies, so as to keep it out of the Mississippi valley and the Gulf of Mexico, where Spain's own colonies lay. Spain was still expanding in North America under Charles III – Los Angeles was founded in 1781. Moreover Spain was genuinely at a loss to see what France thought it could get out of the war. Grimaldi held it to be axiomatic that 'the aim of every war is to keep one's own territory or seize that of another'; his successor, Florida-Blanca, said France's war 'lacked an objective in starting it [and] a plan to prosecute it'.[5] Moreover, the termination of the dispute with Portugal had drawn the sting out of Spain's quarrel with England just at the time when France and England were drifting towards war. This led to a reversal of roles in the alliance: France now became the suitor, with Spain playing hard to get. Spain would make exorbitant demands and distort the conduct of the war.

There was a middle course theoretically available to France. The 'family compact' between the French and Spanish Bourbons stipulated that Spain should supply France with eighteen battleships on demand, and arguably this is what France should have settled for; particularly as the text of the compact seemed to provide that those ships that were captured or in need of their annual refitting should be replaced. This option might have been preferable to suffering the vagaries of combined operations and allowing the objective of the war to be distorted. For that is certainly what Spain intended: 'We do not wish to commit Spain to entering the war merely in order to frighten England into making a peace from which nothing but the independence of the Americans would be obtained.'[6] It was not certain, however, that Spain would supply the eighteen ships, although the treaty was crystal clear that offensive and defensive war were equally covered. For, as Vergennes told the king, Spain 'should already have furnished' the ships.[7]

Furthermore, as Montmorin, French ambassador to Spain, observed, if Spain did grudgingly supply the ships they would probably be 'its worst vessels which would probably be equipped with the least attention and commanded by its most ignorant and least cooperative officers'. So Montmorin advised: give Spain what it wants because 'once committed to the war, their need of us will make them more amenable and we will have the upper hand'. Vergennes proposed that Spain should regain Gibraltar, and Mobile and Pensacola in the Floridas, and that the English should be expelled from Honduras. Spain was to recognize the United States the day she entered the war. Florida-Blanca, apart from adding Minorca and the whole of the Floridas, modified these proposals in two important respects.

First, Spain would not recognize the United States until England did – she merely acknowledged that it was a French war aim and maintained this line throughout the conflict. For instance, the governor of Cuba refused the offer of American assistance in the conquest of English Florida, and Gérard, French plenipotentiary to the American Congress, was not received at court when he passed through Spain in 1780.[8] Spain hoped to give the thirteen colonies an anarchic constitution, such as that possessed by the Holy Roman Empire, in order to keep the new state weak.[9]

Second, whereas Vergennes had merely proposed that the allies should 'make every effort' to achieve these 'objectives', in the final version the allies were bound not to lay down arms until the retrocession of Gibraltar had been achieved. This was a tough nut to crack. Spain generously offered an objective of France's choice to put into this category; it suggested the right to fortify Dunkirk, but France had no intention of fortifying this place, just of expelling the English commissioner. Apart from this, the recognized French objectives were: wider fishing rights off Newfoundland; the right to possess forts in India; recovery of Senegal; and the retention of Dominica. Perhaps the worst feature of the treaty of Aranjuez, signed on 12 April 1779, was the clause which provided for a joint invasion of England that year. Combined with the futile attempt by combined forces to take Gibraltar in 1780–82, this meant that, as far as military operations were concerned, the Spanish tail was wagging the French dog.

Although Louis XV had drawn up a plan for an invasion of England, the moving force now was the Spanish minister, Florida-Blanca. He worked on it in 1778 and the first half of 1779 and insisted on absolute secrecy. Only Louis XVI, Maurepas and Vergennes were to know; the service ministers, Sartine and Montbarey, minister for war, were not told until March 1779; admirals and generals later. Naturally, Marie-Antoinette was excluded.[10] Florida-Blanca held it as axiomatic that Spain did not have the wherewithal to withstand a long war. Metropolitan Spain's backward economy meant the country was more dependent on her colonies than either England or France. Her resource economy as well as her finances would be gravely disrupted by war, especially one that cut her off from the riches of Ultramar.

Florida-Blanca accordingly favoured a combined Bourbon invasion of England, culminating in a dictated peace in London. This had three main advantages: i) that the war would be ended in a single campaign; ii) that with the theatre of war in Europe, Spain's colonies would be relatively safe; iii) that London (or Portsmouth, as was finally agreed on) could easily be exchanged at the peace for Gibraltar, Spain's main objective, which would be difficult to obtain directly, being regarded as almost impregnable.

Vergennes's objections to an invasion of England were, first, that, if successful, it would alarm Europe and might create allies for England (he was surely thinking of Austria); second, that an England so humiliated – and in the Americas Spain wanted to leave England with nothing but Canada – would seek revanche, whereas he wanted to end the war psychosis between the two countries, the seemingly endless cycles of humiliation and revenge; and third, his correct belief that American independence, France's first priority, could ultimately be won only in America. In this he was reflecting the established view of the marine ministry: France should tie up English forces with the threat of an invasion, but actually concentrate her resources in America and the West Indies. This view was especially espoused by Fleurieu, the director-general of ports and arsenals, to whom fell the chief responsibility for planning campaigns and who was highly regarded by his former pupil, Louis XVI.[11] As such, this was probably Louis's own view; but his uncle Charles had him over a barrel.

The invasion was abandoned for lack of a safe harbour in which to regroup after bad weather delayed sailing. England had many such harbours along her south coast but France had few on her channel side. This expensive fiasco cost 100 million *livres* and led to Spanish recriminations accusing France of deliberate sabotage. It led to a many-faceted crisis which marked the lowest point in Louis's reign before the Revolution.

The linked facets of the crisis included the threat of Spanish defection and the possibility of a premature and inglorious cessation of hostilities, which led to a standoff between Maurepas and Vergennes, and a quarrel between the finance minister, Necker, and Sartine over the latter's unbudgeted overspending. Louis had to resolve both these disputes. As Necker was at the heart of these disputes – even negotiating solo with England – and as his was arguably the most disastrous appointment Louis ever made, we will start with the peculiar circumstances of this unconventional and personal appointment by the king.

Necker

We have said something about Necker's early career in France: how he made a fortune out of privileged information, buying English stock just before the signing of the Peace of Paris in 1763; how, by the 1770s, his avarice was being displaced by his vanity and, pushed by his wife, a literary social climber and salon hostess, he sought high office, and this despite the apparently insuperable obstacles of being a foreign national and a Protestant; and, finally, how he sought to overcome these obstacles by a self-proclaimed disinterested use of that wealth, by the salon in which he was tirelessly puffed by his wife, and above all by cultivating the soil of public opinion, manuring it through his skills as a financial polemicist, employing the verbose and lachrymose style made fashionable by Jean-Jacques Rousseau. It will be remembered that he had made a name for himself by attacking Turgot's grain policies just as the Flour War was getting under way, and that Turgot referred to him as 'that joker'. Turgot's picture of Necker was shared by Vergennes and Soulavie (as well as by the writer of this book); but Necker was, at least until 1790, wildly popular and has received critical acclaim from some historians.[12]

On 22 October 1776, five months after Turgot's dismissal, Necker was appointed director-general of the royal treasury – as a Protestant he could not be sworn in as controller-general. The removal of Turgot in May 1776 revealed that he had been a rival centre of gravity to Maurepas within the ministry. Almost immediately after his dismissal, the other ministers invited Maurepas to sit in on their weekly *travail* with the king on a regular basis, to coordinate policy. Shortly afterwards the king appointed him *chef du Conseil royal des finances*. It was a purely decorative title – the *Conseil royal* hardly ever met – but so was the English first lord of the treasury: if the ancien régime had lasted longer, the title might have gathered to itself functions analogous to those of an English prime minister. At all events, it seemed that Maurepas would be able to see out the rest of his days in peace and preponderance. This was not to be the case, partly because Louis, whilst enhancing Maurepas's status, was not prepared to delegate to him any more power than he already possessed; partly also because the problem of royal finance was so central and so intractable that a finance minister of any talent, or even any character, was bound to exert a powerful influence. Turgot was succeeded by Clugny, who revoked his predecessor's reforms, Vergennes being most virulent in his criticism of his late colleague's 'metaphysical' edicts: 'he wanted to create and did not know how to correct'.[13] Clugny, apart from his scandalous lifestyle, is otherwise remembered as the only controller-general of the century to die in office (18 October 1776). It was Clugny's sudden death which led to the most unconventional of Louis's appointments, that of Jacques Necker four days later.

The appointment of such an outsider is attributable to Louis's personal interest in finance and the finance ministry, which he called 'the most sensitive position in the kingdom';[14] but it also sheds light on a controversial aspect of Louis XVI's kingship: his addiction to unofficial channels of information. Louis's tutors had stressed that a king was at a disadvantage in that his exalted position cut him off from information coming from the world outside Versailles and that he should strive to rectify this. Louis needed little prompting and was keen to chat to those menials and peasants who were thrown in his way. He also read the contemporary journals widely, and the English-language ones every day, to see what people thought of him. In 1780 Vergennes tactfully alluded to this practice apropos of a series of pamphlet attacks on Necker: 'Your Majesty is able to judge of the evident effect of such a number of writings, since you have had the goodness to show me, several times, that your majesty was employed in reading them.'[15]

But there was a darker side to this thirst for information. Louis continued Louis XV's practice of reading private mail. His chief source of such information (though it was not through him that Necker was appointed) was the *intendant des postes*, d'Ogny. D'Ogny had a secret bureau of twelve clerks employed in opening intercepted letters and showed Louis extracts from these on Sundays, when he had a regular *travail* with the king. D'Ogny and his *cabinet noir* represented a major breach in Maurepas's system of controlling the information that Louis received; indeed, Maurepas's own wife dared not express herself freely in letters because she knew that d'Ogny read the king extracts from them.

Apart from gaining information from intercepted letters, which, according to Véri, contributed to his indecisiveness, Louis, perhaps because of his physical inaccessibility, was inundated with letters from informers, cranks or men with projects, and it was by this epistolary means that Necker was worked into the ministry. The agent of this manoeuvre was a *littérateur* and former soldier called Alexandre Masson. He was an adventurer, fabricating for himself the bogus title of marquis de Pezay, but he had useful contacts. His father had been an important naval contractor and had had many dealings with Maurepas when he was naval minister; Maurepas had stood godfather to the boy. When he grew up he wrote a book on military history and, presumably through Maurepas's influence, became tutor in military tactics to Louis XVI when he was dauphin – another of Maurepas's pedagogical protégés. Assuredly it was not the accident of a broken spur which had led to Maurepas's appointment. Pezay, in Véri's words, 'created for himself a sort of ministry by writing letters to the king and receiving replies', which admirably defines the essence of a ministerial relationship with the king and shows how easy it was to establish one.

It seems that Pezay recommended Necker to the king some time in 1776 and, reputedly for the sum of 100,000 *livres*, forwarded his financial projects to Louis, who found them interesting. A letter from Necker to Maurepas of August or September refers to 'the analysis of the financial situation which I have made and of which the king has approved'.[16] This suggests that Necker bounced Maurepas into recommending his appointment by giving the impression that the king intended to appoint him in any case. There is some evidence that Maurepas was planning to have Beaumarchais appointed court banker (an equivalent position) to facilitate his funding of the American colonists. Beaumarchais was, with Maurepas's knowledge, working on a scheme that would enable full-scale naval rearmament without a state bankruptcy, which would have been 'infamous in the midst of peace'.[17] Necker's correspondence with the king was probably along these lines and secured the 'approval' of a king who wanted a strong navy, accepted the verdict of both Terray and Turgot that the existing structure would not support additional taxation, but had also eschewed 'bankruptcy' – Vergennes, for example, telling him that he dare not mention the prospect or even the very word, 'Your Majesty, out of delicacy and equity, having proscribed the word from the very day of his accession'.

But could these three conditions – rearmament, no new taxation and no bankruptcy – be reconciled? It would require sleight of hand. This was the great age of the charlatan. Cagliostro and Mesmer (the latter with adherents in the French cabinet, the former favoured by a cardinal and a court banker) were the most famous of them but there were many others. It was also the age of the 'project': the scheme for getting something for nothing, the quest for the philosopher's stone. As in the late twentieth century, the rapid decline of formal religion gave rise to an increase in superstition. As de Tocqueville observed, the French Revolution itself was a displacement activity of this kind. Louis was interested in 'projects' and therefore susceptible to their authors. And in public finance he was particularly vulnerable to them because he too needed to square a circle, to turn dross into gold. How else could he pursue naval rearmament, let alone fight a war, without increasing taxation or declaring a bankruptcy? Turgot had said it could not be done and Turgot was right.

These constraints meant that a future war would have to be financed by credit, and Necker observed, plausibly, that this could more easily be obtained by an ex-banker than an ex-intendant (the usual background of a controller-general). To preserve the forms, it was agreed that an ex-intendant would be made nominal controller-general, but, as the *parlementaire* Lefevre d'Amécourt noted, 'the king at the same time reserved to himself the direction of the royal treasury and nominated le Sieur Necker to exercise it under his own orders with the title ... director-general of the royal treasury',[18] which suggests that Louis felt personally responsible for keeping an eye on his unconventional appointment.

On the choice of a controller-general, Necker arrogantly mused to Maurepas: 'We have still got to find this man in whom I am looking only for very ordinary qualities and I have to say that I myself do not know a single *homme de robe* I can confidently suggest.'[19] Thus Necker questions the adequacy of the classical training of a minister under the ancien régime, i.e., presenting cases in the *Conseil d'État* as a *maître des requêtes* before administering a province as an intendant and finally returning to Versailles as a minister. It was one of his most important contributions to the debate about government, raising an issue relevant to all periods and all regimes: that of the claims of the specialist and the technician, against those of the man with a good general training but no directly relevant experience – the 'Greats man' in the British civil service being a case in point.

The straw-man chosen for controller-general was Taboureau des Réaux, who soon felt that the humiliation of his position exceeded its prestige and resigned in June 1777, Necker becoming director-general of finances. As a Protestant, Necker could not countersign executive orders, so Maurepas had to sit in on all of his *travaux* with the king, however routine. True to his word, Necker did not increase taxes to pay for that war, which cost about 400 million *livres* during his period in office, though he did prolong until 1790 the second *vingtième*, which was due to expire at the end of 1780. Instead he relied on loans, arguing that it was permissible to raise these provided that sufficient money to service them was saved through economies. Good husbandry and individual economies appealed to Louis, who practised them himself, sometimes to a ludicrous extent, as when he told Marie-Antoinette, who remarked on his shabby coat, 'Nevertheless, Madame, it will have to last the summer.'

Necker also appealed to Louis because he was a reformer but, unlike Turgot, he was not an ideologue. Necker, whose principles were eclectic, had read and absorbed the writings of men such as Moreau, who had influenced Louis's intellectual development. Both Louis and Necker wanted to explain the objectives of government to the people but through paternal absolutism rather than enlightened despotism. Both were adepts of the sentimental style of the day.

Consider the words that Necker put into Louis's mouth in a public declaration of 1788: 'For several years I have known only fleeting happiness.... What does spending money do for one's happiness?'[20]

Necker's memory will have to sustain a weight of criticism in this biography, so it is only fair to say at the outset three things in mitigation: i) Louis set the parameters of war without increased taxation or bankruptcy; ii) the rates of interest on his earlier loans were not as crippling as on the later ones; and iii) Necker, like everyone else in government, was gambling on a short war.

That the war was still raging, or rather not raging, in 1780 led to the crisis of that year when the various strands of foreign and domestic politics threatened to converge and reinforce each other in a Dickensian dénouement.

The mid-war crisis of 1780

By the autumn of 1780 France had fought three campaigns and achieved little. As Montmorin put it, they always 'fought in the present year the campaign they should have fought in the one before.'[21] And wise Véri said: 'This is the third campaign rendered totally useless either by waiting for ... [Spain's] alliance or as a result of its conclusion.'[22] The 1779 failed invasion of England ending Spain's hopes of acquiring an equivalent to exchange for Gibraltar meant she had to address herself to acquiring the rock directly. She mounted a blockade with eleven battleships, but, on 18 January 1780, Admiral Rodney relieved the garrison and inflicted a crushing defeat on a Spanish fleet sent to pursue him. The British relief of Gibraltar and the losses inflicted on the Spanish fleet nearly knocked Spain out of the war.

In September Vergennes received an ultimatum from Florida-Blanca: complaining that the provisions in the convention of Aranjuez for combined operations were being systematically ignored, the Spanish minister stated baldly that his country could only support one more campaign and that, unless a large combined expedition were sent to capture Jamaica (which could be exchanged for Gibraltar) and knock England out of the war, she would immediately sue for peace. Florida-Blanca asked France to supply half the forces: 12,000 troops and twenty ships-of-the-line. 'Fine', said Maurepas, 'let her sue for peace'; and on 26 September, after a crisis meeting with Necker, who was the chief proponent of an early peace, Maurepas gave the king an 'alarming' presentation of the financial situation and argued that there was no alternative to France herself suing for peace.[23]

Maurepas would have proposed an *uti possidetis* truce for America with mutual restoration of conquests between France and England. Maurepas confessed to Véri, however, that 'M. de Vergennes is not in favour of a truce',[24] as it would be letting down the Americans. Vergennes wanted instead to meet the Spanish demands halfway. At least by concentrating on Jamaica they would be in the right hemisphere, and after Jamaica had been taken the troops could be transferred to America. But Maurepas overruled him and Vergennes had to give way: 'You absolutely insist . . . I shall obey you because you are the prime minister and the king himself. But under protest'.[25] But Maurepas wasn't the king; Louis XVI was; so Vergennes put pressure on Louis to overrule his 'prime minister'.

Next day he wrote to Louis one of the most eloquent, even grandiloquent pieces of blackmail in diplomatic history. He didn't dispute Maurepas's assertion that the state of the finances was 'truly alarming and seem to offer no alternative to peace and that immediately'. (In fact, the next day he wrote to Montmorin, saying that France could only afford 150,000 *livres* of war expenses for 1781 and that even 'such ruinous efforts' would not be enough to make feasible a major conquest, such as that of Jamaica.)[26] So should he instruct Montmorin to tell Spain to go ahead and sue for peace? Montmorin would make the best of a bad job but, Vergennes continued, 'to admit to Spain that we have need of peace and that we are relying on her to secure it!' – it didn't bear thinking about. 'There is no one, Sire, who could answer for the consequences and assure Your Majesty that his reputation and *gloire* would not be compromised. I only speak of this, Sire, because beside it all other considerations pale into insignificance.' He asked the king to ponder this and 'if need be consult M. le comte de Maurepas', but – and here came the punchline – 'if the conclusion is to make an approach to Spain, then I most humbly beseech Your Majesty to give me the order in writing. The circumstances which have necessitated unfortunate courses of action fade and are soon forgotten, but the bad effects which result from them are felt the more the greater the distance from their cause.'[27]

Vergennes's eloquent blackmail had an immediate effect on the king: Spain was fobbed off with the promise of extra help in the West Indies and the war cabinet – Louis, Vergennes, Maurepas and Sartine – sat down to plan the campaign (possibly first suggested by Montmorin) which would culminate in the decisive and brilliant victory at Yorktown a year later. In retrospect, Vergennes had been wrong to press for war in 1777; but in retrospect he was right to reject peace in 1780. The saving to the exchequer would have been comparatively small, the humiliation for the regime perhaps fatal.

But behind the genuine drama of these exchanges lay a dramatic irony: all the while, and unbeknown to Vergennes though not to Louis, Necker, Maurepas and, yes, Spain were already engaged in secret peace negotiations with the enemy. There are two recorded instances of Necker's contacts with England in 1780: one in July, the other in December. All we know of the July initiative is that Necker approached Lord Stormont, who had been the English ambassador to France before the war and with whom Necker had enjoyed good relations. A bald English cabinet minute dated 3 August reads: 'Declaration delivered this day to Ld Stormont by Baron [*sic*] Necker read, and the answer prepared by Ld Stormont read and approved.'[28]

In July Maurepas also contacted Lord North and George III through the Anglo-Irish amateur diplomat Nathaniel Parker Forth – he whose information Louis thought was unreliable. Again, our knowledge of this comes from George III's correspondence. On 29 July, Lord North, enclosing Maurepas's letter to Forth, comments 'that it is certainly genuine' and that 'notwithstanding the very deceitful character of the writer' Maurepas seemed to want 'an end to the war, at least whilst he was writing the letter'. George, who was also 'well acquainted with the duplicity of [Maurepas's] conduct', authorized Forth to proceed on the understanding that American independence could not even be discussed.[29] This is all we hear of that particular initiative.

After the Spanish crisis, Maurepas and Necker continued their contacts with England, again with the king's knowledge and without Vergennes's. At least Necker wrote on his copy of the letter dated 1 December, which he sent to Lord North, that it had been sent to Maurepas and forwarded with the approval of the king.[30] Its central plank is again the *uti possidetis* truce and it contains the dig that England probably had a better idea of Spain's requirements than did France; for Spain, behind her ally's back, had been in negotiations of her own with George III, who was more hopeful of peace with her than with France. On 18 December, George wrote to Lord North rejecting a truce on the grounds that it was 'the same in reality' as 'independency' for the Americans.[31] Further negotiations between France and England would have to await a resolution of the military stalemate.

The crisis in Franco-Spanish relations, which passed from the acute to its normal chronic condition, intensified again a year later. The marquis de Castries, who had succeeded Sartine, thought that Spain was not pulling its weight and wanted to raise the matter before the king in the council, but Maurepas, 'who finds the presence of the king inconvenient, eluded this presence by saying that it led to delays'. Nevertheless the council met and

M. de Maurepas went in with the ministers and spoke to . . . [Castries] alone for a few minutes. The matter was presented; M. de Vergennes discussed it and concluded that the Spaniards should be given four thousand men without strings [for an attack on Minorca]. M. de Maurepas mouthed in a low voice (for he articulated nothing) that it was necessary to prevent the Spaniards from making their peace without us.

M. de Castries remained silent but the king, who knew his opinion, smiled at him and invited him to speak. M. de Castries said that since the Spanish fleet is giving us no assistance, let us make clear to Europe that our forces are inferior to England's which accounts for our setbacks. "But", said the king, "it was us who dragged them into this war and that is a reason not to put pressure on them". This remark, which was loyal and fair-minded, and which did not seem to have been dictated [by Vergennes or Maurepas] disposed M. de Castries not to press his point too vigorously.[32]

Louis was sensitive to the accusation that he always followed Vergennes's lead and he found it necessary to reassure Castries: 'You can speak frankly [in cabinet] in the knowledge that I take the decisions. It's not M. de Vergennes but me.' To which Castries replied, 'but if Your Majesty always ranges himself with the opinion of M. de Vergennes, it is in effect he who decides'.[33]

Castries's appointment had arisen from a bitter quarrel between Necker and Sartine. 'Unless the king', Véri wrote in 1780, 'reduces departmental expenditure to a sum inferior to the revenue, the post of controller-general is untenable in the long run'. Louis's failure to do this, serious enough in time of peace, became critical during the war because of the large sums of money involved. The problem was expressed in terms of a clash between Necker and Sartine, who, as minister for the marine, was the biggest paymaster during an overseas war. 'No minister', observed the naval intendant, Malouet, 'had as many ships constructed or provisioned the ports better'. But he did this regardless of expense: there is a pleasant cartoon of Sartine bending down by the shore and skimming silver écus across the sea. Necker was not alone in attributing Sartine's extravagance to the 'attention to detail of the bureaucrat' and thinking that a military man, which meant a *grand seigneur*, would be cheaper because of his expert knowledge.[34] Necker's conclusion, never devoid of paradox, would soon be filled with irony: Sartine's seigneurial successor, Castries, would bankrupt the monarchy.

In 1779 Necker allocated Sartine 120 million *livres* for the naval campaign of 1780; judging this to be inadequate, Sartine, without consulting Necker, ordered the treasurer of the marine to issue notes to the value of 21 million *livres*. When he found out, a year later, Necker wrote to Maurepas of this 'thunderclap as unexpected as it is incredible'.[35] Necker was not suffering merely from hurt pride; 21 million *livres* was a substantial sum (one-sixth of the naval estimates) and it forced him to pay 6 per cent instead of 5.5 per cent to borrow money against the tax receipts for 1781.[36] Sartine, in turn, when he was again allocated 120 million *livres* for the 1781 campaign, posed his dilemma neatly: the king had eighty ships-of-the-line, but for that money Sartine could only put sixty to sea. It was a policy decision the king would have to make.

The crisis found the lines of communication between the king and Maurepas cut as Maurepas was confined to bed in Paris with a particularly bad attack of gout aggravated by fever – in a secretary's hand he told Louis, 'I do not have the strength to hold a pen'.[37] On 1 October Necker was therefore able to have his *travail* alone with the king and presented him with an ultimatum: either Sartine or he must go. Louis broached the matter of the 21 million with Sartine, who excused himself by saying that the money was for secret naval operations which could not be disclosed to Necker because he was in treasonable correspondence with England. After such an accusation it is hard to see how Necker and Sartine could serve in the same administration. The king would have called Necker's bluff except for the fact that, 'scanning the *Almanac Royal* with . . . Maurepas he did not find anyone suitable [to be finance minister] in public employment. It was not that he could not find people who wanted the job, just that, as . . . [Maurepas] said only a fool or a knave would want it.'[38]

So, on 2 October, Louis sent Maurepas one of his most characteristic notes: 'Shall we dismiss Necker, or shall we dismiss Sartine? I am not displeased with the latter. I think Necker is more useful to us.' This cynical and graceless communication makes no attempt either to impose a policy decision or reconcile the two ministers. Necker had the audacity to demand that Maurepas show him the king's note, and Maurepas had the weakness to comply; thus Necker temporarily reversed the tables on Maurepas, screening the king's contact with his own leading minister!

The king then decamped to Choisy, where he stayed until 6 October; next day he returned to Versailles, but was at Compiègne from 8 to 11 October. Marie-Antoinette remained at Versailles, where, on 8 October she gave Necker an audience. She affected to take him under her wing and Necker exploited this to tell the sick and isolated Maurepas that the queen had obtained the king's positive word to replace Sartine with Necker's friend the marquis de Castries, a former protégé of Choiseul and fellow director of Necker's in the *Compagnie des Indes*, the French equivalent of the East India Company. When, on 12 October, Maurepas had finally recovered sufficiently for Louis to come

Paris to see him (by convention the king did not visit seriously sick ministers), Maurepas applauded what he mistakenly believed to be a *fait accompli* – just as he had when Necker had duped him into believing that the king had already decided to appoint him in 1776. The queen, who regarded Sartine as her protégé, had not brought him down. On this Castries himself is explicit: 'everything had been arranged with M. Necker before telling the queen'.[39] But it suited both queen and minister to act as if Castries *was* her protégé.

Maurepas consoled himself by telling the king that they could always dismiss Necker as soon as the war was over. When Maurepas next saw Necker he said to him: 'They're saying in Paris that I am trying to have you dismissed just as you were trying to have me dismissed when I was detained at Paris; one is no more true than the other.'[40] Sartine, the scapegoat, delivered himself of a bitter indictment of Louis:

> You will not find any class of citizen in public affairs for whom the king and his family display the slightest affection. They will let the various factions fight each other, if they so desire, and the king will in turn sacrifice them one to the others, beginning with the ministers of whatsoever party. Everyone has now had time to judge the king. The statement by the ministers that a measure represents the king's volition is no longer an efficacious weapon in their hands. The measure is regarded as representing merely the ministers' personal policy, to be contested with every confidence.[41]

Sartine was not exiled, but he was not consoled by being granted a pension so generous it became the yardstick by which colleagues measured their own. Some thought this generosity indicated that Louis was keeping Sartine in reserve to succeed the ailing Maurepas. They were wrong – he acted out of a guilty conscience.

After dismissing Sartine on 13 October, Louis decamped to Marly, where he remained for the rest of the month. But first Louis sent Maurepas the following note, the only one of several written during this crisis to have survived: 'if you see M. de Vergennes, reassure him if he is worried'.[42] This looks suspiciously like Louis leaving Maurepas to pick up the pieces, for, although the move to Marly would have been planned well in advance, the timing of Sartine's dismissal would have been designed to fit in with it.

Vergennes was upset with Louis on several counts. In the first place, Louis had rejected his report to the council, on which Necker as a Protestant did not have a seat, about the differences between Necker and Sartine, which had been entirely favourable to the latter.[43] Second, Sartine was Vergennes's personal friend as well as his political ally; Vergennes believed that a serving minister should cease intimate relations with a disgraced one for reasons of security; so, out of a sense of duty rather than cowardice, Vergennes felt himself obliged to 'drop' Sartine, which he promptly did.[44] In addition, Vergennes had been outspoken in his attacks on Necker. Véri relates that Vergennes 'has always been M. Necker's most determined adversary, badgering M. de Maurepas to dismiss M. Necker on suspicion of treasonable relations with the English for the profit of his bank or some other even worse motive. Is it possible to believe that M. Necker is ignorant of this and doesn't resent it?'[45] Given that both Maurepas and Necker were negotiating separately with England, with Louis's knowledge but not Vergennes's, and given Louis's intimate knowledge of the English political scene, it could have been that the king himself was the driving force behind the negotiations. This would explain the resentful tone of Vergennes's letter asking for a written order to negotiate.

Even when yielding to Necker, Maurepas believed it was the Genevan's plan to 'run all the ministries'.[46] In dismissing Sartine rather than Necker, Maurepas for once rejected the advice of his wife; neither did he consult the other ministers, because he knew they were all solidly behind Sartine, if only out of self-defence. And they were right. In December, Necker followed up his advantage by asking the king to replace Maurepas's cousin, Montbarey, the minister for war, with the marquis de Ségur. Louis was in a quandary, telling Marie-Antoinette, 'M. de Maurepas is old; perhaps he does not have a year to live. I would cause pain to this old man. I don't know what to do.'[47] But he sacrificed Montbarey as he had Sartine.

By no stretch of the imagination could Montbarey's tenure of the war ministry be described as distinguished, though he did have the integrity to oppose entering the American war in spite of the fact that it would 'quadruple' his influence.[48] A prince of the Holy Roman Empire and a grandee of Spain, in France his consideration depended largely on the kinship and protection of Maurepas. Two episodes in his career exemplify Louis XVI's relationships with his ministers. Montbarey had thought that his age (he was forty-eight in 1780), 'although double that of His Majesty, being much closer than that of his other ministers', meant that he would have more in common with the king. Perhaps for this reason he decided to tell not only Maurepas but also Louis of his decision not to take a conventional mistress (who would take up too much time, demand favours and embarrass his wife) but to ask Lenoir, the police minister, to procure him a prostitute and arrange for her to be spied upon to prevent her causing trouble. Louis, 'without exactly approving, agreed with me that this course of action was the least subject to drawbacks'.

On another occasion, Louis smoothed Montbarey's path with the queen, whose interference in military promotions was a source of frequent disputes. After one of these, he ran to the king's apartments, trusting that his superior speed would outweigh the queen's advantage of the secret passage. Outstripping her, he was the recipient of elaborate advice from the king:

> No one knows better than I . . . what you have gone through; calm yourself; I will take it on myself to mention the matter to the queen. But for some time avoid seeing her; and as for the matters of which you are accustomed to give her an account, I will undertake them, and I will tell you when you may and when you ought to present yourself before her. For this await my positive orders. Moreover, rest assured about the possible consequences of this affair; I will take you under my protection and you have nothing to fear.

It was six weeks before Louis judged it right for Montbarey to see the queen. Montbarey told Maurepas of his quarrel with her, but not, at first, of his audience with the king.

Montbarey's replacement by Ségur was, for Maurepas, the deadliest blow he ever received and was compounded by the role Marie-Antoinette played in it. In the twilight of his life he had lost control over the composition of the ministry. Véri signalled that his decline occurred 'as soon as it was believed he no longer had the same influence in decision-making and in the choice of the men he had to work with. It seemed to me, moreover, that he could not expect from the newcomers, appointed against his wishes, the same agreement and harmony he had found in their predecessors.'[49] And he was right; Castries did not invite Maurepas to attend his *travail* with the king and when, as a matter of courtesy, Castries informed Maurepas of the changes he had made to his secretariat (the subject of his first *travail* with the king), Maurepas 'replied drily that he was already aware of them'.[50] The king had naturally told him.

Maurepas's position at this time was complicated. His wife wanted him to resign over Ségur's appointment. But power was keeping him alive. Instead he told the king that the whole of Paris was buzzing with the rumour that he was about to be made prime minister – a return to the charge he had made back in 1774. Louis told Marie-Antoinette this with the comment, 'what stupidity; it lacks common sense.'[51] Castries would not allow Maurepas to sit in on his *travail* with the king, but in return Maurepas was giving alternative naval commands, including sending a naval expedition Castries knew nothing about. But Castries did not want Maurepas to resign. Instead he wanted him to take responsibility for what Castries considered to be Maurepas's war.[52]

Necker's first ministry, 1776–81

Necker's victory was a Pyrrhic one; Maurepas was to have the last laugh, one of many in his life. But first he let Necker have his moment of glory and his king bask in its reflection. In 1780 Edmund Burke – the future scourge of the French Revolution and philosophical father of Toryism, but then a Whig supporter of American independence – praised the French king in the House of Commons:

> By economy Lewis XVI has found sufficient resources to sustain the war. In the first two years of it he has laid no burden whatever on his people. The third year is arrived; still no talk of imposts; and I believe that even those which are common in time of war have not been laid on. I conceive that in the end France must have recourse to imposts but those three years saved will extend their benign influence through a whole age. The French people feel the happiness of having an economical master; economy has induced that monarch rather to retrench his own splendours than the subsistence of his people. In the suppression of great numbers of places he has found a resource to continue the war, without adding to his expenses. He has despoiled himself of the magnificence and purple of royalty; but he has established a navy; he has reduced the number of his household servants but he has augmented the number of his sailors; he has given France such a navy as she never before possessed, and which will immortalize his reign; and he has established it without laying on a penny of imposts. The people under his reign are great, glorious and formidable; they do not groan under the burden of expenses to which our nation must submit to acquire great-ness and inspire fear. This is true glory; this is a reign which must raise the name of Lewis XVI above the boasted reign of Henry IV.
>
> Lewis XVI, like a patriot king, has exhibited great firmness in protecting Mr. Necker, a foreigner without support and without connexion at court, alone indebted for his elevation to merit and the discernment of his sover-eign, who has been able to discover and appreciate his talents. Here is a good example to follow; and, if we wish to conquer France, it is with her own weapons that we must attack her here; it is with economy and reformation.[53]

This is probably the highest praise Louis XVI has ever received. Louis trans-lated Burke's speech into French, and showed it to Necker, ostensibly to ask whether his translation was correct, in fact as a graceful way of letting Necker know of Burke's praise for his ministry.

Burke was completely wrong in saying Necker was 'without connexion at court'; quite as much as his ability to manipulate public opinion, it was the basis of his power. Necker got away with reducing court pensions, which so impressed Burke, because the pill was sweetened by a simultaneous increase in the political power of the military aristocracy. This occurred both at the centre – we have seen the introduction of two military aristocrats as service ministers – and in the provinces, where, in line with the prevailing belief that it was necessary to devolve administration if not political power, he set up two pilot 'provincial administrations' at Bourges and Montauban. In the Bourges assembly, set up in 1778, the original sixteen members were appointed by the king and these co-opted a further thirty-two colleagues: Turgot's planned assemblies were to have been directly elected. Moreover, whereas in Turgot's scheme the members were to be chosen from and by landowners, irrespective of birth, in Necker's membership was allocated, a third each, to the three juridical orders of ancien régime society: clergy, nobility and the third estate. Necker also decided that the noble members should be restricted to those whose family had owned a fief for more than 100 years. This discriminated heavily in favour of the old military nobility, since more recent ennoblements were gained largely through the purchase of legal appointments, with no obligation to acquire a fief. Necker placed bishops as presidents of his assemblies.

This attack on the service nobility, the *noblesse de robe,* lay at the philosophical heart of Necker's project, but there is evidence that it did not find favour with the king. Necker believed that while France was governed by some hundred families of the administrative *noblesse de robe*, who were promoted according to seniority, it was patently absurd to consider that such families had a monopoly of the administrative talent in the kingdom. His particular bête noire was the position of intendant, of whom he wrote in a celebrated passage:

One can hardly give the name administration to this arbitrary volition of a single man who, whether present or absent, informed or incompetent, is obliged to run the most important aspects of the public service, for which he is necessarily unsuited, having devoted his entire life previously to the appellate functions of the council.[54]

Moreover, Necker claimed, intendants spent most of their time intriguing to get back to Versailles as a *conseiller d'état* or a minister. Necker, like Turgot, envisaged his assemblies as ultimately replacing both the intendants and the provincial *parlements* as well as giving the regime a wider basis of support, though in practical terms that meant transferring the basis of support from the administrative nobility to the military one and to the clergy. It should also be said that both Turgot's and Necker's assemblies, whatever their differences, predominantly represented landed wealth rather than trade and industry, though overseas trade was the main generator of new wealth in France and the reason wars were now fought.

Necker's contention that France was run by a hundred administrative families was not controversial. Soulavie thought that it was only fifty, whom he 'religiously preserves' by naming them in a footnote. These men, by their very caution, preserved the systems which had been installed by Richelieu and Colbert, the founding fathers of Bourbon absolutism. 'Such', Soulavie concludes, 'was the form and regularity of the customs that one vigorous mind might preserve inviolate our ancient institutions'[55] – rather like Asimov's *Foundation*. Soulavie may even have got this idea from the king, whose marginal comments on Turgot's project he transcribed: 'I find in the series of administrators, nominated by my ancestors, and in the principal families of the *robe* [lawyer's gown] and even of *la finance* of my kingdom, Frenchmen who would have done honour to any nation of the known world.'[56] These families, coeval with Bourbon absolutism, had created it and in some cases would die for it.

Apart from the service nobility, Louis in the above extract also pays a compliment to Necker's other bugbear: *la finance*. It was a backhanded compliment – qualified by 'even' – but one which implied that on this issue, untypically, he was prepared to take an unpopular stance. What was *la finance*? Was not Necker the financier par excellence? Today all bankers are hated, but in 1794 only the farmers-general were sent en bloc in one 'fournée', or baker's batch, to the guillotine. We have seen from Turgot's attack on them that the tax farmers were an important element of *la finance* – Louis called them 'the columns of the state'.

Like other officeholders such as *parlementaires*, each of the members of *la finance*, one of the most characteristic phenonena of the ancien régime, bought his office, and this represented a loan to the state on which he received 5 per cent interest. The most important members were the *intendants des finances*, who formed a permanent council for the usually transient finance ministers, and the receivers-general of the direct and the farmers-general of the indirect taxes. The *intendants des finances* were unpopular because they decided the tax affairs of individuals in secrecy and without appeal. They also acted as a break on a reforming finance minister and Necker therefore abolished them. Members of *la haute finance*, such as the receivers and farmers-general, employed their own people to collect the taxes and advanced money to the crown against future receipts whose level was contractually guaranteed.

The distinction between public and private was blurred, but so it was in Britain after the bank 'rescues' of 2009. Necker moved from these early-modern arrangements towards the modern system of paying officials a salary to collect taxes, though with an element of bonus, not automatic, as today, but kicking in if the expected receipts were exceeded – this *régie intéressée* replaced tax farming.[57]

Soulavie, however, and Louis defended the traditional financiers as a bulwark of the regime. They paid the crown less than they collected but it was an advance against taxes which, in the case of the *taille*, took two years to collect. Moreover, the financiers would also lend unsecured sums to the king through thick and thin because they were 'tied to the maintenance of the machine'.[58] They lent to the crown because that was their *raison d'être*. They also provided a self-correcting mechanism, providing for the king's legitimate needs, but recoiling if his policies seemed to be going off the rails, as during Louis XIV's minority and dotage. Because they were tied to the regime, they defended it against all comers. How else than by their being 'tied to the maintenance of the machine' could one explain the willingness of the old financiers to lend to the government days before the fall of the Bastille or to the king had the flight to Varennes succeeded? As Malesherbes and his family, for the administrative robe, paid for their devotion on the scaffold, so, for *la finance*, did Magon de la Balue, who serviced the royal debt, as well as the farmers-general. That is why Louis said that 'even the financiers ... would have done honour to any nation of the known world'. Yet, perceiving their utility, he nevertheless permitted the attack on them.

Soulavie contrasts the willingness of the old financiers to lend to their native government with the footloose international capital favoured by Necker, eager to seek out the maximum advantage wherever it was to be found. And again there are modern parallels – after Western bankers withdrew credit from emerging markets in 1998 these countries built up their own reserves. The native system Soulavie dubs 'French' and the foreign one 'Anglo-Genevan'.

The French system, which had prevailed until Louis XVI's accession, also required that extraordinary wartime expenditure should be 'derived only from taxes or loans founded upon them'. The Anglo-Genevan system, orginated and promoted by Necker, countenanced financing war from loans without the collateral of additional taxation. Soulavie argued that Louis was buffeted like a 'shuttlecock' between these two systems, just as he was buffeted between pro- and anti-*philosophe* and pro- and anti-Austrian factions. The two financial systems alternated during the period 1774–94: when the 'French' system was installed in government, the Anglo-Genevan formed the opposition, until it was at length replaced by it. So Turgot (1774–76) told Louis on his appointment that in peacetime there should be neither new loans nor new taxes but that war must be financed by new taxation. He was followed by Necker who, in his first ministry (1776–81), financed the American war by unsecured loans; he in turn was followed by Joly de Fleury (1781–83) who instituted loans secured by increased taxation. That was also the aim of Calonne (1783–87), though his pursuit of the taxation side of the equation was unsuccessful. The alternating cycle continued into the Revolution with the Genevan Clavière versus the native Cambon.[59]

Necker's reforms made enemies – not just among *la finance* but with the king's brothers, who were accustomed to placing their protégés and receiving *croupes* in return. But Necker had a strong following among the *soi-disant* liberal aristocracy at court – people like Castries, who would have preferred an English-style aristocratic system to the, at least theoretically, absolute French monarchy. Necker was nudging France in this direction and later admitted that it was his goal. Moreover, as long as he could finance the war he was invulnerable. In 1780 he had been faced with this paradox: war finance was becoming increasingly difficult, but if his peace feelers were successful he would, as Maurepas told Louis, become expendable.

Wars could never be financed by increased taxation alone; that would have meant either raising the level of taxation by 50 per cent, which would have ruined the peasantry, or making the 500,000 members of the privileged classes bear the whole burden, which would have led to outright revolt as happened in 1787, when far less was demanded of them. It was rather a question of a balance between taxation and loans. However, with each succeeding war in which France was engaged in the eighteenth century, the date at which wartime taxation kicked in was deferred. With Necker delaying taxation so long, creditors, worried that they would not get their money back, began to demand a higher rate of return. Over his time in office Necker borrowed a total of 530 million *livres* at an average rate of interest of 6 per cent. For comparison, the English government, with its borrowing backed by parliament, was able to borrow at about 3.5 per cent. It is not altogether fanciful to say that this discrepancy is enough to explain why there was a revolution in France but not in England.

Even that 6 per cent was an average. At the beginning of his ministry the rate was nearer 5 per cent, and would have been lower but for Terray's 1770 bankruptcy. By 1779 the rate had crept up to 7.5 per cent, and at the beginning of 1781 Necker was obliged to offer life annuities at 10 per cent.[60] Necker's loan of January 1781 met with a lukewarm response, despite the fact that for the first time interest payments were exempted from the normal 10 per cent taxation at source. On top of this there had been a lively pamphlet war against him – one pamphlet, significantly, discussed the theme of taxes versus loans;[61] Maurepas, smarting from the ministerial changes that Necker had sprung on him, encouraged rather than contained it.

This is the background to Necker's celebrated or infamous *Compte rendu au Roi* of February 1781, which purported to be a statement of royal revenue and expenditure and was designed to facilitate another loan by raising Necker's own stature. If his 'account' was 'to the king', why publish it? The answer to that rhetorical question is that Necker needed the publicity. But he broke a centuries' old tradition that royal finances were part of the *arcana imperii* – not for public consumption. Necker thought that by opening up these processes the king would be able to borrow more cheaply, as was the case in England where the government published its accounts. That might have been true if the 'account' had been honest; or rather it would have made matters even worse as was proved when truthful accounts were published in 1787 and 1788. For, seeing the gravity of the situation, the opposition then had the king over a barrel. But in 1781, instead of giving the truth, Necker, if one were charitable, employed the device of *suppressio veri, suggestio falsi*: he claimed that, despite four years of war, with no extra taxation, annual revenue exceeded expenditure by 10.2 million *livres*. In reality there was an annual deficit of about 70 million.

The *Compte* sold extremely well (more than 20,000 copies) and became fashionable reading for ladies at their toilet. But it was a *pièce d'occasion* and did not become a classic; there was no edition after 1781. However, it had served its purpose: the loan which had been sticking was soon fully subscribed – who would not want 10 per cent tax-free interest from a government with a budgetary surplus? Necker was able to close the loan and float another in March: the preamble creating this loan acknowledged that publication of the *Compte* had made this possible.[62] But the long-term damage was irreparable: if books can make revolutions then this one did, for it made it impossible for future governments to plead poverty without attacking the veracity of the idol of a nation in whose fiscal interest it was to swallow the illusion.

Necker claimed that he was publishing figures for an 'ordinary' year, in which revenue and expenditure were fixed in advance – hence his ability to publish figures for 1781 which was only two months old. This was also his excuse for omitting the entire cost of the war. Necker put expenditure at about 254 million *livres*, whereas in 1780 it had been 677 million, the treasury paying

146 million *livres* to the navy alone, not including a sum of maybe 50 million of 'debts in arrears', payment of which was traditionally suspended until peace.[63] Turgot's collaborator, Pierre-Samuel Dupont, in a secret memorandum of August 1783, told the current finance minister that the *Compte* 'contains several mistakes which the author has genuinely overlooked and even more quite deliberate ones'. His economies with the truth had exceeded his financial ones and Necker had 'introduced charlatanism into the administration'.[64]

If Necker's intention had not been to obfuscate, he could have provided fairly accurate figures for both 'ordinary' and 'extra-ordinary' expenditure for the previous year, 1780. Or, if he wanted to predict the outcome for 1781, he could have employed the formula provided by Louis himself at the end of his first year on the throne, 1774, to the departmental ministers:

> Send me as quickly as possible two detailed statements of expenditure for your department for the year 1775, one containing the fixed [i.e., ordinary] expenditure, the other the variable expenditure. By the first I mean what is bound to be incurred, by the second that which, being uncertain, neverthe-less recurs every year and which can be measured by taking the average of the last ten years.[65]

In April, Necker's confidential and highly controversial memorandum on provincial administrations was leaked and published through the treachery of the king's malicious brother, Monsieur, comte de Provence, whose chancellor had taken a copy. It managed to enrage two usually opposed groups – the *parlementaires* and the intendants – and revealed an identity of interest between them. The *parlement* had generally been 'on board' because Necker did not raise taxes. But in his memorandum, Necker envisaged his provincial administrations one day replacing both the thirteen *parlements* and the thirty intendants. And though the *parlementaires* increasingly championed the social and economic privileges of the nobility to which they belonged, they did not want the nobility in general to interfere in administration and politics. That should be left to the *noblesse de robe*, whether members of a *parlement* or of the king's direct administration. There was question in the *parlement* of burning Necker's production as an anonymous work, and Castries tried to have Maurepas forbid the *parlement* to discuss the matter. Naturally, Maurepas offered no assistance.

The intendants tended to be anti-Necker in any case: they had been incensed at the humiliation of the ex-intendant Taboureau des Réaux; and the wittiest and most devastating attack on the *Compte rendu* had come from another of their number, Charles-Alexandre de Calonne, the intendant of Flanders. His

Lettre du Marquis de Caraccioli à M. d'Alembert was a reply both to the *Compte rendu* – Calonne wanted to be controller-general and knew that the *Compte rendu* would make it difficult for the crown to plead poverty – and from an intendant to the memorandum on provincial administrations. The *Lettre* is brilliantly written and has many witty sallies, such as 'to lacerate the intendants and their administration . . . is of no political consequence and is just firing on your own troops'. It also reveals what was to be an abiding obsession with Calonne: his hatred of the clergy, 'sold to anyone who extends its power'. He also notices Necker's symbiotic relationship with the 'liberal' *grands seigneurs* at court, epitomized by his introduction into the ministry of the two military aristocrats, Castries and Ségur: 'Ever since places in the ministry have been given to *grands seigneurs* – who are all equally entitled to believe that they have the same degree of aptitude to fill any of them – they all hungrily eye up these places and have been seized with ministerial mania.'[66] Here Calonne stands on its head Necker's argument in favour of specialists rather than generalists by saying that soldiers are not trained in government and that there is no logical reason why they should restrict their designs to the service ministries; they might even covet the finance ministry, that furthest removed from their competence, provided the seigneurial title of *Surintendant des finances*, suppressed by Louis XIV to deter them, were revived.

Under fire, Necker asked for a mark of royal confidence which, he hoped, would silence his critics. He asked to become a *ministre d'état*, which would entitle him to attend the *Conseil d'État*. Since the start of the reign, most decisions were made in cabinet committees, but the council still had a role in the formulation of the foreign policy which Necker had to finance. Necker wanted to defend his measures in person against his enemies 'who', Soulavie relates, 'pretended not to understand his ideas which the king had the goodness to explain and develop'.[67] So it was a reasonable request. Maurepas, however, objected that the fundamental laws of the kingdom barred a Protestant and even, he mused, a foreigner from entering the council. For that, Maurepas told Necker 'with a smile, "you must make the leap made by Henri IV"' – who had famously said that Paris was well worth a mass. Necker took what Maurepas intended as a joke, albeit a malicious one, as a vile attempt to convert him.[68] Marie-Antoinette, who supported Necker's general position – Maria-Theresa and Joseph had come under Necker's spell – did not, given her sketchy knowledge of the fundamental laws, support him in this particular demand to become a *ministre*, which he made through her twice.

Thwarted in this, Necker came up with an alternative mark of confidence. On 15 May he gave Maurepas a memorandum to give to Louis requesting that control of the treasuries of the marine and war ministries should be entrusted to him, at least for the duration of the war. Next day Castries went to Marly and told the king that he was ready to relinquish the treasury of the marine. The initial reaction of the king, who had to consider the long-term integrity of the naval department, was 'but this separation is impossible'; then he added, 'M. de Maurepas talked to me about all that; he showed me a memorandum of M. Necker's; I'll read it carefully and decide what I have to do in two or three days'. Castries then went to see the queen but was told that she was in bed, though Maurepas was present and in the half hour Castries waited outside, Louis entered her chamber three times. When Castries finally managed to see the queen she warned him that, if Necker's demands were met, he would become 'the most powerful man at Versailles' and 'it is pretty certain that you will not keep your place and that, once degraded [by losing control of its treasury] it will be given to an *homme de robe* and you are against that'.[69]

Finally, Maurepas offered Necker the *grandes entrées* (which conferred the right to sit in the king's closet rather than having to stand in the ante-chamber) and the king's assurance that provincial administrations would be set up in all the provinces, something which had been deferred by the outbreak of war. According to Castries, Necker was tempted to accept, but Maurepas, desperately wanting a refusal which he would not fail to distort, diluted and belittled the concessions. Necker then gave his letter of resignation to Maurepas to give to the king; but Maurepas, as if to emphasize the withdrawal of any residual element of protection, refused to hand it to the king, telling Necker, 'if he did not want to address the king directly' he would have to give it to the queen (which he did on 19 May). Soulavie considered that Necker's letter of resignation to the king was both 'truly republican', because it presumed to make conditions, and insulting, being written 'carelessly on a scrap of paper three and a half inches long by two and a half wide'. Louis locked this letter away in its own drawer.[70]

Had the king refused to accept Necker's resignation, Maurepas would have resigned himself, though he did not put pressure on the king by telling him this. What he had said about the fundamental laws was hogwash: there was only one such law upon which everyone agreed – the Salic Law – and even that had been invented in the fourteenth century to bar Edward III of England's claim to the throne through the female line. Likewise, when Louis said he wanted two or three days to read Necker's memorandum on the treasuries of the service ministries he was more likely occupied in reading another memorandum instead, one he had commissioned from Vergennes, who was increasingly enjoying his confidence. This arrived on 3 May. The theme Louis had set

Vergennes was on the desirability of 'entrusting the most sensitive ministry in the country to a foreigner, a republican [Necker had grown up in the Republic of Geneva] and a Protestant'. Vergennes argued that the *Compte rendu* in particular, and Necker's loans in general, through their dependence on publicity, permanently altered the nature of royal finance and even, he implied, the government of France. Necker had increased the power of public opinion, to which Louis himself already paid great attention: 'Your Majesty has had the goodness to show me several times that he busies himself with reading this mass of literature.' The *Compte*, being rendered not to the king but to the public, inverted a basic principle of absolutism: that the king was the only public persona, the only one to be addressed;[71] and it made a mockery of the king's claim that the *parlements* should not publish their remonstrances. Moreover, Vergennes argued, even given that the monarchy took account of public opinion, that opinion needed to be defined. Why should it necessarily be 'the public opinion of M. Necker'?

> He finds this opinion in the spirit of innovation of the times, in the society of men of letters, of the *philosophes* . . . or again in the plaudits given him by a section of the English parliament . . .; finally in the ideas of reform and humanity which he himself propagates . . . Your Majesty has already made very considerable sacrifices to this spirit of innovation . . . which increases its demands and pretensions with every new favour.
>
> Such, Sire, is the nature of the public opinion which M. Necker calls to his assistance and which becomes his strength . . . since he has been deprived by the nature of his operations of the support of the true public opinion of this monarchy.
>
> If "the opinion of M. Necker" finally wins the day, if English and Genevan principles are introduced into our administration, Your Majesty can expect to see the portion of his subjects which now obeys in command, and the portion which presently governs take or share its place.[72]

Vergennes is not objecting, as an earlier absolutist might have done, to the force of public opinion as such, but to the wrong sort of public opinion, and he had always taken pains to help the right sort, 'the true public opinion of this monarchy', prevail through his own counter-manipulation of the press. Until 1789 there were underground polemical pamphlets but no regular political journals in France. The gap was filled by illegally imported French-language periodicals, such as the *Gazette de Leyde*, published in Holland, and the *Courier de l'Europe*, published in London. Not only did Vergennes turn a blind eye to their introduction, but most of their information came from a semi-official news bureau run by Pascal-Boyer under Vergennes's own direction. It served the purpose of the non-attributable briefing. Vergennes's views coincided with those of the *Gazette de Leyde* over the American war and as such it was the recipient of privileged information. However, the *Gazette* supported Necker; so Vergennes starved it of all information relating to the events leading to Necker's fall and there was a virtual 'news blackout' concerning France from 1781 to 1783.[73] As regards the *Courier,* Vergennes went further. Having ignored the French censor by admitting the journal, Vergennes himself censored the actual production, informing the editor of his wishes in a non-attributable way by employing the word '*on*' to refer to himself (the future revolutionary leader Brissot, one of the correspondents, cracked this device). The editor was severely rebuked for an encomium on Necker, which was not repeated.[74]

Vergennes's memorandum must have worried Louis – it is the only recorded example of this consummate flatterer criticizing his king and not just for consulting public opinion but for appeasing it. He clearly had in mind not just Necker's policies but those of Turgot, which he detested as much, maybe more because they represented friendly fire from an ex-intendant. He was probably also thinking of the recall of the *parlement*, against his own brave advice. And the shaft must have struck home. Louis wanted to be a reforming monarch; the trouble with the recall of the *parlement* was that it was an obstacle to reform. And he too was swayed by public opinion. However, Louis did worry about Necker's attacks on the establishment cadres. Necker's leaked memorandum had excoriated the intendants but Louis himself believed that 'the intendants, give or take the odd abuse, are the best part of my system'. But did Necker respect the system at all? Though Louis himself was fascinated by English institutions, he worried that Necker actually wanted to insinuate them into the French polity – in demanding conditional marks of confidence was he not acting like an English minister? And by attacking *la finance* was he not destroying the 'columns' that held the state up? Would foreign credit answer his needs in an emergency? These were nagging questions. On the other hand, Necker seemed to be the only man who could supply credit for what was becoming an interminable war, though Maurepas had quipped that 'the irreplaceable man has yet to be born'.

It was a finely balanced decision, especially as Marie-Antoinette would have liked to keep Necker. So Louis adopted a middle position: he refused Necker's demands but did not dismiss him. Instead Necker resigned. Louis was angry – ministers simply did not resign, especially in the midst of a war. When Maurepas informed Necker of the king's refusal to accept his conditions, he was so thunderstruck that he could not open the door; Maurepas had to summon a valet, telling him with barely contained relish: 'Help . . . Monsieur . . . Necker . . . through . . . the door!' Necker was ill for weeks afterwards.

Necker's resignation was an error of judgement on his own part: Maurepas's health was clearly failing and his death, at the height of an expensive war, would have made Necker impregnable. Nevertheless, his proud nature had been strained by years of paying court to Maurepas, of 'ascending that dark and long staircase' which, did he but realize it, represented for him the 'refined essence of human vanity' just as much as his cramped quarters did for Maurepas. One way of explaining the ultimate failure of both Turgot's and Necker's ministries is to say that each had had to make a Faustian bargain to achieve office: Turgot had to countenance the recall of the *parlement* which fought tooth and nail against his grain policy and his six edicts; Necker had to finance war without taxes, which swamped his painstaking 'economical reforms' and drove him from office before he had time to set up the nationwide network of provincial assemblies with which, according to the duc de Lévis, 'the monarchy would have been indestructible and the prosperity of the state would have increased indefinitely'.[75]

Of Necker's subsequent conduct, d'Angiviller, director-general of royal buildings, a former *menin* of the king's who remained close to him, wrote: 'Hitherto a disgraced minister . . . so far from meddling in affairs, made it a duty to remain aloof from them, to live in retirement, even to abstain for a while from seeing those of his friends who were so involved and seemed to desire to make himself forgotten.'[76] This essentially paraphrases the instructions usually given to a disgraced minister by the minister of the *Maison* to break his contacts with the outside world. But far from living in the shadows, Necker continued to live in a blaze of publicity which cast its own shadow over the rest of the reign. Forgetting or probably not even aware of the convention that the king never admitted a mistake by reappointing an ex-minister to his old job, Necker schemed tirelessly for precisely that.

Necker was succeeded by the sour and ailing *conseiller d'état* Joly de Fleury who, it was said, resembled neither of his names. The departure of Necker was a ray of winter sunshine for Maurepas in the last months of his life, which had been darkened by his losing control of ministerial nominations and the queen's (albeit exaggerated) role in the same. Marie-Antoinette had not, however, wanted to provoke Maurepas into resigning – not, that is, until her position had been sufficiently strengthened by the birth of a dauphin for her to suggest that her nominee, Loménie de Brienne, archbishop of Toulouse, should succeed him.

A birth, a death and a victory

On 19 December 1778 Marie-Antoinette had given birth to a daughter, Marie-Thérèse-Charlotte. Royal births had to be witnessed to dispel any doubts, such as those surrounding the birth of the Old Pretender, who enemies said had been smuggled into the birthing bed in a warming pan. But there was no need for the huge tide of people that lapped right up to Marie-Antoinette's bed. It was a difficult birth; Marie-Antoinette passed out and she lost some hair, which led to a change in the fashion for hats. The room was stifling and Louis had to use his enormous strength to force open an air-tight window. Nevertheless, Louis invested the clumsy *accoucheur* (the one who had tried to use the queen's pregnancy as a means to get Louis to support Joseph II over his Bavarian claims) with the order of Saint-Michael. Despite his disappointment at not having a son, Louis ordered festivities at Versailles which cost 100,000 *livres*.

Seeing that Louis was at last enjoying conjugal relations, two attempts were made by courtiers to fix him up with a mistress they could manipulate to their advantage. But they failed: Louis, like George III, remained faithful to his wife. The rumour that the daughter of Madame Élisabeth's chambermaid, who was brought up with Marie-Thérèse to give the latter the common touch, was in fact Louis's bastard was just that, a rumour.

The proclamation announcing the birth of Louis's daughter included the words, 'this visible mark of providence makes me hope for the complete accomplishment of my desires and those of my people by the birth of a dauphin'.[77] However, Marie-Antoinette's next pregnancy ended in a miscarriage and people began to doubt whether she would ever produce an heir. The succession was assured because Louis's younger brother, Artois, had sired first the duc d'Angoulême, and then the duc de Berry (Louis's first title). Finally, however, on 22 October 1781, the queen at last gave birth to a dauphin. In his joy the king bursts the narrow confines allotted for the day in his diary with minute details of the confinement. There was less of a press this time, with attendance limited to ten. Louis approached the bed and told Marie-Antoinette, 'Madame, you have fulfilled my desires and those of France; you are the mother of a dauphin.' The boy was given the same names as Louis's long-dead elder brother, the duc de Bourgogne.

Three days before the birth of the dauphin, though the news took a month to reach Versailles, the combined Franco-American forces had pulled off an improbable but decisive victory in Virginia. The English forces were divided under the commands of General Clinton at New York and Lord Cornwallis, who was seeking to extend British-held territory in the south. In 1780 5,000

French troops under Rochambeau arrived at Rhode Island, off New York, and in the summer of 1781 despatches came from Versailles indicating that Admiral de Grasse, commanding the main French fleet in the West Indies, would be available for combined operations against the English, either for a siege of New York or in Chesapeake Bay, Virginia, where Cornwallis had been ordered to create a deep-water harbour at the end of the Yorktown peninsula. After the re-capture of New York in 1776, English forces had moved operations to the south, though Cornwallis's forces were shadowed by another allied army under Lafayette.

Rochambeau told Grasse that he would prefer an attack on Cornwallis from Chesapeake. Grasse obliged and the Spanish fleet in the West Indies offered to protect French shipping so that de Grasse could deploy his whole fleet of twenty-eight battleships carrying 3,000 soldiers to North America. In September de Grasse arrived at Chesapeake Bay where he defeated a British fleet sent to relieve Cornwallis and prevented Cornwallis's army from escaping by sea, whilst the Franco-American forces proceeded to Yorktown by forced marches, having deceived Clinton into believing that a siege of New York was intended. On 14 October they invested Yorktown, and on the 19th, Cornwallis, outnumbered and cut off, surrendered with 10,000 men.

Meanwhile Maurepas lay dying. Shortly after the birth of the dauphin he had his most serious attack of gout yet, and this time there seemed no hope of recovery. As Maurepas lay on his deathbed news reached Versailles that the Franco-American troops had won a great victory at Yorktown which might end the war. Castries, who regarded himself as the architect of the victory, expected to be showered with honours. Instead the king received him 'médiocrement'.[78] Maurepas fared better. Louis, who did not see dying ministers, though he did cancel his hunting, was thoughtful enough to send the duc de Lauzun to go and tell Maurepas the good news. Lauzun ran through the list of prisoners, the 214 cannon and the twenty-two standards taken. After each item Maurepas repeated 'Good, good', but then, turning to Lauzun, he said: 'I am dying and I don't know whom I have the honour of addressing.' On 21 November Louis notes in his diary: 'Nothing. Death of M. de Maurepas at eleven thirty in the evening.' Maurepas's body was allowed to remain in the palace until his funeral on the 23rd – 'a high favour', as Castries notes, adding: 'The king seems really affected – or should one perhaps rather say embarrassed.'[79] Louis said, sadly, that he would no longer hear the sound of Maurepas's cane tapping on the floor above him. Maurepas's monument was to be the future conduct of the king he had trained and of the *parlement* he had recalled. In his lifetime Maurepas had, in Lenoir's words, 'despite his lack of energy, known how to contain [the *parlement*]' and at his death Joly de Fleury 'lamented that the king no longer had the man who directed [it]'.[80]

Marie-Antoinette's 'minders' – her 'reader', Vermond, Mercy-Argenteau, the Austrian ambassador, Maria-Theresa (who had died in 1780) and Joseph II, now sole ruler – had advised her to await this moment of Maurepas's death before making any serious political moves. Her role in the ministerial changes in 1780 was regarded as premature. Now, with the birth of an heir, all the pieces seemed to be in place to propel this faction's candidate, Loménie de Brienne, archbishop of Toulouse, towards becoming not just prime minister, but Marie-Antoinette's prime minister. Brienne was one of a band of 'administrator prelates' who ruled the secular as well as the spiritual life of the Midi. They included Boisgelin, archbishop of Aix, and Dillon, archbishop of Narbonne. All three would play a major part in Louis's story. Spirituality was not their strong point, though those who survived the Revolution discovered it. Brienne was an atheist, or at least a deist, and in refusing to translate him from Toulouse to Paris Louis uttered one of his few *bon mots*: 'But an archbishop of Paris must at least believe in God.'

Shortly after Maurepas's death the queen, at the instigation of the abbé de Vermond, proposed that Toulouse should enter the council as a preliminary to becoming chief minister. This was trebly displeasing to the king: he had no intention of replacing Maurepas, still less with a nominee of the queen's, and least of all with a political priest who, following precedent, would acquire the added prestige of being made a cardinal, which would give him precedence in council. Lenoir, the police minister, was in the apartments of the king's aunt, Madame Sophie, when the king burst in 'in a towering rage' and declared that 'the one [Brienne] must be confined to his diocese, and have his revenues confiscated and the other [Vermond] must be sent away from the queen'.[81] Louis's rage subsided but, though thwarted, the ambitions of Toulouse did not.

Louis XVI and George III

Militarily England could have recovered from Yorktown. But her political will was shattered. Lord North had wanted to resign after Saratoga but George forced him to remain. The continuation of the war was his personal policy. Louis realized this and on the fall of Lord North's administration on 20 March 1782, Louis noted that whatever happened 'cela fera une peine personnelle au roi d'Angleterre' (the king of England will take this personally).[82] North was succeeded by Lord Rockingham and after his death on 1 July by the Earl of Shelburne, but this distrusted intellectual, dubbed the 'Jesuit of Berkeley

Square', did not last long. After Shelburne's resignation on 24 February 1783 George was faced with an 'infamous coalition' between the traitor North and his former arch-enemy Charles James Fox. George tried to avoid swallowing this 'bitter potion', as he put it, by asking the younger Pitt to form a government. Louis wished him success – 'je désire qu'il réusisse jusqu'au bout' (I hope he can see the matter through to a satisfactory conclusion) – even though that success would make peace less likely. When it seemed that George had turned the tables on his opponents Louis drew a parallel with French history – the Day of Dupes, when Louis XIII had saved his favourite, Richelieu, against expectations. The struggle was about the appointment and dismissal of ministers, which had not been a difficulty for the Bourbons in the eighteenth century but was about to become an acute one. Louis fully realized that the English crisis was an epoch in the development of the constitution that held such a fascination for him: 'however this turns out, it must prove to be a turning point in the constitution of the English government'.[83]

George was forced to take his medicine but in 1784 he was able to turn the tables on his enemies, install Pitt and win a general election. The way in which Louis describes these events suggests that he was aware of the parallels between their two countries, the changing role of personal monarchy, or at least that such awareness was dawning on him. If Louis XVI had handled the protracted crisis of 1787–89 as well as George III handled the equally prolonged one of 1782–84, the resultant regimes might have converged even more. That, in the event, they diverged to the extent that at no subsequent period in their history is it meaningful to make comparisons, is merely to say that the French Revolution was unique in the way it chanced to develop after the meeting of the Estates-General in 1789.

There was a good deal of fellow-feeling between Louis XVI and George III. As we have seen, there was no element of *Schadenfreude* in Louis's analysis of George's political predicament – he wished him success 'jusqu'au bout'. This is all the more remarkable because, when Louis was discussing George's *peine personnelle*, the war was still raging with an important naval engagement, the Battle of the Saintes, in the offing. Both monarchs had similar life-styles and personal values. George praised Louis's 'sense of justice, candour and rectitude' and the 'simplicity and purity of his morals and private life'.[84] He seems to have forgiven Louis for his clandestine support of the Americans; perhaps he respected Louis's scrupulous refusal to countenance support for the English opposition.

The victory at Yorktown activated France's end-game and confirmed Spain's worst fears. The North administration had already ceased military action against the Americans when it was succeeded by the administration headed by

Rockingham which was committed to granting the United States not just independence but generous terms, even though England still occupied New York, Charleston and Savannah. Moreover, Admiral Rodney's victory at the Saintes, a group of islands off Guadeloupe, on 12 April 1782, made peace easier by salving England's pride and showing France the risks of prolonging the conflict.

Rodney with thirty-six battleships had defeated a numerically superior Franco-Spanish fleet of forty-seven. The thirty-five ships under de Grasse – the same fleet that had defeated the British in the Battle of Chesapeake – had been joined by twelve Spanish ships carrying 15,000 troops with the objective of capturing Jamaica to swap for Gibraltar at the peace. Seven French ships (including de Grasse's flagship the *Ville de Paris*) were captured or sunk, together with 5,000 soldiers; some 2,000 men were killed. The defeat could have been much worse if Rodney had given chase but it illustrated two things: the fragility of the French war machine and the millstone round the neck that the Spanish alliance represented.

Louis was devastated but defiant: 'the king our master', Vergennes informed Montmorin, 'is in no way downcast, though he is profoundly affected'.[85] He went around saying that they had lost seven ships but would build ten by the end of the year. In fact they built twelve. The officer in charge of construction at Brest told Castries, 'the way in which our master has handled this business is enchanting and inspires me to attempt the impossible. We are all geared up for it. Give me the timber and I'll do the rest.'[86] There was a great patriotic outpouring: the king's brothers offered an 80-gunner and the great and good of the ancien régime subscribed for a replacement for the *Ville de Paris*: these included the Parisian municipal authorities, the estates of Burgundy, the farmers-general and the receivers-general of direct taxes. When de Grasse was released from captivity in England, he proceeded to blame his two seconds-in-command for the catastrophe; and he did this in public – an act which was compared to Necker's publication of the *Compte rendu*. De Grasse sought to defend himself in front of the king, but Castries relayed the following message: 'His Majesty is displeased with your conduct in this particular and forbids you from appearing before him. It is painful for me to convey his intentions and to add the further advice that in the circumstance you should retire to your own province'[87] – internal exile.

De Grasse's original appointment provides an interesting insight into the system. The war cabinet chaired by the king was discussing a replacement for La Touche-Tréville to command the fleet about to sail out from Brest. Castries proposed de Grasse but the king remained silent. After a while Castries made the same proposal but the king 'again' – the word is underlined in Castries's diary – maintained his silence. Taking the king's silence for approval, 'the cabinet ended at this point' and de Grasse was appointed. Louis may have had his doubts – for de Grasse did not win or lose by halves. Meanwhile Marie-Antoinette, that accomplished mariner, chastised Castries for not discussing de Grasse's appointment with her.[88]

The Battle of the Saintes should have facilitated peace between France and England; the remaining colonial disputes between them were low hurdles to surmount. In the twentieth century we became accustomed to total victory and to unconditional surrender, concepts which would have been regarded as uncivilized in the eighteenth century. What then facilitated a negotiated peace was a late victory by the losing side, such as the French victory at the battle of Denain, which redeemed a series of defeats suffered by Louis XIV and gave the allies an excuse to be lenient. The Saintes should have served this purpose. But that was to reckon without Spain. Because Louis XVI set himself high moral standards in foreign affairs, because the family and dynastic link with Spain was important to the king, and perhaps because Maurepas, who did not believe in standing alliances, was dead, France did not consider that she had the option of signing with England and leaving Spain without Gibraltar, the principal Spanish goal in the Treaty of Aranjuez. The Battle of the Saintes having been in effect a proxy battle for Gibraltar, if Spain wanted the Rock, she, aided by a reluctant France, would have to take it by storm.

On 18 September, after nearly three years of siege, what became known as the Great Assault on Gibraltar by 30,000 Spanish troops and 7,000 French began. But, despite the use of ingenious floating batteries, the storm failed. Now Louis felt obliged either to secure the rock for Spain at the negotiating table or to participate in a Franco-Spanish expedition to Jamaica under d'Estaing, now back in favour. Both d'Estaing and Louis were extremely dubious about the prospects of the proposed expedition, a feeling that manifested in Louis an example of what Soulavie called his Cassandra-like quality – he knew it would fail but he had to proceed with it.

As the French fleet lay at anchor at Cadiz at the end of 1782, d'Estaing in Spain, Vergennes and Louis at Versailles and La Muette and Rayneval, Vergennes's *premier commis,* in England, sought desperately to find a solution that would stop the fleet from having to sail to probable disaster and (as it seems to us now) the possible collapse of the regime. Even Castries, a hawk, thought France could not risk an attack on Jamaica, but should recall the fleet to Europe for a defensive campaign.[89] France offered England Dominica and Guadeloupe for Gibraltar; Aranda, exceeding his instructions, chipped in Minorca. The English cabinet was split; they seemed to accept but, perhaps through a misunderstanding, another island was demanded.

Vergennes attributed the English change of heart to the fact that, on 30 November, the American delegates had signed separate peace preliminaries with England, reneging on the one requirement France had inserted into the 1778 treaty of alliance. 'If we can judge the future by what we have just seen,' Vergennes wrote, 'we shall be poorly repaid for our exertions on behalf of the United States of America.'[90] George III, benefiting from but despising this act of treachery, and feeling perhaps a kindred sympathy for Louis, said good riddance to bad rubbish on losing his empire. A few days later Franklin had the cheek to ask for a loan of 20 million *livres* from France, receiving a curt reply: 'You agreed on preliminaries without consulting us . . . you are going to give the impression in America that peace is assured without even bothering to ascertain the state of our negotiations. . . . Do you think you satisfy your obligations to the king? When you are in a position to answer my doubts concerning this, I will ask His Majesty to meet your demands.'[91] Franklin had to be satisfied with a loan (never repaid) of 6 million at 5 per cent – this at a time when France had to borrow at 10 per cent.

A more likely explanation for England's intransigence was the realization that the English government would never get the surrender of Gibraltar through parliament. However, they made a generous counter-offer: if Spain were prepared to drop the demand for Gibraltar, England would cede both the Floridas and Minorca. But Charles III wanted his pound of flesh. Louis's Christmas Day – a working one with councils and commitees – was ruined by the arrival of a despatch from Spain saying that Charles 'has absolutely no intention of giving up Gibraltar and will not ratify any preliminaries which do not provide for the cession of this place'.[92] Louis characterized this news as 'a thunderbolt landing on our head'.[93] Then something happened which will probably never be fully explained: Aranda accepted the English counter-proposal. Vergennes, as he told Montmorin in a letter of 17 December, assumed that Aranda had at least tacit authority to conclude without Gibraltar; otherwise it would have been 'an initiative unique in the annals of diplomacy'; and although Charles III grumbled, he did not repudiate his ambassador.[94]

When peace finally came, the relief of Louis, Vergennes, Montmorin and Rayneval was palpable. Rayneval thought it was nothing short of a miracle: when before, he asked, had two countries signed peace before they were compelled to?[95] Montmorin observed that the peace 'seemed to me all the better for the fact that the campaign we have just fought scarcely strengthened our negotiating position'.[96]

They all dreaded another year of warfare. The results of the 1782 campaign augured badly for another in 1783: 'everything which has taken place in this year's campaign', Vergennes reflected, 'announces an unravelling of our moral and physical forces'.[97] Although there were funds for a campaign in 1783 there were none for one in 1784 and if the war did not end in 1782, Vergennes told Montmorin, 'it would become a fight to the finish because what was at stake was nothing less than the complete ruin of one or the other of the belligerents or rather of both because to ruin the enemy meant destroying oneself.'[98] Again, 'if peace is not concluded before the spring we must fear the prospect of a configuration which will throw everything into confusion'. By this Vergennes meant that Austria and Russia would take advantage of France's preoccupations to partition the Ottoman Empire, her traditional ally, and the place where Vergennes had found his wife.

Yet the French cabinet was split over whether to accept peace terms. Ségur and above all Castries wanted to continue the fight, not for Gibraltar but for India where, even as peace preliminaries were being signed, the French were making conquests or re-conquests. This was largely due to the exploits of Pierre André de Suffren de Saint-Tropez. This intrepid commander had distinguished himself in the West Indies and Sartine had wanted to promote him to the rank of squadron leader. Louis, however, whether because of Suffren's ostentatious homosexuality or, more likely, because he was hidebound by promotion according to seniority, wrote against Sartine's proposal 'can't be done'. Sartine communicated this refusal to Suffren with suitable bureaucratic circumlocution: 'His Majesty regards you as one of the officers most fit soon to command one of his squadrons and his intention is to accelerate your promotion as soon as he can. Meanwhile, to mark his satisfaction at all you have achieved so far, he grants you a pension of 1,500 *livres* and gives you the command of a 74-gunner.'[99] Suffren, by daring exploits and alliances with native rulers in the south of India, managed to re-conquer the French fort of Pondicherry, Ceylon, and he gained control of the Coromandel Coast. When he triumphantly returned to France, Louis more than made up for his previous restraint by investing him with the *cordon bleu* of the Saint-Esprit and making him a vice-admiral.

News of the victories in India began to filter through as the French cabinet was finalizing the peace terms. Castries, whose prestige had been dimmed by the defeat at the Saintes, wanted to restore it by holding out for better terms. Why not keep some of the captured sugar islands, now that Spain had renounced Gibraltar? Above all, why not try to restore equality with England in India such as had obtained before the Seven Years War? In terms of wealth and trade, India in the eighteenth century was incomparably more important than America – indeed its GDP was similar to that of France and England combined. Castries told Louis that the French victories in India should be reflected in the peace terms: ' "Ye-es, Ye-es", said the king and from this "yes" pronounced softly, M. de Castries concluded that it would have no effect.' For, Castries considered, 'the king wants peace at any price'.[100]

In council Castries advocated another campaign. Vergennes asked who would pay for it. Joly de Fleury, Necker's successor, was rather proud of his achievement in securing an additional (third) vingtième in the wake of the defeat at the Saintes and surprised everyone by saying the funds were available and that as far as he was concerned the king could make what military disposi-tions he pleased. Vergennes, according to Castries, 'apparently not daring to assume the whole weight of accepting or refusing' peace terms, turned to the king: 'In the final analysis does Your Majesty want to break off negotiations and renounce peace?' Louis, who had gambled on a short war, been behind the peace moves in 1780 and perhaps the readiness to retrocede the sugar islands, pronounced: 'No, We must have peace'.[101]

So was it all worth it? Most of the French gains, whether in India or in the West Indies, were surrendered at the peace. In India the main gain was an enlargement of the area around Pondicherry so it could act as a self-sustaining unit. In the West Indies, France gave back her conquests of Grenada, St Vincent, Dominica, St Kitts, Nevis and Monserrat, gaining only Tobago. Castries told the king: 'I think Your Majesty would be well advised to stop assembling the cabinet committee since every time it meets it costs you a colony'.[102] At least the English commissioner did not return to Dunkirk and French fishing rights off Newfoundland were marginally improved. Spain was the biggest winner, gaining Florida and Minorca.

The French were soon deceived in their hope of replacing England as the main trading partner of the United States: they simply could not supply the goods the former colonists wanted. By the time of the French Revolution, England's trade with her former colonies had reached 90 per cent of their pre-war level and soon surpassed it. And there was a further irony: America, unshackled from the old colonial system, developed much faster and created a bigger market just as the Industrial Revolution was gaining momentum in England, pouring out the goods the Americans needed. On these grounds both England and France should have stayed out of the war.

Peace was not as miraculous as Rayneval thought. Both countries, England as well as France, were financially crippled by the war. The difference between the two countries was not the financial predicament in 1783 but how each extricated itself from it in the coming years. And the financial predicament implied a political one too. What France recovered at the 1783 Peace of Paris was the elusive quality of diplomatic prestige which, by the same token, England

lost: people as wise as Frederick the Great considered that England could not
exist as a great power without America.

The Dutch alliance

Louis naturally backed Catherine the Great's League of Armed Neutrality of
1780, designed to stop English warships stopping neutrals suspected of trading
with the American colonies. Louis makes much of this affront in both his
manifesto and his letters. One of the neutrals was the Dutch Republic and for
its pains, England declared war on her traditional ally. Dutch colonies were
easy pickings for the English and it was only French action in re-capturing
some of these which restricted Dutch losses at the peace to Nagapatnam in
India.

The Dutch enjoyed a hybrid constitution. The monarchical element
consisted of the *stadhouder*, who also sometimes held the post of captain-
general (commander-in-chief) of the army. He was generally chosen from the
House of Orange, descendants of the French prince of that town, who had led
the revolt of the Netherlands against Spain in the sixteenth and seventeenth
centuries. In 1747 the post of *stadhouder* had been made hereditary. There
were close links with England, not just through William III of Orange; William
V, the current *stadhouder*, was George II's grandson. The republican element in
the Dutch constitution consisted of the estates of each of the seven provinces,
the largest of which was that of Holland, and the States-General for the whole
country.

The disaster of the war, plus the associations of the *stadhouder* with the
enemy, led to a seizure of power by the 'patriot' party, a revolutionary group
which had taken over from the traditional opposition party in the States-General
and now sought an alliance with their old wartime partners the French. Louis
and Vergennes faced a similar dilemma to the one they had faced in supporting
the American colonists: should they support ideological opponents (republicans) for diplomatic advantage? Moreover, poaching England's long-time ally
was not the best way to begin what Vergennes hoped would be amicable relations between the two countries. In the course of their more relaxed table-talk at
his Wiltshire seat of Bowood, prime minister Shelburne held out this thought to
Vergennes's number two, Rayneval, who passed it on to his principal: 'In the old
days no one dared to fire a canon shot in Europe without the permission of
England and France, and now the northern powers want to do something on
their own.'[103] If the two countries acted in concert they could impose a pax
Gallica-Britannica on Europe. In earnest of this France agreed to conclude a

trade treaty with England, even though Vergennes was fully aware that England would be the greater beneficiary. Yet they went ahead with the Dutch alliance.

The French ministers and the king then proceeded to intervene in Dutch politics. They did so individually, as rivals rather than colleagues, and this further destabilized both the Dutch Republic and the French government. Vergennes, Castries, Calonne and Breteuil each had their agents there and candidates for the command of the Dutch armed forces. The most worrying feature was a plan to pervert the defensive alliance into an attempt to oust Britain from India. The Treaty of Fontainebleau between France and Holland had stipulated the reciprocal obligation to provide six battleships and 6,000 men if either party were attacked. Castries proposed concentrating these forces in the Cape and Dutch East Indies so that, if war broke out again with England, they would be strategically placed to end England's dominance in India. Vergennes was worried and told Castries that this deployment under a unified command could easily provoke England into resuming the war. 'The king', he concluded, 'does not want war: the interests and the condition of his kingdom justify his love of peace'.[104] Vergennes had been appointed to Maurepas's old post of *chef du Conseil royal des finances* as a reward for success in the American war. He started attending financial committees and knew how bad the situation was. There are indications, however, that Louis was aware of Castries's plan from the beginning 'and intervened at this point [January 1786] to secure its continuation'.[105]

In 1784, however, the immediate problem was Austro-Dutch hostility. Joseph decided to improve his Belgian territories by opening the Scheldt to shipping. Dutch pressure had led to a clause being inserted into the Westphalian treaties closing the Scheldt in order to prevent Antwerp from becoming a rival to Amsterdam. Vergennes even believed that Austria had picked a quarrel with the Dutch deliberately to embarrass France and (at the last minute) prevent her alliance with the republic from being signed. Be that as it may, on 8 October an Austrian ship, hopefully called the *Louis*, set off from Antwerp amidst applause, intending to sail down the Scheldt and buy wine in France. It was soon intercepted by Dutch frigates, one of which fired across her bows, forcing her to head back. Joseph II demanded reparations for the insult to his flag and the cession of the key fortress of Maastricht; he also asked what help his French ally proposed to give. Meanwhile he assembled his troops for an invasion of Holland.

Marie-Antoinette also mobilized. By 1784, she could not simply be ignored; the mother of the dauphin, she now also had three protégés in the ministry: Castries, Ségur and Breteuil, who had been appointed to the *Maison du Roi* in

1783. Joseph announced that he would drop his claims against the Dutch provided the French would allow the Bavarian exchange to proceed – he was putting pressure on the next heir to forfeit his claim in return for being put in sovereign possession of most of the Austrian Netherlands. Marie-Antoinette thought she had squared Louis on this exchange, writing to her brother on 2 December:

> As soon as I received your letters I went together with M. de Mercy to show the king one of your two letters and the plan for the exchange. Whether he did not want to commit himself on the spur of the moment or whether, because of a very confused recollection of what had been said to him about the exchange at the time of the Peace of Teschen, he did not at first take to this proposal, I have to say that before he had seen M. de Vergennes, further thought had already brought him round to it.

She was deceiving herself, for Louis had devised an elaborate way of outflanking her: he would bolster himself with the authority of the *Conseil d'État* which, partly for reasons of secrecy, had languished during the American war. He told Vergennes: 'You will do well to communicate your important note on the present crisis to each of the other ministers in order to have their advice, as we did last year.'[106] Thus we have the written opinions of each of the ministers.[107] That of Vergennes is most favourable to the exchange; indeed he makes out an excellent case for letting it go through, arguing that if the Low Countries were no longer in the possession of a great power, France would no longer need to maintain an expensive army along the northern frontier. But the other position papers were so hostile that Louis had to remind the council: 'France has only one enemy and it's England.' To Breteuil, the queen's protégé, but also a senior member of the former *secret*, was reserved the role of attacking the exchange outright, including a scathing personal attack on Joseph: 'He seems to think that the man who annexes the most territory will go down as the greatest prince in history.'[108] On 31 December Marie-Antoinette wrote to Joseph: 'M. de Vergennes has communicated to all the minsters of the council his report on the proposals for the exchange. I do not know whether this is a new trick on his part but, according to what the king told me afterwards, his report is more conciliatory than the opinion of several other ministers.'

The council decided that the king should write the emperor a letter in which 'without for the moment dwelling on its conformity with my interests' he would say he would consider only the effects of the proposed exchange on the German Empire and in particular on the king of Prussia – a cynical manoeuvre in view of the predictability of Prussia's response. Vergennes wrote the first draft of this letter, Louis making three amendments. Two Vergennes accepted, but he held out against the third: 'It was with the hope of binding the emperor more tightly that, while applauding his intention of lending himself to a suspension of arms [against the Dutch], I inserted the word "immediately"; but as this adverb is not to be found in the emperor's letter, there is no harm in omitting it.'[109] Louis must have thought that Vergennes was pressing the emperor too far, because the adverb in question does not appear in the final draft.[110]

The formulation of this letter caused Louis a great deal of distress. On 5 January 1785 he wrote to Vergennes: 'You were right to remind me, Monsieur, of your courier; I hadn't forgotten it but for two days I have not been in a fit state to concentrate. I am returning the draft letter [to Joseph II] with a few marginal notes I have made. Give it back to me tomorrow morning, after you have made the changes and explanations I have requested. I will copy it straight-away and it can be sent that day.'[111] Louis's inability to concentrate may be a foretaste of the nervous breakdown we will argue he suffered two years later; another forerunner may have been back in 1774 when tensions within the council between the incoming and outgoing ministers caused him abruptly to leave the room without fixing a date for the next meeting. Another such moment occurred in November 1784, when Castries notes that the king is silent and abstracted.[112]

The letter was difficult to write because Louis had to perform a delicate balancing act – hence the length of the letter. He could not yield to the emperor on essentials and although he had not 'dwelt on his interests' he realized that if the emperor gained Bavaria, with its control of the Upper Danube, Alsace would be wide open to an Austrian invasion should Austria revert to her natural alliance with England. Moreover, public opinion was whispering that completion of the purchase of Saint-Cloud for the queen, which occurred in October 1784, was designed to drain funds away from sending troops to support the Dutch.

Marie-Antoinette compounded Louis's worries, making a rational decision in France's best interest more difficult and demonstrating the drawback to dynastic alliances. On 27 November Marie-Antoinette had hurled abuse at Vergennes in Louis's presence, accusing him of manipulating the council. Vergennes offered his resignation on the spot. Louis tried to calm her down and reiterated his confidence in his minister. Marie-Antoinette then bombarded Vergennes with a series of notes, one of them complaining that the Dutch had opened their dykes to flood the Austrian troops and demanding that Vergennes have them closed.[113] Louis wearily wrote to Vergennes, 'I have given your notes to the queen, who made little objection to them. I hope the matter will end there.' It did not, and both the queen and her relatives worked openly for Vergennes's disgrace. Joseph told Mercy, 'I am absolutely of your opinion that there should be a change in the ministry to benefit the queen . . . in important matters we cannot count on M. de Vergennes'.[114]

Marie-Antoinette's accusation in her tirade that Louis was the 'plaything' of his ministers certainly wasn't true on this occasion. Informing the king of the attack on the *Louis*, Vergennes, with his doubts about the desirability of the Dutch alliance, threw the responsibility entirely on to the king whom 'he begged to be so kind as to indicate the steps that he feels we should follow in this truly thorny and delicate situation'. Louis was actually keener on the Dutch alliance than was Vergennes. So were the other ministers – Castries and Ségur, the war minister, voted to send troops to defend the Dutch if Joseph invaded. But Louis had to decide. And his decision was to be as polite to the emperor as possible, whilst not giving way on fundamentals. Hence the care he took over the letter.

As expected, Frederick blocked the exchange; Joseph resurrected his grievances against the Dutch but was induced to settle for the payment of 6 million florins, some of it provided by France herself. This transaction gave rise to the myth during the French Revolution that Marie-Antoinette was secretly sending funds to her brother.

The Franco-Dutch alliance went ahead. Calonne, now finance minister, described the alliance as 'perhaps the most important that France could have contracted'.[115] Holland held key trading posts particularly on the Cape of Good Hope and in Ceylon. Moreover, in the post-Necker era, Amsterdam had replaced Geneva as the main source for royal loans. The Dutch ambassador presented Calonne with the star of the order of the Saint-Esprit, of which he was *grand trésorier*, set in diamonds. He was destined to wear it for only eighteen months.

The Franco-Dutch alliance, signed at Fontainebleau in November 1785, was arguably the zenith of the reign of Louis XVI. France had successfully mediated between Austria and Prussia, and twice between Russia and Turkey. By her consistent backing for Sweden, culminating in the close alliance of 1784, she had prevented that country from sharing the fate of Poland. She had won the goodwill of nearly every country except Austria, whose empty alliance provided a façade behind which France could effectively operate. Even England signed a commercial treaty in 1786. Commercial treaties were also signed with Sweden (1784), Spain (1786) and finally with Russia on 11 January 1787. It all seemed a fulfilment of the passage in Louis's *Réflexions*: 'A king of France, provided he is always just, will always be the leading *and the most powerful* of the sovereigns of Europe *and may easily become the arbiter between them*.'[116]

France, however, was not allowed to enjoy the fruits of the Dutch alliance for long: the Dutch Republic was unstable internally, indeed on the verge of civil war between the *stadhouder* (egged on by England) and the patriots, with whom the Treaty of Fontainebleau had been concluded. One of Louis's last letters to Vergennes, dated Compiègne 11 September 1786, betrays his anxiety:

> I do not understand how the *stadhouder* could have employed the degree of violence he has; I can well believe that M. Harris [English ambassador] is urging the most violent measures on him but this in itself will not be sufficient: England is delighted to see dissension sown in Holland but she will not lend the *stadhouder* effective aid; it is necessary that the latter should believe that he has the effective support of the new king of Prussia.[117]

The 'new king of Prussia', William II, had succeeded his uncle, Frederick the Great, in 1786 and his sister Wilhelmina was married to William V of Orange. Louis was right: only Prussian intervention could save William V, who had fled The Hague (in the province of Holland, under patriot control) for Nijmegen in the Orangeist province of Gelderland. In 1787 Louis's fears were realized when, hoping to provoke an incident, Wilhelmina ostentatiously set out on a journey from Nijmegen back to The Hague. On 28 June the patriots arrested her and, though they soon released her, the affair, as Wilhelmina had intended, gave Prussia and England the pretext to intervene militarily to restore power to the *stadhouder*, who abrogated the Treaty of Fontainebleau. It was replaced by a triple alliance between England, Prussia and Holland. Louis XVI, weakened by Calonne's revelation of the size of the deficit to the Assembly of Notables, stood helplessly aside. The naval and army ministers protested and resigned. The former plausibly argued that the French, who put national pride before all else, would tolerate increased taxation for intervention in Holland and for that alone. The shame sealed the fate of the monarchy. The Peace of Paris of 1783 had, Vergennes rightly believed, removed the stain of the Peace of Paris of 1763, when India and Canada had been lost. Now it was back.

The bigger picture was that, even after France's fluky victory at Yorktown, the diplomatic edifice was fragile. France's traditional hegemony in Europe, shattered in 1763 and illusorily restored in 1783, was threatened by the emergence of two new dynamic powers: one, England, with an overseas empire, and the other, Russia, expanding in all directions.[118] Two of France's allies were immediately threatened: Holland and the Ottoman Empire, and there was no money to defend either. The abandonment of Holland in 1787 was followed by that of Turkey in 1788, thereby incurring both humiliation and shame.[119] Turgot had warned Louis XVI that if France went to war, the chance to reform the monarchy would be postponed for ten years, perhaps for ever. Now the situation was reversed: unless the monarchy was reformed France would not be able to go to war. For two years France turned in on herself, haunted by the unjustified fear that England would take advantage of France's internal weakness to renew the colonial war.[120] Later she was too divided to have a diplomatic persona.

CHAPTER SIX

THE EMBARRASSMENTS OF PEACE

1783–85

THE DAY AFTER MAUREPAS's death on 21 November 1781, Castries notes in his diary: 'The king assembled a cabinet committee where he spoke more than usual, as one saying to himself: "I want to reign."'[1] Louis was now twenty-seven and he did not appoint a successor to Maurepas. In this he was following the precedents of Louis XIV and Louis XV who had appointed elderly premiers who could be expected to die just as they were ready to take over. On 15 December Castries notes: 'M. de Maurepas's apartment has been divided between M. de Cossé and M. d'Aumont. Thus the whole edifice of the premier minister is destroyed.'[2] Cossé and d'Aumont were just courtiers. What this symbolic act reflected was analysed by the duc de Croÿ:

> The king did not change the slightest thing in his lifestyle and his demeanour. He hunted and had his *travail* with each minister at fixed hours, taking good care not to talk to anyone except on matters relating to their department and pulling them up short if they strayed ever so little beyond it. Moreover he appears pretty firm and decided, so that nothing is lacking in this particular and everyone was reticent. The group called the queen's *société* [the Polignac group], who thought they had much to gain, was astonished to see the king hold himself more in reserve and appear to turn to them less, so that without seeming to show any affection for anyone in particular, he really governed by himself in major matters.[3]

Dealing individually with each minister, the king was the only one who saw the whole picture. This could work as long as the war lasted. Louis knew about naval tactics and diplomacy and the two things at which he excelled now formed a unity. There was probably no one in France better qualified to direct operations. War carries with it a certain elemental simplicity which makes some people nostalgic for it. Decisions can be postponed for the duration, which suits indecisive people such as Louis was. Though, like his grandfather, he bordered on pacifism, he was in his element during a war, especially a naval one. Everything else – finance, relations with the *parlement*, reform – were subordinate while the war lasted. In fact the finance minister, Joly de Fleury, dreaded 'the embarrassments of peace'.

For with peace – preliminaries were signed in January 1783 – came the reckoning. In July the keeper of the royal treasury, Bourgade, presented Joly with a memorandum which established that the *Compte rendu* was erroneous. Bourgade's two main conclusions were, first, that even discounting the extraordinary expenditure incurred as a result of the war, there was an underlying deficit on the 'ordinary' account of 15 million *livres* instead of Necker's 10 million surplus; second, assuming the king wanted to repay the debt over a period of ten years from the conclusion of peace, the annual deficit for that period would be 52 million *livres*.[4] When challenged about the cost of servicing the interest on his loans, Necker claimed that it had been covered by suppressing offices in *la finance* and at court – he claimed that this saved the government 84 million *livres* a year. The internal enquiry put the saving at 47,340,000 *livres*. But that is not the main point: these offices which had been bought were regarded as incorporeal property and Necker intended to repay the capital. Only he omitted this item from the balance sheet.[5] The American war had cost 1.3 billion *livres* which when amortized added 107 million *livres* to annual interest charges, although not all of this was incurred during Necker's period in office. Joly believed that on Bourgade's death in 1784 this memorandum or a copy passed to his nephew and heir, Calonne.[6]

The knowledge, at the highest levels of government, that the royal finances were desperate meant that as soon as the war was over, minds turned to remedies. Hard on the heels of the signature of peace preliminaries came an institutional innovation which suggests that the king was not as effective in coordinating the peacetime departments as he had the war effort. The departments, particularly the navy, which had been given carte blanche to win the war, now had to have their spending reined it. Or that was the idea.

The *comité des finances*

On 23 February the king rewarded Vergennes with Maurepas's title of *chef du Conseil royal des finances* and, with Joly's encouragement, Vergennes decided to make some use of it: on the 26th a *comité des finances* was instituted, presided over by the king and consisting of the *chef*, the finance minister and the keeper of the seals, before which all ministers had to submit their regular accounts as well as plans for future expenditure. It was an elaborate response to what Louis could not or would not do himself: impose a budget.

Nor was Louis totally master in the committee. Joly had originally proposed that its members thrash out their differences adversarially before the king, who would make an informed decision (the theoretical procedure in the *Conseil d'État*). In practice the members had preliminary discussions and presented a united front, Louis invariably adopting their conclusions. Vergennes and Miromesnil justified this on the grounds that it was 'unseemly' to have dissensions in the king's presence – a novel and decidedly English point of view.[7] For, like his grandfather before him, the king had found that ministerial disunity, though weakening the government, strengthened his position within it.

Dissension enough came from those who were summoned to appear before the committee, and this above all represented the revenge of Maurepas's *robin* protégés against the *grands seigneurs* who had been foisted on them in 1780, a 'war to the knife', as Ségur picturesquely put it, 'between the *hommes de robe* and gentlemen like us'.[8] It ran deeper than social and personal antagonisms, however, although Joly, in particular, cordially loathed Castries and Castries detested Vergennes. Having quarrelled violently with Vergennes over France's modest gains at the Peace of Paris, Castries planned to maintain the navy on a wartime footing in readiness for a follow-up war with England which France could not possibly afford. Joly unburdened himself to Véri: 'He never mentioned the sums involved but by his gestures and his eyes indicated that they were enormous.'[9] Castries was in fact planning to spend 100 million *livres* during the first six months of 1783 (Sartine had been broken for wanting to spend 120 million for the whole of 1781); in addition, with the conclusion of peace, the letters of exchange issued by the treasurer of the marine (which, after Necker's fall, was once again independent) came flooding back to Paris for redemption. On 23 February, with the king's backing, Joly suspended their repayment, though the king insisted on paying interest on them at 5 per cent. Joly had hoped by this action to force Castries to resign; when the queen persuaded Castries to stay on, Joly himself resigned.[10] Before he went, however, Joly presented the king with an outline reform plan which was the essence of the one that Calonne presented to the Assembly of Notables in 1787, proposing as it did to 'establish a little more equality between the different provinces in respect of taxation'; 'revise the way in which the *vingtième* and other taxes are levied'; and 'establish a new, simpler and less onerous method of collecting ... customs duties'.[11]

Finally, the committee was able to insist that both Castries and Ségur submit their accounts, thereby making them subordinate ministers and ignoring Castries's claim that there should be no intermediary between a secretary of state and the king and that the two men alone could decide the budget of his department. When Ségur presented his accounts on 31 May, Louis employed silence to deliver him a calculated insult. Véri's account, which is corroborated by that of Castries, runs:

> When the minister [Ségur] had finished his *travail*, without any warning, he saw the three members of the committee file into the king's cabinet. When they had taken their places, the king told M. de Ségur to show him his accounts. In his exposition, he showed that he had spent four or five million less than the original estimate. When he had finished, he remained seated. No one broke the silence and the king got up, went to pick up M. de Ségur's portfolio himself and, handing it to him, indicated by this gesture that he could go. It was only after he had left that the members of the committee praised his administration, afterwards continuing the session for another hour. Nothing could give a greater impression of subordination, and this whole rigmarole has only served to humiliate the minister for war in the eyes of the public.

Naturally, the two ministers wanted to resign, which infuriated Louis, who let Castries know through Madame de Polignac that he considered him ungrateful and that, if he resigned, he would block his son's career.[12]

Having with great difficulty achieved its primary purpose of subordinating the service ministers and establishing a budget, the committee was ultimately destroyed by internal dissensions and an attempt to reform the collection of indirect taxes. Both issues centred on Joly's successor as finance minister, Henri François-de-Paule Lefèvre d'Ormesson, the scion of a rich and powerful *robe* family which shared with the king the distinction of being descended from a saint, though only collaterally: in the sixteenth century they had married into the family of St Francis of Paola. One branch of the family was distinguished in the *parlement* and was to provide its last *premier président*. Henri's branch, as *intendants des finances*, had run the *vingtième* since its introduction in 1748. For some years, d'Ormesson, as intendant of the charitable foundation of Saint-Cyr, had had a *travail* alone with the king and in addition had been giving him a 'résumé of the state of his finances ... every six months' – presumably for some years also. Lazy Joly had been glad of d'Ormesson's assistance, but had d'Ormesson also been reporting secretly to Louis during Necker's ministry? D'Ormesson, at thirty-one the only minister remotely near the king's own age, was Louis's personal appointment, an attempt by him to set a limit on Vergennes's power by blocking the appointment of the latter's cousin de Crosne as successor to Joly de Fleury.[13] Vergennes had wanted to fill Maurepas's place, by sitting in on the other ministers' *travail* with the king – the finance committee was a substitute for this, 'a three-man prime minster'– and by vetting ministerial appointments. He had wanted this arrangement partly out of ambition but also to end what he called 'this kind of anarchy in the ministry' which at times 'consumed his whole attention'.[14]

In addition, the proverbial integrity of the d'Ormesson family – *probe comme d'Ormesson* – was in contrast with Vergennes's cupidity, which Louis found distressing; but Maurepas had been fond of observing that only a fool or a knave could possibly want to be a finance minister and this witticism had passed into governmental thinking, Miromesnil, for example, reminding the king of the rare conjunction of 'probity' and 'talent'.[15] Consequently, d'Ormesson acquired and has retained an unmerited reputation for dullness and was abused by the king on that account; yet his brief ministry and his projects were anything but dull.

D'Ormesson was miserable in the ministry. He had to promise the king that he would never resign and he declined the honour of being made a *ministre d'état* in the hope that by refusing this lifetime appointment he would avoid exile should he be dismissed. Louis's diary refers to neither his appointment nor his dismissal; d'Ormesson's refers to 'the indifference with which he treated me and all too often public affairs'.[16] In their *travail* together, Louis refused to talk about anything but the current state of the royal treasury or to allow d'Ormesson to strike up a general conversation. D'Ormesson, having apologized for a hurriedly prepared *travail* because he had been up all night nursing his dying son, met with Louis's brutal reply, 'C'est fâcheux!' (What a bore!) – leaving in doubt whether he was referring to the lack of preparation or the boy's plight: 'une réponse brusque du Roi', d'Ormesson writes in the margin. Louis's own elder son was to prove a sickly child.

Perhaps as if to break out of the conversational strait-jacket imposed by the king, in August d'Ormesson drafted a radical memorandum which, looking beyond the usual hand-to-mouth measures, focused on the year 1787, which d'Ormesson presented as a time both of crisis and of opportunity:

> Happily the approaching expiry of the last lease of the general farm and of the third *vingtième*, which both occur in 1786, allow us to prepare, by this not too distant date, a better internal order by both changing or modifying

the consumption taxes which may be harmful to agriculture and commerce, and by finally enabling Your Majesty to know the respective wealth of his various provinces, still unknown, by means of a better assessment of the two *vingtièmes*, the only tax which is uniform throughout the whole kingdom and consequently the only one susceptible of establishing a fair basis of comparison between the various provinces.[17]

D'Ormesson minutes this document as being 'suspended by the affair of the Discount Bank'. On 24 August d'Ormesson leant on the *Caisse d'escompte* (Discount Bank) secretly to lend the crown 24 million *livres*. The bank had been set up by Turgot in 1775 to foster commerce by lending at 4 per cent through convertible paper money; to maintain confidence it was essential that the bank should be independent of the government, whose credit was worse than its own. Inevitably d'Ormesson's secret arrangement leaked out and there was a run on the bank, which had to suspend payment. D'Ormesson drew up a decree making the bank's notes legal tender and Vergennes went to Versailles to get the king's signature. Louis had retired for the night so Vergennes issued the decree on his own authority. The drama left the king with a dread of credit crises which was to influence the rest of his reign.

While nerves were still frayed, d'Ormesson embarked on a risky reform. In the early summer he and Vergennes had decided to take the king to one side during the removal of the court to Fontainebleau in October to propose the abolition of tax farming.[18] Farming the indirect taxes – i.e., the crown making their produce over to the farmers in return for an advance – was one of the most characteristic institutions of the ancien régime; it was also one of the most entrenched, with vested interests not just in traditional high finance but at Versailles, where courtiers had stakes or *croupes* in the various syndicates of farmers (see above, pp. 79–80). It was a fashionable way of being associated with money. The idea of abolishing the farm may well have come from Vergennes, who had become both more knowledgeable and more radical in financial matters since his intemperate criticism of Turgot's proposals. His immediate concern was that the farmers, by sending their agents aboard American ships in connection with tobacco, salt and other duties, were driving those ships into English ports.

The proposal was to convert the last three years of the farmers' contract into a *régie intéressée* (i.e., the farmers would be paid a fixed salary plus a proportion of the amount collected over an agreed figure) with effect from 1 January. There would be no immediate saving since the existing farmers would become the *régisseurs* and their profits would remain the same, because the money that they had advanced to the king against them (some 60–70 million *livres*) could not be repaid. However, the exercise would make for an easy transition to a rational system of indirect taxation when the contract was renewed in 1787.

D'Ormesson duly presented his proposals to the king in the finance committee on Friday 23 October. Louis, who normally accepted the committee's proposals automatically, on this occasion 'hesitated for an instant' before ordering the farmers' lease to be rescinded. During d'Ormesson's *travail* the following Sunday, the king complained of the rapidity with which the decision had been embodied in a decree and published on the Saturday. Though Louis can be taken to have supported such a reform, he had been shaken by the run on the Discount Bank and perhaps thought that the timing was bad.[19]

There followed an outcry from the financiers but, since the farmers' promissory notes had the same backing after the council's decree as before, one is inclined to believe d'Ormesson's allegation that their dramatic depreciation was engineered by the farmers themselves to give them a pretext to demand the impossible repayment of their advance. On top of this, d'Ormesson had been betrayed by his colleagues. The royal banker, Bourgade, was promoting the interests of his nephew, Calonne, while Vergennes had come to detest d'Ormesson for his refusal to countenance the sale to the crown, at an exorbitant price, of the feudal rights belonging to his estate of Fravenberg in Lorraine. They persuaded the keeper of the treasury, d'Harvelai, who was the complaisant husband of Calonne's mistress, to write the king a letter saying that, unless the farmers' lease was restored and d'Ormesson dismissed he could not answer for the consequences. Calonne was suggested as the ideal man to restore credit. The king rose to the bait, scribbling the following note to Vergennes:

I received your letter last night, Monsieur, and the papers of *M. le controleur-général* on the general farm and the Discount Bank; since the farmers want an accommodation, we shall have to agree to treat with them, though it would be extremely annoying to give the impression of yielding to them; it was M. d'Harvelai's letter yesterday which terrified me; you will be seeing him today and you will inform me before the council [meets] of all that he said to you and of all the ideas you have been able to muster on the present crisis. I do not doubt M. d'Ormesson's zeal for my service but should credit run out, his good intentions will be no substitute. Inform him along these lines until I have made a final decision.[20]

Vergennes 'hinted' that d'Ormesson should resign, but he refused. D'Ormesson had 'not concealed the fact', as Vergennes informed the king on 31 October, that confident as he is of the soundness of a measure which has received Your Majesty's sanction in his committee, he would consider himself blameworthy if he yielded to the efforts of intrigue which sought to decry it and if he abandoned Your Majesty's service at a moment of crisis. He added that he could not resign with honour unless Your Majesty deigned to give him the order directly, whether orally or in writing.[21]

Louis was 'pained' by d'Ormesson's obduracy and by his further insistence that the king satisfy his honour by saying that he took with him the king's 'esteem'. Nevertheless, on 2 November Louis duly wrote to d'Ormesson, saying that 'the state of affairs obliges me to ask you to hand in your resignation but you retain my esteem and protection'.[22]

Unfortunately, the king's 'protection' did not count for much: d'Ormesson's successor, Calonne, placed two villainous men in d'Ormesson's house to spy on him. After a while d'Ormesson asked the police minister, Lenoir, a close friend of Calonne's, whether these two men could be removed as they were upsetting his wife. Lenoir consented to replace them with two wig-makers who were pleasant-mannered and remained in his service. D'Ormesson stoically remarked that if you had to be spied on it was better to have spies you knew.[23]

D'Ormesson's accusation against Vergennes reached the king and lowered the latter in the king's estimation. Louis, who hated ministers making money on the side, was deeply disturbed when he heard of Vergennes's scheme. Not only was he asking sixty years' purchase for the rights in question,[24] but the Fravenberg estate itself (plus another in Alsace) had been given him by the king as a reward for concluding the recent peace. Vergennes asked Louis to appoint an expert to look into the whole matter but the expert found Vergennes to be in the wrong. Vergennes was reduced to telling the king that he had only wanted to sell the king the exclusive right to sell the salt belonging to the estate to prevent smuggling from Alsace to the rest of France[25] and remove the imputation that he was profiting from it! Vergennes wrote Louis desperate letters: 'My misfortune is extreme because I have caused Your Majesty a moment of pain' and 'I will go into retirement consumed by the misery of having lost the esteem of a master to whom I have always referred everything'.[26] In the end, Louis had to accept Vergennes's explanation. He was too valuable to him: having resisted Marie-Antoinette's pressure to dismiss him he was not going to sack the architect of his foreign policy for a mere peccadillo. So when d'Ormesson, who still had his *travail* with the king as intendant of Saint-Cyr, planned a further denunciation of Vergennes on 4 December, Louis thwarted him by the simple expedient of having all the doors to his cabinet kept open so that d'Ormesson would have to make his accusations before the courtiers. Nevertheless, Vergennes's attempt to be prime minister was over.

Resentment at d'Ormesson's blocking the sale of his feudal rights may not have been the only reason why Vergennes sought his dismissal. Even if d'Ormesson was right in saying that Vergennes had first suggested the attack on the farmers, Vergennes may have come to realize that the government was alienating too many vested interests at the same time: the courtiers thought the finance committee would end financial favours, calling it 'le tombeau des grâces'; the Neckerites were sworn enemies who, in Castries, had a fifth columnist in the government. To attack the native financiers as well as the 'Genevan' would complete the alienation of the entire establishment. And this was Louis's central dilemma – and one still relevant today: how do you reform the establishment without its consent? Castries warned him that it would take 'one hundred thousand armed men'.[27]

Could the king, could a new minister square this circle? Louis told Marie-Antoinette, 'there is not much to choose between all the candidates but at least ... [Calonne] has *la finance* on his side'.[28] Marie-Antoinette herself favoured reappointing Necker. Bourgade reported to Vergennes: 'Last Thursday there was a committee in the queen's apartments to discuss Necker.' Shortly afterwards, however, the queen suffered a miscarriage and was *hors de combat* at this crucial time. Castries worked on the king but he gave a categorical and (he hoped) final refusal: 'Considering the generous way I treated M. Necker and the way in which he left me voluntarily, he must think no more of a return to office.'[29]

Calonne's Indian summer

D'Ormesson had been destroyed by an alliance between high finance and the queen's *société intime*: the Polignac group and the king's youngest brother, the comte d'Artois. This same combination also secured the appointment of Calonne as controller-general. On 3 November, Louis wrote to Vergennes: 'You have only to summon M. de Calonne to Fontainebleau and explain our plans for him and report back when you have seen him. I do not know whether he is at Paris or in Flanders [of which he was intendant] ... the main thing we must concentrate on is the support of credit, to assure the funds for the rest of the year but without taking any precipitate measures.' Louis had been scarred by what he termed himself the 'crisis'.[30]

Louis need not have wondered about Calonne's whereabouts: he had observed every recent change at the finance ministry at close quarters. His appointment, perhaps the most decisive of the reign, had a quality of inevitability about it suggested by the king's slightly cryptic nautical metaphor to a common friend, d'Angiviller: 'There's one arrived safely against wind and tide.'[31] A contemporary has left a striking picture of Calonne: '[He possessed] the vivacity of a young colonel; the elegance of a man of means; a coquettishness ridiculous in anyone but a pretty woman; the pedantry of the magistrate; some of the gaucheness of the provincial.'[32]

This pen portrait presents a series of striking paradoxes which lived together in the same body. They can also be observed in the superb portrait of him painted by Marie-Antoinette's favourite painter, Elisabeth Vigée Le Brun. Calonne was rumoured to be her lover and the portrait must be the product of revelatory intimacy. Beyond the symmetrical contradictions there was a central ambiguity or ambivalence which ran through not just his character but also his policies. He was also the nearest Louis XVI came to having a 'favourite', in the seventeenth-century sense of the word. Consider some of the contradictions: Calonne was a relative *parvenu* (his father had been ennobled) and he retained some of the 'gaucheness of the provincial', but he was the only one of the *robe* ministers to have court manners, that indefinable gloss, that final burnishing of the ormolu which disappeared with the Revolution and cannot now be reconstructed. His social (though not his sexual) life was spent with courtiers, or rather one particular set of them, the queen's 'intimate society', the Polignac set.

Calonne had probably been introduced to the Polignac faction whilst he was intendant of Lille through the prince de Robecq, who was the commandant of the city and a member of the group which included the duchesse de Polignac, governess of the royal children since 1780, and her sister, Madame de Polastron, who was the mistress of the king's youngest brother, the comte d'Artois, who was also part of the set. Calonne paid his debts to the Polignac group; that is, he paid their debts, notably those of Artois, who became his staunchest supporter: one of Calonne's first acts on becoming finance minister was to have the treasury undertake to service the 14 million *livres* the prince owed.[33] In 1784, he increased the Polignac family's income by 100,000 *livres*, which was not a large sum considering that they had to entertain the queen and divert her political ambitions. Vergennes, who formed a close alliance with Calonne, further secured their support by making one of their number, the comte d'Adhémar, ambassador to London, a candidacy the queen had refused to encourage.[34]

This group was to stick by Calonne through thick and thin. Yet, despite his court connections, Calonne denounced the entry of courtiers into the ministry and their arrogant assumption that they were 'all equally capable of exercising any ministry'. He blamed Necker for this trend, and condemned it because he held that the aristocrat ministers – of whom Castries was the supreme example – no longer believed in the absolute monarchy, preferring an aristocratic oligarchy such as England's, with its fig leaf of democracy.

Although, following in his father's footsteps, Calonne had started life in a provincial *parlement* and retained 'the pedantry of the magistrate' underneath the French polish of court manners, he had been at daggers drawn with the *parlementaires* since entering the royal council as a master of requests aged twenty-nine. Men such as he were described as *transfuges* ('defectors'). His early career in the council was marked by two episodes which made him desperate with the *parlements*. In the first, in 1766, he had been the principal draftsman of the speech in which Louis XV, proclaiming that 'le pouvoir législatif m'appartient sans dépendance et sans partage', so lacerated the *parlement* that it came to be known as the *séance de flagellation* (see above, pp. 14–15). In the second episode, Calonne was accused of abusing the confidence of La Chalotais, the public prosecutor of the *parlement* of Rennes, in order to obtain proof that he had been writing poison-pen letters to Louis XV. Calonne was also able to retrieve from La Chalotais a bundle of love letters, tied up with a pink silk ribbon, that Louis XV had written to one of his mistresses. Louis rewarded him with the intendancy of Metz.

No one doubted that Calonne had a brilliant mind. Before embarking on his political career he had been a distinguished student at the École des Quatre-Nations in Paris, winning most of the prizes for Latin and Greek – later he wrote that the only fame that had any appeal to him was that of a scholar. But was this success a result of graft or flair? In the curious potted autobiography he later published, Calonne put these achievements down to hard work,[35] something he felt was necessary because of his reputation for frivolity. For he was witty in an age which admired wit, charming in an age which relished charm, but it was felt that these were not the requirements of a minister of the crown. Talleyrand noted, 'the majority of men like to see the qualities of hard work and prudence in ministers; Calonne was not reassuring on either count.' Calonne concluded that he should have gone around with the furrowed brow of a man weighed down by affairs of state. The duc de Lévis, who knew him well, thought that Calonne trusted too much to his 'extreme facility for work'. However another witness says that his 'frequent trips to Paris' were not, as supposed, for pleasure, for 'his very carriage became an office' and 'back home, shutters closed, legs in the bath, lit by candles, he found in the precious resources of his intellect the means to save France'.[36] Then again, a diplomat claimed he gambled till 3 a.m. and was so exhausted that 'of all the ministers, not excepting M. d'Ossun, he was the one who got in most sleep during the meetings of the *Conseil d'État*'.[37]

So Calonne was controversial. And we have yet to examine his policies. When he was sworn in as controller-general before the *Chambre des Comptes*, the audit office that signed off the king's accounts (fourteen years late), Calonne made a statement of intent:

> As soon as I have completed the arduous task of discharging the war debt, I will apply my mind to the execution of plans of general reform which, grounded in the very constitution of the monarchy, embraces all its parts, regenerates rather than squeezes resources and reveals that the true secret of lightening taxation lies in the proportionate equality of its assessment and in the simplification of its collection.[38]

These words have become famous as trailing his reform programme, but they were scarcely noticed at the time because Bourbon France was enjoying its Indian summer. Talleyrand, Calonne's collaborator, then more famously Napoleon's foreign minister – 'dung in a silk stocking', Napoleon called him – said in old age: 'No one who did not live in the years before 1789 can know the meaning of *le plaisir de vivre*.' In similar vein Pasquier, councillor in the *parlement* in 1787 and in 1837 last chancellor of France, recalled that, 'since the dawn of the monarchy France was never happier than she was then. I have witnessed the magnificence of the empire; and since the [Bourbon] restoration [in 1814] I have seen fortunes arise daily. But in my opinion nothing has yet equalled the splendour of Paris in the years that elapsed between the peace of 1783 and 1789.'[39] Calonne, with his elegance, wit, charm and ostentatious but never vulgar display, was the incarnation of all this; but also, though this was too cruel, 'of every abuse he sought to eradicate'.

Is it just with the benefit of hindsight that periods before great crises acquire their aura, or is there a voluptuous death wish present, as in Vienna before 1914? Was it merely the contrast between these six years and the six that followed – those of the National Assembly, the Legislative Assembly, the National Convention and the Terror – that rendered their memory so poignant? Was it the contrast, the disillusionment of the latter period that made them so bitter? Or, as I shall argue, was it the shattering of the illusion which caused the Revolution? The disillusionment in fact came in 1787 rather than 1789, and marked the start of the revolutionary process. For, in many ways the well-being of the earlier period was illusory, or borrowed, rather like that of the period before the great financial crash of 2008; Calonne himself admitted in 1786, 'that which is artificially maintained cannot last for ever'.[40]

And yet the government deliberately fostered the illusion of well-being. The point of departure for the illusion was Necker's *Compte rendu* of 1781. And since its full title was *Compte rendu au Roi*, it seemed to have official sanction. Yet Maurepas did not believe in it, calling it the 'Conte bleu' – the book had the blue wrappers traditionally used for fairy tales – and a pamphlet attacking Necker's work was so titled. The king also had his doubts about the *Compte* which the internal inquiry into it quickly confirmed. Perhaps one should go back a bit further, to the decision first to rearm and then fight four years of war without additional direct taxation. It is often said that if France had raised additional taxation while rearming, England would have launched a pre-emptive strike. But this view is mistaken: as we have seen, England swallowed even greater humiliation to keep France at least technically out of the war. Since Louis understood the English political system better than his ministers, the failure to realize this must rest at his door.

This decision not to levy additional taxation raised doubts among investors in government stock as to whether their money was safe. The *Compte rendu* was designed to allay these fears: as Calonne scathingly reminded Necker in 1787: 'it doubtless produced the effect you intended'.[41] However Necker was right to reply that it would be dangerous to attack the 1781 *Compte* since 'it had been for a long time the basis of public confidence'. The unsung hero of war finance was Joly de Fleury who, thanks to his contacts in the *parlement* and the defeat at the Saintes, was able to increase indirect taxes by 25 million *livres* and levy a third *vingtième*, bringing in 21 million. Adding these sums to the 'surplus' of 10 million in the *Compte rendu*, people were allowed to form the impression that the government now had an annual surplus of 56 million *livres*. In fact there was an annual deficit of getting on for 100 million *livres* and a debt of 4 billion, which had to be serviced.

This was the dilemma facing Calonne, whose appointment roughly coincided with the signing of the Peace of Paris on 4 October 1783. Normally a long and expensive war was accompanied by a bankruptcy. 'Banqueroute' was understood not as a complete repudiation of royal debt, which would have caused mayhem, but rather a forcible reduction of the rate of interest paid to holders of government stock, such as Terray had perpetrated in 1770. But this would have shattered the illusion and meant that the king would have had to pay a higher rate of interest in future – a default premium. Besides, Louis was keeping his promise to Turgot not to countenance any kind of bankruptcy. Calonne encouraged Louis in this, telling him that a bankruptcy would be 'murderous' – an early example of the heightened language used in the Revolution.

So Calonne had to continue borrowing money. Between 1783 and 1785 he raised loans totalling 488 million *livres* at between 7 and 8 per cent, costing 33 million *livres* a year to service. A loan at 8 per cent almost amounted to a default premium – the English government could borrow at half that figure. The trouble was that people believed Necker's *Compte rendu* when it suited them – i.e., in order to argue the case for no increase in taxation – but were sceptical when it came to placing their own funds. By definition, those taxed only included Frenchmen, but increasingly, and following Necker's example, the raising of loans was international.

Calonne told the *parlement* that these loans were necessary to fund the war debt. This meant re-financing short-term loans or letters of exchange due for immediate redemption with longer dated instruments – that is, extending the maturity of the debt, to use the parlance of the 2008 crisis. To do this Calonne had to persuade the financially illiterate *parlementaires*, who were asked to register the loans, and the public, who were asked to subscribe to them, that funding the debt would solve the problem. He could not at this stage reveal his scepticism about the *Compte rendu* because it 'was the basis of public credit'.

To aid him in this necessarily dishonest task – for what modern finance minister can give advance warning of, say, a devaluation? – he created a *caisse d'amortissement* (sinking fund) which, he claimed, by means of compound interest would pay off a quarter of the debt in twenty-five years. This of course could only work if there was a primary budgetary surplus, otherwise it was robbing Peter to pay Paul. The sinking fund was wound up after two years, but it had served its purpose: by 1786 the debt was 'constituted' but that did not mean it was paid off. A modern analogy would be consolidated credit. With this, someone with a variety of debts – some to loan sharks, demanding repayment at assorted times – has his debts consolidated into one, with provision for regular repayment. That, of course, doesn't mean that the debt has gone away but it may seem like that to the credulous, and Calonne, in dealing with the *parlementaires*, may have sought to give this impression in order to float his loans. What the consolidation does do, however, is to give a clearer idea of the extent of the problem, though this may be worrying in itself.

By 1786, however, the illusion was wearing thin, as Calonne freely confessed to the king. Without additional taxation they would need to 'raise a new loan which would necessarily be considerable and which would surely meet with a lot of opposition from the *parlement* which would be all the more plausible in that the government could no longer claim they needed to fund the war debt'.[42]

At the same time as sustaining the illusion that the royal finances were on an even keel, Calonne aimed to give an air of prosperity to the country at large. Peace of itself brought about a natural increase in trade and industry; but Calonne wanted to give the ormolu regime a further burnish. In an anonymous pamphlet he wrote in 1781, attacking the *Compte rendu*, Calonne had called France 'a kingdom where resources are increased by the very act of expenditure'. This theory has been seen as a precursor of Keynesian pump-priming, or the 'multiplier effect', though it was also at the heart of Physiocratic doctrine. We saw that Louis's education owed some debt to the Physiocrats through Christian agrarianism, though neither he nor Calonne believed in grand theories.

As intendant of two rich provinces, Calonne had been a first-hand witness of the wealth of the kingdom; he now realized that France was a poor state in a rich country and that the country had the potential to be even richer. Her infrastructure was much better than England's, with a superb network of roads and canals, which her rival lacked; perhaps by importing England's industrial technology she could rival or even surpass her. After the peace, many Englishmen were encouraged to set up factories in France. Calonne embarked on a series of great public works, such as the embellishment of towns, construction of canals and improvement of roads, though these were already more than adequate. He found money for the construction of a great port at Cherbourg, provocatively close to England. He built a fine wall round Paris with grand ornamental watch towers at the gates, *decus et tutamen*, as an ornament and as a safeguard against smuggling, which provided a livelihood for many in the ancien régime. He encouraged the crown's bankers and departmental treasurers to invest their own money and the crown's (the two virtually indistinguishable) in commercial and industrial enterprises. Ministers and the high nobility followed suit. Just to include those mentioned in this book: Bourgade developed the Chaussée d'Antin complex in Paris; the duc de Croÿ invested in the mines at Anzin; Castries and the prince de Conti in coal mines; Vergennes and d'Angiviller in a textile mill near Rouen founded by an Englishman; Orléans and Penthièvre had several iron foundries in the Champagne; Artois set up a chlorine plant; Calonne set up a factory at Saint-Omer. And the king personally had a twelfth of the shares in the Le Creusot iron foundry.[43]

These were, in the main, useful projects. The Paris wall, for example, enabled Calonne to negotiate an extra 12 million *livres* a year on the renewal of the farmers' lease. But there was also a speculative element, which Calonne at first tried to contain but then encouraged. This shift coincided with his realization, after the difficult registration of his loan in 1785, that he would not be able to turn to the *parlement* for money again. Instead he gambled on an indefinite bull market on the Bourse, which mostly consisted of stocks in which the government had a large share, such as the India Company or the Discount Bank. The Bourse was very sophisticated – more so than the London Stock Exchange where trading in options was illegal. And since the government had a finger in every pie, any crisis would be a systemic one. The parallels with the seize-up of credit following the collapse of Lehman Brothers is striking.

The attempts to increase Paris's water supply is a saga that illustrates several of these points. Calonne backed the Paris Water Company, which aimed to use the fire pumps invented by the Périer brothers. An advantage of this scheme was that the company could double as a fire brigade. In August 1784 the royal treasury lent it 1.2 million *livres* in return for 1,000 shares at par. Calonne also encouraged the treasurers of the marine and war departments to invest. Meanwhile Breteuil, Calonne's enemy and the minister for Paris, encouraged a rival operation that was claimed to be more hygienic. This aimed to increase Paris's water supply by diverting the course of the Yvette. Faced with competition, the shares of the Paris Water Company began to slide, so in April 1786 Calonne gave the Italian banker Campi 1.5 million *livres* to mount a share-support operation. So successful was Campi that the share price doubled. There is a story, which I like to think is apocryphal, that, at his first *travail* with the king, Calonne observed that he was heavily indebted but that there were always ways for a finance minister to line his pockets. Without saying a word, the story continues, Louis opened his bureau and contemptuously threw a bundle of 230,000 shares in the Paris Water Company at the new minister.[44] If the story was in fact true, it would explain Calonne's need to support the share price.

In April 1786 Breteuil tried to bounce the council into accepting the Yvette scheme. But Calonne, as well as observing that his scheme would supply drinking water to districts hitherto without, deployed the key argument that 'the shares [of the Paris Water Company] were the equivalent of royal bills, which the government had to keep supporting to preserve their credit and that of all the other royal stocks'. Louis came down on Calonne's side, even slapping Breteuil down 'pretty sharply'.[45]

Calonne's main point is one that will be familiar today: the Water Company was 'too big to fail' because its collapse would involve that of other key institutions. Another example of such an institution was the French India Company, which Calonne reconstituted in 1785 with 40,000 shares of stock, each priced at 1,000 *livres*. It was given a seven-year monopoly on all trade with countries beyond the Cape of Good Hope. The new company – and there were many such – had to pay the king for a surety bond known as a *cautionnement*. It was just a money-making exercise: caution itself was thrown to the winds. The largest of these transactions occurred in February 1787 when the Discount Bank made a substantial rights issue in return for giving the government an enormous *cautionnement* of 70 million *livres*. Since the breakdown in relations with the *parlement* on 23 December 1785, which will be examined in the next chapter, the king had been unable to borrow normally on anything like the required scale. But the money he received as *cautionnements* was not new money, not *louis d'or*, but just the same old share certificates churning round the system.

This was not, however, paper money. Ever since John Law and the Mississippi Bubble of 1718–20, France had had a horror of the stuff. But there was now an urgent need to expand its issuance. The Discount Bank issued barely 100 million livres' worth in paper, compared to the Bank of England's 200 million; yet France held half of Europe's stock of metallic currency, according to Necker's calculations, or 3 billion *livres* according to Calonne's. Much of this gold and silver came from foreign subscriptions to loans, since France had a balance of payments deficit, and the inflationary effects were a major cause of the deficit.[46] If the government had printed money – which the National Assembly did with the *assignat* in 1790 – it could have resorted to its own equivalent of quantitative easing: that is, paying off its debt by means of inflation, as had happened with Law and would happen in the French Revolution.

But that solution, if that is the right word, was not used in the 1780s, either because the mechanism was not understood or was deemed to be dishonest or creative of moral hazard, as was felt initially in 2008. In fact it has been argued that the king *did* create a sort of moral hazard by bailing out the Rohan-Guémenée family after its bankruptcy and Choiseul's heirs after his death in 1785, and that the main point of Calonne's Indian summer was to prop up the main court families, who were suffering from declining rent rolls as a result of depressed agricultural prices, because these great families were the constituent elements of the regime.[47] In fact, as we shall see, they were its main solvent.

Eschewing bankruptcy or inflation, the government was left with the problem of circularity, or systemic risk. If the financiers were 'tied to the existence of the machine', as Soulavie put it, was the machine tied to the existence of the financiers? So when Calonne intervened through intermediaries to prop up a company in which the king had shares he was speculating with his own scrip. Something had to give. In the first half of 1787 no fewer than five court bankers defaulted. Stagnating tax receipts were putting pressure on the financiers who lent to the crown on the strength of them. They were already struggling as 1787 began, but the *coup de grâce* was delivered in early February when Calonne recapitalized the Discount Bank. Many of the shareholders were court bankers and Calonne's call for additional money put intolerable pressure on them.

The first bankruptcy was that of Harvoin, receiver-general of taxes for Tours. Next was Baudard de Saint-James, treasurer of the navy, who sought refuge in the Bastille and turned over his accounts to the king. He had been particularly squeezed by Calonne's call on the Discount Bank, of which he was also an administrator. This was followed on 5 March by the highly embarrassing default and flight to England of Bourboulon, anti-Necker pamphleteer and treasurer to the comte d'Artois. Finally, on 1 June, came another major default, that of Megret de Sérilly, one of the two treasurers of the war department, who had been hit by the default of Saint-James. Other government bankers were on the brink and by April there were fears that the treasury itself would have to suspend payment.[48]

So it would be against the background of a systemic credit crisis that Louis would launch his major initiative at reform in 1787. Before that, however, Louis and Marie-Antoinette had to endure the protracted tragi-comedy of the Diamond Necklace Affair.

CHAPTER SEVEN

UNRAVELLING
1785–86

The Diamond Necklace Affair

THE DIAMOND NECKLACE AFFAIR lifted the lid on a can of worms and made the ancien régime resemble one. An out-of-favour cardinal-archbishop who was accused of being a knave was idolized when he turned out merely to have been a fool. The press was scurrilous to an extent that even our kiss-and-tell age would find offensive. The *parlement* was revealed as nakedly political and venal. Ministerial rivalries trumped any loyalty to a king who appeared despotic, arbitrary and vengeful. And the biggest sufferer of all was Marie-Antoinette who, despite the French name of the scandal – 'l'affaire du collier de la Reine' ('The Queen's Necklace Affair') – was the innocent victim. For the kernel of the highly complex Diamond Necklace Affair consisted in the successful attempt by a gang of confidence tricksters to convince cardinal de Rohan, archbishop of Strasbourg and almoner to the king, that the queen's favour was returning and would be complete if he could negotiate the purchase of a 2,800-carat diamond necklace for her in secret and without the king's knowledge. The heist relied on the assumption that the queen would do such a thing. In some senses – though this can be exaggerated – the affair marked the true 'unravelling of the ancien régime'.[1]

The necklace in question wasn't really a necklace at all, rather a series of loops and chains which cascaded down the bodice – hence its alternative names, 'river' and 'slave necklace', because though it appeared to flow, it actually imprisoned its owner – or would have, had it ever been worn. It had been created out of 647 large diamonds by the court jewellers Boehmer, towards the end of Louis XV's reign, and was spectacular for 'the size, whiteness, match and fire of the stones'.[2] It was valued at about 2 million *livres* (though the price came down), or one-fivehundredth of the cost of the American war. Boehmer was hoping that Louis XV would present it to Madame du Barry, but they made three mistakes: they created it 'on spec' without a commission, and they banked on the longevity both of the king and of the style of the piece. Louis died suddenly before he could give it to his mistress – and there is no guarantee he would have had he lived, having already given her the elegant château of Louveciennes. The piece was in the style to which Louis XV gave his name and was unsuited to the classicism to which Louis XVI gave his.

Outdated, it was also vulgar. Paste versions of 'river necklaces' were worn by actresses, despite the physical restrictions they imposed on their performances. Such a necklace may have been considered suitable for an ex-courtesan, but it was not for the only other possible candidate in France after du Barry had been exiled to a convent – Marie-Antoinette. The new queen was known to be fond of diamonds: Louis gave her diamond epaulettes on the baptism of their second son, the duc de Normandie; and it was a standing joke between queen and jeweller that Boehmer would drown himself if she did not take this expensive stock off his hands and save the firm from bankruptcy. However, she advised Boehmer to break up the necklace and sell the stones separately, which ironically became its fate. Louis himself is said to have considered presenting the necklace to Marie-Antoinette after the birth of the dauphin in 1781 and to have had it in his cabinet for four months before abandoning the project on receiving news of the naval defeat at the Saintes.[3] The point to retain about Boehmer is that impending bankruptcy made him credulous. And the heist depended on the despair-induced credulity of the two victims, Boehmer and the cardinal de Rohan.

Louis René Edouard, prince de Rohan-Guémenée, belonged to a clan – or 'tribe' as their many enemies called it – which claimed descent from the semi-autonomous dukes of Brittany. As such they enjoyed a rank between that of the dukes and the princes of the blood. But they were heavily indebted, especially the Guémenée branch, to which the cardinal belonged. His cousin, the duc de Guémenée, had gone bankrupt in 1782 to the tune of 32 million *livres*. Louis had controversially bailed him out by buying the port of Lorient from him at an inflated price but had indicated that he was not amused by stripping his wife of the post of governess to the royal children. The family hoped that the cardinal would rescue its fortunes, but his extravagant lifestyle and a fire in one of his châteaux made this unlikely. His one hope was to become a minister, but this route was blocked by Marie-Antoinette, whose resentments never faded.

Many of her prejudices dated from the time when she was dauphine. Choiseul had arranged her marriage and his protégé (later her own), the baron de Breteuil, was on the point of being nominated ambassador to Vienna (he had already sent ahead carriages and effects characterized by the 'solid magnificence' for which he was known) when Choiseul fell and Breteuil's appointment was revoked. Instead Rohan, allied to du Barry and the new foreign secretary d'Aiguillon, was appointed. Marie-Antoinette's antipathies had been based on flimsier foundations.

While he was ambassador, Rohan insulted Maria-Theresa for her hypocrisy in weeping over the partition of Poland while taking the lion's share of the booty – like the walrus and the oysters, 'with tears and sighs, she sorted out those of the largest size'. On d'Aiguillon's fall, Rohan was replaced by Breteuil, but in 1777, despite being detested by Marie-Antoinette, Rohan was appointed court almoner on the death of cardinal de La Roche-Aymon. On Louis's accession in 1774 his former governess, the 'chère petite maman', Madame de Marsan, of the Rohan clan, had persuaded him to promise cardinal de Rohan the reversion to this post. Marie-Antoinette tried to get Louis to renege on this promise but he refused, consoling his queen with the thought that they need not have much to do with the new almoner. Marie-Antoinette took this literally and never addressed a single word to the cardinal before the affair broke in 1785. When Rohan's relative, the princesse de Guémenée, had been obliged to tender her resignation as governess to the royal children, Rohan was deprived of a channel of communication to the queen. When his arch-enemy Breteuil, appointed minister for the *Maison du Roi* in 1783, formed a dynastic alliance with the new *gouvernante*, Marie-Antoinette's favourite, the duchesse de Polignac, Rohan felt that an 'iron ring' had been placed about the queen. He became 'obsessed by the threat posed to his political existence . . . by Breteuil' – and putty in the hands of Jeanne de Valois, the woman who became his nemesis.[4]

Jeanne de Valois, who masterminded the heist, was the impoverished descendant of an illegitimate but recognized son of Henri II (d. 1558), of the Valois dynasty, which had preceded the Bourbons. This gave the story the added piquancy required by the jaded palate of ancien régime society, though this French Tess of the d'Urbervilles was assuredly not a 'pure woman' – her improbable descent (recognized by the stickler court genealogist, Hozier) was just about the only genuine thing about her. Jeanne, an orphan, grew up in utter destitution, begging for her bread with the plea, 'take pity on a poor orphan of the blood of the Valois'. She was taken under the wing of a court lady and, having satisfied the court genealogist, received a small pension. At court she threw fainting fits in front of the king's sister, Madame Élisabeth, the duchesse d'Orléans and the finance minister of the day. Each gave her money. One day her patron's carriage crossed that of cardinal de Rohan and an introduction was effected. They probably became lovers. Jeanne convinced Rohan that she had become intimate with Marie-Antoinette – who later claimed she had never even met Jeanne, though this is doubtful – and that she was beginning to soften the queen's hostility to the cardinal.

Rohan asked Jeanne to give Marie-Antoinette a letter and Jeanne got her lover, a blond guardsman called Rétaux de Villette, to forge the queen's replies. Rohan treasured the ensuing correspondence of over a hundred letters. Now Rohan wanted to meet the queen. This could have proved difficult but Jeanne plausibly argued that, given the queen's public hostility to the cardinal, the meeting would have to be at night, in a grove of citrus trees the queen was known to frequent. Jeanne found a twenty-three-year-old shopkeeper who bore a passing resemblance to the queen – Habsburg lip, aquiline nose, fair complexion. She was called Leguay, but Jeanne, quite gratuitously since she would be posing as Marie-Antoinette, gave her the name baronne d'Oliva – a near anagram of Valois. One midnight in August 1784 the newly-minted baroness, dressed in the flowing muslins Marie-Antoinette now preferred to formal wear, gave the cardinal a rose as a prearranged symbol of friendship. Then, from the shadows, Rétaux called out to be quick as the king's sisters-in-law were approaching. The fake queen then beat a hasty retreat and the cardinal was hooked.

Hitherto, Jeanne had merely extracted money from the cardinal, but now that he had swallowed the bait she raised her sights and constructed a plan to convince Boehmer that the queen had commissioned Rohan to buy the necklace on her behalf. Rohan was provided with a forged memorandum and a forged letter, purportedly from the queen, saying she wanted to purchase the necklace but was temporarily short of funds. So she was charging Rohan to handle the matter, paying interest on the whole whilst she discharged the capital in four payments starting in July 1785. It was now January. If Boehmer and Rohan's judgements had not been affected by their different but equally parlous predicaments, they would have realized that the queen's signature 'Marie-Antoinette de France' was not one she would have used. She would have simply signed 'Marie-Antoinette' just as the king signed 'Louis'. However, Boehmer didn't just rush into it. He told Rohan that he would be glad to have the necklace off his hands since he was paying interest of 8,000 *livres* a year on the money he had borrowed to construct it. But he would have to square it with the banker Baudard de Saint-James, treasurer of the marine, from whom he had borrowed 800,000 *livres*. No one knew, but Saint-James himself was teetering on the brink of a spectacular bankruptcy which would rock the financial system, as we saw in the last chapter. But Saint-James, who like Rohan was in thrall to the charlatan Sicilian soothsayer Cagliostro, raised no objection and Boehmer handed over the necklace to the cardinal, who bore it in his carriage to the tiny apartment at Versailles which had been granted to Jeanne. There Rétaux arrived, this time dressed in the queen's livery, to take the necklace back, as Rohan supposed, to Marie-Antoinette.

As soon as the cardinal had left, Jeanne and her lover attacked the necklace with a kitchen knife, damaging some of the stones. Then Rétaux proceeded to sell some of the stones, way below market value, to the various Parisian diamond merchants and pawn brokers. These were suspicious, however, and called the police. Rétaux was detained and hauled before Lenoir, the police minister himself. Rétaux told Lenoir that he was acting on behalf of a woman of standing at court, Madame la comtesse de La Motte-Valois (Jeanne had married a guardsman called La Motte, who had fabricated the title of comte). This was all technically true and since no robbery had been reported Rétaux was released without charge. Meanwhile the 'comte' de La Motte took the bulk of the diamonds to London to sell. The perfect crime. He only got 150,000 *livres* for the main stones, perhaps an eighth of their true value, but it was a fortune for someone who had started life as a beggar. The La Mottes bought a substantial house in their province, filled it with bronzes and marbles, and entertained the local notables.

There was one cloud on the horizon: Rohan asked Jeanne why the queen was not wearing the necklace – not even on great feast days such as that of the Purification on 2 February or Pentecost on 24 May. Because she had not yet plucked up courage to tell Louis, Jeanne plausibly assured him. She was aided by the fact that Marie-Antoinette, heavily pregnant with the duc de Normandie, who was to be her favourite child, appeared little in public. But the deadline approached for the first payment, 1 August. Jeanne told Rohan that the queen was having difficulties finding the sum and would be obliged if the cardinal could lend her the money for the first payment. Teetering on bankruptcy himself, Rohan approached the banker Baudard de Saint-James again. Strapped himself, this time Saint-James refused Rohan. Jeanne then tried another tack: the queen now found the necklace too expensive and wanted to return it. Boehmer then reduced the cost by 200,000 *livres* – an irrelevance of course since the necklace no longer existed. The 'queen' then came back with a counter-offer: she would increase the first payment to 700, 000 *livres* provided it could be paid on 1 October instead of 1 August. As a masterstroke Jeanne then came up with 30,000 *livres* from the sale of the stones to cover the lost interest. But she could not stop Rohan from advising Boehmer to thank the queen for her gesture, which he did. Mystified, the queen 'absent-mindedly tore . . . up' Boehmer's letter.

At the end of July Rohan showed Cagliostro the contract for the acquisition of the necklace. Cagliostro may have claimed to have been born on the Nile millennia ago but he saw through it: 'I'll lay money on its being a forgery', he told Rohan, and advised him to make a clean breast of it to the king. 'It's too late to go back', he was told. Imagining she was ahead of the curve Jeanne then told Boehmer's associate Bassenge that Rohan had discovered that the queen's signature was a forgery but that he would compensate the jewellers out of his immense fortune. If Rohan still had an immense fortune Jeanne would have still got away with it. But Boehmer knew he didn't and it was he rather than Rohan who went to the king via Breteuil who, as minister for the *Maison du Roi*, happened to be the minister relevant to the case. Breteuil advised Boehmer to draw up a memorandum enclosing the forged documents but omitting any reference to Jeanne de Valois: he wanted his enemy, Rohan, centre stage. Breteuil gave this memorandum to the queen herself.

Breteuil regarded himself as 'her' minister and put it about that his ambition was to 'make the queen reign'. Breteuil's purchase of the palace of Saint-Cloud from the duc d'Orléans in October 1784 seems to have formed part of his plan to 'faire règner la reine' and he may himself have dreamed of becoming its governor. It was unusual, even mildly scandalous, for a palace to be purchased directly for the queen – rather than for the dauphin – and the impropriety was intensified by the queen's insistence that the servants wear her personal livery and that orders be issued 'by the queen's command'. It was also unusual for a minister to buy an expensive palace without consulting the finance minister. Calonne's anger with Breteuil was uncontained; nor did he bother to contain his anger with Marie-Antoinette. It was the beginning of an implacable enmity between them.[5]

On receiving the memorandum and forged documents, Marie-Antoinette went straight to Louis, whose first reaction was to convene a council of the entire Rohan family. With his keen geographer's eye – an eye for detail which in general policy sometimes distorted the bigger picture – Louis was able to visualize the physical features of his kingdom more clearly than any ruler before the days of aerial reconnaissance. But when he thought of the population that inhabited it, he envisaged a small number of families or clans which he knew intimately and who had to be preserved, chastised, elevated or degraded as occasion demanded, plus his 'peoples' – an undifferentiated mass the more anonymous for being in the plural. Soon he would get to know them better. Talleyrand, on the other hand, saw the country as being made up of a series of 'societies', political and social more than familial, with whom government had to 'reckon'.[6] The Rohan council, however, could not be assembled because the head of the family, the maréchal de Soubise, was absent – surprising since he was a minister without portfolio.

If Rohan had gone to the king, if the family council had been convened, the matter could have been kept within these bounds – like the Guémenée bankruptcy. But now it became a matter of high politics played out in public and involving just about everyone of importance. Monday 15 August was the feast of the Assumption of the Blessed Virgin – she was also the patron saint of the queen, who was called Marie too. There was to be a big service in the chapel royal and the first worshippers were assembling. As a man of importance, the king's ceremonial alter ego, Miromesnil, the keeper of the seals or justice minister, had already taken his place when a messenger summoned him to attend the king. Not realizing why Breteuil was closeted with the king, Miromesnil's legs turned to jelly – he thought he was about to be dismissed, for the minister for the *Maison* was the agent of exile. On this occasion, however, Miromesnil need not have worried. Breteuil was closeted with the king and queen, who had not had time to have her hair done, even though it was sparser after her first difficult confinement and arranged *en nature*. It was 10 a.m. Miromesnil watched silently while Breteuil egged Marie-Antoinette on to seek a dramatic revenge for both of them: Rohan, he said, should be arrested in his full pontificals as he was accompanying the king down the aisle of the chapel. But Louis wanted to act *en connaissance de cause*. He sent for Rohan and (according to Miromesnil's account) 'while they were going to find him, I said to the king "I have an observation to make to you. You are going to perform the dual function of king and judge and I beseech you to forget that it is your wife who is compromised".' Then, in his recollection, he replaced the last words by 'that you are the queen's husband'[7] – advice that should have been heeded.

Rohan arrived and saw on the king's bureau an enormous map of the world charting the progress of La Pérouse's voyage.[8] From this his eyes were directed to Boehmer's memorandum for which the king demanded an explanation. Marie-Antoinette averted her gaze. Rohan confessed that he had been tricked. Louis confronted him with the letter purported to be from the queen and signed by her. Rohan blustered: 'As for the letter I have nothing to say since it is a copy. I only remember a few words from it.' But, insisted the king, 'have you nothing to say to justify your conduct and the guarantee you have given [Boehmer]?' Louis then told Rohan, 'Pull yourself together, remain by yourself in my cabinet and put on paper anything you can find to justify yourself.' While he was doing this, the others debated what to do in the adjoining library.

At this stage, three people thought Rohan was guilty; the queen, naturally; Breteuil – according to Castries, 'it appears that the baron de Breteuil believed from that moment that the cardinal was guilty'; and Louis. He was aware that Rohan had great debts and jumped to the conclusion that the cardinal had stolen the necklace, as is clear from his letter of 16 August to Vergennes: 'You will surely have learned, Monsieur, that yesterday I had Cardinal Rohan arrested; from what he confessed and from the papers found on him, it is proved only too well that he has used the queen's name by means of forged signatures to obtain diamonds from a jeweller to the value of 1,600,000. . . . It is the saddest and most horrible affair that I have ever seen.'[9] So far Louis had not consulted Vergennes and a court lady thought that this was a piece of luck: 'I thank God that you were not present at the council, though that was a misfortune for our masters whose just indignation you would have calmed, thereby avoiding a big scandal but not the punishment of the guilty parties.'[10]

Miromesnil proposed delay for further investigation but the queen continued to demand that Rohan be arrested forthwith. 'But', objected the keeper of the seals, 'surely not in his pontifical robes.' 'You are not Rohan's lackey!' replied the king. Rohan entered the library with his written confession: he had been tricked by an adventuress into thinking that the queen had commissioned him to buy the necklace.

'Where is this woman?' asked the king. 'Sire I don't know', replied Rohan – untruthfully, since he had helped her to get out of Paris and gain her native province. 'Have you got the necklace?' the king resumed. 'Sire, it is in this woman's hands. I'll pay for the necklace . . .' 'My cousin,'[11] the king interrupted, 'in such circumstance I have no choice but to place seals on your house and assure myself of your person. The queen's name is precious to me. It is compromised. I must take every precaution.' Rohan begged the king not to have him arrested in front of the whole court: 'May Your Majesty deign to remember your affection for Mme de Marsan who looked over your childhood, the glory of the maréchal de Soubise [one of the most disastrous generals in French history], the brilliant name of my family.' Another version has him begging the king 'out of consideration for my family not to make a scene'; 'I cannot', said the king, 'either as king or husband.' Then, for the first time in nearly a decade, Marie-Antoinette addressed Rohan: 'How is it possible, Monsieur le Cardinal, that you could have believed that I would have employed you to conclude such a transaction when I haven't spoken to you for eight years?' But 'a few days afterwards she confided to one of her ladies-in-waiting that she had experienced at this juncture a wave of fear, surprise and anger which had nearly made her ill'.

The king then told Rohan to leave his cabinet and ordered the baron de Breteuil to follow him out and arrest him. Breteuil caught up with the cardinal in the Oeil-de-Boeuf and told him he was arresting him: 'But we can't remain stationary here! Can't you guard me as we are walking along?' And with that he proceeded along the gallery. 'Fearing perhaps that he would escape' – disguised as a cardinal? – Breteuil summoned an officer of the guard and ordered him 'in the name of the king to arrest M. le Cardinal and answer for his person'. Breteuil had a more important task: to go to Rohan's house and put seals on his papers. But he was dilatory and Rohan for once thought quickly. He asked the officer whether it was in order for him to write a note: 'Good Lord! Do as you like.' Rohan scribbled four lines in code telling his secretary, the abbé Georgel, to burn his papers. When he was escorted to his apartments at Versailles he gave this to a servant together with the key to the code and instructions to rush to Rohan's hotel. The story goes that the servant made such speed that his horse dropped dead on arrival. Certainly he arrived well before Breteuil. But the cardinal had been too foolish by half: the letters that were burnt – his extensive correspondence with the 'queen' – would have shown that he was a fool, not a knave.

Rohan was moved to the Bastille, but a luxurious annex of the grim fortress, and he was attended by a suite of servants and entertained his many visitors with oysters and champagne. Nevertheless, his supporters wore the colours of red and yellow to symbolize the cardinal in his red robes lying on a bed of yellow straw. Under questioning he admitted that he had given the necklace to Jeanne. She was later arrested at Bar-sur-Aube, but prior to that she had lived in such great state that she had dined at the château of the duc de Penthièvre, prince of the blood and grand admiral of France. She had turned up in a coach-and-six.

Rohan invited Castries and Vergennes to visit him in the Bastille. He didn't want Breteuil to come because that minister, in Castries's word, 'hated' Rohan. Rohan asked them whether they came as friends or ministers. If the former, Castries observed, they would not be able to attend the cabinet committee which would decide his fate. It was this cabinet, held on 25 August 1785, which transformed the Diamond Necklace Affair from an episode of interest only to *la petite histoire* to a defining moment in the history of the regime. The council met to decide whether the cardinal would be tried by administrative law by a panel of the *Conseil d'État* or by *justice réglée*, literally 'regular justice', the

French equivalent of common law. If the latter, it would be heard by the *parlement*. Conciliar justice had come a long way since the Louis XIV period, parodied by Alexandre Dumas, when innocent men could be enclosed in an iron mask at the king's bidding. It was already on the way to being the modern *droit administratif* reserved for cases where the state was involved, and if the state was not involved in the Diamond Necklace Affair, when was it? However, the queen herself wanted to avoid any appearance of the verdict being fixed. Marie-Antoinette had not attended cabinet before but on this one personal issue she was able to insist that the ministers only speak to the king in her presence – which made her, in effect, a prime minister for the conduct of the Diamond Necklace Affair – and, as she told Joseph, 'they have not been able to budge . . . [the king] an inch'. She told the council: 'I am implicated. The public assumes that I have received a necklace without paying for it. I want to know the truth behind a matter in which people have dared to employ my name. The cardinal's relatives want him to be tried by *justice réglée*; he appears to want this too. I want the affair to be judged by this process.'

After the queen had made her impassioned statement, 'a profound silence descended on everyone'. Without being asked, Castries broke it, arguing that since judicial proceedings in the case so far had been 'by exceptional justice' ('par voie extraordinaire') they may as well continue as they had begun. Why not make Rohan and Jeanne de Valois confront each other – after all, council decisions were meant to be taken adversarially. He drew a parallel with the special commission, or war council, which had been set up to answer the various claims and counterclaims arising from the defeat at the Saintes and where the various parties had been made to confront each other adversarially. Rohan had told Castries in prison that he did not fear such a confrontation. Castries came near to accusing his patroness, the queen, influenced by Breteuil, of lying when he said, 'I think I can answer for it that the relatives [of Rohan], though they do not fear regular justice have not asked for it.'

Then Miromesnil came up with a pedantic point, which Louis no doubt considered to be again a 'réflexion de laquais': 'there are tricky procedural problems where a cardinal is involved and it is going too far to bring about a confrontation by administrative procedure'. That, however, did not necessarily mean that Rohan had to be tried by the *parlement*. He observed that Rohan's office of grand almoner – it had been 'grand' only for two centuries! – did not automatically entitle him to trial by the *parlement* since it was not a great office of state like that of chancellor. He recommended that the king send him for trial at the Châtelet, Paris's criminal court, which was less of a theatre than the *parlement*.[12]

'During this discussion M. de Vergennes did not say a great deal and M. de Breteuil never a word.' Having egged the queen on (she needed little egging) Breteuil could leave the rest to her. Vergennes's position was more complicated. He was known to have many links with the Rohan clan and didn't want to be seen to be partial. A part of him may not have been averse to seeing two enemies of his, the queen and Breteuil, slide to disaster – after all, the queen was still trying to get him dismissed. Then again, at this stage, he did not know if Rohan was an accomplice or not. He confided to the French ambassador to Vienna: 'I am delighted by this outcome [Rohan's being tried by the *parlement*] which will dispense me from taking any further part in proceedings. I hope the judges will get to the bottom of the matter. As for me, the more I see of it the less I understand. What is inconceivable is how the cardinal could have been such an innocent dupe as he claims to have been.'[13] Calonne also kept his counsel, though he too, as we shall see, had a vital interest in the case.

So the queen, the de facto prime minister for the case, then effectively took the decision:

> Very well! My opinion is that the cardinal should be given the choice, that he should convene all his family, that he should weigh everything and that he should make a decision, whether to take the path of administrative law or regular justice in the matter; that he should give the king his decision in writing; that the document should be signed by the whole family and that, whatever route is chosen, the matter should be dealt with swiftly because I am compromised.

> The king said to M. de Castries: You will go tomorrow with M. de Vergennes – and the baron de Breteuil will have to go as well – to bring this decision to the cardinal and in three days I will need his reply. When the ministers told Rohan [in the Bastille] that Jeanne had denied everything, he exclaimed 'My God! If I were allowed to confront the woman I am sure I could discomfit her'.

The ministers, however, pointed out to the cardinal that the confrontation could not take place before he had made his choice. According to Castries, easily the most reliable witness, Rohan was in a genuine quandary over whether to opt for trial by the *parlement* or by a special commission of the council. It took him the full three days Louis had given him to opt for trial by the *parlement* and he chose as defence counsel the celebrated advocate Target (Louis was to ask for Target at his own trial). Castries notes that the charges in the letters patent sent to the *parlement* 'contained the phrases "criminal attempt" and "the king's indignation that one had dared to compromise the name of his august wife and companion" – and they seemed too strong'. They were also too vague. Was there still a crime of *lèse-majesté*? Was Rohan being accused of it? Above all, the *parlement* was not an impartial court of law but was highly politicized. This would be a political trial in the public gaze, an anatomical dissection of the political system by a hostile press. A forensic examination by a special commission of the council would have raised the usual mutterings about ministerial despotism, and the exile of the cardinal by *lettre de cachet* some more. But the dirty linen could have been bundled into a basket and incinerated. Castries realized all this but was ignored. Why?

The crucial early stages of the affair were decided by the king, the queen and Breteuil, Marie-Antoinette boasting of this to Joseph II in a letter of 22 August:

> Everything has been concerted between the king and me; the ministers knew nothing about it until the moment when the king summoned the cardinal and interrogated him in the presence of the keeper of the seals and the baron de Breteuil. I was also there and I was genuinely touched by the reason and force employed by the king in this harrowing session. The cardinal begged not to be arrested but the king replied that he could not consent to this either as king or husband.

The queen and Breteuil, whose ministerial department happened to be the relevant one, had persuaded Louis to arrest Rohan without making sufficient preliminary enquiries into the affair. Lenoir, who was forced to resign in mysterious circumstances just after the cardinal's arrest, asked his successor as *lieutenant de police*, de Crosne, why he had not taken steps to arrest La Motte and seize the diamonds in order to discover whether Rohan was a dupe or an accomplice. Lenoir was told that de Crosne's superior, Breteuil, had not wanted the police bureau to have anything to do with the affair but had personally given his orders to the senior police officers and the governor of the Bastille where Rohan was imprisoned.[14]

Castries accuses Breteuil not of suppressing evidence, but of something subtler – that is, not resisting the royal couple's precipitate behaviour. 'The baron de Breteuil put no obstacles in the way of the king's desire to have Rohan arrested which was confirmed', he said, though conceded that 'it would have taken a stronger man than he to oppose' the king's determination. But why give the cardinal the option of being heard by the *parlement*? Clearly Castries believed the business of pressure from the Rohan clan was a cock-and-bull story. Rohan also was clearly undecided about which path to choose – conviction by the *parlement* meant imprisonment. But the apparently magnanimous gesture of Breteuil, in whose office the *lettres patentes* sending Rohan before the *parlement* were drafted, can be explained by the fact that he clearly believed that he could sufficiently manage the *parlement* in what was always going to be a political trial to secure Rohan's conviction. Rohan and his supposed partners in crime would be judged by the members of the *Grand' Chambre* – senior judges, several in receipt of royal patronage – and the *Tournelle* or criminal court sitting together.

Breteuil was relying on the support of the 'ministerial party' in the *parlement* which Miromesnil had built up by means of a judicious use of sticks and carrots, which included d'Aligre, the *premier président*, and d'Amécourt, the king's political agent. But it was not as easy as that: Calonne and Vergennes had their own faction in the *parlement* and were secretly working for Rohan's conviction. Vergennes had strong links to the Rohan clan, whilst Calonne was hoping that failure to have Rohan convicted would lead to the downfall of his rival Breteuil and his ally d'Amécourt, who hoped to supplant Calonne as finance minister.

Calonne and Breteuil were at daggers drawn over a number of important issues. Calonne was furious that Breteuil had negotiated the purchase of the château of Saint-Cloud for the queen without consulting him. Then, in 1785, Vergennes and Calonne asked Lenoir to send key police reports on public opinion directly to the king without informing Breteuil. Lenoir replied correctly that all reports had to go to his hierarchical superior, Breteuil, as minister for Paris. But Lenoir tells us that, unbeknown to all the ministers, the king 'who without exactly having an aversion to the baron de Breteuil did not have much confidence in him' was in fact in the habit of asking Lenoir to send him reports and 'expressly asked him to say nothing to' Breteuil. Breteuil discovered some of this when a royal messenger gave Lenoir a message from the king when he was in Breteuil's cabinet.[15]

Calonne had another reason for wanting to discomfit Breteuil. He calculated that the acquittal of Rohan would lead to Breteuil's dismissal and that he could take his job. As we saw when looking at d'Ormesson's brief ministry, a financial crisis in 1787 was likely, and Calonne was pursuing alternative approaches to it. One was to make a virtue out of necessity and gamble on a comprehensive reform of the financial system that would have enormous political implications. This will be the subject of the next chapter. The other was simply to cut and run by swapping ministries. But for that he had to bring down Breteuil by securing Rohan's acquittal. To do so he mobilized his faction in the *parlement*. We know from a list of the votes compiled by d'Aligre at the conclusion of the trial that seven judges had been directly influenced by Calonne, who had a hold on four of them through suspending payment of their debts to the crown.[16] This group was led by Président Lamoignon, who controlled a further three judges.[17] Lamoignon, who was Calonne's close friend – he would persuade the king to appoint him keeper of the seals in 1787 – had split the *parlement* in 1783 over his attempt to reform criminal procedure and to rationalize the *épices*, or tips which litigants had to give the *parlementaires*. The king had supported Lamoignon's reforms but had been dissuaded by Miromesnil on the grounds that they would need the support of the senior judges for 'important pending legislation'. Vergennes and Calonne had then apparently attempted to displace Miromesnil in Lamoignon's favour but had encountered the king's general satisfaction with Miromesnil's handling of the *parlement* over the previous ten years.[18] Lamoignon's party was working for Rohan's acquittal.

There is no evidence that Calonne wasted any sympathy on the plight of the House of Rohan; but Vergennes did. Whenever the clan was in trouble they turned to him. Vergennes, for example, had allowed Rohan-Guémenée to sell Lorient to the king so it could be used as a free port by the United States: he received for it a life annuity of 480,000 *livres*. He played some part in the proceedings in the *parlement* and a number of the judges paid fulsome tributes to him.[19] Vergennes thwarted the king, however, in such a subtle way that the king seems not to have suspected him or at least not to have borne him any resentment, though the queen did both: Vergennes ensured that the witnesses who could prove Rohan's innocence were available. Rétaux de Villette, who had forged the queen's signature, was extradited from Geneva and, under threat of torture, confessed. It was more difficult to extradite the 'baronne d'Oliva', who had impersonated the queen on the terrace, from Brussels, because the local laws forbade extradition without the consent of the party concerned. In the end Vergennes sent a police inspector to Brussels to 'indoctrinate' – Vergennes's word – the woman into returning voluntarily, which she did. What he promised her is not known, but at the trial she was acquitted.

The case of Jeanne's husband, La Motte, who had gone to London, presented a different problem. For he, like Jeanne, would base his defence on the assertion that Rohan was working for himself. The ambassador to London, Adhémar, wrote to Vergennes, 'Do not forget, I beg you, Monsieur, that the queen ardently desires that the Sieur de La Motte can be heard before the judgment.'[20] And he suggested that the best way to achieve this was to have La Motte kidnapped, even though this was a crime which carried the death sentence in England.

Amazingly Louis fell in with the plan and authorized Vergennes to proceed with the kidnap. La Motte was to be lured to South Shields, 'seized in his bed . . . wrapped in a blanket . . . carried to a rowing boat waiting off shore for the purpose, and from there to a French vessel stationed a short distance away'.[21]

All Vergennes could do was drag his feet in the hope that by the time La Motte was brought back the trial would be over. And he begged the king to be allowed to avoid all contact with La Motte on his return in order to preserve his reputation for impartiality! Not only did the king agree but he assured Vergennes that he had 'conducted himself in this matter, as indeed you should, as a man of honour'.[22] In fact the kidnap plan had to be called off because South Shields was crawling with sailors and customs officials. So La Motte's evidence could not be used in the trial. It may be that the confession of Rétaux made him change his mind, but it is singular that Vergennes went to such lengths for Rohan, despite the fact that his original conclusion was that Rohan could not have been 'such an innocent dupe' as he claimed.[23]

Very few of those concerned believed in Vergennes's or Calonne's impartiality in the affair. While the king turned a blind eye to it, the queen did not. The Austrian ambassador notes that the queen accused Vergennes of 'displaying a partiality designed to save the prelate' at the expense of her reputation. Mercy also suspected that Vergennes and Calonne had calculated 'that if the court was compromised following the trial, blame would inevitably redound to . . . [Breteuil]. People even go so far as to claim that . . . [Calonne] might have employed diverse means of corruption for this aim. Also . . . [Vergennes] is accused of having allowed this finance minister absolute carte blanche for this.' But however much Marie-Antoinette blamed Breteuil for giving her bad advice, she couldn't admit this by having him dismissed. Besides, her real enemies were Vergennes and Calonne, who were 'decidedly against the queen and far from scotching the rumours . . . [against her] they rather took pleasure in stirring them up'.[24]

As a result of Calonne and Vergennes's tireless pursuit of justice, the cardinal was acquitted by twenty-six votes to twenty-three. With what his biographer is compelled to call 'breath-taking hypocrisy', Vergennes informed Adhémar: 'People are generally surprised, and no one more than I.'[25]

After Rohan had been acquitted, Louis compounded his error in sending him before the *parlement* by treating him as if he had been found guilty. Next day, 1 June, he wrote to Breteuil:

Monsieur, my keeper of the seals has just informed me of the *parlement*'s judgment in the necklace affair. Since the queen's name has been found to have been grievously compromised in this affair and since M. le Cardinal has taken part in it as well as Cagliostro, you will proceed to M. le Cardinal's place; you will require him to relinquish his office of grand almoner and his sash as chevalier of my orders.[26] I join herewith a *lettre de cachet* ordering him to leave within three days for his abbey at La Chaise Dieu where it is my intention that he see few people; from now until his departure he must only see his relatives and his legal advisers.

Cagliostro will leave Paris within three days and my kingdom within three weeks.

In writing this letter, Petitfils says that Louis's 'mind was so greatly troubled, his emotion so intense that he made an error rare for him: instead of dating the letter 1 June, he wrote "Le 1er Sept. 1786".'[27] The truth is more prosaic: Louis simply dates his letter 'Le 1er' and a different hand has added 'Sept. 1786' in a darker ink.* There are, however, other signs of confusion or illogicality in this vengeful and vindictive letter. 'Since the queen's name has been found to have been grievously compromised in this affair and since M. le Cardinal has participated', he wrote and yet the *parlement* had 'found' precisely the reverse.

When it became apparent that Rohan might be acquitted, the public prosecutor had asked that Rohan should apologize before the *parlement* to the king and queen, resign his offices and give alms to the poor. According to Castries, 'these conclusions were so singularly biased, so evidently dictated by and for the court that the *parlement* reacting in the opposite sense did not pronounce a single word against the cardinal for his culpable credulity . . . and in short for all that he suspected and admitted it possible for the queen to have done'.[28] Because of the pressure Louis and Marie-Antoinette personally had put on the public prosecutor to have Rohan at least censured, people said that 'they had lost their suit'. 'They were', as Castries noted, 'all the more outraged by the judgement in that having declared that the queen's honour had been compromised, the king had a right to expect the *parlement* to take this statement into consideration and at least pronounce a censure'.

Since he felt he had been denied justice, Louis took it into his own hands. The result was a comedy of errors. The verdict had been delivered on a Wednesday. On Thursday Louis wrote his letter to Breteuil. But on Thursday evening, on leaving the council, Louis pretended to ask Vergennes's advice on how to handle the *parlement*'s verdict. Vergennes replied that, as far as he was concerned, 'the judgment ended the matter and the king made no comment'. Meanwhile the cardinal was pondering whether to anticipate the king's action

*Letter in the author's possession.

by resigning his offices, thereby hoping to avoid internal exile. But he dithered, which was a mistake: When Louis was later asked what his reaction would have been if Rohan had resigned, he replied, 'I feared and expected it; and I would have relented over the exile'. Louis was afraid that Rohan's apology would deny him his justification for vengeance.

At one o'clock on the Friday a sick Breteuil was taken in a sedan chair to Rohan's hotel to give him the king's *lettre de cachet*. Rohan told Breteuil that he was suffering from a pain which 'alternated between his nose and his knees' and 'insisted that he be allowed to go to Flanders or Artois rather than the Auvergne'. Breteuil icily replied: 'My remit is simply to convey the king's orders'.[29]

Rohan had by now written a letter to the king resigning his offices but he had 'lost twenty-four hours' and by the time Vergennes gave the letter to the king at two o'clock Breteuil had accomplished his mission. Louis again pretended to ask Vergennes's advice on whether to exile Rohan and 'the minister replied that he thought it would play badly in Paris'. 'The deed is done', said the king. Vergennes was a little disconcerted. 'I think', wrote the baron de Staël, the Swedish ambassador, 'that ... [Vergennes] is a chameleon and it was a trap laid by the king to get his opinion before he had given his'.[30] Staël was Necker's son-in-law and, like him, he prioritized public opinion – that is, liberal metropolitan susceptibilities, the Genevan's weapon of choice.

Castries has an interesting variant: when Vergennes gave him Rohan's letter, 'the king said he had changed [his mind?] and that he had been exiled. To which he added, "they always move too fast".[31] This is the *reductio ad absurdum* of indecisiveness: a positive order should not be implemented in case it is counter-manded. The implication of Louis's reflection is presumably that he had given Breteuil his orders without specifying when they were to be carried out, and that Breteuil had rushed in before Louis had time to change his mind – which he might have done on receipt of Rohan's letter. It is as if he had been making a gesture – possibly to pacify his wife – but didn't really want to go through with it.

Castries thought that Louis had a right to take justice into his own hands (Miromesnil profoundly disagreed) since the *parlement*'s actions had been purely political: 'it is a principle of justice that a private individual in the queen's situation would have the right to compensation with interest and the king has merely made up for what the tribunal through automatic opposition to the court had not done'. But he thought Louis had been harsh. In the letter which Vergennes gave the king, Rohan had

reminded ... [the king] that when he had been arrested he had told him that "it is necessary both for you and for the queen that this matter be cleared up in a regular fashion. I want you to justify yourself and I hope that you can". Based on these expressions of justice and kindness M. le cardinal de Rohan had a right to expect not to be exiled and, holding the scales of justice in his hand, the king should have left it at dismissing him from his office of grand almoner, banning him from anywhere he was or was likely to be, that is Versailles and Paris, and commanding him to be careful what he said.[32]

Instead Rohan had been exiled to one of the remotest spots in the country: Chaise-Dieu is situated in the Puy-de-Dôme in the Auvergne, at an altitude of 1,082 metres. This recalled Maupeou's treatment of exiled *parlementaires* in 1771 and even, to a public saturated in Roman history, the *relegatio ad insulas* practised by the Julio-Claudian emperors. Rohan's progress to his remote abbey was a stately triumph: by speeding the cardinal on his way, the public could display their hostility to the court. But for some, how Rohan should be treated presented a dilemma. The bishop of Nevers jumped fully clothed into his bath to avoid displeasing the court by receiving Rohan as he passed through his diocese on his way into exile.

The king extended his displeasure to the whole Rohan clan: the aged maréchal de Soubise, whose redundant presence at the *Conseil d'État* Louis had tolerated out of respect for the memory of Louis XV, was made to feel unwanted.[33] In December, Castries relates, 'the king turned his shoulder away from . . . [Soubise] during an entire session of the council'. But Soubise did not take the hint. Louis complained to Castries, 'how can he not see for himself that he is out of place here?' Then he asked Castries to tell Soubise not to attend the council. 'Ah! Sire, [Soubise] is overwhelmed by the misfortunes of his family. Surely Your Majesty does not want to add to his pain, and I beg you not to give me such a cruel commission'. In the end Louis agreed to write Soubise a letter for Castries to give him in which the king said 'that he consented' to Rohan's absence for the duration of the trial.[34] He never returned.

A possible explanation for Louis's vindictiveness is that he remained convinced that Rohan had played a role in stealing the necklace as well as compromising the queen's good name. If we recall his first letter to Vergennes on the subject, he said 'from what he confessed and from the papers found on him, it is proved only too well that he has used the queen's name by means of forged signatures to obtain from a jeweller diamonds to the value of 1,600,000'. The account which Louis asked Rohan to draw up has been lost, as were 'the papers found on him'. According to Madame Campan, writing long after the event, Louis consoled Marie-Antoinette by saying, 'in this affair people have only wanted to see the prince of the church and the prince de Rohan, whilst in fact he is just a man who needed the money'. Jeanne de Valois had then tricked him and made off with the spoils. 'Nothing could be clearer and you don't have to be Alexander to cut this Gordian knot.'[35]

The other character upon whom Louis exercised vengeance was Cagliostro. Cagliostro, real name Giuseppe Balsamo, born at Palermo in 1743, had many acolytes: Badaud de Saint-James we have mentioned, but there was also the duc de Chartres, the duc de Montmorency-Luxembourg and Madame de Polignac. Cagliostro stayed at Rohan's château at Saverne, where they indulged in magic séances and performed transmigration of souls. Cagliostro had the ambition of uniting all the branches of freemasonry (which he claimed to have founded) and hoped that Rohan's influence would persuade the pope to revoke the anathema placed on masonry in 1738. But it is difficult to see what he had done to call down on him the vengeance of the king. True, he had prophesied that Rohan would return to Marie-Antoinette's good graces, but he had also been the first to point out to Rohan that her signature had been forged. If Rohan could believe that Cagliostro had met Noah and Jesus Christ, it was but a small matter to believe that the queen wanted him to buy the necklace.

The political and judicial functions of the *parlement* were normally kept separate, and management in the former case was legitimate. The trial of Rohan can be likened to an impeachment, such as that of Warren Hastings in 1795. And maybe precisely because they were acting as political judges, the *parlementaires* were able to sort out the political in the case (Rohan) from the criminal (Jeanne) and the irrelevant (Cagliostro) and to let the woman who had impersonated the queen off scot-free. And to give the right verdict. Perhaps the most surprising and disturbing feature is that no fewer than twenty-three out of the forty-nine judges voted for Rohan's guilt. Jeanne de Valois was sentenced to a public flogging and to be branded on the shoulder with a 'V' for *voleuse* (thief). Unfortunately the public executioner was so nervous (or stimulated by Jeanne's *petite* beauty) that his hand slipped and Jeanne was branded below the left breast. She had been sentenced to life imprisonment but escaped under mysterious circumstances two years later and settled in London, where the publication of her memoirs created a sensation. Rétaux de La Villette, who had forged Marie-Antoinette's letters, got off with lifetime banishment. La Motte was sentenced in absentia to the galleys for life.

The breakdown in relations between crown and *parlement*

It may well be that the most lasting consequence of the Diamond Necklace Affair was that the king never forgave the *parlement*, an institution which he had recalled to life in 1774, and that this resentment fuelled the fight to the finish between king and *parlement* in 1787–88. The *parlement*, as Castries observed, had exonerated Rohan simply because the king wanted him to be censured.

We have not heard much of the *parlement* since Turgot's troubles with it and his dire warning to the king in 1776. Indeed the relations between the absolute monarchy and the *parlement* in the last fifteen years of the existence of both presents a paradox to the historian. The mutually destructive crisis in the relations between them in 1785–86, which degenerated into open warfare in 1787–88, was preceded by over ten years of stability. Whether this stability was due to the fact that the *parlementaires* returned chastened from their 1771–74 exile, or to the regulations that Maurepas and Miromesnil put in place in 1774, or simply to the fact that the government avoided controversial legislation is a moot point. An important consideration also was that, in time of war, the *parlement* exercised a patriotic self-restraint, particularly if additional taxation was not sought.

Over the years Miromesnil had patiently built up a body of senior judges, nicknamed the *parti ministériel*, who would see through royal legislation, except that which Miromesnil disliked, in particular Turgot's six edicts, though Louis forced these through by *lit de justice*. So, in effect, Miromesnil could exercise a secret veto (though Malesherbes knew what he was up to) by informing the *parti ministériel* of his opposition or divisions in the government, but Louis could override this veto by his use of the *lit de justice*.

In fact very little legislation which Miromesnil (or the *parlement*) disliked was presented to the *parlement* in the years 1774–85. Necker didn't raise taxes and his loans were accepted. Besides, hostilities were suspended in wartime. Miromesnil became rather smug about his success, which was really based on not trying conclusions too furiously. In 1782 this stability was celebrated by the two men responsible for securing it, Miromesnil himself and Étienne François d'Aligre, the *premier président* of the *parlement*, whose installation costs of 80,000 *livres* had been met by the king; he also enjoyed an annuity of 20,000 *livres* a year, with one of 8,000 for his wife. Miromesnil told Véri that though people blamed him for being soft with the *parlement*, 'nevertheless the magistrature have not caused any trouble whilst I have been in office'; d'Aligre told Vergennes that 'since the king's accession, he had not experienced any difficulties on the part of the parlement. They have always registered everything immediately.'[36]

The occasion for these self-congratulatory remarks was the registration of an additional *vingtième* tax. This made three in total and meant (in theory) that everyone but the clergy paid a tax of three-twentieths of their income. But the circumstances of the registration were exceptional – the catastrophe of the Saintes – and it was in fact the last new tax instituted under the ancien régime. The topical nature of the tax was made clear by the finance minister, Joly de Fleury, in a letter to the king of 23 June 1782: 'The recent naval reverses . . . have already prepared opinion for this tax and it could prove very inconvenient to give it time to cool off.' And the *rapporteur du roi*, Lefevre d'Amécourt, the man who guided royal legislation through the *parlement*, could use the argument that the tax would shorten the war 'by making our enemies see that one reverse . . . does not exhaust French national resources'. The third *vingtième*, which was to last for the duration of the war and three years thereafter, was discussed at a meeting between Joly, Vergennes and Miromesnil for the government, and d'Aligre and d'Amécourt for the *parlement*. Afterwards, Louis made a special effort with d'Aligre, addressing him kindly in his cabinet and bringing tears to the old magistrate's eyes; but Miromesnil was still worried that the king would lose his temper unless the edicts were registered 'purely and simply' with any *remontrances* following.

In this same year, 1782, Miromesnil claimed that he had never bought votes in the *parlement*, only given money to some magistrates 'on account of domestic misfortunes'; and he added, 'I know that often the finance ministers have adopted this method; it should not be that of a chancellor'.[37] In fact, they both did; the publication of Turgot's papers after Calonne's death in 1782 caused embarrassment by the revelation that even this virtuous minister had indulged in the practice.[38]

So too did Breteuil, who, as minister for Paris, had many official and unofficial dealings with the *parlement* of that city. And this was the Achilles' heel of the system: if the ministry was united, as it was under Maurepas, or there was a strong king, such as Louis XIV, the *parlement* could be managed. If not, the *parlement* acted like a sounding board that magnified ministerial rivalries and divergent interests, which is exactly what happened when the Diamond Necklace Affair moved to the *parlement* for its theatrical dénouement.

But the atmosphere had already been soured by the circumstances of the registration of Calonne's loan of 80 million *livres* the previous December. For the *parlement* had accompanied the registration with the rubric 'at the king's express command'. This was the formula employed in registrations by a *lit de justice* (though this hadn't been one) and it gave investors the impression that the registration had been forced.

Louis and Calonne were beside themselves with anger and on 23 December Louis summoned a delegation from the *parlement* to Versailles. The night before, the Polignac group, Calonne's staunchest supporters, were greatly agitated. The duc de Polignac, 'pacing up and down', neglected his guests; 'the duchess only arrived when supper was served'. M. de Vaudreuil collared her immediately; 'anger flashed from the eyes of this outspoken friend of the controller-general'.[39] When the *parlement* arrived for the audience Louis deliberately snubbed the deputation by only opening one of the double doors to his audience chamber.

This session has not achieved the celebrity of Louis XV's *séance de flagellation*, because it was held in camera at Versailles rather than in the Palais de Justice at Paris. One thing the two had in common, however, was Calonne. He had written the core of Louis XV's speech; now he was the central subject of Louis XVI's. But there was this difference between the two sessions: Louis XV had formulated an imposing statement of royal sovereignty; Louis XVI's only contribution to the debate was a petulant outburst which would be typical of him in the years to come. From the king's exasperation *parlementaires* should have read the signs that ten years of fine weather were now darkening. D'Amécourt, the principal object of Louis's wrath, has left an eye-witness account of the king's concentrated anger. Louis began chastising the *parlementaires* for publishing remonstrances which were intended for his own, not public, consumption and for abusing his kindness to the point of 'criticizing my administration at all times and all places . . . I want you to know that I am contented with my controller-general'. Did Louis need to say this?

Calonne was embattled. The *parlement* hated him for his antecedents and did not see the need to borrow money in peacetime. Apart from personal and jurisdictional conflict with Breteuil, he was fighting a running battle with Castries over the naval estimates. However, the key peacetime ministers, Vergennes and Miromesnil, formed a governing triumvirate sometimes called the 'comité de gouvernement' which ran general policy with the king. Miromesnil considered that Breteuil's incompetence could be ignored 'now that we have the master [Louis] on board'. All the same it is strange that Louis felt the need to tell the *parlement* that he was 'contented' with his finance minister, the same word he had used when asked for his first impressions of Marie-Antoinette back in 1770. But so strong was the impression that Louis held his ministers in low esteem that this statement was necessary. We noted Sartine's bitter verdict: 'The statement by the ministers that a measure represents the king's volition is no longer an efficacious weapon in their hands. The measure is regarded as representing merely the ministers' personal policy, to be contested with every confidence.'[40] There is another example of this enervating attitude of the king's: Louis was chatting with the police minister, Lenoir, about rumours doing the rounds in Paris that he was about to dismiss Miromesnil 'whom I greatly esteem'. In that case, Lenoir asked, did he have permission to use his network to spread it about that the king esteemed his justice minister? The time would soon come, however, when a close identity between king and minister would be viewed as a liability.

After telling the *parlement* that he was 'contented' with Calonne, Louis said: 'I am going to annul a decree which is as ill-considered as it is disrespectful.' Then he took a piece of paper out of his pocket and ordered the chief registrar to record everything he had just said. To make quite sure, Louis repeated: 'Is that quite clear; the decree must be printed as it now stands?' – that is, without the rubric 'at the king's express command', though 'at the king's command' was precisely what it now was. For Louis, this was the central event of the audience, as his diary entry makes clear: '23 December: audience with the *parlement* to score out its registers.'

As the *parlement* was leaving, the king called back the *premier président*, d'Aligre, to tell him, 'I no longer want M. d'Amécourt as the reporter of my affairs; you will give the keeper of the seals an alternative and he will report to me.' D'Amécourt, the king's political agent, was meant to argue the case for royal legislation, but not only did he want to replace Calonne as finance minister, he was in league with Breteuil. As such, instead of defending Calonne's loan, d'Amécourt had 'verified the falsity' of Calonne's accounting and 'gone so far as to criticize with studied sarcasm . . . the various declarations in the preamble'. That evening the canopy of Calonne's bed fell on him, burying him beneath '40 pounds weight' so that he was unable to reach his bell. Rescued at last, he had himself bled twice – perhaps as a precaution, perhaps as a publicity stunt. Wits saw symbolic significance since 'ciel' can mean either sky or canopy.[41]

On 29 December d'Aligre provided Miromesnil with 'a list of those gentlemen . . . whom he considers to be most suitable to carry out the duties of reporter'. Louis found none of them satisfactory. As d'Amécourt maliciously records, 'we were a long time without a reporter. . . . Finally the abbé Tandeau was appointed'.[42] Another casualty of the episode was d'Amécourt's mistress, who was so shocked by Louis's harshness that she collapsed and died.[43] The public prosecutor of the *parlement*, Joly de Fleury, brother of the ex-finance minister, tried to patch things up between crown and *parlement*, but there was little appetite for a reconciliation on the part of the *parlement*, who felt Louis had brutally insulted them. D'Amécourt warned Miromesnil that there was talk of formally protesting against the king's actions, but Miromesnil warned him that if this happened he would advise the king to summon the whole *parlement* to Versailles and once again 'score out with his own hand such a disrespectful ruling'. Miromesnil shared his concern with the king: 'I confess, Sire, that I am in a considerable state of anxiety, not out of fear of what will happen (because those who fear the *parlements* do not know or do not wish to know how little they are to be feared) but because I am pretty uncertain of the good faith of those with whom I have to deal.'[44] All this must have impacted on the trial of Rohan six months later.

Moreover, as Louis had implied, the *parlement* had not confined its criticisms of Calonne's policies to his loans. And they displayed innumeracy as well as ill will in their criticism of the recoinage he carried out in 1785. The ratio between gold and silver – fixed by the royal mint in 1726 at 14.4:1 – had become too low, with the result that gold coins were being exported.[45] The lack of specie had underlain the crisis at the Discount Bank in 1783. Calonne raised the ratio to 15.5:1 and consequently reduced the weight of the gold coinage by one-sixteenth, which had the desired effect. For d'Amécourt and his ilk, however, either the king, or Calonne personally, was simply pocketing the difference. The *parlement* remonstrated and made its remonstrances public. The king, who was known to respect confidences and require the same of others,[46] was furious. The matter was aggravated because information was leaked by the councillor of state, Foulon, who had oversight of the royal mint and a son in the *parlement*. Hoping to supplant Calonne, he launched a series of attacks in the *parlement* and published an anonymous pamphlet attacking the recoinage. For this Louis exiled Foulon in March 1786.[47] Three years later, at the time of the storming of the Bastille, he finally achieved ministerial status, only to be lynched by the mob.

D'Amécourt dismissed, Foulon exiled; of Calonne's enemies only d'Aligre was left standing. Could Calonne persuade Louis to dismiss d'Aligre too, perhaps enabling Calonne to wrest back control of the *parlement*? Apart from the money officially given to d'Aligre, successive governments had turned a blind eye to two considerable debts of his to the crown. One was for 50,000 *livres* to purchase the office of councillor in the *parlement* for his son; the other was for 200,000 *livres*, the capital on a life annuity from the loan of 1781, on which he had already received 81,000 *livres* interest. As the king had not been informed, the potential for blackmail was considerable.

But the sword of Damocles had not been sufficient to secure d'Aligre's support over the 1785 loan or the recoinage, so, in July 1786, Calonne got his mistress's husband, d'Harvelai, the royal treasurer, to give d'Aligre an official reminder that he owed the king a quarter of a million *livres*. Calonne then obtained a decree from the council annulling d'Aligre's contract for the life annuity. Miromesnil tried to get Calonne to insert into the decree d'Aligre's admittedly feeble excuse that his failure to pay the two large debts to the crown was down to the death in rapid succession of two of his notaries, who he thought had paid the money.

Miromesnil then went to see d'Aligre, who was furious at the way Calonne had resurrected his debt and omitted his excuse from the decree. All the same it is clear that, chronically ill, humiliated and dishonoured, d'Aligre wanted to resign and that Miromesnil persuaded him to hang on. His long and tortuous account to the king smacks of falseness. Miromesnil claimed that he had communicated to d'Aligre 'all my fears about the impression the matter of the life annuity had made on your [the king's] mind; that I was well aware of Your Majesty's insistence on the principles of strict financial rectitude; that in this particular Your Majesty's impressions always ran very deep'. He assured the king that he had told d'Aligre that it was well-nigh impossible to serve in such an important post as head of the *parlement* without the king's confidence. However, he continued, 'it is not possible to force a *premier président* to retire; for that one would have to put him on trial and whatever M. d'Aligre says, I see that at present he has no intention of handing in his resignation'.

This was nonsense. Unlike the chancellor – we saw that Maupeou had refused to resign – the *premier président* held a revocable commission from the king which was necessary if the king was to retain any control over the *parlement*. The ordinary councillors in the *parlement*, like d'Aligre's son, either bought or inherited their offices, which gave them a large degree of independence, but the key players – the *premier président*, the public prosecutor and the attorney generals, together with the king's political agent, the *rapporteur* – had to be dismissible, or the king would have no control over the *parlement* – and d'Amécourt had been dismissed. What made it worse was that Miromesnil conceded that d'Aligre's opposition to Calonne was 'implacable', as he had demonstrated during the discussions over the 1785 loan and the recoinage, and Calonne was 'fully aware how disadvantageous it will be to have at the head of the *parlement* a leader always disposed to undermine his legislation. He ardently desires that M. d'Aligre should go and I cannot blame him.'

A week later, Miromesnil went to Paris to report the king's reaction. He told d'Aligre, 'in conformity with Your Majesty's instructions, that Your Majesty had not explicitly ordered me to tell him that you wanted him to resign his post, but that I could not hide the fact that all that had happened for some time had made a very deep impression on Your Majesty'. In other words, it was not just d'Aligre's unpaid debt but his entire conduct of the *parlement* that had angered Louis. Miromesnil conceded that if d'Aligre 'does not retire, M. de Calonne will think that it is I who have persuaded him to stay on'.[48] He did, and rightly so, and the quarrel between Calonne and Miromesnil, those two pillars of the government, hitherto friends who staged amateur dramatics together in their homes, would rip the regime apart. Miromesnil had bamboozled the king, and six months later the penny would drop.

The sea itself

For most of his life the sea had lapped the shores of Louis's imagination and yet he only saw it for the first time on 23 June 1786, at 3.30 a.m. It was at Cherbourg where an ambitious new military harbour was being constructed and he had to be there at low tide. At Louis's accession, Cherbourg had been merely a fishing village and one in ruins, for in 1759 the place was occupied and destroyed by the English in an attempt to prevent its further development. Situated at the end of the Cotentin peninsula, it was only three hours' sail from Portsmouth, the object of the 1779 invasion for which which a safe harbour would have been useful. Louis envisaged creating an artificial harbour. It was a massive project which took a century, off and on, to complete. Cherbourg is still the second-largest artificial harbour in the world.

Two plans were put forward. Building a huge sea wall was the simplest. The plan that was chosen, however, envisaged sinking a line of ninety vast cones, 142 feet in diameter and linked by a lower structure of chains, to enclose the new harbour area. The first cone had been placed in 1784 in the presence of Castries. The eighth was witnessed by Louis's brother Artois in May 1786. Calonne suggested to Louis that he supervise the sinking of the ninth cone. It was a welcome diversion, as the *parlement* had just acquitted Rohan. Vergennes had been right, exiling Rohan did not 'play well in Paris': the queen was greeted with hostility, Louis with bemused resentment. Marie-Antoinette stayed behind as she was carrying their fourth child, Sophie; when she was born Louis noted sourly that there were no festivities. He was glad to shake the dust of court and capital from his red-heeled shoes.

The mayor of Harfleur, which Louis visited after blessing his cone, has left an account of Louis's three-day Norman excursion, and this provides the basis for the present description.[49] Though written in an ecstatically reverential style, albeit tempered with references to *l'opinion publique*, italicized, the account has a poignancy which is only partly due to the dramatic irony that this joyous episode, maybe the happiest in Louis's life, was preceded by months of frustration and succeeded by continuous crisis – a crisis that would last for the rest of his life. The account was written up immediately after the visit, when the memories of the people from all walks of life Louis had encountered were fresh and untainted; 'various obstacles delayed publication' until 1787, however, by which time Louis's world was falling apart.

Castries and Ségur accompanied the king, as befitted service ministers. Calonne stayed behind. He was working hard on his great reform project. But he planned every detail of the expedition to make sure that it went smoothly and that Louis was well received. For the journey, on information provided by the intendants of Caen and Rouen, Calonne provided Louis with a digest of the latest maps of Normandy, together with historical, architectural and economic data of this, his richest province. Calonne always paid Louis delicate attention, as when he presented the dauphin, who was proving to be a worryingly sickly child, with a small coach drawn by donkeys. Was he compensating the king for his trials at the hands of the *parlement*, Rohan's acquittal being in no small part due to Calonne himself? Or was he trying to fortify the king for the trials he knew lay ahead?

The royal party, restricted to fifty-six, left Rambouillet at 5.15 a.m. on 21 June. On the same day, at the same time, five years later, in a much bigger coach, Louis would be travelling on his only other journey of equal length, the only other one beyond the ring of royal palaces – a journey interrupted at Varennes. If he had gone to Normandy instead, as Mirabeau counselled, the outcome could have been very different.

Everywhere in Normandy Louis mixed with ordinary people, returning with interest the kiss a peasant woman had planted on him, pardoning six naval deserters who had been sentenced to death, remitting taxes. Once, he was seized by the pangs of hunger in the midst of the countryside. Bayeux was a few miles off but Louis could not wait. He ordered his coach to stop at the first village they came to and dropped in to the modest local inn. The keeper and his family fled. But Louis summoned them and put them at their ease. 'Have you any fresh eggs?' 'Yes and they are still warm.' 'And butter?' 'Straight from the press.' 'That is excellent.' For bread, the essential accompaniment of every French meal, then as now, Louis contented himself with a huge home-made loaf. 'Then he sat down on a wooden bench and had himself served on the same table used by travellers.' A crowd assembled and a pregnant peasant girl whose lover would not marry her asked the king to intervene. Louis replied, 'Your condition can be criticized but your request is legitimate. I want you to be married by the time I return and I will give you a dowry.'[50] The village bell was rung 'to announce to the neighbouring hamlets the joy and admiration with which the king's justice and goodness had just filled everyone's heart'.

Back in his coach, he asked himself why he was receiving such unaccustomed displays of affection. He concluded that in court and capital he was maligned. He scribbled a note for the queen: 'My people's love has touched the depths of my heart. Judge if I am not the happiest king in the world.' The Norman *bocage*, which provided feed for livestock, had been badly affected by drought. Thousands of animals had had to be put down and people were starving. Charitable institutions were overflowing and Louis gave two of them 8,000 *livres*. Calonne had proposed 10,000, but charity and poor relief was already a big item of expenditure, rising from 5.4 million *livres* at the start of the reign to 33.3 million by 1788 – more than the cost of the court.

They reached the outskirts of Cherbourg late on the 22nd and dined at the abbey. Lafayette, with the possible exception of Necker the greatest self-publicist of his age, who had milked to the limit his exploits fighting in the American war, just happened to be there. He was not in favour at court, he was not a sailor and his native province was the Auvergne. Also present, though of right as the military commandant of the port, was Dumouriez, who had championed the cones as against the dyke. Both men would soon cast their shadow on the king.

After hearing mass at 3 a.m. next day Louis went out to supervise the sinking of the ninth cone. The engineers and naval officers were presented to him. Calonne had provided him with fiches containing all their personal details. They were enchanted. He was rowed out in a canoe manned by twenty oarsmen and was the only one of the party not to be seasick. He was wearing the scarlet uniform of a naval lieutenant-general, embroidered with gold fleurs-de-lys. It got sea-stained, but was cleaned, kept and stowed in the royal carriage on 21 June 1791. He intended to wear it again. The king, meticulous as usual, noted that the sinking of the cone had taken precisely twenty-eight minutes. Louis, watching the spectacle through his lorgnette, saw a workman struck by a cable which had become detached. He tugged at a nearby doctor's sleeve to alert him but the man died. Louis naturally provided his widow with a pension.

Later they boarded a new 74-gunner called *Le Patriote* – patriotism was not an invention of the French Revolution nor, as Louis later remarked, the monopoly of radicals. He was greeted by the squadron leader, Albert de Rioms, who had distinguished himself in the late war. Louis sometimes paid compliments slyly, as when he had asked Necker to check his translation of Burke's encomium. This time Louis told Rioms, 'There's something missing from *Le Patriote*.' 'What would that be, Sire?' 'Why the flag of a lieutenant-general which I order you to hoist.' In this way Louis informed Rioms of his promotion.

An astounded Rioms gazed at the king's red-and-gold uniform and thought, 'I can wear that now.'[51]

The next two days were occupied with naval reviews and manoeuvres – the latter an innovation of Louis's reign. Louis, watching from Le Patriote, asked the newly promoted lieutenant-general why his ship was not taking part. Rioms replied that 'etiquette forbade the firing even of blanks on a ship which ... [the king] honoured with his presence'. As we have seen, Louis slavishly adhered to etiquette at Versailles; for example, he did not see Maurepas and Vergennes on their deathbeds, though he would dearly have liked to have shown them this kindness and to have received their parting advice. But in Normandy Louis emerged from this court carapace. 'Ignoring this usage' – even the mayor of Harfleur was slightly shocked – Louis told Rioms that 'he wanted to observe the ship's movement at the point of firing, and the ricochet effect of cannon shot on the sea'. A somewhat reluctant Rioms 'humoured the king with a few cannonades'. At the dinner that evening Louis again broke with etiquette when he invited the comtesse de Fauduas to join the company even though she had not been presented at court.

The second day was interrupted by bad weather. Louis asked Rioms the direction of the wind. From England, he was told. 'Oh! I'd happily go there!' he replied. 'The English would not receive me badly and in that country people do not deceive kings.'[52] And yet here he was creating a harbour whose only function could be as a base for the invasion of England – a country, ironically, which he deeply admired, and the language and political institutions of which he understood, the home of his hero Captain Cook, whose voyages inspired him to send out La Pérouse. Englishmen of rank asked to be presented to the king at Cherbourg, including, the mayor of Harfleur notes reverentially, 'the nephew of Milord Duc de Richemond'. The celebratory cannon-fire could be heard from the Isle of Wight.

After the exercises, there was a state banquet on board Le Patriote. The naval officers were reliving the glories of the American war but they got some of the details wrong and Louis felt the need to correct them: 'The king cited the dates, the names of the vessels, the officers who commanded them and the slightest particulars of the circumstances in question.' Amidst all the refined delicacies which covered the table, the king spotted a pâté which seemed to be shunned. He asked what it was made of. 'From salt fish; it's the sailors' staple at sea.' The monarch wanted to try it and announced, 'I prefer it to all those at Versailles.'[53] At Versailles, Louis was stilted; he could not find the words to thank a returning ambassador or general, and ministers had to write out banal compliments for him to learn. On Le Patriote, among sailors, he relaxed. At the inn he displayed the common touch, on the ship kingly grace. 'His Majesty chose this occasion to deploy royal magnificence by distributing rich presents to some, recompensing others with favours, encouraging this man with the hope of rapid promotion, and bestowing on others those favours which compensate the French for everything, those of being singled out for a word, a look, by royal approval.'

From Cherbourg, he passed to Lisieux and then on to Honfleur. From an eminence above the port he gazed out at the Seine and the Channel. He stood there for three-quarters of an hour, lost in thought. Then he said that he wished he had brought with him the naturalist abbé Dicquemare, who had surveyed the area on many occasions. Gazing out at the sea he 'exclaimed twenty times, "nothing is finer" '. Two children presented him with a basket of oranges, which he said he would take home for the queen.

The final stop was Rouen, capital of Normandy. News of the king's charming behaviour had travelled quickly and a vast crowd assembled, consisting 'not just of the inhabitants of the town but people from the extremities of the province'. There, Louis made a promise: 'that he would make up for his short visit by promising to return soon' and this time accompanied by the queen, who he could not wait to tell of his reception.[54] If he had kept his promise he might have kept his throne.

Later, he summed up the experience: 'I have never tasted the delights of kingship more than at my coronation and later when I was at Cherbourg.'[55] Though euphoric, these are carefully chosen words. Louis does not say 'the happiest days of my life', though as dauphin he must have known few. In any case he is not talking about private happiness but the joys of kingship. There must, he implies, have been few of those. In his will he was to apostrophize his son, 'should he ever have the misfortune to reign'.

He returned home via Vernon, Meulan and Saint-Germain. Lafayette wangled an invitation to share the king's carriage. As he neared Versailles, Louis noticed that the cheering grew sparser. 'I can tell from this that I am approaching Versailles. Never mind, I will leave it more often and I'll stray further than Fontainebleau.' His valet-de-chambre, Thierry, noted that the king came back 'full of joy'.[56] He had told the naval commandant of Brest, who travelled with him, that he planned to visit all his ports in the same way.[57] He never saw the sea again.

Despite his upbringing, Louis possessed the common touch – too common his courtiers thought. At Cherbourg he overheard a naval officer employing coarse language to a sailor. The officer apologized to the king but Louis replied that it was just naval talk and he would have used the same language himself.

He could chat with the tilers on the roofs of Versailles or peasants on the estate. When he was forced to live in Paris, he could manage the new class of people he had to deal with. What he couldn't do was make small talk with courtiers or address crowds.

The cones turned out to be a white elephant. Because of the expense, their number was reduced from ninety to sixty-four and the wider gaps put pressure on the chains, some of which became detached. The cones collapsed. The project was abandoned in 1789. It had cost 28 million *livres*. In 1800 Napoleon's engineers surveyed the scene, still with an eye to invasion. There was only one cone intact – the ninth: the one blessed by Louis.[58]

CHAPTER EIGHT

ROYAL REVOLUTION

THE ASSEMBLY OF NOTABLES OF 1787

Calonne's reform programme and its adoption by the king

THE FRENCH REVOLUTION BEGAN not as an attack on a prison or a palace but as a programme of reform submitted to the king by one of the most devoted and orthodox servants the monarchy ever possessed: the controller-general of finance, Calonne. The importance of the programme lay not only in its comprehensiveness and audacity, but in the enthusiasm with which the king embraced it and made it his own.

Hitherto, outside the fields of foreign and naval policy, Louis had not exhibited any distinctive, personal policy beyond seeking to establish a new moral tone in public affairs, symbolized by his rejection of bankruptcy. He had taken a detached view of the operations of many of his ministers, even, Véri wrote in 1783, 'himself setting the example of showing contempt' for them.[1] For their part, his ministers had sometimes sought to shift direct responsibility on to the king, as Maurepas had during the Flour War; this was a tendency which was to increase with the regime's difficulties. Calonne, however, achieved such ascendancy over Louis – based partly on the intellectual satisfaction the king derived from his minister's attractive presentation of financial matters but also on a shared dislike of *parlementaires* and political priests, and on a shared belief in the continuing viability of the administrative monarchy – that Louis's personal identification with his minister came to be as much of a constitutional embarrassment as had been his previous detachment.

On 20 August 1786 Calonne presented the king with a memorandum which, under the unassuming title *Précis d'un plan d'amélioration des finances*, announced an administrative and fiscal revolution with political and even constitutional implications. The measures were to be endorsed by an Assembly of Notables before being sent to the *parlements* for immediate registration by *lit*

de justice. Assemblies of Notables were nominated by the king from fixed categories of people, whereas Estates-General were elected by the three orders of
the kingdom: clergy, nobility and the third estate (commoners). The last
Assembly of Notables had met in 1626 and represented an attempt by Richelieu
to outflank opposition in the *parlements*. In 1786, this was again the motive, as
Calonne told the king: 'Assemblies of Notables . . . though without the inconve-
niences of the Estates-General . . . possess like them the advantage of sparing
government the protests of the sovereign courts [*parlements* etc.] and of
denying them the pretext of treating everything that does not meet with their
immediate approval as surprises to the king's religion.'[2]

The *parlements* could not be entirely excluded from the process; but the
notables' endorsement of the measures would replace the preliminary and
protracted discussion before registration. So, Calonne calculated, the day after
the closing ceremony of the Assembly of Notables the edicts could be registered by the *parlement* of Paris and, when the relevant personnel had returned
from the Assembly to their provinces, by the provincial *parlements*, all by *lit de
justice*. 'This would be the work of twelve to fifteen days and the whole thing
could be wrapped up by 15 March.' In this way, 'the king would have completed
in three months all that his predecessors had desired (or should have desired)
to do'.

A journalist reported that when Calonne told Vergennes that he wanted to
convoke an assembly of the elite of France, Vergennes was shocked

> that he should choose the period of France's maximum glory, through the
> recent peace, the flourishing state of the navy, the humiliation of her rival
> and the creation of a new power in America, to employ a measure which
> suggested either great weakness in the monarch or a great financial crisis.[3]

The report was wrong – Vergennes was on board – but it vividly conveys
the impression of disquiet, even shock, that the announcement made on a
people accustomed to a sense of prosperity at home and preponderance abroad
(an illusion, as we have seen, deliberately fostered by the government). Nor,
though Calonne writes as if Assemblies of Notables had a fixed place in the
political firmament, was there any call for such an 'unwonted apparatus', to use
Louis's phrase, though there had been some pressure for a meeting of the
Estates-General since the Maupeou coup.

There are two, not necessarily contradictory, views as to why Calonne
should have dropped this bolt from a seemingly cloudless summer sky. One,
the narrower, sees the monarchy in general, and Calonne in particular, as being

in a tight corner in 1786. There was little chance that the *parlement* would extend the life of the third *vingtième*, due to expire at the end of the year, or even endorse another annual loan in December, particularly after Calonne's unsuccessful attempt in August to break d'Aligre. This view, which was commonly held at the time, suggests that if Calonne had managed to move to a more sheltered ministry, taking over the *Maison du Roi* from Breteuil after Breteuil's failure to have Rohan convicted, nothing more would have been heard of the Assembly of Notables. Furthermore, since Calonne's quarrel with the *parlement* was essentially a personal one, he should have resigned with or without another ministry to go to; he had had three years as controller-general (the average for the reign being fifteen months) and although he would have to endure a period of 'internal exile' on his estates in Lorraine, it would be sweetened with the pension of a *ministre*.

Such a view ignores the fact that if an exemplary servant of the crown is embattled with the *parlement* because of his very services, his fate cannot be merely personal. It also disregards the ambiguity of human motivation: that Calonne would have switched to a safer ministry if he could does not diminish his sincerity in telling the king 'I would indeed have no regrets if I were the victim of the enterprise'.

Nor was the enterprise merely a desperate improvisation. The convocation of the Notables can be seen as the culmination of the work of the *comité de gouvernement* through which Louis had ruled since the death of Maurepas in 1781. The period 1781–87 has a unity that is symbolized by Vergennes, the *chef du Conseil royal des finances*, who, Calonne suggests, was behind the convocation of the Notables.[4] Minds had been concentrated by Joly de Fleury's report to the king in July 1781 on the falsity of Necker's *Compte rendu*, whilst a perspective on 1787 had been opened by d'Ormesson's memorandum of August 1783, which presented the simultaneous expiry of the third *vingtième* and the lease of the general farm as a chance to reorganize direct taxes in such a way that the king would be able to ascertain the relative taxable capacity of the various provinces, and to reorganize indirect consumption taxes by abolishing customs barriers between provinces. This was the essence of Calonne's proposals. Indeed, d'Ormesson provides a link between Calonne's reforms and the period of reforming zeal at the start of the reign: a bundle of his papers is entitled 'Mémoires et projet d'édit pour l'établissement d'une subvention territoriale dressés en 1775 par M. d'Ormesson à la demande de M. Turgot'.[5]

The centrepiece of Calonne's measures was, similarly, an *impôt territoriale* ('land tax') which would replace the two remaining *vingtièmes* and be payable by all landowners without exception or evasion, thus yielding more than the three *vingtièmes* put together and answering the king's imperative that the poor should not pay any extra. It was to be paid in produce rather than money and as a percentage of the crop rather than a fixed amount, which would prevent its yield from being eroded by inflation. The only variation admitted was between richer and poorer agricultural districts, land being divided into four categories on the basis of its rental value. This classification was to be carried out, in the provinces which had not retained their estates, by a three-tier system of assembly, being the parish, district and provincial levels.

Calonne felt that if the provincial assemblies were composed of the three orders sitting distinctly, as in the provincial estates, they would be dominated by the clergy and the nobility, who would rig the assessment. This, he told the king, was a weakness in Necker's provincial administrations, which in addition were presided over by a bishop. Therefore, in the proposed assemblies the sole criterion for membership would be the possession of land. In the parish assemblies there would be one vote for each 600 *livres* of landed income, while the president of the provincial assembly would not be the man with the highest social rank but the delegate of the district which contributed the most taxation. In earlier drafts, half the seats were to be reserved for the clergy and nobility; in the memorandum presented to the Assembly of Notables this concession was omitted.

In the third estate, which included many prosperous non-noble land-owners, merchants, lawyers and so on, Calonne saw a vast untapped source of support for royal authority, as he told the king in November: 'If there is a clamour from vested interests, it will be drowned by the voice of the people which must necessarily prevail, particularly when, by the creation of the assemblies, ... the government has acquired the support of that national interest which at the moment is powerless and which, well directed, can smooth over all difficulties.'[6] Calonne (like Necker) envisaged that the provincial assemblies would gradually take over the political and administrative role of the *parlements* but (unlike him) not that of the intendants. He may have intended to go further: a draft he made in November provided for a deputy from each provincial assembly, having received authorization from the secretary of state for his province, to go to Versailles once a year to liaise with the government. This was the vestigial remnant of Turgot's plan for a 'national municipality' which, if the deputies had all arrived at the same time, at the end of their session, it might have resembled – or grown into: a modernized form of the Estates-General. Perhaps for this reason, this feature was dropped at the last minute from the final version, probably at the king's insistence.[7]

The church was also threatened by the proposals. Not only were the clergy to pay the land tax at the same rate and in the same manner as everyone else (they had forced Louis XV to allow them to increase their self-assessed *don gratuit* instead of paying the *vingtième*), but the king sought to undermine the corporate independence of the church by obliging it to pay off the debt it had incurred as a painless way of raising the said *don gratuit*. Since the whole machinery of the Gallican Church existed largely to service the clerical debt, its redemption would cause the separate administrative existence of the church – a veritable *imperium in imperio* – to wither away unbidden. It also seems likely that Calonne envisaged some kind of dissolution of the monasteries.[8]

In addition to these measures, Calonne proposed the abolition of internal customs barriers and their replacement by a national tariff at the frontiers and the free circulation and, with certain safeguards, export of corn. The *corvée* (forced peasant labour on the national highways) was to be commuted and the *gabelle* (salt tax) and *taille* (poll tax paid by non-noble country dwellers) were to be reduced as a prelude to their eventual replacement by the new kind of tax. Other measures included: the extension of the stamp duty to bring in an extra 25 million; the sale of the crown lands, with the king retaining their feudal rights (*inféodation de la domaine*); re-scheduling of debt repayment over twenty rather than ten years (some of the loans Necker had contracted were due for repayment in 1787 and shortly thereafter); and conversion of the *Caisse d'escompte* (Discount Bank) into a National Bank.[9] Finally, Calonne planned to consolidate the various departmental treasuries into one. This last was more than an essential administrative reform: it presupposed the emergence of a co-ordinating first minister, which, if the measures succeeded, Calonne would inevitably have become.[10]

The precise authorship of the various measures is often difficult to determine. In 1787 Dupont, the main collaborator of both Turgot and Calonne, was the principal architect but others were also involved, first of whom was another friend of Turgot's, the *conseiller d'état* Bouvard de Fourqueux. Talleyrand claimed paternity, with Nicolas de Saint-Genis, a specialist in church law, of the proposal to repay the clerical debt.[11] Chaumont de la Millière was responsible for the *mémoire* on the *corvée*, and the baron de Cormeré that for internal customs barriers. Calonne's friend, the *conseiller d'état* Lenoir, gave general assistance on commercial matters.

Calonne also proposed that Protestants should be given a 'civil status', that is to say that their wills and marriages should be recognized at law, which they had not been since 1685 when Louis XIV had revoked the tolerant Edict of Nantes. Louis told Calonne that the matter fell within the jurisdiction of Miromesnil. Miromesnil stonewalled, much to the irritation of the king, who probably would have liked to grant toleration to the Jews also[12] but who nevertheless felt a psychological need (in 1787 as in 1789) to carry the conservatives with him.

In sum, Calonne's proposals, exemplified by the following passage from his memorandum on the land tax, amount to a rejection of the spirit and mechanism of the ancien régime:

The most glaring anomalies vitiate the tax system. . . .

There are towns which have bought exemption, those which have settled for a lump sum; some provinces have their taxes farmed out, others collect them through their own estates, whilst yet others have bought exemption.

One cannot take a step in this vast kingdom without encountering different laws, conflicting customs, privileges, exemptions . . . rights and claims of all kinds; and this dissonance, worthy of the barbarian centuries or those of anarchy, complicates administration, clogs its wheels . . . and everywhere multiplies expense and disorder . . .

In this credo Calonne located the field where he and his opponents would join battle: the question of uniformity. Against Calonne will be arrayed all the forces of particularism, whether regional or social; all with the same basis of legitimacy, deriving from usage. It will be a battle of ideologies quite as much as of politics: utilitarian versus legitimist.

The measures Turgot had actually presented were the tip of an iceberg; Calonne's, though without the full Physiocratic rhetoric, revealed its full mass. Even so, they were not original, being, as he put it, the product of the best minds within the royal administration over the century, and in this lay their appeal to Louis's unspeculative cast of mind. If they were revolutionary, it was the Revolution of Napoleon (to whom Calonne was to offer his services in 1800) rather than of the *Rights of Man*: the hand of equality was extended, that of liberty withheld. This was to lead Calonne's opponents to accuse him of 'ministerial despotism', for the ancien régime's conception of individual or corporate liberty was anchored in that very variety that Calonne so eloquently denounced. It is not clear whether Louis, or Calonne for that matter, realized just how much power would be unleashed by the destruction of the *pouvoirs intermédiaires* – those bodies such as the *parlements* that mediated between the king and the people and the people and the king – and by inflation-proof taxation and the manipulation by government of public opinion through the provincial assemblies. In view of his analysis of the subsequent phase of the Revolution, it is likely that another of Calonne's collaborators, Mirabeau, understood the immensity of this power, which was to become the power of the modern state.

From the outset Calonne made it clear to Louis that the 'essential condition' of his project was the need for unswerving royal resolve. He alluded to the careers of Turgot and Necker, but it was more likely the fall of d'Ormesson, which was both more apposite and also the occasion of his own elevation, which prompted him to voice his fears about how Louis would behave in a crisis. So he cautioned the king: 'Archimedes said that he needed only one lever to move the world. To move and put the machinery of state back on its feet needs only the firm resolve of Your Majesty'. However, he could 'guarantee success' only if the king 'gave him that unshakeable resolve without which it would be better to attempt nothing'. Again Calonne stressed the need for the king's 'sacred word'. For his part, Calonne assured his king that he 'would sacrifice himself without hesitation to secure success and if the price of that success were his downfall then he would think it one worth paying'.[13]

We know that the king kept his word. Never before or since did he identify so wholeheartedly with the policies of a minister. Whether the Bourbon monarchy had the strength of the Archimedean lever would soon be known. Calonne did not exaggerate when he told the notables 'that the king had made the measures entirely his own through the close attention he has paid to every single one of them before adopting it'.

However, the king's initial reaction when Calonne first broached the matter was one of scepticism. Indeed it has recently been claimed that these objections 'were tantamount to a refusal'.[14] It is more accurate to say that he was enthusiastic about the objectives but doubted whether they could be achieved. Louis was a reforming monarch – demonstrated by his support for Turgot and Necker, whom he blamed for deserting him – but he had witnessed the opposition which even their limited reforms had encountered. Calonne answered with a paradox: these ministers had failed precisely because their reforms were piecemeal: wholesale reform was easier, as its parts were self-buttressing. In this sense Calonne was vindicated when in 1789 the National Assembly carried Calonne's reforms to their absurd reduction.

Discussion of Calonne's programme

Louis's doubts were practical rather than theoretical and it has to be said they were well grounded. He asked whether the programme could not be implemented without resurrecting the 'unwonted apparatus' of an Assembly of Notables. He was concerned that such an assembly could metamorphose into an Estates-General; indeed, two insiders claimed that Calonne only asked for an Assembly of Notables because the king had 'categorically refused' to convoke the Estates-General of the kingdom.[15] Calonne assured Louis that there was a big difference between the Estates-General, which were elected and had a mandate, and Assemblies of Notables, whose members were appointed by the king, who also set the agenda.

Louis also queried (as the notables and Miromesnil would) whether the extra revenue could be found solely from taxing the 'privileged' without also being 'at the expense of the peoples . . . [on whom] the slightest addition would make the burden intolerable'. He also feared that the reforms would cause 'an insurrection of the clergy, the great landed proprietors and all those who have a vested interest in opposing them', placing him in a dilemma: yielding, which 'would compromise his sovereign dignity in the eyes of the whole of Europe'; or 'having to put down eternal resistance'. Louis also wondered whether the proposed provincial assemblies were compatible with the monarchical constitution and made the typically dry observation that, since Necker's experiment in that field 'had been confined to two provinces, there is reason to believe that they did not produce the desired benefit'. These doubts suggest a variation on the Cassandra legend: a man who foresees the dangers but doesn't heed his own warning.

Louis also thought that the project should be implemented in stages because 'so vast and important a plan' required 'the necessary time' not just to consult 'the people most worthy of his confidence' – his ministers or the council – but 'even to gauge general opinion on the topics which are susceptible of being confided to a public discussion'.

This placed Calonne in a quandary. The publication of Necker's *Compte rendu* had made it hard to argue that the nation had no right to discuss government finance: now it was 'necessary that the nation should be disabused before a National Assembly', as he qualified the Assembly of Notables.[16] However, the revelation of the existence of a deficit was market-sensitive information and must be accompanied by the remedy or there would be a financial catastrophe. Consequently it would be difficult to 'sound out' public opinion as the king desired. The number of experts to whom 'state secrets could be entrusted is very circumscribed'.

Preliminary discussions were held without the king between Calonne, Vergennes and Miromesnil – Vergennes an ally who had witnessed the near-collapse of the fiscal military state and realized that reform was necessary to maintain an effective foreign policy, and Miromesnil the conservative whose hands needed to be dipped in the blood. Calonne wanted the decision in principle to be taken during the court's removal to Fontainebleau (scheduled for 9 October–15 November) after which the king would order the drafting of the measures to be placed before the Notables, whose convocation would be announced for early December.

On 9 October the king, Calonne, Vergennes, Miromesnil and Dupont, whose appointment as *conseiller d'état* would be made there,[17] together with half the court, arrived at Fontainebleau, some thirty-eight miles to the southeast of Versailles. The château was being extensively refurbished, particularly the royal apartments. The work was suspended during the *voyage* and continued after the royal entourage left for Versailles on the 15th. The money was wasted since the king was only to spend five more days at the château in his life, 5–9 November 1787. The *voyage de Fontainebleau* was a mournful occasion: the place was deserted and the king had to command court officials to spend the night there and even to forbid absences of more than four hours at a stretch. Even the plays and operas staged at Fontainebleau failed to find favour.[18] However, the reduced state of the court that toured the smaller châteaux with the king was more conducive to decision-making and the more intimate atmosphere meant that it was easier for a minister to closet the king. Important decisions were therefore often taken away from Versailles: the decision to recall the *parlement* in 1774 was taken at Compiègne, that to rescind the lease of the general farm in 1783 at Fontainebleau and that to intervene in the proceedings of the Estates-General with a *séance royale* in 1789 at Marly. The budget for the following year was usually set during the autumnal removal to Fontainebleau.

This time, however, nothing was decided at Fontainebleau. Indeed Louis was distracted when Castries presented him with a long memorandum attacking every aspect of Vergennes's foreign policy.[19] But Louis now joined in the discussion himself by presiding over a series of committees – long meetings, according to Castries – consisting of Calonne, Vergennes and Miromesnil. Vergennes's support for the reform programme was assured; concerning Miromesnil, Louis was later to make a curious remark to Malesherbes: 'It was not those two [Calonne and Vergennes] who most influenced my decision but M. de Miromesnil, who disavowed this advice throughout the meeting of the Assembly; that is what determined me to part company with him.'[20] Clearly Louis did not mean that convoking the Notables was Miromesnil's idea but rather that Calonne and Vergennes had an identity of views with his own because they were among the last ministers to serve him who believed in the continuing viability of the classical administrative monarchy. Their opinions therefore merely reflected his without adding light or power to them: they were in the ministry because the king trusted them, not because they represented a group he had to accommodate.

The king of France, however, was now not the only power in the state and did not, of himself, have the ability to implement a programme of the magnitude of that presented by Calonne, who admitted as much when he lamented to Castries in December: 'There is no one in France strong enough to carry through all that is necessary.'[21] Miromesnil was in the ministry as the representative of the *parlement* with which Louis, at the beginning of his reign, had been prevailed upon to govern. If Miromesnil endorsed the programme, it might succeed.

It was disingenuous of Louis, however, to say that Miromesnil *had* endorsed the programme. Rather, over a period of three months, Louis attempted to browbeat Miromesnil in the *comité de gouvernement*, where he was in a minority of one, just as he had himself been isolated in a committee by Maurepas before the recall of the *parlement*. Yet however much Louis may have deceived himself, Miromesnil remained totally unconvinced: witness the lengthy and anguished letters which he wrote to the king and which constituted his only means of free expression.[22] Miromesnil disagreed with Calonne both on the role of the Assembly and the programme that should be submitted to it. Whereas Calonne wanted a puppet assembly, Miromesnil thought there was no point summoning one at all unless it was allowed to make 'de très humbles représentations' – a phrase which must have reminded Louis of the 'très humble remontrances' with which the *parlements* were allowed to delay the passage of his legislation. An Assembly of Notables armed with the powers and staffed with the personnel suggested by Miromesnil could, by a perversion, become an instrument of aristocratic revolt against the royal reform initiative.

The fundamental divide between Miromesnil and Calonne can be most clearly seen in the former's discussion of the proposed land tax. He tells the king that their committee had dealt with this matter 'only very superficially' and had left out of the discussion the whole variety of regional variations to be accommodated. This was not, however, 'superficiality' on Calonne's part, as a man of Miromesnil's infinite subtlety must have realized: the disparate nature of the regime, making general legislation for the whole country impossible, was precisely what Calonne was trying to end. The passage from Calonne's memorandum on the land tax quoted above is at total variance with Miromesnil's considerations, which were as follows:

How to raise the land tax throughout your states [plural]. The difficulties it may encounter when applied to Brittany and Languedoc, bearing in mind that you have just allowed these two provinces to settle for a lump sum [*abonnement*]. The measures to be taken in respect of Burgundy and Navarre and the little Estates of the provinces adjoining Navarre such as Bigorre. Provence, which has its own individual regime, Flanders, Artois, the Cambrésis, in short all those of your provinces which have Estates or their equivalent.[23]

Miromesnil sought reinforcements. Knowing that the other secretaries of state (Castries, Ségur and Breteuil) would support his conservative gloss on the constitution, on 28 December he wrote asking the king to include them in the discussions, thereby acknowledging the demise of the *comité de gouvernement*.

Louis, however, ignored both this letter and Miromesnil's treacherous suggestion that the king show it to Vergennes privately and 'make whatever use of it you see fit'. Instead Louis announced that 'a *Conseil des Dépêches* would be extraordinarily assembled' for the morrow when, Castries bitterly continues, he would be officially informed of the convocation of the Notables, 'like a *maître des requêtes*'.

The council did not take minutes but in the extraordinary session on Friday 29 December Louis made this simple announcement with no discussion:

> I am occupied with extremely important measures designed to ease the lot of my peoples, to eliminate several abuses and to restore order to my finances. Before ordering their implementation, I have decided to consult an Assembly of Notables. I have chosen its members. Each secretary of state must without delay send out letters of convocation, based on the one which the keeper of the seals will supply, to the people included in his department.[24] . . . The proposals I will successively lay before the Assembly will be examined in advance by my council.[25]

To add insult to injury the king tossed this bombshell casually at his ministers at the end of the council.[26] Did Louis XIV ever act in so high-handed a manner? That night the king could not sleep but, as he confided to Calonne, it was for joy.

Castries felt his exclusion as keenly as Miromesnil his intimidation: 'Your Majesty has determined the most important event of his reign without deigning to test my loyalty.' Louis replied, with lame and technical rectitude, that they were dealing 'only with the arrangements to be made for the assessment of taxation which had absolutely nothing to do with anything but finance'. Castries's *patronne*, the queen, feebly assured him 'that for eight days the king had been seeking an opportunity to impart his plans to him without being able to find one'.[27] Besides, as a journalist noted, Castries's 'opinions given at council make the king yawn whereas Calonne's command his attention'.[28]

Of course there was more to it than that. Castries talked of his loyalty, but he did not really have any (except of the kind that delights in purveying unpalatable 'truths'), either to the king personally (whom he called an 'implacable master') or to the absolute monarchy – taking a leaf out of the *Compte rendu* of his friend Necker, he concluded his letter to the king by reflecting that 'at least I will be able to give an account to the nation of the functions with which Your Majesty has deigned to honour me'. Castries and Breteuil favoured an aristocratic, constitutional monarchy.

Aristocratic attitudes challenged the king's attempts, which he made in the interests of efficiency and fairness, to equalize taxation. Aristocrats also envisaged devolution of power to bodies such as provincial estates and, increasingly, the Estates-General, which they hoped to dominate. The process of aristocratic infiltration into the ministry, encouraged by Necker and denounced by Calonne in 1781, had seemed harmless as long as the king was pursuing socially and politically neutral policies. In the period 1781–86 he had been able simply to ignore the new ministers in the making of general policy, attempting to contain their higher departmental extravagance through the *comité des finances*. When, however, the king was putting forward a programme like Calonne's, he could hardly expect men such as Castries to transcend the limitations of their class.

Castries said of his exclusion: 'The king prefers unanimity (which allows him to sleep peacefully) rather than resistance leading to a better course of action.'[29] He was right in saying that the king had created an artificial and temporary ministerial unity by exclusion and pressure. Nevertheless, the king's dilemma was insoluble: if he had consulted the other ministers, they would have tried to block the measures; excluded, they were to intrigue with the notables against them. If all the ministers and the interests they represented had supported the proposals, he would not have needed to turn to an Assembly of Notables in the first place. An early biographer of Louis XVI considered that Necker would have had the prestige to implement Calonne's programme without the king's needing to convoke the Assembly of Notables.[30] But Necker's programme would have been very different.

Necker

It was Castries's continuing association with Necker that most disturbed the king and since Necker was to play the role of *deus ex machina* in the Assembly of Notables we must touch on his conduct since his resignation in 1781. The *comité* over which Louis presided was engaged in examining the sixty-three financial statements that Calonne had given the king in November;[31] these necessarily involved a refutation of the *Compte rendu* and it was certain that if Castries had been included he would have leaked the discussions to his friend.

In January 1784 Necker had published, without seeking the king's permission, *De l'administration des finances*, based on archival material he should have given to the king when leaving office. Louis told Vergennes that the correct procedure (and Louis was 'infinitely sensitive to procedure') was 'to send the manuscript of his work to his successor'. Since that successor was Calonne, Necker rightly guessed that the king would refuse permission to publish; so he went ahead, in Vergennes's phrase, 'because he wanted to nourish his faction' with an injection of publicity.[32] The book was a very thinly veiled attack on Calonne's administration. It has been argued that, but for this publication, Calonne would have introduced his reforms in 1784, when Louis's prestige was still shining from the peace.[33]

Vergennes assembled several conferences of all the ministers except Castries in his apartments, and they all signed a letter advising the king to exile Necker, a step which was necessary 'to give your ministers the consideration they need to serve you well' since 'the partisans and associates of M. Necker flatter themselves that they can realize in his favour his theories about the empire of public opinion'. Though he knew that Necker was destabilizing his government, Louis correctly judged that stern action would serve only to increase Necker's celebrity.

The following year, 1785, Marie-Antoinette asked Louis to allow Necker to return from Lyon, where he was residing, nearer to Paris to consult his doctors. Louis gave his permission on condition that Necker avoided the capital itself. At the same time, the king wrote to Vergennes,

> I sent for M. de Castries and told him ... that he should bear in mind that on the occasion of M. d'Ormesson's departure two years ago I told him formally that neither M. Necker nor his friends must dream of his ever returning to office; that provided M. Necker kept a low profile and his friends did not get him talked about, I would leave him alone. But that if ... he undermined the operations of the government, I should regard it as a personal attack and then I would send him back to Geneva never to return to France. I leave it to your discretion how much of this you want to tell M. de Calonne. I expect to discuss the matter with him on Thursday.[34]

For some time Castries was reduced to writing letters to the king on the subject of Necker, knowing that Louis would not hear him out.

More trouble from the *parlement*

If Louis had any doubts as to the necessity of the step he was about to take, two incidents in December 1786 must have served to dispel them. Even on the brink of the abyss, Breteuil continued his intrigues in the *parlement*, planning to bring about Calonne's fall by having him denounced for leaving his loans open after they had been fully subscribed, thereby exceeding the amount stipulated in the edicts (the *rentes* of the loan were backed by the Hotel de Ville and, as minister for Paris, Breteuil had access to the certificates). This was too much even for Miromesnil, who informed the king but insidiously added that if Calonne had indeed exceeded the amounts, it was a betrayal of faith to a public already cynical towards the ministers – though again this was a matter for the king, not the *parlement*. He suggested that:

> It would be desirable for Your Majesty to ask M. de Calonne next Sunday whether the sums . . . have been exceeded and to tell him to give you the statements. It would also be necessary for Your Majesty to tell M. le baron de Breteuil that he would like to have these statements checked secretly and to ask him whether he does not have people in the Bureau de la Ville who could obtain secret information for him, at the same time recommending the greatest discretion.
>
> M. le baron de Breteuil, flattered by such a confidence and happy to enlighten Your Majesty's 'religion' himself, will in all likelihood prevent M. d'Amécourt and his emissaries from acting.[35]

Presumably this complicated manoeuvre succeeded, for no more is heard of the denunciation in the *parlement*.

When Calonne realized (because of the king's procrastination) that he would not get his measures passed in 1786, he had fallen back on the rather forlorn hope of detaching two of them – extending the stamp duty, and alienating the crown lands – and getting the *parlement* to register them in December so he would have something under his belt. Miromesnil advised the king – and Louis was never to forgive him for this piece of counsel[36] – that there was no hope of getting these measures through the *parlement*, so the attempt was not made. Miromesnil was right, but his advice hammered home to the king that the ruling partnership between the monarch and the *parlement*, the cornerstone of the ancien régime, was at an end.

It has been argued that 'the crisis began in 1787 because Calonne thought the consent of the *parlements* would not be enough to win general confidence for his proposals'.[37] The very reverse is the case. It began because a situation had been reached in which the keeper of the seals, the minister responsible for seeing royal legislation through the *parlement*, had to advise the king that there was no point even attempting to get just two of Calonne's measures through. Calonne advocated an Assembly of Notables, as he had told the king, 'to spare the government the objections of the sovereign courts', couched as ever in the paradoxical language of hyper-loyalty – *plus royaliste que le roi*. Paradox, however, was no longer a viable basis for government.

Personal relations between Louis and the *parlements* – not just the *parlement* of Paris but the provincial ones as well – turned even more sour between the convocation of the Assembly of Notables on 31 December and its opening on 22 February. The *parlementaires* were well aware that the Assembly was an attempt to outflank them, as Castries noted: 'The *parlement*, uneasy and resentful, says that the intention is to deprive it of its right of registration and that this step will lead to the Estates-General.'

In choosing the notables, Calonne had warned the king that, since the *parlementaires* and clergy would be inclined to oppose the projects, the number of the nobility (he thought the court nobility would be favourable or at least susceptible to patronage) and the third estate combined 'must be large enough for the wishes of the king to prevail'. However, perhaps under Miromesnil's influence, Louis included all the *premiers présidents* and *procureurs-généraux* of the *parlements*, and three extra *présidents* from Paris were summoned, making a total of 37 out of the 144 summoned to the Assembly. There was only a handful of commoners. Louis decided to follow precedent and overruled Calonne's attempt to pack the Assembly. Even so, a cartoon depicted the notables as turkeys with the caption, 'With what sauce would you like to be eaten?' to which the turkeys replied that they did not want to be eaten at all. Nor did giving the *parlementaires* generous representation in the Assembly of Notables in any way placate them.

Miromesnil informed Louis on 3 January that d'Aligre had warned him that there was a move afoot in the *parlement* to pass a resolution giving their five deputies to the Assembly of Notables a mandate and obliging them to report back to the *parlement*. This mandate was probably to the effect that they could not bind the *parlement* in any way or even commit their individual votes when it came to registration. Miromesnil told d'Aligre that if such a resolution were passed, he would advise the king to summon the whole *parlement* to Versailles to score it out, as in 1785. The question of the 'mission' or mandate was clearly still not resolved on 1 February since Miromesnil had to raise the matter with the king again. But he reassured Louis that the *parlement* had not as yet got wind of any of Calonne's measures, 'except the [sale of the] crown lands . . . and that in an uncertain manner'. However, he had already told the king that the plan to extend the stamp duty had 'leaked out' and he 'had no doubt that there were many intrigues afoot both in Paris and at court' to bring rival candidates into the ministry.[38]

Louis was already furious at what Miromesnil called the 'faults' of the *parlements* of Besançon, Dijon and Grenoble, all of which were in dispute with the crown over a variety of issues. The *parlement* of Dijon drew the king's especial displeasure for ordering the arrest of the local intendant. Louis summoned fourteen of their number to Versailles, kept them standing for five hours, crossed out their registers and, in a refinement of cruelty, refused to allow the *premier président* and *procureur-général*, who were to attend the Notables, to stay on: they had to make a double return journey and had not yet got back to Versailles by the time of the scheduled opening ceremony. Similar treatment was meted out to the *premier président* of the *parlement* of Besançon.

Such harshness created a bad impression. Coeurderoi, *premier président* of the sovereign court (*parlement*) of Nancy, who had arrived at Versailles for the Notables, was shocked to see the ashen faces of his colleagues of Dijon.[39] One journal thought it ironical that at a time when the king was trying to 'reanimate patriotic spirits' and inaugurate 'a new regime of liberty' by summoning the Notables, he should 'flagellate three or four *parlements* for having defended the feeble vestiges of the nation's rights'.[40]

Moreover, Miromesnil was worried that, capitalizing on the king's bad mood, 'those who do not like the *parlements* – and their number is fairly large' would act as *agents provocateurs* and 'secretly seek to goad the *parlement* of Paris into taking some senseless course of action in order to turn you against the magistrature'. Miromesnil probably meant that Louis, on Calonne's advice, would attempt a re-run of Maupeou's coup d'état and he warned the king that it was his 'primary duty' to maintain 'the constitution'. A month later Castries would warn the king, 'If you want to constrain the *parlements*, you will have to break them', which, he added, would take 'one hundred thousand troops'.[41] It would not be as easy as in 1771, because the loyalists, 'the king's good servants', had been disillusioned by Louis's treatment of them in 1774.

If such a coup was contemplated and if Castries is right that it would require 100,000 armed men, it demonstrates a decline in royal confidence from the time when Maupeou carried out his coup without the need to deploy any troops – a facility which contemporaries found shocking in itself. However, Maurepas advised the young king to use troops frequently and linked this to the recall of the *parlements*.[42] Troops had been used heavily in the Flour War of 1775 and would be again in the period 1788–89.

The death of Vergennes

The opening of the Assembly was postponed from 29 January to 7 February, then the 14th and finally the 22nd. Calonne had fallen ill through overwork and Vergennes was dying of it. Calonne had to be carried to the *Conseil d'État* because the quack blister cure he was undergoing made it painful for him to walk.[43] Despite another quack diagnosis – of 'repressed gout' – it was probably hard work that had caused the progressive deterioration of Vergennes's health throughout 1786. He was seventy and still worked a ten-hour day, despite the king's plea that he slow down – Louis told him to leave the running of the foreign ministry in his deputy Rayneval's capable hands and 'as for the great internal matter [the Assembly of Notables], I will hold all the committees religiously so there will be no delay'.[44] Vergennes's eldest son, Constantin, wrote that 'the glory and interest of the king were all that concerned him. His only thought in all his suffering was to be in a fit state to attend the Assembly of Notables'.[45]

On 6 February, he seemed to rally and the *Correspondance secrète* notes, touchingly, that he was going to retire, but 'would not leave the king and would accept M. de Maurepas's apartments', which, tenanted and divided as they were, still retained their symbolic significance.[46] On the 13th, however, he died, affirming that he saw the whole heavens opening before his eyes.

Protocol dictated (when did it not?) that Louis not attend Vergennes on his deathbed, but he gave orders that all the ministers were to go to the funeral. Even the queen, who viscerally loathed him, felt obliged to cancel her concert. The *Correspondance secrète* has the king receiving the news of his minister's death 'just as he was about to set off for the hunt. "There will be no sport today", His Majesty said, "I have lost the only friend I could count on, the only minister who never deceived me"'.[47] These were indeed the king's sentiments, but the news was broken to him not as he was mounting up but at daybreak in his chamber by d'Angiviller, his director of works who, on Louis's orders, was in Vergennes's apartments the night that he died (at 3 a.m., Louis recorded).

D'Angiviller, trading on their childhood association, made bold to advise the king 'to cancel the Assembly [of Notables] and put it off till another time'. He was 'exposing himself to a danger which was all the greater for the loss of the one man in whom he had confidence'. Calonne 'had not sufficiently measured the forces of opposition' and, precisely because he was so talented, had 'overestimated his powers'. D'Angiviller did not advise the king to dismiss Calonne (who was a close friend) but he did say that the king 'should put himself in charge of all the reforms; that it was known that it was he who wanted them and was driving them forward'. The king, however, 'persisted in telling me that it was too late, and he believed it'.

D'Angiviller then gave a selective account of this conversation to Calonne:

I saw real tears flow from his eyes at the loss of the man to whom he was subordinate in [the king's] confidence. I saw him moved by the king's predicament and burning with a desire to sacrifice himself entirely to extricate him from it; but what is the use of the resolutions of frivolous men who abandon themselves to circumstances and are ruled by them?[48]

In this vignette is a microcosm of the whole adventure: the king's fatalism, and Calonne's overconfidence and genuine readiness to sacrifice himself for the king's service.

Calonne's grief for Vergennes was sincere and heartfelt. The following July he wrote to d'Angiviller:

What would he say today, that worthy and much-lamented friend whose last and only too prophetic words I shall never forget? Would that he had himself been able to execute the commission he bequeathed me! He would have spoken better than me; perhaps the plots he had run to earth would not have materialized if he had lived; or in any case if the king had kept him he would not have been deprived of all the ministers who were truly loyal to him [*vraiment à lui*].[49]

The 'plots' may refer to those in the *parlement*. By the last clause, Calonne meant that, apart from himself, Vergennes was the last minister to share Louis's conception of the absolute monarchy and that no other was to give wholehearted support to the programme he was to lay before the Notables in the king's name.

Vergennes's death undoubtedly affected the outcome of the Assembly of Notables; but his influence could have cut two ways. He had a group of supporters in the Assembly[50] and he might have kept Miromesnil 'onside'; as the English ambassador put it, Miromesnil 'appeared to approve' Calonne's plans until Vergennes's death, 'when he immediately chang'd his ground and has since uniformly opposed him on every occasion'. Louis himself acknowledged, in a curious appreciation he inserted in the official record of the Assembly of Notables, how much he had been relying on the dead minister's 'business skill and prestige' to manage the Assembly. Another insider suggests Vergennes might have advised the king to jettison Calonne if his difficulties risked compromising the monarchy.[51] That is precisely what he had done, under less pressure, with Calonne's predecessor, d'Ormesson.

Vergennes was succeeded as foreign secretary by the comte de Montmorin, who had been ambassador to Spain and was a former *menin* and personal friend of the king's. After no more than a decent interval Castries asked the king for Vergennes's post of *chef du Conseil royal des finances*; the king's refusal can hardly have surprised him, but it enabled him to give a warning: 'If you give the post to M. de Calonne it will be to the detriment of the interests of the state.'[52]

The Assembly of Notables

The Assembly of Notables was to meet in a newly constructed hall in the Hotel des Menus Plaisirs, in the town which had grown up round Versailles. Louis himself made an inspection of the work, asking sniffily what all the galleries and boxes were for. On being told they were for the queen, her attendants, the courtiers and the public, he replied that it was not a 'public entertainment'; that 'the queen was perfectly free to attend if she so desired but on her own' and that 'his own retinue would be the bare minimum to support the royal majesty'. His decision came as a great relief to the organizers, who were being solicited for tickets.[53]

But the king had little control over court ceremonial, which was elaborate when he opened the Assembly on 22 February 1787. Seated on a throne covered in purple velvet strewn with gold fleurs-de-lys, beneath a canopy of purple satin, both feet resting on cushions, he was flanked on the dais by his brothers, Provence and Artois, and the princes of the blood, but was not accompanied by the queen, who had found this way to distance herself from the proceedings.[54] At a quarter to twelve the king doffed and replaced his hat and delivered himself of a short speech. It was a compilation of the king's and Calonne's words.[55]

Gentlemen, I have chosen you from among the different orders of the state and I have gathered you around me to intimate my plans to you.

This is a usage which has been employed by several of my predecessors and notably by the first of my branch [Henri IV], whose name has remained dear to all Frenchmen and whose example I shall always take a pride in following.

The plans which will be communicated to you in my name are great and important. On the one hand they [aim at] improving the revenue of the state and assuring a stable surplus by a more equitable assessment of taxation; on the other, at freeing commerce from the various impediments which restrict its circulation, and so far as circumstances permit me, in alleviating the poorest section of my subjects. Such, gentlemen, are the measures which have exercised me and which I have decided upon after a thorough examination. As they all tend to the common weal and as I know the zeal for my service of you all, I have no fear in consulting you about their implementation; I shall listen to and examine your observations carefully. I trust that your opinions, all tending towards the same goal, will easily harmonize and that no sectional interest will stand out against the general.

It was customary on these occasions for the keeper of the seals to 'develop the king's thoughts more fully', but Miromesnil's speech was short and ambiguous and on this occasion the task fell to Calonne who gave a speech lasting an hour and six minutes. There was a résumé of his proposals but the notables were most struck by his treatment of the deficit and by his very opening words: 'The measures which His Majesty has ordered me to present . . . to you have become entirely his own through the extremely close scrutiny His Majesty has brought to bear on each before adopting them.' This intrusion of the king's personality, like that of an author, was an embarrassment, angering and frustrating his opponents by blocking the constitutional escape-route of the 'surprise to the king's religion', the French equivalent of the English king's being 'misled by evil advisers'. Calonne said that the deficit had existed for centuries: when Terray had taken over the finances it had stood at 74 million *livres*, and at 40 million when he had left office; when Necker took over it had been 37 million, and on Calonne's appointment it had been 80 million. Mindful that Necker's supporters were present in strength in the Assembly, Calonne had, in so far as possible, heeded the Genevan's request not to criticize the *Compte rendu*, though to reveal the size of the deficit without criticizing Necker's denial of its existence was not easy. The king himself questioned whether the 'section on the deficit was not calculated to instill alarm'. Nevertheless, he told Calonne, 'I will keep my fears to myself: one must not show fear lest one inspire it.' He was trusting that Calonne would be able to 'maintain general confidence', by which he meant 'calm the markets'.[56] He was right to sense danger from that quarter.

After Calonne's speech, the session was quickly concluded and the king left at half past one. On his way out, he was heard to say: 'This is my work and I will see it through.'[57]

At the following day's plenary session, Calonne read out the six memoranda of the first of the four divisions which comprised his work. The notables were then to meet next day in seven bureaux or working committees, each presided over by a prince of the blood, and to have a week in which to discuss the memoranda of the first division, including the two most important, those on provincial assemblies and the land tax. But, from the start, the clergy and Necker's supporters made a dead-set at Calonne, 'falling on him', as Castries puts it, 'like a quarry they wanted to devour'; they seemed likely to mangle the provincial assemblies beyond recognition and reject the land tax outright.

The *parlementaire* members of the Notables, fearful of what the king might do, initially took a back seat. But Miromesnil is reported to have held secret meetings with them to concert opposition, each *premier président* also sending his local *parlement* information about decisions taken so that when the edicts came to be registered, opposition would be uniform.[58] Calonne described to d'Angiviller the opposition he encountered: 'A combination of every kind of obstacle, a coming together of all the vested interests; the baneful preponderance of the clergy; the manoeuvres of a fanatical sect [Necker's supporters]; the perfidy of my main collaborator [Miromesnil]; the best intentions denigrated; a war of word-splitting; unseemly railing against the minister.'[59]

The clergy, who had most to lose from Calonne's proposals, being hitherto undertaxed, led the attack, the queen's protégé, Loménie de Brienne, archbishop of Toulouse, acting almost as a leader of the opposition. Men of his ilk, prelate-administrators like Boisgelin, archbishop of Aix (who hoped at least to get the blue ribbon of the order of the Saint-Esprit out of the business), set the tone for a revamped defence of clerical and other privilege. When one old duke got up to rehearse the argument that, since the church lands had been given to God by pious benefactors they should not be subject to taxation, a clerical deputy leant forward and whispered to him: 'We don't say that any more.' The casuistry and word-splitting bemoaned by Calonne were the product of the clerical mind; Brienne, for example, found it possible to distinguish between 'equality', which he accepted, and 'uniformity' which he abhorred.[60]

The notables' objections to the provincial assemblies were, first, that the 'confusion of ranks' was humiliating to the first two orders who, according to Brienne, 'would not attend if they risked being presided over or even preceded by citizens of an inferior order and that then the assemblies would become tumultuous'; and, second, that the assemblies were too dependent on the intendant: 'democracy or despotism' – both equally repugnant.[61]

Their objections to the land tax occasionally followed an old path: that the priest should give the king his prayers, the nobleman his blood and the commoner his money.[62] Generally, however, the notables shifted the ground from the basis of assessment (with which it was difficult to quarrel without seeming to favour the 'sectional interests' which the king had denounced) to the very nature of the tax. They held that the land tax was 'unconstitutional' because, instead of its being related to a specific need, its duration and amount were open-ended. Their underlying objection was based on the concept of 'no taxation without representation' which had been enunciated by the American colonists. Not only were the nobility and clergy being asked to surrender their fiscal privileges, but even the 'simulated' consent provided by the *parlements* and provincial estates was being diluted by the prospect of a perpetual, inflation-proof tax, whilst the proposed provincial assemblies threatened to give the king formidable new powers and influence by harnessing the support of the expanding commercial and legal classes. A sense of disquiet at the prospect of fundamental change comes over in Brienne's phrase 'democracy or despotism' and the 'republicanism and despotism' used by one of his colleagues. The selfish exercise of their privileges blocked the extension of central power, which, unfortunately for the king, was widely if temporarily unpopular. It has recently been argued, against the weight of historiography, the view of the author of this book and the evidence of their behaviour in 1788 and 1789, that the notables were not selfishly defending their financial privileges but rather were prepared to exchange them for political power, as in England.[63] But they knew that the patchy incidence of taxation was a block to the further expansion of the Bourbon state, just as in the Revolution the National Assembly regarded the deficit as a national treasure with which to bind the king.

Many of the contradictions and paradoxes in the notables' position, summarized by the phrase 'aristocratic constitutionalism', come together in the person of Marie Jean Paul Motier, marquis de Lafayette. His exploits in the American war had given him a taste for fame or, as we would say, 'celebrity'. Louis preferred understated conduct and set the example himself: Castries had to prevail on the king to include Lafayette, who, as ever, was determined to make his mark. Lafayette started from the position that 'we should not lightly tamper with a constitution under which France has existed so gloriously for nearly eight hundred years' (1787 was actually the 800th anniversary of the election of Hughes Capet, the founder of the dynasty). He quickly realized, however, that the king was in difficulties and that the attempt to increase his power would actually lead to its diminution, concluding that he should not be allowed to escape until the country had acquired a new constitution.

In the bureau of which he was part he observed that the second *vingtième* was due to expire in 1791 and added: 'It strikes me that we ought to beseech His Majesty to determine here and now on the convocation of a truly national assembly for that time.' Artois, blunt but displaying far more intelligence in the Assembly than he did when he became king in 1824, having to battle long hours, often-single handed, for Calonne's measures, stepped in and 'asked whether . . . it was the convocation of the Estates-General he was requesting. He [Lafayette] replied that this was precisely the object of his request.'[64]

None of these arguments impressed the king, as he made clear to Castries, taking the notables' part, on 28 February:

> *Castries*: All the orders of the state summoned to hear the proposals of your controller-general are all, unanimously going to bring their disapproval to the foot of the throne; all privileges have been overturned ... ruin and disorder [brought] to every part of the kingdom ... Does Your Majesty want to constrain the *parlements*? If so, he must destroy them. Does he want to arm one hundred thousand men, does he want to leave a stain on his reputation? Your monarchy is absolute but not despotic.
>
> *Louis*: Hah! you know perfectly well that I do not intend to govern like a despot but I disagree with you and I have thought about it a lot: the land tax is the most just and the least onerous of taxes.
>
> *Castries*: Perhaps in the state of nature you would be right, Sire. But so many agreements, rights, abuses if you will, have arisen that what would then have been justice would not be so today. The collection of a tax in kind would be impossible and would cost a quarter of its yield.
>
> *Louis*: But I assure you, you are absolutely wrong on all of this.

Another matter of fundamental disagreement between the king and the notables was the question of the deficit. The bishop of Langres, among many, observed that in 1781 a minister of the crown had published a detailed statement showing that there was a surplus, to which Artois had to reply: 'The *compte* of M. de Calonne is in print as well as that of M. Necker and it benefits from an approval on the part of the king which is the fruit of a long [elsewhere he says 'six-month'] scrutiny.' When Langres observed that 'one of them is false', Artois agreed: 'Yes, certainly one of the two and today's strikes me as safer than the other.'

Calonne had told Necker that he had only said what he had been forced to say and had made no specific mention of the *Compte rendu* of 1781;[65] but on receiving Calonne's letter Necker had 'turned visibly pale and trembled'. Though Calonne had pulled his punches in his speech, what he really thought was contained in a draft letter he thought better of sending to Necker. The draft included the following:

> As for the balance between income and expenditure which is placed at the end of the *Compte* you gave the king in 1781, which results in a surplus of about ten million, I have recognized and demonstrated the error by evidence which is so incontrovertible that I could not make it the basis for the calculations which I was obliged to show the king.

1 Louis XV cream ware bust. Barnave said: 'Frenchmen combined such submissiveness with such contempt for their master that they seemed ready to suffer everything'. He chose power rather than popularity. But the kindly king became a second and better father to Louis-Auguste.

2 Louis' father, the gloomy and repressive Louis-Ferdinand, school of Roslin. Taken shorty before his death in 1765, his uniform hangs loosely off the once corpulent dauphin. He scolded Louis XV over his capitulation to the *parlements*; to which the king replied, 'My son, you should wish me a long life for you don't yet know how to behave'.

3 Louis as duc de Berry, c. 1765, pastel by Quentin de la Tour. His aunt Adélaide said 'speak at your ease, Berry; exclaim, bawl out, make a noise like your brother Artois; dash my china to pieces and make yourself talked about.' Aged ten Louis is plump and pretty; with puberty he became thin and gangling before becoming stout and strong with maturity.

(a)

(b)

(c)

(d)

(e)

4 A life in medals: (a) Louis-Auguste as dauphin bronze plaque c. 1774 this must have been cast shortly before Louis' accession as his face is beginning to fill up; (b) lead medal of Louis opening 1787 Assembly of Notables; this 'royal revolution' was the turning point of his life and reign; (c) and (d) struck pewter medals by. B. Andrieu of the storming of the Bastille and the king's arrival at Paris on 6 October (first two in a projected series); (e) reverse of copper struck medal 1793 by C.H Kuchler for Mathew Boulton of Birmingham: the executioner holds Louis' severed head aloft.

5 Louis' surviving siblings. Gold, enamel and lapis lazuli snuff box, 1776, later inset on the base with a miniature of Provence, Artois and Elizabeth. Clever Provence subtly undermined Louis both before and during the Revolution but became a surprisingly effective king as Louis XVIII (1814–24); Artois, loyal before the Revolution, especially during the Assembly of Notables, compromised Louis by his Counter-Revolutionary activities. Elizabeth stayed in France to be with her brother and looked after his children in prison until her own execution in 1794. But her identification with the Counter-Revolution 'made home life Hell', as Marie-Antoinette put it.

6 Marie-Antoinette. Gold, hardstone and simulated pearl snuff box by Neuber, c. 1780. 'Never has a queen of France been less popular; and yet no act of wickedness can be laid at her door. We are decidedly unjust to her and far too severe in punishing her for, at most, a few examples of frivolity' – Marquis de Bombelles, 1789.

7 Armand-Thomas Hue de Miromesnil, Keeper of the Seals, 1774-87, marble bust by Jean-Antoine Houdon, 1775. The archetypal conservative, Miromesnil was the biggest single obstacle to reform. Malesherbes had no doubt that Miromesnil had 'hidden contacts among the *parlementaires* to undermine Turgot's operations' by informing the *parlement* 'with a hundred turns of phrase' of divisions within the ministry.

8 Anne-Robert Turgot, finance minister 1774-1776, pastel by Joseph Ducreux. Louis opened himself up to no other minister in the way he did to Turgot. But he overstepped the mark so that Louis said, 'M. Turgot wants to be me and I don't want him to be me'.

9 Chrétien-Guillaume de Lamoignon de Malesherbes. Minister and Louis' defence counsel, marble bust by A. D. Chaudet. Malesherbes, a strategic thinker with no grasp of detail, could perhaps have fused the old with the new, but said he feared office next to a mortal illness. At Louis's trial Malesherbes addressed the King as 'Sire' and 'Your Majesty'. The deputy Treilhard rebuked him: 'So what gives you the effrontery to use expressions proscribed by the Convention?' 'Contempt for you and for life!'

10 Louis's nemesis: Jacques Necker, finance minister 1776-81 and 1788-90; Wedgwood jasper ware c. 1780. Unfortunately, Louis and Necker each reinforced the other's tendency to indecisiveness. Malouet said of Necker (in words that could equally be applied to the king): 'He had a rare talent for appreciating both in the most minute detail and in perspective the vices and disadvantages of every proposal, and it was these endless ramifications which so often made him indecisive.'

11 Benjamin Franklin, souvenir Sèvres coffee can c. 1780. Franklin charmed Marie-Antoinette and ran rings round Vergennes. Franklin affected a fur cap like Rousseau, and like Rousseau he abused the hospitality he received. He signed separate peace preliminaries with England – reneging on the one requirement France had inserted into the 1778 treaty of alliance.

12 The dramatis personae in the Diamond Necklace Affair, Cardinal de Rohan, Jeanne de Valois, the 'baronne d'Oliva' and the comte de la Motte, from *Les mystères de la science* by L. Figuier, 1893. This celebrated heist relied on the assumption that the queen would buy a 2,800 carat diamond necklace without the king's knowledge. In some senses the affair marked the true 'unravelling of the ancien régime'.

24 Louis about to mount the scaffold is exhorted by his confessor: '"Fils de Saint-Louis ascendez au ciel."' Contemporary painting by Charles Benazech. His last words were, 'I die perfectly innocent of the so-called crimes of which I was accused. I pardon those who are the cause of my misfortunes. Indeed, I hope that the shedding of my blood will contribute to the happiness of France and you, unfortunate people...' These words may have been broken off by Santerre, by the drum-roll or by the descent of the axe.

22 Louis accepts the constitution, contemporary coloured etching. Louis told his brothers: 'The nation likes the constitution because the lower portion of the people see only that they are reckoned with; the bourgeoisie sees nothing above them. Vanity is satisfied'. He told a minister, 'My opinion is that the literal execution of the constitution is the best way of making the nation see the alterations to which it is susceptible' – a numbingly negative approach.

23 Joseph Ducreux, pastel highlighted by chalk of Louis taken shortly before his execution. This haunting picture shows a prematurely aged king, 'a man of sorrows acquainted with grief'. He said, 'after all that I have suffered death is not so difficult'.

16 (a and b) Silver wine-taster, Paris 1786–89, the base inset with a gold double *louis d'or* dated 1789 and the handle with a half louis of Louis XIII dated 1643, engraved with the arms of France and Lamoigon (Keeper of the Seals 1787–1788) and inscribed, 'Don de royale amitié offert à M. Chr [étien] Fr[ancoi]s de Lamoignon 1789'. Louis' reluctance to dismiss Lamoignon is confirmed by this opulent gift.

17 Early optimism. Representatives of the three estates pay homage to Louis and Necker. The third estate is represented by a peasant though only one sat in the Assembly. In fact the deputies for the Third Estate were required to wear black, which contrasted with the plumes and damask of the nobility and clergy. French school, 1789.

18 Lacquer snuff box, 1789. Louis is doffed in a cap of liberty. The inscription round the edge reads, 'Vive Louis le roi citoyen'. The reverse shows the old lilies of France but Louis' cap displays the tricolour cockade.

19 Lafayette as commander of the Paris National Guard, portrait by P. L. Dubucourt. This vain self-publicist was in 1790 the most powerful man in France. In 1792, Marie-Antoinette said, 'I will not owe my life to that man twice'; but Madame Elizabeth countered that Lafayette was 'the only man who by placing himself on a horse can give the king an army'.

20 Honoré-Gabriel Riquetti, comte de Mirabeau, bust in biscuit porcelain showing his pock marks. Mirabeau argued that the Revolution had completed the modernising mission of the monarchy and that its errors should be corrected by civil war. Louis replied: 'one can never accept that civil war is necessary, but one can imagine the possibility that it becomes inevitable; [and] provided it comes about neither through the actions or [even] the wishes of the king, he will prepare himself to accept it, without fear or remorse'.

21 Engraving depicting Louis' coach being stopped on the bridge at Varennes. On the other side were enough troops to ensure the royal family's safety and escort them to their ultimate destination, Montmédy.

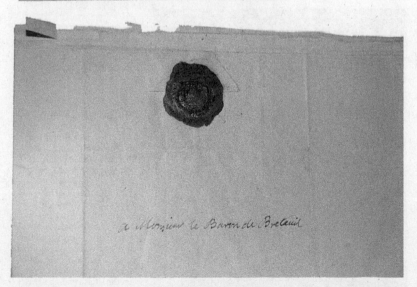

13 After Rohan had been acquitted, Louis compounded his error in sending him before the *parlement* by treating him as if he had been found guilty. Louis' letter to Breteuil orders internal exile for Rohan and deportation for Cagliostro. It is dated 1 [June] – a later hand has added 'Septembre 1786.'

14 Louis mingles with the people of Normandy on his way to Cherbourg. Printed cotton c. 1786. Louis asked himself why he was receiving such unaccustomed displays of affection and concluded that in court and capital he was maligned. He scribbled a note for the queen: 'My people's love has touched the depths of my heart. Judge if I am not the happiest king in the world.'

15 Charles-Alexandre de Calonne, finance minster 1787–1787, oil painting by his reputed mistress Louise-Elizabeth Vigée-Lebrun. Architect of wide-ranging reforms, Calonne told the king 'I would indeed have no regrets if I were the victim of the enterprise'. When he was, the Austrian ambassador wrote 'The king's authority is all the more grievously compromised by the abandonment of the former controller-general in that the latter's plans had been so openly approved by the king that he had scarcely left himself any way of disowning him'.

Having observed that he had not attacked the *Compte* in 1781 (technically true since his pamphlets had been anonymous), Calonne added, acidly, that 'it doubtless produced the effect you intended' – in other words the *Compte* had been a purely political text designed to bolster royal credit in general and his own in particular.[66]

Necker also sent Louis a letter for which Castries was hauled over the coals on 11 March. Louis said in an animated voice as soon as he saw Castries: 'M. Necker has just sent me the most extraordinary letter, have you seen it? I find its tone extremely singular . . . I forbid him to make any public justification or to print anything. . . . He seems to think that M. de Calonne's figures are wrong but I have seen them and I am sure they are right.' The king wanted Castries to bring him Necker's evidence, but Castries refused unless his friend was present.

In the face of this rapidly deteriorating situation, on 26 or 27 February Calonne wrote a very anxious letter to the king. Fearing the outright rejection of the land tax, he drew up 'a *supplément d'instruction* along the lines Your Majesty has already indicated'.[67] The *supplément d'instruction* was read out by each prince to his committee on 28 February. It laid down certain principles concerning the land tax which the king did not regard as being 'open to discussion': that the tax should apply to all land without exception, was to vary with the yield of the crop and was not to be susceptible to any *abonnements* (exemption in return for a lump sum payment). In his own bureau Artois added that a tax payable in kind seemed the only way of meeting these conditions.

The initiative for another attempt to defuse the crisis came from Louis himself, who contacted the archbishop of Narbonne with a view to a meeting between Calonne and his archiepiscopal opponents which took place on the evening of 1 March. In a letter to the king Calonne tries to pass it off as going well – 'clouds of misunderstanding were dispersed' – and says that, although there was strong opposition to a tax in kind, the clerics no longer insisted on *abonnements* or their own *don gratuit*.[68] 'I was particularly pleased', he writes with unconscious irony, 'with the conduct of the archbishop of Toulouse. I owe him the justice of saying as much.'

Next morning, Calonne met five deputies from each committee in a conference presided over by Monsieur, the comte de Provence. Its purpose was again to 'disperse some clouds' – over the land tax and the disparity between Necker's calculations and his own. The king provided Calonne with a memorandum outlining how the minister was to conduct himself at the conference for which Calonne gave him fulsome thanks:

I shall follow to the letter the course Your Majesty prescribes, inspired as it is by the most judicious wisdom. Your Majesty's letter removes all doubts as to what I should say. When a king takes the trouble to enter into such details concerning his affairs and to offer his ministers personal guidance, he is sure to be well served, etc.[69]

Calonne argued his case for nearly six hours on end, broken only by his leaving three times to consult the king.[70] Maybe Calonne was pleading with Louis to allow him to let the conference examine the sixty-three financial statements which he had given the king in November, to demonstrate the falsity of the *Compte rendu*. Louis was reluctant because 'nothing would have been more scandalous than an enquiry as to whether the king had authorized a mistake in 1781 or in 1787'.[71] The king's reluctance compromised Calonne's already slim chances of winnng over the conference, and, despite a virtuoso performance in which, according to d'Angiviller, 'he left everyone stunned by such extraordinary talent and fluency',[72] he failed utterly in his attempt to win endorsement for the land tax in kind or vindication in his dispute with Necker over the deficit.

The Easter crisis

Castries believed that Calonne was beaten and that only 'the king's *amour-propre* still protects him'. Far from resigning to the inevitable, however, the king and his minister deliberately raised the stakes. An appeal to the people, who Calonne had said would be 'enraged' by the rejection of the measures, had always been implicit in what he had said to the king. Now, as the Notables passed the month of March in captious debate, the appeal was prepared. The memoranda of the first two divisions were published, preceded by a detachable *Avertissement* (which can be translated either as 'Preface' or 'Warning') drafted by the barrister Gerbier on the instructions of Calonne, who wrote the first two paragraphs and gave the flier its title. It was also probably corrected by the king.[73] Brienne credited the rumour that 'the king had not only read this *Avertissement* but had even made some alterations; it is [Calonne's] way of making everything that he does personal to the king'.[74] It has been suggested that the king's changes were designed to make the publication less offensive to the notables.[75]

In the *Avertissement* the work of the notables was ironically praised and there were provocative passages such as: 'People will doubtless pay more – but who? Only those who do not pay enough'; and 'Privileges will be sacrificed ...

yes, as justice and necessity require. Would it be better to heap even more on to the non-privileged, the people? There will be loud squeals ... that was to be expected', etc. On Palm Sunday, 1 April, the *Avertissement* was read out from the pulpit by all the curés in Paris and distributed in large numbers in the provinces.

Yet this *appel au peuple*, as many notables, including Lafayette and Miromesnil, characterized it, fell strangely flat. Perhaps its ironical salon tone restricted its appeal. And what did Calonne expect the people to do – surround the Hotel des Menus Plaisirs? President Coeurderoi accused Calonne of wanting to 'cause the mob to riot against the notables in favour of his proposals' but noted with satisfaction that the 'people' were not 'taken in by his charlatanism', so that his actions 'served only to turn the notables and even all respectable society against him'.[76] The people were not prepared to turn out for the king, but by this appeal Louis contracted an engagement to help the people were he ever in a position to do so.

On 2 April, Castries bearded the king over the *Avertissement*:

Castries: I do not know if Your Majesty realizes what is going on, the way in which M. de Calonne's scandalous pamphlet has been distributed throughout Paris and the indignation it has caused?

Louis: Yes, I know all that has been exaggerated.

Castries: How can one exaggerate the seditious distribution of it to all the curés of Paris and dissemination of it among the people? Would Your Majesty not be alarmed to see his subjects worked up against each other? I must warn Your Majesty that things are going to get more and more difficult for him because of the increasing outcry against his controller-general.

Louis: All that is the work of intrigue.

Castries: But is it Your Majesty who is causing M. de Calonne to act so imprudently?

Louis: I have eight days.

The king's evasive 'I have eight days', in response to Castries's suggestion that Louis himself was the driving force behind Calonne's imprudence, refers to the recess of the Notables during Holy Week when it was rumoured that the king's opponents were to be imprisoned by *lettre de cachet*. Calonne wined and dined the provincial mayors furiously, believing them to be closest to the principal beneficiaries of his measures, the people.

Miromesnil also saw the king that day, coordinating his action with Castries.

Miromesnil: If Your Majesty had consulted me [before publishing the *Avertissement*] I would have taken the liberty of making a few observations.

Louis: I am old enough [he was thirty-three] to judge for myself; I read it and approved it.

Miromesnil: If that is the case then I have no more to say.

Louis: (a minute later) What are your reasons then? See what is said about the Notables at the end.[77]

Miromesnil: Since Your Majesty permits, may I ask him to consider the preceding phrase ... 'in the end patriotism and honour will win out'. So they haven't yet.

Louis: Maybe not.[78]

Miromesnil also accused Calonne of lying when he had said that there would be no increase in taxation except for the privileged: 'that is to deceive the people in your name'. 'That caused me pain', replied Louis, who entertained similar doubts himself. Castries noted contemptuously, 'the king listened to all this about his controller-general, appeared to feel no ill will towards the man who said it, did not disown him [Calonne] and retains him'.[79] In the evening, Miromesnil called on Calonne and gained the impression that he wanted to dissolve the Assembly prematurely.

Miromesnil was mistaken. For at this time Calonne presented the king with a long memorandum descriptively entitled, 'Prospectus de ce qui reste à faire et de la marche à suivre pour terminer l'opération' ('Prospectus of what remains to be done and the steps to be taken to bring to a conclusion the business of the Assembly').[80] It was the last attempt by Calonne to prevent his programme and ministerial career from being submerged by the tide of opposition the *Avertissement* had unleashed.

Calonne proposed submitting his evidence in refutation of Necker's *Compte rendu* to twenty-one hand-picked notables. He also proposed some concessions to them: 'The organization of the provincial assemblies would preserve the distinction of ranks, as the notables desired' and the land tax would be paid in money unless a particular province asked to pay in kind. The king would then attend the closing session 'not later than the 30th of the month'. Votes would be taken in reverse order of precedence, starting with the mayors, who would be sure to approve the proposals and 'who would be followed by all the others, or at least the great majority, and the opinions could be collected very quickly'. 'If,' however, 'the issue appeared to be doubtful, one could close the Assembly after the résumé without taking votes and with a phrase from king dismissing the Notables.'[81]

In the *Prospectus*, Calonne fleshed out the idea of central treasury control, to which he had alluded in his opening speech of 22 February. He proposed the amalgamation of all the separate treasuries of the various ministries and lesser spending agencies into a single royal treasury, to be housed in the Louvre. The financial role of the treasurers and head clerks would pass to a 'chef de bureau' for each department, who would sit in 'adjacent' rooms in the Louvre with his staff and receive money from the central treasury *ad hoc*. Calonne reminds the king that he has 'yet to give his decision' to the principle of a central treasury. One can see why: Louis could hardly have warmed to his minister's approving references to English accounting practices, especially since these presented a further possibility: Calonne sitting in the Louvre together with a sizeable chunk of the royal bureaucracy would have been the equivalent of a first lord of the treasury.

So pressure on the king was now building, both from Calonne and from Calonne's enemies. Calonne had proposed writing a letter to Necker 'asking him to defend himself before the Assembly of Notables or before anyone of his choice'. The king had been furious, exclaiming that 'he did not want that scamp appearing in the Assembly'. Instead, he told Calonne to write to Necker's successor, Joly de Fleury, for his views on the *Compte rendu*,[82] which Calonne did. Calonne made no objection, since Joly had discovered the falsity of the *Compte rendu* soon after taking office. However, Joly had been stung by Calonne's references to his administration in his opening speech and now denied that there had been a deficit when he had taken office. Calonne sat on this information, but, by a masterstroke of revenge, Joly sent Miromesnil a copy of the correspondence in the sure knowledge that he would bring it up with the king. Miromesnil told Louis that 'M. de Fleury asserts that he very much doubts that there was a deficit when you entrusted him with the administration of the finances, as he has recently indicated to M. de Calonne'.

Miromesnil went on to say that when he and Vergennes had gone through Calonne's figures they had lacked the necessary expertise – a fine time to make such a confession – and that some impartial experts should be consulted, 'since M. de Calonne should not fear the light of truth from whatever source it comes'. He concluded this, his last letter to the king as a minister, with a section portraying Calonne in opposition to the whole establishment:

> I fear that he wants you to dismiss the Assembly without concluding anything and perhaps without giving it the time to present you with its final observations.

I see that he is trying to turn you against the bishops, against the nobles, against your ministers. He is making a kind of appeal to the people which may have dangerous consequences. Finally I see alarming consequences for your happiness and for the rest of your reign.[83]

On Maundy Thursday, 5 April, Louis confronted Calonne with Joly's correspondence. But Calonne replied with an ultimatum, the third Louis had received from a minister, the other two being from Necker.[84] Calonne told Louis that he 'had to decide whether to dismiss [Miromesnil] or himself' because 'It was hardly surprising that the Notables rejected everything ... when they were supported ... by a faction in the ministry'.[85] Calonne supported his demand with police evidence that Miromesnil had been conspiring with d'Aligre and other *parlementaires*. He even 'claimed that the pamphlets decrying his operations with which the notables were inundated were printed under his [Miromesnil's] auspices'.[86] The king made no difficulties, for he had a list of grievances of his own against Miromesnil: the rebellious conduct in the Assembly of his reputed bastard son de Néville, intendant of Guyenne, Miromesnil's specious letters; but above all the king blamed him for his advice not to send the stamp tax and lease of the crown lands before the *parlement* before the meeting of the Notables, which rendered him dependent on the Assembly.[87]

In his terrible isolation (the phrase is Castries's) Louis had no one he could turn to. Vergennes was dead and Louis is said to have wept at his grave, lamenting 'he would have spared me all this'. He believed his policies to be right – and many historians would agree – yet they had been universally rejected. He had appealed beyond the political elite to the people; there had been no flicker of a response. He believed that the intendants, who were to have a supervisory role over the provincial assemblies, were 'the best part of my system', and few historians would dissent from this view either, but no one had defended them among the notables; indeed, some intendants had even spoken against the institution themselves.[88] He could only turn to Calonne.

'Calonne, alone with the king at Versailles, conceived the audacious plan' – Castries is writing – 'of overthrowing the ministry and filling it with ministers of his own choice'.[89] For Calonne had accused not just Miromesnil but a 'faction within the ministry' of orchestrating opposition among the notables. Calonne's main ally in the *parlement*, Lamoignon, was to be keeper of the seals, Lenoir to replace Breteuil at the *Maison du Roi*, Puységur to replace Ségur at the war ministry and Admiral d'Estaing, who had outspokenly defended the *Avertissement*, was to replace Castries. Only Montmorin, the new foreign secretary, would be left standing.

Castries and the queen could see no further than Calonne's 'detestation' of Miromesnil and 'malignity' towards Breteuil. Marie-Antoinette's essentially trivial mind could not get beyond personalities and see that Calonne was advocating a new principle: that ministerial unity in order to get the king's business through a hostile assembly should replace the old notion of maintaining division among the ministers to preserve the king's independence of action. Calonne was running great risks and, as had happened in England, felt he had the right to ask for a ministry of his choice – to be in effect a prime minister in the English sense, as the prospectus had implied. The pressure of an assembly forced Louis at last to contemplate making such an appointment. Louis agreed not only to dismiss Miromesnil but to replace him with Lamoignon, who was informed by Calonne's private courier.

Next we learn from Lenoir, who was to have succeeded him, that Breteuil 'was dismissed momentarily and the order had been given to M. de Montmorin to go and ask him for his resignation as well as M. de Miromesnil's' – Montmorin's agency was necessary because the minister for the *Maison* could not exile himself. 'Then the queen caused the part of the order concerning M. de Breteuil to be revoked.' The queen ranted and raved and 'would not leave the king until she had saved M. de Breteuil and overthrown the controller-general'.[90] Marie-Antoinette had not forgotten Calonne's role in the Diamond Necklace Affair.

Calonne told the English diplomat, Lord Holland, that he had complained to the king that the queen was openly criticizing his projects. Louis's 'immediate reaction was to shrug his shoulders at the idea that the queen (a *woman* as he called her) was capable of forming or venturing an opinion on this matter'. But when Calonne insisted that this was indeed the case, Louis summoned her on the spot and told her not to meddle in men's affairs. Then, to the amazement of Calonne, he 'took her shoulders and frog-marched her out of the room like a naughty child'. Calonne was appalled and 'said to himself, "I am undone"'. As Calonne's biographer observes, he 'had the misfortune to witness a scene such as no woman, let alone Marie-Antoinette, could forgive'.[91]

At the end of his life Calonne told Napoleon that he had been brought down by 'an abominable intrigue encouraged by the woman who should have been the first to defend my endeavours and promised to do so'.[92] The first part of Calonne's assertion was true, the latter typical of his wishful thinking – Marie-Antoinette had made no such promise. Later, however, she confessed that her opposition to Calonne had been a grave mistake. At the time Besenval accused her of 'protecting the mutiny of the notables', to which she replied: 'No, I was completely neutral', earning Besenval's rebuke: 'C'était déjà trop!' – 'In such circumstances being neutral is not enough ... You should be in no doubt,

Madame, that the king's *gloire* or discredit will always redound on you.'[93] Pressed by Mercy-Argenteau, she was working to bring Brienne into the ministry.

Calonne fought tooth and nail to preserve the king's confidence, never once leaving Versailles, despite the fact that, as Brienne observed, the attractions of Easter in Paris would in normal circumstances have proved irresistible to a sybarite like Calonne. His doctor had told him never to let the king out of his sight. It remained to be seen whether this advice would prove better than the blister cure he had prescribed in January. Similarly, Calonne's enemy Miromesnil could not even take time off to see his daughter, who was dying on his estate just a few miles away.[94] They could have given themselves up to their respective pleasures and grief, for Louis never saw a minister he was thinking of dismissing. Calonne had been unable to see the king since Thursday the 5th. He had tried to see him on Saturday and Sunday morning, employing the services of their common friend, d'Angiviller, but to no avail. When the king refused a second time, 'alleging his Easter devotions', Calonne knew the game was up.[95]

And the king was fooling them all. No order of appointment or dismissal had been made. Louis was waiting for a reply to a letter. On Good Friday, the 6th, the day after agreeing to Lamoignon's appointment, Louis took time off from his 'Easter devotions' to offer the finance ministry to Chaumont de la Millière, the intendant of bridges and roads. He told him that the 'good of his service' required that he dismiss Calonne, but that he had

> absolutely no intention of withdrawing the plans for the amelioration of the finances which I caused to be presented to the Assembly of Notables; I intend to prosecute the execution of the measures with firmness [that word again], whilst allowing such reasonable changes as [the notables'] representations may present.

He would take personal charge of seeing these measures through to the statute book:

> my intention is to assemble a committee of the council over which I will regularly preside. Here the representations [of the notables] will be discussed and here I will decide what answer to make to them and the manner of implementing the plans.

Chaumont's role 'at this present juncture' would be confined to 'examining the state of the funds in the royal treasury and with maintaining funding in the interval before the reforms kick in'. As regards the reform programme, the king would be his own minister. Calonne had exploited the fact that the king had 'made the measures his own'. So be it. Louis concluded the letter: 'Give me your reply, Monsieur, through the same channel and keep my secret until I tell you otherwise.'[96] But that night Louis 'felt so frustrated and angry that he didn't want any supper and went to bed at nine o'clock. The queen wept in a corner of her husband's chamber.'[97]

It seems that Chaumont did not respect the king's request for secrecy, for Castries, Brienne and his brother, the comte de Brienne, refer to it in their diaries almost immediately. These three were important members of the opposition and it is possible that Chaumont was sounding out support. From Paris Chaumont replied to the king the next day, Saturday 7 April, asking for an audience during which he would quickly be able to demonstrate that he would be 'betraying the trust of Your Majesty if I were to accept a post whose duties I am absolutely incapable of fulfilling'.[98] This audience took place on the evening of Easter Sunday, 8 April; Chaumont needed only a quarter of an hour to convince the king 'that he was just about able to run his two departments, but that he had no grasp of the ensemble [i.e., finance and home affairs] and he had a sort of incapacity for figures'.[99] The queen, on whom Louis was increasingly relying as the crisis deepened, was also present.

This left Louis without a finance minister in the middle of the biggest crisis of his reign, for he decided to press ahead with the dismissal of Calonne in any case. At 10 p.m. he gave Montmorin – the only minister present at Versailles, and the only one standing above the fray – two letters of dismissal, one for Miromesnil and one for Calonne. In the morning Montmorin went to see Miromesnil in Paris and was at first denied admission because Miromesnil's daughter had just died. Montmorin had already informed Calonne on Easter Sunday night. The wags said he had died on the Day of Resurrection. Calonne was intrigued to know who his successor might be. Was it Necker? No, replied Montmorin. Or Brienne? Same answer. Or Néville? No again, and no more questions! He did, however, add 'that he was authorized to say that his successor would not be displeasing to him and that he would not be the only one dismissed'.[100]

That successor was the *conseiller d'état* Bouvard de Fourqueux. Calonne had entrusted to him the drafting of the proposals of the third division, on the royal domain, so that his appointment perfectly reflected Louis's desire for continuity and was certainly 'not displeasing' to his predecessor. The king let Bouvard de Fourqueux know 'that he would not brook a refusal'. This was backed up by a lecture from Montmorin. Castries notes that Bouvard, 'who knows only profound submission to the king's orders reluctantly accepts and presents to the public merely a man of straw'. Castries's belief that obedience to the king is matter for criticism is typical of the man. Castries added that Bouvard's appointment 'proves that nothing is to be expected from the king's reflection'. Yet the intellect of Bouvard, preferred as his successor by Turgot, the greatest French economist of the century, was far greater than Castries's. Whatever the causes of the French Revolution, the intellectual incapacity of the king and his ministers was not one of them.[101]

On 15 April Calonne received a letter from Montmorin which, though formulated in a polite if slightly sinister vein, constituted an internal exile under strict conditions:

> The king, who knows, Monsieur, that you intend to proceed to Hannonville [Calonne's estate in Lorraine] as soon as you have handed over to your successor the memoranda [of the fourth division] with the explanatory notes that His Majesty has ordered you to give him, considers that as soon as you have done this you should effect your planned departure; and just as at Berny [Calonne's estate near Paris] you only wished to receive a few of your relatives and close friends, he counts on your also following this course at Hannonville, where you will reside until further orders.[102]

Calonne was to brief his successor and then depart to the eastern frontier, as far away from Versailles as possible. As with Rohan's exile, the distance was finely calibrated to match the depth of disgrace.

The duc de Luxembourg wrote that Calonne 'took with him the regrets and friendship of the monarch and the worries of a business that he alone could see through'.[103] The first part is true – exile was just a systemic cruelty – but Louis had taken Calonne at his word: since he had made the reform plans his own, perhaps the only way of implementing them, given Calonne's unpopularity, was to ditch the pilot and steer the ship to harbour himself, as d'Angiviller had suggested. This is precisely what he told Chaumont that he was going to do; and the period of Bouvard's brief ministry (9 April–1 May) was that of the king's greatest involvement in the day-to-day running of government; for though Bouvard was not a straw man, he was a sick one, suffering from gout and dyspepsia. Louis had told Chaumont that he would take personal charge of relations between the government and the notables, presiding regularly over the necessary *comités*.

This he did, with a committee every day, sometimes more,[104] and there was more of a sense of cabinet government than in the Calonne phase of the

Assembly, though Castries and Ségur were not consulted. Relations between the king and Castries remained execrable, largely because of Castries's relationship with Necker. Castries had been ill in bed in Paris, but after recovering, he stayed on for a further three days as a silent protest at being excluded from the decision-making process. He only returned to Versailles when the king dropped him a note saying, that 'he would be very put out if he continued his absence and that he was required not only for the council but for the *comité* which preceded it'.[105]

The return to cabinet government, however, did not lead to unified policy. As he was to do with the National Assembly during the Revolution, Louis now pursued conjointly twin policies in relation to the Assembly of Notables, with separate sets of agents at his disposal. One policy, backed by Bouvard, Dupont and Lamoignon, was to dissolve the Assembly of Notables before the situation degenerated further with demands for the accounts and for institutional limitations on the king's power. The reform edicts would then be presented simultaneously to the *parlements* for registration by *lit de justice*, whatever the degree of endorsement by the notables. These 'hawks' were all ex-Calonne men. That is why Calonne had to be exiled. The 'doves', represented by Montmorin and Breteuil, Castries and Ségur, argued that it would be unseemly and counterproductive to dismiss the Assembly before its mission had been accomplished and that the chances of the *parlements* registering the edicts would be less than if the Assembly had never been convoked in the first place.

On one occasion the question of dissolving the Assembly was put to a vote in the ministerial committee. Bouvard and Lamoignon were for dissolution and Montmorin and Breteuil against, employing the arguments presented above. The convention was that the king should abide by a majority vote, whatever his own opinion, unless there was a tie, when he had the casting vote. Louis inclined towards the 'doves' but he did not want to take the responsibility for the decision.[106] So he took the extraordinary step of summoning Ségur, who was out of favour and whose dismissal was rumoured, to ask him to vote, knowing full well that he would vote for continuing the Assembly and presenting the memoranda of the fourth division.[107]

The appointment of Loménie de Brienne

At the same time, and without consulting his ministers, the king made epistolary contact with Brienne: their exchange of memoranda amounted to a negotiation for his entry into the ministry. Louis's marginal comments on Brienne's first memorandum, dated 18 April, and his own memorandum would be sufficient in themselves to dispel the notion that the king was stupid and ill-informed.[108] His remarks are precise, clear, at times sardonic, and display a thorough mastery of the complex financial and administrative issues involved. Brienne says the king must be absolutely sure that an extra 70 million *livres* of taxation are necessary and receives the sharp rejoinder: 'Naturally the king is far from desiring such a load of taxation if it is not necessary; on the contrary, he would be delighted to lower existing taxation; but remember what is said at the beginning of the [Calonne's] memorandum about palliatives being worse than the disease.'

Furthermore, even if the new land tax were to bring in more money than was needed, the answer was not to reduce *its* yield but that of the less equitable and efficient taxes, such as the *taille* and the *corvée*. Brienne naïvely suggests that money can be saved by lowering the rate of interest on government stock and is wearily reminded: 'Of course there is a substantial saving to me made by lowering the rate of interest but that can only be done when your credit is good and when you have enough money to dictate terms to the market' ('pour faire la loi aux capitalistes'). Louis, again wearily and, as it turned out, accurately, suggests that Brienne's estimate of what economies can be effected is wildly optimistic: 'All in all, you'll be lucky to save twenty million without retrenching on the army and navy.' The navy was sacrosanct; Louis eventually agreed to reduce the army estimates by a derisory 8 million *livres*.

Louis's comments, however, were not entirely negative. What he was trying to do with this man, who seemed to be able to manipulate the Assembly, was salvage as much as possible of the programme of reforms. He conceded that the presidency of the provincial assemblies would always go to the clergy or nobility, but the third estate was to have as many members as the other two combined and voting was to be individual rather than a block vote by order – a ruling little remarked upon at the time. Louis was able to insist that the powers of the intendant remain substantially those envisaged by Calonne. The amount brought in by the land tax would be raised from the 54 million *livres* brought in by the existing two *vingtièmes* to about 80 million; it would not be open-ended but the Assembly might 'examine ways of establishing equality on a given base that could be increased or diminished according to recognized needs' – to allow for inflation or a new war. The amount paid by the clergy would be worked out in the provincial assemblies, but its collection would be left to clerical officials.

On Brienne's advice, though he was not yet a minister, the king, accompanied by the king of arms and four heralds,[109] re-opened the Assembly in person on 23 April. He made the concessions hammered out with Brienne and indeed

Louis lifted his speech almost verbatim from one of Brienne's memoranda.[110] But despite ministerial pressure, Louis refused to impose significant economies – only 15 million where even Calonne had mentioned 20 million, though he said he would demolish his châteaux of La Muette and Choisy and had already given orders to remove the furniture.[111] The announcement that La Muette and Choisy would be sold only led to a demand for a moratorium on the king's entire building work, including the new harbour at Cherbourg; though others thought that this should be covered by a special loan paying 10 per cent.

Given the king's mood, the fate of the Assembly of Notables stood on a knife edge again. Louis had gone along with Brienne's advice to the extent of using his very words in his speech and he expected tangible results from what he considered to be major concessions. He gave the notables financial statements in confidence and they leaked them to the underground press. Louis's anger was fanned by Lamoignon and Bouvard. According to Brienne, Bouvard 'told anyone who cared to listen that the king was anxious to rid himself of the Assembly'. On 27 April there was another ministerial *comité* to discuss the future of the Assembly, but this time the king inclined to dissolution. An initiate notes on that date, 'I learned from an unimpeachable source [Montmorin] that there was a *comité chez le roi* to prevent him from acting intemperately ['prendre de l'humeur']'[112] – in other words, dissolving the Assembly.

The same day there was a further ministerial *comité*. Panic was beginning to take hold. Government stocks had been falling for weeks. Lamoignon showed Brienne a letter from the keeper of the royal treasury, saying 'that he was at his wits' end and that there was only a week's supply of money left'.[113] Brienne's journal entry for 30 April notes that 'the stock market goes from bad to worse'. With these words Brienne closed his diary: he had no time for it since the king appointed him, on 1 May, *chef du Conseil royal des finances*, the largely honorary title enjoyed by Maurepas and later Vergennes, the leading ministers of the reign.

Brienne's appointment was logical in some ways, and surprising in others. Logical, because he had already written the king's 'speech from the throne' on 23 April. But the very fact that the king mechanically transcribed, word for word, what Brienne intended only as ideas perhaps suggests that Louis was already assuming what would be his revolutionary mode of behaviour – distancing himself from the acts of his ministers. Moreover, Brienne's own stock was sinking: on 28 April even his ally, Boisgelin, observed that he 'was master neither of his own bureau nor the Assembly'.[114] The opinion of Pierre Chevallier, who published the negotiations between the king and Brienne, was that the archbishop's proposals were slipshod and dishonest in their optimism and that Louis quickly saw through them.[115]

Allied to this dawning realization that Brienne might not be able to deliver what he had promised, Louis had personal and professional reasons not to appoint him. He did not like prelate-ministers, partly because he believed they should reside in their dioceses curing souls, but also because, if they became cardinals, they would take precedence in council. Moreover, the king disliked Brienne's manners: Castries relates that Louis was offended by Brienne's habit of resting his elbows on the council table, though he was himself too polite to say anything. As for Brienne's health, it was scarcely better than Bouvard's; he was confined to a diet of bread and milk and was so covered with eczema that the king had to have all documents emanating from him dusted.[116]

So why did the king appoint him? Louis told Brienne quite candidly, when he asked that Necker be made finance minister under him, 'that he [Brienne] had only been appointed to avoid Necker'.[117] Seeing Bouvard's ministry collapsing, his colleagues, Lamoignon, Montmorin and Breteuil, had been pressing Necker's candidacy on the king. Louis, worn down rather than persuaded, had finally said: 'Oh well, I suppose there is nothing for it then, we'll just have to recall him.' But he said it so sadly and so irritably that Breteuil was able to have Brienne appointed instead. Louis warned them all that Brienne was ambitious and restless and that they might live to regret the choice.[118] Once again Louis's Cassandra-like qualities came into play: within four months Castries and Ségur would resign rather than serve on Brienne's terms, to be followed by Breteuil a year later.

Brienne was sometimes described as the leader of the opposition in the Assembly and, if he had been, there would have been a logic in the king's appointing him. However, the real leader of the opposition, albeit *in absentia*, was Necker. The only way Louis XVI could have placated the notables would have been by appointing him. They would then have endorsed a programme which would have been registered by the *parlements*. However, it would have been an aristocratic caricature of Calonne's proposals, a perversion or inversion which would have resulted in the English-style constitution Necker and his courtier allies had always wanted.

This is clear from the diary of Castries, Necker's ally and 'openly the patron of the *frondeurs*'.[119] 'The truth of the matter is', he notes, 'that there was such a momentum in the bureaux [of the Notables] to give rise to the fear that they would demand the appointment of M. Necker'. 'The mood' in the bureaux, he adds, 'tends to restrain authority in such a way that monarchical government will no longer be able to reconstitute itself'. Castries, who 'has known the public mood for a long time realized this from the . . . day' the Assembly opened, and considered that institutional restraint on government 'will give the people the security of not having to give the sweat of their labours to an implacable master'.[120] Such venom from a minister of the crown! And where had the 'sweat of their labours' gone? On Castries's overspending department.

Necker, however, was in exile. Just as there had been the joint dismissals of Calonne and Miromesnil, so there had been the joint exiles, on the same day, 13 April, of Calonne and Necker. Louis had both an ostensible and an underlying reason for the exile of Necker. The ostensible reason was Necker's publication, despite the king's formal prohibition delivered through Castries, of his defence against Calonne's attacks. Necker's pamphlet carried neither author nor title but began, 'I was a minister of the crown for five years'. Necker had it printed but kept it under wraps. He read it out in Madame de Buffon's salon and she advised delaying publication at least until the end of the Assembly.[121] But, such was Necker's hubris, he also sent a copy to the king and queen. Marie-Antoinette received a covering letter blandly assuming that the king would not take this 'defence of his honour and reputation amiss'. She did not reply, but when Louis told her to forbid Necker from publishing, she refused.[122]

Then, on 10 April, with incomparably bad timing, not realizing that Calonne had been dismissed on the 8th, Necker released the edition. As with his 1781 resignation, he realized his mistake too late. 'M. Necker', Brienne notes, 'is desolated that the disgrace of the minister should have preceded the publication . . . [saying] "no one is more put out than me [Necker] by the timing of M. de Calonne's dismissal"'.[123] By the time of Brienne's appointment, Necker's pain had subsided sufficiently for him to affect philosophy. His daughter, Madame de Staël, recorded with filial piety the pious words of Necker on hearing, from his exile, of Brienne's appointment: 'Please God this new ministry may serve the state better than I could have done! It is already an enormous undertaking in the present circumstances; but soon it will surpass the strength of anyone'. His daughter commented with the benefit of hindsight, 'there were still [in 1787] enough resources to save the state from a revolution, or at least the government could have ridden the tiger'.[124]

Castries was summoned to the royal presence over Necker's publication and subjected to a series of outbursts: 'He has published his book without my orders. He has published a letter he wrote to me when it would have been good manners to notify even a private citizen. . . . He has cast doubt on my justice when I told you I would look into the whole matter.' This last particularly rankled with the king, who was sensitive to accusations of unjust action when he had punished cardinal de Rohan despite his acquittal by the *parlement*. Necker was exiled outside a radius of twenty leagues (sixty miles) from Paris. (One can imagine Louis getting out his compasses.) Only the intervention of the queen, arguing the illness of Necker's wife and the pregnancy of his daughter, had prevented Louis from sending Necker clean out of the country and back to Geneva.

However, the deeper reason for the exile was that the king wanted Necker out of the way whilst the Notables were in session. This Louis admitted to Castries on 4 May when he agreed that Necker could return to Paris 'when my business is finished'. When Castries raised a quizzical eyebrow, the king explained, 'after the Assembly'.[125] The king would not be pressurized by the Assembly into appointing the man who, he believed, had destabilized his government for the past six years. This motive was confirmed when on 4 June, a week after the end of the Assembly, and without informing Castries, Louis told Breteuil to notify Necker that he could return to Paris. Castries, believing he should have been the first to be informed, confided to his diary that 'it would be too distasteful to serve such a master if one were serving him alone and not the state as well'.[126]

The end of the Assembly of Notables

The last weeks of the Assembly of Notables lack the drama of the Calonne phase. Yet it was a period of greater danger for the monarchy. In the Calonne phase the objectives of the notables had been negative: to defeat his plans and (if not before the *Avertissement* then certainly after) to drive him from office and even to put him on trial. Boisgelin wanted to have him hanged. Their victory in at least the first two aims emboldened them to pursue a counter-offensive. They now sought institutional checks on the king's activity. The most dangerous demands were those for regular meetings of Assemblies of Notables and for a finance committee to supplement/replace the shadowy *Conseil royal des finances*, which seldom met. The *chef* of the *Conseil royal*, who was Brienne, would preside over the new body, but its composition might include representatives of the *parlements*, chosen by them and not by the king, and lay members from outside the administration. These would be chosen by the king but designated by public opinion, a very Neckerian concept which would have led to a further articulation of the society of orders which was now set to dominate the provincial assemblies.

The committee would meet at least twice a year to examine the state of the treasury. It would draw up a prospective budget at the start of every year and, at the end of the year, audit the final accounts, which would be published. Ministers would be bound by this budget unless they obtained dispensation from the committee – the signature of the king or controller-general would no longer be sufficient. No financial operation could take place without having been examined by the committee and no loan raised without registration by the *parlement* and without an indication of the collateral for its repayment. The finance committee might have served as a permanent committee of the Assembly of Notables supervising the king between sessions.

This was the notables' reasoning: believing (or affecting to believe) that Necker's *Compte rendu* was accurate, it seemed to follow that Calonne, with the king's connivance or lack of supervision, had squandered a lot of money. They had uncovered evidence of where some of this money might have gone and how it could be concealed by the 'exemptions from audit'. Money had gone on supporting the stock market and on buying or exchanging the estates of favourite courtiers, or of distressed ones such as the Rohan family. Even Vergennes had been a beneficiary. Larger sums had gone on paying the debts of the king's two brothers, and the king himself had been extravagant.

These abuses contributed only a tiny portion to the deficit – the main culprit was the navy – but to the suspicious minds of the notables there seemed to be an inescapable logic to the sequence: the *Compte rendu* is accurate; there is a large deficit; one-sixth of royal expenditure is unaudited; therefore the evidence of fraud we have uncovered must be the tip of the iceberg; therefore institutional steps must be taken to prevent a recurrence. 'But', as one observer put it, 'if the king acquiesced in all the Assembly's demands, he would be put in tutelage'. 'So what', was the answer, 'isn't he a minor' who must be restrained from 'committing the same faults again'?[127]

Louis did not accept this analysis: the *Compte rendu* was demonstrably fraudulent, his brothers had debts because (unlike all their predecessors) they had not been given a sovereign estate (*appanage*) to support their dignity; the stock market had to be supported during a political crisis; but perhaps, with the benefit of hindsight, buying Rambouillet for himself and Saint-Cloud for the queen had been a little foolish. So he refused to grant a finance committee independent of his control.

Given the king's reluctance to make what they regarded as meaningful concessions, the notables were equally reluctant to give unequivocal backing to his proposals, even though these had met many of their previous demands. As Castries put it, 'they enveloped their half-acceptance in so many words that those who refused and those who accepted are indistinguishable and one has to unravel their opinions in fifty pages of print'. And this was likely to be insufficient to overawe the *parlement* when the government came to present the measures for registration. The Assembly of Notables was dismissed on 25 May 1787. It ended in disaster for its architect, Calonne, and its sponsor, the king.

The onset of Louis's depression

Not only was Louis forced to dismiss Calonne, he was forced to do so by an assembly – the first of the Revolution – whose 'leader of the opposition', Brienne, became the head of government. Brienne himself said 'there is some glory in regarding the fall of the minister as satisfaction due to the Assembly'.[128] Yet never, perhaps, since the days of Richelieu, had a king so publicly identified himself with his minister. As Mercy wrote to Joseph II on 19 May: 'The king's authority is all the more grievously compromised by the abandonment of the former controller-general in that the latter's plans had been so openly approved by the king that he had scarcely left himself any way of disowning him.'

This was an embarrassing situation for the ministers, for an 'absolute' monarch of sorts was still required. The fiction that the king's religion had been surprised by an evil adviser was not enough; the king had actually to believe it; his 'dear' controller was transformed into his 'expensive' controller. Louis had to be re-educated, as he had when he recalled the *parlement* in 1774, and this would affect his mood. The clerical mind of Brienne was ideal for the task. Calonne was accused of peculation on a heroic scale – the difference between Necker's *Compte rendu* and his own: 4 billion *livres*. A commission was set up to investigate his administration and prevent the recurrence of such 'abuses'; Calonne wrote bitterly: 'In M. d'Ormesson, who has not been brought into this *comité* without design, they are sure of having a *rapporteur* who has thoroughly made up his mind against me in advance.'[129] And though honest d'Ormesson ultimately exonerated him, it came too late for Calonne.[130]

On 17 June Brienne wrote to Calonne:

Far be it from me to disturb the repose you have planned for yourself. However, you cannot be ignorant of the fact that considerable sums of money have left the royal treasury without the king's authorization; you do not know what became of them and you should not be surprised by His Majesty's displeasure. It would have been wrong for me to conceal from him that of which the interest of his service requires that he be informed; and, as there is no doubt, I have not sought clarification from you.[131]

The money to which Brienne refers was spent supporting the Bourse at the critical juncture of the meeting of the Notables, a task made doubly difficult because Breteuil was supporting a syndicate of 'bear' speculators. Calonne admits to d'Angiviller that, under pressure of work, he had not always observed all the accounting formalities, though most of his predecessors had used such *acquits de comptant*.

If it had not been for Brienne's earlier assurances, he would have sent the king a memorandum defending his administration:

> I have every confidence in the king's justice. No one knows him better than I and when I can be heard no one will submit himself with greater abandon to his judgment and his virtues. He knows better than anyone what I have done for his service, why I have done it and to what I exposed myself in doing it . . . but I hurl defiance at the prelate-minister who has rent my heart by wresting the king's esteem from me . . . and I scorn the hatred of his organization [the clergy] to which he is not strongly attached but would happily sacrifice me.

Calonne perceptively observed that his enemies needed to treat him as a criminal in order to justify 'surprising the king's religion'. The last use of the old formula was also its least conventional. The forcing of the king's mind was symbolized by Calonne's having not only to resign from the order of the Saint-Esprit but to return the insignia to the king, including the star set in diamonds presented to him by the Dutch after the conclusion of the 1785 alliance. Amelot, former minister of the *Maison du Roi*, had the unenviable task of asking Calonne for the insignia, Breteuil having been denied or having forgone the pleasure. Amelot broke through layers of protocol to say, 'I cannot adequately express the pain I feel at being instructed to announce such devastating news to you.'[132] The only other occasion on which such an extreme step had been contemplated – and rejected as suggesting too much 'disorder' in the finances – had been when Terray had been dismissed in 1774, when also the mind of the king had been forced.

Calonne left France, which meant exile proper. 'How can I remain in this kingdom', he wrote, 'where by this rigorous treatment [being stripped of the insignia] I seem to be treated as a criminal?' He retired, first to Holland, then, in August, to England, which he hated. In his absence he was impeached by the *parlement*. On learning that Calonne had left the country, Louis said sadly: 'He need not have worried, I would certainly not have allowed him to be harassed.'[133]

Calonne's friends, however, stuck by him: Artois and the Polignacs worked assiduously for his recall. Calonne's mistress, Madame de Chabannes, of the Talleyrand clan, followed him to Lorraine, breaking the conditions of Calonne's strict exile. When he crossed the Channel, she 'did not blush at looking him up in London'. When she asked for the king's consent through Breteuil, the minister for exiles, Louis replied: 'She can go and f--- herself'. 'I take it then', replied M. de Breteuil, 'that I can tell Mme de Chabannes that Your Majesty grants her request'. Nevertheless, on her return, she was forbidden to appear at court. Calonne had gone to London to write his defence against Necker. In February 1788 the Paris police impounded 400 copies.[134]

The sinister way in which Louis's mind had been worked against the man in whom he had put his trust, much as it had been worked against Maupeou, coupled with the defeat and denigration of his cherished plans and the blows to his authority all wrought a profound change in the king. It is from this time that people note an insouciance about affairs in him, an apathy which is often engendered by depression. His hunting increased perceptibly: whereas in the early period of the Assembly it had been infrequent, in the fortnight after Calonne's fall he hunted on 11, 14, 16, 19, 21 and 24 April.[135] During one of these hunts he was discovered alone, sobbing in a forest glade, his face bathed in tears. Mercy writes to Joseph II on 14 August: 'Against such ills the king's low morale offers few resources and his physical habits diminish these more and more; he becomes stouter and his returns from hunting are followed by such immoderate meals that there are occasional lapses of reason and a kind of brusque thoughtlessness which is very painful for those who have to endure it.'

On 19 May Mercy reports that Louis comes to the queen's apartments every day and weeps at the critical state of the kingdom. This is in marked contrast with Louis's extreme reluctance to discuss politics with Marie-Antoinette before 1787. Dependence is also frequently associated with depression. In short, most of the characteristics, good and bad, which are commonly attributed to Louis XVI – irresolution, dependence on Marie-Antoinette, sentimentality, kindness – emerge only after the Assembly of Notables, which marks the great watershed in his life and reign. The precise point at which the ancien régime ended and the Revolution began is a matter of debate, but in the history of Louis XVI the ancien régime ended with his decision to convoke the Notables and the Revolution began when he was forced to sacrifice Calonne.

Louis had received no support from his ministers, Miromesnil, Castries and Breteuil, who sided with the 'mutiny' of the notables. They had ceased to be the agents of the crown in its secular struggle with the nobility and had become an undifferentiated part of the privileged orders. If Vergennes had lived, he would probably have sacrificed Calonne, as he had earlier sacrificed d'Ormesson, rather than have him remain in office until his retention or dismissal was equally damaging to the monarchy; which would have been a safer if more ignoble outcome. Louis's Cassandra-like cynicism increased, typified by his warning that the ministers would live to regret the appointment of Brienne – as if there were prizes in politics for being right.

Louis had also been betrayed by the queen. But she lost her circle of friends. The Polignac group had remained loyal to Calonne and the king throughout. They were punished for their loyalty to the king by a period of exile. They spent two months in England, including six weeks taking the waters at Bath. As governess of the royal children it was something of a dereliction of duty on Madame de Polignac's part, compounded by the death of Louis's infant second daughter, Louise. News of this brought Madame de Polignac back and she returned to Versailles on 2 July.[136] On 17 July, the princesse de Robecq wrote to Calonne that 'it is very lucky that in your misfortune Mme de Polignac should have returned' and adds that she 'tells the queen every time she receives news of you: she wants to retain the right to speak to her about you'.[137] Relations with the favourite were patched up, but things were never the same and the split, represented at the ministerial level by the continuing rivalry between Breteuil and Calonne, was to weigh heavily on royalist reactions to the Revolution.

CHAPTER NINE

THE ROAD TO THE ESTATES-GENERAL

MAY 1787–MAY 1789

The ministry of Loménie de Brienne: May 1787 to August 1788

THE APPOINTMENT OF BRIENNE marks the beginning of Marie-Antoinette's sustained involvement in politics. Hitherto, that involvement had been fitful, tangential, concerned with personalities rather than policy, but Brienne was her protégé and she had to support him in default of a disheartened, confused and resentful king. She started attending ministerial *comités*; and her increased influence was noticed by the public. The diplomat Bombelles noted on 19 July 1788, when the crisis had deepened further:

> The archbishop . . . [Brienne] went to the Petit Trianon at nine o'clock in the evening. The king followed closely, but whilst the principal minister was closeted with the queen in her cabinet, the king remained in the salon. When the queen joined him there it was clear that she had been crying. Sadly her vexations have further to go and her true servants believe that she is bringing new ones on herself by having herself admitted to cabinet committees because since the public know that she takes part in them she is held responsible for all the harsh decisions taken there.

Though he pitied her, Bombelles thought she had only herself to blame because 'instead of remaining satisfied with the fine role of queen of France, she wanted to be its king as well'. As a diplomat, Bombelles also blamed her for trying to further her brother Joseph's expansionist ideas, and blamed her mother, Maria-Theresa, for placing her brood of feisty daughters on half the thrones of Europe with the same aim in view. Given that, until recently, Austria had been the national enemy, Marie-Antoinette should have bent over backwards not to interfere.[1]

These underlying causes were intensified by her reputation for flightiness and extravagance. Her unpopularity, already evident at the time of the Diamond Necklace Affair, became pronounced in the summer of 1787, when she was first called 'Madame Deficit': these two strands fused in the popular belief that she had a room at Versailles paved with diamonds. During disturbances in August 1787, Breteuil begged the king not to let her go to Paris.[2]

All the king's horses

Louis, too, was losing some of his popularity: Malesherbes, who had been minister of the *Maison du Roi* between 1775 and 1776 and was now recalled as a minister without portfolio to give general advice, thought the king was losing the propaganda war. He gave Louis a memorandum on economies. Whilst conceding that structural reform of the budget would take time and not make an immediate impact, he told Louis that he should have suppressed a host of useless offices the moment the notables had been dismissed, and curtailed his building programme and his excessive use of horses. 'There is no point concealing from the king', Malesherbes chides,

the surprise that the notables coming up from the provinces felt whilst hearing tell of an enormous deficit and at the same time beholding with their own eyes at Versailles, Paris and all around, buildings going up on all sides for the king's household and those of the princes; and when on top of this those who travelled via Compiègne, Fontainebleau and Rambouillet compared notes on the simultaneous constructions all at the same exorbitant cost.

Instead of making a big symbolic gesture at the end of the Assembly of Notables, 'all that was heard was the sale of a few horses which, so far from appeasing the public, served only to irritate them because they saw this merely as an accounting trick, just the usual replacement of horses no longer fit for service with better ones'. Trivial as it may seem to discuss the origins of the French Revolution in terms of horse-trading, we know from Castries's diary that the topic of new stables and horses was the subject of heated discussions in the council.

Why, Castries, asked when they were discussing the *parlement*'s remonstrances against financial legislation, did the king need 3,000 horses when Louis XIV had managed with 1,000? On 19 July Castries notes the following discussion in the council:

Duc de Nivernais: '... we cannot hide from Your Majesty that the public mood is bad.' 'But why so?' said the king. No one replying, [Castries] spoke up. 'Because the public views with some surprise that at the same time as Your Majesty prepares to place new burdens of taxation on the people, he makes no personal sacrifice; that whereas he has made a bad choice [of Calonne as minister] which has led to the ruin of his finances, he seems disposed to make his subjects pay the price; that his building continues on all sides ...'

And chief among these buildings he lists the 'ruinous' stable blocks at Rambouillet, Saint-Cloud, Saint-Germain and Sèvres. Whereas the king was erecting these grandiose edifices, 'Louis XIV had made do with an ordinary house'. The king testily replied, 'But I don't have too many horses for the summer and it seems to me that although one could retrench during the winter one really can't be buying and selling horses every six months.' Finally Brienne, realizing that there was no point flogging a dead horse, wound up this part of the discussion. Nevertheless, the number of horses (which were used for all forms of government transport) was reduced from 2,215 to 1,195.[3]

The general point that Malesherbes is making is that the king was, as we would say, bad at public relations and that in the new situation this mattered. Having described the provincial notables' goggle-eyed amazement at the king's building works and contrasted it with the talk of economy from both Calonne and Brienne, Malesherbes asks, 'How could ... [the notables] not have drawn the conclusion that it was for pleasure palaces that the *parlements* were being asked to register new taxes? And what sort of account would one expect these notables to give to their provinces of what they had witnessed during their sojourn at court?' And yet this was not an accurate picture, for 'in his heart of hearts the king really wanted to lighten the burden of taxes on his people'. 'But', Malesherbes continues, 'what is deplorable is that the public either does not believe it or considers that the king's good intentions will have no effect'.

The other ministers who, according to Malesherbes, 'sincerely desired a serious reduction in expenditure' encouraged him to write his memorandum and 'spare no blushes'. He presented it to the king just before a council meeting – the only opportunity he got – and Louis 'received it graciously. I know that he read it carefully, but he never spoke of it to me again'. The reason: 'I believe that it was the premier minister's policy that I should have no private conversations with the king.'[4]

Brienne promoted

In his state of apathetic depression, Louis was induced to appoint Brienne, on 26 August 1787, *ministre principal,* a form of words designed to spare the king's susceptibilities, since he had declared that he would never have a *premier ministre.* Brienne was not given a formal *brevet* of appointment,[5] but on 27 August a circular letter informed each minister that 'the present situation demanding that there should be a common centre in the ministry to which all parts relate, I have chosen the archbishop of Toulouse as my *ministre principal*... consequently my intention is that you give him prior notification of important matters about which I need to be informed either by you and him together or in your *travail* with me.'[6] In this way a position painfully worked out by trial and error over thirteen years was codified in an almost casual way as a response to a crisis. But it was not to endure, since the constitution of 1791, with its obsession of pinning down individual responsibility, outlawed the post of prime minister.

Castries and Ségur took the opportunity to resign. Personal relations between the king and Castries had remained bad and, on Brienne's advice, Louis had rejected Castries's plea for armed intervention in the Netherlands to repel the threatened Anglo-Prussian invasion: 'Present the idea of *la gloire* to Frenchmen and you will affect the most useful ... diversion from the present turmoil. Give the appearance of necessity to taxation, the mood will calm and perhaps you will see government recapture a part of what it is ready to lose.'[7]

All in all, Castries's resignation should have come as a relief to both men, yet when Louis learned that Castries wanted to go, he sought to avoid him – as ever in the king's eyes resignation showed ingratitude. When it finally came, Castries's resignation was accompanied by two observations to the queen which show the gulf between him and Louis XVI. The first was that 'if there could be any question of an *homme de robe*'s succeeding me, I should feel obliged to tell the king that his navy would be ruined'. Thus he rejected the class of royal administrators who had built the absolute monarchy and whom the king most trusted – including the brilliant Sartine who had created Louis's navy. His second observation revealed divided loyalties which must have made being a minister a strain: 'As a Frenchman, I want the Estates-General, as a minister I feel bound to tell you that they could destroy your authority.'[8]

Brienne benefited from the resignations of Castries and Ségur (who was replaced by his own brother, the comte de Brienne) and, with his enhanced status as *ministre principal,* was able to create the ministerial unity that had been lacking throughout Louis's reign. In particular, central control was established over departmental spending, whilst in March 1788 France's first budget in the modern sense was drawn up and published. Nevertheless, the general position of the government was so weak, and the use to which Brienne put his new authority so inconsequent, that the changes were largely of symbolic importance, opening a chapter as the book was closing. For Louis, though, inheritor of the Sun King, Louis XIV, the new dispensation marked a partial eclipse. Indeed he is obscured from sight for much of this period and one is left wondering at his relationship to the events of his reign. On one question, however, his ministers could always count on the smouldering king to flicker into life: that of combating the pretensions of the *parlement.* Indeed the central theme of this period is the mutual destruction of the crown and the *parlement,* the constituent parts of the polity of the ancien régime.

The *parlement* asks for the Estates-General

The notables dispersed, taking despondency to the provinces and leaving behind them criticism of the king's proposals but no authority to implement even their own suggested modifications. The only chance now was to register the measures – representing the compromise thrashed out between the king and Brienne – in the *parlement* en bloc. The early historian of the reign, Joseph Droz, writes: 'It was known that Louis XVI wanted Calonne's projects implemented, regarding this as essential alike for the maintenance of his authority and for the prosperity of his people. All Paris believed that these projects, translated into edicts, were about to be brought to the *parlement* in a ... [*lit de justice*] when they would be registered. The news from Versailles varied only as to the day fixed for this.'[9]

Brienne, however, chose to present the modified edicts individually, starting with the least controversial. Those on the grain trade, provincial assemblies and the *corvée* were registered in June. Assuredly, Calonne had not fallen on account of these. On 6 July the edict extending the stamp duty was rejected by the *parlement,* which demanded a statement of royal revenue and expenditure and declared that only the Estates-General were competent to grant a permanent tax. Even the qualification 'permanent' was removed when the modified land tax was presented in July, despite the efforts of a repentant d'Amécourt to secure a fair hearing for the new tax.[10]

Many have found this demand by the *parlement* for the Estates inexplicable – it represented political suicide, since the *parlement* exercised a fiduciary political role only in the absence of the Estates. It has been suggested that the *parlement* abdicated its political role because it felt powerless to resist royal 'despotism'.[11] A more likely explanation (for we are not about to observe a display of *parlementaire* weakness) is spite. Louis XVI, by convoking the Notables, had unilaterally shaken the structures of the ancien régime and had created in the minds of the *parlementaires* a condition of doubt as to the continuance of their political role: if the king could summon the Notables, the *parlement* could go one better and demand the estates.

But the best 'clue to the enigma', as he puts it, is provided by Malesherbes. During the past 'forty years',[12] he told the king, a 'spirit of independence unknown to our ancestors' had arisen 'among all the nations who communicate their thoughts by the written word'. Indeed, 'there is not a single private individual who does not examine under what conditions obedience is due'. This process had accelerated recently. The American War of Independence had played a part, but a much smaller one than the revolt of the Austrian Netherlands against the Emperor Joseph II, because those lands were 'much easier to reach from the French provinces'. But the main catalyst had been the Assembly of Notables, which had just ended. Consequently, 'the situation of France in 1787 bears no relationship even to France in 1786, because the Assembly of Notables produced events which have no parallel in our history'.

The first event was the revelation of an enormous deficit for which thenceforth the king would be held personally accountable. The second way in which summoning the Notables had permanently altered the landscape was the creation of the provincial assemblies in the *pays d'élection*, which, unlike the provincial estates in the *pays d'états*, 'will assemble regularly every year'. Calonne had thought that these new assemblies would be a channel for the benedictions of the people to flow 'to the foot of the throne'. But what, Malesherbes countered, 'if the people thought it had grounds to complain?' Then, he continued, 'the king's conduct will be subject, through these assemblies, to the censure of the entire nation'.[13] The Turgot/Dupont memorandum on provincial assemblies had come into Louis's hands in February 1788. It advocated a national assembly formed of elected deputies from the provincial assemblies. We saw that an early draft of Calonne's envisaged a watered-down version of this.[14]

By the end of the Assembly of Notables, Malesherbes argued, all sides agreed that the meeting of some form of national assembly was inevitable. The decision was merely between the Turgot version and a resurrection of the Estates-General, which had not met since 1614. According to Malesherbes, and this is confirmed by Brienne's memoirs,[15] the government, with the consent of the king, intended to set up a national assembly co-opted from the provincial assemblies, which started to function at the end of 1787. For it was 'impossible' that 'this coping stone would not soon be placed on the edifice' since otherwise the government would have the worst of both worlds: criticism from provincial assemblies without the authority possessed by a national body to grant taxation. But this 'plan of 1787' had been derailed by the *parlement*'s demand that the estates should be elected in the traditional way.[16]

First of all, some provincial *parlements* had refused to register the edicts creating provincial assemblies in their jurisdiction – that of Bordeaux had even been exiled for its opposition – and thus had undermined and delayed their universal adoption in the *pays d'élection*. Their motive, according to Malesherbes, was simply that the *parlements* feared the rivalry of bodies that represented the people better than they, representing as they did no one but the king. The *parlement* of Paris, with such a large jurisdiction, did not entertain this fear and so registered the edict creating provincial assemblies. But regarding representation at the national level, it had exactly the same fears as its provincial brethren: it did not want a truly representative national assembly which would have a greater legitimacy than its own, representing as it did only the king. So when the *parlement* first called for the Estates-General, when the stamp tax was presented for registration, it demanded that the estates should be 'regularly convoked'. The *parlement* did not add, as it famously did after Necker ended its exile in September 1788, 'and that according to the forms of 1614', but that was what it meant: the Estates-General should be a weak body dominated by the aristocracy. The organization of the Estates-General is and was usually discussed only when the *parlement* revealed its intentions more clearly, though still in code, with the 1614 ruling, but its motives were integral to its demands for the estates from the outset, as Malesherbes realized. It takes one to know one. And he came from the most distinguished *parlementaire* family, the Lamoignon.

The *parlement*, then, was well aware of the limitations of previous Estates-General, as to both real power and genuine representation – the two were linked. The Estates-General had no legislative power. They could only raise grievances (*doléances*), which the king could embody or discard in edicts he laid before the *parlement* for registration after the estates had gone home. The estates had no standing committee, such as the provincial assemblies and even the provincial estates possessed, to watch over their affairs between meetings. Indeed there were no scheduled meetings: each session of the estates was a discrete entity, no provision was made for a further meeting and the gap between estates could be as much as ... 175 years. So, once the estates had ended, 'the *parlements* . . . re-entered upon all their rights, without any fear of contradiction from the nation's representatives'.[17]

Then there was the imperfection of representation. The clergy, the first 'order', the nobility, the second, and the third estate, the rest, each had roughly (for it varied from meeting to meeting) one-third of the votes. Voting was by order but this did not make a big difference as the third estate would not have had the majority even if voting had been by head. With noble and clerical privilege a burning issue in 1787–88 – though not as ardent as that of supposed royal despotism – the third estate, if the format of 1614 were to be repeated in 1789, would be in a permanent minority of one on the issue that most concerned them as an order.

So, according to Malesherbes, the *parlement* calculated that, if the estates could be convened according to traditional forms, its own influence within the estates would be considerable, as it was the only section of the nobility with experience of participation in public life at the national level. But, more importantly, the estates themselves would not be a threat and when they were not in session the *parlements* would continue to exercise their role as the only *permanent* representatives of the nation. And the *parlementaires* enjoyed their power. Some relished the chance to 'flaunt their zeal for the rights of the people', whilst others 'were not displeased that those distributing [government] favours needed their votes'.

Indeed, at heart, and paradoxically, many *parlementaires* were more attached to preserving the absolute monarchy than was Louis XVI himself. They wanted to scare him to increase their price but they had not forgotten that they had originally been created by medieval kings seeking to spread their writ over the newly acquired provinces of France. In short they simply 'couldn't believe that it was the king himself who was voluntarily renouncing the constitution under which France had been so flourishing under Louis XIV. And when they stuck to resolutions tending to make the effects of the coming estates illusory, they thought they were being the king's most loyal subjects'.[18] In all of this the *parlementaires* miscalculated: they did not commit suicide, they were killed, many of them literally.

The public, who, as Malesherbes observed, were not as learned in political history as were the judiciary, did not at this stage take in the full implications of the *parlement*'s pronouncement on the Estates-General. For the *parlementaires* 'had a better understanding of what they are asking than the public but would not explain as frankly what they want'.[19] So the public mood became ugly: when the comte d'Artois arrived to register the edicts in the *Cour des Aides*, which regulated taxes on alcoholic drinks, he was attacked by a crowd which had to be driven off at sabre point. Artois returned to Versailles ashen-faced and trembling and went straight to bed.

Brienne's response was to have the *parlement* exiled to Troyes (15 August–20 September). After its refusal to accept the finality of the *lit de justice* establishing the new land tax, the king and the duumvirate (at it was beginning to be called) of Brienne and Lamoignon made the descision. There was a *comité* before the council took the formal decision, but, Malesherbes notes, 'the discussion was singularly short both in the *comité* and in the council which immediately followed it'. Malesherbes wrote a memorandum criticizing the exile or 'translation' to Troyes but he did not present it and adopted the stance that 'the policy which was adopted was doubtless excellent since it was adopted', but whether this tautological statement was ironical or philosophical is unclear. In any case the government negotiatéd. A leading part in the negotiations was played by d'Amécourt, who was now rewarded by being restored as *rapporteur du roi*.[20] A compromise was hammered out whereby the king would abandon his new taxes in return for a massive loan of 500 million *livres* staggered over a period of five years, at the end of which the Estates-General would meet. Malesherbes wrote scathingly – and his memoranda were given to the king: 'The deal, by which the *parlement* was allowed back' and, in return for the prorogation of the unreformed *vingtièmes*, 'the land tax (which I have always regarded as being the only good measure in this field) was abandoned, was no more to my taste than the authoritarian measures which had preceded it.'[21]

Louis's views on this transaction, which entailed the abandonment of his attempt to reform taxation, are not known. Marie-Antoinette was more worried about the promise to convoke the Estates-General – she told Joseph II on 23 November that this promise 'caused her a lot of distress'. The compromise was to be solemnized in the *parlement* on 19 November. Brienne thought he had secured enough support to allow a free vote (the best way to ensure the success of the loan) and indeed the queen believed that during the debate 'the majority of opinions was for registration'.[22] There were, however, some intemperate speeches and the keeper of the seals, Lamoignon (Brienne had no seat in the *parlement*), either losing his nerve or thinking it was time to reassert royal authority, whispered to the king, who, without counting the votes, pronounced: 'Having heard your opinions, I find it necessary to establish the loans provided for in my edict. I have promised the Estates-General before 1792; my word should satisfy you. I order the edict to be registered.'

At this point the king's cousin, Philippe, duc d'Orléans – first prince of the blood and the richest man in France; close to the throne yet for that very reason denied the naval career he sought or any other; condemned by the king to be a *frondeur* – stood up, hesitated a moment, then stammered out: 'Sire ... this registration strikes me as illegal ... it should be stated that this registration has been effected by the express command of Your Majesty' (the form used for a *lit de justice*). Louis, a little shaken, retorted: 'Think what you like, I don't care ... yes, it is legal because I want it.'[23] Shortly afterwards the king left and the *parlement* declared the proceedings null and void. Orléans was exiled to his estates at Villers-Cotterêts by a *lettre de cachet* delivered personally by Breteuil, whose obligations to the House of Orléans did not enable him to mitigate the rigours of a five-month exile with no visitors allowed. Here, surely, was an authentic victim of 'ministerial despotism'.

Louis, or Lamoignon, took the view that in the king's presence there was no need to count heads, as the king represented the general will, as he explained to a *parlementaire* deputation: 'If a majority vote in my courts constrained my decision, the monarchy would no longer be anything but an aristocracy of magistrates as detrimental to the rights and interests of the nation as to those of the sovereign.'[24] Here Louis enjoys the distinction of being the first to use the word 'aristocrat' in the specific, pejorative sense in which it was used during the Revolution.

According to Malesherbes, the reason why the *parlement* objected to the measures presented in the *séance royale* of 19 November 1787 was that estates promised in five years' time was the last thing they wanted. Sensing that a national assembly was inevitable, the *parlements* wanted to pre-empt the debate and bounce a form of estates on to the king and the public before they had time for reflection. Indeed 'the sooner the estates met the sooner they could get rid of them' and the sooner they met the less chance the provinces would have to articulate their view.

Louis's conduct over the *séance royale* (as it was termed) of 19 November raises several questions. In the first place, the hybrid form – between a free registration and one by *lit de justice* – existed only in the antiquarian's mind of Lamoignon. Orléans was right in saying that this attempt by the king to 'have his cake and eat it' was illegal, i.e., without legal form, though whether he was right to say it is a different matter. Louis's petulant outburst, 'it is legal because I want it', was pure despotism, the arbitrary and formless will of a single man contradicting all he had written as a child in his *Réflexions*. It can be put down to the temper he was known to possess, the stress he was undoubtedly under, or the accumulated frustration of thirteen years of dealing with the *parlement*. Whatever the reason, he must have felt thoroughly ashamed when he got back to his apartments.

The exile of Orléans gave people pause: if this could happen to the highest in the land, who was safe? Two *parlementaires* considered to be in league with

Orléans, Fréteau and Sabatier, were conveyed to state prisons. Nor were these blows struck with ringing authority, Marie-Antoinette confessing to Joseph, 'It is irksome to have to take authoritarian measures; unfortunately they have become necessary and I hope they will inspire respect.' Joseph, who never found authoritarian measures irksome, must have detected his sister's anxiety and also something of the paralysis of will that was beginning to affect the government. The whole episode showed the royal government at its worst – indecisive, capricious and bad-tempered.

From the bungled *séance royale* to a final confrontation with the *parlement* was only a matter of time. The first clear details of the plan – and this is the measure of her new involvement in government – comes in a letter of Marie-Antoinette to Joseph of 24 April 1788:

> We are about to make great changes in the *parlements*. . . . The idea is to confine them to the function of judges and to create another assembly which will have the right to register taxes and general laws for the [whole] kingdom. I think we have taken all the measures and precautions compat-ible with the necessary secrecy; but this very secrecy involves uncertainty about the attitude of large numbers of people who can make or break the operation . . .

The idea of removing the judiciary from politics and conferring their powers on a new body (a *cour plénière*) was radical: Maupeou had merely changed the personnel of the *parlement*. It also, as Marie-Antoinette says, would have enabled the king to make uniform laws for France rather than see the twelve local *parlements* try to modify them in accordance with the local constitutions. Not only would the *parlements* be confined to their judicial functions but even these would be reduced, since the vast jurisdiction of the *parlement* of Paris – nearly half of France – would be carved up and distributed among local *grand bailliages*, which would make justice more accessible. It would also be cheaper since the *épices* – the gratuities litigants were obliged to give the judges – were abolished. But Brienne routinely planned to staff the new body with ex-notables, though in fact the court only met once and Brienne did not even bother to appoint all its members.

Lamoignon offered judicial reforms that were better worked out and his reform of criminal procedure represented the work of a lifetime. He sought to diminish the *parlements*' hold over the people by confining the cases they dealt with to the rare civil cases involving sums of more than 20,000 *livres*, criminal charges against nobles and a few specialized cases. He abolished the *question préalable*, by which a condemned man was tortured to reveal his accomplices, and virtually abolished seigneurial justice by insisting that a manorial court be equipped with a strong prison and a graduate judge.[25]

Malesherbes was sceptical about the plenary court: either no one would accept service in it (which proved the case) or, if they did, it would be 'even more formidable than the *parlements*', given that its composition was very similar to that of the Assembly of Notables, which the king had felt obliged to dissolve. Then again, the creation of extra courts, though a boon to their localities, was divisive and intended to be so – pitting the candidates for the *grands bailliages* against the *parlements* whose functions they were usurping, as, indeed, the latter held they did, and forcing those candidates to choose between their ambition and their loyalty and honour. Malesherbes did not think the measure would succeed, though he does not give the main reason why it would fail: fear of *parlementaire* reprisals.[26] But his main objection was the military force deployed by the government.

For the sake of form, the measures were submitted both to the committee and to the council for a rubber stamp. The king even asked everyone, including Malesherbes, for his individual opinion. But he was only allowed 'a rapid reading of one of the edicts'. And he had no time to take soundings concerning how the new *grands bailliages* would work and how they would be received in the provinces. 'Nevertheless, I said enough for the king to realize, as we left the committee, that I should no longer remain in his council'.[27]

Resigning, however, was not so simple. 'Some time' after the coup d'état carried out on 8 May, Malesherbes told Brienne that he really had to speak to the king about his resignation. He was not allowed to see the king alone, but, before the council the king took him on one side, though still in Brienne's presence, and said 'with great kindness that he knew that I really wanted to quit, that he was sorry for it, but that he insisted that I must stay for a while longer'. (Afterwards, Brienne explained that 'a while' meant until September.) 'After these few words the king rushed away giving me no chance to reply, just enough to say that I would take the liberty of giving him a written exposé of my reasons for leaving'. He gave the paper to the king again at the start of the council, 'which was the only time I approached him'. 'The king received it kindly, put it in his pocket and never mentioned it again'.

The government did not proceed towards its coup with the confidence of a Maupeou and employed far more troops than he had considered necessary. A preliminary skirmish with the *parlement* justified Marie-Antoinette's 'uncertainty' about the loyalty of 'large numbers' of key players. On 3 May, aware of the impending blow and unsure whether they would ever meet again as the

parlement, the *parlementaires* had finally enunciated the content of the fundamental laws, or unwritten constitution of the kingdom, whose obscurity they
had hitherto exploited. This list, very much a *pièce d'occasion*, included irre-
movable magistrates, the sanctity of the capitulations between the king and the
various provinces at the time of their incorporation into France, and no taxation without the consent of the estates. On 6 May, for their part in drafting the
fundamental laws, Duval d'Eprémesnil and Goislard de Monsabert were
arrested by armed force, but not before – according to two sources[28] – a secretary of state, who can only be Breteuil, had tipped off d'Eprémesnil and given
him time to seek refuge in the *parlement*; upon which the nineteenth-century
historian Chérest remarks: 'In default of the loyalty of its principal servants, the
monarchy could not even count on their professional discretion.'[29] Having
failed to prevent the arrest (but ensuring it the *éclat* of taking place in full
parlement), Breteuil proceeded to throw responsibility for it directly on to the
king by insisting that he send him a copy, entirely in his own handwriting, of
the blank order, signed 'Louis', which Breteuil had filled in and despatched in
accordance with normal procedures.[30]

On the eve of the monarchy's last offensive the troops – the French Guards
and the Swiss Guards – were loyal, but those responsible for giving them their
orders, i.e., Breteuil, as minister for Paris, and the duc de Biron, colonel-in-
chief of the French Guards, wavered, through fear of *parlementaire* reprisals
should the king lose.[31] On 5 May Biron told Breteuil that without direct orders
from the king he could not put detachments of French Guards at the disposal
of Breteuil's subordinate, the police minister: 'If things turn out badly the
parlement could take me to task and I could only defend myself by exhibiting
the king's orders.' Ministerial instructions were not enough, he had to 'know
the king's personal intentions' ('avoir le secret du Roi') and despite his eighty-six
years and the state of his health – he died in October – he wanted to go to
Versailles to discover these.[32]

Calonne's impeachment by the *parlement* in 1787 had made ministerial
responsibility a reality. Furthermore, in a council meeting to discuss that
impeachment, two ministers at least – Castries, of course, and Malesherbes –
had stated that such responsibility was desirable.[33] But the practical application
now made by ministers was not that the king 'could do no wrong' but that he
must take everything on his own head – a sign perhaps that the regime itself
and not just the government of the day was being called into question.

On 6 May the members of the *parlement* received *lettres de cachet*
summoning them to Versailles on the 8th. There, after telling them that 'there
was no transgression they had not committed over the past year', the king

registered the edicts and ordered the *parlement*, without protesting, to go into vacation until the new order had come into being. They complied. Paris remained calm. Indeed, on 26 May Biron complained to Breteuil of the excessive deployment of troops, 'considering the calm which obtains ... throughout Paris'.[34] Louis and Marie-Antoinette felt able to visit the Invalides and Artois the royal gardens and the royal family spent a few weeks at the newly acquired château of Saint-Cloud, on the outskirts of the capital.

In the provinces, however, the May edicts led to a period of serious disorder. Some hardliners suggested that Louis put himself at the head of his troops and crush the disturbances in the worst affected province, Brittany, 'without fearing the consequences of civil war',[35] a course Louis was consistently to reject, though in the past he had been happy enough to use troops to suppress an *émeute* such as the Flour War. In July the Breton nobility sent a twelve-man deputation to Versailles to protest against the edicts. They were arrested in the dead of night and conveyed to the Bastille. They had been dining in the Marais at a reception given by their supporters. One of these was the comte de Boisgelin, brother of Archbishop Boisgelin, who had played a major role in defeating Louis's 1787 reform initiative. The comte was master of the wardrobe, a plum court office, which made his rebellion all the more heinous in the king's eyes. On 15 July Louis took his revenge: 'Given your conduct over the past fortnight, it will come as no surprise that I am asking you to resign your office of master of the wardrobe ... and that I forbid you to appear at court. It is from those who are in closest attendance on me and serve my person that I am entitled to expect the greatest zeal and loyalty'.[36] He was replaced by the duc de La Rochefoucauld-Liancourt, who proved to be no more loyal. Another of those at the reception was the ubiquitous Lafayette (who had no links with Brittany) – he was demoted. The ambassador to Portugal, Bombelles, commented: 'As for M. de Lafayette, a lot of people are asking why he wants to be mixed up in everything, given that he is intrinsically nothing'.[37]

Breteuil refused to sign the *lettres de cachet* committing the Breton deputies to the Bastille and resigned (on 25 July). He no longer believed in the system he had played such a large part in undermining and had for some time been advocating a written constitution.[38] It may be that his resignation was designed to bring about the fall of the Brienne–Lamoignon duumvirate and his own elevation to *chef du Conseil royal*. Certainly his friends were working for this.[39] He refused the queen's request that he continue attending council as a minister-without-portfolio.[40]

It is hard to assess the scale of revolt in the provinces; did it extend much beyond Brittany and the towns boasting a *parlement*? However, the king was told that 'the four corners of the kingdom were on fire' for, according to Bombelles, Louis was 'surrounded by a faction [Artois and the Polignacs] opposed to the archbishop'. Madame de Polignac assured Marie-Antoinette that she was not 'pushing any of her friends [i.e., Calonne] but merely wanted to rid the court and the nation of a man who had never had a settled strategy'. But, Bombelles continued, 'it is not the people who are in revolt. . . . The people are well aware that they are not being stirred up for the defence of their hearths and the scraps of comfort remaining to them. All the hostility comes from the seigneurs and the *parlementaires* who, in a new regime, would have (by a fairer distribution of taxation) to pay the money they have always refused to give to the public treasury'.[41] One of the great enigmas of the period 1787–88 is why the king was unable to get this fairly simple message across. Somehow the 'seigneurs and magistrates' were able to convince the people, who nevertheless saw through them, that liberty was more important than equality. Soon that would change. They would want both, and also *fraternité* – being treated as human beings of equal worth.

Whatever its extent, the provincial unrest took its toll on royal finances, and by August the treasury was empty. No one would provide 'anticipations' against future taxes whose payment could not be guaranteed. The declaration of 16 August suspended all payments for a fortnight, after which they would be resumed, half in government paper, half in coin.

Malesherbes had not been consulted and only learned about what he considered a 'bankruptcy' at Paris. Feeling that his honour has been stained by the measure, he sought an audience with the king, which was not granted until 24 August when he renewed his request to resign. This time the king accepted the resignation but made typical restrictions, which were tantamount to the exile usually imposed on disgraced ministers. Malesherbes puts the king's words in indirect speech without quotation marks, but they are so typical of Louis that they can be put back into direct speech as his own:

> Since you are determined to go, I will detain you no longer but you mustn't mention it to anyone. I gather that you are due to visit your sister's country estate so all you have to do is stay there, without returning to the council. I will tell you when I allow you to tell anyone about your *retraite*.[42]

Louis's use of the construction 'vous n'avez que' to make light of something difficult is typical of the man. Malesherbes said that after the Lamoignon coup d'état, 'I regarded my presence in the council as like being in the Bastille – by *lettre de cachet*'. This was a figure of speech. But his detention at his sister's amounted to a real if verbal *lettre de cachet*. To preserve his enforced cover, next day Malesherbes paid court to the royal family and attended their public banquet. Then he left for his sister's and that evening a courier informed him that Brienne had fallen and been replaced by Necker.

Brienne left in secret with hired horses for the country seat attached to his new and lucrative see of Sens. He avoided Paris, where his effigy was burnt. 'He proposed shortly', Bombelles comments, 'to go to Pisa where perhaps he will run into M. de Calonne, and then they will have a good old laugh together over the public's madness and their own'. As a leaving present Marie-Antoinette gave Brienne a gold box with her portrait studded with 'superb diamonds'.[43]

Marie-Antoinette was instrumental in recalling Necker, widely regarded as the only man who could restore credit. The recall was preceded by a bout of courtly shadow-boxing.[44] Brienne told Mercy, who acted as go-between, that 'for some time' he had wanted Necker to serve as finance minister under him. Necker was reluctant, or seemed so; first, because he had (as Marie-Antoinette put it) been 'lacerated by the way the king had always treated him'; and second because he didn't know the current state of the finances – he sent Mercy the corrected proofs of his 'triumphant' refutation of Calonne's version of the deficit. The king did not want Necker back. The queen wanted Necker to know he owed his appointment to her. And Necker did not want to serve under Brienne. So on 18 August she told Mercy:

> I greatly fear that the archbishop will be forced to disappear from the scene completely and then whom can we choose to have overall direction? Because we must have someone, especially with M. Necker. He needs to be restrained. The personage above me [the king] is in no fit state for this; as for me, whatever people say, I am only the second fiddle and despite the confidence of the first, he often makes me feel it ... the king is extremely reluctant [to appoint Necker]; the only way to get his consent is to promise only to sound [Necker] out without making any commitment.

On the 25th she confided: 'I tremble ... that I am bringing him back. My fate is to bring misfortune.'

What did Marie-Antoinette mean by saying that Louis 'was in no fit state' to restrain Necker? Was it just that Louis was too feeble? But he had had sufficient strength to thwart all her attempts to influence foreign policy for fourteen years. No, she was referring to Louis's mental and possibly physical state. A month later, on 27 September, Bombelles recounts an episode which was carefully hushed up: 'our best court sleuths will not get to the bottom of what goes on inside ours':

Today, when the king was out hunting, he was brought a bundle of letters. He retired to a copse to read them and soon he was seen sitting on the ground with his face between his hands and his hands on his knees. His equerries and other people, hearing him sobbing, fetched M. de Lambesc [the grand equerry]. He approached the king. The king told him brusquely to go away but he insisted. Then the king, turning towards him a face bathed with tears repeated, but this time kindly, "leave me alone". Shortly afterwards His Majesty needed to be lifted on to his horse, where he seemed to be suffering from some malady. A chair was brought for him to sit on, but he was ill a second time. Finally he returned to Versailles, having recovered his senses and external composure as well as his good health. This adventure has been kept secret but the secret will not be well kept with so many people in the know.

Bombelles did not know what the letters contained that had such an effect on the king: 'I am reporting a fact; a distressing fact. But I have no idea what caused it.'[45] One hesitates to offer a medical diagnosis at this distance – was his malady psychosomatic? Maybe this is why he felt it necessary to address Marie-Antoinette's concern that he would not be able to 'restrain' Necker, by drafting a detailed set of parameters to be used by Mercy in negotiating Necker's return to the ministry. A copy has survived in Marie-Antoinette's hand:

So far M. de M.[ercy] has only spoken to M. N[ecker] as if on his own initiative . . . but now he can tell him that the king has been informed of the negotiation and sanctions it; that he desires to put M. Necker at the head of the finances again; that he will have a seat in the council [the point over which he had resigned in 1781] and will have carte blanche in his department; that the king thinks that after a disagreeable operation [the 8 May coup] but one that was necessary in the circumstances, whatever M. N. proposes can only be approved by the public and that he will restore confidence; that the king is firmly resolved to summon the Estates-General at the time indicated and to work with them on ways to end the deficit and make sure it doesn't recur. That the king cannot in advance undertake to restore the *parlements*, but that he will work on doing this at the end of their vacation, whilst at the same time preserving the benefits gained by the people from greater access to justice [the *grands bailliages* carving up the *parlement*'s jurisdiction]. If M.N. can think of further economies [on top of Brienne's] he can rest assured that the king is ready for any personal sacrifice.[46]

Louis could not bear to negotiate directly with the man who had undermined his government for the past six years and, as Necker had handed his 1781 resignation to Marie-Antoinette, so she handled his return. (She had also received communications from Brienne before the king negotiated his entry into the ministry.)

The king told Brienne that he 'could not abide his [Necker's] manners or his principles but that he did not want Necker to know this' – a task assisted by the Genevan's vanity. But, as during the crisis over the farms in 1783 and during the Notables, the fear of a collapse of credit – a blow to both Louis's pride and his honour – again unnerved him. On 25 August he appointed Necker *directeur-général des finances* and on the 27th vindicated his resignation in 1781 by granting him, as a *ministre d'etat*, entrée to the council, which was to enjoy a renaissance as a decision-making body during Necker's second ministry. Since the king had granted toleration to Protestants in 1787 the obstacle which in 1781 had debarred him from the council had been removed. There was no one placed over him and indeed, during his second ministry, Necker seems to have possessed the essential attribute of a prime minister under Louis XVI: that the other ministers had to apprise him of important matters before raising them with the king.[47] But Louis did it all with a bad grace, and the new attitude of cynical compliance noted when he appointed Brienne is encapsulated in his remark: 'I was forced to recall Necker; I didn't want to but they'll soon regret it. I'll do everything he tells me and we'll see what happens.'[48] Louis secured Brienne a cardinal's hat and Brienne confessed that his 'character was not made for stormy times'. His parting advice to the king was not to surrender unconditionally to the *parlement*. Riotous rejoicing greeted the news of Brienne's departure and Louis ordered Biron, commander of the French Guards, to repel force by force. There were several deaths.

After the fall of Brienne, that of Lamoignon was probably inevitable. He negotiated with individual *parlementaires* through the *conseiller d'état*, Foulon, in an attempt to save his judicial reforms at the price of abandoning the *cour plénière*.[49] Necker, however, whether fearing a rival in Lamoignon or believing that nothing less than the unconditional restoration of the *parlement* would restore credit, scotched the transaction. The king had promised Lamoignon a *lit de justice* maintaining the reforms, the *parlementaires* had been summoned to Versailles and the usual orders given to the household troops. The hall was still being decorated at eleven o'clock on the morning of the 14th. Then the whole thing was called off. Louis's diary gives the bare facts: '14 September: resignation of M. de Lamoignon. 15 September: There was to have been a *lit de justice.*'

Right up to the last minute there had been a desperate struggle for the king's ear between Necker and Lamoignon. On 12 September Bombelles notes: 'The present state of crisis cannot last. The queen is in a filthy mood [*d'une humeur cruelle*]. Yesterday she inveighed against all the ministers in a *comité* which was discussing how to restore the *parlement* to its functions.' Necker was trying to persuade the king to restore the *parlement* unconditionally, the one thing Brienne had urged him not to do. Lamoigon argued that the *lit de justice* would pass off peacefully. Necker said it would cause a riot. As evidence he gave the king a copy of some proposals of the junior chambers of the *parlement*, including: the king could not move troops from one province to another; could not retain ministers who had incurred the *parlement*'s displeasure; or hold a *lit de justice*. This shook Louis, though none of the motions had been adopted by the senior *Grand' Chambre*.

At this juncture the military commandant of Brittany arrived seeking fresh orders to deal with the revolt from Villedeuil, the new minister for the interior. He was scared to take it on his head to give them. The intendant of Brittany, Bertrand de Molleville, had already fled back to Versailles, jumping over his garden wall to escape the crowds. The ministers spent the whole of the 13th closeted together, 'alternating between hope and fear' as to how the *lit de justice* would pass off. The king alternated between panic and apathy. Bombelles, attending the king's *coucher* on the 12th, saw him 'in fine good humour' and wondered if he realized how far his authority had been 'sapped'. Louis wanted a blow-by-blow account of Bombelles's sister-in-law's accouchement. It took a long time (to happen and recount) and 'since she was happily delivered of a little girl the conversation took a festive turn.' When Louis's own son, now dying, had come into the world, he had overflowed the allotted space in his diary to record all the details of the confinement. Facts and figures.

The whole scene of chaos is symbolized by what happened to the actual seals of state after Lamoignon had resigned them. Louis had decided to be his own keeper of the seals till he chose a successor, so he needed physical possession of the seals to impress them into the hot yellow or green wax of documents. But the delivery of the seals descended into a farce which, Bombelles considered, 'proves how far M. de Lamoignon had lost his head'. He sent them to Montmorin, his friend the foreign secretary, via a municipal officer who travelled in a blue sedan chair. On arrival, this man asked Montmorin what he was supposed to do with the seals. Montmorin had no more idea than the young officer, 'so he sent him straight round to the king' – without the seals. Happily, as he was about to barge into the king's cabinet, flouting every rule of etiquette, 'he encountered M. de Villedeuil on his way out, who went back in to take the king's orders. These were to the effect that the seals were to remain with M. de Montmorin until the hour appointed for the council, 'when they should be brought in and handed over to His Majesty'.[50] Louis only kept the seals for four days – his diary entry for 19 September reads: 'Swearing in of M. Barentin' as keeper of the seals. The reactionary protégé of Miromesnil, Barentin had been successively *avocat-général* in the *parlement* and *premier président* in the *cour des aides*. He was to prove a more determined opponent of Necker than Lamoignon had ever been.

Lamoignon's fall was celebrated in Paris by riotous rejoicing in which, 'despite the restraint of the troops ... over thirty lost their lives'. 'These commotions', Bombelles observed, 'recur too often and it is very disturbing that the people are becoming acclimatized to them.'[51] Lamoignon retired with a vast pension and the promise of a dukedom and an important embassy for his son. People thought such generous treatment unmerited; yet for the king's cause the head of the leading *parlementaire* family had irrevocably quarrelled with his corps; a future career in the *parlement* for his son was out of the question – hence the embassy. On leaving office he made a prophecy: 'The *parlement*, the nobility and the clergy have dared to resist the king. Before two years have elapsed the *parlement*, the nobility and the clergy will be no more.'[52] But Lamoignon did not live to see this prophecy fulfilled. For in May 1789, at the time of the opening of the Estates, Lamoignon was found dead in the grounds of his château at Bâville, a rifle by his side. He was the last true servant of the old monarchy.

Necker's second ministry

Necker's appointment brought confidence that the Estates really would meet and the struggle for mastery of that body began in earnest. The genesis of that struggle, dating to the last weeks of the beleaguered Brienne ministry, was the king's declaration of 5 July lifting censorship and inviting advice from all sides about the composition of the estates. The declaration stated that the king was prepared to modify the old regulations concerning the Estates-General in accordance with the changes that had taken place in society since their last meeting in 1614, thus launching the debate that was to dominate political life for the next twelve months: the number of deputies the third estate was to send to the Estates-General and the voting arrangements of that body. The third estate, by 1788 the bulk of the population in wealth and numbers, claimed *doublement*, i.e., representation equal to that of the other two orders, the clergy and nobility, combined and, to make this effective, individual voting *(par tête)* rather than block voting *par ordre*.

The king's declaration was not intended to inaugurate a dispassionate enquiry after the truth: issued at the height of the *révolte nobiliaire,* it was an attempt by Brienne to prevent the nobility from dominating a body, the Estates-General, whose meeting they had forced the king to concede. Some viewed it as a policy of divide and rule; others, less cynically, as one of alliance with the third estate; both were traditional royal policies. Either way, the declaration succeeded where the *Avertissement* had failed – it roused the third estate out of its saecular slumber (*le réveil du tiers*). Brienne's wide-ranging and uncluttered radicalism is clear from the following extract from his memoirs:

> . . . my preference was for a double representation for the third estate and voting by head – as I had established in the provincial assemblies and was doing in all the provincial estates that were being set up . . . those for Dauphiné had been agreed and after my time were set up along the lines I indicated. . . . Part of the kingdom would have been divided among provincial assemblies, with double representation and voting by head; they would have nominated their deputies to the Estates-General; elections by the *bailliage* would not have taken place . . .[53]

We saw in the memoranda that Malesherbes gave the king the full implications of elections by the provincial assemblies rather than by the old electoral unit of the *bailliage* and why the parlement preferred the latter. The assemblies would elect a National Assembly – Malesherbes uses the phrase – with deputies representing the whole nation, rather than an Estates-General with deputies representing the separate orders. Brienne and Malesherbes thus cast doubt on the continuance of the separate existence of the orders, at least at the political level. At all events, the Brienne ministry seemed to be establishing a framework in which competing interests were balanced and the king's independence of action secured by support from the third estate. This bold and experimental phase of royal policy-making was abruptly terminated by the appointment of Necker, who advanced the meeting of the Estates-General, but deferred the triumph of the third estate.

If Necker had been a statesman he would have issued – and to the sound of trumpets – a royal proclamation maintaining Lamoignon's reforms and at the same time granting the third estate *doublement.* Elections to the estates would have been conducted through the provincial assemblies and these, as Calonne had intended, would have been encouraged as vehicles for royal policy and propaganda. Instead, the provincial assemblies were put into hibernation and the *parlement* was recalled unconditionally. On his return to office, Necker saw the situation thus: the king had promised to convoke the Estates-General and there was no going back on this promise; first and foremost because public opinion demanded it; second, because it would have dishonoured the king to renege on a promise; but – equally importantly – because the *parlement* had stated that it was no longer competent to authorize taxation or loans. It was, as Necker graphically put it, 'as if Atlas had suddenly declined to shoulder the burden of the world'.

As it was, true to the guiding principle he enunciated in *De la Révolution française* – act only out of necessity but make your actions seem spontaneous – he now advanced the date appointed by Brienne for the opening of the Estates-General (1 May 1789) to 1 January. However, in registering the royal declaration concerning the estates, the *parlement* took a step which seemed to throw Necker off course, by ruling that the estates should be organized 'according to the forms employed in 1614', which implied not only a rejection of *doublement* but also the retention of the old electoral unit. It represented a riposte to the declaration of 5 July and an attempt to foil the king's attempts to modernize the estates.

The *parlement* lost its popularity overnight, never to recover it, something which Necker was slow to register, perhaps because the *parlement* was echoing his own doubts. His reappointment represented, after all, the triumph of the *révolte nobiliaire* just as his first ministry had advanced the ministerial aspirations of the aristocracy. He may have been 'born in the dust of the counting-house and married to a woman of the same estate',[54] but he had got to the top under the old order and married his daughter to the Swedish ambassador, the Baron de Staël. People born to the purple sometimes rebel against the system, those who have worked their way to the top rarely, almost never. He was later to write: 'All my contacts, all my habits had been contracted among the order of society which rejected *doublement*'.[55]

If Necker had chosen to face down the *parlement*, he would have found the king receptive. Louis had not given Brienne the degree of active support Calonne had enjoyed, but where the *parlement* was concerned Brienne, like all his predecessors, had not found the king wanting. Louis had also been stung by the *révolte nobiliaire,* as Necker himself relates: 'I have not forgotten that on my return to the ministry the king, personally affronted by the conduct of the nobility of Brittany, believed that he should buttress his authority with the loyalty of the third estate'.[56]

Thus the king did not influence Necker's response to the *parlement*'s pronouncement on the Estates-General, which was to restore the date of their opening to 1 May in order to allow time for consultations with the Assembly of

Notables, which met again between 6 November and 12 December. The queen, still smarting from the *révolte nobiliaire* against her minister, was against reconvening the Notables because, as Brienne said, 'A new Assembly of Notables, composed of the privileged whose mentality I well knew, could, in assembly, only be disposed against the third estate and therefore dangerous.'[57] But Necker had been the darling of the first Assembly of Notables which had sought to bring him to power in 1787. And keeper of the seals Barentin thought that Necker had planned to reconvene the Notables even before the *parlement*'s declaration.[58]

Indeed, Necker's action is more comprehensible if one does not assume he had decided on *doublement*. Castries, now an ordinary notable and strongly against *doublement*, asked Necker what line he would like the notables to take and was told 'that he had neither advice nor an opinion [to give] and that he would decide solely on the advice and opinions of the notables'. That advice, by six of its committees to one, was against *doublement*, the dissenting committee being that presided over by Provence.

On 5 December, while the Notables were still in session, the parlement 'interpreted' its original declaration, stating that 'no law or fixed usage stipulated the respective number of deputies'. There is evidence that this declaration was got up by Necker in the belief that the the privileged orders' prior consent to *doublement* was necessary or equitable. If, however, he thought that the authority of the *parlement* still counted, he was singularly out of touch with the public opinion he so vaunted. Louis read the situation better and took the measure of the *parlement*. Now he took his revenge for all he had suffered at its hands over the years. When a *parlementaire* deputation came to Versailles to present the declaration on the Estates-General, together with a request for certain constitutional guarantees, the king snubbed both them and Necker with brutal relish: 'I have no reply to make to my *parlement*; it is with the assembled nation that I shall concert the appropriate measures to consolidate permanently public order and the prosperity of the state.'[59] The *parlement* was seeking a post-1787 *modus vivendi*, asking the king to grant a constitutional charter which it would then register, but it received the neat reply that if it was not competent to register taxation, *a fortiori* it was not competent to modify the constitution given that he himself could only do this in conjunction with the representatives of the nation.

Advice also came to the king from another quarter, the Polignac group, often referred to as the queen's *société intime* but in reality the king's ally against her past political pretensions and increasingly a haven of intimacy and relaxation for the king himself. Recently they had given the king and their ally

Calonne strong support in the first Assembly of Notables and had quarrelled with the queen over this. By December 1788, though, they had realized that what had started the previous year as a necessary and desirable administrative and political revolution was fast becoming a social one. This is made clear in two publications associated with the group, Calonne's *Lettre au roi* (published in London) and the *Mémoire des princes*, signed by five of the princes of the blood (not Provence or Orléans), headed by the comte d'Artois, whose chancellor, Montyon, prepared the draft.

Calonne and Artois defended the consistency of their position: throughout they had stood for the maintenance of royal authority and equal taxation; Calonne had never attacked a single legitimate right – for abuses such as tax evasion were not rights; or, as Artois put it, 'all that was at issue was repairing not destroying'. Louis was not moved by such reasoning in December but, coming from a group that had provided both political support and friendship, it may have sown a seed of doubt, though the *révolte nobiliaire* had soured the soil in which it grew.

Finally, with the benefit, such as it was, of the notables' opinion, that of the *parlement* and the *Mémoire des princes*, the king came to decide the question of *doublement* and related issues in his council, which emerged from fourteen years in the shadows to shine in meridian splendour *because Necker could not make up his mind*. Some have seen indecisiveness or detachment in the very nomenclature of the ruling that finally granted *doublement* on 27 December: *Résultat du conseil touchant les états généraux* (*arrêt* – 'decision' or 'decree' – being more usual).

Malouet describes his friend Necker's havering: 'The *doublement* of the third estate was pronounced and I make no secret of the fact that I favoured it even against the opinion of M. Necker, who resisted it for a long time, foresaw the disadvantages and only yielded to the impression that the voice of public opinion always produced on him. No one outside his intimate circle knew how much he hesitated over the famous *Résultat du conseil* or with what misgiving he promulgated it . . .'[60] The archbishop of Bordeaux saw a printed first report by Necker refusing *doublement* and merely giving the major towns some extra deputies.[61]

The king did not share these doubts. Both the protagonists in the council – Necker tending towards *doublement* and Barentin decidedly against – attest, the latter resentfully, to the king's prejudice against the nobility and clergy; but Louis could not bring himself to pass up the opportunity for a thorough discussion. Indeed it has justly been observed that 'never perhaps was a royal decision subjected to a more thorough scrutiny'.[62] The method the king adopted was to preside over a series of cabinet committees consisting of the adversaries, Necker and Barentin, plus two further ministers. Since Barentin tells us that the latter two were different every time, we can calculate that the king wore out twenty pairs of ministers in sessions lasting from four to five hours each – totalling maybe a hundred hours of discussion. The king took an almost academic delight in the minutiae of the organization of the Estates-General and 'never seemed to tire of the discussion'. 'His Majesty made frequent observations but it was impossible to divine his opinion.'

Finally, a double session of the *Conseil des Dépêches* was convened on 27 December. Exceptionally, the queen was present. She had attended ministerial *comités* under Brienne in 1787–88 but never the council. Barentin continues:

> It seemed that the king, having heard and digested everything, had only to pronounce. Nevertheless, he wanted to count the votes again. I adhered to my original opinion as did M. de Villedeuil; M. de Nivernais was less firm, playing the subtle courtier and not coming to a positive conclusion. M. de Puységur wavered. The king pronounced for *doublement*. The queen maintained total silence; it was easy, however, to see that she did not disapprove double representation for the third estate.

Such is the account of Barentin, who was present; but Lenoir, the ex-*lieutenant de police*, was voicing a widely shared belief when he said that, in adopting *doublement*, the king had 'despotically' overridden the majority view of the council by which he was supposed to abide.[63] The king may have brought indirect pressure to bear – notably through the presence of Marie-Antoinette – and two ministers had changed their minds during the final discussion; but even according to Barentin the basic disposition of the council was five to four for *doublement*, whilst Necker says it was eight to one.

Apart from Barentin, Necker's main opponent had been Laurent de Villedeuil, Breteuil's replacement at the *Maison du Roi*. A former intendant, he had followed a classical career within the royal administration. A rare bird now in the ministry, he was an unrepentant defender of the tenets of the administrative monarchy. He proposed that, given the unrest in the country, the meeting of the estates should be shelved and instead 'an assembly of the nation without distinction of orders' should be summoned. The king would choose the 'deputies' from nobility, clergy and magistrates 'as well as from the third estate'. According to Barentin, this proposal 'made a profound impression on His Majesty'. Necker and Montmorin, the foreign secretary, however, insisted that the question of whether to call the estates could not be reopened.[64]

Another important decision was the venue for the Estates-General, which in the past had been held in several provincial cities as well as Paris. Candidates were Orléans, with the king residing at the château of La Source; Amiens; 'but above all Tours, with His Majesty residing at Chanteloup and his ministers at Amboise'.[65] Necker favoured Paris, centre of finance and of his popularity, but he was overruled by a majority in the council and had to settle for Versailles as the next best option. Even this, however, according to Louis's intimate friend d'Angiviller, was 'despite the personal and private opinion of this prince'.[66] D'Angiviller does not say which town would have had Louis's preference, but his future conduct suggests it may have been Soissons, with himself residing at nearby Compiègne.

The *Résultat du conseil* consists of five short paragraphs providing: i) that there should be 'at least a thousand deputies' in the estates; ii) that the electoral unit should be the *bailliage*, the number of its deputies being determined by its population and taxation; and iii) *doublement*.

This is followed by Necker's lengthy report, which had formed the basis of the council's discussions. It was redrafted for popular consumption when the *Résultat* was published as a twenty-six-page pamphlet. The report emphasizes that by granting *doublement* there is no intention of prejudging the question of voting by head or by order (which the minister seems to favour). In the last section Necker has the king thinking aloud with his ministers and promising to become a constitutional monarch. His pledges include regular meetings of the estates, their consent to taxation and control over the budget (including the king's personal expenditure), and consultation with them on *lettres de cachet* and freedom of the press. The whole is punctuated with sentimental asides from the king, characteristic of the times: 'For several years I have known only moments of happiness', and 'What does spending money do for one's happiness?' The duc de Luxembourg thought the king granted 'more than the Estates-General on bended knees would have dared to hope for'. Calonne lamented the dismemberment of royal authority and wrote prophetically: 'A revolution followed by a counter-revolution [*une révolution contraire*] is the worst calamity that can befall a nation.'[67]

The *Résultat*, however, seems to have satisfied the tacticians of the third estate and there was public rejoicing throughout the kingdom, reflected in this letter: 'The *Résultat du conseil* has been rapturously received by the citizens of Paris. People embraced and congratulated each other and called down blessings on Louis XVI who had given them victory over the enemy. On parting they exclaimed: "Vive le roi et le tiers état!"'

The chief criticism of Brienne is that his policies were half-baked: he had had some good ideas – the *cour plénière*, electoral alliance with the third estate and the modernization of the estates – but he had failed to think them through. Necker is said to have lamented, 'Had I but had the fifteen months of the archbishop of Toulouse!' by which he meant that royal authority had declined so far by the time of his recall that he had no scope for initiative. His lament therefore was also a confession. His only policy was to put the monarchy into the official receivership of the estates and let them decide everything. There was early evidence of this approach when he advanced the date for their meeting to 1 January, a date before which it would have been difficult to have elaborated a royal programme. He had also given an ominous indication of his views on the management of assemblies when he told Castries that he had 'neither advice nor an opinion' to give the notables. This approach was all the more dangerous in that he was not confiding the destiny of the monarchy to a proven cog in the constitutional machine but to an antiquated body that had been racked with internal dissension.

Necker blindly accepted the *parlement*'s rejection of Brienne's plans to modernize the estates: the *Résultat*, though it granted *doublement*, did not make structural changes – in particular it retained election by the *bailliage* – and thus was to the political system what Necker's first ministry had been to the financial: tinkering. Indeed it may be that the *Résultat,* though hailed by the third estate as cementing the king's alliance with them, was in fact the unperceived turning point when, in accepting the old format for the estates, the king first allowed a body, the nobility, which had lost its power, to dictate the agenda.

Unfortunately, Louis and Necker each reinforced the other's tendency to indecisiveness. In the context of the *Résultat*, Malouet said of Necker (in words that could equally be applied to the king): 'He had a rare talent for appreciating both in the most minute detail and in perspective the vices and disadvantages of every proposal, and it was these endless ramifications which so often made him indecisive.'[68] In the case of Louis, his indecisiveness was not only reinforced by Necker, but institutionalized by the mechanisms of the *Conseil d'État*. Having systematically neglected the council as a policy-making body throughout his reign, Louis now saw fit to amplify its procedures. The *Résultat* is a textbook case of a judgement arrived at adversarially; but the introduction of pairs of ministers arguing, perhaps to make up the numbers, a brief in which they did not believe, whilst over a space of a hundred hours the king luxuriated in his indecisiveness, was a joyous embellishment of Louis's own devising. The highly irregular appearance of Marie-Antoinette was the icing on the cake. These protracted discussions almost suggest that Louis's long resistance to formal advice was because, like an addict, he feared that once he started taking it he would never be able to stop.

A Bourbon king was only as good as the advice he received. Louis rarely took personal initiatives, but he had shown himself capable of responding to bold measures, in particular those of Turgot and Calonne. In 1788, his perception heightened by hostility, Louis was quicker than Necker to sense that the *parlement* had shot its last bolt and he was readier for a more imaginative approach to the estates. It was unfortunate that he did not possess a bolder minister.

Malesherbes might have been such a man. He gave the king insightful memoranda. Of the first, on economies, Malesherbes said, 'I know that he read it carefully'; but the most important one runs to 153 pages of printed text. Did he read that? Malesherbes confessed that he 'didn't have the gift of brevity'.[69] If he had possessed the beguiling lucidity and eloquence of a Calonne, which even his enemies admired, he might have made more impact on the king. If he had possessed these gifts, Malesherbes could have reduced his analysis to a few simple 'bullet points': i) the situation in 1787 was a world away from that of 1786 because the king had convoked the Notables, revealed the deficit to them and opened a Pandora's box by instituting provincial assemblies; ii) the benign effects of the king's liberal policies were negated by their being dribbled out rather than announced in a solemn statement backed by the council on convening a national assembly and by their being accompanied by 'authoritarian measures' – exiles, imprisonments and troop deployments; iii) this had enabled the *parlement*, despite the hypocritical selfishness of many of its members, to set the terms of the debate on the defining political event of the day: the convocation of the Estates-General.

Until 1786, Malesherbes argued, the *parlement* had whipped up public opinion; thereafter it merely reflected it. Another way of looking at the question is this. The *parlements*, in the words of one of their number, 'only exercised a secondary and fiduciary power in the absence of the Estates-General'.[70] The moment that, with Necker's return, people thought the estates really would meet their abolition (in 1790) was already accomplished in idea. Louis realized this. Necker did not. The *parlements* were a spent force. So was their counterparty, absolute monarchy. Necker also saw the nobility as strong and to be placated – 'a great weight in the balance'; Louis saw them as weak and in need of protection – 'I will not desert my nobility.'

Malesherbes's views on the royal authority were complex, even paradoxical. He wanted the king to use the remnant of his absolute power to secure the nation's liberty. Few contested the king's right to determine the electoral units and number of the deputies. But Malesherbes controversially argued that the king should veto any attempt by the estates to perpetuate its organization in the next assembly. He also thought that the king, as the incumbent, could and should establish 'red lines' over which the estates could not encroach when the relative powers of king and nation were being settled. The Estates-General were not a sovereign body, they did not possess what Siéyès called the dictatorship of constituent power. Malesherbes warned the king that the estates would try this on but they must be resisted. He warned, 'they will successively strip you of several of your prerogatives. It is up to you, in your council, to draw up a definitive list of what you will never surrender.' 'I think like you', the king replied, but what could they do when 'we see even the courtiers, who live off the monarchy, turning to opposition.'[71] The comte de Boisgelin had been typical. And Malesherbes was led by his own 'puerile'[72] distaste for office to refuse the king's request that he succeed his Lamoignon cousin as keeper of the seals – the minister with overall responsibility for the holding of the estates.

And what were Louis's views on the Estates-General? We know from Calonne's memoranda that he did not want them in 1786. But by 15 February 1788 at the latest he began to contemplate the possibility. For in an *obiter dictum* on Turgot's memorandum on provincial assemblies he commented: 'the idea of forming perpetual Estates-General is subversive of the monarchy which is only absolute because authority is not shared.'[73] The key word here is 'perpetual'. This can be taken to mean either 'regular', with elections at fixed intervals, such as those provided for by the English triennial act. Or it could mean 'continuous', which seems the natural interpretation. No diet or parliament, however, in the eighteenth century was perpetual in this sense; for example, the English parliament only met for a few months of the year, which left the executive with considerable scope. The 1789 Estates-General which transmuted into the National Assembly on 17 June did, however, become *perpétuel*, meeting every day with no vacation. This partly explains how it arrogated to itself virtually all the powers in the state.

Both Malesherbes and the king took a very gloomy view of the future. In October 1788 they discussed Hume on Charles I, Malesherbes concluding that Louis would not share the fate of the English king because in France 'the political quarrel is luckily not aggravated by a religious one'. 'Very luckily', the king said, squeezing Malesherbes's arm, 'so the atrocity will not be the same.'[74] The day before the *Résultat du conseil* was announced, Louis, on entering his private *cabinet*, found that the portrait of his grandfather had been replaced by one of Charles I. Indeed, there is at this time a fatalism about the royal entourage; Mercy, for example, noting the declining health of the dauphin, concluded illogically that although his younger brother, the duc de Normandie, was 'robust . . . this kind of constitution is always dangerous for the cutting of teeth' and that he would probably go the same way.[75] Notwithstanding, Marie-Antoinette took comfort in the health and beauty of the duc de Normandie, her favourite, her 'chou d'amour'. She liked to show him off, making him perform the nursery songs she had taught him. But Bombelles, a victim of her motherly pride, noted that 'the princes of the House of Bourbon are not distinguished by the beauty of their voice'.[76] Louis XV had been an exception.

But there was little hope for the dauphin, who had contracted tuberculosis – the curse of his family – and had been ailing since 1785, when he was four. His variety of the disease affected the bones, and in February 1788 Marie-Antoinette informed her 'dear brother' Joseph that one of the boy's shoulders was higher than the other and that his spine was deformed. The doctors recommended that he be sent to Meudon for the air, where Louis himself had been sent as a frail and probably tubercular boy. Since he was obviously dying it was cruel to separate the child from his family. As it was, Louis visited his beloved son more than forty times between February and December 1788. The ambassador, Bombelles, saw the dauphin in June, and noted, 'I would have cried had I dared, seeing his lamentable state, bent like an old man . . . he fears the world and is ashamed to be seen'. The doctors' diagnoses differed for, as Bombelles observes, 'our children of France [children and grandchildren of a king] are often the victims of these differences of opinion'.[77]

The pessimism in the royal entourage extended to the ministers, where it was sometimes accompanied by cynicism. La Luzerne, the naval minister, was 'the first to think that at the present moment high office was to be feared rather than desired'. When Brienne's brother, the comte de Brienne, war secretary, was made a *ministre d'état*, he simply complained about having 'four hours taken out of his week' sitting through meetings of the council. And when he was made a knight of the Saint-Esprit, the highest order of chivalry, and was told that the installation and vigil on New Year's Day 1789 would be in freezing weather, he replied that the honour 'was not worth getting a cold for'.[78]

CHAPTER TEN

THE SILENT KING AND THE
THIRD ESTATE

WE NOW COME UPON the central tragedy of the reign: the misunderstanding between the king and the third estate in the Estates-General which led to the collapse of royal authority and a damaging and widespread belief in the king's duplicity. Having virtually called the third estate into existence as a political force, the king was perceived to have betrayed their trust and thrown in his lot with the nobility; the truth was more complicated, but the perception was what mattered.

The third estate was an artificial social-political entity revived by Calonne and his king to preserve the monarchy's independence of action. It was a divisive move, as Miromesnil and Castries had bluntly told the king, and created the elements of a contest. At first the royal policy had fallen flat, the *Avertissement* elicited little response, but at some time between the summer of 1788 and that of 1789 the nobility ceased to be a threat to the monarchy, so there was no need to make it further concessions. The focus of political debate shifted from the question of royal 'despotism' to a struggle between the orders: in other words, belatedly, the royal policy had succeeded. Louis, and his principal adviser, Jacques Necker, did not recognize this turning point and, as late as April 1789, Necker called the nobility 'still a great weight in the balance'. Neither did they have a clear idea of how to respond to this change; the *Résultat du conseil* suggested no great clarity of vision on the part of the government.

Moreover, this confusion of aims was further clouded, for anyone trying to interpret it, by the king's inaccessibility and by a formidable development of his silences. Silence was now not just *to* questions but *on* questions. Louis made no attempt to influence the elections to the Estates-General, either by indicating suitable candidates or by drafting model *cahiers de doléances* or mandates to be adopted by the electoral bodies: in previous Estates-General these had formed a basis for royal legislation. His reticence went further: the nobility of the *bailliage* of Clermont-en-Beauvaisis had imposed on their deputy, the duc de Liancourt, a mandate to limit the king's power. Mindful that Boisgelin, his predecessor as master of the wardrobe, had been dismissed and exiled for supporting the Breton rebellion, Liancourt thought it prudent to ask: 'If Your Majesty thinks I have contracted obligations which could displease him, would Your Majesty be good enough to inform me?' He would then have resigned; Louis gives him the illuminating reply: 'When I ordered the convocation of the Estates-General I permitted all my subjects to make any suggestions tending to the good of the state. When the estates meet I will treat with them of all the great matters there presented. Until such time I must not reveal my attitude towards individual deliberations provided they have been conducted in accordance with the regulations.'[1]

A straw in the wind about Louis's attitude was provided by his response to the Réveillon riots of 27–28 April. Réveillon was a wallpaper manufacturer who advocated a lowering of wages, though apparently without seeking to apply his theories to his own employees. When a mob burned down his house and his factory for his pains, Louis assumed that this riot, like the more limited ones of the previous year, had been instigated by the *parlement* and deprived it of cognizance over the affair. This was the last occasion on which the king was seen to act in terms of the old politics.

But there were counter-currents: a strong movement to persuade the king to replace Necker with the baron de Breteuil and reassert the royal authority. This was made possible by a reconciliation between Breteuil and the Artois-Polignac set, who had always sided with Calonne in his bitter dispute with Breteuil. Their long-term aim was to bring back Calonne and exploit any situation that could 'sooner or later restore him to office'.[2] But for the moment they gave Breteuil to understand that not only would they not oppose his recall but would 'welcome' him back 'as being the only man capable of maintaining the rights of the crown'.[3] But when, on 30 April, Artois asked Breteuil what was to be done, he replied, 'Nothing, except to keep calm, always remain faithfully attached to the king and to the country and to look to the tutelary genius of France for that which one can no longer expect from the sensible measures which should have been taken.'[4]

This was hardly encouraging for the would-be counter-revolution. Artois tried an alternative approach: to persuade Louis to create a special council to deal with the Estates-General on which all the princes of the blood would have a seat – most of them had signed the letter to the king back in December

condemning double representation for the third estate. The king was not interested. Then Artois suggested that maybe just he and Provence could be
members; to which 'His Majesty replied coldly that he would summon them
occasionally if he felt he had need of their advice'. Then, on 28 April, Artois and
Provence tried another tack: Louis should replace the ministers with ones
better able to 'defend the rights of his sceptre'. Apart from Breteuil, La Vauguyon
(son of Louis's appalling governor) was to be foreign minister and the hated
Foulon was to have something. Unfortunately Louis detested all three. So he
replied that he was 'very happy with the members of his council, that all,
without exception, were serving him very well and above all were suited to the
circumstances because of their gentle and prudent conduct'.[5]

This is the account of an initiate, Breteuil's lieutenant, the diplomat
Bombelles, who thought Breteuil would receive the call 'despite His Majesty's
prejudices against him'.[6] But tidings quickly spread beyond the inner circles. On
the same day, 28 April, two Breton deputies wrote home about an attempt by
Artois and the Polignacs to persuade the king to dismiss Necker and cancel the
meeting of the estates. 'The other ministers as well as the princes of the blood
were thoroughly involved' in the plot. A deputation from the *parlement* apparently promised funds for the adventure but, as in the previous December, Louis
gave them all a dusty response: 'the conspiracy was discovered and the king flew
into a frightening rage, abusing all the ministers, above all M. de Villedeuil,
from whose suit he tore two buttons'. A third deputy adds that the king 'in his
usual energetic manner' would have dismissed Necker's ministerial opponents
if 'M. Necker had not convinced him of the inconvenience of such a change at
the moment at which the Estates-General was about to begin'.[7] Thus there was
nothing to diminish the high hopes of the deputies of the third estate as they
gathered at Versailles throughout April for the opening of the estates.

Only protocol dampened their spirits. Before the estates opened the deputies for the three orders were presented to the king. It was said he did not want
to receive the deputies for the third estate at all because no one knew the correct
procedure or even most of their names, exceptions being Target, who had
defended Rohan, Bailly the astronomer and the comte de Mirabeau, Calonne's
hired pen, who had not been able to stand for the nobility in his native Provence
because he did not own a fief. When the members of the nobility and clergy
were ushered into the king's cabinet to be presented, both wings (*battants*) of
the doors were opened, but for the members of the third estate one remained
firmly shut – in their face it must have seemed. And Louis must have known
the full significance of this slight because he had recently inflicted it on the
refractory *parlement*.

On 4 May, the day before the opening of the estates, there was a procession and solemn mass. Louis looked radiant but Marie-Antoinette's 'brow was troubled, her lips tight-set and she made vain attempts to hide her agitation'. Any cries of 'Vive la Reine' Bombelles noted were stifled. He continued: 'Never has a queen of France been less popular; and yet no act of wickedness can be laid at her door. We are decidedly unjust to her and far too severe in punishing her for, at most, a few examples of flightiness.'[8] She looked anxious again during the opening ceremony on the 5th.

The king was accompanied by his brothers and the princes of his blood, with the exception of the duc d'Orléans, first prince of the blood. He had stood for election to the estates and opted to sit among the deputies rather than by the king. Louis, for whom such grandstanding was tasteless as well as insulting, asked him twice to take his rightful place. Refusing, he protested his loyalty. Louis replied tartly, 'The proof of that will lie in your conduct.' With Orléans's embellishments the king's reply became 'Your person will answer for your conduct'; and with Chinese whispers, 'Your head will answer for your conduct.'[9]

Orléans was already seated with the noble deputies when the king's retinue entered. They wore brightly coloured costumes with plumes in their hats. The clergy wore clothes of sombre magnificence. These first two orders were allowed in first, before the deputies for the third estate, in regulation plain black clothes and plumeless hats, were finally admitted. Hats led to further acrimony. Louis having doffed and replaced his own, which bore, as well as ostrich plumes, the huge diamond known as the Régent, the nobility replaced theirs. So too did some of the third estate, who were supposed to remain uncovered. Some had done this in ignorance of the rules, others in defiance of them. But Louis resolved the impasse by doing what in any case he had been itching to do in the summer heat amidst 1,200 bodies: ostentatiously mopping his brow, he removed his own hat and fanned himself with it. Everyone had to follow suit, and was glad to do so. Other problems could not be solved so neatly.

Proceedings were opened by three speeches from the king, from Barentin and from Necker, extending respectively to three, ten and sixty pages of print. Louis's speech was an anodyne compilation of draft speeches from Necker, Barentin, Montmorin, Rayneval, the *premier commis* of the foreign office, and two ministers-without-portfolio, the duc de Nivernais and the comte de Saint-Priest. There also exists a draft by Marie-Antoinette – symbolizing her increased influence over the king. In addition to the speech he actually delivered on 5 May, there are also two drafts in the king's hand.[10] But the king's final draft, the speech he actually delivered to the Estates-General, simply lifts four paragraphs from Montmorin's draft (apparently the last submitted to him) and follows them with four of Necker's. The first and last paragraphs of anodyne sentimentality are the king's own. Only in the first of his three drafts, in which he vents his frustration at the opposition to his reforming plans in 1787–88, does Louis offer his own explanation for the impasse: 'I have often been thwarted in my policies but my goal has never changed. I will be greatly in your debt, Messieurs, if you will give me your full support in accomplishing them.' Marie-Antoinette suggested that Louis delete this passage, which he did. But Louis's speech was 'splendidly articulated'. It was well received and put him in a good mood.[11]

Necker's two-hour speech was mostly taken up with technical details about the financial crisis, which he both claimed to have solved and thought should be the deputies' priority. To get any inkling of general royal policy we need to look at the elaboration of this speech. A starting point is the curious section in the *Résultat du conseil*, after the regulations for the elections to the estates, in which Necker has the king thinking aloud. But the status of his thoughts is unclear. The king has told his ministers – perhaps formally in council – that he will act as a constitutional monarch, needing the consent of the estates to raise taxation, etc. The king would also 'lend a favourable ear to ... [the estates'] suggestions on how to give these provisions permanence and stability'. But what does that mean?

In a draft of his speech Necker proposed to reinforce the king's promises with 'legislative authority'. But Louis objected; and he had obviously raised this matter before, because Louis writes that he '*still* insists on changing the phrase' that endows his promises with legislative authority. Maybe Louis is saying no more than that his word should be taken as his bond. But maybe he is also saying that he does not want these pledges to be given constitutional status. An indication that the king was already being held to his pledges is afforded by the protest by the electoral assembly of Paris at government attempts to prevent the publication of proceedings in the estates.

Louis also picks Necker up on his general views about the legislative process. Necker believed that the Estates-General could make laws – elsewhere he wrote 'with the opening of the estates, legislative power begins'. Not only that but 'the king, while speaking of the new constitution, should pronounce only on the suitability indeed the necessity of maintaining [*sic*] a bicameral legislature. For the rest, he should content himself with the arrangements presented to him' by the estates. This was anathema to the king. But he politely put Necker's error down to sloppy wording: 'At the beginning I have added "at the request" of the estates because ... they cannot make law on their own.'[12] The phrase 'on their own', however, does mark the king's recognition that the 1789 estates, unlike those of 1614, will have a role in the legislative process.

Barentin thought that the king was overly 'indulgent' in putting Necker's error down to a mere 'slip of the pen'. Rather, Necker had 'smuggled in what he did not want to be noticed for the moment, but could use as ammunition if needed'. Even the king's change to 'at the request of the estates' was too mild for Barentin. Louis should have told Necker roundly that laws were made by the king after the estates' 'doléances, supplications [or] representations'. Barentin also thought it was a mistake for the king to concede (whether by promise or legislation) 'periodic' estates because it 'stripped him of the right of convoking and dissolving them and above all of not assembling them at all'.[13]

This was the heart of the matter, but it was temporarily obscured by wrangling in the estates over whether voting should be by order or by head. On this the government speeches said little either. It was difficult to disentangle from them any marked preference, let alone a decision for one or the other. Barentin seemed to favour voting by order, Necker a mixed system depending on the matter to be discussed. And he let out, inadvertently – by referring to *two* or thee orders – that ultimately he favoured a two-chamber system, as in England. This was 'slipped in' (twice) and this time Louis did not remove it. Perhaps he hadn't noticed it – no one else did, or has subsequently. Necker was leaving it to the estates to sort out their own voting procedures. These, however, were essentially technical matters, if ones with political implications, which the king could and should have resolved, though precedent and public opinion were against his doing so.

The first seven weeks of the estates (to 17 June) were occupied by procedural wrangles designed to pre-empt the question of voting by order or head. The deputies of the third estate insisted that the credentials of all the deputies should be 'verified' in the third's chamber, refusing to constitute themselves as a separate order, as the nobility and clergy quickly did. The king offered a futile arbitration service and many suspected that the lack of a resolution would give him an excuse to dissolve the estates. We have found no evidence of this intention, but the fact that, in January, the king had dissolved the estates of Provence after just six days because of disputes between the orders is at least suggestive.

Malouet, a naval intendant and advocate of a strong constitutional monarchy based on alliance with the third estate, strongly believed that the king should perform the *vérification des pouvoirs* himself and present the estates with a programme: 'The subversive idea of a constituent assembly was born of the passive and uncertain state of the monarch, who effaced himself before the new power he had called to consolidate but not annul his own.' But he had to admit that he was alone in his beliefs: 'All the deputies I was able to see before the opening of the estates . . . [of every political complexion] all, to my great astonishment, shared M. Necker's belief that the king should neither propose any plan nor adopt any regulatory procedure; that it was necessary to see the first deliberations of the estates; that it was for them to pronounce on their organization.'[14]

Meanwhile, the deputies for the third estate of Brittany sought guidance from Bertrand de Molleville, who had been intendant of Rennes at the time of the *révolte nobiliaire*, intending, as they put it, 'to do everything for the king to re-establish his authority so that the nobility and the *parlements* could never damage it again'. They asked Bertrand 'to be their interpreter with M. Necker and transmit them his instructions which they would always follow strictly'. Bertrand found it impossible to see Necker, but his *premier commis*, Coster, gave him the message that 'the minister declined all private communication with those deputies as repugnant to the purity of his principles, since it might be considered as . . . a species of corruption'. These royalist deputies were radicals, their Breton club becoming the nucleus of the Jacobin Club.[15]

If communication with Necker was difficult, with Louis it was well-nigh impossible. Although Necker was de facto prime minister, the minister with overall responsibility for the running of the Estates-General was the keeper of the seals, Barentin, who took it upon himself to regulate the king's contacts with the deputies, much in the manner of Maurepas. On 22 June he writes to Louis: 'I think I should point out to Your Majesty that when deputies are instructed to approach you, you might think it best if they address themselves to me so that I can fix an appointment with Your Majesty. Otherwise you might be exposed to being interrupted by requests at any time. Moreover, some requests might occur which require that Your Majesty be given prior notification.' And on 12 June: 'I replied to the *doyen* [of the *tiers*, Bailly] that I would take Your Majesty's orders but that it was not proper to present you with anything you had not been apprised of in advance; that it was therefore necessary for him to give me the speech or address.' On 1 July Barentin considers that the king should admit a deputation, but only to tell them 'that he is going to assemble his council immediately to enable him to decide what course of action he thinks he should adopt'. Spontaneity is thus excluded.[16]

Unfortunately Barentin operated his system in a partial way, and his hostility to the third estate, already evident at the time of the *Résultat*, underwent a crescendo in a series of seventy-six letters to the king between April and July: on 19 June, for example, he advises the king to see a deputation of the nobility because they had behaved well, but not one of the third estate. In fact

Barentin could never find time for Bailly, who urgently needed to seek clarification from the king and explain his order's hopes and fears, namely that the king was 'sold to the magnates' (as Mirabeau put it) or had all along planned this, the same paralysis that had wrecked the estates in 1614. Above all, Bailly would have been able to explain the steps by which the third estate was being driven to assume powers that properly belonged to the king.

On 3 June the third estate declared that it could not 'recognize any intermediary between the king and his people', on the strength of which Bailly asked Necker to get him an audience on the spot. He remained in the apartments adjacent to the Oeil-de-Boeuf whilst Necker went in to see the king, but Necker came back with the message that Bailly would still have to make an appointment with the keeper of the seals. It seems that Necker, as de facto prime minister, could prevent Barentin from seeing the king alone – hence all those letters – but Barentin could prevent Bailly from seeing the king alone. Louis, of course, instead of allowing himself to be trapped in a labyrinth of highly political protocol, should have knocked all their heads together, but he had always found it difficult to disentangle the status of conventions. So Bailly once more had to go to Barentin, who was out but finally transmitted the king's message: 'In my present situation it is impossible for me to see M. Bailly this evening or tomorrow morning or to fix a day to receive the deputation of the *tiers*.'[17]

Unfortunately, Bailly had chosen a bad day: the dauphin had died at one in the morning. The third estate deputies, who were often given to sentimentalism in their relations with the king, had on this occasion shown extreme insensitivity. One deputy had said, 'for Heaven's sake his son is not as sick as the state'. Unable to force their way into the king's cabinet, the third estate deputies tried to waylay the king on his approach, thronging the Oeil-de-Boeuf, the gallery, and the *levée* chamber. Louis had felt it necessary to double the guards and make them arrive early 'in the fear that they would force the door of his cabinet'.[18]

Louis was devastated – he never loved anyone as much as his eldest son. At a quarter to eight he heard mass in private – which he also did on the 5th and the 6th – and then he shut himself off. Only on the 7th does he note, 'La messe et le monde à l'ordinaire'. Louis had to make all the funeral arrangements himself: the dauphin's heart was buried at Val-de-Grâce, his body at Saint-Denis. The Feuillant monks said the service at Meudon, where the boy had died, and Bombelles thought their intoning sounded like the underworld scenes in Gluck's opera *Orfeo*. Everyone went into two months' mourning save only the king, who was obliged by protocol to dress normally. Villedeuil, as minister for the *Maison du Roi*, informed the little duc de Normandie that he was now dauphin and he was invested with the cross of the order of Saint-Louis. He cried because his elder sister, now eleven, was crying. The new dauphin was a vigorous young boy whom Marie-Antoinette thought had peasant vitality – only studied cruelty would kill him – but such was the pessimism at court that Bombelles thought that 'his spine was bent and he would end up a hunchback'.[19]

The deputation of the third estate, exceptionally, managed to see the king on the 6th, but their importunity had drawn from him his celebrated remark: 'There are no fathers then among the third estate.' Thus tragedy is mixed with farce, reality with formalism. On 15 July Louis was to announce that in future access to him would be direct, without intermediary, but 'it had taken nothing less than the storming of the Bastille to bring down this barrier'.[20]

The difficulty in obtaining a private audience with the king was all the more disconcerting because of his total public silence, yet many believed that this was the correct constitutional stance. D'Eprémesnil, former leader of the *révolte parlementaire*, even 'observed that a letter entirely written in the king's hand could infringe the liberty of the chamber [of the nobility] and the private and personal opinion of the king must necessarily restrict free debate and therefore should not be read out'.[21]

On 3 June, a full month after the opening of the estates, Véri asks:

What are the king's views and those of Necker, his solitary guide in this maze? I do not know. This is what I have learned. The duc de Nivernais, deeply affected by the partisan struggles in the estates, asked for an audience of the king with whom he unexpectedly found Necker. He strongly represented to him the necessity of taking a line in the debates between the third estate and the other two orders and said that only his decision could bring about harmony in the main business of the estates. No reply from the king. The duc insisted once more: still silence from the king. And finally Necker came in with: 'it's still too early'.[22]

It wasn't; it was too late.

Necker was finally coming round to the idea of a royal intervention but before he could act, on 17 June, the deputies of the third estate unilaterally declared themselves to be the National Assembly. Moreover, as d'Angiviller noted, 'it declared null and void all hitherto existing taxes and established the principle that even in the past, the tacit consent of the nation had not been sufficient to legitimize a tax, that its formal consent was necessary and that registration by the *parlements* had not been a substitute'.[23] The ancien régime,

1614–1789, had never been a legitimate one. The abbé Siéyès said that 'on this day of the 17th we jumped forward two centuries'.[24] He had in fact led his troops across the Rubicon a week previously, on 10 June, when, on his proposal, the third estate had voted to issue one last appeal to the other estates to join them and then proceed to verify their powers in the name of the whole Estates-General.

During this crucial period (14–21 June) the king was based at the royal château of Marly, four miles to the north-west of Versailles. By suggesting that Louis withdraw to Marly to mourn the dauphin, Necker's enemies had provided themselves with a congenial milieu in which to work on the king. It had always been easier for a small group to manipulate the king in one of the smaller châteaux than at Versailles, where ministers had automatic access to him. Necker later wrote that 'the visit to Marly had been arranged to make it easier to surround the king and to work his mind against the plans of the ministry'; Vaudreuil, Madame de Polignac's lover, advised, 'Let us make sure that nothing contrary to us reaches [the king and queen] and leads them to turn towards the nation either from prudence or from weakness.'[25] Montjoie wrote: 'A vast silence reigned about the king; access to the throne was difficult.'[26]

One source says that Louis had not wanted to go to Marly and cut down the length of the stay. And at first Necker's enemies had not found the king receptive; one of their group, the comtesse d'Adhémar, writes:

We never ceased repeating to the king that the third estate would wreck everything and we were right. We begged him to restrain them, to impose his sovereign authority on party intrigue. The king replied: "But it is not clear that the *tiers* are wrong. Different forms have been followed each time the estates have been held. So why reject verification in common? I am for it." The king, it has to be admitted, was then numbered among the revolutionaries: a strange fatality which can only be explained by detecting the hand of providence.[27]

The declaration of a National Assembly annoyed Necker (who seriously considered blowing up their chamber)[28] more than it did the king, who merely remarked, 'It's only a phrase.' But Louis was sufficiently alarmed to return to Versailles on the 17th, where he presided over several *comités* and held the *Conseil des Dépêches*, which lasted until 9.30 p.m. Here Necker outlined his plan to intervene in the proceedings of the Estates-General by a *séance royale*. He argued that the main battle was lost and all the king could do was cover his retreat. He should deploy the panoply of a *lit de justice* to command the first two orders to join the third in discussing matters of general interest, including the crucial one of the organization of future estates. Hopefully that would give the king enough credit to make conditions for his surrender. These were: i) that the feudal and honorific privileges of the nobility should not be discussed in common; ii) that the king would not accept a single chamber legislature; iii) that the public should not be allowed to attend sessions; iv) that the king 'reserved to himself the full exercise of the executive power, especially the administration of the army'.[29] Necker wanted to 'pass over' the declaration of the National Assembly in the hope that, once voting procedures had been settled, it would go away.

Barentin, however, immediately seized upon the implications of the declaration of the National Assembly. To his legalistic and precedent-bound mind – and he rightly surmised to the legalistic minds of the lawyers who dominated the third estate – as long as the Estates-General had remained the Estates-General, they would never have dared to usurp the legislative power, which previous Estates-General had never exercised.[30] This act, the assumption of the title National Assembly, was, for Barentin, the primary cause of the council meetings which culminated in the famous *séance royale* of 23 June, when the king for the first and last time attempted to intervene in the proceedings of the estates. Barentin wanted the king to annul the third estate's act. A further meeting of the council was arranged for the 19th back at Marly to finalize details for the *séance royale*. Necker's account suggests that this was a mere formality, but the *conseiller d'état* Vidaud de la Tour, who played a key role in drafting the final text, told d'Angiviller that Necker's memorandum was merely 'taken into consideration'.

Necker travelled to Marly in the same carriage as his ministerial allies Montmorin, La Luzerne and Saint-Priest. On the way he read out his memorandum in full but it was lost on Saint-Priest because of the 'jolts of the carriage on the pavings'.[31] When they arrived, the queen summoned Necker and, together with Artois and Provence, tried to dissuade him from reading his memorandum to the council. Marie-Antoinette, having originally supported the third estate, was now vacillating between the king and Artois. A gap in her correspondence with Joseph II makes it difficult to speak with certainty about her views in May and June, but during that time Necker's son-in-law, the baron de Staël, wrote of Artois's confidence 'now that he has won over the queen',[32] and Mercy describes her as having been momentarily 'swept along by the infernal plot directed against the finance minister'.[33]

At all events, Necker refused her request and at the council no substantive objections were raised. The king had remained silent but, according to Necker, was about to terminate the session by approving the proposals, and the portfolios were already closing when suddenly we saw an official in attendance enter; he approached the king's fauteuil, whispered to him and immediately His Majesty rose, instructing his ministers to remain where they were and await his return. This message, coming as the council was about to finish, naturally surprised us all. M. de Montmorin, who was sitting next to me, told me straight out: 'Everything is undone; only the queen could have allowed herself to interrupt the *Conseil d'État*; the princes must have got round her and they want, by her intervention, to postpone the king's decision.'[34]

When the king returned, he adjourned the council and indeed postponed the decision.

Such is Necker's account. But d'Angiviller has a different take:

> Far from being adopted . . . [Necker's proposal] gave rise to so many reflections that it was thought necessary on a matter of such gravity to consult the most enlightened magistrates [the *conseillers d'état*]; that several of them be summoned to the council to examine . . . [Necker's proposal]; that it seemed a matter of such importance that the two princes, the king's brothers, who did not have the *entrée* to the council were likewise summoned and, unless I am deceived, several princes of the blood, but my recollection of this is not as clear as it is over the other facts. I was at Marly.[35]

The next day, 20 June, was the crucial one. Necker was detained in Paris by the grave illness of his sister-in-law, Madame de Germany, but, realizing the pressures the king would be under, he sent him an urgent note: 'Several drawbacks to a *séance royale* which I had missed have been pointed out to me and it is thought that a simple letter of invitation [to the orders to sit together] would serve better.' This may be because he felt his plan would be distorted; or because he feared that even his own version would be rejected by the Assembly. He would have been informed of its mood by the stream of deputies, including the radical barrister Target, d'Angiviller noted entering Necker's house, which was directly opposite d'Angiviller's own.

But orders had already been given to the troops in preparation for the *séance royale* to bar entry to the hall in which the Assembly met. The *séance* was announced for the 22nd but crassly, just by wall posters, not even a royal message. The Assembly, wrongly concluding that the king intended a dissolution of the estates, took a further, decisive, step: repairing to an indoor real tennis court, they took the famous oath not to separate until they had given

France a constitution (20 June). For Louis, this was the critical move: he had already shown his concern over legislative arrangements during the drafting of Necker's opening speech; ultimately he would be driven to contemplate flight in order to secure a say in the framing of the constitution.

And it was in this charged atmosphere that the council met again at Marly. The chevalier de Coigny, one of the Polignac group, writes to the bishop of Soissons:

> This morning the queen and his brother [presumably Artois] went to see the king and asked him what he was planning to do; he seemed as usual very uncertain and said that really the matter was not worth worrying about; that since previous Estates-General had not all acted uniformly in procedural matters one could let them arrange it as they liked.
>
> 'But look,' they replied, 'the *tiers* has just declared itself the National Assembly.' 'It's only a phrase.' 'It has passed a resolution declaring the present form of raising taxation illegal in future.' 'Heavens,' the King replied, 'he who pays the piper calls the tune and since they are the ones paying taxes it does not surprise me that they want to regularize the way it is raised.'
>
> A deputation from the Parlement having failed to move the King, M. le Cardinal de la Rochefoucauld [*président* of the Clergy's deputies] accompanied by M. l'Archévêque de Paris appeared in their turn. Turning on the emotion, they threw themselves at His Majesty's feet and besought him in the name of Saint Louis and the piety of his august ancestors to defend Religion, cruelly attacked by the philosophes who counted among their sectaries nearly all the members of the *tiers*, etc.
>
> This appears greatly to have shaken the King, who asked in an emotional voice where they had learned so much . . .
>
> Then Mme de Polignac wheeled in the royal children and the queen . . . pushed them into the arms of their father, beseeching him to hesitate no further and to confound the plans of the enemies of the family. The king, touched by her tears and by so many representations, gave way and intimated his desire to hold a council on the spot. The princes were sent for and the council met immediately without summoning [Necker] . . . who knows nothing of this. Everything is settled: the king will issue a declaration which will satisfy the nation, will order the deputies to work in their respective chambers and will severely punish the meddlers and intriguers. You may rest assured that he will not budge and a *séance royale* is announced; it is there that the plan that I tell you of will be unfolded . . .[36]

This second council at Marly met on the 20th, with the king's two brothers and four *conseillers d'état* present and Necker absent. Although there were to be two further meetings of the council at Versailles, on Sunday 21 June and on the 22nd, the presence once again of the king's brothers on the 21st convinced Necker that the game was up, though the king's unease is shown by his asking Saint-Priest and Montmorin before the meeting on the 22nd for written opinions, which he knew would be favourable to Necker's case. Saint-Priest, however, offered no guarantees that Necker's plan would succeed: 'I fear that the third estate in its present state of exaltation will reject those absolutely just restrictions to be imposed on deliberating in common. I even fear that it will complain about the sovereign intervention of Your Majesty at this juncture'.[37] The king would then have to appeal to the country – how is unclear – but that resource was 'as slow as it is uncertain'. And there was no money in the treasury to pay for military sanctions. Louis liked his ministers to guarantee success, and this uncertainty and lack of a clearly defined position, coupled with the 'tennis court oath', emboldened Barentin, Artois and the Polignacs to attempt to capture the mechanism of a *séance royale* and fill it with the spirit of their own proposals.

As Necker's draft has not survived, it is hard to say exactly what changes were made. But Vidaud de la Tour, who made the final version, told d'Angiviller, in whose coach he travelled to the *séance royale*, that the changes 'were not considerable but essential'. He continued, 'you will find [at the *séance*] that the king is abandoning much – too much – of his authority. It distresses me and I see with sadness that they want to destroy everything and that the state is lost. All I could hope to do was to preserve the basis of legislation [*la base des loix*], that was the only aim I set myself, in the hope that in calmer times experience and reason may replace them'.[38] These somewhat fugitive words seem to mean that Vidaud hopes he has reserved to the king sufficient legislative power to reverse bad laws when the climate permits.

In its details, the final version may perhaps represent a compromise effected by the king between the position of Necker and that of Barentin, but the changes were more than an already doubtful enterprise could bear. Voting in common on matters of general interest was retained, but the king suggested that motions should only be carried by a two-thirds majority and insisted that the organization of future estates should be decided by the orders sitting separately. The king promised provincial estates and approval by the Estates-General of taxation, loans and even the royal budget – all in all a recipe for an aristocratic, decentralized, constitutional monarchy. This compromise of royal authority would not have been necessary if Necker had not allowed the case for an active alliance with the third estate to go by default. An important difference between Necker's and the final version was that Necker's promise of a 'career open to talents', e.g., no requirement of nobility for commissioned entry to the army, was omitted. For the third estate deputies, social differences were as important as political ones: they resented the fact that the noble deputies disdained to sit next to them in the same chamber quite as much as the political implications of this.

The deliberations leading to the *séance royale* had taken as long as those preceding the *Résultat du Conseil*, but as they lacked form so they had led to a bad decision. For rule by counsel to be effective, it is essential that advice be taken in an orderly and formal way by people who are authorized to give it, i.e., the ministers. It was disastrous for the king to be taken out of his natural setting at Versailles, cut off from his official advisers and closeted with people such as the archbishop of Paris or even his brothers (Louis XV had not had a brother, while Louis XIV had always excluded his from affairs).

The *séance* itself, in which, for the last time, the king appeared in his full regalia, was a fiasco. Along the streets of Versailles, Louis was himself treated to complete silence – the 'lesson of kings', as the phrase went. The use of Lamoignon's unfortunate terminology – *séance royale* – suggested that the king was treating the Estates-General with no more respect than a disobedient *parlement*. In his *discours-programme,* similar in form to those he had recently pronounced in the *parlement,* reference was made to the king's *volontés,* whilst the first clause began 'le roi veut'; even the nobility, the beneficiaries of the *séance,* jibbed at forms which would have been regarded as highly irregular at the height of the ancien régime. As for the third estate, they simply refused to obey the king's order to 'disperse immediately and proceed tomorrow morning each to the chamber allocated to his order'. To the master of ceremonies, Mirabeau addressed his famous apostrophe about only moving at the point of the bayonet. The versions of Louis's reactions to this are at total variance, ranging from 'No, not bayonets' and 'So they want to stay? Damn it let them', to 'Clear them out!' The very criers refused to proclaim the new laws, claiming that they had colds.

Up to this point, the third estate deputies' thinking about the king's intentions towards them had been wishful. If they had had eyes to see, or if they had not covered them with rose-tinted spectacles, they might have realized that, as early as the *Résultat du conseil* back in December Louis's attitude had been equivocal. Even as they began to have their doubts, they could not make up their minds whether his silence was due to indecisiveness or divided counsels. Either or both were possible. But now on 23 June, Louis, in his robes and with a metaphorical crown on his head, had actually spoken *ex cathedra*. And his words were peremptory. Even so, some deputies tried to extract crumbs of comfort from the bitter bread, and notably from the fact that Necker was still in office.

Necker had absented himself from the *séance*, which refurbished his fading popularity; this is ironic because, as Saint-Priest suggests, his version of the *séance royale* would probably have been rejected as well. Necker had not informed the king, who arrived at the ceremony to find the other ministers and state councillors in place but the finance minister's chair empty. Louis waited a little for him to arrive, looking round myopically, but Necker was sitting in his carriage. He was in a quandary: to resign before the *séance* would have caused a riot. On the other hand to attend the *séance* would be to endorse policies of which he disapproved. So he sat in his carriage with the horses harnessed up and dithered until his daughter, the feisty Madame de Staël, told him it would be dishonourable to attend.

After the *séance*, as rumours of his resignation swirled through the streets of Versailles, a vast populace poured into the palace, reaching the doors of the royal apartments, where, on this occasion, the bodyguards were able to halt them. Marie-Antoinette summoned Necker and for twenty minutes begged him not to resign. Then he went to see the king, who was heard through the door 'shouting at the top of his voice: "It is I, Monsieur, who am making all the sacrifices, making them with all my heart, whilst you take all the credit; you want to take all the thanks yourself." ' This scene took place in the king's inner cabinet but was overheard in the council chamber next door by d'Angiviller who was with two courtiers.

Necker emerged, looking 'pensive and worried'. A more sensitive man, d'Angiviller reflects, would have been mortified by the king's words. D'Angiviller begged Necker not to descend to the crowd, whose cheers were an insult to the king. He told him to leave via the glass door that gave on to the galleries 'to which I had the key in virtue of my office'[39] and offered to escort Necker back to his house. But Necker would not forgo his triumph. D'Angiviller told one of the courtiers present, 'My dear count, if I had not feared for the king's safety, it would have been through this window that . . . [Necker] would have rejoined the mob.'[40]

D'Angiviller's account is true but unfair. Necker was descending to enjoy his triumph but also to pacify the crowd by telling them he had agreed to stay on. As well as shouting at him, Louis had also begged Necker not to resign. Necker made the same demand Calonne had made in 1787: to rid himself of Barentin and Villedeuil and remodel the ministry with like-minded men; that is, to be a prime minister in the English sense. The king refused and Necker weakly or responsibly agreed to stay. He added that if at any time his services should cease to be agreeable to the king he would retire to his estates as discreetly as possible. Louis replied, 'I will take you at your word', but he said it in such a kindly tone that its significance did not sink in. By not attending the *séance*, Necker had signalled that the ministry was divided and this he believed would win the king sympathy and permit a climb-down.

The hardliners blamed Marie-Antoinette for her conciliatory tone, as Artois's friend Vaudreuil, recounts:

> 'Dare I ask the queen,' I said bowing respectfully, 'whether M. Necker accompanied the king to the Assembly?' 'No,' she replied with an air of surprise and annoyance, 'but why this question?' 'Just that if the principal minister is not put on trial today, tomorrow the monarchy will be destroyed.' Hardly had I pronounced these words when a severe gesture from the sovereign ordered me to leave. I bowed even lower to show even greater respect: 'I am pained to see that I have incurred the queen's displeasure but I will never hesitate between favour and duty.' After a third bow, even lower than the others, I retired and was not recalled.[41]

According to Mercy, the union of the three orders in one chamber, effected by royal command on 27 June, was brought about by the 'moderation and wisdom of her counsels'.[42] As likely she was just scared. She knew she was hated, protected only by the king's gravity-defying popularity. On the previous Friday and Saturday, whilst the council was discussing intervention, the dwellings of even moderate nobles, such as the marquis de Ferrières, had been painted with a black P for 'proscrit'.

Louis's order to the nobility to sit with the third estate and the clergy, who had already gone over to them, was obstructed by Barentin, who gave the duc de Luxembourg, president of the nobles' chamber, to understand that it could be discounted.[43] The order had to be repeated and followed by a direct request from Artois, which must have cost him dear. Luxembourg had begged the king not to give in to the third estate, telling him that the division of the estates into three chambers 'put a brake on their freedom of action' and preserved the king's; but Louis took his arm and in Cassandra mode replied, 'You insisted on them, these Estates-General. Well now you're stuck with them'! This was needlessly rubbing it in, for in April, even before the estates had opened, Luxembourg freely confessed he had been wrong to demand them as a peer in the *parlement*.[44] The king told Luxembourg, 'My mind is made up. I am prepared to make any sacrifice. I do not want a single man to perish in my quarrel. Tell my faithful nobility that I am asking them to join the other two orders. If that is not enough, I order it. As their king, I desire it.'[45] Yet such was the suspicion among the deputies of the third estate that a rumour was credited that at midnight on the 26th artillery had been ordered from Saint-Cloud in order to bombard the National Assembly. It had been countermanded at the last minute by a 'committee of the royal family', which decided instead to order the nobility to sit with the other orders.[46]

Barentin continued to regard the articles enunciated in the *séance* as law, even after the union of the orders, and since Villedeuil, as minister for the *Maison*, was effectively minister of the interior, they were able to promulgate them all over France. In an attempt to cover himself, however, Barentin did not seal the declaration with the formal yellow seal or countersign the version sent to the *imprimerie royale*. For his part, Louis, in persuading Necker to stay, told him that he did not insist on the articles which had angered the *tiers*, and Necker was sure that 'his views were the same as mine'.[47]

Nevertheless, an important concomitant of the *séance* was not countermanded: the concentration of troops round Paris. On 22 June, the day Necker's version was finally jettisoned, Louis signed the first order, for the Swiss Reinach regiment to leave Soissons and arrive at Paris on the 26th. On the 26th, the day before he ordered the nobility to sit in the National Assembly, further orders were given, so that by 14 July there were some 30,000 troops assembled in the Paris region. This was far short of the 100,000 intended – the figure, it will be remembered, Castries had thought necessary to subdue the *parlements*. Of the ministers, Louis at first only consulted Puységur, the minister of war, and then, with the promise of the Saint-Esprit and the governorship of Calais, Louis asked him to step down in favour of the aged maréchal de Broglie, whom he summoned from Normandy: 'I need with me, M. le Maréchal, someone whose loyalty I can trust; someone who knows how to command my troops.'[48] On 4 July these troops were put under the general command of Broglie, with the baron de Besenval, lieutenant-colonel of the Swiss Guards, his field commander in Paris.

At this time, in a ministerial committee, Necker confessed he was embarrassed by his popularity, which was eclipsing that of the king, and offered to resign without fuss. Louis was touched by the offer and, pressing his advantage, Necker asked him to withdraw the troops. Broglie objected, but was only supported by Villedeuil and Puységur. Nevertheless, Louis did not see fit to cancel the orders to the troops.[49] Naturally the National Assembly was also concerned about the troop build-up. On 8 July, after an angry speech in which

Mirabeau denounced the 'warlike preparations of the court', the Assembly petitioned the king to withdraw his troops from the Paris region. At 6 p.m. the archbishop of Vienne entered the king's cabinet to ask him to receive the Assembly's petition. Louis prevaricated and, Bombelles records, Broglie 'felt obliged to enter the king's cabinet to fortify His Majesty' against this scandalous request.[50]

But what were the troops summoned for? Most people at the time (and since) have assumed that the king's intention was to throw off the mask of conciliation, dissolve the National Assembly and subdue Paris by force of arms. There is not a shred of evidence for this assumption. The king's instructions to Besenval give the general tenor of the military operations contemplated: Besenval must 'give the most precise and the most moderate orders to the officers commanding the detachments you may have to employ that they should only act as protectors and should take the very greatest care not to get into a quarrel with or to engage in any combat with the people, unless they are inclined to arson or to commit riot or pillage which threatens the safety of the citizen'.[51]

The duc de Broglie was given wide powers: generalissimo as well as war minister, he commanded not only the troops-of-the-line but the royal bodyguards, an exceptional infringement of the prerogative of the king who, unmartial though he was, must have been hurt as the kings had always retained personal command of their military household. Even so, Broglie's use of these powers was extremely cautious. In a series of letters to Besenval, he outlines his strategy.[52] There is no mention of offensive measures and even defensive ones are restricted. On 1 July he writes:

> The king consents that you assemble all the forces on which you can rely to safeguard the royal treasury and the Discount Bank and that you confine yourself to defending these two positions . . . at a time when we are unfortunately not in a position to look to everything. I shall authorize the marquis d'Autichamp to remain in his command at Sèvres and then, if it becomes necessary, to bring up the Salis regiment as reinforcements to protect Versailles, falling back on the palace if necessary.

On 5 July he tells Besenval to replace the garrison of the Bastille and 'as soon as the artillery regiment arrives you must send a small detachment of gunners to examine whether the cannon are in good order and to use them if it comes to it, which would be extremely unfortunate but happily is wildly improbable . . .'

Why was Louis so cautious? We have quoted his remark to Luxembourg about not wanting 'a single man to perish in his quarrel'. But that remark could have been embroidered by time. To understand Louis's views on bringing force to bear on the National Assembly we must once again return to his reflections on Turgot and Dupont's 1775 memorandum on 'municipalities' (provincial assemblies). Louis made these annotations in February 1788, in the light of the promise he had just given to convoke the Estates-General. He assumed that Turgot's proposed national municipality, elected by the provincial municipalities, would be 'the assembly of the French people' in a way that the *parlements* and even the traditional Estates-General could never be. With such a truly national assembly 'there would no longer be any intermediate agency between the king and the nation but that of an army'. Troops could and had been employed against, say, a refractory *parlement*, and in the Flour War, but 'it is a horrible and painful extremity to entrust to an army the defending of the authority of the state against the Assembly of the French people.' It would be legitimate to use force, if absolutely necessary, against the traditional Estates-General, such as Louis had summoned and strove to preserve in the *séance royale*. Such a body was a congeries of interests which could be played off against one another – balanced, reconciled and coerced, if need be. But if Louis considered that Turgot's proposed national municipality, which was based on a narrow landed franchise, was 'the assembly of the French people', how much more so was the real National Assembly? 'National Assembly' was not 'just a phrase' and, despite his glib quip, Louis knew it. Yet Louis faced a paradox or conundrum: the more 'representative' the Assembly became – by reflecting more accurately the real power in the country – the less he would be inclined to use force against it; yet by the same token, the need to do so was greater, because, on 17 June, in Necker's phrase, 'it had arrogated to itself an exorbitant authority'.

And the problem of law and order, for which Louis had never been shy of using troops, was getting worse. The harvest of 1788 had been late and poor and it was the critical stage of the year called the *soudure* – the 'gap' between consuming the old harvest and gathering the next. The harvest of 1789 did not promise to be much better: the weather was cold and dry – even in late April the leaves on the chestnuts were barely showing.[53] Grain prices were high (20 per cent higher than in November) and there was pillaging of the markets, which added to the political tensions in the capital. The number of riots (over grain or wages) had risen during Louis's reign: numbering 200 in the years 1735 to 1739, they had risen to 670 in 1770 to 1774 and 869 in 1785 to 1789.[54] Moreover, economic troubles were spilling over into political ones, as the Réveillon riots back in April had demonstrated.

The king's reply, on the 10th, to the Assembly's request to send back the troops, picked up on this, stressing that they 'were only intended to . . . maintain law and order'. If, however – and here a new theme is introduced – the Assembly found their 'necessary presence' offensive he would, 'at the request of the Estates-General [*sic*]', transfer the Assembly to Noyon or Soissons and install himself in the nearby château of Compiègne to maintain contact with it. This offer has been variously regarded as a gibe 'tipped with irony' (Lord Acton), insulting or sinister. Godechot considered that it 'redoubled' the 'apprehensions' of the Assembly.[55] If so, it was because the translation of the Assembly would remove the pressure of Paris on the king. That was why he made the suggestion, in a letter which he drafted himself. Paris was the Assembly's secret (or rather tacit) weapon. Louis intended to deprive them of it, the Assembly to bring it to bear. That, in a nutshell, is the history of the next two years. But it was a Faustian bargain: in the end it was Paris against the Assembly as well as the king.

We have seen that Louis had not wanted the estates to meet at Versailles, only twelve miles from Paris, and we will see that in 1791 he escaped from Paris with the intention of installing himself at Compiègne and summoning the National Assembly to nearby Soissons. But that was also the plan in July 1789. Far from being a gibe tossed like a bone to the mongrel Assembly, Louis was perhaps rashly revealing his plan, concerted with the ministry with which he would replace Necker's.

For some time d'Angiviller had found the king distracted, 'dreamy', unsure of Necker's loyalty. D'Angiviller urged the king to escape with his family from the 'fermenting hotbed' around him. For a long time Louis 'listened but kept his counsel'. Then 'one day' he said that he was recalling Breteuil and turning to the financier-deputy, the baron de Batz, to raise money. On 1 July Breteuil had written to the king offering his services. Louis replied immediately, inviting him to 'continue the correspondence, and . . . to find by restoring public confidence ways of putting the prodigious amount of money locked up in Paris back into circulation by means of a loan'. Louis told Breteuil to 'hold himself in readiness for a *retraite* [either dismissal or resignation] or other event, and His Majesty's phrase was sufficient indication that he was referring to the forced or voluntary resignation of M. Necker'.[56] However, for a long time Louis was reluctant to commit himself to Breteuil or even see him in person. As late as 8 July Bombelles notes that Provence and Artois 'were having to employ all that their attachment to the king dictated to them to engage His Majesty to see the baron de Breteuil and, aided by his counsels, display sufficient firmness to bridle the audacity of the so-called National Assembly'. The day before, Breteuil had felt it necessary to write to the king urging him not to listen to the 'siren voices' asking him to withdraw the troops.[57]

D'Angiviller thought Breteuil was a disastrous choice but, knowing he was the queen's, merely observed that Machault would have been preferable. Louis had considered him at the start of the reign, but he was now ninety and did not interview well. He did, however, provide the *mot juste* on Necker: 'a man as dangerous to keep as awkward to dismiss'.[58] Louis asked d'Angiviller to put up Breteuil in his own house on his arrival so as not to arouse suspicion, though d'Angiviller lived opposite to Necker.

Arriving at d'Angiviller's on 12 July, Breteuil asked him to join the new ministry, which he declined. He told him that the king was going to Compiègne and that the Assembly would be 'translated' to Soissons. They had already sent Thierry, the king's valet-de-chambre and intendant of the crown jewels, ahead to Compiègne with the king's diamonds, valued at 20 million, to serve as collateral for a loan. Batz had formed a syndicate with other financiers to raise 100 million, but Breteuil 'had neglected to ascertain whether this sum would be provided in gold and silver, and he discovered that it was not an engagement of this nature that they had contracted and that instead of ready cash, they were only offering paper' – the same depreciated scrip we noted in 1787, only even more depreciated. To their amazement there was not an écu in the royal treasury – which d'Angiviller put down to Necker's treachery, though Saint-Priest had warned the king of the situation in his letter of 22 June.

Breteuil asked d'Angiviller whether there was any money left in his department (royal buildings) but d'Angiviller said that, on the king's orders, it had all gone on charitable gifts to people in the Duchy of Rambouillet whose crops had been flattened by freak hailstorms – a meteorological phenomenon which seems to have particularly afflicted the late ancien régime. What about the *domaine de* Versailles, Breteuil asked. There were 60,000 *livres* left there: 'And that was the sum total of the resources at his disposal to save the king and his whole family, to snatch them from the imminent danger which threatened them, to pay for travel costs and for the troops needed to escort them and to guarantee their loyalty which was already proving to be shaky'.[59] Breteuil did also plan to raise a loan of 150 million *livres* at 7.3 per cent, but as was his habit, he left the details to others: La Vauguyon (son of Louis's former governor) who was to be foreign secretary, a former first secretary at the finance ministry, and the diplomat Bombelles.[60]

Indeed, of all the ministerial appointments ever made by Louis XVI, that of Breteuil, who received the title *chef du Conseil royal des finances*, is perhaps the most surprising. He had been a dangerous *frondeur* in the ministry in 1783–88, and advised Marie-Antoinette badly during the Diamond Necklace Affair, though she had restrained Louis from dismissing him during the Assembly of Notables. After the coup d'état of 8 May 1788 (which he opposed),[61] Breteuil, as minister for Paris, had asked for holograph orders from the king in order to shift responsibility onto him, and had later resigned rather than take a more repressive line. Knowing the king's aversion to violent measures, one would not expect Breteuil to be more resolute, more prepared to take responsibility for subduing a city in arms than he had been in 1788 for containing relatively minor disturbances with the king's full co-operation. Nor was it an idle fear, for later in the year Barentin, Broglie and Besenval were put on trial for the new crime of *lèse-nation*. Small wonder then that Breteuil 'paid a great deal of attention to installing himself in his hotel and in forming his secretariat'[62] – and did nothing.

La Vauguyon drew up for Artois a prospectus for the new ministry: Bombelles's comments on this sum up the whole enterprise: 'It is well presented but does not indicate with sufficient precision what would have to be done in the present crisis. The combined talents of Richelieu, . . . Sully and . . . Mazarin would not have been superfluous . . . I count more on the faults . . . of [our] enemies than on the adequacy of the means employed for the restoration of peace and of the royal authority'.[63] And did Breteuil even want the job? Bombelles avowed that 'he did not fear to take the helm, but he desired it less than when he saw more chance of doing any good'.[64] And we have seen that in April he had advised doing 'nothing, except keep calm'.

There was more to it, however, than mere inactivity. The princes in bringing back Breteuil had simply mistaken their man. In their political stance, Breteuil and Necker represented the right and left wings of a liberal-aristocratic coalition, which shows the fine point on which the *séance royale* turned and how far Louis's options had narrowed. Breteuil was not a plain reactionary like Artois, who probably did want to subdue Paris by force of arms. One of Breteuil's intimates said that he 'had thwarted all the plans of the maréchal de Broglie'. Later, when he was Louis's plenipotentiary in 1790–92, one of his chief tasks was to be that of thwarting the princes' plans for counter-revolution. All in all, it is extraordinary that the replacement of Necker by Breteuil should have been the signal for an armed rising in Paris.[65]

Dinner – *le dîner* – was taken by the upper classes in the mid-afternoon. Necker was sitting down to his, *en famille*, on Saturday 11 July when at three o'clock La Luzerne, the naval minister, was announced with a letter from the king. It was possibly the gentlest letter of dismissal Louis ever sent a minister:

When I engaged you, Monsieur, to remain in place you asked me to adopt a plan of conduct towards the Estates-General and you have shown me on several occasions that a plan of extreme complaisance was the one you preferred. Since you did not believe you would be of use in executing other plans, you asked for permission to resign if I adopted a different course of action. I accept your offer to leave the kingdom during this moment of crisis and I count on your departure being as you promised prompt and in secret. It behoves your reputation for integrity not to give rise to any disturbances. I hope that when things have calmed down I will be able to give you proof of my sentiments towards you.[66]

There are several curious features about this dismissal. First, the last sentence of Louis's letter seems to give him a loop-hole for asking Necker back. Second, Necker notes: 'The king did not order me to leave the kingdom because from this period he doubted whether he had the legal power to exercise such an act of authority towards anyone'[67] – the world of exile by *lettre de cachet* had at last come to an end. Finally, Necker, not one to miss an opportunity for publicity, nevertheless executed an extremely prompt and secret departure.

When he received the king's letter Necker did not interrupt his meal and said nothing about it either to his brother or to his daughter, Madame de Staël. After they had gone, Necker left, accompanied by his wife, and although they were going to Switzerland, they went via Brussels so as to cross the French border as quickly as possible and avoid being seen in Paris, Burgundy and Franche-Comté. They did not even change out of the clothes in which they had been dining. Saint-Priest and Montmorin were also dismissed and La Luzerne, having given Necker the king's letter, also resigned.

News of Necker's dismissal became public on the 12th when the sporadic disturbances caused by the price of food as well as the political situation coalesced into a general insurrection. The day before, Broglie had told Besenval: 'If there is a general insurrection we cannot defend the whole of Paris and you must confine yourself to the plan for the defence of the Bourse, the royal treasury, the Bastille and the Invalides.' Besenval's response to the rising exceeded even the caution of his orders. A man said to be better fitted for the service of Venus than of Mars, he did not even try to prevent the crowd, led by deserters from the French Guards (Breteuil's response to the desertions was to look up precedents for granting an amnesty),[68] from seizing the arms from the Invalides with which, on the 14th, they stormed the Bastille (there is evidence that right up to this event Breteuil was negotiating with the

Assembly).[69] Needless to say, its garrison had not been replaced nor its cannon refurbished. And yet a study of the royal army suggests that it could and should have been used with good hopes of success and that the failure to do so destroyed its morale.[70]

What gave the Paris rising an institutional rather than a merely riotous character was that control of the situation had been seized by the central committee of the electoral college of Paris which had (illegally) continued to meet even after it had performed its original function of choosing the Parisian deputies to the Estates-General. On 25 June some radical assertions were made in the committee: i) that the king had recognized that they retained 'an active power'; ii) that the 'pretended municipality' nominated by the king should only continue their functions 'provisionally' until elections for successors had been held; iii) that the king was only 'the sovereign implementer of the general will'; iv) that instead of royal troops a 'bourgeois guard' of 48,000 men should be formed to maintain order in Paris.[71] Ludicrously, after the fall of the Bastille, Louis tried to impose a general staff from the regular army on what now became the National Guard.

The head of the 'pretended municipality' was Flesselles, the *prévôt des marchands* or mayor, directly answerable to the king through Villedeuil, minister for Paris. The other key royal agent was Crosne, *lieutenant-général de police*, also answerable to Villedeuil. But not only were these key royal agents being superseded by revolutionary new entities even before the fall of the Bastille, but they collaborated with them. So the hard-line Villedeuil had no control over his subordinates. Flesselles told the central committee on 13 July that 'the only authority he desired to exercise was that which had been conferred by the inhabitants of the capital'.[72] And he joined the central committee in its opposition to the troops deployed by the government of which his superior was a leading member. He also helped organize the storming of the Bastille, even though Besenval had ordered its governor to resist 'to the last man'.[73] Ludicrously, again, on 15 July, the king talked of concerting operations with Flesselles even after the fall of the Bastille and even after Flesselles had been, unfairly, murdered on the false accusation of withholding ammunition.[74]

Meanwhile, Crosne ignored an order on 24 June from Villedeuil to stop the circulation of the National Assembly's resolutions of 17 and 20 June. He also could or would do nothing to prevent the circulation of a 'scandalous pamphlet', *Premier coup de Vêpres*, which had been drawn to the minister's attention by 'une personne auguste' – the conventional way ministers referred to the queen.[75] Whether as a protest against Necker's dismissal or because his own position had become untenable, Crosne handed in his resignation to the king, was thanked by the electors' committee and instructed by them to continue his functions in so far as they related to 'subsistances'.[76] The king had already lost control of Paris some time before the fall of the Bastille made this manifest. The troops merely skated on the surface.

'Rien', Louis famously wrote in his diary on the 14th. No hunting. There had been a lot of entries like that. Louis was shutting himself off, whether at Versailles or Marly. When occasionally he did go hunting, d'Angiviller was relieved. Not only did the king need the exercise – his days as a svelte youth were long past – but remaining closeted gave a misleading impression of cowardice, a term which more justifiably could have been applied to his brother, Artois.

The Bastille was stormed; its governor slain; its stones turned into souvenirs. At first no one dared to tell the king about the events in Paris, but on the night of 15/16 July, an emergency meeting of the council was held at which Breteuil advocated flight to Metz, which had a strong citadel; Artois went down on both knees begging Louis to go, whereas Broglie and Provence were for staying – a divided council. Louis was meant to decide but, as with the fateful decision to enter the American war, he didn't want to: 'So, Messieurs, we have to decide: do I go or do I stay? I am ready for either.' In the end he stayed, obsessed as he was by the fear of civil war or of his cousin Orléans seizing a vacant throne. Whatever the grounds for the latter fear, Barentin, no less, told the royal historiographer, Moreau, at two o'clock on the morning of the 16th: 'I believe we must have recourse to another dynasty'.[77] Louis came to regret his decision to stay, musing in February 1792: 'I know I missed my opportunity; it was 14 July. We should have gone then and I wanted to; but what could I do when Monsieur himself begged me not to go and the maréchal de Broglie, the commander-in-chief, replied to me: "We can certainly go to Metz but what do we do when we get there?" I was abandoned by everyone.'[78]

As for Breteuil, his advice rejected, he fled alone, disguised, it is said, as a monk. Alone of the new ministers he never resigned, perhaps because the *chef* of a non-existent *Conseil des Finances* was too nebulous for the National Assembly to comprehend, let alone include in its demand for dismissals. Possibly, in his haste, he simply forgot to resign and possibly it was at the king's insistence. For Louis's legalistic mind endowed the status of Breteuil with an embalming sanctity; it was his last 'free' appointment, as the declaration of 23 June was his last 'free' utterance; no matter if both had been made under pressure and no matter if two bad decisions were being carved on tablets of stone.

Necker, Montmorin, Saint-Priest and La Luzerne returned, Louis profiting in his letter to Necker of the 16th from the escape clause he had left himself in the previous one: 'I wrote that when things had calmed down I would give proof of my sentiments towards you.'[79] 'Nearly all the people', Droz writes, 'who had taken part in the projects which had been so speedily overthrown emigrated or retired to the provinces.'[80] Artois, his mistress Madame de Polastron, his friend Vaudreuil, Vaudreuil's mistress Madame de Polignac, the Bourbon-Condé, all packed up and left the country. With moist eyes, Louis told Madame de Polignac, who had been his friend as well as the queen's, 'I have just ordered the comte d'Artois to leave. I now give you the same order. Pity me, but don't lose a moment. Take your family with you. You will always be able to count on. me. I will not fill your offices.'[81] The emigration had begun. Louis told them that he feared for their safety, but Lafayette, commander of the newly formed National Guard, claimed that Louis forced the emigration of Artois and Condé, who 'shed tears of rage' at having to go.[82] There was certainly an element of exile: as the situation worsened, internal exile was being replaced by exile proper – first Calonne, then, briefly, Necker, now the Polignacs. Either way, all those who in a very real sense had 'surprised the religion of the king' in the period 19 June–14 July were removed.

On 17 July Louis went to Paris to show his acceptance of what had happened. Marie-Antoinette, fearing that he would be detained or murdered, begged him not to go, but he burst out: 'No, no! I will go to Paris; numbers must not be sacrificed to the safety of one. I give myself up, I trust myself to my people and they can do what they like with me.'[83] Provence was given the title of lieutenant-general of the kingdom during his absence. In fact Louis was deeply hurt by the Parisians' response to his gesture. In his 1791 declaration, the manifesto he left behind when he escaped from Paris, he was to write: 'People stationed along the whole route took great pains to prevent those shouts of *vive le roi* which come so spontaneously to Frenchmen, and the speeches that were delivered to him, instead of testifying gratitude, were filled only with bitter irony'; poor Bailly, the new mayor, had referred tactlessly to Paris conquering its king. When he returned to Versailles, Besenval writes,

the unfortunate king found himself almost alone. For three consecutive days he had no one with him except M. de Montmorin and me. The very valets served him as they pleased. ... On the 19th I had entered the king's apartments, all the ministers being absent, to get him to sign an order giving post-horses to the colonel of the Évêchés regiment. Just as I was presenting this order to him a footman interposed himself casually between the prince and me to see what he was writing. The king turned round, noticed the insolent fellow and made to seize a pair of tongs. I checked his movement, prompted though it was by very natural anger; he squeezed my hand to thank me and I noticed that there were tears in his eyes.[84]

A few days later Saint-Priest, who had been given the portfolio of the *Maison du Roi*, 'ayant le département de Paris', went with Necker to 'put himself in possession of the municipal administration of the said town'. But there had been a municipal revolution in Paris. The murdered *prévôt des marchands* had been ousted by the elected mayor, Bailly. At the Hôtel de Ville, two seats had been prepared, but Bailly offered one to Necker and sat down on the other himself. Saint-Priest, who had to find a seat among the aldermen, notes bitterly: 'For the sake of peace I had to suffer this insolence on the part of the mayor, hitherto my subordinate, as replacing the *prévôt des marchands* who took his orders from the minister for Paris. But royal authority had already ceased to exist in Paris.'[85]

As he sat alone at Versailles, without ministers and badly served by the valets, Louis must have wondered what had happened since he lay awake, in 1786, unable to sleep from the joy of thinking of his plans to reform France. Calonne had said he would not mind if he were the victim of the enterprise; now Louis was himself. He thought of the coalition of vested interests that had defeated him, the miserable and unsuccessful compromise with Brienne, and Necker's total negativism. He was abandoned by everyone; even Malesherbes, who could perhaps have fused the old with the new, had said he feared office next to a mortal illness. Louis had been accused of raising the hopes of the *tiers* in 1787–88 and dashing them in the Estates-General, but things had become so embittered. Ought he not now to reconcile rather than divide? Had Calonne been right about revolution and counter-revolution? And the *tiers* wanted so much, not just fair taxation but, judging by the 'tennis court oath', political power at his own expense and the destruction of the social privileges of the nobility – these were largely honorific, but honour mattered so much; it was all about vanity. His brother Artois, loyal ally in 1787, had been warning him of this for more than six months; perhaps he was right, but he was surely wrong in wanting to subdue Paris by force. That was out of the question. Louis had used force to subdue the Flour War in 1775 – and his own *lieutenant de police* had thought it excessive. Maurepas had taught him that the police must act frequently. But you cannot hold down a city or a country, as Charles I had found; and he had been executed for levying war against his peoples – Louis would never do that. Nor would he leave Versailles as Charles had left London – a fugitive king!

We do not know what went through Louis's mind because, though he was to give an analysis of the later phases of the Revolution, he spoke very little of the period from 1787 to 1789. His conduct, however, provides the best clue to the striking feature of the events of the summer of 1789 – their radicalism, as graphically captured in Malouet's description of the aftermath of the fall of the Bastille: 'If the court had been at Paris instead of Versailles, it would have been the ministers, the princes who would have been slaughtered instead of Foulon, his son-in-law Berthier [intendant of Paris] and de Launay [governor of the Bastille]. It was as the agents of the government that they were pursued ... here was a ferocious populace in search of victims and it would have taken them alike in the street or on the throne.'[86]

This mood had been created by a sense of betrayal by the king. It has even been suggested that this sense of betrayal, intensified by the fear (however misplaced) that their very lives were in danger, induced in the third estate deputies a clinical trauma.[87] At all events the hope at the opening of the estates had turned to malaise and, with the *séance royale,* to anger. The troop concentrations had added the ingredient of fear so that, combined with the well-known murderous proclivities of the Parisians, most of the elements of the Terror were already present, including a touch of the macabre, as when grass was rammed into the mouth of the aged Foulon in answer to his reputed quip, 'Let them eat grass', and as when, prior to being killed, his son-in-law Berthier was made to kiss Foulon's 'pale and bloody' severed head. A chilling postscript to a letter home from Maximilien Robespierre, a young poor-man's lawyer sitting for Arras, runs: 'M. Foulon was hanged yesterday by a decree of the people.'[88] Ever punctilious, Robespierre accords the hated minister his 'Monsieur', the same as he accords (instead of the then obligatory 'Citoyen') the man who kindly dabbed his bleeding jaw on 9 Thermidor. But the key word is 'decree'. By using it Robespierre gives a theoretical, legal basis for a lynching: decree ('arrêt') was a precise legal term being used by a lawyer.

At the political level, the king's volte-face had effected, to his disadvantage, a synthesis between two strands of thought that might otherwise have remained separate: on the one hand, the *parlementaire* rejection of monarchical self-sufficiency and stress on the need for the consent of the governed; on the other hand, the traditional monarchical advocacy of equality and uniformity, and of reason rather than precedent as the spirit of legislation. This fusion led, among other things, to the idea that the 'nation' could design a constitution from scratch, which assigned to the king merely the role of 'first functionary'. Quickly, the National Assembly acquired the tone implicit in Siéyès's phrase 'the dictatorship of constituent power'.

It is harsh to be judged by action (or inaction) rather than by intentions, but with the king silent and inaccessible it was difficult to do otherwise. Also, by any normal standards he had displayed inconsistency. By his *appel au peuple* in 1787 Louis had contracted obligations which were remembered in 1789. He had sown dissension and, when it finally bore fruit, left it rotting in the fields. Had he gathered it, his constitutional concessions might not have been necessary; as it was, they were insufficient.

CHAPTER ELEVEN

THE INVASION OF A PALACE

Louis XVI in the Revolution

A FTER THE FALL OF the Bastille, the reign of Louis XVI is but one aspect of the French Revolution, a vast movement of which only the briefest outline will be given here. The king became a *roi fainéant*, with far less theoretical and actual power than the king of England. For, allied to the new personal distrust of Louis XVI, there was the deep theoretical distrust among eighteenth-century political thinkers of what they termed 'the executive power'. Political theory had played little or no part in the fall of the ancien régime, but these ideas rushed into the vacuum of power and experience caused by the collapse of royal authority in the summer and gave the Revolution a further impetus.

If Louis was feared or reckoned with, it was because of the residual authority which some deemed that he derived from God and from his ancestors. The proponents of absolute monarchy, however, were virtually non-existent. Louis's brother Artois, in exile first with his in-laws at Turin and later at Coblenz, was an exception, but he had to dissemble to humour his émigré troops; for the aristocrats' part, whether sitting on the right wing of the National Assembly or forming the émigré armies at Coblenz, they wanted to subject the king to the tutelage of *parlements*, provincial estates, and the whole panoply of an aristocratic constitution.

Not only was Louis's role reduced, but his voluminous official pronouncements and much of his ministerial correspondence present little interest: they rarely reflect his true political position and will be summarily treated here. In particular, neither the Assembly nor (if only for their own protection) the ministers were privy to what became his central policy: to secure by flight from the capital, where he was installed in the Tuileries on 6 October 1789 and regarded himself as a prisoner, an equal role for himself with the Assembly in the formulation of the new constitution.

It is also perhaps necessary to state that Marie-Antoinette's letters to her Austrian relatives during the Revolution, as before it, were not Louis's letters: it is indeed difficult to know precisely what, if any, part Louis played in her secret diplomacy, given that only a handful of his letters in this connection have survived and that the authenticity even of these has been questioned. In general, it can be said that, though her influence was greater than it had been before 1787, political divergence between the king and queen continued right up to the fall of the monarchy.

Given Louis's diminished role, we now dwell on his personal response to the Revolution and the deepening of his human and political sympathies, which are enlarged by his suffering. The main sources for this period are the manifesto *Déclaration du Roi, addressée à tous les Français, à sa sortie de Paris*, which he left behind when he escaped from Paris on the night of 20/21 June 1791, and his secret letter to his brothers of 15 September explaining his acceptance of the constitution.

* * *

On 12 October 1789, Louis wrote a letter to his Bourbon cousin, Charles IV of Spain:

> I owe it to myself, I owe it to my children, I owe it to my family and all my House to prevent the regal dignity which a long succession of centuries has confirmed in my dynasty from being degraded in my hands ... I have chosen Your Majesty, as the head of the second branch, to place in your hands this solemn protest against my enforced sanction of all that has been done contrary to the royal authority since 15 July of this year and at the same time my intention to implement the promises which I made by my declaration of the previous 23 June.[1]

It is significant that Louis did not send this letter on 15 July but on 12 October. Though he alludes to the fall of the Bastille, his real target was the October Days, the horrific events of 5th and 6th of that month during which his wife narrowly escaped assassination and he ended up as the prisoner of Paris. Some argue that Louis's mind froze on 23 June; more likely his blood froze on 6 October. For Louis, the October Days projected a shadow onto the previous episodes of the Revolution, as we will see from the extracts from his 1791 manifesto, our main guide to his innermost thoughts from the opening of the Estates-General to his flight.

During August and September, the National Assembly sought to institutionalize the political gains it had made in June and July and to fulfil the 'tennis court oath' through establishing the outlines for a new constitution and prefacing them with its *Declaration of the Rights of Man*. Already, however, the Revolution had been enlarged beyond the political dimension by a revolution in the countryside. The failure of the 1788 harvest led to tension as the *soudure* approached, and this was heightened by hope that the seigneurial regime would be ameliorated and by fear – *la grande peur* – of aristocratic reprisals, which the peasants imagined would be carried out by bands of marauding 'brigands'. The peasantry responded to these pressures by burning châteaux, destroying records of feudal dues and simply ceasing to pay them.

The breakdown of order in the countryside was both product and result of the collapse of the royal bureaucracy throughout France. For a fortnight there was no one to direct it, even assuming they would have been obeyed. Necker, who had taken the long way back to Switzerland to save the king embarrassment, did not return to Versailles until the night of 28/29 July and the appointments to his third administration were not completed until 4 August. When he had finally been contacted at The Three Kings at Basel, he had seriously wondered if he should return, his wife against, his virago daughter for. When he arrived back at Versailles, Marie-Antoinette told him that his zeal for the king's service should be redoubled by gratitude for his recall. Necker replied that zeal went with the job but that 'nothing obliged him to feel gratitude' – his would prove indeed to be a thankless task. In the hiatic period of Necker's absence, Louis could only turn to his childhood friend Montmorin, but though he had been an able ambassador to Spain he was out of his depth in the Revolution and inclined to turn towards the prevailing wind.

Necker had been recalled to restore the finances, royal or national – the dividing line had been crossed. But given the chaos in the country, revenue collapsed and Necker was thrown back on his old standby, the loan. On 7 August he asked the National Assembly to endorse a loan of 30 million *livres*. The Assembly grudgingly accepted but three weeks later less than 3 million had been raised. Necker tried another loan, this time for 80 million with a high rate of interest, but it met with little more enthusiasm. At the end of his tether, Necker proposed a one-off payment of 25 per cent of income by every taxpayer plus a portion of their gold and silver: 'the wife of an ordinary peasant will give her wedding ring if necessary'. Instead of patriotic cheers, this proposal was greeted by 'a mournful silence' until Mirabeau said the alternative was bankruptcy. Louis offered to melt down his silver vessels, but Mirabeau responded that he was 'not moved by the porcelain of the powerful or the crockery of kings' – an assonant but silly sally. But the orator's underlying point was the rejection of Louis's assumption that 'the expenses and revenues of the state ... [were] indistinguishable from his own'.[2] The 25 per cent 'patriotic contribution' was a flop.

The collapse in revenue resulted from a disinclination to pay and an inability to collect, for the royal administration in the provinces had collapsed. The municipal revolution in Paris was replicated in every city, town and village in France, the royal *prévôt des marchands* or equivalent being replaced by a popularly elected mayor and council. At the same time the regional administration, based on the unit of the *généralité*, thirty of them, each ruled by an intendant with half a dozen *subdélégués* under him, also disintegrated, the incumbents no doubt paralysed by the murder of Berthier, the intendant of Paris. The intendancy structure had been the jewel in the king's crown, 'the best part of my system' as Louis himself put it.

Far from this breakdown of the machinery of government being a usurpation of power by the National Assembly, most of its members deplored the state of affairs, for many of the deputies for the third estate were substantial landowners who desired the restoration of order as much as anyone. Indeed, one complained, 'There is no longer any governing authority; Louis XVI is no more king than you are'.[3] Even the new, elected mayor of Paris, Bailly, had been unable to prevent the slaughter of the intendant of Paris, despite promising to put him on trial – for what crime? Instead Bailly was presented with the intendant's heart on a pike, whilst the onlookers struggled to infuse coffee with his heated blood.

Given the collapse of civil authority, the natural solution would have been to employ the military. However, the Assembly members dared not entrust the king with the restoration of order lest, job done, he turn the troops on the Assembly itself. Consequently they sought to defuse the crisis by a stratagem. The Breton club got up some prominent liberal nobles to renounce their seigneurial privileges on the night of 4/5 August and this inspired a spirit of emulation on behalf of their more intransigent brethren who sat on the right wing of the Assembly. In its enthusiasm the Assembly declared that it 'entirely abolishes the feudal system'. What it meant was that serfdom, or what was called *servitude personnelle*, i.e., anything which implied that the seigneur had some ownership over his peasants, was abolished outright. It was in fact already rare and, where it existed, much attenuated by 1789. Louis had abolished it on his crown lands in 1779 together with *mainmorte*, which prevented the serf from transmitting his land to any but his children. Dues on peasant properties, which were really the equivalent of rent, were to be redeemed. There was a grey area between servitude and rent which was never defined; nor was the rate of compensation for dues. Seigneurial justice was also abolished.

The August decrees also saw the entire implementation of the 1787 programme; indeed, in some respects it went further, with the abolition of privilege in taxation, tithes, sale of office, and the different privileges of the towns and provinces of France. The entire 'corporate' organization of France disappeared overnight, though a customs union was not achieved until 1791. Not surprisingly the king, in his message to the Assembly of 18 September, found little to criticize, only making five observations of substance.[4] He thought that where serfdom had in the past been replaced by a money payment, this should not be abolished without compensation; seigneurial justice should remain until, as Lamoignon had provided in 1788, something had been put in its place; if tithes were abolished, they should be replaced by a tax payable to the state. Otherwise the operation would merely result in the random redistribution to landowners of 60–80 million *livres* that the treasury could well use. He naturally accepted free trade in grain, which he himself had introduced but, scarred by the Flour War of 1775, did not want it to be applied in a doctrinaire fashion.

Finally, Louis stressed the implications for foreign policy: the Treaty of Westphalia guaranteed the seigneurial rights of foreign princes with possessions in the former German province of Alsace, the 'princes possessionés' and Louis informed the Assembly that they had already lodged strong protests. Also the pope needed to be consulted over the suppression of *annates* – a fee due to the papacy when a see changed hands. Foreign policy was Louis's expertise: the Prussian ambassador thought that his main reason for convoking the Estates-General was to have the money he needed to conduct it effectively.[5] Now Louis was confronted with ignorance: Robespierre, for example, cheerfully admitted his complete ignorance of international treaties, believing that foreign policy could be derived from the principles enshrined in the *Declaration of the Rights of Man*. He was asked how he could speak on the German princes' rights 'without ever having ... read anything on the subject'. 'But you are at least familiar with the Treaty of Ryswick?' 'No.' 'Have you studied German public law?' 'No. Public law and treaties don't come into it, only the law of peoples.'[6] And when Robespierre entered the governing committee of public safety in 1793 his portfolio was foreign affairs! One can see what Louis was up against. The Venetian ambassador wrote that Louis's 'very pertinent' observations on the August decrees as a whole 'clearly demonstrate that the sphere of expertise of this Assembly is very limited'.[7]

The Assembly's reception of Louis's observations symbolized the role that it was to assign him: only Lally-Tollendal thought it appropriate for the king to make any comment whatsoever. The president was instructed to ask Louis simply to promulgate the decrees. Louis described this treatment in his 1791 manifesto: 'The Assembly . . . not content with degrading the monarchy by its decrees, even affected contempt for the king's person and received his observations on the decrees of the night of 4/5 August in a manner which can hardly be described as showing respect.' The king saved face by saying that, since the decrees were statements of intent rather than finished legislation, he would *publish* rather than *promulgate* them.

Louis was not merely objecting to instant legislation, which he had been brought up to believe was arbitrary and formless. He was objecting to his exclusion from the legislative process. This exclusion operated at two levels. As regards ordinary legislation, the Assembly discussed giving Louis a veto, but over the articles of the constitution itself, none. They would draw what one member termed a 'religious veil' over this usurpation by according him the right of *acceptance* but not of *sanction* – in other words he could take it or leave it but not affect its validity. But for Louis the 'religious veil' was not a blindfold; Louis, who in May had reminded Necker that the estates 'cannot make laws by themselves', was to complain bitterly of this treatment in his 1791 manifesto:

When the Estates-General, having styled themselves the National Assembly, began to occupy themselves with the constitution of the kingdom, remember the memoranda which the men of faction had sent in from several provinces and the agitation in Paris tending to make the deputies renege on one of the main clauses in all their *cahiers* providing that *legislation would be carried out in conjunction* with the king: in contempt of this stipulation, the Assembly has denied the king any say in the constitution by refusing him the right to grant or withhold his assent to the articles which it deems constitutional, by reserving to itself the right to place such articles in this category as it sees fit.

The main factions in the Assembly (from right to left) were: the 'noirs' or 'purs' who wanted a restoration of the ancien régime or at a minimum the declaration of 23 June – some had emigrated, many would follow; the *monarchiens*[8] who favoured a strong constitutional monarchy based on England's; and what may be called the 'soft left', the logic of whose position was a republic but who found it more comfortable and/or acceptable to keep Louis as a figurehead deprived of any real power, executive or legislative. These last were led by the 'triumvirate' of Duport, an ex-*parlementaire*, one of the few who had secured election to the estates, Barnave who had made his name in the Dauphiné revolt in 1788, and Alexandre de Lameth, one of the many disgruntled courtiers who were annoyed that Marie-Antoinette's favours went to the Polignacs rather than themselves.[9] On the extreme left were men like Pétion and Robespierre, though even as late as 1791 Robespierre said (darkly) that the declaration of a republic would be 'aristocratic'. He believed that the *Declaration of Rights* should be the litmus test for all policy. He was not yet influential but (until his nervous breakdown in the spring of 1794) had a superb strategic sense. He was perhaps the first to realize the full implications of the fall of the Bastille by which 'the nation recaptured the legislative power'.[10]

The group nearest to the Necker government were the *monarchiens*, who dominated the Assembly's first constitutional committee. The *monarchiens* had led the third estate's struggle against the first two orders but had become disturbed by the enlargement of the Revolution and feared lest its new social dimension would threaten the political gains of the early summer. They wanted to stop the Revolution at this point and felt that only the king could fill the vacuum created by the retreating nobility. A year later the 'triumvirs' would come to the same conclusion. Theoretically this current, with constant recruits from the left, should have strengthened the king's position. Instead they were just extra passengers overloading a sinking ship. For the revisionist tide encountered an even stronger counter-current of popular politics outside the Assembly, which was exploited by the far left within it, men such as Robespierre and Pétion.

The *monarchiens* sought to concentrate the powers of the executive branch by means of an absolute veto and dilute those of the legislative branch by the creation of a second chamber, largely nominated by the king. The debate on these two measures symbolized the conflict between the *monarchiens*, who wanted to use a strong executive to suppress popular politics and preserve property rights, and those on the left, who were prepared to exploit popular disturbances to bring pressure on the king and on the Assembly itself.

The *monarchiens* were not a homogeneous group; Mounier, for example, had led the revolt in Dauphiné the previous summer and was only driven to see the need for a strong executive by the collapse of order. The dominant tendency of the group, however, may be termed Briennist: the three prelates, Boisgelin (Aix), Champion de Cicé (Bordeaux) and La Luzerne (Langres) had been Brienne's close collaborators and Malouet shared his views. Their theme was a strong monarchy in traditional alliance with the third estate. When the king, in his silence, had been thought to be favouring the nobility, Malouet, left without a doctrinal position, had remained silent himself for six weeks. In September he spoke again, rebuking the Assembly for droning on about the rights of man whilst France was lapsing into political and social disintegration. Louis now discussed matters with Malouet, though he did not give the *monarchiens* as a bloc any formal support.

Their Briennist position largely accounts for their failure, for it alienated the right wing, the intransigent nobility on whom they counted but for whom the policies of Brienne had been anathema: they likened the second chamber to the *cour plénière* and thought that its adoption would lead to *despotisme*. In any case they did not expect to be given seats in any second chamber and feared that one might help consolidate a constitution they detested. For, in pursuance of their *politique du pire*, they preferred total collapse which might lead to an aristocratic version of the ancien régime. Throughout the life of the National Constituent Assembly, the noble right, like the *émigrés*, had no care either for the restoration of an effective monarchy or for the personal fate of Louis XVI. On the occasions in August and September when the far and moderate right did cooperate, they were the strongest grouping in the Assembly, for logically the union of the orders should have led to a dilution of the radicalism of the National Assembly, a point which some third estate deputies bemoaned.

Apart from the August decrees, the Assembly considered three measures which it considered to be constitutional: the *Declaration of the Rights of Man*; whether there should be an upper and lower chamber; and whether the king should be given a veto over ordinary (but not constitutional) legislation.

An upper chamber was Necker's hobbyhorse and was favoured by the *monarchiens*. Louis seems not to have been interested either way: Necker later wrote that Louis had finally come round to his way of thinking about the desirability of an English system 'but only when it was too late'. In any case only 89 out of a possible 1,200 deputies voted for a second chamber on 8 September. The Assembly then turned its attention to the king's veto over legislation.

The debate turned on whether Louis should have an absolute veto (as the English king had), a delaying or 'suspensive' veto or no veto at all, as Siéyès argued. Necker wanted to present the Assembly with a memorandum saying that the king was prepared to accept a suspensive veto provided it lasted for at least two legislatures; using his daughter as an intermediary Necker negotiated with the 'soft Left' to this effect. The *monarchiens*, however, who wanted the king to have an absolute veto, blocked the reading of Necker's memorandum until after the vote on the grounds that a minister of the crown had no right to have any influence in the drafting of the constitution. Their real motive, however, was that their case would have been fatally undermined if the king himself had already sold the pass.

In fact he hadn't: in his manifesto he characterized a suspensive veto as 'purely illusory'. To him the absolute veto symbolized the irreducible minimum share in legislation acceptable, given that he had reasonably assumed, in common with Malouet but practically no one else, that legislation would proceed as before: the king in his council would draw up *lettres patentes* which would be debated by the Assembly (rather than the *parlements*) and, with appropriate modifications, become edicts. In his manifesto he was to complain that he had been 'denied the right formally to initiate legislation'. This was actually more important than the veto; for if the king introduced the legislation (as in England) the veto didn't matter. In not standing up for the absolute veto, Louis seemed to be following the maxim announced (but not strictly adhered to) when he recalled Necker in August 1788: 'I'll do everything he tells me and see what will happen'; and Necker to be following his maxim of giving way in advance to irresistible pressure. The result of this comedy of errors was that the principle of a veto was accepted by 733 votes to 143, but the absolute veto was rejected by 673 votes to 329.

The next question was the duration of the suspensive veto – whether it should last for one, two or three legislatures – and here the Assembly wanted to tie the king into a package. Louis had not yet commented on the decrees of 4 August and it was rumoured he would reject them. On 18 September he gave the response we have examined and, pressed for clarification, on the 21st told the Assembly that he endorsed the 'general spirit' of the decrees and made the distinction between publication and promulgation, the latter having to await the formal drafting of the measures. This was enough to satisfy the Assembly and by the massive vote of 728 to 224 it granted the king a suspensive veto for three legislatures (Necker's memorandum had only asked for two). Assuming a legislature lasted two years this meant a delay of up to six years – hardly 'illusory', provided the king dared to use it, a consideration which no one raised at the time.

Whilst these debates were going on, ideas were evolving about how long a legislature should be in session. This question of 'permanence', which Louis had raised as early as February 1788, was absolutely crucial to the king's role: the Hanoverian kings retained substantial powers by dint of the fact that parliament only met for a few months a year. The question was decided empirically by the Assembly's imagining that it was in a permanent state of crisis and therefore must sit every day of every year and sometimes through the night. As Saint-Just said, the price of liberty was eternal vigilance. No wonder nerves became frayed.

But this matter was not uppermost in people's minds and on 21 September an acceptable *modus vivendi* seemed to have been reached with the king. The atmosphere had soured, however, by the time (2 October) the Assembly submitted to the king the *Declaration of the Rights of Man and of the Citizen* and, following this preamble, the first nineteen articles of the constitution itself. Louis's response, on 4 October, was made against a background of mounting popular pressure on him and on the Assembly itself, to some degree orchestrated by its left wing. Alarmed, the moderate deputies had asked the king to withdraw to Compiègne and propose transferring the Assembly to nearby Soissons – when Louis had himself proposed this to the Assembly on 12 July, it had enraged these same deputies.

But now, on 30 August, Louis himself refused to move. It would have been only human, especially for Louis, to say 'I told you so'. The bishop of Langres asked Necker why and received the 'impatient' reply: 'Monsieur, if you want to know the truth understand that our role is very arduous. The king is good but difficult to persuade. His Majesty was tired . . . he slept through the council', an affectation he used to 'conceal his agitation'.[11] 'We were for translating the Assembly but the king woke up, said "No" and withdrew.' Malouet comments: 'The king, who had a passive courage, saw a kind of shame in withdrawing from Versailles; he was perfectly aware of the danger but he flattered himself he could avoid it by a display of force, though if it came to using it, he could never decide to draw his sword against his subjects.'[12] This, not 15 July, was the chance Louis should have taken. On 15 July he would not have had a party. But he had now demonstrated his willingness to compromise and shown his opponents to be intransigent. People would have flocked to Compiègne.

The force to which Malouet alludes was the Flanders regiment. After the withdrawal to Compiègne had been abandoned, Saint-Priest, as minister for the *Maison*, had summoned this loyal regiment for the king's personal protection: only a thousand strong, it could have no aggressive effect – the Assembly later gave Louis a guard of 1,500. Saint-Priest had thought that the *Gardes du Corps*, the royal bodyguard of 1,800, all nobles, officers and men, needed reinforcement. But on the night of 1 October this ultra-loyalist regiment gave a banquet for the Flanders regiment at which imprudent toasts were drunk. They also sang the air 'O Richard! O mon roi! L'univers t'abandonne' from Grétry's *Richard Coeur de Lion*. It was reported that some drunken officers had trampled underfoot the tricolour cockade which had been adopted in July – red and blue for Paris, white for the dynasty – and even sported a black Habsburg one. But this is a stock episode whose importance has been exaggerated: weeks before the banquet, a Paris crowd had set off to bring Louis back to Paris, on this occasion stopped by the National Guard at the gates of the city.

We know what Louis really thought about the *Declaration of Rights*. In his manifesto he was to inveigh against 'a metaphysical and philosophical government which cannot work' and one can see why it would not appeal to one of his practical bent. The *Declaration* was obviously inspired by the American version which Lafayette, who corresponded with Jefferson, would have preferred simply to have translated into French; but it aimed to be universal. Salient articles were: i) 'All men are born and remain free and equal in rights'; iii) 'Sovereignty resides essentially in the nation'; vi) 'The law is the expression of the general will. Everyone has the right to participate in its formulation, either in person or through freely elected representatives . . .'

The Enlightenment in general – what Louis meant by 'philosophical', after the *philosophes* – and Rousseau in particular were the main influences but article six flouted Rousseau's basic principle in *Du contrat social* (1762) that sovereignty could not be represented; only direct democracy, as in ancient Greece, would qualify. It has been suggested that Louis was given a veto because it was an *appel au peuple* and it afforded a channel (however corrupt) for the sovereign people to override its 'mandatories', as the representatives were termed, for sovereignty could not be represented.[13]

Louis was by no means the only person to dub the *Declaration of Rights* as 'metaphysical and philosophical'; many, even on the left, concurred. One said they had not been elected to 'write philosophical treatises' and pass their days debating 'superfluous issues of abstract metaphysics'.[14] They were practical lawyers, not *philosophes*. Many had the same mind-set as the king. There has been endless debate about the role of Enlightenment ideas in the origins of the Revolution. They played little part; but from July onwards they were used to validate the seizure of power from the actual man, Louis, whom they had empirically come to distrust; and the extent of popular sovereignty happened to fit the extent of the distrust of Louis as perfectly as a *palais royal* kid glove. People started boning up on the *Social Contract*, which is abstruse, but short.

But on 4 October Louis contented himself with the observation that a declaration of principle should not precede its practical embodiment. Similarly with the constitution itself: he accepted the nineteen articles provisionally but thought that the constitution could not be judged piecemeal but only when it had been finished,[15] which remained his position during the two years it took to draft. Moreover, he added, even his provisional acceptance was given 'only on the positive condition, from which I will never depart, that the general result of your deliberations is to leave executive power entirely within the hands of the monarch'.[16] This was also the intention of the Assembly – at least in theory; but Louis's tone was peremptory.

Things might have rested there but for the intervention of the sovereign people itself, or at least the Parisians who, in Robespierre's phrase, 'stood proxy' for it. At about ten o'clock next day, 5 October, Saint-Priest received intelligence that an armed force had left Paris and was making for Versailles.[17] It was a motley crowd, containing mainly women, and it demanded bread and the king's sanction to the Assembly's decrees. Saint-Priest sent a message to Marie-Antoinette to return to the palace from the model village at the Petit Trianon. The courier found her in the grotto, resting after feeding her ducks and goldfish and she returned immediately.

Louis had just left to go shooting – not hunting as is usually stated. He had not hunted since 17 August, since it is harder to make contact with a hunt in full cry than a shoot. His diary notes: 'Monday, 5th, shot at the Porte de Châtillon [in the woods above Meudon]. Killed eighty-one head. Interrupted by events. Rode there and back.' He reached Versailles at about three o'clock, galloping with his retinue down the Grande Avenue to the palace, and, without changing, held the council. It proved to be its last set-piece debate. Normally the chamber was hermetically sealed, but on this occasion people came and went at will. The ministers kept sending out couriers for information, but none returned.

Saint-Priest proposed withdrawing to Rambouillet and was supported by the maréchal de Beauveau, La Luzerne (Marine) and La Tour de Pin. All four, as Saint-Priest observed, had been soldiers. The civilians – Necker, Montmorin (though a camp-marshal, he had not seen active service) and the archbishops of Vienne and Bordeaux – were opposed, Necker warning that if the king abandoned Paris there would be no money to pay the *rentes* or the troops.[18] In addition, they were under the mistaken impression that England would exploit such a situation to launch a naval attack. On 2 October La Luzerne had asked for 1.5 million *livres* to lay in salt beef so they could mobilize the fleet at a moment's notice: 'The king felt the weight of these arguments but, given the penury of the finances, he decided that only 300,000 would be spent on extra provisions.'[19]

With the council, as so often, evenly divided, the king cast his vote for staying. In his manifesto he stated that he had 'sufficient warning to be able to withdraw where he pleased; but he feared that this step would be exploited to set alight civil war' – the likely consequence, Saint-Priest concedes. A factor in Louis's decision was that mid-way through the council meeting he had met a deputation of five of the women, given them wine and promised to rush in grain supplies to Paris. Won over, one of them asked to kiss his hand. 'I can do better than that', he said and kissed her on both cheeks, a *souvenir de Cherbourg*. The deputation left shouting 'Vive le roi!' and were nearly strangled by their companions. However, Louis gave orders for bread to be brought in from Senlis and Lagny, which seemed to satisfy them. Most prepared to traipse back to Paris.

But at six o'clock a message arrived from Lafayette, commander of the Paris National Guard, that he was marching to Versailles at the head of his troops. This force posed more of a threat than the women: the citizens' militia formed to preserve order during the July disturbances also incorporated the former French Guards who had carried out the attack on the Bastille. The debate in the council now veered towards flight. Orders were given for the carriages, which had been waiting ready-harnessed in the Grande Écurie, to be brought round, but the crowd cut the traces. The officers on duty could have stopped them but they had overheard the king pacing up and down the council chamber, exclaiming, 'A fugitive king! A fugitive king, never!'[20] This, thought Louis, is how civil wars start. He had been reading Clarendon's *History of the Rebellion and Civil Wars of England*. 'I am menaced by the same fate', he thought, 'the only way to avert it is to do the exact opposite of everything that unfortunate monarch did'.[21] When he left London to raise his standard, Charles had already made parliament as many concessions as Louis had made the National Assembly.[22]

At eight o'clock confused firing was heard and Louis ordered the carriages to be readied again, but this time the grooms refused. The Assembly took the opportunity to ask the king for his acceptance 'pure and simple' of the constitutional articles. At ten o'clock the king told their president, Mounier, that he would accept their articles. The irony of the situation was not lost on Mounier, who had no more liking for the articles than had the king. Dutifully, Mounier asked the king to put his sanction in writing. Louis 'went to his desk, [and] wrote it out in full: "I accept, purely and simply, the constitutional articles and the *Declaration of the Rights of Man* which the National Assembly has presented to me"'. Then 'he handed his sanction to him, weeping'.[23] As Necker was to observe: 'We had to yield, but posterity will never forget the moment that was chosen to consecrate the theory of the rights of man and to insert the cornerstone of the temple of liberty'.[24] Duty done, Mounier shortly afterwards seceded from the Assembly and tried to raise his native Dauphiné against it – a commoner, but a gentleman. Louis did not have the luxury of retiring from the Revolution.

Fearing the sinister loyalty of Lafayette, Louis told Mounier to assemble as many of the deputies as he could in the palace. Mounier ordered a drum roll and rustled up 200 deputies, but Lafayette had already arrived by the time they turned up at about 1.30 a.m. On his arrival the 'hero of two worlds' exclaimed, 'Sire, I thought it better to die at your feet than pointlessly perish' trying to stop the National Guard from marching on Versailles.[25] Louis must have winced at such fatuous grandiloquence. When the deputies arrived, Louis told them, 'I wanted to be surrounded by the nation's representatives and profit from their advice when I received M. de Lafayette; but he has come before you and I have nothing to say to you except that I had no intention of leaving and that I will never be separated from the National Assembly.'[26] Ambiguous words – did he mean leaving for Compiègne or for Paris? Louis knew that Lafayette, whilst protesting his loyalty too much, would be trying to bully him into residing in Paris and had hoped the deputies would stiffen his resistance. Having tried to soften Louis up, an exhausted Lafayette finally left the palace at 5 a.m. and went to his grandfather Noailles's town-house in Versailles. Then he threw himself onto a sofa and fell into an exhausted sleep. In view of what happened next he was dubbed 'General Morpheus' and accused of 'sleeping against his king'. But this is unfair: no one suspected what was about to happen. Louis went to bed at 2 a.m., Marie-Antoinette having already retired to her separate apartment with two ladies-in-waiting.

About half an hour after Lafayette's departure, daybreak on a misty autumn morning, a portion of the crowd broke into the palace, made for the queen's apartments and hacked down two of her bodyguards outside the door, shouting, 'We want to cut her head off, and fry her heart and liver and it won't stop there'. One of the bodyguards just had time to reach the queen's apartments and shout to a lady-in-waiting, 'Madame, save the queen, her life is in danger.' Then he was cut down and left for dead. Behind the queen's bed, concealed in the panelling, was a door opening onto a secret passage leading to the king's apartments. Constructed in 1775 to preserve Marie-Antoinette's political life, it now preserved her actual life. Some accounts have the furious populace, disappointed of their prey, slashing the mattress of the queen's bed to ribbons. But she was not safe yet, for when she reached the king's apartments she found the door locked: Louis had gone down another passage to the dauphin's chamber, followed by a domestic with a chamber candlestick. He picked up the sleeping boy in his arms, but soon after the candle went out. Feeling his way in the dark he told the servant: 'hold on to my dressing-gown'. Louis's twelve-year-old daughter was found to be safe with Madame de Tourzel, their new governess (after Madame de Polignac's emigration). But for ten agonizing minutes the queen hammered on the door, whilst the mob pursued her from another direction, through the Hall of Mirrors towards the Oeil-de-Boeuf, loyal guards closing the doors of the *enfilade* behind them. That day Marie-Antoinette's blond hair went white at the temples. Finally, the whole family were reunited in the Oeil-de-Boeuf, from which, fifteen years before, the courtiers had thundered out to announce his accession to the new king.

With daylight the crowd gathered in the Cour de Marbre and clamoured for the king. He appeared on the balcony outside his bedroom, followed by the queen and the two children, the four-year-old new dauphin, standing on a chair saying he was hungry, as the rioters had been until they scoffed the buffet laid out for the National Assembly. 'No children!' went up the cry, 'the queen on the balcony alone!' She had to consent. Then, Saint-Priest relates,[27] a new shout went up: ' "To Paris, to Paris!" ' was endlessly repeated, and the king, in a profound stupor, kept going on the balcony, maintaining his silence, and returning to throw himself into an armchair in his room to rest. I took the liberty of telling him that by not consenting to leave he was exposing himself and the royal family to the utmost danger; that he must regard himself as a prisoner, subject to the laws imposed on him.' Marie-Antoinette agreed: 'You couldn't make up your mind to go whilst there was still time; now we are prisoners. . . . As for me, I put myself in God's hands.' To Necker's wife (the minister had not uttered a word) Marie-Antoinette said in a horrified whisper, 'They want to force us, the king and me, to go to Paris with the heads of our bodyguards carried before us at the end of their pikes.' Lafayette egregiously told the crowd that the queen had learned from her mistakes and the whole family appeared with him on the balcony as for a curtain call. The whole episode burned in Louis's memory when he came to write his manifesto: 'God alone prevented the execution of the greatest crimes and saved the French nation from a stain which would have been indelible.'

Louis told La Tour du Pin, the governor of Versailles: 'You will remain in charge here. Try to save my poor Versailles.' But already the place was emptying, 'and the only noise that could be heard now in the château was that of the closing of doors and shutters, inside and out'.[28]

The royal family were taken to Paris in a vast, grotesque procession, the heads of their bodyguards indeed held aloft on pikes. Louis-Philippe, duc de Chartres, son of the duc d'Orléans, witnessed that 'these monsters, noticing that the ribbon on one of these heads was out of place, made a wig-maker rearrange it and repowder it'.[29] It took seven hours to cover the twelve miles from Versailles to Paris, during which time Louis did not utter a single word. Fishwives shouted abuse and gesticulated at Marie-Antoinette's window. Even that was not the end of it. On arrival at Paris they had to appear on the balcony of the Hôtel de Ville before finally, at nine o'clock, being installed in the palace of the Tuileries. The next day and for some days afterwards Marie-Antoinette had to appear in the gardens staring down her tormentors with the inbred Habsburg pride which both infuriated and silenced her enemies. Then the novelty of a new arrival in the zoo wore off. It took, however, until 12 February 1790 before Louis ventured outside the palace gates. He was scared and sullen – felt a prisoner and wanted to demonstrate the fact.

The Tuileries, 'a long brown building in the west of the city', had been begun by Catherine de Medici and finished a hundred years later by Louis XIV.[30] Set in its vast gardens, one side of the Renaissance structure faced the Louvre and the other the Champs-Élysées. Burned down during the siege of Paris in 1870, all that remains are the gardens, with their marble statues. The little dauphin said, 'It's very ugly here, Maman.' But Marie-Antoinette replied, '*Mon fils*, Louis XIV lived here once and found it very comfortable.'[31] But she neglected to add that the boy-king Louis XIV had escaped from Paris with his mother during the rebellion known as the *Fronde*. And that as soon as he reasserted his authority he started building Versailles at a comfortable distance from his capital. Built as a protest against Paris, Versailles continued to stand as a reproach, symbolized by the fountain where the rebellious Parisians are shown morphing into frogs. The Tuileries had last been occupied by the court during the minority of Louis XV, from 1715 to 1722, and Louis was to complain that 'the disposition of the rooms [368 of them] was far from affording the comfort to which he was accustomed in the other royal residences and which any private individual with a competence may enjoy'.

Louis, however, had reason to complain of more than private discomfort. The October Days destroyed the last vestige of his independence of action. They also came widely to be regarded as the first great breach of legality in the Revolution. It was this that prompted Mounier's secession, together with several of his followers, and even those who had profited from the affair affected regret. There were dark aspects to the October Days that will probably always remain obscure, despite the committee of inquiry instituted at the Châtelet: Lafayette, Orléans, Mirabeau, any or all of them could have conspired to have the king and the queen assassinated. Louis stood in the way of all three: of Mirabeau, celebrated orator, pockmarked sexual athlete, attacker of a monarchy in which he profoundly believed, especially with financial inducement, who wanted a modern absolutism based on alliance with the third estate; of Orléans and his dynastic ambition; of Lafayette, who with cool contempt told Marie-Antoinette that he put the fate of the Revolution before that of the king and that he would have her divorced on grounds of adultery[32] – there were strong but unfounded rumours that the father of the new dauphin was not the king but the comte de Fersen, a handsome young Swede attached to the court of France in general and to Marie-Antoinette in particular but not, at least at this stage, carnally.

Louis attributed many of his difficulties to Orléans and his fear of leaving him a vacant throne had been a further reason against flight. According to Necker: 'The king, inspired by personal notions which I never shared, feared the effects of this hot-house of plots [Orléans's residence, the Palais-Royal] more than the outcome of any upheaval.'[33] Lafayette made Orléans the scapegoat by having him sent on an empty diplomatic mission to England, which amounted to exile.

In his diary, Louis tried to anaesthetize himself to the impact of the October Days by reducing them to the banality of some of his other entries. Thus the entry for 6 October runs: 'Left for Paris at twelve thirty. Visit to the Hôtel de Ville. Had supper and slept at the Tuileries.' The ordeal is treated as just another journey – 'soupé et couché à Rambouillet' is a frequent entry for the period 1784–89. In the recapitulation for the year 1789 we read:

Excursions in 1789.
Marly 14–21 June
Paris 6 October–31 December
Nights that I slept away from Versailles 93

It is a way of assimilating the terrifying to the mundane.

Slightly more ambiguous – keeping up appearances, or nostalgia – is Louis's maintaining his hunt intact and recording its activities, though in a different form, to denote his absence: for instance, on 12 October, 'le cerf chassoit à Port-Royal', the form used when he was present being 'chasse du cerf à . . .'. This was kept up for nearly a year until, in the entry for 14 September 1790, we read: 'le cerf chassoit pour la dernière fois'. As a silent protest against the October Days, Louis shut himself up in the Tuileries, which he scarcely bothered to furnish, and refused to hunt, though with his tendency to *embonpoint*, he needed the exercise. People asked: 'Why does the king not hunt?' It had become a political question.

For, despite the form of face-saving in his diary, Louis did consider that the October Days had brought about a radical change in his position. His letter to Charles IV with which we began this chapter inaugurates a dual attitude: that there are different orders of promises, and those made under duress are not binding. This would soon lead to a dual policy.

CHAPTER TWELVE

THE REVOLUTION
CARICATURES ITSELF
OCTOBER 1789–JUNE 1791

The Tuileries

T HE PROGRESS OF THE French Revolution resembled that of the tuberculosis which killed both of Louis's parents and his son. There were periods of remission, even periods when the patient had the illusion of feeling better than before he contracted the disease; but before long there was a little, and then much coughing of blood. Foulon had been savagely slain and his son-in-law the intendant of Paris made to kiss his severed head; but only two bodyguards had been killed on 6 October – the one who had time to warn Marie-Antoinette, though left for dead, miraculously revived. Lafayette managed to save the rest of the bodyguards, who were simply disarmed and forced to march behind their decapitated colleagues. Most amazing of all, Besenval, after six months catchless trawling for evidence that he planned to massacre the Parisians, was actually acquitted by the Châtelet, Paris's central criminal court. So too, *in absentia*, was Barentin, who published a defence based on the argument that before the Revolution the king was responsible for the collective ministerial advice he acted on (rather than vice versa, as in a constitutional monarchy).[1] The Châtelet even went on to investigate the role in the October Days of the left-wing members of the National Assembly, especially Orléans and Mirabeau. After all, most of the deputies for the third estate were lawyers, and for a short period the rule of lawyers seemed to have brought about the rule of law. This, however, was the high-water mark of a political reaction against the October Days, though one wonders how far it would have gone if the attempted assassination of Marie-Antoinette had actually succeeded.[2]

So the period between 6 October 1789 and 20 June 1791, when the royal family fled Paris, was one of up and downs within a declining trajectory. This is how Louis put it in his manifesto:

As long as the king could hope to see the return of order and prosperity to the kingdom result from the measures employed by the National Assembly and from his residence near that Assembly in the capital of the kingdom, he did not count the cost of any personal sacrifice. If this hope had been fulfilled, he would not even have argued the nullity with which his total lack of liberty tainted all his undertakings since the month of October 1789.

This passive acceptance of the Revolution remained Louis's policy until the end of 1790, when the Assembly's civil constitution of the clergy and the rapid deterioration of the political situation finally caused him to contemplate flight and resistance.

The 'personal sacrifice' refers to the king's prerogative power, not his personal convenience. For though he was to complain in his manifesto that the Tuileries was uncomfortable, the Assembly granted him plenty of money with which to rectify the situation and was almost aggrieved that he did not do so. In order to support the 'splendour of the throne', the king was granted the level of civil list he had requested, 25 million *livres*.[3] But the royal domain had been nationalized and Louis regarded the 25 million as no more than its just equivalent. Indeed, as he was now without any landed property, in August 1790 he publicly demanded that the Tuileries–Louvre complex be put in his name, plus Versailles, Saint-Cloud, Fontainebleau, Compiègne, Saint-Germain and Rambouillet, together with the revenue from their estates. Marly was to be sold. His demand was left pending. But even though, as he complained in his declaration, military and political pensions were later assigned to the civil list 'even after its size had been determined', it was still a decent sum, similar in size to George III's.

The crucial point, however, was that Louis was now a state pensioner. Before the Revolution he had enjoyed two independent revenue streams: that from taxation, the most important element of which, the *taille* (at least until 1781), didn't even have to be negotiated; and that from the royal domain. Having been central in the Middle Ages it was now tiny, but the loss of it symbolized the end of the concept that Louis XIV, though he didn't use the actual words, nevertheless believed: 'L'état c'est moi'.

La vie endure. Life goes on. For Louis was the prisoner of routine as well as of Paris. He rose early as usual, heard mass, and had breakfast *en famille* – a simple repast of yoghurt, fruit and fresh bread, though the Tuileries food bill was as high as that at Versailles, what with the hangers-on and the waste. But his days dragged, without hunting or much executive activity. The conduct of foreign policy had taken up much of his time at Versailles but now it was contentious. His warnings about the *princes possessionés* had been ignored; and now, as a colonial dispute arose between England and Spain, he wanted to honour the family compact which entitled Spain to automatic assistance. The Assembly jibbed at this and the wider debate led to Louis's loss of control even of this, the only trade (apart from locksmithing) he had ever been taught. So he read some twenty newspapers or journals a day and spent more time with his family, watching them idle away their time too, playing billiards or sewing. He silent, Marie-Antoinette tearful, Madame Élisabeth avowedly counter-revolutionary, egging on her exiled brother Artois, to the annoyance of the king and queen.

Still, court life revived, expanded, adapted, and Paris became a court-capital again. Half the 1787 number of court officials moved into the Tuileries (only twelve of the twenty-eight in senior positions emigrated), whilst the ranks of courtiers were supplemented by recruits from a broader social spectrum. Bailly, the new mayor of Paris, was given the *entrées de la chambre*, as was the public prosecutor of the new *département* of Paris. Lafayette, who already had these *entrées*, received in addition those of the king's cabinet. The abolition of titles of nobility in June 1790 meant *a fortiori* that one no longer had to have proof of nobility stretching back to 1400 to enjoy the *honneurs de la cour* – that is, to be individually presented to the king and queen.[4]

Louis had taken vetting applications for presentation very seriously, covering them with his annotations and giving the general guideline that the débutants and débutantes should not be 'as young as previously'. Presentation of men encountered two (entirely unrelated) problems in the Revolution: democrats both loathed and mocked the whole rigmarole and the king no longer hunted. After their genealogies had been accepted, the débutants, wearing the embroidered tailcoat known as the *habit habillé*, were presented to the king at his *lever*. But the main event occurred the following day, when the débutant would be given a horse from the royal stables and would join the hunt. Everyone waited to see whether the king would compliment the beginner on his horsemanship. But obviously, if the king no longer hunted, he could not judge the performance. Instead, bizarrely, the successful candidate was given a certificate stating that if the king had still hunted the débutant would have been allowed to ride to hounds with him.

The presentation of women, however, continued, as it did in Britain well into the reign of Elizabeth II. The last to be presented was the wife of Saint-Priest, who, as minister for the *Maison du Roi*, must have got wind of its ending and squeezed his Greek-born wife in before the shutters came down with the abolition of the *honneurs de la cour* on 4 June 1790. The abolition of presentation was connected logically and politically with the Assembly's decree of 19 June, which had abolished titles of nobility and armorial bearings, yet pompously protected those on public monuments as belonging to sacred property rights. It was logically connected, because if nobility no longer existed it no longer mattered when the nobility of a family had begun. And it was politically so, since both the abolition of presentation and the decree were sops to public opinion – albeit futile, given dispensing with the *honneurs de la cour* 'merely made the radicals bolder in their demands'.[5] In fact, Louis secretly continued the practice of the presentation of débutantes throughout 1790 and into 1791, when he annotated one request to the effect that he would have granted it but for the political climate. So débutants would have been presented if 'the king resumed his wonted pleasures' (Assembly-speak for hunting) and débutantes if the political climate improved – which came to the same thing.

Related to the questions of nobility and presentation was that of the orders of chivalry.[6] In Britain today the orders of chivalry still soldier on long past their fighting age, but in France, with one exception, the chivalric orders were abolished in July 1791, a year before the fall of the monarchy and in May 1792 their archives were publicly burned in the Place Vendôme. The exception was the order of Saint-Louis, because, from its inception under Louis XIV, it had always been based on merit, not birth. Louis XVI missed a trick in not expanding and sponsoring the order of Saint-Louis because this and its civilian equivalent, the Saint-Michel, could have been developed into a *légion d'honneur*, except that in 1793 all holders were required to hand in their insignia or be subject to the dire penalties of the law of suspects.

The most prestigious order was the Saint-Esprit which, like its English equivalent, the garter, was only replenished by filling dead men's shoes. This did not happen in the Revolution. Not that men did not die, even those protected by the Holy Spirit, but Louis did not want to convey this most personal and prestigious honour in his gift on men who had brought him to his present predicament, whilst it would have been politically unwise to reward loyal adherents. This is made clear by his annotation on one petition for the honour: 'I shall never forget the remarkable zeal which [the applicant] displayed in my service but I cannot make any promises in advance to bestow the *cordon bleu* [of the order] and I believe that in the present circumstances the reward will prove more damaging to him than beneficial'.[7] The depth of Louis's feeling about this order, whose blue ribbon he had worn in public since childhood, is shown in a letter to Charles IV of Spain announcing that he would no longer wear the insignia either of the Saint-Esprit or of the Spanish equivalent, the Golden Fleece: 'I shall always consider myself attached in heart and soul to the knights of this order'.[8]

To fill the vacuum created by emigration (given a boost by the October Days) and anti-noble legislation, new groups paid their court – the *corps des marchands* and representatives of the new electoral districts of Paris, the focus of popular politics. The expensive silk *habit habillé* was no longer obligatory and a more simple tailcoat or *frac* could be worn. Radicals and conservatives attended the king's *lever* and *coucher*. In a sense, the court had always been politically neutral, or rather the politics of the courtiers had not mattered to the kings as they did not play a political role. Most court officials had opposed Louis XV's attack on the *parlements*, but kept their jobs; most were disloyal during the pre-Revolution (only two were dismissed); and many were radicals at the beginning of the Revolution, such as the duc de Liancourt, master of the wardrobe, and Lafayette's cousins the ramified Noailles family.[9] Liancourt, it will be remembered, had been told by Louis during the elections to the estates that he had no need to resign over his politics provided he observed the electoral regulations. But, paradoxically, the political complexion of the court mattered more under a constitutional than under an absolute monarchy (witness the bedchamber crisis at the start of the reign of Queen Victoria), and plans were drawn up, one in the king's hand, to reimburse the *charges* of the existing officials and remodel the court as a 'constitutional' household. These, however, were shelved for lack of funds on the outbreak of war in 1792.

It has been argued that Louis's maintenance of his old-style court, the one area where he still had a measure of control, demonstrated his bad faith well before the flight to Varennes confirmed it. Allied to this was the matter of diplomatic receptions. At Versailles the king generally received the diplomatic corps every other Wednesday, but at the Tuileries this was increased to twice a week, on Sundays and Thursdays. There are several ways of interpreting this. Did Louis use these receptions to keep his brother monarchs informed of his predicament so that he could ask for their intervention if needed?[10] – after all, Austria, Prussia, England, Spain and Piedmont would all sooner or later enter a coalition against revolutionary France. Or could it simply be that Louis was reassured to be with people who still regarded him as His Most Christian Majesty, King of France and Navarre by the grace of God? An empirical explanation would be that now he no longer hunted he had more time on his hands – his diary shows that at Versailles hunting and diplomatic receptions were sometimes interchangeable alternatives.

Just as diplomatic receptions quadrupled, mourning time for foreign rulers almost trebled. Perhaps Louis was making a statement, but his gloomy parents had loved mourning, dark clothes and funerary tapers, and perhaps in his deep distress he took comfort in reverting to type. Amazingly, the court went into mourning for Emperor Leopold II weeks before France declared war on his successor. Louis's logic was impeccable: Leopold was his wife's brother and when Leopold's widow also died there had to be mourning for her too because she came from the Spanish branch of the Bourbons. Louis would actually have gone into mourning for Leopold even if their two countries had been at war. Only France was no longer 'his' country.

Under the ancien régime Louis had spent his summer holidays away from Versailles in one of his smaller châteaux, such as Compiègne, and a part of every autumn was spent at Fontainebleau. The summer of 1790 was no exception: to sustain the illusion of normality, the royal family was allowed to spend the period 4 June–30 October 1790 at the queen's newly acquired palace of Saint-Cloud 'at the gates of Paris', as Marie-Antoinette put it, or in its suburbs, but (unlike the Tuileries) well away from the poorer, radical Faubourgs of Saint-Antoine and Saint-Marcel. The royal coaches were accompanied to Saint-Cloud by the Cent-Suisses bodyguards and 300 National Guards, an impressive if temporary fusion of the old and the new.

At Saint-Cloud receptions for the diplomatic corps were even more frequent than at the Tuileries and, in the last week of July, Marie-Antoinette received the ambassadors every day and entertained them every evening. The public was deeply suspicious of the king's activity at Saint-Cloud, so to reassure public opinion Louis returned twenty-two times to Paris, where he presided over the *Conseil d'État* on Sundays. Also, the president of the Assembly travelled out to Saint-Cloud for his weekly *travail* with the king, no longer the sole preserve of ministers.

Political deterioration

The royal family had been allowed to stay at Saint-Cloud because it furthered the impression of business as usual which the leaders of the Assembly wanted to promote. Louis played along with this and, as the extract from his manifesto states, may at first have been sincere. Under Necker's aegis he took several steps publicly to identify himself with the Revolution. On 4 February 1790, he went down to the Assembly and made a speech in which he 'placed himself at the head of the Revolution', swore to uphold the constitution and, according to Élisabeth, the soul of the counter-revolution within the Tuileries, 'lost whatever crown was still left on his head'.[11] Of this proceeding, however, which amounted to a speech unaccompanied by a policy, it has justly been observed: 'If one merely utters sentimental phrases one obtains only fleeting applause. . . . Necker raised a peristyle which did not lead to any building.'[12] The king's request that the Assembly attend to the deficit was ignored. When Malouet, seeking to profit from the enthusiasm produced by the king's speech, asked the

Assembly to confirm the king as head of the army and the administration, the Assembly did not even vote on his proposals. Still, medals were struck, one calling him 'the best of kings' and the raising of statues proposed at Lyons and Marseilles – appropriately, for, as he was stripped of powers, Louis became, in Soulavie's phrase, 'a royal statue'.

Mirabeau was scathing about the king's 'peculiar speech', calling it 'empty rhetoric' and 'pantomime'.[13] Louis was acting 'with anything but good faith' and 'compromising his power'. And the worst of it was that his attempt to score the fleeting and 'artificial ... plaudits of Paris ... will not be without consequences in the provinces'. In the provinces lay Mirabeau's main hope of rescuing the monarchy, and in this he was at one with the king, with whom he entered into secret contact in the spring through the Austrian ambassador Mercy-Argenteau. But Mirabeau's moment had passed (though we shall have more to say of him) because of the very fact that he was suspected of advising the king. His moment had been July 1789 when he was denouncing him.

The man of the moment now was Lafayette, the most powerful man in the kingdom. Like Robespierre in his red summer of 1794, Lafayette's power stemmed from dominating both the Paris municipality and the Parisian National Guard, which was in 1790 'the most formidable police and military force then available in all of France'.[14] Louis detested this pompous, vain, self-publicizing ladies' man with his yellow-dyed wig; this man who had 'come to die at his feet' on 5 October but carried him off to the Tuileries where 'it seems safe to assume that ... he considered these pseudo-soldiers [the National Guard] to be little more than gaolers'.[15] Marie-Antoinette considered him little more than an accomplice to her attempted assassination. She never bothered to conceal her hatred of the man. Louis had to placate him, but he had subtle ways of showing what he really thought.

On 12 February a Te Deum had been held in Notre-Dame to give thanks for the king's speech, but Louis pointedly did not attend a further Te Deum which featured the general staff of the National Guard. Louis confined the National Guard to patrolling outside the Tuileries. Internal security was given to the 2,000 Swiss Guards who, as the event would prove, were ready to lay down their lives in its defence. Many of the courtiers visiting the palace were ex-bodyguards – the regiment was left in limbo until it was dissolved on 25 June 1791 – and they showed their contempt as they passed by the National Guard.

Louis betrayed his feelings about the National Guard in other ways too. He had given up hunting as a protest at being taken away from his familiar haunts. Denied the exercise, his face had acquired a waxy, not to say prison complexion, and a worried and embarrassed Lafayette urged him to hunt in the Bois de Boulogne; but Louis reminded him that he had only assured his personal safety within the precincts of the Tuileries. 'Sire,' Lafayette replied, 'I should have the honour of accompanying Your Majesty with the elite of the National Guard.' Louis suavely replied, 'I do not wish to disturb such a large number of useful citizens.'[16] When in 1790 he did ride (not hunt) in the Bois de Boulogne and the Champs-Élysées, he refused to be accompanied by the duty commander of the National Guard, only allowing the duc de Cossé-Brissac, commander of the crack unit of the Cent-Suisses, to play this role. Similarly, on his rare visits to Parisian sites, he refused to allow any senior officer from the National Guard into his carriage.

The brightest light on his innermost feelings is provided by his letter to Philippe-Louis de Noailles, prince de Poix. Poix was an officer in the body-guard, but unlike most of his confrères, his politics were similar to those of his cousin, Lafayette. He advised the king that he should wear the uniform of the National Guard at a review. Worse, his advice was given in public, causing Louis intense embarrassment. Louis wrote Poix the rudest of any of his surviving letters:

> Regardless of the confidence I may have in M. de Lafayette, and his advice on how I choose to dress, it should be noted that I may have good reasons for not seeing eye to eye with him on this matter. . . . You, on the other hand, do not have my confidence in any way; you learned quite by chance of his [Lafayette's] request and you have taken it upon yourself to mention it to all the officers of the National Guard, stressing the unfavourable impression which my refusal to wear their uniform would make; not content with this, you use my own people to spy on my household and criticize the orders I may give from time to time. . . . I know that some silently disapprove of the actions which circumstances force me to undertake, but they do not condemn my behaviour.[17]

What Louis is saying is that whilst people to the left blame him for not doing more to please the crowd, those to the right, including most of his courtiers, blame him for doing too much (such as the speech of 4 February), but at least they don't say anything to his face. Not only does Poix do this – and in public – he gets the minority of left-liberal courtiers to spy on him and to report back when he, Louis, gives vent to his true feelings in private. Soon the word 'de-popularizing' would be applied to Louis's conduct. The irony is that (when it didn't matter) Louis had been obsessed with popularity and delighted to see decorative memorabilia at the start of his reign emblazoned with the words, 'Louis le populaire'.

Lafayette, attempting to persuade Mounier to resume his seat in the Assembly, pointed out that the only external signs that the king was not free were his refusal to hunt and the absence of his personal bodyguard. He did not add that the new guard, the Paris National Guard, was under his command, which made him a latter-day mayor of the palace and the king a *roi fainéant,* for whom the costly court merely represented, as Louis put it, 'the vain shadow of royalty'. 'Fainéant' can be translated as 'do-nothing' or 'nothing doing' and both apply to Louis's situation: 'do nothing' in the sense that, until the new constitution was completed (September 1791) and he was allocated a few crumbs of authority, he was both in theory and in practice powerless; 'nothing doing' in the sense that Louis could not possibly accept this situation for long.

The king and his ministers were called 'the executive power' and it was viewed with distrust, a hangover from the days of 'ministerial despotism' reinforced by memories of Breteuil's 'ministry of the hundred hours'. Some ministers had been chosen from 'the legislative power', i.e., the National Assembly, in the summer of 1789, but the experiment had failed through suspicions that the ministers would be corrupted by the 'court' – a vague but persistent code-word for the occult forces which were supposed to be operating on the king. These suspicions contributed to the fatal decree of 7 November which stated that no member of the Assembly could be a minister, though the measure was primarily directed against Mirabeau, whose ministerial ambitions were well known. This shoddy piece of *ad hominem* legislation had lasting consequences beyond the obvious one of forcing Mirabeau to work for the king clandestinely. For it made co-operation between the executive and the legislative very difficult and prevented the development of parliamentary government along English lines. It also reduced the standing and calibre of ministers available to the king.

Ministerial office was in any case a poor thing after the October Days, although one of the ministers, Bertrand de Molleville, remarked to the king that there were still more applicants than vacancies. In July, to humiliate the king, the assembly had feted the returning Necker ministry but, as Louis observed, 'subsequently it treated them no better for that'. They were cut off both from the king and from the Assembly. Whereas the *cour des ministres* had been at the heart of Versailles, ministers, symbolically, did not have offices or apartments in the Tuileries. There was not much for ministers to do and they operated in a world of unreality. On the one hand, they were not privy to Louis's ultimate plans, and on the other, the Assembly duplicated the work of their departments by the creation of its own committees.

Lameth accused the executive of 'playing dead'. Louis, for example, was accused of pursuing a *politique du pire*, letting the Revolution caricature itself by not resisting mad decrees, like the one of June 1790 abolishing titles of nobility and obliging nobles to use their family name: Orléans ostentatiously called himself Capet. Lafayette, whose grandstanding had contributed to the passing of this decree, tried to row back. He had the gall to turn up to cabinet to support Necker in asking Louis to veto the decree. He refused, taking a grim satisfaction in the symbolic demise of the aristocratic constitutionalism which had defeated his reform programme in 1787 and launched France on its revolutionary journey – a defeat in which both Necker and Lafayette had played leading roles.

Besides, it was far from clear that the Assembly recognized that Louis even had a veto before the Assembly's completion of the constitution ended the state of flux and its own dictatorship of constituent power – witness the reception accorded to his modest observations on the August decrees, a proximate cause of the October Days. Another explanation for the king's inactivity is that both Louis and Marie-Antoinette were as traumatized by the invasion of their palace as the deputies had been by the king's volte-face in June–July and that it took a year for them to recover from an actual, not just an imagined, threat to their lives.

Lafayette and Mirabeau, sometimes collaborating, though with mutual suspicion, both worked to bring down the Necker ministry. Mirabeau, from his days of working with Calonne, had always regarded Necker as a charlatan, and one moreover who had refused his overtures at the opening of the Estates-General. On 1 September 1790 Mirabeau told Louis that Necker 'no longer governed public opinion. People expected miracles from him', and that his response to the crisis was 'routine'.[18] Louis agreed. When it was suggested that Mirabeau would have to concert action with the existing ministry, Louis exclaimed, 'Ah! Nothing can be done on this point with M. Necker. Everything that we do with M. de Mirabeau must also stay completely secret from my ministers and I rely on you in this respect.'

On 2 September the suppression of a mutiny at Nancy by General Bouillé provoked a rising in Paris which threatened to march on Saint-Cloud. Lafayette advised a terrified Necker to 'seek refuge with a friend'. Instead Necker fled to his estate at Saint-Ouen, sent in his resignation to both the Assembly and the king and retired to Switzerland, having lost all control over the direction of the Revolution. Madame Élisabeth commented: 'Have you heard the great news that does not cause a stir in Paris? M. Necker is gone. He took such a fright at the threat of being hanged that he was unable to resist the tender solicitations of his virtuous wife to take the waters. The Assembly, on reading this phrase, laughed and passed to the order of the day.[19] Necker's dismissal had caused the storming of the Bastille, his resignation merely laughter. Lafayette wanted Louis to appoint the compliant foreign secretary, Montmorin, as *chef du Conseil royal des finances*. Louis refused, possibly because in Breteuil (who had fled before he had time to resign) he considered that he already possessed one.

After the fall of Necker, the Assembly assumed responsibility for finance. It had already made substantial incursions into the king's use of the executive by setting up its own committees to shadow government departments: as the king's manifesto was to say, the Assembly 'by means of its committees constantly oversteps its own self-appointed limits . . . and thus combines all the powers'. Its control over finance, however, was the unkindest cut because Louis considered that he had acquired considerable expertise in this field: 'The king understands the problems of this department, yet if that were possible he has been rendered more of a stranger to it than to the others.' And how did it tackle the 'famous' deficit which had sparked the whole thing off? By putting the church lands 'at the disposal of the nation' – Assembly-speak for confiscation.

The land was to be sold in small lots to give as many people as possible a vested interest in the new regime, though ultimately there were only 80,000 purchasers. Meanwhile the land served as collateral for an issue of bonds known as *assignats*. The royal (now national) debt was estimated at 2 billion *livres*. The first issue of *assignats* was for 400 million *livres* bearing interest of 5 per cent; the second, issued in March 1790, was for 800 million, this time with no interest – fiat paper money. By the fall of the monarchy in August 1792, 3.2 billion were in circulation. By the fall of Robespierre on 27 July 1794 the total was 11 billion. Hyperinflation was the inevitable consequence. It is easier for its elected representatives to cheat the nation than it is for its king. And (then as now) inflation is more bearable than bankruptcy because its effects are insidious rather than brutal and the intention can be (and always is) denied. Louis had surrendered his absolute power rather than declare a bankruptcy, which he had always believed would have been dishonourable. All his ministers, from Turgot to Calonne, had eschewed and condemned bankruptcy. Brienne had fallen because he had paid in paper money bearing interest at 5 per cent. The National Assembly had not even done that. Louis's ironic bitterness was intense. The state of the economy was also desperate, and not just because of the collapse of authority and the rebellion in the rich sugar island of Haiti, where the slaves also wanted the Rights of Man. There was a price to pay for equality: the luxury trades collapsed as the emigration of nobles increased. Six hundred men lost their jobs when Louis gave up hunting. Louis was petitioned by many skilled craftsmen who complained that their livelihoods had been destroyed by the Revolution. One such petition, signed by eighty craftsmen, urged the king to reassert his authority, offering armed assistance. They complained that wages had not kept up with inflation, about the disappearance of specie and the loss of the colonies.

The reaction to Necker's departure symbolizes the rapid deterioration of the political situation of the monarchy. After the October Days, Malouet had founded the Club des Impartiaux as a centrist counterweight on the Assembly to the Jacobin Club. His centre-right friends were joined by those from the centre-left, including Lafayette, La Rochefoucauld and Liancourt. Soon, however, they fell into disagreement over Malouet's insistence that the Assembly should define the constitutional powers of the executive immediately, before the revolutionary torrent eroded it any further. La Rochefoucauld replied that the executive was merely 'the keystone which could only be put in place when the other parts of the edifice had received their form and disposition'.[20] In other words, they differed over the question of whether the king or the Assembly should be invested by the constitution with ultimate supremacy. Yet even when Malouet, Lafayette and Mirabeau acted in unison, as in the debate of 15–22 May 1790 over the royal prerogative of declaring peace and war, their proposals underwent such substantial modification that, as the king was to put it in his declaration: 'With [peace] treaties having to undergo revision and confirmation by the Assembly, no foreign power will be willing to contract engagements which could be broken by others than those with whom it was negotiating: in which case all the powers would be concentrated in the Assembly.'

Louis was to attribute this deterioration largely to the influence of the Jacobin Club. The development of the network was arguably the biggest political development of 1790–91, restoring the dynamic to the Revolution at a time when former radicals, such as Barnave, thought they could stop it like a taxi. In his declaration, Louis, who recognized the enemy, compared the network, with its 'mother society' in Paris corresponding with affiliates throughout the country, to the *parlementaire théorie des classes* whereby the concerns of one are the concerns of all:

In nearly all the cities and even in several country towns and villages associations have been formed with the name *Société des Amis de la constitution* [the Jacobin Club]. In defiance of the laws, they do not permit the existence of any other clubs that are not affiliated to themselves, thus forming an immense corporation even more dangerous than any of those which previously existed.[21] Without authorization, nay in contempt of the laws, they deliberate on all aspects of government, correspond with each other on all subjects, make and receive denunciations, and post up their resolutions. They have assumed such a predominance that all the administrative and judicial bodies, not excepting the National Assembly itself, nearly always obey their orders.

The Jacobin network, Robespierre's most original creation, which transformed this obscure provincial deputy into a household name and a force throughout the land, pressurized the Assembly by collective petitions and posted 'slates' of candidates for the elections which were now held for most offices. It was the unexpected rise of these clubs which was responsible for the rapid deterioration of royal authority in the months preceding the king's flight. The Jacobins were a minority and a ginger group – maybe the first ever – and were not universally popular. The artisans who had petitioned Louis and offered their armed support begged the king 'above all to dissipate and punish those seditious persons who in the name of being "friends of the constitution" are its most cruel enemies'.[22]

The king needed to counter the influence of the Jacobins in the formation of a public opinion which he still believed to be sovereign. This aim is at the heart of his relations with La Porte and Mirabeau. Louis appointed Arnaud de La Porte, like Malouet, a former naval intendant, as intendant of the civil list when it was set up in 1790. The list was never part of the *Maison du Roi* and Louis had personal control of its considerable funds in a way he never had over the six departmental ministries. La Porte was the king's agent within the context of the constitution, conducting negotiations over the formation of ministries, buying support, subsidizing pamphleteers, trying in general (and in vain) to direct public opinion. La Porte told the king that Mirabeau was 'the only man who, in the present circumstances, which are most critical, can really serve Your Majesty'.[23] Mirabeau advised extending La Porte's activities by mounting an elaborate propaganda and secret service machine which, with its complex network of agents, ignorant of each other's activities, would have appealed to Louis's love of secrecy for its own sake.

Mercy-Argenteau contacted Mirabeau in May 1790 through their common friend the comte de La Marck, with a view to obtaining the orator's services. It was agreed that his debts would be paid, he would have a pension of 5,000 *livres* a month and a million *livres* at the end of the session of the National Assembly if his conduct had been satisfactory. On the strength of this Mirabeau moved into a fine apartment in the fashionable new Chaussée d'Antin complex, which raised suspicious eyebrows. Though he was paid for his services that did not make Mirabeau corrupt, for corruption consists not simply in receiving money but in changing conduct as a consequence. And even Lafayette, who was no friend, conceded, 'he would not for any sum have maintained an opinion which would have destroyed liberty and dishonoured his mind'.[24]

Mirabeau's political beliefs were almost identical to Malouet's, though there was no formal collaboration between them. Both his apostrophe to Dreux-Brézé on 23 June about only moving at the point of the bayonet and Malouet's silence were motivated by the same sense of the king's betrayal and by despair that the nobility had captured the monarchy. Mirabeau's ambition was to be the modern Richelieu and carry the monarchy forward to the next decisive stage of its development: its transformation into what would become the Napoleonic system. In a series of fifty 'notes for the court', he offered a stylish analysis of the Assembly's legislation which vindicated the consistency of his career as one who had collaborated with Calonne on the drafting of his projects, offered to defend Lamoignon if he was impeached by the *parlement*, and advocated alliance with the third estate. The National Assembly, he argued, had achieved what Louis had been seeking in 1787: the Revolution, properly understood, by destroying the *pouvoirs intermédiaires* 'facilitated the exercise of power' – notably, on 3 November 1789, the Assembly had 'buried alive' the *parlements* by indefinitely prolonging their summer vacation, finally abolishing them on 7 September 1790. 'Richelieu', he adds, 'would have been pleased by the notion of forming just one class of citizens.' Mirabeau distinguished between the destruction of the corporate organization of the ancien régime, an irreversible achievement which could only strengthen monarchical authority, and the new constitution, which shackled it but could still be modified.[25]

The civil constitution of the clergy

For Louis the gravest manifestation of the political deterioration, because it affected not just his royal prerogative but his Christian conscience, was the civil constitution of the clergy, what Talleyrand was to call 'perhaps the biggest political blunder of the Assembly'.[26] It would have been difficult for the French clergy to have been more conciliatory towards the Revolution. On 4 August they had renounced that separate corporate status they had defended so doggedly against Calonne. They accepted the loss of their lands and their tithes, and, being paid by the state, now God as well as Caesar were rendered salaried state functionaries. On 12 July 1790, however, the Assembly issued its civil constitution of the clergy, which introduced popular election of bishops and *curés*. It was not this doctrinaire measure, though, which led to difficulties but the new boundaries for the bishoprics, which were to be co-extensive with the new *départements* that had replaced the old provinces. As there were 135 old bishoprics and only eighty-three *départements*, some bishops would have to resign and others be assigned new sees. This change required papal institution.

Pius VI was hostile both to the French Revolution in general and to the civil constitution in particular. Although formal condemnation did not come until his briefs of 10 March and 13 April 1791, he had already sent Louis a warning letter on 9 July 1790: 'Do you think that a purely political body can change the doctrine and discipline of the church, scorn the opinions of the Holy Fathers . . .?'[27] One can imagine Louis's unease when on 22 July he gave his sanction to the civil constitution.

Popular hostility to the king's prolonged stay at Saint-Cloud was also growing, fanned by newspaper reports of rudeness to the National Guard and by a curious episode on 29 June when two respectably dressed men attempted to deliver a letter to Louis from the Blessed Virgin Mary, assuring him that a heavenly host would restore him to his ancestral rights.[28] The royal family returned to Paris on 30 October, just as the civil constitution issue was entering its toxic phase with the Assembly's decree on 27 November that all priests must swear an oath of allegiance to the constitution, including the civil constitution, or resign their livings. Louis postponed giving his sanction whilst he desperately and in vain urged the pope to baptize the civil constitution and thus save France from schism.[29] Then, on 26 December, with 'death in the soul', Louis finally sanctioned the decree. About half the *curés* took the oath, but only seven bishops did so, including Brienne, who received a stiff letter from the pope and returned him his cardinal's hat. Schism was thus a reality, with France divided into jurors and non-jurors. In his last testament, Louis was to 'ask God to accept . . . my profound repentance for having put my name (albeit unwillingly) to decrees which may be in conflict with . . . the Catholic Church to which I have always remained sincerely attached'.[30]

Louis's aunt Adélaïde tortured him with a reproachful letter, dated 18 January 1791, telling him that, by sanctioning the decree, 'you have deprived yourself of the only thing that could give you strength courageously to resist all the afflictions you have been made to suffer'. She asked for permission for herself and her sister Victoire to retire to Spain or Rome 'until the persecutions end'.[31] The aunts left for Rome on 19 February, creating the impression that this was the start of an exodus of the royal family. They were detained by the local Jacobin Club at Arnay-le-duc, and while the National Assembly debated what to do, Adélaïde and Victoire played piquet with the local priest. Finally they were allowed to leave.

The oath to the civil constitution also had practical implications for the exercise of Louis's personal devotions. Having sinned by sanctioning the decree, he wondered whether he had the right to make his Easter communion. In his perplexity, he wrote an anguished and confused letter to the bishop of Clermont seeking guidance:

> May I receive communion and must I do it within the fortnight? You know the unfortunate predicament in which I find myself through my acceptance of the decrees on the clergy; I have always regarded my acceptance of them as acting under duress, having never hesitated as regards my personal concerns to deal with Catholic pastors always, and being fully resolved, if I come to recover my power, fully to restore Catholic worship. A priest I saw thinks that these sentiments may suffice and that I can make my Easter communion. However, you are in a better position to see what the church in general thinks ... whether on the one hand this may not scandalize some and on the other, I see the men of faction – a reason admittedly which cannot weigh in the balance – already speaking almost threateningly. I beg you to consult such bishops as you see fit about this, ones on whose discretion you can count. I desire also that you give me your reply tomorrow before noon and that you return my letter.[32]

The bishop's reply was crushing. The king's sanction of the decrees 'has had the most disastrous consequences for religion'. The bishop understood that the king had yielded to duress, but added: 'Your Majesty knows that it was only resistance to force which produced the martyrs.' He concluded that the king should postpone making his communion that Easter.[33]

A further complication was that Louis wanted to receive communion from a non-juring priest, the only valid ones in his eyes. The conventional view is that Louis decided to spend Easter at Saint-Cloud to secure the services in secret of a proper priest, but there are flaws in this explanation. On 20 April La Porte wrote to the king: 'This evening I am going to try to dispel [this] notion in the Cordelier club', the more radical rival of the Jacobin Club dominated by Danton.[34] The 'notion' was that the king had already made his communion secretly in his private chapel, which he probably did on the 16th, the day before he was due to leave for Saint-Cloud. That day Louis was publicly denounced in the same Cordelier club for having received communion at the hands of a non-juring priest. The spies Louis complains about in the Tuileries could easily have discovered the fact.

If he had already made his Easter communion, the purpose of the visit to Saint-Cloud may have been different. Louis had been very ill in March and daily bulletins had been posted for a week concerning his health. He had been coughing blood and may have feared a return of the tuberculosis from which he suffered in his youth – so he may simply have wanted fresh air to recuperate. But April was an unusual time to be leaving what was now the seat of government – he never left Versailles at this time and in 1790 had not left for Saint-Cloud until June.

That is what the conspiracy-minded Parisians thought, and on 18 April 1791, as Louis prepared to set off for Saint-Cloud, a suspicious crowd turned back the carriage in which the royal family was sitting in the very courtyard of the Tuileries. It has convincingly been argued that 'the religious issue' was merely a 'pretext': the crowd simply did not want the king to spend another prolonged period away from Paris. But it may be more than this: the Parisians were the more suspicious of the king's motives for leaving precisely because he had already taken communion and therefore betrayed the Revolution. And they must have suspected that, having got to Saint-Cloud, the royal family would not stop there.

Despite the pleas of Lafayette and the mayor, Bailly, the National Guard mutinied and did nothing to drive back the crowd. One of them accused Louis of giving asylum to refractory priests and Louis shouted back: 'Wretch, who made you judge of my conscience?' After two hours sitting in the carriage and seeing that Lafayette was powerless, Louis took his family back into the palace and they abandoned their plans. The crowd, led by the grenadiers of the National Guard, entered the vestibule of the palace and tried to follow Marie-Antoinette to her apartments. But Louis, still furious, shouted: 'Grenadiers! Stop right there!' And, as Fersen relates, 'they all stopped as if they had had their legs cut right off'. Inside, Louis is reported to have said, 'I am well aware that they want to murder me like they did Henri IV [assassinated in 1610], but a better crown awaits me above.'[35] This is a conscious echo of the last words of his ancestor, Charles I, whose portrait by Van Dyck he had made a point of having sent over from Versailles: 'I go from a corruptible to an incorruptible crown.' Next day Louis went down to the Assembly to complain and received a wince-making reply from the president: 'riots are inseparable from the progress of liberty'.

The 'Saint-Cloud departure', as it is called – though departure was the one thing it wasn't – was a turning point. As Marie-Antoinette wrote to Mercy on 20 April, it 'has confirmed us more than ever in our plans [for flight]'. It was also symptomatic of the galloping consumption in the body politic. Whereas the Club des Impartiaux had been founded in 1789 to strengthen the executive, its successor, the Club Monarchique, founded by Clermont-Tonnerre and Malouet the following autumn, was instituted, according to its historian, quite simply 'to save the monarchy'.[36] Popular pressure forced it to change address no less than four times before it finally closed after being stormed in a popular rising on 28 March 1791. At this time a deputation from the Jacobin Club descended on the Tuileries to demand that the king sack all his top court and church officers.[37] To cap it all, on 2 April Mirabeau died aged forty-two, *in mediis rebus*, suspected by 'patriots' but still a powerful force in the National Assembly.

The king, as his manifesto makes clear, was well aware of the deteriorating situation and how it was reflected in the ongoing drafting of the constitution: '. . . the nearer the Assembly approached to the end of its labours, the more the wise men were seen to lose their influence and there was a corresponding daily increase of clauses which could only make government difficult, even impossible, and inspire contempt for it.' Among these clauses, the king specifically mentioned that passed on 8 June depriving him of the prerogative of mercy and several detailing the responsibility – criminal rather than political – of ministers.

Such troubles seemed to deepen the king's depression. Madame de Tourzel, the new governess to the royal children, notes that the king and queen returned from Easter communion 'in a state of extreme depression. This state of mind was indeed habitual in the royal family.' In August 1790 Mirabeau had talked of 'the kind of torpor to which misfortune reduces people' and the following January, Montmorin 'said sadly . . . that when [the king] spoke to him about his affairs and his position it seemed as if he were talking to him about matters concerning the emperor of China'. Both Élisabeth and Marie-Antoinette believed that his recent illness, which lasted several weeks, was as much mental as physical in cause. Marie-Antoinette writes on 19 March: 'You already know how much I have been worried about the king's health; it was all the more disquieting because it is really the overflowing of his cup of sorrows which has made him ill.'[38]

Eighteen months of going along with the Revolution had led to a deeper captivity, a deeper depression. There must have seemed to him little to lose by flight. Moreover, France was now divided along religious as well as political lines: the crumb of comfort held out to him by Malesherbes in 1788 – that the absence of religious quarrels differentiated Louis's position from that of Charles I – had been taken away. And Malesherbes's other prophecy had come to pass: 'they will successively strip you of several of your prerogatives. It is up to you ... to draw up a definitive list of what you will never surrender'. This he was about to do.

CHAPTER THIRTEEN

THE FLIGHT TO MONTMÉDY

Escape plans

FLIGHT FROM VERSAILLES HAD been proposed in the council and rejected by the king on three occasions before the move to Paris. On each occasion, Louis had experienced a sense of shame at departing: 'A fugitive king! A fugitive king!' he had exclaimed on 5 October. The king's virtual captivity in the Tuileries removed that shame: escape was more honourable than flight, almost an obligation. Captivity also put the king at an obvious disadvantage – his residual power could be used against him – which his escape would redress. For flight can be considered as a variant of the instrument of exile, whose essence had been absence from the king, just as hell is said to be absence from God. Escape from the Tuileries was, however, more dangerous than flight from Versailles, as the aborted journey to Saint-Cloud demonstrated. Flight, though, still risked civil war.

Shortly after the October Days, Mirabeau advised Louis's brother Provence, who unlike Artois had not emigrated, that the royal family should leave under armed escort for Normandy. But Provence said he would never be able to bring the king round: 'to give you some idea of what . . . the king . . . is like, imagine trying to hold oiled billiard balls together'.[1] Louis did, however, have an escape plan of his own on which he worked 'for nearly six months' with his closest remaining friend, d'Angiviller. D'Angiviller had emigrated after the fall of the Bastille because he had been in discussions with the Breteuil government, though he had refused to join it. But the king had kept up 'a fairly continuous correspondence' with him in his exile. Even from prison in 1792, Louis continued to write to this boyhood friend, 'l'ami du duc de Berry' as Louis's father had called him, inserting his messages between the lines of ones written by a servant who smuggled them out to Mannheim. D'Angiviller sat out the

October Days but returned to France during the false dawn of January 1790. He immediately became 'obsessed' by the idea that the king should seek safety outside Paris. 'I was confirmed in this single idea', he continues, 'when in the month of June 1790 the king charged me with trying to procure a million *livres* secretly which he told me he needed to win over to his party some of the most influential' *fédérés*.

The *fédérés* were the delegates of municipalities and national guards who came from all over France to celebrate the first anniversary of the storming of the Bastille at a grand, open-air ceremony in the Champ de Mars. Many delegations asked Louis to visit their region. If Louis had accepted the Normans' request, fulfilling his promise of 1786 to return to Rouen because his visit after inspecting the dyke at Cherbourg had been so fleeting, it would have been politically embarrassing for Lafayette or the Assembly to stop him, though a mob might have mysteriously materialized to do the job, subject afterwards naturally to a judicial whitewash. The *fédérés* were so enthusiastic that Louis maybe didn't need a million *livres* to win them over. D'Angiviller, who was shocked that the king had not felt able to ask a minister for this sum managed to find him 400,000. He gives no more details of Louis's plan, though it clearly involved flight within the interior of France, rather than to its frontiers or abroad, and was linked to the federation. If this plan had been implemented, d'Angiviller confidently asserted, 'we would not have witnessed the horrors consequent on the one which was adopted without my knowledge' – the Flight to Varennes.[2]

Marie-Antoinette got wind of d'Angiviller's plan and didn't like it, telling Mercy: 'I've just had a conversation with M. d'Angiviller. It was as long as it was painful. He still sticks to his idea of . . .'[3] The ellipsis is Marie-Antoinette's, but what word does she want to conceal? Internal flight? Civil War? Marie-Antoinette herself wanted to rely on the resources of her Austrian family. She also distrusted d'Angiviller because of his friendship with Calonne. Mercy thought that Calonne 'could be implicated in the negotiations' of d'Angiviller to bring Mirabeau into contact with the court.[4]

Mirabeau wanted d'Angiviller to be the sole channel of communication between him and the king because he was the king's confidant and 'because of the mutual friendship between M. Turgot and . . . [d'Angiviller]'. Turgot had been the main inspiration for Calonne's programme. Mirabeau approached d'Angiviller with a view to offering his services to the king and terms were discussed. D'Angiviller was even prepared to travel to Madrid to lodge a bond with the king of Spain promising Mirabeau a lump sum at the end of the session of the National Assembly. But it was done through intermediaries to avert suspicion. And in the end d'Angiviller pulled out because he believed that his dealings with Mirabeau would inevitably get out and undermine Mirabeau's effectiveness. For the same reason d'Angiviller did not discuss with Mirabeau the king's plan to buy the support of the *fédérés*, even though the two plans had much in common. Mirabeau advised that the king should make Rouen instead of Paris the capital of the kingdom. Then (as Henry V found) with Normandy in his possession, and with it control of the Seine, 'he would exert a stranglehold on the food supply of . . . [Paris] the only centre of resistance worth considering'.[5]

After d'Angiviller pulled out, Mercy negotiated the deal with Mirabeau, which involved a change of emphasis: Mirabeau would now be working for the queen – and paid by her. Some of the expressions employed by Mirabeau in his 'notes for the court' suggest that Louis was not meant to read them; e.g., 'The queen . . . must have a clever agent about the king under her secret influence.'[6] But it was a question of emphasis rather than conflict. Louis, as well as Marie-Antoinette, met Mirabeau just once and in great secrecy, at Saint-Cloud on 3 July 1790; a recently discovered position paper which can confidently be attributed to the king shows that Louis was more closely involved with Mirabeau than has been supposed.[7]

This paper, dated 18 August 1790, reflects the evolution of Louis's thinking in view of the deteriorating political situation, and particularly the Assembly's ecclesiastical policy. Louis was gradually moving away from his passive acceptance of or passive resistance to the Revolution. The paper is in Mercy's hand but unsigned. It has been suggested that Mercy composed it himself on Marie-Antoinette's instructions or ('most likely') that Louis himself dictated it to Mercy. It is indeed most probable that Louis dictated the letter, but to Marie-Antoinette rather than to Mercy, with whom Louis never had close relations. A parallel is to be found in the negotiations culminating in Necker's return to office in 1788: the king dictated his position paper (and the one in question here is a position paper) to Marie-Antoinette, who gave it to Mercy to conduct the negotiations because the king did not want to be directly involved. The memorandum is worth quoting *in extenso*:

The king has amply demonstrated that he will shrink at no personal sacrifice which he judges might benefit his people's happiness. Guided by this principle the king is resolutely determined never to provoke the most disastrous scourge which could threaten the monarchy: one can never accept that civil war is necessary, but one can imagine the possibility that it becomes inevitable; [and] provided it comes about neither through the actions or [even] the wishes of the king, he will prepare himself to accept it, without fear or remorse; and it is in line with this thinking that he would like to see a plan worked out which combines everything which foresight, wisdom and the probability of success might require in such critical circumstances.

The preparatory measures proposed by M. de M[irabeau] are praiseworthy and one is very tempted to adopt them, but it is necessary to discuss ways and means. The impact of events still too obscure to foretell will greatly affect the necessary calculations and combinations. The working out of these details can only be done verbally and this must only be done by taking the precautions which have become necessary as a result of recent incidents.

This letter displays many of Louis's characteristics: the need to be assured of success; the need for foresight – Vergennes's watchwords were 'prévenir et prévoyer'; and the love of secrecy (necessary now). His readiness to make 'personal sacrifice' is found in the extract from his manifesto quoted above. But what is quintessentially Louis is his sophistical attitude to civil war: 'provided it comes about neither through the actions or [even] the wishes of the king, he will prepare himself to accept it, without fear or remorse'. His contorted attitude has an almost Shakespearean complexity, and one unsuited to an age which prized transparency. He must not provoke civil war, which (despite his impotence in the Tuileries) he could unleash by simply raising his little finger in virtue of the residual, traditional loyalty which most Frenchmen still had for him. He must not even want it. But (and this is the contradiction) he must get ready ('se préparer') for it by taking appropriate measures for which he gives Mirabeau an amber light. Louis's attitude was exactly the same as that which governed the flight to Varennes in 1791 and the declaration of war against Austria in 1792. In both, his position was highly nuanced but nonetheless fatal to the monarchy.

Louis considered two specific escape plans. Both were centred on General Bouillé, whose army in the east was considered to be the only reliable one. Its reliability, however, was only relative: after all, Bouillé had come to Louis's attention by dint of suppressing a mutiny – that of the garrison at Nancy, in August 1790. This was a serious business involving three regiments, one of which, the Châteauvieux, was Swiss. There had been 100 killed and forty were hanged as an example. But Bouillé had diplomatically employed both troops-of-the-line and National Guards to quell the mutiny.

'Plan A' involved Bouillé marching on or towards Paris to rescue the king. 'Plan B' (the one finally adopted in April 1791) involved the king escaping from

Paris and joining Bouillé in Lorraine, in the hill fortress of Montmédy. Mahomet or the mountain. 'Plan A' would have been an internal French matter. 'Plan B' involved the employment of Austrian troops and money. Louis considered both plans in tandem, only finally plumping for 'B' and committing himself to flight at all after the death of Mirabeau and the Saint-Cloud departure. The link with the departure is made explicit the same evening by Marie-Antoinette's telling Fersen, who was to organize the Paris end of the escape, 'the king gives you carte blanche'.[8] As the political situation deteriorated there was an elision between the two plans, with Bouillé himself requiring Austrian involvement.

'Plan A' involved a grand coalition of Mirabeau, Calonne and even (briefly) Artois, then staying with his in-law, the king of Sardinia-Piedmont, at Turin. Calonne even visited his old enemy, Breteuil, in Switzerland on his way from London to Turin, and Mirabeau hoped to include both former ministers in his coalition.[9] The plan was very complicated: the grand-sweep simplicity of Mirabeau's political thought was matched only by the complexity of its execution. He elaborated Louis's plan to buy support in the provinces into a grand plan for the eighty-three *départements* to petition the king to dissolve the National Assembly on the grounds that it had exceeded its mandate and convoke a new Assembly to Compiègne. The king would proceed there in broad daylight – escorted by Bouillé's troops. The aim was basically to set up an English-style government, as had been advocated by the *monarchiens* and in Calonne's recent book *De l'état de la France présent et à venir*. From Turin Calonne sent his aunt to sound out Bouillé and she got the impression that Calonne was to be 'a form of chancellor of the exchequer'. The king was to have the initiative in legislation and an absolute veto. It was a daring idea and would have had the virtue of ending the threat of counter-revolution by bringing Artois back into the fold, his council concluding that 'however frightful a coalition of this sort may be, it is preferable to civil war'. Artois would have brought with him most of the émigrés, except die-hards such as the intransigent prince de Bourbon-Condé, who thought the scheme was execrable. Artois and Calonne were men of principle but also men of power, and for this reason sometimes had to humour the rank and file of what became an expatriate army who wanted a restoration of the ancien régime, warts and all.

Mirabeau thought he had won over thirty-six of the eighty-three *départements* to petition for the dissolution of the National Assembly but such consultation could not be kept secret and so many rumours were circulating it was suspected that Mirabeau's opponents had poisoned him – in fact he died of tuberculosis exacerbated by his unregulated lifestyle. Mirabeau died on 2 April, and with him the rainbow coalition evaporated as rainbows do. Bouillé and Calonne had overestimated Mirabeau's ascendancy over the Assembly, but with his death Calonne moved towards outright counter-revolution, now that he was no longer offered a swift return to power. And, as during the 1787 Assembly of Notables, he and Artois were inseparable.

Plan 'B' centred on the baron de Breteuil, head of the disastrous 'ministry of the hundred hours' which had presided over the fall of the Bastille. In Britain today, when a minister is forced out of office, he routinely says that he wants to spend more time with his family, even if he hates them. The ancien régime equivalent was to leave for health reasons, often to take the waters, the reason Necker gave in 1790. Calonne asked permission to go to the Spa town of Bagnières after his fall in 1787 and his allies, the Polignacs, went to Bath. The convention reached sublimity when Breteuil wrote to Louis on 8 November 1789: 'I feel I owe Your Majesty an account of the use I made of the permission he granted me to travel outside the kingdom for as long as my health required. I have taken the waters at Spa and Aix-al-Chapelle. I have been [in Switzerland] since the fourth of last month and plan to spend the winter here.'[10] The purpose of his letter was to ask the king if he could resume his diplomatic career, preferably as ambassador to Rome, when that post became available. Louis turned him down, but the request shows that, at this stage, Breteuil was prepared to work with or at least derive an income from the new regime.

However, eighteen months later he had become the most reactionary of all the players: a recently discovered memorandum which he intended to be delivered to the king on his arrival at Montmédy advocates a restoration of the ancien régime *tout court* – it even rejects the compromise of the *séance royale* of 23 June and questions whether the Estates-General is needed at all. And Breteuil's is usually considered to be the acceptable face of the counter-revolution! The discovery of this document makes more pertinent the question of the authenticity of another document, in which the king offered him plenipotentiary powers, which Breteuil claimed the king had sent him in November 1790:

Monsieur le Baron de Breteuil, knowing the extent of your zeal and fidelity and desirous of giving you a new proof of my confidence, I have chosen you to be entrusted with the interests of my crown. As circumstances do not permit me to give you my instructions on such and such an object, to have a continuous correspondence with you, I am sending you these presents to serve as plenipotentiary powers and authorization vis-à-vis the different powers with whom you may have to treat on my behalf. You know my intentions and I leave it to your discretion to make what use of them you consider necessary for the good of my service. I approve of all you do to attain the aim I have set, which is the restoration of my legitimate authority and the happiness of my peoples.[11]

If this document is genuine, then a die-hard reactionary may be said to be speaking in the name of the king, though once the king appeared in person, Breteuil's delegated powers would cease; and Breteuil confessed to Fersen as late as 29 May, 'I don't rightly know what His Majesty is planning to do.'[12]

Moreover, the same scholar who discovered Breteuil's reactionary programme has concluded, after consulting two handwriting experts, that the plenipotentiary powers were indeed forged.[13] This possibility was first pointed out by P. and P. Girault de Coursac, the scholarly hagiographers of Louis XVI, who suggested that Marie-Antoinette and Fersen commissioned the forgery. So Breteuil remains what he had always been, the queen's minister. This does not, however, mean that the wilder assertions of the Girault de Coursacs are valid, since for them the forgery is just the coping stone of an elaborate edifice constructed to demonstrate that Louis was a patriotic king with a sincere desire to be a constitutional monarch. They claim that Marie-Antoinette kept everything from the king; that she had originally planned to leave Louis behind in Paris as an encumbrance; that she planned to escape with the dauphin, who would be proclaimed King Louis XVII with herself as regent; and finally that Louis only resolved on flight after the Saint-Cloud departure in order to demonstrate that he was free and to induce the nation to accept the reforms of the National Assembly whose good work would otherwise be wasted.

Only at this point, the de Coursacs argue, did Louis contact Bouillé. For six months Bouillé had been working on the details of the queen's escape plan in the mistaken belief that the king was privy to it. Now he had to put the original plan to the king as something newly devised, but, in order to prevent the king from finding out what he had put his pen to (reader, prepare to take a sharp intake of breath), Bouillé caused the escape to miscarry by making sure Louis ended up in a cul-de-sac at Varennes.

Wild as this general thesis is, the de Coursacs demonstrate from several *lapsus* in Marie-Antoinette's correspondence – such as 'I' crossed out and replaced with 'the king' – that in speaking for the king, she is really putting forward her own ideas. That the queen wished to conceal matters from the king is clear from the following letter to Fersen: 'The bishop [of Pamiers, Breteuil's agent] should have told you already about the problems of writing to me. Only today, M. La Porte, who shows everything to the king, gave him your packet.'[14] The packet contained a long memorandum of Fersen's on the general situation and some skeleton letters for the queen to write to foreign rulers. Clearly most of the correspondence concerning plan 'B' was conducted by the quartet of Marie-Antoinette, Fersen, Mercy and Bouillé. The de Coursacs also observe that, apart from the plenipotentiary powers, there is only one extant letter of the king's with a bearing on the escape: a letter to the Emperor Leopold II dated 20 June 1791, which may have been tampered with.

But to say that Louis did not give Breteuil carte blanche is not to say they had no contact. In September 1790 Breteuil sent the king a memorandum via the bishop of Pamiers, who was returning to France from Switzerland. In this memorandum Breteuil, who regarded himself as Louis's last freely chosen minister, stressed the 'urgency of adopting any plan whatsoever' rather than drifting, which 'inspired general mistrust in all parties'. The best plan was for the king 'to leave Paris ... in order to withdraw to a safe place *within the kingdom* and surround himself with the forces of General Bouillé.'[15]

Of Bouillé, who was impatient with such labels as revolutionary or counter-revolutionary and preferred to call himself a 'royalist', La Marck observes: 'Administrative reforms had always struck him as necessary and, as for improvements in the political structure, his opinions tended towards a form of constitution similar to England's. The king was not unaware of this viewpoint and that did not prevent his designating him the officer most worthy of his confidence, which proves once again that Louis XVI had sincerely opted for a constitutional system of government.'[16] After Bouillé's suppression of the mutiny, Louis had sent him a nice letter with, rare for him, a gracious postscript such as Louis XIV might have written: 'I know that one of your favourite horses was killed under M. de Gouvernet; I am sending you one of mine which I have ridden and which I beg you to keep for love of me.' In the body of the letter Louis had told him: 'Look after your popularity; it may be very useful to me and the kingdom; I regard it as the sheet-anchor which may one day be the means of restoring order.'[17] Lafayette tried desperately to win Bouillé over but, failing, made Louis write him a letter recalling him to Paris; but Louis sent Bouillé a secret letter countermanding this and he stayed put.[18]

So everyone thought of Bouillé, who was indeed devising a plan of his own (which envisaged the Assembly, suitably petitioned, asking the king to go and repel a preconcerted Austrian invasion from Luxembourg), when he received a visit from the bishop of Pamiers, returning to Breteuil after seeing the king and bearing letters of credence dated Saint-Cloud 23 October.[19] Pamiers had found the king receptive; the October Days and above all the civil constitution had shaken his hope that the storm could be outridden. Bouillé did not like the plan outlined by the bishop, considering in particular the escape from Paris too risky: he preferred Mirabeau's rival plan for an open departure.[20] Nevertheless, he put himself at the king's disposal and understated his objections lest he seem disloyal, for 'the king had learned by experience of the perfidy of men which had made him distrustful and suspicious'.[21]

Louis asked Bouillé to propose a fortified town to which he could withdraw in safety with his family, Bouillé offering him Valenciennes as well as Besançon and Montmédy. Louis also asked Bouillé for a route and Bouillé suggested the shortest one – via Rheims and Stenay. Louis rejected Rheims because he had been crowned there and feared recognition. So Bouillé suggested entering Austrian Flanders via Chimay then crossing the Ardennes to reach Montmédy via the back way.

> But the king displayed even more reluctance for crossing the emperor's territory to reach Montmédy than for going via Rheims, being set against leaving the kingdom ... the king, who had read a lot of history and during the Revolution preferred to read that of England, had remarked that James II had lost his throne because he left his kingdom and that Charles I's death warrant had been grounded on the fact that he had levied war on his subjects. These reflections, which he often communicated to me, instilled in him an extreme repugnance for leaving France to put himself at the head of his troops or to cause them to move against his revolted peoples.[22]

So the Belgian route by which Monsieur was successfully to escape was ruled out and a very circuitous one was chosen instead, via Châlons, Sainte-Ménehoulde, Varennes (about which Bouillé was anxious as it was not a relay-station) and Stenay. Thus, so far from planning to leave the country, the king chose a poor route rather than leave France even momentarily.

One feature of Bouillé's own plan was retained, albeit in an attenuated form: that the Austrians should assemble a body of some 8,000 troops on the Luxembourg frontier to give him a pretext for his own troop concentrations. By April 1791 Bouillé was becoming concerned about the loyalty of his own troops. They were mostly German-speaking (four regiments from German states, two from Switzerland) but Alsace and Lorraine were still largely German-speaking and they were stationed in some of the most ultra-revolutionary areas. On 18 April he wrote to Fersen:

> The troops are on the point of mutiny which will lose us those who still remain faithful ... [I] therefore strongly wish that from the beginning of

May there should be a corps of ten to twelve thousand Austrians around Luxembourg . . . with orders to join up with the king's army as auxiliaries if required . . . everything will become impossible if we let May slip by.[23]

Marie-Antoinette undertook to arrange for the deployment of Austrian troops, but communications between her and Vienna were slow and imperfect – as late as 22 May 1791 she would tell Emperor Leopold, who had succeeded their brother Joseph II who had died of tuberculosis on 20 February 1790, 'I am astonished you should know so little of our real intentions.' Imperial councils were divided between backing the plans of Louis and Breteuil, backing those of Artois, Calonne and the émigrés for an armed uprising in the Midi to restore the ancien régime, and doing nothing. Artois met Leopold at Mantua and had a distorted transcript of their meeting delivered to the Tuileries. It said that Leopold was preparing to back an émigré invasion of France with 35,000 troops on 15 July and that the royal couple should sit tight in the Tuileries and await deliverance. Apart from the obvious personal danger of remaining (the same faced in August 1792), the last thing Louis wanted was to exchange subjection to the Parisians for subjection to the émigrés. For 'the king, reduced to the neutral and passive role of a hostage, would lose the character of arbitrator and pacifier that he wanted to assume'.[24] Marie-Antoinette sought desperately for confirmation or denial from her brother of what is known as the 'Mantua forgery' – a denial was sent on 12 June but it arrived after they had left Paris. As for her own request for Austrian troops to be moved to the Luxembourg border, Mercy, now adviser to the governor of the Austrian Netherlands, was resolved to turn a blind eye to any order from the emperor to mobilize. The 8,000 troops never materialized.[25]

'What do we do when we get there?'

More important than the respective roles of the king and queen in the escape plans was, assuming they could reach Montmédy, what to do when they got there. It was the same dilemma as Broglie had posed when flight to Metz was considered after the fall of the Bastille. The short answer is that Louis would have changed into the red-and-gold uniform he had worn when inspecting the dyke at Cherbourg, harangued the troops (though he was poor at public speaking) and raised Bouillé from the rank of lieutenant-general to that of marshal of France. He could not ask the minister for war to supply a baton for the ceremony because he was kept in the dark about the flight. But the duc de Choiseul-Stainville offered his father's old baton instead. Then what?

Timing was crucial to Louis's calculations. For Bouillé the end of May was the deadline because of the condition of the troops. But for Louis July was a sort of triple witching month: i) he had to forestall the imagined invasion on 15 July; ii) the Assembly was expected to finalize the constitution in July, so Louis had to get out of Paris before that date or be forced to accept it as it stood;[26] iii) finally, there was the question of the elections to the Legislative Assembly, the successor assembly to the Constituent. Primary assemblies for these elections had already begun and the final round was due to start on 5 July. As the historian of the Jacobin Club puts it, 'never before had Jacobin intervention in the electoral process been so flagrant' – putting up 'slates' of candidates and applying pressure.[27] As a result, Louis gloomily noted, 'if one can detect any disposition on the part ... [of the primary assemblies] to go back on anything it is in order to destroy the remains of the monarchy and set up a metaphysical and doctrinaire form of government which would not work'. Louis's flight had the desired effect of suspending the meetings of the primary elections.

As the individual constitutional articles had been drafted they had been presented to the king for his 'sanction'. But the process was a solemn farce. On the one occasion when he offered constructive criticism, his palace was invaded. As Prudhomme puts it in *Révolutions de Paris*, 'the king was no more than a herald-at-arms patiently waiting outside the legislature to learn what decrees he had to proclaim'.[28] If he read this – and we saw that Louis whiled away his enforced leisure reading journals – he might have reflected that in the old days he had employed heralds to proclaim *his* legislation, and to the sound of trumpets.[29]

So, from a place of safety, Louis hoped to renegotiate the constitutional articles with the Assembly. Bouillé lost his optimism about a settlement with the Assembly after Mirabeau's death on 2 April, but there were many deputies ready for an accommodation and Louis sought to strengthen their hand. The duc de Choiseul (nephew of Louis XV's minister), who was responsible for providing troop detachments to escort the king's carriage between Châlons and Montmédy, was optimistic about a settlement. Louis told Choiseul that he would have 'accepted reasonable proposals from Paris [for a revision of the constitution] and he would have imposed obedience on Coblenz', where the émigrés were now concentrated. Once a constitution had been agreed, Choiseul informs us, Louis planned to install himself at Compiègne 'for a long time' and summon the Assembly to him, only returning to Paris once the constitution was bedded in. A receipt exists for furniture for Compiègne 'for the estates' dated December 1790.[30]

The best contemporary analysis of Louis's timing came from an enemy, Robespierre, who in March had proposed the 'self-denying ordinance' making members of the Constituent Assembly ineligible to sit in its successor.[31] Four times he employs the rhetorical refrain, 'why did he choose this precise moment' to go? And answers: 'he chose the moment' when the primary assemblies were in progress and when there was the prospect of a Legislative Assembly more radical than its predecessor which was prepared to 'revoke a portion of its measures'.

Robespierre did not think that the king's flight was meant to bring about the restoration of the ancien régime. Nor, Robespierre adds, 'could it have been upon Leopold and the king of Sweden and on the army [of émigrés] beyond the Rhine, that he placed his hopes'. No, Robespierre argued, something more dangerous because more insidious was afoot: the king intended to do a deal with the National Assembly which would enable the émigrés to return voluntarily to France. (Louis mentions this objective in his manifesto.) The triumvirs, Barnave, Duport and Lameth, according to Robespierre, would 'at first ask for very small sacrifices to bring about a general reconciliation'; and they would have little 'trouble in inducing a weary people to accept a deal, a halfway compromise'. 'You will have observed', he added, 'how [the king] distinguishes [in his manifesto] between those things in the constitution which he finds offensive and those he deigns to find acceptable.'

Robespierre believed, without firm evidence, that the 'triumvirs' and Lafayette colluded or connived in Louis's escape. 'The king', Robespierre proclaimed, 'fled with the consent of Lafayette'. He had seen how the 'triumvirs' had striven to revise the constitution in order to strengthen the executive and had witnessed the measures they had taken to attack the Jacobins. At the beginning of March 1791 the king was given the right, in certain circumstances, to replace local officials – to the chagrin of the local Jacobins who had often been instrumental in their election. On 11 May Le Chapelier introduced a law banning wall-posters and collective petitions, which, as Robespierre's unsuccessful intervention made clear, was aimed at the Jacobin Club.

Robespierre's guesses about the king's intentions are as good as any, given that the two men who should have known most, Bouillé and Breteuil, said respectively, 'I never knew what course the king would have adopted at Montmédy', and 'I don't rightly know what His Majesty is planning to do'. The only authentic document we have is Louis's 'Declaration to all Frenchmen on leaving Paris' which would have been his manifesto if he had recovered his liberty. One by no means friendly publicist treats the manifesto as a living text and speculates on its status 'if the king persisted in his declaration', that is didn't disavow it. Intriguingly, he argues that though Louis should have no say in the framing of the constitution, once he had accepted it he could apply his suspensive veto retrospectively to those articles he disliked.[32]

Louis's action in leaving his declaration behind is generally considered foolish – he should have waited until he had reached safety. Breteuil thought any announcement of the king's measures would be premature.[33] But Louis specifically instructed La Porte to deliver the manifesto immediately to the Assembly and he must have felt an imperious need to speak his mind at last. He told La Marck 'that he saw in the execution of this . . . project only a means of being free to address to the nation the language of reason and paternal benevolence'.[34] He told the Parisians that he would 'return to their midst when he had freely accepted a constitution which would enforce respect for our holy religion, establish government on a stable footing . . .' Any hostages to fortune were given with a sense of relief in what was in any case hardly a compromising document. For it offers not a wholesale repudiation of the Revolution but rather a detailed, at times rather boring critique of a constitution Louis wants to modify, not reject. The declaration, on which Louis worked for over six months, is unique in that the king had no recourse to the advice of his ministers, since none was privy to his plans for flight. After hearing it in stony silence, the Assembly suppressed it and few have bothered to read it through, but when a normally silent man speaks out he deserves an attentive hearing.

The declaration, of curious form, begins and ends with a personal potted history of the Revolution. The middle section beginning, 'Let us examine the various parts of government', is a critique of the new institutions, in theory and in practice, tending to show that government needs to be strengthened. Apart from his claim for an equal share in the legislative process, Louis criticizes the excessive decentralization established by the Assembly and the fact that all the new bodies are 'elected by the people and do not depend on the government'. Louis also criticizes specific policies of the Assembly, particularly those on finance. The Assembly had not yet published an exact budget; it had abolished the old taxes without providing viable replacements – 'the ordinary taxes are greatly in arrears and the extraordinary resource of 1.2 billion *assignats* are almost spent'. In other words, the Assembly had signally failed to solve the financial crisis for which it had been summoned. The general conclusion of the declaration is that the Assembly by its incompetence has thrown away the patient fruits of his reign. The finances are in chaos, France's diplomatic hegemony destroyed and religious schism established.

Louis's manifesto is above all that *appel au peuple* which the suspensive veto did not allow him to make. He felt that the National Assembly had bamboozled the people, run ahead of the *cahiers de doléances* and wrapped up the deceit in 'high-falutin' sophistry. And many from all sides of the Assembly agreed that this had happened, that a 'religious veil' had been drawn over this usurpation. Alexandre de Lameth, one of the 'triumvirs', had coined the phrase 'religious veil', and another, Adrien Duport, told the Assembly that had the king refused his sanction to any of the constitutional articles: 'you would have declared ... that you had no need for any sanction on the king's part to establish your constitution'. But the king's refusal would have been embarrassing because his sanction had smoothed the passage of legislation which the country would otherwise have regarded as too radical since it was not yet 'ready to trust its destinies to your zeal'.[35] This view was also held on the extreme left. Jérôme Pétion, Robespierre's associate but soon to be his deadly enemy, wrote in a private letter to Brissot: 'The people would complain if the king were stripped of all his prerogatives. There aren't twenty *cahiers* which don't instruct the deputies to make laws in conjunction with the king. The suspensive veto only leaves him with the appearance of power which I think it is impossible that he can abuse given permanent assemblies.'[36] Louis's appeal is over the head of the Assembly directly to the people. And, as its title implies, it is an indictment of Paris before all Frenchmen. But his appeal was never allowed to reach them.

Though Louis's criticisms are of a negative, sometimes peevish nature, one can derive from them a programme for a constitutional monarchy with a strong executive. Apart from an input into framing the constitution, Louis asks for the right to initiate legislation, an absolute veto and, possibly, the right to dissolve parliament – i.e., the English system. He wants the power to negotiate peace treaties subject to ratification by the assembly – again, as in England. But he accepts the loss of the power to declare war as a corollary of the surrender of the power of the purse, which he intended to make to the Estates-General before they opened. He wants to negotiate the religious settlement with the pope and end the schism. And he wants a bodyguard to protect him from pressure from the crowd.

Louis's programme is in marked contrast to the positively stated if rudimentary one contained in Marie-Antoinette's letter to Mercy of 3 February.

The king is busy now collecting together all the materials for the manifesto which he must necessarily issue as soon as we are out of Paris. It will be necessary first to explain his flight, pardon those who have merely been led astray, flatter them with expressions of love; to except from the pardon the revolutionary leaders [*les chefs des factieux*], the city of Paris unless it returns to the old dispensation, and everyone who has not laid down his arms by a certain date; restore the *parlements* as ordinary law-courts without their ever being able to meddle with administration and finance. Finally, we have decided to take as a basis for the constitution the declaration of 23 June as necessarily modified by circumstances and events. Religion will be one of the great points to bring to the fore. We are now grappling together with the very difficult choice of the ministers we will want to appoint [*personnes que nous voudrons appeler près de nous*] when we are free. I thought it would be preferable to have one man at the head of affairs, as M. de Maurepas was formerly. In this way the king would avoid working with each minister separately and affairs would proceed with less fluctuation. Let me know what you think of this idea. The man is not easy to find and the harder I look the more disadvantages I find in them all.

This letter and the king's declaration afford the rare chance of making a direct comparison between the political thinking of the queen and that of the king at this time. Louis's declaration is simply not based on the principles the queen outlines here. The queen's version is not just shorter but cruder, more immature and more vengeful. Louis does not mention pardons, let alone punishments; the declaration of 23 June is mentioned but is not central. Also Louis would never have exploited the religious schism as Marie-Antoinette here proposes. Louis simply intended, as he told the bishop of Clermont, 'fully to restore Catholic worship if he came to recover his power'. Though neither of them desired it, Marie-Antoinette's approach would inevitably have led to civil war. In her reference to Maurepas, Marie-Antoinette shows that she does not think that Louis is up to his job, whilst Breteuil would not have been pleased to read the last sentence of his patron's letter. Not only did he want to be prime minister but 'to have [the ministry] in his hand to avoid inconsistency'. He also planned to nominate all the other ministers: La Gallissonière for war, du Moutier for the marine, La Porte for the *Maison*, Barentin to return to the seals, and his close collaborators Bombelles and the bishop of Pamiers to have foreign affairs and finances, respectively.[37]

When Marie-Antoinette purports to speak in the king's name or to outline his intentions, as in her version of the manifesto, she either gives a garbled account of his views or adds some of her own. In particular, her views on foreign policy are wild and crude. For example, some of the proposals for the cession of French territory to buy foreign support revealed in her correspondence with Mercy-Argenteau are not only treasonable but fanciful in the extreme; indeed, so fanciful that they amount to proof that the king, with his excellent grasp and long experience of diplomacy, could have had no knowledge of them. Their premise is that the post-1787 alliance of England, Prussia and Holland would not allow Austria to restore the power of the French monarchy. England, therefore, must be bought off by territorial concessions – the West Indian sugar islands or all the French possessions in India, leaving only trading counters, are suggested. Alternatively, an alliance of Spain, Sardinia and Denmark (!) must be formed, by means of smaller concessions, to contain the triple alliance. The king is said, in this correspondence, to be unhappy about these concessions. It is more likely he had never heard of them.

The financial arrangements which she credited to the king and which Fersen sent to Breteuil may have been Louis's. She did not have the technical expertise to devise them. 'The king thinks', Fersen said, 'that the church should get back its lands by purchasing the 1.2 billion *assignats* in circulation at their current value of 20 per cent below par', that is, 1 million payable in silver. Those who had bought church lands would be reimbursed. This should be accompanied by a partial bankruptcy, that is, a forcible reduction in the rate of interest paid to creditors, like Terray's in 1770. This was a step Louis had hitherto resisted.

It is sad to relate but true that Marie-Antoinette spent no more time telling Mercy, in Brussels, about her political programme than she did arranging with him how to send on ahead a travelling dressing-case fitted with silver boxes. In order to avert suspicion the queen's sister, Christina, governess of the Austrian Netherlands, asked to have a similar one made. Next, the queen's cipher was removed from all the pieces and finally this *nécessaire de voyage* was sent to Brussels. These details are given by Marie-Antoinette's chambermaid, Madame Campan, and without the queen's letters to Mercy would scarcely be credible. Nor would Campan's statement that the queen was 'determined to have a complete wardrobe with her' if we did not have Mercy's letter to Kaunitz in which, with horrified incredulity, he tells the chancellor of whole crates of the queen's belongings reaching him by public transport.[38] Most extraordinary of all, Marie-Antoinette's hairdresser, Léonard Antié, was sent ahead in his own cabriolet with instructions to join the royal party at the staging post of Pont de Sommevel.

The royal party were to travel in disguise, with passports issued to a Baroness Korff, the widow of a Russian colonel. Marie-Antoinette posed as the governess to her children, Amélie and Aglaé (the dauphin had to be dressed as a girl). Their real governess, Madame de Tourzel, reversed roles with Marie-Antoinette and posed as Madame Korff. Madame Élisabeth wore the plain dress and cap of a maid. Louis was acting as Madame Korff's steward, but he directed: 'you will put in the carriage box . . . the red coat with gold lace that I wore at Cherbourg'. This detail evokes from Michelet one of his most purple passages: 'What he thus hides in the box would have been his defence. The dress the king of France wore when he appeared against England, amidst his fleet, was better calculated to consecrate him than the holy ampulla of Rheims. Who would have dared to arrest him if, throwing open his dress, he had shown that coat? He ought to have kept it, or rather kept his French heart, as he then possessed it.'

Louis's disguise as a servant also enables Michelet to make a brilliant point:

> This disguise, which appeared so unseemly, placed Louis XVI in the private condition for which he was formed. Judging from his natural abilities he was calculated to become, doubtless not a valet – for he was educated and accomplished – but the servant of some great family, a tutor or a steward, dispensed – as a servant – from every kind of initiative; he would have been a punctual and upright clerk, or a well-informed, strictly moral and conscientious tutor, as far, however, as bigotry admits. A servant's costume was his most appropriate dress; he had till then been disguised in the inappropriate insignia of royalty.[39]

If leaving in disguise was unregal, so, Mirabeau considered, was escaping in the dead of night. He warned La Marck, his interlocutor with the court: 'Remember ... that you must never under any pretext be an accomplice or even a confidant in a secret escape [*évasion*] and that a king must leave in broad daylight if he wants to remain king.'[40] Instead Louis went 'at night like a broken king' – the words T. S. Eliot applied to Charles I in 'Little Gidding'.

The flight

So, on the night of 20/21 June, the shortest one of the year, the king and queen, Madame Élisabeth, the royal children and their governess, Madame de Tourzel, left the Tuileries – separately to avoid recognition. They were to reassemble at the Petit Carrousel where Fersen was waiting with a two-horse carriage to drive them out of Paris. The queen left last; as she went from the palace Lafayette's carriage, with blazing torches, passed so close that she could touch it with her cane. She pressed herself against a wall and then continued but got lost in the maze of small streets around the Tuileries. Some say she even crossed the Seine by the Pont-Royal before finding her way back and arriving half an hour late. Louis had been more fortunate. A fortnight previously the Chevalier de Coigny, who resembled the king, had left the palace at night wearing clothes similar to the ones the king was to wear. Accordingly, the king, after chatting with

Lafayette and Bailly at his *coucher*, was able to leave the palace by the grand staircase and the main entrance. 'So completely was he at ease', Louis told the rest of the party, 'that his shoe having become undone, he put it right without attracting attention.' When the queen finally reached the waiting carriage and was safely inside, the king 'took her in his arms, kissed her, and said over and over again "How glad I am to see you here!" They all kissed each other; all the royal family did me [Madame de Tourzel] the same honour.'[41]

Fersen then drove the carriage out of Paris to the Barrière Saint-Martin, losing another half-hour by making a detour. Too much is made of these and other delays and mishaps and of the *specially constructed carriage* – the horrified italics are Bouillé's – which was waiting to take the royal family on the rest of their journey to Montmédy. 'What has not been said', it has been asked, 'about this berline?'[42] – 'the hearse of the Monarchy', as Fréron dubbed it. The journalist Mercier even called it 'a miniature Versailles, lacking only a chapel and orchestra'. That it was big is undeniable, for it had to take six people and the provisions for an extended journey. People even quarrel about its colour, some insisting that it was grey, others inclining to the opinion that it was brown. In fact it was dark green with a black undercarriage and yellow wheels, and travelled at seven miles per hour – fast for the time. But such are the accidents of failure, not its substance. Had the voyage succeeded, the carriage would have been of shining silver.

Fersen conducted the berline as far as Bondy, where a relay of six post-horses was put in. Why he left at this point is not clear. Perhaps he did not want to lend weight to the suspicions that he was having an affair with the queen. He galloped off alone to Belgium with the Great Seal in his saddlebags, planning to take it to the king at Montmédy, where a house, still standing, in the lower part of the town had been prepared. At Bondy they were joined by two waiting-women in a yellow carriage which was to precede the berline. An ordinary postilion took Fersen's place, with two disguised bodyguards sitting on either side in case of trouble. 'Adieu, Madame de Korff!' Fersen shouted to Madame de Tourzel.

At Meaux, twenty-six miles from Paris, the sun rose; and with it their spirits: '"Here I am," said this good Prince, "outside that town of Paris where I have experienced so much bitterness. You may be quite sure that once I am firmly seated in the saddle I shall be a very different person from the one you have seen hitherto."' They broke into the provisions Fersen had provided: *boeuf à la mode*, cold veal, a bottle of wine and five of water. They had no cutlery or plates, which made it difficult to attack the *boeuf à la mode*, which is a casserole. At eight o'clock Louis consulted his gold precision watch and observed, 'right now Lafayette will be in a pretty pickle'. As the king's berline rattled along the fine roads his grandfather had constructed, Louis, the keen cartographer, applied himself to his map as the towns and villages flashed by: La Ferté-sous-Jouarre, Montmirail, Vauchamps, Loges. This was only the second journey of his life of any distance.

At Chantrix (ninety miles from Paris) the postmaster recognized the king but he was loyal and refused to accept payment for his service. Louis presented him with two silver *écuelles* (two-lugged broth bowls) which have been handed down in the family. But just outside the town one of the wheels of the carriage bumped against a bridge; the horses reared and their traces were broken. It took an hour to repair them and by the time they reached Châlons-sur-Marne it was five o'clock.

At Châlons the king was recognized by at least one person – accounts differ – but it was a loyal town and the carriage was not stopped. 'When we have passed Châlons we shall have nothing further to fear,' said the king. 'At Pont de Sommevel we shall find the first detachment of troops and we shall be safe.' The area of Bouillé's command began at Châlons and Louis had insisted, against his general's advice, on having detachments of cavalry placed in the towns between Pont de Sommevel and Montmédy. But when they reached Pont de Sommevel at six in the evening there were no troops to meet them. Louis turned white as a sheet and 'felt that the very ground was giving way beneath his feet'. The berline was two hours late and the duc de Choiseul, after waiting until a quarter to six, concluded that the escape had been postponed and withdrew his forty hussars. The hussars were not the only absentees: Marie-Antoinette's hairdresser failed to materialize also. Choiseul had given him a note to tell the detachments further along the route that the escape had been cancelled. Some stayed put, some got drunk, some fraternized with the inhabitants, some were arrested, some ended up at Varennes.

When the berline reached Sainte-Menehould at eight o'clock, the troops were there all right – forty dragoons under Captain d'Andoins – but their presence had aroused so much suspicion in this ultra-revolutionary town that their captain had felt unable to use them: as luck would have it the local peasants had just lost a lawsuit against their seigneur and they thought the troops had been sent to enforce the judgment. D'Andoins 'rode up to the carriage for a moment and said to [Madame de Tourzel] in an undertone: "The arrangements have been badly made; I am going away in order not to arouse suspicion."' And he told the bodyguard posing as a postilion, 'Leave immediately; hurry or you are lost.' Furthermore, the king was again recognized and this time by an enemy – Drouet, the postmaster at Sainte-Menehould, who recognized the king from his portrait on the new *assignats* (the one on the coins still portrayed him as young and slim). But by the time Drouet had convinced the authorities and set off with a companion in pursuit of the royal family, they had a start of an hour and a half.

They thus safely reached Clermont at nine-thirty. Here again the relay of troops was present – a hundred dragoons under Colonel Damas – but again the town was seized by a panic and would not let the troops leave with the carriage. Even more ominous, when Damas ordered his men to force their way out, the troops, who had been fraternizing with the inhabitants, refused to obey. Only Damas knew who was in the carriage, but one doubts whether this knowledge would have made the troops any more obedient.

Just outside Clermont, the king's party turned left off the main road, taking a minor road to Montmédy, via Varennes. They had been advised not to take the main road through the ultra-revolutionary Verdun. Unfortunately, Drouet had asked at the posting-house at Clermont (where the horses had been changed) which route the berline was taking – otherwise he would naturally have shot past the turning and on to Verdun. By cutting across country, Drouet was able to reach Varennes at about the same time as the king.

Since Varennes did not boast a relay-station, Bouillé had made private arrangements for a change of horses, but they could not be found. In what must have been a state of blind panic, the king and queen went down the street knocking on doors. Varennes is in two halves, divided by the river Aire. The postilions could not be persuaded to continue their journey with tired horses, which had covered the last two stages at ten miles per hour, but they finally agreed to drive over the river and see if the relay was there. It was, and also another detachment of cavalry. But while Louis had been knocking on doors, Drouet had had time to assemble a small posse which stopped the berline under an arch in the town walls leading to the bridge. Passports were demanded and produced. Nevertheless, the *procureur* of the town, a small grocer aptly named M. Sauce, asked the occupants to step into his house above the shop. They agreed. The use of force by the two bodyguards would quite possibly have enabled the carriage to cross the river.

At first Louis insisted that he was not the king. Finally, he declared in a loud voice: 'Yes, I am your king; here is the queen and the royal family. Surrounded by daggers and bayonets in the capital, I have come to the provinces to find the liberty and peace you all enjoy in the midst of my faithful subjects: I could not live in Paris without perishing, my family and myself. I have come to live among you my children and I will not forsake you.' He was very moved and embraced everyone present. They too were moved. He said he only wanted to go to Montmédy and was prepared to be escorted there by the local National Guard. He appealed to Sauce, but the *procureur* was scared.[43] He was a small man, standing in for the mayor who was away in Paris as a deputy to the National Assembly. The queen appealed to Madame Sauce, who wept but replied: 'What would you have me do, madame? Your situation is very unfortunate; but you see that would expose M. Sauce; they would cut off his head.'[44]

Then Choiseul and Goguelat arrived with the forty hussars who should have been at Pont de Sommevel. The crowd outside was not yet large, but growing. Choiseul and Goguelat were able to go in and see the king. 'Right!' said Louis, 'when do we start?' 'Sire, we await your orders.' Choiseul suggested that the king mount up with the dauphin in his arms and the rest of the party mount up also. Then, surrounded by the hussars, they should try to break out. 'But can you answer for it,' said the king, 'that in this unequal struggle a bullet will not hit the queen, or my sister or my children?' The plan was abandoned. At five in the morning another officer, Deslon, arrived with sixty dragoons, but there was now a crowd of 10,000 around the shop, summoned by the tocsin. Deslon was allowed in alone to see the king. He explained that his sixty men could do nothing but that Bouillé was on his way. But 'the king was in such a state of prostration that ... [Deslon] feared that His Majesty had not heard him, though he repeated himself three times'. Finally he asked him what he should tell M. de Bouillé. 'You can tell him that I am a prisoner, that I fear he can do nothing for me, but that I ask him to do what he can.' Deslon then asked the king for his orders, but Louis bitterly replied: 'I am a prisoner and have none to give.'[45]

Bouillé was the last hope. Word had been sent to him at Stenay, less than thirty miles away but over mountains, where he was with the Royal Allemand regiment. Louis played for time. But at six o'clock there arrived not Bouillé but Lafayette's aide-de-camp Romeuf, with orders to intercept the king. It remains a mystery why Bouillé did not get there first. Romeuf's orders did not say that Louis should be returned to Paris but that is what the crowd were demanding. Louis read the order and placed it on the bed of his sleeping children and said, 'There is no longer a king in France.' Marie-Antoinette picked it up and flung it on the floor: 'I don't want it defiling my children.'

At half past seven the berline headed on its mournful way back. Bouillé arrived at 9.30, but the horses were exhausted and the berline was in any case surrounded by 6,000 National Guards and an immense crowd. Even if Bouillé could have caught up with the king, his intervention would have provoked a general massacre. So he withdrew to Stenay and immediately crossed the border. Later he received an emotional letter from the king:

You have done your duty, monsieur; stop blaming yourself; you have dared all for me and my family and have not succeeded. God has permitted circumstances which paralysed your measures and your courage. Success depended on me; but civil war horrified me and I did not want to shed the blood of my subjects, whether deluded or faithful. My fate is bound up with that of the nation and I do not want to rule by violence. You, monsieur, have been courageous and loyal: I wanted to express my thanks; and perhaps one day it will be in my power to give you a mark of my personal satisfaction.[46]

'Success depended on me' – what a curious expression. All Louis had to do was sit in a carriage. 'But civil war horrified me' suggests that Louis didn't try very hard, was deliberately indecisive, if one can be. He said in his position paper for Mirabeau that he could 'accept' civil war, provided that it was offered to him on a plate, as it were. But Louis by his flight had initiated a chain of events whose likely outcome would have been civil war. That is why the National Assembly proclaimed that he had been 'abducted', though they knew that this was not true. But Louis might not even have been able to muster a civil war since the little town of Varennes – a village really – became, on 21–22 June, a microcosm of France: if Louis couldn't pass Varennes there was no point in passing it. The fact that Louis was stopped at Varennes suggests that his whole enterprise might have failed.

The return to Paris was squalid. The berline was surrounded by a crowd so dense that it raised a thick cloud of dust like a fog. Though the sun was blistering, the occupants were not allowed to draw the blinds. Often the crowd compelled the berline to go at walking pace. Someone spat in the king's face. A priest who had ridden up to greet them was hacked to pieces in front of their eyes. Madame de Tourzel writes: 'It is impossible to give any idea of the sufferings of the royal family during this unfortunate journey – sufferings both moral and physical: they were spared nothing.' At Clermont and Sainte-Menehould they were subjected to officious insults. At Épernay the mayor presented the king with the keys to the town but said: 'You should be grateful to the town for presenting its keys to a fugitive king!' Only at Châlons were they treated well: they were housed in the former intendance where, twenty-one years before, the young Archduchess Maria Antonia had been rapturously received on her way to wed the dauphin. At the little town of La Ferté-sous-Jouarre the wife of the mayor served the royal family herself, dressed as a servant. She knew that otherwise the king would invite her to join them and did not want to invade their momentary privacy. This little gesture, with its delicate respect for fallen majesty, was one of the most affecting of the whole journey.

Just outside Épernay the royal family were joined by three commissioners from the National Assembly – Barnave, Pétion and La Tour-Maubourg – who were to escort them back to Paris. La Tour-Maubourg travelled with the waiting-women in the other carriage – he was close to the king and queen and didn't want to witness their humiliation; Barnave and Pétion squeezed into the berline, bringing its complement to eight. Pétion, a blond, big-nosed lawyer from Chartres, was consistently rude, talked of republics and regretted that France was 'not yet ripe for one'. On his return he asked the National Assembly to put the king on trial.[47] He has left an account of the journey which is replete with naïve presumption.[48] We are told that Madame Élisabeth was falling for his charms when he asked himself: 'What if this was a trick to buy me? Had Madame Élisabeth agreed to sacrifice her honour to make me sacrifice mine? Yes, at court no price is too high, one is capable of anything; the queen could have planned it.' Pétion's feelings were ones of forced contempt mixed with a good deal of superstitious awe for royalty. He was amazed that during the twelve hours it took them to reach Paris from Meaux none of the royal ladies had needed to relieve herself. Of Louis, he writes:

> The king tried to strike up a conversation. . . . He asked me if I was married, I said that I was; he asked me if I had any children. I told him I had one who was just older than his son. I said to him from time to time: 'Look at the countryside, is it not fine? . . . What a fine country France is! There is no kingdom in the world that can compare with it.' I let out these ideas deliberately; I examined the impression they made on the royal physiognomy, but his expression is always cold, unanimated to a devastating degree and, truth to tell, this mass of flesh is insensible.
>
> He wished to speak to me of the English, of their industry, of the commercial genius of that nation. He formulated one or two phrases, then became embarrassed, noticed it and blushed. This difficulty in expressing himself gives him a timidity I noticed several times. Those who do not know him would be tempted to take this timidity for stupidity; but they would be wrong: very rarely did he let out anything misplaced and I did not hear him utter anything stupid.
>
> He applied himself greatly to following his maps and he would say: 'We are in such and such a *département* or district or spot.'

The royal family were clearly wasting their time with Pétion. With Barnave, however, it was different. Whether he was converted on the road to Paris is doubtful. This mission, for which he had proposed himself in the Assembly, was, unlike Paul's, not one of persecution. Barnave was a gallant and handsome young man, only twenty-nine, and he was undoubtedly stirred by Marie-Antoinette's misfortunes to a personal devotion to the queen. But the radical of 1789 had in any case for some months been convinced that the Revolution must be 'stopped', as he put it, before it turned into an attack on property and that for this an *entente* with the court was necessary.

It must have been difficult for Barnave to talk politics with Pétion sitting there, all suspicion, but he took time off to drink, throw chicken bones out of the window and tease the dauphin. The dauphin, having eaten beef casserole with his fingers, thought it was all right to relieve himself in his trousers; but Louis unbuttoned his flies for him and provided him with a silver chamber pot, which Barnave held for the boy. The party spent a night at Dormans – where Louis records in his diary that he 'slept for three hours in an armchair' – and another at Meaux before arriving back in Paris at eight in the evening of Saturday 25 June.

The Champs-Élysées was densely packed, but there was total silence. Everywhere placards sententiously proclaimed: 'Whoever applauds the king will be thrashed; whoever insults him will be hanged.' Everyone left their hats on. The arms of the National Guard were reversed, as for a funeral, drums gratuitously rolled – ritual humiliation. The king was taken back to the Tuileries and placed under the strictest house arrest. A few minutes later, Pétion went into the king's bedroom: 'Already all the valets had preceded there in their usual costume. It seemed as though the king were returning from a hunting-party; they did his toilet. Seeing the king, contemplating him, you never could have guessed all that had just happened: he was just as phlegmatic, just as tranquil, as if nothing had happened. He immediately put himself on show.'

'He put himself on show', externally and internally; that is the clue. It was partly a matter of conditioning, the life on display he had known since a small child, partly a way of holding himself together. The flight to Varennes appears in his diary as an ordinary voyage. The detail is meticulous: there was no *coucher* at Dormans because there was no bed. He had slept in a *fauteuil*. Written across his diary for the month of July are the words: 'Rien de tout le mois: la messe dans la Galérie.' For August: 'Tout le mois a été comme celui de juillet.' He seems to be saying: 'What a boring month!' – in fact he had been suspended from his functions and was kept under such close surveillance that he was not allowed to go to the chapel to hear mass. His sanction was no longer required for bills to become law: the minister of justice applied the seal on the instructions of the Assembly.

The aftermath: suspension and revision of the constitution

During the three months of his suspension Louis lived in total seclusion, never so much as venturing into the Tuileries gardens until he resumed his functions on accepting the completed constitution in September. Madame de Tourzel tells us that 'Madame Élisabeth and the queen made the king play billiards every day after the *dîner* so that he might get some exercise'. Indeed, as a substitute for the hunting diaries, Louis kept a record of his games against his wife and sister between July 1791 and July 1792.[49] It provides an interesting parallel chronicle to the political events, for, though he usually won, in moments of crisis his game tended to fall away.

Yet from his seclusion Louis exercised an influence greater perhaps than at any time since the opening of the estates and these months also offered the best chance since then of effecting a lasting settlement in France. For it is not exact to say that the king's flight weakened the monarchy: rather, it polarized opinion concerning it. On the one hand his flight gave birth to the first serious expressions of republicanism – among a handful of deputies, men such as Pétion and Buzot, who were later to be known as the Girondins; and more widely in the political demi-monde centred on the Cordelier club and the electoral wards or *sections* of Paris. The Cordelier club got up a republican petition and on 17 July took it to the Champ de Mars to collect signatures. On the other hand, the forces of order or of respectability rallied round the throne and the municipality replied to the petition by declaring martial law, in token of which Bailly, Lafayette and the National Guard arrived on the scene accompanied by a red flag. One shot was fired from the crowd and Lafayette ordered his men to open fire, killing some fifty of the petitioners. The popular leaders, men like Danton, Camille Desmoulins and Santerre, went into hiding and popular politics was dead for some months. All but a handful of the deputies in the Jacobin Club, Robespierre being the most celebrated, seceded and joined the more moderate Feuillant club. The Massacre of the Champ de Mars, as it became known, was a watershed. The National Guard had fired on the people for the first time and in defence of, not against, the king. The dividing line now was between Parisian popular politics and the Assembly backed up by the essentially bourgeois National Guard.

Who made up the popular movement? Its personnel has been described as constituting a 'crowd' rather than a mob.[50] It has long been known that they were artisans, skilled craftsmen, shopkeepers rather than what the fastidious nineteenth-century French historian Taine called 'la dernière plèbe', who would not have had the leisure to riot or indulge in the tedious and patient work of radical politics, staying up after your opponents thought it was time to retire to bed. They came to be known as the 'sans-culottes', because they wore trousers rather than the knee britches favoured by members of the establishment. Originally a term of derision, it soon became a badge of honour. The sans-culottes were the motor of the Revolution until the Jacobins themselves became the establishment in 1793–94. It was an irony that Louis loved to consort with them as individuals – talking with tilers on the roofs of Versailles, or discussing the prospects for harvest on the route to Varennes – and was maybe happier or more himself with them than with courtiers, but en masse he could never see them as representing the true France he idealized.

The National Assembly and the popular movement represented two rival legitimacies, each claiming sovereignty. The National Assembly claimed a sovereignty, rather like the English king in parliament. The popular movement claimed that the Assembly members were merely its 'mandatories' – the Estates-General with their *cahiers de doléances* had represented an archaic form of this – and the sovereign people could show its will by cheering or booing from the galleries or invading the sitting. And, in order to keep their mandatories up to the mark, the electoral unit of the *section* refused to comply with the law obliging them to disband after the election. The Assembly saw the maintenance of the king as the essential prerequisite for their interpretation of sovereignty, which was ironic since his suspension had shown he was not necessary.

After the discovery of the king's flight, Lafayette did, for a fleeting moment, consider the declaration of a republic. A meeting of deputies was hastily assembled at the house of his friend, the duc de La Rochefoucauld, but its sense was decidedly against such a move and Lafayette did not insist. Rousseau had said that republics only worked in small countries and in 1791 it was widely assumed both by advocates, such as Buzot, and opponents, such as the queen, that a French republic would be a federal one. Moreover it was generally assumed that the declaration of a republic would be accompanied by a second revolution, one against property. Barnave encapsulated this fear in a brilliant speech. 'Are we going to terminate the Revolution or are we going to start it up again? What you have accomplished so far is good for liberty and equality. If the Revolution takes a further step, it cannot do so without danger. The next step towards further liberty could entail the destruction of the monarchy and the next one towards equality an attack on property.'

Barnave's speech had been given during the debate on the king's fate on 13 July. It had not prevented the king's suspension from his functions but it could have been worse: the extreme left, led by Robespierre, Pétion and Buzot, had wanted even sterner treatment for the king, ranging from trial (Pétion), through presumed abdication (Vadier) to a referendum (Robespierre). This grouping consisted of some thirty deputies who had a coherent ideological position based on applying the Rights of Man to everything. This consistency enabled them to punch above their weight, though Madame Roland, for now supporting Robespierre, thought 'there were no more than forty for the good cause'. They may have been only thirty voices, but they acted as a geared lever on the well-organized popular movement. The other ideologically pure group was the far right, who wanted a return to the ancien régime. As a protest against the king's suspension (but disastrously for the king) they abstained from voting, attending the Assembly and merely sitting on their hands.

By this stage, despite or perhaps because of the king's flight, there was a large natural majority in favour of restoring some of his authority to the king, or would have been but for suspicion and personal rivalries. This majority represented what would in the nineteenth century be called the 'notables' – the sort of upper bourgeoisie who had roses named after them, like Madame Alfred Carrière or Souvenir du Docteur Jamain, often bred by their gardeners; one might call them the 'new revolutionary establishment'. Louis was invited to join it – on its terms. The National Assembly, which had been elected on virtual manhood suffrage, imposed a stiff property qualification of one silver mark or nineteen days' labour for election to the successor assembly, the Legislative (i.e., non-constituent) Assembly. In the nineteenth century this new establishment held all the cards, but in the period 1791–92 there was all to play for.

Establishment sentiments found expression in two moves by the Assembly to preserve the monarchy, the initial one highly formal, the other, by its constitutional committee, more creative. The immediate response of the Assembly was to stage-manage the measures taken in the wake of the king's flight so as to preserve both the throne and its present occupant; it employed a version, or rather the *reductio ad absurdum*, of the ancient convention of the 'king's religion being surprised'. Only because people were accustomed to the convention could such a blatant subterfuge have been contemplated. Even so, the relationship between convention and reality was strained to breaking point when the nation was immediately asked to believe that the king had not fled but had been abducted by General Bouillé, who soon obliged by sending the Assembly a letter of confirmation. That this version also made the king appear an imbecile would not have troubled the Assembly, though Bouillé did not help his case by saying that if any harm were done to the royal couple not a stone of Paris would be left standing.

After couriers had been despatched to the provinces with this official version, the gates of Paris were closed. When the king and queen had been brought back, commissioners from the Assembly helped them to make prepared statements in which the king said that his journey had revealed to him the extent of support for the constitution in the country; this part of the story at least was true, for Marie-Antoinette confessed to Mercy on 31 October that her journey had convinced her that 'there is not a single town, not a regiment on which we can rely'. Nevertheless, to make absolutely sure that the royal couple should have time to concert their 'story', it was arranged that the queen should be in the bath when the commissioners arrived – she gave them her statement the following day.

Behind the formality and the farce, however, the conviction was growing among a good number of deputies that many of the criticisms levelled against the constitution in the king's declaration were justified and that it was in no one's interests to have a morose monarch. At the very least, Varennes concentrated minds and gave the Assembly an enforced pause: on 24 June, elections to the Legislative Assembly were suspended, which would have pleased Louis, since in his declaration he had complained of the unsuitable candidates the primary assemblies were throwing up. And his flight also, in spite of his recapture, did further his objective of assisting the movement to revise the constitution. The starting point for this had been Le Chapelier's proposal of 23 September 1790 that seven new members be added to the Assembly's constitutional committee to give a coherent final draft to a constitution whose articles had been voted piecemeal over the past twelve months. Among the seven were Barnave, Alexandre de Lameth and Adrien Duport – the 'triumvirs' – who quickly established control over the committee. These men had been leaders of the left in 1789 but now they wanted to consolidate the revolution and in the spring of 1791 they had made contact with the court. Though they did not actually meet the king and queen, there had been exploratory talks through third parties. Montmorin, Mirabeau, Barnave and Alexandre de Lameth had certainly met together to discuss business, whilst the triumvirs' associates, Beaumetz and d'André probably saw the king in person on 19 April, the day after the Saint-Cloud departure.[51] Their complicity in the king's flight was widely assumed, though without hard evidence, and their reaction to his recapture is epitomized by Alexandre de Lameth's lament: 'What a disaster! In my terror at the speed with which public order is disintegrating, I hoped that a negotiation with the king, from a position of demonstrable and complete independence, could, through reciprocal concessions, give France the rest for which I seek in vain except through such a conjuncture.'[52]

According to some accounts, the constitutional committee had chosen commissioners to go and treat with the king at Montmédy and these were sitting in a coach ready to depart when news arrived of his recapture.[53] Indeed, of the commissioners actually sent, one, Barnave, as we have seen, saw no reason to change his brief just because the king had been stopped. In snatched conversations on the return journey, Barnave and Marie-Antoinette worked out an agreement of which the queen later sent him a résumé: the Assembly would revise the constitution in the light of the king's criticisms provided that the king would then frankly accept it, prevail on the emperor to 'recognize it by any act' and conclude a new treaty with France, and finally induce 'the Princes and the émigrés or at least some of them' to return to France.[54] Nor was this merely a transaction: the points are naturally linked in a key passage in the declaration: 'He [the king] placed his confidence in the wise men of the Assembly . . . when speaking about the intended revision of the decrees. . . . They recognized the need to give this government and the laws which ought to assure everyone's prosperity and place in society enough consideration to induce all those citizens to return to the kingdom who had been compelled to expatriate themselves.' Since this agreement answered Louis's central complaint, that he had been denied any say in the framing of the constitution and would have achieved the objective of his flight, there is no reason to doubt its sincerity as long as the revision stood a chance of success.

Louis told Malouet, 'We have been very satisfied with Barnave', whilst he remained grateful to the triumvirs for scotching a move in the Assembly, immediately after his flight, to replace him with his brother Artois, presumably on the grounds that a frank enemy was better than a false friend – a very Robespierrist position. Louis preferred Barnave to Duport (an ex-*parlementaire*) and Lameth (a renegade courtier). The detailed negotiations were conducted by Marie-Antoinette, who believed that the flight had actually strengthened the monarchy. Her sincerity at this stage of her dealings with Barnave is clear from the following letter of 12 August to Leopold:

My ideas are always the same: I do not think I am deceiving myself about the sincerity of some of those who were once our most dangerous enemies. One of them [Barnave] is endowed with the most animated and captivating eloquence and his talents exercise a very great influence on the Assembly. I have already witnessed to some degree the effect of his eloquence in winning back opinion and in making it resume confidence in the purity of our intentions. It has been for a long time the only resource we have. It is, I fear, too late to try others and they have become useless and dangerous.

The constitutional committee made the king's declaration the basis of its operations.[55] Indeed, the original plan was to give Louis all the powers of the king of England (putting it this way may serve to bring home how little power the constitution left him) – for example, the right of dissolution and the initiation of legislation; there was also to have been a bicameral parliament. These schemes foundered on the rock of intransigence represented by the right wing. Despite pressure from the court – a rare occurrence in the constitutional context – its 250 deputies preferred, in Ferrières's words, 'to risk the destruction of the monarchy and their own rather than surrender the hope of restoring the ancien régime'.

The committee had to content itself with the support of fifty from the moderate right, led by Malouet and Cazalès. This was insufficient for a frontal revision of the constitution and the committee had to employ the expedient of re-classifying certain constitutional decrees as ordinary unentrenched legislation subject to repeal. The civil constitution of the clergy was put in this category, which meant that the king could in good conscience swear to uphold the constitution but not the ecclesiastical settlement which everyone knew he detested; so also was the abolition of the king's prerogative of mercy on which Louis had also dwelt at length in his declaration. But without the support of the right, the committee was unable to have these decrees simply repealed, nor did it even manage to re-classify the decrees forbidding the king to command the army in person or move more than twenty leagues from Paris.

In addition, the committee proposed new measures in answer to the king's declaration. Notably, it was successful in obtaining for him a bodyguard of his choice, 1,200 infantry and 600 cavalry, whose purpose, the debates made clear, was to protect him from insurrection as, during the October Days, had the one whose disbanding he had lamented at length in his declaration. The committee's attempts to enhance the prestige or diminish the perils of being a minister were largely unavailing, though it managed to introduce a clause allowing ministers to appear before, though not to be members of, the Assembly (a generous concession, Robespierre considered). In addition, through a procedural manoeuvre which failed, Le Chapelier proposed legislation against the clubs which virtually paraphrased Louis's declaration, answering his criticisms point by point: affiliation and correspondence between clubs was to be prohibited – the same analogy with the old *parlements* being drawn – as was the publication of their resolutions. On 26 August the committee's proposal to restore the initiative in fiscal legislation to the ministers was rejected. Finally, the king was declared 'hereditary representative of the nation' instead of merely its 'first functionary', which went some way to placing his theoretical authority on a par with that of the Assembly. But there was no disguising the fact that the revision had substantially failed. On 13 August Barnave told the Assembly that the previous evening the committee had discussed whether it should resign in view of the Assembly's recent decrees.

Marie-Antoinette, cut off though she was in the Tuileries, conducting everything by correspondence, and unable to use her charm, realized something of what was going on. On 16 August she writes to Mercy of 'the leaders who for the last eight days have realized that they are absolutely beaten'. It is at this point that the tone of her correspondence changes. For Barnave had failed to deliver his side of the agreement; the constitution remains 'a tissue of absurdities'.[56] Barnave limply and disingenuously tries to convince the queen that 'account has been taken of several things contained in [the king's] memorandum'.[57] The queen is amazed: 'These gentlemen say that "the constitution is very monarchical"; I confess that I have need of enlightenment on this point . . .'[58]

Moreover, a last hope that the revision of the constitution could be enlarged by observations from the king prior to his acceptance was dashed by Robespierre's withering speech of 3 September warning the triumvirs against attempting such a move and accusing them of wanting to become ministers. The triumvirs failed to defend themselves, whilst the right laughed. Louis made himself ill with indecision about what to do, though the only alternative to acceptance was abdication. Finally he accepted the constitution in a letter to the Assembly of 13 September, which, though largely drafted by Barnave and Montmorin, forms a pendant to his declaration. It was a skilful letter highlighting the improvements to the constitution made since his flight, to which, it was insinuated, they were attributable. 'You have shown a desire to restore order', the deputies were told, 'you have considered the lack of discipline in the army; you have recognized the necessity for curbing the licence of the press'. He ended with a flash of candour: 'I should, however, be telling less than the truth if I said I perceived in the executive and administrative resources sufficient vigour to activate and preserve unity in all the parts of so vast an empire; but since opinions are at present divided on these matters, I consent that experience alone shall decide'.[59] Next day, as king of the French rather than king of France and Navarre, wearing the red cordon of the Saint-Louis, the only order left, Louis took the oath to the constitution before the Assembly, he standing, they, with the solitary exception of Malouet, seated with their hats on.[60]

With the failure of the revision, Marie-Antoinette took up an idea which had briefly crossed her mind in June 1790, that of an 'armed congress' of the great powers to put pressure on the Assembly or its successor – 'not war but the threat of war', as she put it. Her earlier letter to Leopold had characterized such measures as 'too late ... useless and dangerous' whilst she had steadfastly rejected the advice of Mercy and Fersen that there should be no negotiations with the Assembly. The idea of a congress was the hobby-horse of Marie-Antoinette and Breteuil alone: after Varennes, Mercy and Fersen advised her that the king should send Monsieur plenipotentiary powers, rescind those of Breteuil and subordinate him if need be to the prince's adviser, Calonne.[61] Whether or not Marie-Antoinette forged Breteuil's *pleins pouvoirs* he was essentially 'her' minister as he had been ever since she had secured his appointment in 1783. In advocating a congress, Breteuil may well have been beguiled by his success at the Congress of Teschen in 1777, mediating the first Bavarian crisis. There is no clear evidence of Louis's views on a congress – he probably thought it was a waste of time but humoured his wife.

Breteuil and the congress, however, were anathema to the king's émigré brothers Provence and especially Artois, and to their 'prime minister' Calonne. In part this was merely a continuation of the personal rivalries of 1785–87. Calonne took great delight in writing to Catherine II of Russia: 'After the catastrophe of Varennes, one might have expected that the baron de Breteuil, desolated by the fatal consequences of his counsels, would have refrained from giving them, and would have ceased making use of the "powers" which he surprised from His Majesty['s religion]. These 'powers' lapsed with the plan which occasioned them.'[62]

It was also, however, a matter of policy: Artois favoured direct military intervention in France by the powers. On 27 August, while Louis was debating whether to accept the constitution, Artois procured the Declaration of Pillnitz from the emperor and the king of Prussia, which stipulated that, provided the other powers assisted, the co-signatories would intervene to restore the king of France to his rightful position. The emperor knew perfectly well that English determination to remain neutral removed any obligation on his part to intervene in France. All Frenchmen, however, from the king down, were misled by the belief that England was itching to avenge the defeats of the last war. Accordingly, Louis wrote a secret letter to his brothers complaining of the impossible position in which they had placed him:

> I was deeply hurt to see the comte d'Artois go to that conference at Pillnitz without my consent ... do you really have to serve the fury of the men of faction by having me accused of carrying war into my kingdom? ... For how can I persuade them that this declaration is not based on my request? Will anyone ever believe that my own brothers are not carrying out my orders? Thus you portray me to the nation as accepting [the constitution]

with one hand and soliciting [intervention] from the foreign powers with the other. What virtuous man could respect such conduct? And you think you are serving me by depriving me of the respect of decent folk.

I hope you will come to your senses. Understand that victory is nothing if you cannot then proceed to govern and consider that one cannot govern a great nation against the current orthodoxy [*son esprit dominant*].

These lines were penned by Louis as a postscript to a longer letter explaining to his brothers why he had accepted the constitution. As he was finishing it he received a printed copy of an open letter from his brothers, written by Calonne and assuming that his acceptance of the constitution was forced and invalid. Louis considered that the procedure of publishing private advice was as disrespectful and insulting from his brothers as it had formerly been from the *parlements*. Lest his brothers continue to say that they were representing his real wishes – again like the old *parlements* – Louis had a second copy of his memorandum to his brothers sent to the emperor, who was thus able to give the lie to the king's brothers: 'Not only do I believe that my brother-in-law the king has genuinely [*sérieusement*] accepted the constitution, and is against [*répugne*] any idea of counter-revolution, but I have positive proof. So do Your Royal Highnesses: he has communicated his real intentions to you in a secret memorandum which contains arguments for the decision he has taken which outweigh those advanced against.'[63]

The king's memorandum is a moving document including a brilliant analysis of the mentality of both the revolutionaries and the émigrés; but, above all, it is a passionate and prophetic plea against war which, the king believes, his rejection of the constitution would entail. Monarchical authority, he argues, can only be restored by force or by 'reunion' – by which he means allowing the people time to judge the defects of the constitution for themselves. He first considers force:

This can only be employed by foreign armies – the émigrés by themselves are capable only of exercising a suicidal revenge – and this means recourse to war. The émigrés flatter themselves that the rebels will capitulate immediately before such immense forces, thus avoiding war [an implicit rejection by Louis of the utility of an armed congress]. But the leaders of the revolution, those who control the levers of power both in Paris and in the provinces, are committed up to the hilt to the Revolution. They will use the National Guards and other armed citizens and they will begin by massacring those who are called aristocrats.

War will be inevitable because it is in the interests of all those in authority to fight; it will be terrible because it will be motivated by violence and despair. Can a king contemplate all these misfortunes with equanimity and call them down on his people? I know that kings have always prided themselves on regaining by force that which people have sought to snatch from them, that to fear in such circumstances the horrors of war is called weakness. But I confess that such reproaches affect me less than the sufferings of my people . . .

[So there would be no capitulation but a bitter war. Probably the foreign armies and the elite of the nobility would defeat] National Guards and regiments without officers. But these foreign troops could not settle in the kingdom and, when they were no longer here, how could one govern if insubordination began anew? I know that my émigré subjects flatter themselves that there has been a great change in people's attitudes. I myself for a long time thought that this was happening but I am now undeceived. The nation likes the constitution because the word recalls to the lower portion of the people only the independence in which it has lived for the last two years and to the class above [the bourgeoisie] equality. The lower portion of the people see only that they are reckoned with; the bourgeoisie sees nothing above them. Vanity is satisfied. This new possession has made them forget everything else. . . . The completion of the constitution was all that stood between them and perfect happiness; . . . time will teach them how mistaken they were, but their error is nonetheless profound. . . . One can never govern a people against its inclinations. This maxim is as true at Constantinople as in a republic; the present inclinations of this nation are for the Rights of Man, however senseless they are.

[And even discounting these considerations, how would one govern through the aristocracy?] Is the aristocracy which you say would be the support and refuge of the monarchy even united among itself? There are as many parties on this side as on the other. One wants the old order; another the Estates-General and yet another an English-style government. What real strength could the government derive from these different parties which would be even more divided among themselves if they won and several of which would rather treat with the Jacobins than with another faction of the aristocracy?

. . . I have therefore thought that [war] should be rejected and that I should try once more the sole means remaining to me, namely the junction of my will to the principles of the constitution. I realize all the difficulties of governing a large nation in this way – indeed I will say that I realize that it is impossible. But the obstacles that I should have put in the way [by refusing to accept the constitution] would have brought about the war I sought to avoid and prevented the people from properly assessing the constitution because it would only have seen my constant opposition. By my adopting its principles and executing them in good faith, they will come to know the cause of their misfortunes. . . . Let the princes conduct themselves in such a way as to spare me the decrees against them that the Assembly may present for my sanction; let the conduct of your entourage be such that I cannot be suspected of intentions contrary to the plan that I am going to follow. The courage of the nobility . . . would be better understood if it returned to France to augment the forces of the men of goodwill. . . . The true nobility would then have a splendid opportunity of regaining all its prestige and a portion of its rights. What I say of the nobility could equally be applied to the monarchy.[64]

The interception of this letter would have done the king's cause a lot of good – particularly the last sentence, in which the king limits his ambition to regaining, peacefully, 'all his prestige' but only 'a portion of his rights'. Here, like Cassandra, Louis predicts all that will follow war: the *levée en masse*, the proscription of the nobility (now called, pejoratively, aristocrats) and the 'popular' legislation he will be forced to veto. Like Cassandra he was not believed.

The escape from Paris – the flight to Varennes – was Louis's first major personal initiative since the convocation of the Notables in 1786; his declaration, a manifesto in all but name, his first personal statement. In the interval he had drifted, following the impulsion of advisers in whom he did not believe. His initiative was the subject of hostile propaganda from the start – killed by condescension in the Assembly from those very members who sought to preserve the monarchy, stifled at birth and yet made the basis of the revision – and this has set the tone by which historians have continued to judge it.

Yet Louis did not write it in a vacuum but kept abreast of events; the lengthy section on the prerogative of mercy must have been written only days before the flight. And for the first time since the Revolution began, he seems to be swimming with the current, for in his manifesto he catches a revisionist tide, which was to reach its high-water mark in Barnave's passionate speech of 15 July – 'il est temps de terminer la Révolution' – before retreating for three years, submerged by an ocean of blood. The constitution was, as Marie-Antoinette observed, 'a tissue of absurdities' because many of its clauses were either too general to be applicable or too topical to endure.

If the intransigence of the right, as baleful an influence in 1791 as in 1789 and as little mindful of the monarchy and the monarch, had not prevented the adoption of the king's suggested modifications, France would have had not only a more workable constitution but one which would have worked better because it would have been freely accepted by the king.

All Louis's opponents who came into close political contact with him, from Brienne through the triumvirs to Dumouriez, ended up appreciating his predicament, and the moment this happened, authority melted from them. Brienne had said he would be a 'notable in the ministry'; he was nothing of the sort. For, as Mirabeau observed, a Jacobin in the ministry was not the same thing as a Jacobin minister; but neither was he as influential.

CHAPTER FOURTEEN

PLAYING BY THE BOOK OF
THE CONSTITUTION
13 SEPTEMBER 1791–10 AUGUST 1792

Nᴏᴛ ᴏɴʟʏ ᴡᴀs ᴛʜᴇ constitution of 1791 defective, it was never given a chance, the conduct of everyone involved in its implementation, from the king downwards, being characterized by cynicism, irresponsibility and gross miscalculation. In his speech accepting the constitution, Louis had made no bones about its imperfections but had 'consented that experience alone should decide'; to Bertrand de Molleville, minister for the marine, he confided the cynical variant to this approach which was to be his touchstone: 'My opinion is that the literal execution of the constitution is the best way of making the nation see the alterations to which it is susceptible.'[1] He had outlined this approach in the secret letter to his brothers, but the generosity of spirit there displayed was cancelled by the word 'literal'. Marie-Antoinette's view was that nothing could be expected from the internal forces of the monarchy: the revision had failed and 'there was not a single town, not a regiment on which they could rely', though if her attention had not been focused exclusively on the radical east, she might have detected in the Catholic west the first rumblings of what within eighteen months would be a general royalist insurrection. As it was, she pinned her hopes on her 'armed congress of the powers' putting pressure on France, which the king, as mediator, would relieve at a price; it was a variant of Bouillé's original scheme to enable the king to profit from solving an artificial crisis.

Among the politicians a similar sense of unreality prevailed. The new assembly, the Legislative, which met on 1 October, was more radical than its predecessor. This was not the intention: the Constituent Assembly, in the teeth of opposition from Robespierre, had imposed a property qualification for electors and elected, those eligible being called 'active citizens', those not eligible 'passive citizens'. However, only 25 per cent of those eligible voted and this played into the hands of the Jacobins, who knew how to get their vote out. The results were to justify Marie-Antoinette's observation to Barnave of 31 August: 'Despite the decrees, the constitution and the oaths, who can guarantee that [the next legislature] will not want to change everything and that the republican party will not regain the upper hand? If that happens, where is the force to prevent it?' The self-denying ordinance rendering ex-constituents ineligible for seats in the new Assembly worked against continuity. The aristocratic right wing entirely disappeared, many to join the princes at Coblenz, and there were only about twenty nobles in the Legislative Assembly. The new right was made up of the constitutional monarchists, whether followers of Lafayette or of the triumvirs. Theirs was the most false and hopeless position of all, defending a constitution in which no one believed, in which they did not believe themselves, many of them hoping to modify it through a foreign adventure which would tend to strengthen the executive, though Lafayette would have severely restricted the personal role of Louis XVI. Of the new deputies, 264 joined the Feuillant club, to be joined by a further seventy by the end of the year.

The left wing was numerically inferior – 136 joined the Jacobin Club – but they tended to include the more eloquent speakers, notably a group of lawyers from the *département* of the Gironde, headed by Vergniaud; they were allied with Brissot and the ex-Constituants Pétion and Buzot. A smaller group, including Danton, Couthon and Saint-Just, were to acquire the name Montagnards because they sat on the extreme left of the Assembly where the seats banked steeply; they were suspicious of everyone else. Things got off to a bad start when the crippled deputy Couthon, soon to be the inseparable companion of Robespierre, proposed that the Assembly should no longer employ the terms 'Majesty' and 'Sire' when addressing the king. The motion was carried but when Louis refused to appear before the Assembly on these terms, it was withdrawn. From the outset the Girondins sought a confrontation with the king: by introducing savage legislation against the émigrés and the refractory priests and by seeking war with Louis's brother-in-law the emperor, they aimed to manoeuvre him either into identifying himself with their interpretation of the Revolution or appearing a traitor. Some were republicans, all wanted to capture the ministry. The fragility of the position of the constitutional monarchists was demonstrated in November when Pétion, who had tormented the king during the return from Varennes, defeated Lafayette in the elections for mayor of Paris on the resignation of Bailly.

The king and the constitution

Like his grandfather before him, Louis had always tended to evade responsibility for individual difficult decisions (this was reciprocated by his ministers).

With the appointment of Brienne in 1787 the note of 'don't blame me' emerges and with his acceptance of the constitution this becomes his settled view. The full text of his conversation with Molleville about the constitution runs:

> Here then is what I think: I am far from regarding the constitution as a masterpiece. I think that it has great defects and that if I had been permitted to make some observations some useful changes might have been made. But it is too late for that now: I have sworn to maintain it, warts and all, and I am determined, as indeed I should, to keep my oath rigorously. My opinion is that the literal execution of the constitution is the best way of making the nation see the alterations to which it is susceptible.

In this task Louis was aided by the fact that 'the constitution was not very well known by the public', whereas he had an 'amazing memory' and carried a pocket-sized edition around with him everywhere.[2]

Roederer, the public prosecutor of the *feuillant département* of Paris (the authority for greater Paris), describes the exasperation of the constitutional monarchists at this attitude: 'In accepting the good offices of La Rochefoucauld, of Lafayette, of the departmental administration, of the general staff of the National Guard, he did not assist with any of his resources nor fortify them with any of his personal adherents nor with any conclusive act testifying to his sincerity; he did not encourage them by any mark of gratitude or of confidence.'[3]

The members of the departmental administration of Paris resigned in discouragement in July 1792, tormented, Roederer adds, by the 'secret anxiety or rather the intimate conviction of his political bad faith, a conviction repressed only by his need to hide it from themselves'.[4] In the same spirit Barnave asked that 'the king resume his wonted pleasures [hunting] and furnish his palace of the Tuileries'.[5] The general problem is put succinctly by Orléans's son, Louis-Philippe, in his memoirs. Louis XVI, he argued, possessed two kinds of authority: that derived from the constitution and that derived from God and his ancestors, which no legislation could abolish overnight. His failing was in not putting the latter at the disposal of the former.[6]

The most striking example of Louis's detachment concerns ministerial appointments. On 31 October Montmorin tendered his resignation as foreign secretary and du Moutier was asked to succeed him but, Marie-Antoinette writes to Fersen, 'he has refused . . . and I even dissuaded him. He is a man to put by for better times.'[7] Writing to Mercy, La Marck elaborates on this: 'It appears that it is out of esteem for M. du Moutier that they [the king and queen] have not wanted him in the ministry. I also know that they have said that they regretted appointing M. Bertrand [de Molleville] because they are satisfied with him.'[8] This attitude, however, can partly be explained by the perils which the constitution attached to the office of minister, especially the provisions relating to ministerial responsibility, which is conceived of as criminal rather than political: in November 1791 Isnard told the Assembly, 'by [ministerial] responsibility we mean death'.

Article XXVII of the constitution, which stipulated that there should be no prime minister, stemmed from the Constituent Assembly's obsession with pinning down individual ministerial responsibility. On the same grounds two of his colleagues objected when Montmorin, after his resignation, wished to continue attending the council as a minister-without-portfolio.[9] Thus the ancien régime notion of a *ministre* as a life appointment and the late development of the office of prime minister ended for reasons quite extraneous to their origins. Also stemming from the desire for precise ministerial responsibility was the stipulation that there should be a 'cabinet secretary' to keep minutes of council meetings – a practice which, to the regret of historians, did not obtain under the ancien régime. Louis deferred making this appointment until June 1792, when he bowed to pressure from the Girondins in the Assembly.

If, however, the perils of the king and his ministers were now greater, their position had a solidity in relation to the Legislative Assembly it had not possessed in relation to the Constituent. For though the political situation continued to deteriorate, to the point where many dared not accept ministerial office, the king's constitutional position was rescued from the shifting sands of the period when the legislature also possessed the 'dictatorship of constituent power'. Louis fought doggedly for his constitutional rights, in particular through his fearless use of the veto, which in a normally functioning system would not have been necessary.

For if Louis sought to discredit the constitution by the literal application of its provisions, the Girondins sought to destroy the compromise on which it was based by introducing divisive legislation. On 9 November they had a decree passed enjoining all émigrés to return to France within two months upon pain of being considered suspect of conspiracy, having their lands confiscated and being punished by death. On 29 November another decree declared that priests not taking an oath to the constitution within eight days were to be 'considered suspect of revolt against the law and of evil intentions towards the Fatherland'. They were to be stripped of their pensions and held responsible for all religious disturbances in their neighbourhood.

These two decrees were the negation of the rule of law and prefigured the National Convention's law of suspects, for it does not follow that simply by being an émigré or a non-juring priest one is a traitor. Their main purpose was to embarrass the king, who used his suspensive veto on both decrees. The veto on the émigré law was accompanied by a second letter from Louis to his brothers which he wanted to be communicated to the Assembly. However, as he wrote on the projected speech, 'On n'a pas voulu l'écouter'[10] – the Assembly decided that the king was not allowed to give his reasons for applying his veto. On the decree concerning refractory priests, the *feuillant département* of Paris smoothed his path by requesting him to use his veto. The *département*'s address was written by Duport and Barnave[11] and was Barnave's last service for the court before retiring, disillusioned, to his native Dauphiné in January, no longer able to blind himself to Marie-Antoinette's political bad faith and realizing that all sides were moving towards a war with Austria which would destroy the fragile basis of the constitutional monarchy.

The outbreak of war

The key to understanding foreign affairs in 1791 and 1792 – and one vouch-safed to none of the parties in France – is that Austria and Prussia, for fifty years mortal enemies, had come to a solid understanding which was ratified by a treaty of alliance on 7 February 1792.

Emperor Leopold's initial response to the French Revolution had been one of cautious welcome. As grand duke of Tuscany, he had granted a constitution to his subjects and after he succeeded his brother Joseph as emperor in 1790 his consistent advice to Louis had been to give the constitution a chance. But in 1791 Frederick William II of Prussia gave him to understand that he would no longer oppose the Bavarian exchange, provided Leopold would allow him to pick up Danzig (Gdansk) in a second partition of Poland. This meant that Leopold could no longer overlook the trouble being fomented by French revolutionary emissaries in Belgium, since the elector of Bavaria could hardly be expected to swap his country for one in turmoil. Leopold believed that there could be no permanent pacification of the province until the revolutionary ferment in France itself had been bottled up. Accordingly, by January 1792 at the latest, he had decided on armed intervention in France – not merely a congress – delaying only to conclude his alliance with Prussia and for the campaigning season to begin.[12]

This knowledge makes a nonsense of the secret diplomacy of Marie-Antoinette who, for all the good it did, might have spared herself the 'prodigious fatigue' of her voluminous correspondence, carried on under the most arduous circumstances, employing a back-breaking code, often written in invisible ink, depending on the chance availability of a safe courier, sometimes sewn into a hat-lining, sometimes placed in a crate of tea. The attraction of an armed congress for her was not just the avoidance of war by the threat of it but also the hope that the powers – especially Prussia – would restrain her brother Leopold's very real designs on the German-speaking provinces of France, particularly the patrimony of their father, Francis, duke of Lorraine. Louis probably set little store by this secret diplomacy, but on 3 December 1791 he did write a letter to the king of Prussia, with whom Breteuil, still acting as his plenipotentiary, enjoyed good relations. Louis referred to the idea of an armed congress 'at the moment when, despite my acceptance of the new constitution, the men of faction openly display their aim of completely destroying the remains of the monarchy' – he most likely means the decrees on the émigrés and the priests.[13] By the time this letter reached Frederick William, he had already decided on joint action with Austria.

Also unaware of the imminent Prusso-Austrian alliance was the king's uncle, Louis, comte de Narbonne, illegitimate son of Louis XV, lover of Necker's daughter, Madame de Staël, appointed in December minister of war in the *feuillant* ministry and quickly becoming its driving force. Narbonne's plan was to secure the benevolent neutrality of Prussia, thereby isolating Austria and enabling France to conduct a military promenade through the territories of the electors of Mainz and Trier, who were accused of harbouring concentrations of émigré troops. The victorious French army would then be used to close the Jacobin Club and restore monarchical authority. Narbonne received no support from the king, who, through Breteuil, repudiated Narbonne's envoy to Frederick William, the comte de Ségur. When the matter was discussed in the council on 9 December, Louis left after twenty minutes during which he did not open his mouth.[14] Louis did, however, announce on 14 December that he would summon the elector of Trier, on pain of war, to disperse the émigré formations before 15 January 1792; to reinforce this ultimatum, Narbonne announced the formation of three armies under Luckner, Rochambeau and Lafayette, who had relinquished his command of the National Guard to run as mayor.

At the same time Louis's trusted foreign secretary, de Lessart, explained the king's true position in a private letter to Noailles, the French ambassador to Vienna, dated 16 January: 'As you can well believe, the king is at the head of those who are against it [war]; his excellent mind, in conformity with his heart, seeks to reject the very idea. Even were it successful, he regards it as a calamity for the kingdom and a scourge for humanity.'[15] And to avert this scourge, Louis sent a special envoy to Trier, Bigot de Sainte-Croix, to make sure the elector did comply with the summons and so avert war. In fact Bigot was pushing on an open door, for the elector felt in any case that the émigrés had outstayed their welcome: as Bigot told de Lessart, 'the French émigrés are now the masters of the electorate'.[16] Accordingly, the elector immediately complied with the French ultimatum even though Breteuil, acting on his own initiative, urged the elector to resist it. Bigot was relieved for he realized what damage the émigrés were doing to the king's cause. He considered that the emigration achieved the dual purpose of creating both 'an imaginary connivance [on the king's part] with those who aspired to save the king' and 'the external threat which was necessary in order to propagate terror at home'.[17] Bigot supervised the evacuation of the electorate by the émigrés. His mission accomplished, he wanted to return; but de Lessart told him to stay put to give the lie to any Girondin claims that the émigrés had returned.

That should have ended the matter, but the emperor's new attitude ensured that things did not rest there, for whilst he accepted the dispersal of the émigrés, Leopold saw fit provocatively to guarantee the elector's territories from French attack. This enlarged the scope of the conflict and enabled the Girondins, who favoured an ideological war of nations, to persuade Narbonne to raise his sights from the elector to the emperor himself. In the Assembly, Gensonné questioned whether the emperor's declaration was compatible with the 1756 alliance and on 25 January the Assembly asked Leopold to clarify this point before 1 March, otherwise France would be obliged to go to war. The Girondins wanted war in order to smoke out the queen's presumed treason when confronted with war with her brother. As Brissot put it in December 1791, 'I have only one fear; it is that we won't be betrayed. We need great treasons; our salvation lies there, because there are still strong doses of poison in France and strong emetics are needed to expel them.'[18]

Narbonne's alliance of convenience with the Girondins led to conflict both with his *feuillant* colleagues in the ministry, especially the foreign minister de Lessart, and with the king. Louis dreaded war – witness his letter to his brothers – but, as ever, his position was ambivalent, for there were possible advantages which could accrue to him either from an unlikely French victory, which would tend to strengthen the executive, or from defeat, which would give him a role as mediator. He had told the king of Prussia on 14 December that 'there remains war if it becomes inevitable', a stance similar to that with which he had 'prepared himself' for the possibility of civil war in 1790 – provided he had not worked for either eventuality. This comes over most clearly in a letter to Breteuil: 'Instead of a civil war it would be a foreign war and things will be all the better for it. The physical and moral state of France make it impossible that she should support even a half-year's campaign. It is not I who wanted war . . . my conduct must be such that in its misfortune the nation sees no other resource than to throw itself into my hands' – as mediator.[19]

As much as war itself, however, Louis feared taking responsibility for its outbreak. De Lessart, who was desperately trying to dilute the acidity of the exchanges between France and Austria, posed the question of responsibility in a letter to the king of 19 February:

> Yesterday I went to the diplomatic committee [of the Assembly] to give them some idea of the state of relations with the court of Vienna. I saw that everyone regarded war as inevitable and that the majority ardently desired it; but at the same time they were all for leaving to the king the whole burden of this great decision. They said that the king should make full use of his initiative and that the National Assembly should take no part and that it was better to risk everything [meaning, not to go to war?] than explain itself on this particular.[20]

Meanwhile, Narbonne sought to put pressure on the king by threatening him with the joint resignations of Generals Lafayette, Luckner and Rochambeau and by introducing them into the council in a quasi-ministerial capacity. 'On Friday 2 March', Molleville notes, Narbonne 'brought them into the council despite the king's repugnance for such an extraordinary proceeding.' They each remained standing to report on the state of their armies. The king then gave them a sign of dismissal and 'seemed pleased to have thus avoided their presence at the council'. The generals, however, wanted to read a memorandum and 'since it seemed too long to be read standing, His Majesty sat down and invited the generals to do the same'. The memorandum was totally unimportant but the point was that, under the ancien régime at least, to be asked to sit down in the *Conseil d'État* was to be made a *ministre*. As if to underline the point, next day Lafayette turned up to a *comité* of ministers – meeting without the king, in a room adjoining that of the council – in place of Narbonne to rebuke the ministers for their quarrelling. This is the occasion when Lafayette is credited with saying to the keeper of the seals, 'we shall see which of us, the king or myself, has the majority in the kingdom'.[21] Finally, when Narbonne tried to break the king's favourite minister, Molleville, Louis dismissed Narbonne on the grounds that he was trying to be a prime minister, a post that, as Marie-Antoinette maliciously observed, was now forbidden by the constitution.

The Girondins threw their weight behind Narbonne and, though he was not reinstated, were able to bring down the *feuillant* ministry by impeaching de Lessart and having him sent before the national high court at Orléans to stand trial for the crime of *lèse-nation*, which had replaced that of *lèse-majesté*. On this occasion Vergniaud told the Assembly that 'presumption [of guilt] is suffi-cient to ground a decree of accusation'. He also made a scarcely veiled threat to Marie-Antoinette: 'All the inhabitants [of the Tuileries] should be aware that only the person of the king is inviolable.' Since the queen was not 'inviolable' a committee was held at the house of the mathematician Condorcet, now a leading Girondin, to discuss sending the queen herself to the high court at Orléans on twenty-three trumped-up charges. Among those present were Lafayette, Pétion, Brissot, Narbonne and Siéyès – an overarching rainbow coalition in favour of war.

Louis – whether out of fear for his wife or as a Machiavellian manoeuvre – now appointed a ministry not just of Girondin complexion but one which would indubitably be identified with the Girondins in the Assembly and would throw responsibility for the consequent declaration of war squarely on to them. This is the gist of an extremely obscure letter to the king from his agent Radix de Sainte-Foy, who had been negotiating the Girondins' entry into the ministry: 'They [the Girondins] prefer Lacoste to Kersaint for the marine. As for us, we think that the latter [as more closely associated with the Girondins] would suit the circumstances better. This is not hard to comprehend since this is a kind of gamble which is being proposed to the king and the praise or blame for it [war] must necessarily redound to its prime movers.'[22] (Lacoste was appointed.) At the same time Louis issued a proclamation making clear his views on the change of ministry: the former ministers had 'earned the respect of public opinion for their honourable conduct' whilst their replacements were only 'accredited by popular opinion', a neat distinction. One source has Louis contemplating abdication.[23]

As expected, the new Girondin ministry recommended a declaration of war against Austria. In the council Louis, according to Madame Roland, the formi-dable wife of the new minister of the interior, 'delayed the decision for a long time' and only yielded to 'the unanimity of his council'.[24] Louis insisted not only on the unanimous advice of the ministry but on retaining the signed, holo-graph opinion of the individual ministers – a variant of the tactic he had employed when relations were sensitive with Austria in 1784–85. On this occa-sion, though, he had the opinions published by the *imprimerie royale* together with the précis he had made of the position paper of the new foreign secretary, Dumouriez, who Louis had met in 1786 as commandant of the port of Cherbourg.[25] Then, on 20 April, as prescribed by the constitution, the king went to the Assembly to propose war on the king of Bohemia and Hungary, Francis II, son of Emperor Leopold who had died suddenly and mysteriously in March. The king's proposals were ecstatically accepted, with only seven dissenters. Louis was pale and stammered and there were tears in his eyes; he delivered his speech in a monotone, 'in the same tone of voice as if he had been proposing the most insignificant decree in the world', as if to distance himself from his words, as in a modern 'speech from the throne'. And the words themselves were impersonal: 'I have come in the name of the constitution formally to propose war'. On 3 August he was to tell the Assembly that 'my former ministers know what efforts I made to avoid war'.[26]

The war, in Reinhardt's words, 'revolutionized the Revolution'. The historiography of the French Revolution has for some decades been dominated by the question: was the Terror implicit in the Revolution from the start or was it created by the national emergency of war? In a sense these views are anticipated by two contemporary analyses. Louis himself in his letter to his brothers had predicted that the *levée en masse* and the proscription of 'aristocrats' would follow from war. The diplomat Bigot de Sainte-Croix, who had organized the dispersal of the émigrés from the Electorate of Trier, argued that 'without the war France would not be a republic'. But his central thesis is that as early as 1789 there was a faction conspiring to destroy the monarchy. The result of its efforts was that 'The first Assembly had deprived the king of the power to resist the incursions of the second.' In order to further their designs, the assemblies 'invented a raft of new oaths in order to supply the legislators with acts of resistance to punish or perjuries to presume'. This created the climate in which the Terror could flourish.[27]

Either way, a king who thought that constitutional rectitude marked the limit of his duty to France was not acceptable at a time of national danger; nor was a queen suspected of betraying the French war plans to the enemy. Isnard accused her of this in the Assembly on 15 May but without the proof we possess. On 26 March, before the declaration of war, she had given Mercy a résumé of the campaign being planned in the council, while on 5 June she wrote to Fersen: 'Luckner's army has been ordered to attack immediately; he is against this but the ministry wants it. The troops are lacking in everything and in the greatest disorder.' On 23 June she writes again to Fersen: 'Dumouriez leaves tomorrow for Luckner's army; he has promised to rouse Brabant to rebellion.' It is arguable that her action was prompted less by treachery than by her fear that if Austria lost Belgium, and with it the Bavarian exchange, Austria would seek compensation at the expense of France's eastern provinces. Fear of Austrian expansion was becoming an obsession with Marie-Antoinette and stands in marked contrast with her views before the Revolution. It is echoed in Fersen's letter to her of 21 June:

The emperor plans a dismemberment [of France] ... but there is perhaps a way of preventing it; it is to give the king of Prussia a written undertaking for the payment [of his expenses]: he wants it but the king's signature is necessary. I still have one blank seal left which I have not mentioned to the B.[aron de Breteuil]. Do you want me to make use of it if it might be of use in assuring us of the king of Prussia's opposition to any dismemberment? ... It would be good to have three more [blank seals].

On 3 July the queen sent the seals and, a surely unrelated event, Prussia duly entered the war. This reassured Marie-Antoinette. It was also a more serious threat to France: the French offensive against Austria in the Low Countries collapsed wherever it met with resistance, but the Austrians had not embarked on a major counter-offensive. Prussia, however, with a formidable army and with one eye on a further partition of Poland, offered a swift and intense campaign.

The fall of the monarchy

If the king thought that he could make the Girondins behave responsibly by giving them power he soon learned that he was mistaken. The Girondins acted as an opposition party in power,[28] and continued to devise decrees which would embarrass Louis. Between 27 May and 8 June Louis was asked to sanction a decree abolishing his constitutional bodyguard, which had only been set up on 16 March, a second placing him thus unarmed at the mercy of a new camp of 20,000 *fédérés* or provincial National Guards near Paris, and a third ordering the deportation of refractory priests. Louis wanted to veto the decree abolishing his constitutional guard, a useful force of 1,800 men (1,200 infantry and 600 cavalry) who were for the most part loyal, but since none of his ministers was prepared to countersign his veto he was obliged to give his sanction.[29] The colonel of the guard, the *ci-devant* duc de Cossé-Brissac, was sent before the high court but his cavalry adjutant proposed marching on the Jacobin Club and even the Assembly. Though this could have been justified on the grounds that provision of his guard was part of the constitution (Section 1, Article 12), the king declined the offer.

Thus disarmed, however, Louis did not intend to deliver himself up to the mercies of the *fédérés*; nor had he any intention of sanctioning the deportation of what he regarded as the only Catholic clergy in France. Exploiting a split which had developed within the ministry, on 12 June he dismissed the most intransigent, Roland (interior), Servan (war) and Clavière (finance), retaining

Dumouriez, Duranthon, the keeper of the seals, and Lacoste at the marine. Dumouriez may have suggested this manoeuvre – he had not been informed about the camp of *fédérés* and drew his sword on Servan in the council. But when Dumouriez himself pressed the king to sanction the decrees, Louis dismissed him too on 16 June – Louis's diary specifically refers to a *renvoi*. Dumouriez was shocked – he didn't know Louis had it in him, but Louis said, 'don't imagine you can frighten me with threats, I have made up my mind.'[30] Dumouriez left to take up a command at the front. It was hard to find replacement ministers. One who accepted, Mourges, resigned after twenty-four hours when he realized that countersigning vetoes was to be part of his job. On 18 June Louis finally persuaded Duranthon to countersign the vetoes, but he advised the king to conceal this fact until after the presentation to the Assembly of the two *feuillants* who had finally been prevailed upon to accept the departments of war and foreign affairs. The strain plunged Duranthon into nervous depression; he told the king that 'public affairs are necessarily suffering from the state of stupor into which I have fallen.'[31] In early July, the king let him go.

Louis must have smiled inwardly, for he was in a similar condition himself. The impeachment of de Lessart – which was compared with that of Strafford in the lead-up to the English Civil War – shook his composure, and the false position in which he was placed by the declaration of war must have been a great strain. His silences became more and more protracted. Madame Campan writes: 'About this time [May] the king fell into a state of despondence which amounted almost to physical helplessness. He passed ten successive days without uttering a single word, even in the bosom of his family; except, indeed, in playing backgammon with Madame Élisabeth after dinner, when he was obliged to pronounce the words belonging to that game. On one occasion he failed to recognize his son and asked who the child was.'[32] The activity involved in his use of the vetoes seems to have shaken him out of this fit of blank despair.

The dismissal of the Girondin ministers, amid a growing conviction that the king was planning to seize control of Paris before the arrival of émigré or allied troops, provoked a reaction similar to (and as unfounded as) that caused by the dismissal of Necker in 1789. A petition was due to be presented to the king asking him to withdraw his veto to the two decrees on 20 June, the double anniversary of the tennis court oath and the flight to Varennes. Apprehensively, Louis wrote to his confessor, M. Hébert, on the 19th: 'Come and see me; I have never stood in so great a need of your consolations. I have finished with men; I look to Heaven. Great misfortunes are expected tomorrow; I shall have courage.'[33]

Fortified by the last sacrament, Louis, who expected to be assassinated and, according to Montmorin, 'for some months had been acting like a man preparing himself for death', had the courage to endure not the orderly presentation of a petition, but the occupation of the Tuileries for four hours by a mob drawn from the radical *sections*. During this ordeal Louis stood on a window-seat with nothing between him and the mob but a table and a handful of grenadiers. Before him were paraded the bleeding heart of a calf with the inscription 'heart of an aristocrat' and bloodthirsty, misspelt placards, such as 'tremble tyrant your hour has come' and 'down with Monsieur Veto and his wife'. Louis humoured the crowd by wearing a cap of liberty and toasting the nation from a bottle of wine – a drunken Louis swigging from a bottle, his head engulfed in an enormous Phrygian cap, became the subject of a popular cartoon. But he would not give his sanction to the decrees: 'I am your king. I have never swerved from the constitution,' Louis said. 'We'll come back every day until he sanctions the decrees', was heard from the crowd. 'Sire, do not be afraid,' said a grenadier. 'I am not afraid; put your hand on my heart, it is pure and calm' – and he thrust the soldier's hand on to his chest.

Marie-Antoinette took refuge in the council chamber with her son. She barricaded herself behind the great table around which so many decisions had been made or deferred and she endured the insults of the mob. Madame Élisabeth suffered the most, with the tip of a sword pressed against her throat, but then she was the most hostile to the Revolution: her chidings against Louis and Marie-Antoinette for being too soft on the revolutionaries and her indiscreet support for Artois rendered family life 'a living hell', as Marie-Antoinette put it.

The authorities – Pétion, the mayor, and Santerre of the National Guard – let it go on for hours. Arriving on the scene, Pétion said: 'Sire, I have just this minute learned of the situation you are in.' 'That is very surprising,' replied Louis, 'this has been going on for two hours.' The crowd finally left at eight in the evening. 'Pétion is my enemy', Louis had told Dumouriez, and when next day Pétion tried to justify his conduct, Louis told him to 'shut up; go and do your duty; I will hold you personally to account for good order in Paris. Goodbye.' Then Louis turned his back on him. Marie-Antoinette feared that this would do the king damage.[34] She herself smuggled out a message to Fersen written in sympathetic ink: 'I am still alive but it is a miracle. The *journée* of the 20th was appalling. I am no longer their main target, it is the life of the king himself they seek. He displayed a firmness and courage which overawed them for the present, but the danger can recur at any time.'[35]

Louis's passive courage temporarily rekindled support for the monarchy. Petitions expressing outrage flowed in from provincial authorities, including that of Varennes. A petition condemning the *journée* was signed by 20,000 Parisians, each of whom would fall foul of the law of suspects in 1793. A judicial enquiry censured Pétion, who was suspended from his functions on 6 July. Baffled, the Girondins now had either to accept defeat or to overthrow the throne. For there was gridlock between the Executive and the Legislative, as happens today in that other eighteenth-century constitution founded on distrust of the head of state, the American; but with this difference: the Girondins' measures had nothing to do with the good of the country. The camp of 20,000 *fédérés* was designed purely to overawe the king; paid more than the troops at the front, they should have been fighting there. To break the deadlock in early July an orchestrated campaign was initiated for Louis's dethronement (*déchéance*): the Assembly was flooded with petitions from clubs, *sections*, from town and country. Vergniaud explored the constitutional possibility of overriding the royal veto if 'the Patrie was in danger' which it was proclaimed to be on 11 July when Pétion's suspension was lifted.

The 'Patrie en danger' decree had several important consequences. It called up for national service everyone capable of bearing arms. On the same day the commune decreed that everyone with a pike could enter the National Guard. Hitherto entry had been restricted to 'active citizens', those who had the vote. Now 'passive citizens' could enter and this changed the tone of the National Guard, which lost its bourgeois and (constitutional) monarchist character. Administrative authorities were ordered to be *en permanence* – that is to meet daily. On 25 July the Legislative, under pressure from the electoral *sections*, decreed that the *permanence* be applied to sectional meetings and that in this emergency 'passive citizens' could participate. The *journée* of 10 August was made by far from 'passive citizens'.

On 31 July the Mauconseil *section* declared that it withdrew its allegiance from the king. 'The *journée* of 20 June forebodes another', said Marie Antoinette,[36] while on 27 July Louis entered in his diary: 'alert the whole day'. Meanwhile, on 25 July, the duke of Brunswick, generalissimo of the Prussian army, issued a manifesto which threatened Paris with total destruction if the royal family was harmed or the Tuileries invaded again. Marie-Antoinette had been pressing for such a declaration and Fersen had a hand in drafting it,[37] but its very vehemence was counterproductive and increased rather than diminished the perils of the royal family.

Meanwhile the king had to endure another of those interminable festivals which for him commemorated a defeat: the third anniversary of the storming of the Bastille. The celebrations lasted from 10 a.m. to 7 p.m. and the royal family all had their roles assigned for this ritual humiliation. Madame de Staël witnessed the events:

To support such a situation required the character of a martyr from Louis XVI, something which never deserted him. His way of walking [the Bourbon waddle] and his countenance had something distinctive. On other occasions one could have wished that he displayed more grandeur but on this occasion all he had to do was to remain just himself in every way to seem sublime. From afar I followed his powdered perruque bobbing up in the midst of those black-haired heads; his clothes, still braided as formerly, contrasted with the costume of the populace who pressed around him. When he ascended the steps of the altar [to the nation, to swear to uphold the constitution] methought I saw a saintly victim voluntarily offering himself up as a sacrifice.[38]

There was a bonfire of the vanities – feudal deeds, mitres, cardinals' hats, genealogical proofs of nobility, the arms of the former historic provinces, now replaced by *départements* with no resonance, all piled up. The president of the Assembly invited the king to light the touch paper, but he declined and looking fixedly at him said, 'feudalism no longer exists'. *Fédérés* had come from all over France to join in the celebrations, after which they were supposed to head for the front. But Robespierre's Jacobins persuaded them (with offers of free hospitality) to disobey both government and Assembly (which were not inclined to subsidize revolt) and stay on to lend a hand in bringing down the monarchy.

Faced with the imminence of a second rising, this time to dethrone him (the first had merely been orchestrated to bring the Girondins back into the ministry and was frowned on by Robespierre for that reason), the king had two choices. One was to try to hold out in Paris until the Prussians arrived (Marie-Antoinette had their itinerary; by the end of August they reached Verdun, the last fortress between them and Paris). This plan would involve doing some kind of a deal with the Girondins (themselves engulfed in a wider movement they could no longer control), spending money lavishly on buying support in Paris and putting the Tuileries in some sort of defensive posture. The other choice was to try once more to escape from Paris.

Indeed there were rumours that the queen had already gone. On 13 July Montmorin wrote:

During Wednesday to Thursday night a rumour spread round the National Guard on duty that the queen had left and the commander was obliged to wake the king at two in the morning and beg him to make the queen show herself which was the only way to satisfy the Guard. You will see from this that they are as well guarded to prevent escape as they are badly defended against those who would violate their sanctuary. Nevertheless there has been serious question of getting them out of Paris. Some want them to trust themselves to Lafayette who, as you can well imagine, would be only too delighted to have ... [the king] in his clutches and would risk anything to get hold of him.

Élisabeth thought that Lafayette was 'the only man who by placing himself on a horse can give the king an army'. Relations between the queen and Lafayette, however, remained desperate, though by the summer, Molleville notes, the king's mistrust for Lafayette 'had largely been dispelled'. Lafayette in turn believed that the king's technical adherence to the constitution was sufficient, since it allowed him only 'the exercise of a very limited and scarcely dangerous power'.[39] In this frame of mind, Lafayette made two attempts to save the constitutional monarchy on his own terms. First, on 28 June he left his army and appeared before the Assembly to denounce the *journée* of 20 June. Next day, according to Louis's diary, 'there was to have been a review of the second legion [of the National Guard] in the Champs-Élysées'. Lafayette planned to review this loyal legion with the king, harangue it and march with it to close down the Jacobins. Lafayette claims that the queen told Pétion, as mayor of Paris, to countermand orders for the review. She said, 'M. de Lafayette wants to save us but who will save us from M. de Lafayette.'[40] Louis merely told him, 'this is all useless' and he was right – only a few guards turned up and Lafayette returned to his army. Lafayette, only a year before the popular idol, was burnt in effigy – but, to Robespierre's fury, the Assembly refused to censure him.

Lafayette's second attempt, in conjunction with the 'triumvirs', was a plan to get the king out of Paris. It had been arranged that Lafayette's army of the Rhine and Luckner's army of Flanders should exchange positions. This meant that at one point, at Compiègne, Lafayette's army would pass within twenty leagues of Paris. The constitution stipulated that the king could not step outside this limit and Louis, who wanted to play by the rules, insisted on strictly observing this.[41] Lafayette was to arrive in Paris and announce to the Assembly that the king was going to his palace of Compiègne, as was his entitlement under the constitution. They would leave under the escort of the Swiss and loyal units of National Guards. Lafayette would have kept Louis as a puppet king but Adrien Duport persisted in his post-Varennes ambition of getting Austrian backing for an English-style constitutional monarchy with a bicameral parliament and the restoration of a titled nobility without material privileges.[42] We know this from several letters found on him, in which the plan is outlined in code: the 'invalid', i.e., the king, must 'choose a healthy place for himself on his estates – he has

plenty to choose from – but the airiest and most exposed to the north wind
[i.e., Compiègne] would be best'. His accommodation must be able to accommodate 'a spare room', i.e., a second chamber, and his restoration to health
would be aided by 'Swiss herbs', that is Swiss troops.[43]

On 11 July Marie-Antoinette wrote to Fersen: 'The Const.[itutionalists] in
conjunction with Lafayette and Luckner want to conduct the king to Compiègne
the day after the federation [15 July]. For this purpose the two generals are going
to arrive there. The king is disposed to lend himself to this project; the queen is
against it. The outcome of this great venture which I am far from approving is still
in doubt'. This brief, coded note reveals a clash, in extremis, between the king and
the queen which is not just a tactical one of whether to leave Paris or stay put; not
just a matter of personalities – Marie-Antoinette's 'it would be too appalling to
owe our lives to that man [Lafayette] twice', the first time being the October Days
– but a symbolic clash over whether to rely on the Prussians or on the internal
forces of the constitutional monarchy. For Lafayette intended that the king should
issue a proclamation from Compiègne forbidding his brothers or the foreign
troops to advance any further.[44] Mercy[45] and Fersen had both urged Marie-
Antoinette to stay put in Paris, Fersen specifically warning: 'If you do [risk flight]
you must never summon Lafayette, but the neighbouring *départements*'.[46] In the
end, it was Marie-Antoinette's opinion that prevailed rather than that of Louis,
who informed Lafayette, politely, that his plan was not practicable.[47]

Apart from his wife's opinion, two further considerations must have
weighed with the king. The first was that Lafayette intended, as in 1790, to
reduce him to the role of *roi fainéant*; as a foretaste of what he could expect
from Lafayette, the *feuillant* ministry offered its collective resignation on 10
July – a move concerted with Lafayette to throw the king on his mercy and
make him accept the escape plan.[48] The second consideration was that, if he
abandoned Paris before the Prussians arrived, they might put one of his
brothers forward as king. Lafayette has him saying: 'I do not want to fall foul of
my brothers by going to Compiègne.' He stayed put as he had in 1789, when he
feared that Orléans would seize a vacant throne. As Lafayette said: 'He feared
the victor whoever it was.'[49]

The closest contemporary account of Louis's thinking is given in the
memoirs of Bigot de Sainte-Croix, who, on 10 July, was appointed minister of
the interior and interim foreign minister – interim that is until anyone was
brave enough to volunteer for the job. Louis told Bigot:

> Whatever the outcome of a war I did everything to prevent, I will resist the
> attempt by any foreign power to impose a form of government on France.

My intention is to support the constitution until the nation itself releases me from the oath I have taken to uphold it. . . . No one wished more for the destruction of abuses than me. I wanted the bases of a free constitution and its principles have always been close to my heart. My efforts are well known. I have no doubt that any fair-minded man will do me that justice. However I am aware of the dangers surrounding me . . . and I submit my fate to the Sovereign Master of the Universe.[50]

These ideas are the same as those outlined by Louis in a letter to his brothers regarding his motives for accepting the constitution and his speech on that occasion. He was banking on a counter-revolution of the mind in his misled subjects. This was his settled view, in so far as a man of his mutable temperament – one recalls Provence's analogy with the oiled billiard balls – may be said to have had one.

Having rejected Lafayette's escape plan and also another for a withdrawal to Normandy,[51] Louis had to secure his position in Paris as best he could. He had 7 million *livres* in cash from his civil list and borrowed another million from a M. Chavelet. Laporte distributed money lavishly. On 16 June alone, Louis spent 377,000 *livres*. The wealthy brewer Santerre, a colonel in the National Guard, who had orchestrated the petition on the Champ de Mars, received 50,000 *livres*, though he later denied it. Danton was also approached. Assembly member Ribes received 800,000 *livres* to distribute among fellow deputies and made a speech in the king's defence. A lot of the money went to journalists – the editors of the *Logographe* received 90,000 *livres*. Placards and brochures were subsidized, carrying such titles as *The King at his Desk* (3,000 copies), *With a King We Have Bread* (3,000 copies), *No More Jacobins* (2,000 copies) and *Second Denunciation of the Jacobins* (7,000 copies). Pétion probably accepted the king's money.[52]

The Girondin deputy Guadet haughtily refused to take the money but he and his colleagues Gensonné and Vergniaud did negotiate with the king through the court painter Boze and the keeper of the seals Dejoly. Vergniaud reminded the king that 'he had been sadly deceived if he had been led to believe that not to depart from the letter of the constitution was to do all that he should'. He suggested that the king should enlarge his council by including three popular ex-Constituants; also that he should take a personal initiative to bring about a cease-fire. The king's reply said nothing about enlarging the council and that the cease-fire could only be effected by 'les moyens généraux', i.e., official diplomacy. Louis acidly observes that 'we owe the declaration of war entirely to the self-styled patriot ministers'. Dejoly considered that this reply 'would not satisfy either a friend of liberty or a man of ambition. It is dry and negative.'[53]

Nevertheless, the Girondins, ever hopeful of storming the ministry a second time and pursuing their tactic of 'threatening the court and attracting it to them',[54] staved off the impending insurrection three times before it broke with the dawn on 10 August.[55] At midnight on the 9th the bells of the Paris churches began to ring out their tocsin one by one and everyone in the Tuileries rushed to the windows to pick out the distinctive tones of each and its patron saint – Saint-Laurence, Saint-Roche, Saint-Eustache, Saint-Germain-des-Près, Saint-Étienne-du-Mont – until the whole sky was filled with their noise. At 4 a.m. Madame Élisabeth brought Marie-Antoinette to the window to see the dawn. Louis, who had grabbed a few hours' sleep on a sofa, joined them. His wig was flattened on the side where he had been sleeping.

The palace was in a far better state of defence than it had been on 20 June, for there had been ample warning: the Assembly had been told that unless they abolished the monarchy there would be a rising on the 10th. The 1,000 Swiss Guards, absolutely loyal, had been brought back from their barracks at Rueil and Courbevoie and there were 1,000 mounted police and 2,000 National Guards. There were also about 300 armed nobles – 2,000 had been summoned – who did more harm than good by antagonizing the National Guard. Montmorin was there and Malesherbes, who was not used to wearing a sword and was terrified of tripping over it and breaking his neck.[56] Both had contributed to the outbreak of the Revolution, as had the king, and they were staying in Paris to die with the monarchy. Otherwise, they feared their ministerial careers would be misunderstood.[57] It was the highest sense of ministerial responsibility, not political or criminal, but moral.

These forces, Reinhard considers, were 'enough to contain the insurrection, perhaps to crush it'. The king had been told that 20,000 men were surrounding the palace, whereas the numbers of the two forces were numerically equal. But all depended on the attitude of the National Guard, Parisian and provincial – the *fédérés* who were going via Paris to a camp at Soissons whose formation Louis had allowed. In prospect was an internecine struggle both within the National Guard – one battalion turning out for the king, one against him – and within a single battalion: the grenadiers maybe for the king and the gunners against. But the balance was tipped during the night by the replacement of the municipality, from which the National Guard took its orders, by an 'insurrectionary commune' comprising delegates from the *sections*, which gave the orders to march on the Tuileries next day. Mandat, the loyal commander of the National Guard, having been summoned to confer with the old municipality, was murdered by the new one.

It was thus a dejected king who went down to review his troops at six o'clock. He was silent and depressed; his ingrained timidity stood him in bad stead; this was not physical fear. He said, 'after all that I have suffered death is not so difficult.'[58] He scorned to wear the *gilet* padded with fifteen layers of taffeta Marie-Antoinette had provided, but, as she said, 'he fears above everything else speaking to assembled men'; he could find no rousing words. The most loyal troops had been placed nearest the palace – they shouted 'Vive le Roi!' – but as he progressed, his reception became cooler. 'My God, they are booing the king!' shouted a minister. 'What the devil is he doing down there? Let's go and fetch him quickly.' He was brought back.

Roederer, of the *département* of Paris, advised that resistance was impossible and that the royal family should take refuge in the Assembly. Bachmann, the major of the Swiss Guards, said, 'If the king goes to the Assembly he is lost.' The king looked at his ministers, his last council, and said, 'Come, gentlemen, there is nothing more to be done here', and, raising his hand, 'let us go and make this last sacrifice to the nation.' The queen said nothing but turned green with chagrin. Louis said to the maréchal de Mailly, whom he had put in charge of the Tuileries, 'We shall be back – once calm has been restored.'

Roederer led the little procession, the royal family, the ministers, the departmental officials, along a double hedge of soldiers to the Assembly. From the king's bedroom Madame de Tourzel's daughter saw this sad procession pass on its way: 'The idea of a funeral procession came to mind; it was indeed the cortège of the monarchy.' In the night there had been a fall of leaves and the gardeners had put them in piles along the route the procession took. The dauphin kicked them carelessly. 'The leaves are falling early this year,' Louis said to Roederer. It had been predicted in a radical journal that the monarchy would fall with the leaves.

On leaving the palace, Louis had omitted to countermand the orders to defend it. This the Swiss Guards did, killing or seriously wounding about 300 insurgents. When Louis, at about ten o'clock, finally gave orders to the Swiss to stop firing, they were butchered almost to a man.

The rising was as much against the Assembly as against the king; and it may be that if it had pronounced Louis's suspension or dethronement sooner the attack on the Tuileries might have been called off, though the prospect of looting was probably too enticing. But the Assembly did as much for the king as it dared under mob pressure. Louis was suspended from his functions, not deposed: his fate was to be decided by a new assembly, a National Convention, voted by manhood suffrage. Vergniaud even proposed that the dauphin's governor, M. de Fleurieu, be replaced, from which Louis took some negative comfort.

The royal family spent the day crowded together in the reporters' box. At two in the morning they were transferred to the neighbouring Convent of the Feuillants, where they remained for three days. The precise point at which the king, who after all had sought refuge in the Assembly, became a prisoner is hard to discern. To Louis it seemed to come on 11 August, when his attendants were ordered to leave the Feuillants: 'I am in prison then, and less fortunate than Charles I, who was allowed to keep all his friends with him to the scaffold.' Knowing that the king was penniless, his courtiers emptied their pockets, but Louis said: 'Keep your purses, gentlemen, you will need them more than we shall, as you will have longer to live, I hope.' Louis frame of mind was now, as it had been for some time, that of a man with a terminal illness.

There was a dispute between the Assembly and the commune over the final destination of the royal family, the Assembly preferring the Luxembourg, former home of Provence, the Commune the Temple, the grim medieval habitation of the former Knights Templar. Its massive central tower, with pointed roof, walls nine feet thick and mere slits of windows, looked like a prison. The Commune, now the real power in the land, got its way. And on 13 August, at six o'clock in the evening, Pétion called to take the royal family away. There were nine in the carriage and someone wondered if they would be too squashed. 'Not at all,' the king said with a wry smile, 'M. Pétion knows full well that I can endure a longer journey in cramped conditions.'[59] The royal family were driven, through immense and hostile crowds, to the Temple. The carriage crept along at a snail's pace as only two horses had been provided. It stopped at the Place Vendôme, where Louis contemplated the equestrian statue of Louis XIV which had been thrown down from its pedestal. 'That, Sire,' said the municipal officer, Manuel, with studied insolence, 'is how the people treats its kings.' 'Let us hope,' replied the king, who like many a fallen monarch was beginning to find the right words, 'that it confines its attention to inanimate objects.' 'Saddest of all' for the king 'was that no one dared even to show compassion.'[60] Night was falling when the party reached the Temple, where they were met by the officials of the Commune – hats on heads, addressing the king as 'Monsieur', not 'Sire' – which had assumed responsibility for their custody.[61]

CHAPTER FIFTEEN

THE PRISONER IN THE TEMPLE

THE TRANSITION FROM PALACE to prison was not as abrupt as it could have been. Louis had been virtually under house arrest since the October Days and literally so during his suspension. And there were other similarities. Though sequestered from the general public, in prison Louis led a life on display similar but with even less privacy than the one he had lived at Versailles. In his palace he was dressed in public, but he had already dressed in private; he dined in public, touching little, then supped alone; he processed through halls of mirrors and gilded salons, but also through a warren of secret passages and staircases. In the Temple the municipal jailers observed his every waking and even sleeping act, and reported his actions to a press avid for news. In this respect the *Moniteur* picked up where the *Gazette de France* had left off.

In the Temple, no less than at Versailles, Louis's life was governed by a daily routine. He rose between six and seven o'clock, shaved and dressed himself. Then he retired into a little side-turret which served as an oratory (he followed the church year in the breviary used in the diocese of Paris) and study. Before he was moved to the Great Tower, he had access to the library of the knights of Malta, which contained some 1,500 volumes, of which he read 250. One day, pointing at the works of Rousseau and Voltaire, he whispered to Hue, the dauphin's valet-de-chambre, 'Those two men have ruined France.'

The main purpose of his reading was to prepare himself to educate the dauphin and in particular he sought to brush up his own Latin. He talked about the various Latin authors to one of the municipal officers, who adds perceptively: 'He struck me as very anxious to demonstrate that he is informed.'[1] On 22 November he applied to the Commune for a further thirty-three French and Latin authors: poets (Horace, Ovid and Virgil) and historians (Sallust,

Suetonius and Tacitus). One member of the council objected: 'The prisoner was scarcely sure of a fortnight's existence and the books he was requesting would be enough to occupy him for a very long life.' Another thought his reading should concern the crimes of kings (the Saint-Bartholomew massacre) or works dealing with the American Revolution and the life of Cromwell. Ironically he was at this very time polishing his translation of the 'crimes' of a king – Horace Walpole's *Richard III*. In the end his request for more books was granted in full.

At nine o'clock the family came up to the king's room for breakfast, which would consist of coffee, chocolate, fruit, bread and milk foods. At about ten o'clock they all went up to the queen's room on the third floor, where the ladies sewed whilst Louis instructed his son, mainly in Latin and geography; but, as the king's valet-de-chambre, Cléry, notes, 'it was the new geography of France that the king showed him'.[2]

At noon the family walked outside to give the children some air and exercise, returning at two o'clock for the *dîner*, which was quite an elaborate affair with two main courses and dessert, and red and white wine. The king usually drank half a bottle of champagne and a glass of liqueur with dessert. This food cost 80,000 *livres* a month and was provided by two chefs and eleven sous-chefs taken straight from the *bouche* or kitchen of the Tuileries.[3]

After the *dîner*, Louis and Marie-Antoinette would play piquet or backgammon until four, when the king had a nap. At six, Louis gave his son more lessons or played games with him. After supper, at nine o'clock, the king retired to his study and read until midnight.

This ordered life was punctuated by various privations and alarms. On the night of 19/20 August, the royal family were deprived of Madame de Tourzel and the princesse de Lamballe, the queen's companion and kinswoman. They were imprisoned in La Force. On 2 September, Hue was arrested. Soon the prisoners were left with only Cléry. The queen and Madame Élisabeth mended the king's clothes whilst Marie-Antoinette asked Cléry to teach her daughter how to do her own hair, finding this preferable to being attended by the wives and relatives of municipal officers.[4]

Events from the outside world filtered through, sometimes slowly, sometimes with brutal immediacy – the royal family craned at the windows to catch the cries of the newspaper sellers. The Prussian advance continued, throwing into doubt the result of the insurrection of 10 August: the municipal officer, Mathieu, mindful of Brunswick's threat to demolish Paris, asked one of Louis's servants: 'Beg him [the king] to write to . . . [the king of Prussia] to halt his march and save himself and the town.'[5] The fortress of Longwy fell on 23 August and on

1 September news reached Paris that Verdun, the last fortress between the Prussians and Paris, was about to capitulate. At four o'clock on the 2nd the populace responded by breaking into the prisons and starting to massacre the inmates. The slaughter continued uninterrupted until the 7th, by which time about half the prisoners had perished – roughly 1,200 people, only a third of whom were political prisoners.

Montmorin perished (Laporte had already been guillotined on 23 August) and another obvious target for the *septembriseurs* was the princesse de Lamballe. The mob took her corpse and severed head to the Temple and sought admittance, hoping to kill the king and queen as well but they were kept out by the expedient of stretching the tricolour sash of one of the municipal officers across the main entrance (Cléry had to find forty-five sous for the sash). Not to be thwarted, the mob lifted the princess's head aloft on the end of a pike so that it was visible from the windows of the Tower. A dispute arose between the municipal officers and the National Guard as to whether the royal family should show themselves at the windows. Louis asked a Guard what was going on, receiving the brutal reply: 'Very well, Monsieur, since you want to know, it's the head of Mme de Lamballe they want to show you. I advise you to show yourselves unless you want the people to come up.' The queen fainted. The king replied: 'We were ready for everything, Monsieur; but you could have dispensed with telling the queen this appalling news.'[6]

One of the first acts of the National Convention was the proclamation of the Republic on 21 September. To the sound of trumpets a municipal officer read the proclamation in the courtyard of the Temple. Inside, Louis's jailers watched for his reaction, but he pretended not to hear and continued reading his book. They now multiplied opportunities for calling him 'Monsieur' and sat down in his presence. His jailers submitted him to a series of petty indignities: one of them, called Rocher, knowing that the *ci-devant* king had an aversion to pipe-smoke, took delight in blowing it in his face.[7] They stopped his son's mathematics lessons and his wife's embroidery, in case their work contained codes. They did not allow him to shave himself in case he committed suicide – an insult to a devout Christian. But gradually his gentle submissiveness won them over despite themselves; and superstitious atheists that they were, they sought his personal possessions, such as his gloves and cravat, as relics.

Despite having to endure these petty vexations, Louis found in his settled life, free from responsibility, bounded by welcome family duties and religious observances and lived from day to day, a serenity he had rarely experienced since 1787. Nor at first were the new masters of the country disposed to alter this state of affairs, though the king himself had long believed that his trial was

inevitable. It was brought about by a change in the fortunes of the war and by
the discovery, in the panelling of the Tuileries, of an iron document-safe, the
famous *armoire de fer.*

On 22 September Dumouriez, after brilliant manoeuvres, checked the
Prussians at Valmy, very near Varennes, and allowed them to retreat. He then
turned on the Austrians in Belgium, defeated them at Jemappes, near Mons, on
6 November, and a week later entered Brussels. These victories robbed Louis of
his status as a valuable hostage, and though Dumouriez personally favoured a
restoration of the monarchy, this only served further to endanger the life of the
king.

Then, on 20 November, Roland, the minister of the interior, made his
dramatic announcement to the Convention concerning the discovery of the
armoire de fer. Louis had constructed this himself after the insurrection of 20
June but he had had to employ the services of one Gamain to fit the lock. Louis's
joinery had been so skilful that, but for Gamain's belated delation, the *armoire*
might never have been found. The majority of the 627 documents in the iron
safe did not justify the space they took up. Most were letters Louis had received
– not sent – including seventy-six from priests complaining about their
proscription. The documents found in ordinary desks and cupboards during
the sack of the Tuileries were actually more incriminating as they showed that
the king had continued paying his bodyguards even after they had emigrated
and joined the princes at Coblenz. They showed also that Louis had subsidized
the Feuillant club and the *Logographe,* the journal of the Legislative Assembly.
The new discoveries did not provide any proof of dealings with foreign powers
– Louis and Marie-Antoinette systematically burned such papers – that proof
came only when the papers of their correspondents became available. Soboul
in *Le Procès de Louis XVI* claims that 'the papers in the *armoire de fer* brought
proof that Louis XVI was conducting a correspondence with Calonne'.[8] In fact
they prove only that Calonne wrote letters to the king: on one of them Louis
wrote 'point répondu' and Calonne received no letters from the king, to his
great grief.[9] His rival Breteuil had fared better and the Convention had at its
disposal letters found on the Prussians which hinted at Louis's relations with
him, though the lead was not followed up.[10]

What the documents in the iron safe – and those captured in the sack of the
Tuileries – do demonstrate is Louis's relations with Mirabeau, Lafayette and
Dumouriez, and also his spending considerable sums of money to win over
public support at the level of popular politics and through subsidizing the
royalist press. The captured documents show that Louis and his agents, notably
La Porte, the intendant of the civil list, were engaged in political management

typical of the eighteenth century: La Porte was playing Robinson to Louis's George III – though with conspicuously less success. But what should have been taken as evidence of Louis's sincerity in trying to rule as a contemporary constitutional monarch was, in the puritanical climate of the Revolution, considered instead to be conclusive proof of his duplicity and secretiveness. For in this climate, secrecy was equated with conspiracy and Roland built up the drama by claiming that the safe had a special key, whereas in fact it was the same one which fitted three other cupboards.

The discovery of the iron safe meant that the Girondins could no longer prevaricate about bringing Louis to judgment – the very minimum that their opponents to the left, the Montagnards, would accept. The Montagnards' preferred line, as outlined by Robespierre and Saint-Just, was that Louis had already been 'judged' by the *journée* of 10 August and should be put to death without more ado. Paradoxically, the Girondin leaders, most of whom wanted to spare the king a trial or at least his life, had a personal dislike of the king, stemming from having served in government under him; they had also advocated a republic before Robespierre had. And whereas the Girondins' dislike of the king was personal, that of the Montagnards was abstract, as instanced in Saint-Just's famous apophthegm, 'Kings cannot reign innocently'.

Both Robespierre and Louis had thought it would be better for the country if a trial were avoided, Robespierre thinking that the king should simply be executed in accordance with the 'verdict' of 10 August, and Louis preferring and expecting to be assassinated: he had expected this to happen on 20 June and again expected it on his way to the Convention for his second appearance on 26 December. His reflections on the life of Charles I had convinced him that he must above all avoid a formal trial, because that would make the whole nation culpable, a thought which had been developed by Montmorin, in conversation with Molleville in August: 'If the king is tried and formally condemned, you will not see a monarchy for a long time.' Expecting to be assassinated on the 26th, Louis made his will on Christmas Day.

Its opening has a pathos and consciously archaic grandeur about it:

In the name of the Holy Trinity, Father, Son and Holy Ghost. This day, the 25th day of December, one thousand seven hundred and ninety-two, I, Louis, of that name the 16th, king of France, having been for four months imprisoned with my family in the Tower of the Temple in Paris by those who were my subjects and deprived of any communication whatsoever, even (since the 11th of the current month) with my family; moreover involved in a trial whose outcome is impossible to predict, given the passions of men, and for which no pretext or procedure can be found in any existing law; having only God as witness of my thoughts to whom I can address myself, I declare here in his presence my final wishes and sentiments.

Louis still regards himself as king, and not just king of the French (the revolutionary and pre-Louis XIV title) but king of France. However, in the only overtly political passage in the will, his advice to his son 'should he have the misfortune to be king', he paraphrases the words he had used in accepting the constitution. He 'can only work for the happiness of his peoples if he reigns according to the laws, but at the same time a king cannot make them respected . . . unless he has the necessary authority' – otherwise 'he does more harm than good'.

The trial

The trial began with a preliminary hearing on 11 December. At eleven o'clock in the morning Louis was instructing the dauphin as usual when two municipal officers entered and took the boy away without explanation – as 'co-conspirators' Louis's family were to be denied access to him. On 15 December he was told that he could see his children but only on condition that neither saw their mother or Aunt Élisabeth so long as the trial lasted. Naturally Louis refused. He was particularly upset that he was not allowed to see his daughter on her fourteenth birthday.

At one o' clock Chambon, who had succeeded Pétion as mayor, was announced and told the King that,

He had come to see him in order to conduct him to the Convention in virtue of a decree [providing] . . . that 'Louis Capet should be brought before the bar of the Convention'. 'I am not called Capet,' said the King, 'it is the name of one of my ancestors. I could have desired, monsieur, that the commissioners had left me my son during the two hours I have spent waiting for you. In any case this treatment is in accordance with what I have experienced here for four months. I am going to follow you, not in obedience to the Convention but because my enemies are in possession of *force majeure*.'

Louis was brought to the bar, wearing a brown coat, hat under arm, stout and, his razor having been confiscated on 7 December, unshaven. He was only thirty-eight but looked to be in his late fifties, as can be seen from the white chalk portrait done of him in prison by Joseph Ducreux, formerly painter to the queen. But he emanated grace. In stripping the king of his dignities, the Convention and the Commune had unexpectedly revealed his dignity. The president, the honey-tongued Barère, the Anacreon of the guillotine, addressed him: 'Louis, the French nation accuses you. The National Assembly decreed on 3 December that it would try you . . . you will be read the indictment containing the crimes of which you are accused. You may sit down.'[11] The indictment consisted of thirty-two composite charges, some of them going back to 1789, leading to the general accusation of 'conspiring against liberty and an attempt against the safety of the state'. The general accusation was virtually meaningless, certainly not susceptible of legal proof or disproof. Furthermore, the constitution of 1791, under which France continued to be governed until 1795, envisaged only three acts for which the king was responsible: retracting his oath to uphold the constitution, leading an army against the forces of the nation and leaving the kingdom. Louis had done none of these things and had, in any case, already incurred the only penalty provided – dethronement. The trial was going to be a political one. The president put each charge separately to Louis and he was required to give an immediate reply. Some took him by surprise;[12] but he answered well, showing considerable presence of mind, over four hours of questioning.

And this was all the more impressive in that Louis, without a lawyer, and held incommunicado for over three months, had to improvise a defence. This was a novel situation for him because the Bourbon kings had always acted on formally delivered advice; as Louis had written when dauphin, 'counsel is of the essence of monarchy'. This conditioning made spontaneous action difficult for him in the new situations where it was required. That, apart from the fact that he was entitled to one by law, was why Louis repeatedly asked for a lawyer.

He did not follow the example of Charles I in challenging the competence of the court but offered a defence based on the laws in force at the various times when he was supposed to have committed the crimes. Many historians and contemporaries, of various political complexions,[13] believed that Louis's adoption of Charles I's line would have been the only way to salvage the prestige and mystique of monarchy and the best way to secure its speedy restoration. If, they argued, the king descended to bandying words with the Convention in answer to the individual accusations, he would be legitimating the process. For, as one of Brissot's collaborators on the *Patriote française* put it, 'be it weakness, be it reason, be it the hope of making his cause better', Louis had rendered homage 'to the national sovereignty'.[14]

In fact Louis did consider following the example of Charles I. On 17 December, between the preliminary hearing and the trial proper on the 26th, Louis wrote a letter to Malesherbes along these lines. 'I am under no illusions about my fate', he wrote,

> The ingrates who have dethroned me will not stop in midflight. They would be too embarrassed to see their victim constantly before them. I will suffer the fate of Charles I and my blood will flow to punish me for never having shed any. . . . The National Assembly numbers within its ranks those who have wrecked my monarchy, my denunciators, my judges and probably my butchers. Such men cannot be persuaded, they cannot be rendered just. Still less can their hearts be melted. Might it not be better to put some spirit into my defence, considering that weakness will not save me? My thinking is that my defence should be addressed not to the Convention but to the whole of France which will judge my judges and restore me to the place in my people's hearts that I never deserved to lose. [As for the Assembly] I will maintain a dignified silence and, in condemning me the men who call themselves my judges will be merely my assassins.[15]

For some reason this letter did not reach Malesherbes until 4 April 1793, when it was all over and Louis reverted to his original plan of defence.

In accordance with the legalistic plan of defence Louis adopted, he replied to the charge 'you caused an army to march against the citizens of Paris' (in June–July 1789): 'At that time I could order troops to march where I pleased.' For the period between the fall of the Bastille and his acceptance of the constitution, he relied on the amnesty for political offences issued at that time. For the period when the constitution of 1791 was in force, he invoked ministerial responsibility where appropriate. The charges were badly framed and, as Marat observed, there were too many of them. Some were banal: e.g., 'You vetoed [the decree of 29 November against refractory priests]. What have you to answer?' This charge received the obvious reply: 'The constitution allowed me the free exercise of a veto on decrees.' Some were illogical: e.g., 'After your arrest at Varennes your exercise of the executive power was suspended yet you continued to conspire. On 17 July the blood of the citizens was shed on the Champ de Mars.' Others were downright silly, as the accusation that he had pretended to be ill in the spring of 1791 so that a sympathetic public would allow him to go to Saint-Cloud. To this Louis replied: 'This accusation is absurd.' Louis's replies were characteristic: solid but legalistic, negative, unimaginative. Louis only really comes alive when accused of shedding blood at the Champ de Mars and notably on 10 August. At the latter charge, tears sprang to his eyes.

He did not offer his own interpretation of the events of the Revolution. For example, he might have observed that one could not condemn him for corresponding with men such as Mirabeau and Lafayette, the heroes of 1789, or Dumouriez, the saviour of France at Valmy, without condemning the Revolution itself. It is unlikely, however, that the National Convention would have appreciated such an argument, since its response to learning of Louis's dealings with Mirabeau was to smash the bust of him in its precincts, remove his body from the Pantheon (reserved for heroes of the Revolution) and chuck it into a common grave. As for Dumouriez, he was, for the moment, too useful to the war effort. So the Convention hypocritically turned a blind eye to a letter of one of the king's agents, dated 14 June, saying, 'I am sure I can come to an understanding with M. Dumouriez over everything concerned with His Majesty's service'.[16]

After the charges, Louis was presented with the evidence in the form of documents he had written or received. These he claimed not to recognize. This was pointless and lacking in dignity, but he was being presented with the evidence without warning,[17] and as he later observed, some of it could have been counterfeited.[18] On Louis's letter to the bishop of Clermont concerning his Easter communion, even the impassive Barère had to ask: 'Don't you recognize your signature?' 'No.' 'The seal bears the arms of France.' 'Lots of people had it.' At first Louis tried to vary his answers: 'I don't recognize it'; 'Not in the slightest'; 'No more than the last'. Then it was just 'No'. Finally he began to lose patience: 'No, no! No, sir, no!' So did the Convention. When Dufriche-Valazé said, 'There are many other pieces; I think it would be superfluous to communicate them to the National Convention', the minutes note, 'Expression of agreement on all the benches'. Louis finally said: 'I request counsel' and retired. The Montagnards wanted to refuse Louis's request; when they were firmly in the saddle in 1794 they were to deny the accused counsel by the infamous law of 22 Prairial in the revolutionary calendar (10 June 1794). Pétion argued that to deny Louis counsel was against the laws of humanity – he felt it necessary to bend over backwards to be fair to a personal enemy. The Montagnards, who had no personal animus against the king, felt no such compunction. After a violent debate, Louis was granted legal representation.

After his appearance, as he was waiting in the conference room of the Convention for the mayor's coach to take him back to prison, Louis tried to strike up a conversation with a guard. Being rebuffed he took out his edition of the constitution from his pocket, though he already knew it by heart.

Chaumette, the *procureur* of the Commune, took a piece of bread and some brandy from a guard and started to eat, and Louis, who had eaten nothing since breakfast, said: 'My dear Chaumette, I have had no more to eat than you. Do let me have a bit of bread, please.' Chaumette obliged and Louis was munching his bread as he got in the coach. But another official took the bread from the king's hand and threw it out of the window. 'Ah!' Louis told him, 'It is not good to throw bread away, especially when it is so scarce.' The king had missed his *dîner*. When he arrived back at the Temple he ate six cutlets, a chicken and some eggs and went straight to bed.[19]

Louis chose as his defence counsel Target and Tronchet, two of the most celebrated barristers of the 1780s. They had both helped draft the constitution and by choosing them Louis indicated the line his defence would take. Target declined the honour, signing his letter to the Convention, 'le républicain Target'. He did, however, publish a pamphlet saying the king's life should be spared.[20] Tronchet, who had been one of the commissioners who had examined the king after his return from Varennes, accepted, but in the coolest, most grudging terms.[21] Before he saw the king, an attempt was made to strip-search Tronchet 'even in the most intimate places', but Tronchet refused and was still let in. Others, including Malouet and Mounier, who had both taken refuge in London, wrote to the Convention offering the king their services; and among those who risked their life in this way it is good to be able to note Miromesnil.[22] Malesherbes also wrote: '. . . I have been summoned twice to the council of the man who was my master at a time when this function was coveted by everyone: I owe him the same service when it is a function which many people find dangerous.'[23] Louis accepted the services of Malesherbes as well as Tronchet.

When Malesherbes was admitted to the Temple, Louis was reading Tacitus. With tears in his eyes he embraced the old man with the words: 'Your sacrifice is all the nobler because you are exposing your own life without being able to save mine.' Malesherbes reassured him that they would both be all right. But Louis was right, on both counts. 'I am sure they will kill me,' he replied, 'they have the power and the will. Never mind, let us work on my trial as if I were going to win. And win I shall, since the memory I shall leave behind will be without blemish.' At this stage Louis was allowed to see the evidence against him. A municipal officer notes: 'When the members of the [Convention's] committee . . . brought him the 406 documents relating to his trial, he received them like a grand seigneur receiving the accounts of his steward.'[24]

Malesherbes and Tronchet were appalled by the mound of paper they had to go through and told the Convention that, being in their seventies and sixties respectively, they could not cope. Their request for a third counsel was accepted and they enlisted the services of de Sèze, who had successfully defended Besenval in 1789, to deliver the king's defence. 'Looking at de Sèze's emotional peroration,' Louis said, 'we must delete it; I don't want to soften them.'

On 26 December Louis made his second appearance before the Convention. He and his counsel were kept waiting outside the main hall of the Convention. Malesherbes addressed the king as 'Sire' and 'Your Majesty'. The deputy Treilhard rebuked him: 'What then gives you the effrontery to use in its very precincts expressions proscribed by the Convention?' 'Contempt for you and for life!'[25]

De Sèze's defence developed the same arguments Louis had employed at the time of his first appearance. He spoke for three hours and Louis was so concerned for him that he wondered if he could have a substitute – like Necker at the opening of the Estates-General! There was something of an emotional peroration, including the words: 'The people wanted liberty, he gave it to them.' There were murmurs from the left and from the galleries, and de Sèze crossed out the offending sentence. He ended by reminding them: 'History will judge your judgment and its verdict will be that of centuries to come.'

Louis then delivered a short speech:

> You have just heard the arguments for my defence; I shall not repeat them. Speaking to you perhaps for the last time I declare to you that my conscience reproaches me with nothing and that my counsel has told you nothing but the truth. I have never feared a public examination of my conduct; but my heart is rent at finding in the indictment the imputation that I wished to shed the blood of the people and above all that the misfortunes of 10 August should be attributed to me.
>
> I confess that the manifold proofs I have given at all times of my love for the people and the manner in which I have always conducted myself seemed to me sufficient proof that I took little heed of exposing myself to spare their blood and to remove such an imputation from me for ever.[26]

After some further questions about the keys to the *armoire de fer* Louis retired. On his way back to the Temple he heard some confused shouting. The guards raised the windows. 'I thought they were shouting "Vive Lafayette!"' Louis mused. 'That would be stupid.' When Malesherbes told him of such a plan to rescue him, Louis replied: 'Tell them that I will not pardon them if there is a single drop of blood shed for me. I did not desire it to be shed when it might perhaps have saved my throne and my life. I do not regret this.'[27]

The Convention did not proceed immediately to a vote. For a fortnight the parties manoeuvred. Many of the Girondins, obscurely aware that the king's death would enlarge the conflict at home and abroad, devised ways of saving his life – an appeal to the people organized in primary assemblies; a diversionary attack on the duc d'Orléans, sitting in the Convention as Philippe Égalité. Dumouriez came to Paris to put his laurels discreetly at the king's service, but his intervention was counterproductive. Danton is said to have guaranteed to save the king's life if Pitt would give him 2 million *livres*, and Pitt to have refused.[28] According to another version Danton said, 'I will expose myself if I see any chance of success but if I lose all hope I will be among those who condemn . . . [the king], since I don't want my head to fall with his.'[29] Louis himself believed that 'the majority of deputies could easily have been bought'. He had been lent money for the purpose but was scrupulous about using it for corruption. The civil list, he told Malesherbes, had been a different matter, 'being only the rightful equivalent of the money from my domains'.[30]

Finally, between 14 and 20 January, the Convention voted on four motions and they did it by *appel nominal*, which meant that individual votes were recorded. This obviously favoured those who wanted to kill the king and was soon used as a basis for proscription. The first motion was phrased: 'Is Louis Capet, former king of the French, guilty of conspiring against liberty and an attempt against the safety of the state? Yes or no.' The result was that 691 voted 'yes', with 27 abstentions. No one dared vote against the motion. The second motion, proposed on 15 January, concerned the appeal to the people. The voting was 287 for, 424 against, with 12 abstentions. The third motion was on Louis's punishment – death, banishment, imprisonment or whatever. The voting lasted thirty-six hours and could not have been closer: out of 721 voters only 361 voted unconditionally for death – a majority of one. Given the closeness of this vote, a fourth motion was put, whether there should be a reprieve, but this was rejected by a majority of seventy. The Convention decreed that Louis should be notified 'within the day' and executed twenty-four hours after this notification. The Convention rose at three o'clock on the morning of 20 January 1793.

Malesherbes wanted to break the news to the king himself. All morning he hung around outside the Temple but was several times denied admission. He had, however, told Louis of the third vote, that of the death penalty, and saw him for the last time on the 19th. On taking leave of the king, Malesherbes says: 'I could not hold back my tears. "Tender-hearted old man," said the king squeezing my hand, "don't cry: we shall meet again in a happier life. I regret leaving behind such a friend as you. Adieu! As you leave the room, control yourself; you have to remember that they will be watching you ... Adieu! Adieu!"' When he had gone, Louis told his valet, 'The grief of this old man moved me.'[31]

At two in the afternoon, Garat, the minister of justice, informed Louis that he would be executed within twenty-four hours. Listening to the Convention's decree, Louis displayed no emotion except at the words 'conspiring against liberty', when a 'smile of contempt' played on his lips. He pointed to article eight of the Declaration of Rights pasted on the wall: 'the law should only prescribe punishments which are strictly and evidently necessary: no one should be punished except in virtue of a law passed and promulgated before the offence is committed'. Garat was astounded at the king's 'superhuman courage'. This stemmed from his religious faith. For much of his life he had been a pragmatist thrown among ideologues, but for its last act he had an ideology fitted to the occasion. After Garat had read out the decree, Louis produced a document from his portfolio. In it he requested 'a three-day stay of execution to prepare myself to appear before the presence of God', the right to see a priest of his choice and to see his family 'without witnesses'.[32]

The Convention rejected the first but granted the other two requests. Garat then returned to the Temple at six o'clock, bringing with him the abbé Edgeworth de Firmont, Madame Élisabeth's former confessor, who had been advised by Malesherbes of the king's choice of a man 'whose obscurity may save him from persecution'.[33] The king conferred with his confessor until half past eight, when the abbé withdrew to one of the side-turrets so as not to alarm Louis's family, who were now admitted for the first time in six weeks.

His daughter, Madame Royale, has left this account of their meeting:

> We found him greatly changed. He wept for our grief but not for his death. He told my mother about his trial, excusing the scoundrels who were bringing about his death. He repeated to my mother that people had wanted the primary assemblies but that he had not because that would have disturbed France. Then he gave sound religious teachings to my brother; above all he commanded him to pardon those who were about to cause his death. He gave his blessing to my brother and myself. My mother desperately wanted us to spend the night with my father. He refused, having need of tranquillity.[34]

As they parted from the king, their screams could be heard on the staircase, through the massive doors. His daughter was carried out fainting. Cléry who witnessed the scene through a glass door noted, 'it was easy to see from their gestures that ... [the king] himself had told them of his sentence'.

Louis turned to his confessor: '"Ah! Monsieur," he said to me throwing himself into a chair, "what an encounter I have just had. Must I love and be loved so tenderly? But that is done, let us forget everything else in order to concentrate on the one matter, it alone at this moment must occupy all my love and thought." '35

At eleven o'clock Cléry proposed supper. Louis 'hesitated a moment; but on reflection accepted the offer'. Cléry has left this description of the king's last meal: 'The king ate, with a good appetite, two wings of a chicken and a few vegetables, drank two glasses of wine mixed with water and, for dessert, a little finger-biscuit and some Malaga wine.' Then, accountant to the last, he made an inventory of the 250 books he had read in prison.

After supper Edgeworth suggested – what Louis had hardly dared hope for – the possibility of celebrating mass in the morning. The municipal officers not only acceded to this request, but scoured the neighbouring churches for the necessary accoutrements. Louis went to bed at about half past twelve: 'I [Cléry] undressed the king and as I was about to curl his hair, he said to me: "It's not worth it!" Then, lying down, as I was closing his curtains: "Cléry, you will wake me at five o'clock!" ' It was the Eve of St Agnes, when new knights kept a vigil, but Louis slept soundly, no doubt with that 'continuous and most extraordinary snoring' for which he was noted.36

In the morning, just before nine, Louis left the Temple with the commander of the National Guard, Santerre, and Edgeworth, who was permitted to accompany him to the scaffold. He had wanted Cléry to cut his hair, to facilitate the task of the executioners, but they were refused scissors: 'These men see daggers and poison everywhere, they fear I will kill myself. Alas they know me very badly; to kill myself would be weakness. No, since die I must I will die well!' As he went out of his room he fought his last battle of etiquette: the National Guards' 'faces were anything but assured. They all, however, had their hats on their heads. The king noticed it and asked for his own.' He asked for his will to be given to the queen – 'to my wife', he corrected.37

He was taken to the place of his execution – the former Place Louis XV – not in a tumbril but in a bottle-green carriage belonging to the minister of finance – a security measure perhaps but one which helped the king to die with dignity. Snow still lay from a heavy fall during the night and the three-mile journey, in freezing fog, took an hour and a half to complete. Lining the streets were 130,000 men, practically the whole armed force of Paris. From an upstairs window the proto-feminist Mary Wollstonecraft saw the king's carriage pass by. Louis looked 'pensive but not downcast'. On the way Edgeworth and the king recited alternate verses from the psalms for the dying.

When Louis descended from the carriage, three executioners rushed forward and tried to take his coat off. He pushed them aside, removed it himself and unfastened the collar of his shirt. He was further outraged when they sought to tie his hands behind his back. He looked to Edgeworth for guidance: 'Sire, in this further outrage I see only a final resemblance between Your Majesty and the God who will be his recompense.' 'Assuredly . . . nothing less than His example would make me submit to such an affront.' Then, turning to the executioners: 'Do as you please, I will drain the chalice to the dregs.'[38]

Louis then mounted the scaffold hesitantly, supported on Edgeworth's arm: the steps were steep, his hands were tied behind his back and he was stout and lacking in exercise. At this point Edgeworth is credited with saying: 'Fils de Saint-Louis, ascendez au ciel.' Whatever he said must have given Louis courage, for he rushed forward to the front of the platform and tried to address the crowd. Santerre had ordered a drum roll; Louis commanded silence. How many drums stopped beating we do not know; nor how many people heard Louis's words; nor indeed what exactly those words were. The most characteristic version, that of the *Semaines parisiennes*, runs: 'I die perfectly innocent of the so-called crimes of which I was accused. I pardon those who are the cause of my misfortunes. Indeed, I hope that the shedding of my blood will contribute to the happiness of France and you, unfortunate people . . .' These words may have been broken off by Santerre, by the drum roll or by the descent of the axe.[39]

All his life Louis had been haunted by the fate of Charles I and now, as he embraced it, he displayed the same mesmeric dignity – so that the words Andrew Marvell applied to the Stuart king could equally be applied to him:

> He nothing common did or mean
> Upon that memorable scene,
>   But with his keener eye
>   The axe's edge did try;
> Nor call'd the Gods, with vulgar spite,
> To vindicate his helpless right;
>   But bow'd his comely head
>   Down, as upon a bed.

The last couplet was less appropriate as Louis's neck was too fat to fit into the groove properly and the back of the neck and jawbone were 'mangled horribly'. It is doubtful if this caused Louis any pain, but it produced a lot of blood for which the spectators were literally thirsty. 'It tastes quite good,' some said. 'No,' others opined, 'it's horribly salty.' Others rubbed their hands in the blood to revenge 'what the wife of the tyrant had said after the Revolution about wanting to wash her hands in the blood of Frenchmen'. Since people wanted to dip handkerchiefs, pikes and envelopes in the blood which had collected in the trough under the guillotine, Sanson, the head executioner, suggested: 'Wait, I'll get you a bucket and then you can dip in more easily'. Not everyone behaved like this. An eighteen-year-old National Guard called Philippe Morrice nearly fainted and had to be revived with brandy. 'Luckily for me,' he relates, 'they were all decent chaps near me and, like me, they found no cause for merriment there.'[40]

Edgeworth made his way through the vast crowds, which parted for him like the Red Sea, to give Malesherbes the news. He was waiting at the house of his sister, Madame de Senozan, in the Rue Saint-Honoré, the same street where Robespierre lived and the Jacobin Club was situated. Two years later all three –first Malesherbes and his seventy-year-old sister and then Robespierre – would be guillotined and the Jacobin Club closed down.

Louis's body was taken to the local cemetery, that of the Madeleine, and placed in an anonymous grave. 'Let them take him where they like', wrote the deputy Choudieu, echoing perhaps the great hurt of 1789. 'What's it to us? We always wanted him; he never wanted us.'[41]

Conclusion

In some respects the picture of Louis XVI which has emerged is very different from the conventional stereotype of the stupid, lazy and impassive king – a stereotype, held by Louis's contemporaries as well as his historians, which stems not from Marie-Antoinette's propagandists but from his own uncommunicative nature, which his bizarre education served to develop rather than correct. Louis was in fact fairly intelligent and fairly hard-working – even in prison he had sought to improve himself in order to instruct his son. Moreover, his particular aptitudes, for finance, law and foreign affairs, were suited to the areas with which he was expected to deal.

This correction restores to the story of the Revolution an element of tragedy that is absent if one shares with many Pétion's view of its central character as an 'insensible mass of flesh'. Ironically if Louis had conformed to the stereotype there would have been no appointment of Necker, no intervention in the American war, no Assembly of Notables, just perhaps a drift towards an English form of government.

For the character of Louis, the *dévot-philosophe* was complex and this complexity was an essential ingredient in the revolutionary mix. If he hadn't been a *philosophe* there would not have been the revolution we recognize; if he hadn't been a *dévot* he might have let it run its course unhindered for, arguably, he only acted when the Civil Constitution disturbed his Christian conscience. His views on when it was legitimate to use force were sophisticated and they certainly hampered his actions, involving as they did the distinction (not always easy to draw) between a riot and a rising. And because he accepted the legitimacy of a truly representative National Assembly he was reluctant first to summon and then recognize one. He was comfortable dealing with individuals from his 'peoples' but uncomfortable with sovereign people; he found it hard to make small talk with nobles but wanted to preserve those of their privileges which did not interfere with equity and the running of the state. He loved peace but made war; he loved England, yet fought it almost to a standstill. He could display occasional flashes of brilliance (foreign policy) and consistent dullness (the diary), generosity of spirit and insight (his letter to his brothers on accepting the constitution) and self-defeating pettiness (his attitude to implementing the same constitution). He could be uncannily prophetic: his prediction (as early as February 1788) of the effects of permanent assemblies; or (in August 1791) of the effects of war; or that England and her colonies should be left to their mutual destruction. But he failed to act on his insights. Provence's quip about the 'oiled billiard balls' applies not just to others' grip on him but his grip on himself. It is perhaps these contradictions, quite as much as the deteriorating political situation, which account for what I have ventured to describe as periods of nervous collapse after 1787, though there may have been indications before.

His reputation for indecisiveness, however, remains intact, though it should be recognized that its character was partly institutional, being determined by the tradition of ruling by counsel and counting votes in the council. Over the three big decisions at the start of the Revolution (the *Résultat du conseil*, the *séance royale* and the question of flight to Rambouillet) the council was split down the middle; in the case of the *Résultat* one source, Lenoir, considered that Louis had acted *too* decisively, to the point of being despotic. However, although consulting the council was the correct procedure, Louis was not above disregarding it, as over the convocation of the Notables in 1786, and on that occasion he wasted five crucial months making the decision. Over the recall of the *parlements* in 1774 the problem was rather different: the council favoured one solution and his personal adviser, Maurepas, another.

This leads to the conclusion that, except during the heyday of Maurepas's *ministère harmonieux*, the council was itself divided and on issues relating ultimately to the reform of the regime: these divisions were too fundamental to be explained in terms of Louis's failure to hold a cabinet together. Moreover, the king did not have untrammelled control over the composition of ministries: ministers often represented pressure groups which could not be disregarded, and ministries were in a sense coalitions. The *reculades* – the precipitate withdrawal of measures introduced with all solemnity – with which Louis was taxed were one natural consequence; the interests which had been ignored regrouped. The surprising thing about a measure such as d'Ormesson's abolition of tax-farming was perhaps not that it was shot down, but that it ever got off the ground.

Soulavie, however, links Louis's indecisiveness to a lack of will-power. With privileged access to Louis's mind, he distinguishes between 'a man who *knows* and a man who *wills*. The first of these qualities is very extensive and varied. But in great matters of state, the man who wills and commands is almost never to be seen.' Of course too much information can lead to indecisiveness. But Louis was also paralysed by a fatalism tinged with a voluptuous morbidity, an *amor fati*. This is linked to Soulavie's second insight: 'he was endowed with a spirit of foresight' and 'alone beheld from a distance the destiny and ruin of France' so that he became 'the Cassandra of the nation.' No one foresaw the consequences of war better or even as well as Louis expressed them in his letter to his brothers explaining why he had accepted the constitution, despite all the imperfections he highlighted. War, he warned, would bring the proscription of the 'aristocrats' – a word which, ironically, he had been the first to use in its pejorative sense, applying it to the *parlementaires*. The revolutionary forces would not crumble for the entire nation would arm in what would be called the *levée en masse*. Louis also predicted that love for the monarchy would return, though it could not be forced: as early as 1797 a royalist majority was returned in national elections though it was forcibly overturned by the government of the Directory. Too often, though, Louis's prophecies were of the 'I told you so' variety which compounded the problem.

As well as his reputation for indecisiveness, the other negative quality attributed to him – duplicity – also survives critical examination. One may grant that a measure of dissimulation was necessary during the Revolution – though circularizing his ambassadors to say he was delighted with the Revolution when he had already determined on flight seems an excessive smokescreen. But his conduct before the Revolution also raises questions: assuring the *parlement Maupeou* that its fears were groundless when he had already decided to abolish it springs to mind; and, more obviously, his secret help for the American colonists. This suggests that his duplicity was in some degree there from the start.

The immediate cause of the fall of the ancien régime was the deficit. For all his understanding of finance, Louis contributed to its increase by his repudiation of bankruptcy, his failure to impose departmental budgets, his promotion of naval rearmament and his decision to enter the War of American Independence. His repudiation of bankruptcy and the associated increase in the use of loans also implied a greater participation of the governed, or at least of the subscribers, in the process of government. From an absolutist standpoint he should be criticized for this. The failure to impose a budget was an unqualified one, for the regime could possibly have absorbed the cost of the war if Castries had not been so profligate. Calonne certainly thought so. It seems, with the benefit of hindsight, that America would have achieved her independence even without French help. Even so, whether France would then have acquired the same diplomatic prestige is another matter.

In his memoirs, Talleyrand referred scathingly to 'ce *fameux* déficit', by which he implied that the deficit was not the cause of the Revolution. Certainly it often disappeared from view during that event, and cynics suggested that the Assembly refused to tackle it so that it could keep the king in tutelage. Moreover, the deficit was endemic under the ancien régime and at certain times had been much greater, notably after Louis XIV's wars. The very fact, however, that it was endemic suggested that it represented something deeper than bad accountancy that the king should have corrected. It stemmed from the lack of consent to taxation, which Louis implicitly recognized by his turning to provincial assemblies, the Assembly of Notables and finally the Estates-General. Louis grasped this nettle rather than resorting to the 'cop-out' of abandoning a foreign policy (as Louis XV had done at the end of his reign) or doing a deal *in extremis* with the *parlements*.

In attempting to tackle the deficit, Louis discovered, during the Assembly of Notables, that the ideological basis for the absolute monarchy no longer existed. Calonne's measures were rejected out of hand precisely because they would have rejuvenated the system: the land tax was important not so much for the money it would have raised, not even as the collateral for a big loan, but as symbolizing that the regime had not lost the initiative. It is not easy to say why precisely support for the old monarchy had drained away. Perhaps it had been undermined alike by Maupeou's coup and by its reversal; perhaps by *parlementaire* remonstrances which may have had more immediate practical impact than the *philosophes*. What can be said with precision is that before 1787 the rot had reached the king's immediate agents of execution, the ministers, few of whom believed in the system. This could be simply explained by the failure of intendants to reach ministerial rank, so that they were outnumbered by military aristocrats who favoured a devolution of power to the aristocracy as their price for paying taxes. It is noteworthy, however, that the intendants, attacked in the Assembly of Notables, did not have the will to defend themselves, even though Louis thought they were 'the best part of my system'.

To a large extent, then, an assessment of Louis depends on the intractable question of whether the collapse of the ancien régime was inevitable. The same consideration applies to the outbreak and course of the Revolution. We have suggested that the principal ingredient in its outbreak in 1789 was Louis's perceived volte-face in dealing with the third estate: this injected a poison into the body politic to which even the death of the king did not provide an antidote. It created the climate of distrust from which Louis never recovered. The image of 'Le Roi parjure, le Roi Janus' was established. What his precise motives were in 1789 we have not fully succeeded in establishing – he seems to have suffered from confusion of aims himself: certainly he did not analyse the situation in 1789 with the same clarity as in 1791.

The struggle in 1789 was not primarily about the extent of his prerogative power, for in the Résultat he had already conceded 'more than the Estates-General on bended knees would have dared to ask' and was to concede even more in the séance royale of 23 June. The struggle was, however, about his right to make this renunciation voluntarily or at least in free discussion with the estates. This was the principle on which his brother Provence, restored as Louis XVIII in 1814, issued his charter. This free renunciation was also at the heart of his defence of the nobility – without which his sacrifice of power may not have been necessary. He seems to have believed that only free renunciation would be fair and only free renunciation would be lasting. For as Calonne predicted, nothing could be worse for France than a revolution followed by counter-revolution. Although Louis had pursued divisive policies in 1787–88, symbolized by the Avertissement, thereafter he sought to prevent divisions, between orders and classes, émigrés and restants, jurors and non-jurors, and finally over his own fate – the appel au peuple – because it would have imposed a further division.

The failure of such an approach in a revolutionary situation was perhaps inevitable. It is symbolized by the title of a study of Malouet, Le Centre perdu.[42] Before the fall of the monarchy, there were three attempts to 'stop the Revolution': that by the monarchiens in August–September 1789, that by the Feuillants in 1791, with which Louis's escape from Paris coincided, and finally by the Girondins before the dix-août. They all failed, and failed easily. Then, when least expected, Robespierre and the system of Terror, whose spirit at least had been present in 1789 and had sent de Lessart before the high court in 1791, suddenly collapsed. Louis knew that one day it would, as he told his brothers; meanwhile one could not govern a country against its *esprit dominant*. He thought he could detect signs of a change in 1790, but in despair that the 'reasonable men' had lost control of the Assembly, escaped in 1791. On his return he knew he would have to wait, but the politically motivated outbreak of war denied him this chance.

Louis left a will but no political legacy. This was partly due to his uncharismatic personality, his difficulty in expressing himself – and especially his feelings – in public; in short his inability to win adherents; and it was partly due to his lack of a clearly defined position. Absolutism was to return, in brasher guise, under Napoleon and remain part of the mainstream of French politics, but the Bourbons abandoned it in 1789. During the Revolution, Louis's centrist position earned him the distrust alike of the émigrés and the politicians at home. Truly, as Lafayette said, 'he feared the winner whoever it was'. The revolutionary authorities made sure no miracles were performed at his grave. They could have spared themselves the trouble. No real cult emerged of him either as martyr or as king. In 1795 the dauphin died from the studied neglect of his jailers after the execution of Marie-Antoinette and Madame Élisabeth. Louis XVIII, who had shed few tears at his brother's execution, raised a polite *chapelle expiatoire* on the site of his burial. That is all.

The House of France

Hugh Capet
(987–96)

|

(7 generations)

Louis IX
(St Louis)
(1226–70)

(9 generations in the junior Bourbon line, none of them kings)

Henri IV
(1589–1610)

Louis XIII
(1610–43)

Louis XIV
(1643–1715)

Louis,
called Le Grand Dauphin, d. 1711

duc de Bourgogne, d. 1712

Louis XV
(1715–74)

Louis-Ferdinand,
dauphin, d. 1765

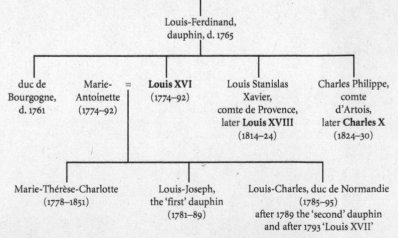

| duc de Bourgogne, d. 1761 | Marie-Antoinette (1774–92) | = | **Louis XVI** (1774–92) | Louis Stanislas Xavier, comte de Provence, later **Louis XVIII** (1814–24) | Charles Philippe, comte d'Artois, later **Charles X** (1824–30) |

Marie-Thérèse-Charlotte
(1778–1851)

Louis-Joseph,
the 'first' dauphin
(1781–89)

Louis-Charles, duc de Normandie
(1785–95)
after 1789 the 'second' dauphin
and after 1793 'Louis XVII'

The direct descent of Louis XVI from Charles I of England

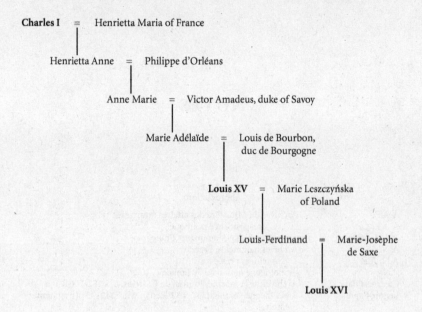

Charles I = Henrietta Maria of France

Henrietta Anne = Philippe d'Orléans

Anne Marie = Victor Amadeus, duke of Savoy

Marie Adélaïde = Louis de Bourbon, duc de Bourgogne

Louis XV = Marie Leszczyńska of Poland

Louis-Ferdinand = Marie-Josèphe de Saxe

Louis XVI

NOTES

Abbreviations

A.A.E.	Archives du Ministère des affaires étrangères
A.A.E. CP	Correspondance politique
A.A.E. MDF	Mémoires et documents France
A.N.	Archives nationales, France
A.N. A.P.	Archives privées
B.N.	Bibliothèque nationale de France
Castries Diary	Archives de la Marine, Journal de Castries, MS 182/7964, 1–2
Lenoir Papers	Bibliothèque municipale d'Orléans, MS 1421–3 (fragmentary memoirs)
D'Ormesson Papers	Archives nationales 144, Archives privées 130–3
Véri Papers	Archives Départementales de La Drôme (Valence), MS Journal (unclassified)

Preface

1. J. Hardman and M. Price, eds, *Louis XVI and the comte de Vergennes: Correspondence, 1774–1787*, Oxford, 1998 (henceforth cited as *Louis XVI–Vergennes Correspondence*).
2. J.-L. Soulavie, *Mémoires historiques et politiques du règne de Louis XVI*, Paris, 1801, 6 vols; Louis XVI, *Louis XVI, Marie-Antoinette et Mme Élisabeth, lettres et documents inédits*, ed. F. Feuillet de Conches, 1864–69, 6 vols.
3. M. Price, *The Fall of the French Monarchy: Louis XVI, Marie-Antoinette and the baron de Breteuil*, London, 2002; A. Caiani, *Louis XVI and the French Revolution 1789–1792*, Cambridge, 2012; B. Shapiro, *Traumatic Politics: The Deputies and the King in the Early French Revolution*, University Park, PA, 2009; J.-C. Petitfils, *Louis XVI*, Paris, 2005; J. Hardman, *Overture to Revolution: The 1787 Assembly of Notables and the Crisis of France's Old Regime*, Oxford and New York, 2010.

Chapter 1: A Dark and Difficult Childhood

1. Miromesnil to Louis XVI, A.N. K163 no. 8.20.
2. Louis-Ferdinand, dauphin, *Choix de lettres addressées à M. de Nicolaï, évêque de Nancy par le Dauphin . . . (1750–1767)*, ed. A. de Boislisle, Nogent-le-Rotrou, 1875, 16.
3. Petitfils, *Louis XVI*, 25.
4. Cited in J. Félix, *Louis XVI et Marie-Antoinette*, Paris, 2006, 25.
5. A.N. K144.17.

6. Sorel, A., *Europe and the French Revolution: The Political Traditions of the Old Regime*, trans. and ed. A. Cobban and J. W. Hunt, London, 1969, 244.

7. L. Dussieux, *Le Château de Versailles*, Versailles, 1881, I, 457–8.

8. Soulavie, *Mémoires historiques et politiques*, II, xxix and 41.

9. Abbé Proyart, *Vie du dauphin*, Paris, 1872, 171.

10. P. Girault de Coursac, *L'Éducation d'un roi, Louis XVI*, Paris, 1972, 66.

11. 'Reconnaissance des environs de Versailles faite par Monseigneur le Dauphin en 1769', B.N. Rés. Geo. C4349.

12. Louis XVI to Vergennes, 13 January 1775, in *Louis XVI–Vergennes Correspondence*, 179, where he talks of 'the value of money at that time [1559]'.

13. See the king's annotation of a memorandum of Loménie de Brienne, pointing out that government cannot dictate the rate of interest it pays on loans unless it doesn't need the money: comte de and Loménie de Brienne, *Journal de l'Assemblée des Notables de 1787*, ed. P. Chevallier, Paris, 1960, 79–83.

14. Louis XVI, *Réflexions sur mes entretiens avec M. le duc de la Vauguyon*, ed. E. Falloux, Paris, 1851.

15. F. Furet, *The French Revolution, 1770–1814*, trans. A. Neville, Oxford, 1996, 28.

16. Cited in S. Padover, *The Life and Death of Louis XVI*, London, 1965, 16.

17. P. Burley, 'Louis XVI and a New Monarchy', unpublished PhD thesis, London University, 1981, 92; J.-N. Moreau, *Les Devoirs du prince*, 1773.

18. D. Van Kley, *The Religious Origins of the French Revolution . . . 1560–1791*, New Haven and London, 1996, 282–4.

19. Quoted in R. Lacour-Gayet, *Calonne*, Paris, 1963, 23.

20. Moreau, *Devoirs*, 192.

21. Moreau, *Devoirs*, 179 and 181.

22. Petitfils, *Louis XVI*, 51.

23. Padover, *Louis XVI*, 23.

24. H. Walpole, *Règne de Richard III, ou doutes historiques sur les crimes qui lui sont imputés*, trans. Louis XVI, ed. Roussel l'Épinal, Paris, 1800.

25. Girault de Coursac, *L'Éducation d'un roi*, 194; C. Duckworth, 'Louis XVI and English History: A French Reaction to Walpole, Hume and Gibbon on Richard III', *Studies on Voltaire* 176 (1979), 385–401, at 393.

26. G. Lamblin, 'Louis XVI angliciste', *Études anglaises* 22 (1969), 131.

27. Padover, *Louis XVI*, 25.

28. *Louis XVI–Vergennes Correspondence*, 90.

29. *Louis XVI–Vergennes Correspondence*, 89.

30. Proyart, *Vie du dauphin*, 171.

31. Girault de Coursac, *L'Éducation d'un roi*, 73.

32. Cited in Padover, *Louis XVI*, 18.

33. Girault de Coursac, *L'Éducation d'un roi*, 88.

34. Petitfils, *Louis XVI*.

35. Quoted in Girault de Coursac, *L'Éducation d'un roi*, 98.

36. Louis XVI, *Réflexions*, 49, 10th Reflection.

37. I omit the *Réflexions*, which are paraphrases, and the Richard III book, which is a translation.

38. Louis XVI, *Journal*, ed. L. Nicolardot, Paris, 1873; *Louis XVI–Vergennes Correspondence*.

39. L. Trotsky, *The History of the Russian Revolution*, trans. M. Eastman, London, 1967, I, 101.

40. Abbé Proyart, *Oeuvres complètes*, Paris, 1819, II, 137.

41. Girault de Coursac, *L'Éducation d'un roi*, 263–5.

42. M. Antoine, *Louis XV*, Paris, 1989, 923–4.

43. Louis-Auguste, dauphin, *Description de la forêt de Compiègne, comme elle étoit en 1765, avec le guide de la forêt*, Paris, 1766.

44. Padover, *Louis XVI*, 17.

45. Soulavie, *Mémoires historiques et politiques*, II, 40–1.

46. Soulavie, *Mémoires historiques et politiques*, II, 26.

47. Abbé de Véri, *Journal, 1774–1780*, ed. J. de Witte, Paris, 1928–30, I, 221.
48. Cited in Félix, *Louis XVI et Marie-Antoinette*, 124.
49. Castries Diary, Journal de Castries, Archives de la Marine, MS 182/7964, 1–2, I, f. 110.
50. *Louis XVI–Vergennes Correspondence*, 388, letter of 26 September 1786.
51. Petitfils, *Louis XVI*, 52–3.
52. *Lettres de Louis XV à son petit-fils*, ed. P. Amiguet, Paris, 1938, 156–7.
53. Duc de Croÿ, *Journal, 1718–84*, ed. vicomte de Grouchy and P. Cottin, Paris, 1906–07, III, 135, 134.
54. D. Echeverria, *The Maupeou Revolution*, Baton Rouge, LA, 1985.
55. Lenoir Papers, Bibliothèque municipale d'Orléans, MS 1421–3, mélanges, 43.
56. A. de Tocqueville, *The Ancien Régime and the French Revolution*, ed. H. Brogan, London, 1966, 207.
57. Letter of 24 June 1772, published in Malesherbes, *Nouveaux documents inédits*, ed. P. Grosclaude, Paris, 1964.
58. J.M. Augeard, *Mémoires secrets*, ed. E. Bavoux, 1866, 39.
59. Quoted in W. Doyle, 'The Parlements of France and the Breakdown of the Old Régime, 1771–1788', *French Historical Studies* VI (1970), 415–58, 163.
60. See for example L. Laugier, *Un ministère réformateur sous Louis XV: Le Triumvirat (1770–1774)*, Paris, 1975.
61. Lenoir Papers, MS 1423, mélanges, 28.
62. Letter of 22 September 1784.
63. P. and P. Girault de Coursac, *Louis XVI et Marie-Antoinette: Vie conjugale, vie politique*, Paris, 1990, 20.
64. Girault de Coursac, *L'Éducation d'un roi*, 285.
65. Cited in Petitfils, *Louis XVI*, 61.
66. Girault de Coursac, *Louis XVI et Marie-Antoinette*, 24–5.
67. Joseph II to Marie-Antoinette, 29 May 1777, A. von Arneth, ed., *Marie-Antoinette, Joseph II und Leopold II: Ihr Briefwechsel*, Vienna, 1866, 6.
68. Quoted by D. Beales, *Joseph II*, I, Cambridge, 1987.
69. A.N. K163 no. 5, 12.3.
70. Cited in Antoine, *Louis XV*, 990.
71. Cited in Antoine, *Louis XV*, 991–2.
72. Louis-Auguste to Terray, 10 May 1774, in *Louis XVI, Marie-Antoinette et Mme Élisabeth*, I, 28–9.
73. Antoine, *Louis XV*, 987.
74. Cited in Félix, *Louis XVI et Marie-Antoinette*, 99.
75. Louis XVI to La Vrillière 13 May 1774, published in *Louis XVI, Marie-Antoinette et Mme Élisabeth*, I, 33–4.
76. Barnave, *Introduction à la Révolution française*, ed. G. Rudé, 1960, 53.
77. 'Le Temps refusé' is the title of the last section of Antoine's great biography of Louis XV.

Chapter 2: Youth on the Throne

1. Croÿ, *Journal*, III, 115.
2. Louis XVI to Vergennes, 6 December 1774, *Louis XVI–Vergennes Correspondence*, 170.
3. The king to La Vrillière, 11 May 1774, *Louis XVI, Marie-Antoinette et Mme Élisabeth*, I, 32–3.
4. Véri, *Journal*, I, 93.
5. Louis XV to his daughter, the duchess of Parma, cited in Antoine, *Louis XV*, 723.
6. E. Faure, *La Disgrâce de Turgot*, Paris, 1964, 18.
7. From Lefèvre d'Amécourt's unpublished 'Ministres de Louis XVI', D'Amécourt Papers, B.N. nouv. acq. fr. 22111 f. 1.
8. D'Angiviller, *Mémoires*, Copenhagen, 1933, 64.
9. Paris, B.N. MS Fr. 6572, f. 55; cited in J. Flammermont, *Le Chancelier Maupeou et les parlements*, Paris, 1883, 554.

10. Véri, *Journal*, I, 93–8.

11. The *dépêches* which gave the council its name were the despatches sent in from provincial officials, intendants, governors, etc. Most of the council meetings consisted of the reading of these despatches, so they could be tedious. Similarly, the meetings of the foreign affairs council, the *Conseil d'État*, consisted mainly in the reading of ambassadors' despatches.

12. Véri, *Journal*, I, 99.

13. Lenoir Papers, MS 1421, Section 2, Réligion.

14. J. Rogister, *Louis XV and the Parlement of Paris, 1737–1755*, Cambridge, 1995, 30–1 and 64.

15. Véri, *Journal*, I, 70–82.

16. Véri Papers, MS Journal, cahiers 157 and 109.

17. Lenoir Papers, MS 1421, Section 2, Réligion.

18. Véri, *Journal*, I, 99.

19. Girault de Coursac, *Louis XVI et Marie-Antoinette*, 530.

20. Initially, Vergennes restrained Gustavus, who was urged on by d'Aiguillon, but once Gustavus had decided on the coup, Vergennes told him there could be no half-measures: J.F. Labourdette, *Vergennes: ministre principal de Louis XVI*, Paris, 1990, 69.

21. Véri, *Journal*, I, 188.

22. Véri, *Journal*, I, 111.

23. Véri, *Journal*, I, 188.

24. Véri, *Journal*, I, 160

25. Véri, *Journal*, I, 115

26. In his declaration of 20 June 1791.

27. Cited in Padover, *Louis XVI*, 58.

28. The best example is Necker's letter to the king at Marly on 20 June 1789, A.N. K163, dossier 13 no. 1.

29. Croÿ, *Journal*, III, 144.

30. M. Antoine, 'Les comités des ministres sous Louis XV', *Revue Historique de Droit* (1951), 228.

31. Véri, *Journal*, I, 188.

32. Véri, *Journal*, I, 160

33. Véri, *Journal*, I, 134.

34. Véri, *Journal*, I, 151.

35. The *travail* (work) was the weekly session in which a minister presented the king with papers to sign or matters to be discussed.

36. Véri, *Journal*, I, 185.

37. K.M. Baker, 'Politics and Public Opinion', in *Press and Politics in Pre-Revolutionary France*, ed. J.R. Censer and J.D. Popkin, Berkeley, CA, 1987, 246.

38. *Journal historique*, 8 November 1774, quoted in Echeverria, *Maupeou Revolution*, 32.

39. A.N. 0354 no. 202, letter from the minister for the *Maison* to the keeper of the seals, 17 October, returning Maupeou's letter.

40. Véri, *Journal*, I, 183.

41. Miromesnil, *Correspondance politique*, ed. P. Le Verdier, Paris, 1899–, I, 171.

42. Joly de Fleury, 1781–83, and Necker, 1788–89.

43. Véri, *Journal*, I, 160.

44. *Annales historiques de la Révolution française* (1931), 198–201.

45. The king to La Vrillière, 25 August 1774, published in *Louis XVI, Marie-Antoinette et Mme Élisabeth*, I, 50.

46. Soulavie, *Mémoires historiques et politiques*, II, 195–6, cited in M. Price, *Preserving the Monarchy: The Comte de Vergennes, 1774–1787*, Cambridge, 1995, 18.

47. A.A.E., Mémoires et documents France (MDF) 1375 and 1628; there is also a plan in the A.N., K695 no. 24.

48. Véri, *Journal*, I, 202.

49. Véri, *Journal*, I, 204–5.

50. Soulavie, *Mémoires historiques et politiques*, II, 56.

51. Soulavie, *Mémoires historiques et politiques*, II, 209
52. Soulavie, *Mémoires historiques et politiques*, II, 195.
53. Antoine, *Louis XV*, 929.
54. A.J.R. Turgot, *Oeuvres*, ed. G. Schelle, Paris, 1913–23, IV, 81.
55. J. Swann, *Politics and the Parlement of Paris under Louis XV, 1754–1774*, Cambridge, 1995, 352–68.
56. Swann, *Politics*, 368.
57. Soulavie, *Mémoires historiques et politiques*, II, 208.
58. J.N. Billaud de Varennes, *Despotisme des ministres de France*, Amsterdam, 1789, 205–9.
59. Véri, *Journal*, I, 162.
60. K.M. Baker, *Inventing the French Revolution: Essays in Political Culture in the Eighteenth Century*, Cambridge, 1990, 112.
61. P.-A.C. de Beaumarchais, *Correspondance*, ed. B.N. Morton and D.C. Spinelli, Paris, 1969–78, III, 82.

Chapter 3: The Bright Beginning

1. Mercy-Argenteau, *Correspondance secrète du comte de Mercy-Argenteau avec l'empereur Joseph II et le prince de Kaunitz*, ed. A. d'Arneth and J. Flammermont, Paris, 1891, II, 195.
2. Véri, *Journal*, I, 445
3. Maurepas in conversation with Véri, 7 September 1775, Véri, *Journal*, I, 338.
4. Louis-Philippe, *Memoirs*, ed. and trans. J. Hardman, New York, 1977, 17.
5. Cited in Petitfils, *Louis XVI*, 242.
6. Duc de Lévis, *Souvenirs et portraits, 1780–1789*, Paris, 1815, 17.
7. To be presented at court you needed nobility going back to 1400, or to be the relative of a minister.
8. Véri, *Journal*, II, 7.
9. P. Mansel, *The Court of France, 1789–1830*, Cambridge, 1988, 3–4.
10. Croÿ, *Journal*, IV, 40.
11. Croÿ, *Journal*, IV, 214.
12. Petitfils, *Louis XVI*, 246.
13. Quoted in E. Lever, *Louis XVI*, Paris, 1985, 255.
14. Quoted in comte de Luçay, *Les Secrétaires d'État en France depuis les origines jusqu'à 1774*, Paris, 1881, 265.
15. Véri, *Journal*, II, 395.
16. Marie-Antoinette, *Correspondance secrète entre Marie-Thérèse et le comte de Mercy-Argenteau*, ed. A. d'Arneth and M.A. Geffroy, 2nd edn, Paris, 1875, II, 356.
17. Baron de Besenval, *Mémoires*, ed. S.A. Berville and J.F. Barrière, Paris, 1821, I, 324.
18. Mercy Argenteau, *Correspondance secrète*, II, 454.
19. Véri, *Journal*, I, 388.
20. Marie-Antoinette, *Correspondance secrète*, II, 356–7.
21. Besenval, *Mémoires*, I, 329–30.
22. Marie-Antoinette, *Correspondance secrète*, II, Marie-Antoinette to Maria-Theresa, 22 June 1775.
23. Marie-Antoinette, *Correspondance secrète*, II, 13 July 1775, 362.
24. Véri, *Journal*, I, 299.
25. Véri, *Journal*, I, 314.
26. The *Cour des Aides* dealt with litigation arising from taxes on alcoholic drink.
27. Véri, *Journal*, I, 128.
28. Véri, *Journal*, I, 318.
29. F. Hue, *Dernières années du règne de Louis XVI*, 3rd edn, Paris, 1860, 442.
30. Letter of 2 June 1776, published in P. Grosclaude, *Malesherbes: Témoin et interprète de son temps*, Paris, 1961, 134. Half the French provinces (mostly on the periphery) had retained their ancient estates, which gave them a measure of control over the levelling

and collection of local taxation, whereas the central provinces, known as the *pays d'élection*, lacked these institutions and their taxation was imposed centrally and administered by the intendant.

31. Marie-Antoinette, *Correspondance secrète*, II, 367.
32. D.L. Wick, 'The Court Nobility and the French Revolution: The Example of the Society of Thirty', *Eighteenth-Century Studies* XIII (1980), 263–84, 272.
33. Mme de Polignac had a place as *dame d'honneur* to the comtesse d'Artois, her husband the survivance as *premier écuyer* to the queen.
34. D'Ormesson Papers, Journal, A.N. 144 A.P. 130.84–6.
35. Marie-Antoinette, *Correspondance secrète*, II, 437.
36. Marie-Antoinette, *Correspondance secrète*, II, 466.
37. In 1780, when they backed Necker's candidates for the marine (Castries), and war (Ségur); they probably hoped thereby to increase their influence on military promotions.
38. Marie-Antoinette to Joseph II, 22 September 1784, in Marie-Antoinette, *Correspondance secrète*, III, 40. By this date the queen's influence was greater than in 1775.
39. Marie-Antoinette to the comte de Rosenberg, 17 April 1776, in Marie-Antoinette, *Lettres de Marie-Antoinette*, ed. M. de la Rocheterie et le marquis de Beaucourt, Paris, 1895–96, I, 87–9.
40. Padover, *Louis XVI*, 90.
41. Véri Papers, MS Journal, cahier 112.
42. Véri, *Journal*, I, 160.
43. Véri, *Journal*, II, 147.
44. Soulavie, *Mémoires historiques et politiques*, III, 153.
45. The material on the general farm is based on Turgot, *Oeuvres*, IV, 150–8.
46. Véri, *Journal*, I, 371–3; Burley, 'Louis XVI and a New Monarchy', 456.
47. Turgot, *Oeuvres*, V, 322.
48. A.N. 144 AP133 dossier 3.2.
49. For a discussion of physiocracy and its relationship to Louis XVI's education, see above, 24–5.
50. Turgot was not so dogmatic on this last point and would have allowed representatives of trade and industry in his projected provincial assemblies.
51. Véri, *Journal*, I, 154–6; Félix, *Louis XVI et Marie-Antoinette*, 147.
52. Petitfils, *Louis XVI*, 196.
53. Véri, *Journal*, I, 290.
54. Véri, *Journal*, I, 288
55. Berthier de Sauvigny, intendant of Paris. He would be brutally slain following the fall of the Bastille.
56. The king to Turgot, 2 May 1775, published in Turgot, *Oeuvres*, IV, 415–16.
57. All the following troops formed part of the king's military household.
58. F. Métra, *Correspondance secrète ...*, London, 1787–90, I, 3 May 1775; J.-F. Georgel, *Mémoires pour servir à l'histoire des événements de la fin du XVIIIe siècle*, Paris, 1820, I, 424.
59. The king to Turgot, 4 May 1775, published in Turgot, *Oeuvres*, IV, 417.
60. His views are expounded in a letter of 5 May 1788, A.N. 0354 no. 54.
61. Véri, *Journal*, I, 192.
62. Turgot to the king, 30 April 1776, transcribed in Véri, *Journal*, I, 455.
63. Turgot to Lenoir, 7 a.m., 4 May, published in Turgot, *Oeuvres*, IV, 425–7.
64. Turgot, *Oeuvres*, IV, 431–2.
65. The *prévôté des maréchaux*, instituted by Francis I to try vagabonds and rioters.
66. The king to d'Aligre, Turgot, *Oeuvres*, IV, 420.
67. Véri, *Journal*, I, 396–7.
68. The king to Turgot, 6 p.m., 6 May, published in Turgot, *Oeuvres*, IV, 428.
69. Turgot, *Oeuvres*, IV, 429.
70. A.N. K164 no. 3, letter of 15 July 1775.
71. Véri, *Journal*, I, 291.

72. The king to Biron, November 1775, published in *Louis XVI, Marie-Antoinette et Mme Élisabeth*, I, 74–5.
73. Turgot to Necker, 23 April 1775 and Necker to Turgot, 24 April, published in Turgot, *Oeuvres*, IV, 412–13.
74. Louis XVI to Turgot, Rheims, 10 June 1775, published in Turgot, *Oeuvres*, IV, 554.
75. The king to La Vrillière, 31 May 1775, published in *Louis XVI, Marie-Antoinette et Mme Élisabeth*, I, 69–70.
76. Véri, *Journal*, I, 175.
77. From a letter to the king of 5 August 1786, A.N. K163 no. 8.14.
78. Véri, *Journal*, I, 420.
79. They are published in Turgot, *Oeuvres*, V, 163–200.
80. Turgot, *Oeuvres*, V, 5.
81. Véri, *Journal*, I, 451 and 459.
82. Véri Papers, MS Journal, cahier 109.
83. Véri, *Journal*, I, 395–7.
84. Marie-Antoinette had been incensed because Turgot had demanded that the queen's protégé, the comte de Guînes, be recalled as ambassador to London. Turgot objected to de Guines telling the Spanish ambassador that France would not support Spain in her quarrel with Portugal over the boundary between their respective South American possessions if England did not support her Portuguese ally.
85. P. Grosclaude, *Malesherbes*, Paris, 1961, 117–18.
86. Véri, *Journal*, I, 447–8.
87. Véri, *Journal*, I, 460.
88. Turgot, *Oeuvres*, V, 2; Véri, *Journal*, I, 454.
89. Véri, *Journal*, I, 319.
90. Turgot to Véri, 10 May 1776, in Véri, *Journal*, I, 430.
91. Turgot to Véri, 14 May 1776, in Véri, *Journal*, I, 431.
92. Turgot to the king, 30 April 1776, transcribed in Véri, *Journal*, I, 457.
93. Véri, *Journal*, I, 430.

Chapter 4: Drift Towards War

1. The *chambre des comptes* of Dijon.
2. Castries Diary, Journal, MS 182/7964, 1–2, I, f. 218.
3. Louis XV, *Correspondance secrète inédite*, ed. M.E. Boutaric, 1866, 2 vols, II, 424.
4. Jeudy to Vergennes, 13 June 1782, A.A.E. MDF 1392 ff. 126–7, cited in Labourdette, *Vergennes*, 196.
5. D'Ormesson Papers, Journal, section 82, A.N. 144 A.P. 130; L. Petit de Bachaumont, *Mémoires secrètes pour servir à l'histoire de la République des Lettres*, London, 1777–89, XXXIV, 309.
6. Véri, *Journal*, I, 354.
7. Guines had assured England, on his own initiative, that if she refrained from assisting her ally Portugal in her dispute with Spain over the boundaries of Brazil, France would not help Spain.
8. A.N. K164 no. 3, 1776, no. 5, 23 February.
9. A.N. K164 no. 5, 1785, 6 February.
10. The best account of the relationship between Louis XIII and Richelieu is in O. Ranum, *Richelieu and the Councillors of Louis XIII*, Oxford, 1963.
11. Louis XVI to Vergennes, 27 May 1776, in *Louis XVI–Vergennes Correspondence*, 228.
12. *Louis XVI–Vergennes Correspondence*, 348.
13. *Louis XVI–Vergennes Correpondence*, 353–4.
14. D'Ormesson Papers, Journal, A.N. 144 A.P. 130.
15. Labourdette, *Vergennes*, 196–7.
16. Castries Diary, Journal, II, 242.
17. D'Ormesson Papers, Journal, A.N. 144 A.P. 130.

18. In the Diamond Necklace Affair, see below, 344.
19. See, for example, his compliment to Necker on 247.
20. Broglie to the king, 14 June 1774, in Louis XV, *Correspondance secrète inédite*, II, 404.
21. Louis XV, *Correspondance secrète inédite*, II, 475, memorandum of 1 March 1775.
22. Louis XVI to Vergennes, 4 February 1778, *Louis XVI–Vergennes Correspondence*, 256. Louis XV, *Correspondance secrète inédite*, II, 428.
23. A.N. K164 no. 3, 1776, no. 5.
24. Louis XV, *Correspondance secrète inédite*, II, 428.
25. Louis XV, *Correspondance secrète inédite*, II, Broglie to the king, 14 June 1774.
26. J.-N. Moreau, *Mes souvenirs*, ed. C. Hermelin, Paris, 1898–1901, I, 321.
27. *Louis XVI–Vergennes Correspondence*, 190–1.
28. Louis XVI to Vergennes, 11 April 1775, *Louis XVI–Vergennes Correspondence*, 190.
29. Proyart, *Oeuvres complètes*, II, 160.
30. Louis XVI to Vergennes, 6 December 1774, *Louis XVI–Vergennes Correspondence*, 171–2.
31. A.N. K164 no. 19, 1775.
32. Louis XVI to Vergennes, 11 April 1775, *Louis XVI–Vergennes Correspondence*, 190.
33. A.F. Bertrand de Molleville, *Mémoires secrets pour servir à l'histoire de la dernière année du règne de Louis XVI, roi de France*, London, 1797, I, 232–3.
34. Vergennes to Ossun, French ambassador to Spain, cited in Labourdette, *Vergennes*, 94.
35. *Louis XVI–Vergennes Correspondence*, 81.
36. J. Dull, *The French Navy and Independence: A Study of Arms and Diplomacy, 1774–1787*, Princeton, NJ, 1975, 36, n. 2.
37. *Louis XVI–Vergennes Correspondence*, 227.
38. Quoted in Padover, *Louis XVI*, 108.
39. Beaumarchais, *Correspondance*, II, 48–58.
40. Beaumarchais, *Correspondnce*, II, 134–5.
41. The king to Vergennes, 25 November 1775, *Louis XVI–Vergennes Correspondence*, 214.
42. Beaumarchais, *Correspondance*, II, 155–7.
43. Louis XVI to Vergennes, 15 October 1775, *Louis XVI–Vergennes Correspondence*, 208.
44. *Louis XVI–Vergennes Correspondence*, 217.
45. Louis XVI to Vergennes, 20 November, 1775, *Louis XVI–Vergennes Correspondence*, 213.
46. Louis XVI to Vergennes, *Louis XVI–Vergennes Correspondence*, 214.
47. J.-L. Soulavie, *Historical and Political Memoirs of the Reign of Lewis XVI from his Marriage to his Death*, London, 1802, III, 413.
48. Soulavie, *Historical and Political Memoirs*, III, 349–50.
49. Véri, *Journal*, II, 42.
50. *Louis XVI–Vergennes Correspondence*, 239.
51. L. de Loménie, *Beaumarchais et son temps*, Paris, 1856, II, 110–11.
52. Quoted in Padover, *Louis XVI*, 109.
53. Louis XVI to Vergennes, 30 August 1775, *Louis XVI–Vergennes Correspondence*, 206. Véri, *Journal*, I, 444 for Turgot's dissent.
54. Sartine to d'Orvilliers, 27 April 1776, cited in R. Lacour-Gayet (père), *La Marine militaire de la France sous le règne de Louis XVI*, Paris, 1905, 82; see also Dull, *French Navy*, 44–56.
55. Archives de la Marine B4 126, cited in L. Laugier, *Turgot*, Paris, 1979, 196.
56. Louis's instructions, the *Mémoire du Roi*, are in Archives de la Marine B4 83, 111–14. Lacour-Gayet and Doniol assume that Louis merely transcribed these instructions, but I have argued that there is every reason to believe that the king wrote them himself: see *Louis XVI–Vergennes Correspondence*, 70–1.
57. A.A.E. CP Angleterre 521 f. 53.
58. A.A.E. MDF 556 f. 257, cited in Laugier, *Turgot*, 199.
59. *Louis XVI–Vergennes Correspondence*, 236–7.

60. H. Scott, *British Foreign Policy in the Age of the American Revolution*, London, 1990, 250–1.
61. Dull, *French Navy*, 86.
62. Vergennes to Louis XVI, *c.* 3 January 1780, *Louis XVI–Vergennes Correspondence*, 281–2.
63. A.A.E. CP Angleterre 526 f. 49.
64. E.S. Corwin, 'The French Objective in the American Revolution', *American Historical Review* 21 (1915/16), 35.
65. *Louis XVI–Vergennes Correspondence*, 252–3; H. Doniol, *Histoire de la participation de la France à l'établissement des États-Unis d'Amérique*, Paris, 1886–89, II, 51.
66. A.A.E. CP Espagne 587, ff. 315–17.
67. Corwin, 'French Objective', 37.
68. A.A.E. CP 588 f. 17.
69. A.A.E. CP Angleterre 528 no. 2 bis.
70. Véri, *Journal*, II, 82.
71. A.N. K164 no. 2, 1778.
72. A.A.E. CP Angleterre 528 f. 83.
73. A.A.E. CP Espagne 588 no. 11.
74. Corwin, 'French Objective', 37, n.16
75. *Louis XVI–Vergennes Correspondence*, 258.
76. Dull, *French Navy*, 92.
77. R. Hudson, *The Minister from France: Conrad-Alexandre Gérard, 1729–1790*, Euclid, OH, 1994, 78.
78. Vergennes to Montmorin, 3 April 1778, A.A.E. CP Espagne 589 f. 4. Louis's commentary is written at the foot of the copy he made of Charles III's letter, A.N. K164 no. 3, 1778; the king endorses his copy 'À.M. de Vergennes'.
79. Padover, *Louis XVI*, 112.
80. Croÿ, *Journal*, IV, 78–9.
81. P. and P. Girault de Coursac, *Guerre d'Amérique et liberté des mers 1778–83*, Paris, 1991, 190.
82. Girault de Coursac, *Guerre d'Amérique*, 185.
83. Véri, *Journal*, II, 94.
84. A.A.E. CP Espagne 589 f. 124.
85. A.N. K164 no. 3, 1778, no. 7, letter of 22 July.
86. Véri, *Journal*, II, 95.
87. Véri, *Journal*, II, 94 and 97.
88. A.N. K164 no. 3, 1778, no. 7, 22 July.
89. Petitfils, *Louis XVI*, 395.
90. Marie-Antoinette to Maria-Theresa, 12 June 1778, in Marie-Antoinette, *Correspondance secrète*, III, 213.
91. Mercy to Maria-Theresa, 18 February 1778, in Marie-Antoinette, *Correspondance secrète*, III, 168–9.

Chapter 5: American Liberty and Royal Debt

1. Doniol, *Histoire*, III, 238.
2. Doniol, *Histoire*, II, 337.
3. Vergennes to Conrad Gérard, 29 October 1778, A.A.E. CP États-Unis 5 f. 43.
4. *Louis XVI–Vergennes Correspondence*, 269.
5. CP Espagne 582, f. 21 and 587, f. 125.
6. A.A.E. CP Espagne 592, f. 309.
7. Vergennes to Louis XVI, 5 December 1778.
8. R. Morris, *The Peacemakers: The Great Powers and American Independence*, New York, 1965, 45–6.
9. Montmorin to Vergennes, 10 April 1778, A.A.E. CP Espagne 588 no. 157.

10. Morris, *Peacemakers*, 445–7.
11. A.T. Patterson, *The Other Armada: The Franco-Spanish Attempt to Invade Britain in 1779*, Manchester, 1960, 37–9.
12. See especially J. Bosher, *French Public Finances 1770–95*, Cambridge, 1970; and R.D. Harris, *Necker: Reform Statesman of the Ancien Régime*, Berkeley, CA, 1979.
13. Price, *Preserving the Monarchy*, 50.
14. Soulavie, *Mémoires historiques et politiques*, IV, 153.
15. Soulavie, *Mémoires historiques et politiques*, IV, 149–59.
16. A.N. K163 no. 13.8, unsigned and undated but Necker to Maurepas, August or September 1776.
17. *Louis XVI–Vergennes Correspondence*, 50–1.
18. D'Amécourt Papers, Journal, B.N. nouv. acq. fr. 22110 f. 34.
19. A.N. K163 no. 13.8, unsigned and undated but Necker to Maurepas, August or September 1776.
20. In the 'Résultat du conseil', December 1788, A.P. I, 496–8.
21. Montmorin to Vergennes, 30 October 1780, A.A.E. CP Espagne 601 f. 97, Doniol, *Histoire*, IV, 515.
22. Véri, *Journal*, II, 345.
23. Vergennes to Louis XVI, 27 September 1780, *Louis XVI–Vergennes Correspondence*, 291–2.
24. Véri, *Journal*, II, 388.
25. Véri, *Journal*, II, 354.
26. A.A.E. CP Espagne 601, f. 17.
27. Vergennes to Louis XVI, *Louis XVI–Vergennes Correspondence*, 291–2.
28. George III, *The Correspondence of King George III from 1760 to December 1783*, ed. Sir John Fortescue, London 1927–28, II, no. 3115.
29. George III, *Correspondence*, no. 3113, 30 July 1780.
30. Harris, *Necker*, 211, n. 13.
31. George III, *Correspondence*, II, no. 3207.
32. Castries Diary, Journal, I, ff. 87–9, 26–29 August 1781.
33. Castries Diary, Journal, I, f. 127.
34. Véri, *Journal*, II, 380.
35. A.N. K161 no. 12.
36. See Harris, *Necker*, 206–9.
37. Maurepas to the king, 8 October 1780, A.N. K163 no. 13.
38. D'Angiviller, *Mémoires*, 118.
39. Castries Diary, Journal, I, f. 42.
40. Castries Diary, Journal, I, f. 46.
41. Véri Papers, MS Journal, unclassified, cahier 100.
42. Private collection, published by P. Girault de Coursac, 'Louis XVI et Vergennes', *Revue d'Histoire Diplomatique* 3–4 (1987), 278; Véri, *Journal*, II, 392.
43. Lescure, ed., *Correspondance secrète inédite sur Louis XVI, Marie-Antoinette, la cour et la ville de 1777 à 1792*, 1866, I, 323.
44. Castries Diary, Journal, I, f. 170.
45. Véri, *Journal*, II, 394–5.
46. Véri, *Journal*, II, 388.
47. Castries Diary, Journal, I, f. 45.
48. Prince de Montbarey, *Mémoires du prince de Montbarey*, Paris, 1826–27, II, 250, 197 and 327–8 and III, 25.
49. Besenval, *Mémoires*, II, 115; Véri, *Journal*, II, 417.
50. Castries Diary, Journal, I, ff. 46–7.
51. Castries Diary, Journal, I, f. 48.
52. Castries Diary, Journal, I, ff. 46–53.
53. Published by Soulavie, *Historical and Political Memoirs*, IV, 176–7.
54. Cited in J. Egret, *Necker*, Paris, 1975, 128–9.

55. Soulavie, *Mémoires historiques et politiques*, IV, 17–18.
56. Soulavie, *Mémoires historiques et politiques*, II, 154.
57. On this see Bosher, *French Public Finances* and Harris, *Necker*.
58. Soulavie, *Historical and Political Memoirs*, IV, 252.
59. Soulavie, *Historical and Political Memoirs*, IV, 241–56.
60. Félix, *Louis XVI et Marie-Antoinette*, 258.
61. *Lettre sur l'emprunt et l'impôt*, cited in Félix, *Louis XVI et Marie-Antoinette*, 259.
62. Harris, *Necker*, 133.
63. J. Hardman, 'Ministerial Politics from the Accession of Louis XVI to the Assembly of Notables, 1774–87', unpublished DPhil thesis, Oxford University, 1972, appendix 1, 313.
64. Dupont to d'Ormesson, 13 August 1783, D'Ormesson Papers, A.N. 144 A.P. 131 dossier 4 no. 11.
65. *Louis XVI–Vergennes Correspondence*, 167, Vergennes's copy of a circular letter written by the king to all the spending departments.
66. *Lettre à d'Alembert*, anon but C.-A. de Calonne, 1787. For the attribution see H. Carré, *Quelques mots sur la presse clandestine*, Paris, 1893, 13.
67. Soulavie, *Historical and Political Memoirs*, IV, 202.
68. Véri Papers, MS Journal, cahier 130.
69. Castries Diary, Journal, I, ff. 72–5.
70. Soulavie, *Mémoires historiques et politiques*, IV, 204.
71. See e.g., Baker, 'Politics and Public Opinion', 304.
72. Published in Soulavie, *Mémoires historiques et politiques*, VI, 149–50.
73. See 'The Gazette de Leyde under Louis XVI', in J.R. Censer and J.D. Popkin, eds, *Press and Politics in Pre-Revolutionary France*, Berkeley, CA, 1987, 95–6.
74. Labourdette, *Vergennes*, 201.
75. Lévis, *Souvenirs et portraits*, 12.
76. D'Angiviller, *Mémoires*, 114.
77. A.N. K163 no. 13.12, cited in Padover, *Louis XVI*, 103, n.
78. Castries Diary, Journal, I, ff. 91–2.
79. Castries Diary, Journal, I, ff. 91–3.
80. Lenoir Papers, MS 1421–3, mélanges, 27; Véri Papers, MS Journal, cahier 102.
81. Lenoir Papers, MS 1423, mélanges, 39.
82. Louis XVI to Vergennes, 30 March 1782, *Louis XVI–Vergennes Correspondence*, 301.
83. Louis XVI to Vergennes, 28 March 1783, *Louis XVI–Vergennes Correspondence*, 320.
84. *Louis XVI–Vergennes Correspondence*, 94.
85. A.A.E. CP Espagne 607 f. 175.
86. Cited in Petitfils, *Louis XVI*, 425.
87. Petitfils, *Louis XVI*, 426.
88. Castries Diary, Journal, I, entry for 11 February 1781.
89. Castries Diary, Journal, I, 144.
90. Doniol, *Histoire*, V, 192.
91. Doniol, *Histoire*, V, 191.
92. A.A.E. CP Espagne 609, ff. 421–2.
93. Louis XVI to Vergennes, 25 December 1782, *Louis XVI–Vergennes Correspondence*, 314.
94. A.A.E. CP Espagne 609 ff. 176 and 441–2.
95. Rayneval to Vergennes, 24 January 1783, A.A.E. CP Angleterre 540, ff. 258–60.
96. Montmorin to Vergennes, 13 February 1783, AAF CP Espagne 610 f. 5.
97. Vergennes to Montmorin (draft approved by the king), 9 November 1782, A.A.E. CP Espagne 609, f. 157.
98. Vergennes to Montmorin, 6 November 1782, A.A.E. CP Espagne 609, ff. 293–5.
99. Petitfils, *Louis XVI*, 429–30.
100. Castries Diary, Journal, I, ff. 148 and 131.
101. Castries Diary, Journal I, ff. 143–4.
102. Castries Diary, Journal, I, f. 147.

103. *Louis XVI–Vergennes Correspondence*, 85.
104. Price, *Preserving the Monarchy*, 201.
105. Price, *Preserving the Monarchy*, 210; Soulavie, *Mémoires historiques et politiques*, V, 43–4.
106. Louis XVI to Vergennes, 6 November 1784, *Louis XVI–Vergennes Correspondence*, 343.
107. A.N. K164 no. 3, 1784, no. 4, 5 November (the opinions of the ministers); see also Castries Diary, Journal, II, f. 191 for his appreciation of the manoeuvre.
108. A. N. K164 no. 3, memorandum of Breteuil, 11 November 1784.
109. A.N. K164 no. 3, 1785, no. 1, 5 January 1785.
110. Louis XVI to Joseph II, 6 January 1785, *Louis XVI–Vergennes Correspondence*, 355–7.
111. *Louis XVI–Vergennes Correspondence*, 353–4.
112. Castries Diary, Journal, II, f. 258.
113. Marie-Antoinette to Vergennes, 30 January 1785, *Louis XVI–Vergennes Correspondence*, 358.
114. Price, *Preserving the Monarchy*, 196.
115. A.N. 297 A.P. 3.122.
116. Quoted in Girault de Coursac, *L'Éducation d'un roi*, 152, author's italics to indicate Louis's additions to Moreau's text.
117. *Louis XVI–Vergennes Correspondence*, 385–6.
118. On this see B. Stone, *The Genesis of the French Revolution: A Global-Historical Interpretation*, Cambridge, 1994, 111–47; also T. Skocpol, *States and Social Revolutions: A Comparative Analysis of France, Russia and China*, Cambridge, 1979, 60–4.
119. In abandoning Turkey, an ancient ally, the shame was especially great. See T. Kaiser, 'From Fiscal Crisis to Revolution: The Court and French Foreign Policy, 1787–1789', in T.E. Kaiser and D.K. Van Kley, eds, *Unleashing the Deluge: Essays on the Origins of the French Revolution*, Stanford, CA, 2011.
120. Such was the view, presented to the council, of Castries's successor La Luzerne: B.N. nouv. acq. fr. 9434 ff. 172, 213–14 and 209.

Chapter 6: The Embarrassments of Peace

1. Castries Diary, Journal, I, f. 92.
2. Castries Diary, Journal, I, ff. 91 and 96.
3. Croÿ, *Journal*, III, 239–40.
4. Joly de Fleury Papers, B.N. fonds nouv. acq. fr. 1438 ff. 217–23.
5. J. Hardman, *French Politics 1774–1789*, London, 1995, 138–9.
6. Joly de Fleury Papers, B.N. 1438 f. 32.
7. Joly de Fleury Papers, B.N. 2487 f. 139; D'Ormesson Papers, Journal, A.N. 144 A.P. 130, sections 22, 55 and 59,
8. Besenval, *Mémoires*, II, 125.
9. Véri Papers, MS Journal, cahier 114.
10. Castries Diary, Journal, I, ff. 147 and 192; Véri Papers, MS Journal (unclassified), cahier 114; Mercy-Argenteau, *Correspondance secrète*, I, 161, n. 1; Joly de Fleury Papers, 1441 f. 142.
11. Joly de Fleury Papers, 1442 f. 39.
12. Véri Papers, MS Journal, cahier 114; Castries Diary, Journal, I, ff. 181–2; Besenval, *Mémoires*, II, 145; minutes for the seventh session of the committee, A.N. 144 A.P. 131 dossier 5.
13. D'Ormesson to the king, 2 March 1783, A.N. 144 A.P. dossier 4.3; on Vergennes and de Crosne see Price, *Preserving the Monarchy*, 85; d'Amécourt also believed that 'the choice of M. d'Ormesson was made by the king alone', d'Amécourt Papers, B.N. nouv. ac. fr. 22111 'Journal du règne de Louis XVI', f. 96.
14. Véri, *Journal*, II, 157; Mercy-Argenteau, *Correspondance secrète*, I, 227.
15. Miromesnil to the king, 27 May 1785, Miromesnil Papers, A.N. K161 no. 28 bis.
16. D'Ormesson Papers, Journal, A.N. 144 A.P. 130, section 58.

17. A.N. 144 A.P. 131 dossier 4.4.
18. D'Ormesson Papers, Journal, A.N. 144 A.P. 130, sections 60–3 and 68–73; his account is challenged by G.T. Mathews, *The Royal General Farms*, New York, 1958, 260–1, which considers that d'Ormesson acted rashly but is substantiated by Véri Papers, MS Journal, cahier 118, 'M. d'Ormesson is no liar.'
19. This was a technical crisis resulting in part from a faulty ratio between what the bank paid for gold and for silver, resulting in a dearth of gold coins: piastres had to be hurriedly and expensively imported from Spain.
20. Louis XVI to Vergennes, 1 November 1783, *Louis XVI–Vergennes Correspondence*, 325.
21. *Louis XVI–Vergennes Correspondence*, 324.
22. Castries Diary, Journal, I, 20–4; d'Ormesson Papers, Journal, section 72. For the fall of d'Ormesson, see Hardman, *French Politics*, 68–73.
23. D'Ormesson Papers, Journal, 83.
24. Castries Diary, Journal, I, f. 208.
25. As a former member of the Holy Roman Empire, Alsace had a customs border with France, not Germany.
26. Vergennes to Louis XVI, 10 November and 12 December 1784, *Louis XVI–Vergennes Correspondence*, 328–30.
27. Castries Diary, Journal, I, ff. 346–7.
28. Castries Diary, Journal, I, ff. 204–5.
29. Castries Diary, Journal, I, ff. 294–5; A.A.E. MDF 1395 f. 158.
30. Louis XVI to Vergennes, 3 November 1783, *Louis XVI–Vergennes Correspondence*, 326.
31. D'Angiviller, *Mémoires*, 113.
32. Auget de Montyon, *Particularités sur les ministres des finances les plus célèbres*, Paris, 1812, 253.
33. H. Lüthy, *La Banque protestante en France*, Paris, 1959–61, II, 686–711; L. Blanc, *Histoire de la Révolution française*, 1847–63, II, 151.
34. Marie-Antoinette, *Correspondance secrète*, III, 348.
35. C.-A. de Calonne, *Réponse de M. de Calonne à l'écrit de M. Necker, publié en avril 1787*, London, 1788, 185, n.
36. Comte de Hézecques, *Page à la cour de Louis XVI, Souvenirs*, Paris, 1987, 277.
37. Marquis de Bombelles, *Journal*, ed. J. Grassion, F. Durif and J. Charon-Bordas, Geneva, 1978–98, II, 107.
38. H. Gomel, *Les causes financières de la Révolution française*, Paris, 1893, 2 vols, II, 82.
39. Pasquier, *Souvenirs du chancelier Pasquier*, ed. R. Lacour-Gayet, Paris, 1964, 30–1.
40. Cited in Félix, *Louis XVI et Marie-Antoinette*, 362.
41. A.N. 297. A.P. 3. no. 59; for Necker's account see, J. Necker, *Mémoire*, 6 March 1787, 176–81.
42. H. Glagau, *Reformversuche und Sturz des Absolutismus in Frankreich (1774–1788)*, Munich, 1908, 349.
43. Petitfils, *Louis XVI*, 460–1.
44. The story originates with Montyon, *Particularités*, 279. Lüthy, *La Banque protestante*, II, 694 gives it credence.
45. Bombelles, *Journal*, II, 133; Castries Diary, Journal, II, entry for 1 April 1786.
46. Lacour-Gayet, *Calonne*, 165.
47. Lüthy, *La Banque protestante*, II, 710–13.
48. On all of this see Bosher, *French Public Finances*, 183–96.

Chapter 7: Unravelling

1. The term was originally applied by D. Van Kley, *The Damiens Affair and the Unravelling of the Ancien Régime, 1750–1770*, Princeton, NJ, 1984.
2. Bombelles, *Journal*, I, 193–4.
3. Bombelles, *Journal*, I, 194.

4. R. Browne, 'The Diamond Necklace Affair Revisited', *Renaissance and Modern Studies* 33 (1989).

5. Hardman, *French Politics*, 209.

6. C.M. de Talleyrand, *Mémoires*, ed. duc de Broglie, Paris, 1891–92, I, 63.

7. Véri Papers, MS Journal (unclassified), cahier 140.

8. The main source I have used for Rohan's interrogation is Castries's eye-witness account: duc de Castries, *Papiers de famille*, Paris, 1978, 388ff.

9. *Louis XVI–Vergennes Correspondence*, 376.

10. Madame de Longchamp to Vergennes, 1 December 1785, A.A.E. MDF 1399 f. 308, cited in Labourdette, *Vergennes*, 295.

11. The king addressed everyone with the rank of duke and above as his cousin, though Rohan was not related.

12. Miromesnil told Véri that Castries and Vergennes supported this proposal: Véri, Ms Cahier 136.

13. Vergennes to Noailles, 10 October 1785, A.A.E. C.P. Austria, 350 f. 228, cited in Labourdette, *Vergennes*, 295–6.

14. Lenoir Papers, MS 1423, mélanges, 31–9.

15. Lenoir Papers, MS 1423, mélanges, 3–5.

16. The seven were présidents de Gilbert, Rosambo and Lamoignon, and conseillers Oursin, Pasquier, Delpeche and Barillon.

17. Lepeletier de Saint-Fargeau, Saron and Glatigny.

18. Mercy-Argenteau, *Correspondance secrète*, II, 32–6.

19. Mercy Argenteau, *Correspondance secrète*, II, 32–6.

20. A.A.E. CP Angleterre 556 ff. 282–3, cited in Labourdette, *Vergennes*, 299.

21. Report of the police inspector Quidor, 6 June 1786, A.A.E. MDF 1400 f. 226, cited in Price, *Preserving the Monarchy*, 179.

22. Louis XVI to Vergennes, 4 June 1786, *Louis XVI–Vergennes Correspondence*, 382.

23. Vergennes to Noailles, 18 October 1785, A.A.E. CP Autriche 350 f. 228, quoted in Price, *Preserving the Monarchy*, 181.

24. Labourdette, *Vergennes*, 300–1.

25. Vergennes to Adhémar, 5 June, A.A.E. CP Angleterre, 556, f. 294, quoted in Labourdette, *Vergennes*, 299–300.

26. That is the *cordon bleu*, the sash of the highest French order of chivalry, the Saint-Esprit.

27. Petitfils, *Louis XVI*, 512.

28. Castries, *Papiers de famille*, 396; B. Stone, *The Parlement of Paris 1774–1789*, Chapel Hill, NC, 1981, 74–5; Petitfils, *Louis XVI*, 510–11.

29. Bombelles, *Journal*, II, 143–4.

30. Baron de Staël-Holstein, *Correspondance diplomatique*, ed. L. Léouzon Le Duc, Paris, 1881, 29–30.

31. Castries, *Papiers de famille*, 397.

32. Castries, *Papiers de famille*, 397.

33. Browne, 'The Diamond Necklace Affair', 33–4.

34. Castries Diary, Journal, I, 309, entries for 16 and 17 December 1785.

35. J.L.H. Campan, *Mémoires sur la vie de Marie-Antoinette par Mme Campan*, Paris, 1849, 25.

36. Véri Papers, MS Journal, cahier 109; d'Aligre to Vergennes, 9 July 1782, A.A.E. MDF 1392 f. 170; Joly de Fleury Papers, B.N. 1438 ff. 204–7.

37. Véri Papers, MS Journal, cahier 109. Miromesnil was technically not chancellor but had the survivance or right to succeed the exiled Maupeou on his death.

38. Véri Papers, MS Journal, cahier 109.

39. Bombelles, *Journal*, II, 96.

40. Véri Papers, MS Journal, cahier 100.

41. Bombelles, *Journal*, II, 97.

42. D'Amécourt Papers, Journal, B.N. nouv. acq. fr. 22111, f. 74. Miromesnil to the king, 28 December 1785, A.N. K163 no. 8.7.

43. Bombelles, *Journal*, II, 102.
44. Miromesnil to the king, 6 January 1786, A.N. K163 no. 8.7.
45. Mainly to England, which paid too much for gold. The result was that England had few silver coins in circulation and France few gold ones.
46. For example Bertin told Vergennes, 'vous connoissiez sa discretion', letter of 16 July 1783, B.N. n.a.f. 6498.
47. D'Amécourt, Journal, f. 74.
48. Miromesnil's account is given in his letters to the king of 5 and 11 August 1786, A.N. K163 nos 8, 14 and 15.
49. Le Tellier, mayor of Harfleur, *Voyage de Louis XVI dans sa Province de Normandie*, Paris, 1787.
50. Le Tellier, *Voyage*, 26–8.
51. Le Tellier, *Voyage*, 45.
52. Lescure, ed., *Correspondance secrète*, II, 55.
53. Le Tellier, *Voyage*, 49–50.
54. Le Tellier, *Voyage*, 88.
55. Girault de Coursac, *Guerre d'Amérique*, 25.
56. Girault de Coursac, *Guerre d'Amérique*, 25.
57. A.N. Marine B3–76, cited in Petitfils, *Louis XVI*, 530.
58. S. Schama, *Citizens: A Chronicle of the French Revolution*, London, 1989, 59.

Chapter 8: Royal Revolution

1. Véri Papers, MS Journal, cahier 122.
2. A.N. K677.103, Calonne to the king, late August 1786.
3. Bachaumont, *Mémoires secrètes*, XXXIV, 22.
4. See n. 49; Lescure, ed., *Correspondance secrète*, II, 127.
5. A.N. 144 A.P. 132 dossier 3.2, 24 February 1775; on Calonne's fall the memoranda were requested by Brienne (dossier 3.3).
6. A.N. K164.4, Objections et réponses.
7. A.N. K677 no. 138; Glagau, *Reformversuche und Sturz*, 375; Assemblée des Notables de 1787, *Procès-verbal*, Paris, 1788, 106.
8. Such I take to be the point of Miromesnil's warning to the king not to imitate the ecclesiastical policy of a power (probably Joseph II's Austria) 'which is certainly very respectable but whose estates in no way resemble your own': A.N. K163 no. 8.22, letter of 28 December.
9. This project had been discussed with Mirabeau, the future 'tribune of the people' in the Revolution, who in 1786, as on his deathbed in 1791, passionately believed in a strong popular monarchy. In a letter of 5 July he praised Calonne for exposing Necker's comforting fraud and thus 'determining the king under the spur of necessity' to 'give France a national credit and consequently a constitution'. H. Welshinger, *La Mission secrète de Mirabeau à Berlin (1786–1787)*, Paris, 1900, 103. Curiously, though no friend to Necker, Mirabeau shared his belief in an evolution towards an English-style constitution through the establishment of similar financial institutions.
10. Drafts of Calonne's proposals are to be found among his papers at A.N. 297 A.P. 3 nos. 91 and 97.
11. Talleyrand, *Mémoires*, I, 105–6.
12. A.N. K163 no. 8.20.
13. Calonne, *Réponse*, 88–9.
14. Félix, *Louis XVI et Marie-Antoinette*, 364.
15. Comte de Saint-Priest, *Mémoires*, ed. baron de Barante, Paris, 1929, I, 194–5; P. Filleul, *Le duc de Montmorency Luxembourg*, Paris, 1939, 265; Véri Papers, MS Journal, cahier 146; Véri confessed, however, that he no longer had inside knowledge of ministerial discussions, Véri Papers, cahier 145.
16. Calonne, *Réponse*, 188.

17. Dupont to Edelsheim, Fontainebleau, 10 November 1786, in Dupont Papers, B. Erdmannsdorfer, ed., *Politische Correspondenz Karl Friedrichs von Baden 1783–1806*, Heidelberg, 1888, I, 264–5.
18. Bachaumont, *Mémoires secrètes*, XXXIII, 153.
19. Soulavie, *Mémoires historiques et politiques*, V, 1–96. Soulavie believed that Castries actually read this memorandum, by Grimoard, to the council but it is unlikely that Louis would have permitted this. He did, however, annotate the memorandum. See Price, *Preserving the Monarchy*, 210ff.
20. Fragment of the abbé de Véri's journal, ed. duc de Castries, *Revue de Paris* (Nov. 1953), 84–5.
21. Castries Diary, Journal, II, f. 335.
22. A.N. K163 no. 8.
23. A.N. K163 no. 8.22, letter of 28 December.
24. Each secretary of state, for general matters not grouped thematically by department, administered a bundle of provinces.
25. 'Projet d'annonce de l'Assemblée des Notables à faire au Conseil du roi', A.N. K677.111.
26. Lacour-Gayet, *Calonne*, 176–7.
27. Castries Diary, Journal, II, 337–8.
28. Bachaumont, *Mémoires secrètes*, XXXIII, 196.
29. Castries Diary, Journal, II, f. 335.
30. J.F.X. Droz, *Histoire du règne de Louis XVI*, Brussels, 1839, 2 vols.
31. Calonne, *Réponse*, 82, note.
32. Soulavie, *Historical and Political Memoirs*, VI, 283–4.
33. Lacour-Gayet, *Calonne*, 102–6.
34. The king to Vergennes, 23 May 1785, published by Soulavie, *Historical and Political Memoirs*, VI, 291.
35. Letter of 28 December, A.N. K163 no. 8.22.
36. Brienne, *Journal de l'Assemblée des Notables*, 46 and 50.
37. W. Doyle, 'The Parlements', in *The French Revolution and the Creation of Modern Political Culture*, I, *The Political Culture of the Old Regime*, ed. K.M. Baker, Oxford, 1987, 165.
38. A.N. K163 nos. 8, 23 and 26.
39. M.-T. Allemand-Gay, and J. Coudert, *Un Magistrat lorrain au XVIIIe siècle: Le premier Président de Coeurderoy (1738–1800) et son diaire*, Paris, 1997, 350.
40. Bachaumont, *Mémoires secrètes*, XXXIV, 70.
41. Castries Diary, Journal, II, 346–7.
42. Lenoir Papers, MS 1421, section 2, Réligion.
43. Lescure, ed., *Correspondance secrète*, II, 106; Calonne to Nicolaï, premier président of the Chambre des Comptes, undated but 11 February, A.N. 297 AP 3 no. 71.
44. *Louis XVI–Vergennes Correspondence*, 390.
45. Assemblée des Notables de 1787, *Procès-verbal*, 36–7; Price, *Vergennes*, 228.
46. Lescure, ed., *Correspondance secrète*, II, 104, entry for 7 February.
47. Lescure, ed., *Correspondance secrète*, II, 108.
48. D'Angiviller, *Mémoires*, 169–70.
49. A.N. 297 A.P. 3 no. 19.
50. Price, *Vergennes*, 228–9; Labourdette, *Vergennes*, 303.
51. Besenval, *Mémoires*, II, 279.
52. Castries Diary, Journal, II, ff. 343–4.
53. Bachaumont, *Mémoires secrètes*, XXXIV, 69.
54. Castries Diary, Journal, II, f. 342; further references to this diary are cited in the text by date.
55. A.N. 297 AP 3 no. 61.
56. Louis XVI to Calonne 27 [*sic* for 21] February 1787; published in *Louis XVI, Marie-Antoinette et Mme Élisabeth*, I, 181.
57. Castries Diary, Journal, II, f. 344.
58. Bibliothèque de l'Arsenal, MS 3978, 212, Besenval, *Mémoires*, II, 213–14.

59. A.N. 297 A.P. 3.119 f. 5.
60. Arsenal, MS 3978, 212.
61. Arsenal, MS 3978, 212.
62. See, e.g., a speech by Angran d'Allerai, Arsenal MS 3978, 215–16.
63. V. Gruder, *The Notables and the Nation: The Political Schooling of the French, 1787–1788*, Cambridge, MA, and London, 2007, 11–88. I have challenged her view in Hardman, *Overture to Revolution*, esp. 129–30.
64. Arsenal, MS 3976, 948.
65. Calonne to Necker, 28 February, A.N. 297 A.P. 3. no. 166.
66. A.N. 297 A.P. 3. nos 58 (copy) and 59; for Necker's account see Necker, *Mémoire*, 6 March 1787, 176–81.
67. Calonne to the king, undated but 26 February, A.N. 297 A.P. 3 no. 65; A.N. K677 no. 141.
68. Calonne to the king, 2 March, A.N. 297 A.P. 3 no. 74.
69. Calonne to the king, 2 March, A.N. 297 A.P. 3 no. 74.
70. Staël-Holstein, *Correspondance diplomatique*, 43.
71. A. Auget, baron de Montyon, *Particularités sur les ministres des finances les plus célèbres*, Paris, 1812, 267. Montyon was an intendant.
72. D'Angiviller, *Mémoires*, 125.
73. A.N. 297 A.P. 3 no. 95; Brienne, *Journal de l'Assemblée des Notables*, 44.
74. Brienne, *Journal de l'Assemblée des Notables*, 44.
75. O. Ilovaisky, *La Disgrâce de Calonne*, Paris, 2008, 132.
76. M.-J. Coeurderoi, *L'Assemblée des Notables de 1787 et l'esprit de réforme: Les réflexions de Michel-Joseph Coeurderoy*, ed. M.-T. Allemand-Gay, Paris, 2008, 69.
77. 'It would be wrong that reasonable doubts, that observations inspired by zeal, that noble expressions of candour should give rise to the idea of a malevolent opposition.'
78. Brienne, *Journal de l'Assemblée des Notables*, 63.
79. Castries Diary, Journal, II, 354, entry for 2 April.
80. A.N. 297 A.P. 3 no. 91.
81. This formula was to be employed in the *séance royale* of 19 November 1787.
82. Bachaumont, *Mémoires secrètes*, XXXIV, 385.
83. A.N. K163 no. 8.32.
84. In 1780, when Necker had demanded the resignation of Sartine, and in 1781, when he had demanded that he be made a *ministre d'état*.
85. Montyon, *Particularités*, 293.
86. Lacour-Gayet, *Calonne*, 240; Bachaumont, *Mémoires secrètes*, XXXIV, 386.
87. Brienne, *Journal de l'Assemblée des Notables*, 61.
88. D'Ormesson Papers, A.N. 144 A.P. 133, dossier 6.4.
89. The following account is based on the version of Castries (Castries Diary, Journal); Lenoir (Lenoir Papers, MS 1423, mélanges, 39); and Brienne, *Journal de l'Assemblée des Notables*, 60.
90. Brienne, *Journal de l'Assemblée des Notables*, 59.
91. Lacour-Gayet, *Calonne*, 239.
92. Lacour-Gayet, *Calonne*, 239.
93. Besenval, *Mémoires*, II, 261.
94. Brienne, *Journal de l'Assemblée des Notables*, 52 and 63.
95. The preceding account of Calonne's fall is based on Castries Diary, Journal, II, 354; Lenoir Papers, MS 1423 mélanges, 39; Brienne, *Journal de l'Assemblée des Notables*, 60; Coeurderoi, *L'Assemblée des Notables de 1787*, 71.
96. A.N. K163 no. 7.1.
97. [Ruault], *Gazette d'un Parisien sous la Révolution . . . 1783–1796*, ed. E. Vassal, Paris, 1975, 84.
98. A.N. K163 no. 7.2.
99. Brienne, *Journal de l'Assemblée des Notables*, 60.
100. Brienne, *Journal de l'Assemblée des Notables*, 58 and 63; Coeurderoi, *L'Assemblée des Notables de 1787*, 73.

101. Castries Diary, Journal, II, 355, 9 April 1787; Brienne, *Journal de l'Assemblée des Notables*, 59; Turgot to Véri, 30 April 1776, in Véri, *Journal*, I, 430.
102. A.N. 297 A.P. 3 no. 110.
103. Filleul, *Montmorency-Luxembourg*, 266.
104. Coeurderoi, *L'Assemblée des Notables de 1787*, 74.
105. Castries Diary, Journal, II, 358–9, entry for 16–17 April.
106. The same situation had arisen over the decision to enter the American war, but Maurepas had forced him to take responsibility.
107. Bachaumont, *Mémoires secrètes*, XXXV, 28–9, entry for 27 April.
108. These memoranda have been published in Brienne, *Journal de l'Assemblée des Notables*, 79–83.
109. A.N. K677 nos 168–71.
110. Brienne, *Journal de l'Assemblée des Notables*, 95–6.
111. Brienne, *Journal de l'Assemblée des Notables*, 94–5.
112. Gérard, diary of the 1787 Assembly of Notables, A.A.E. MDF 1402 f. 66.
113. Brienne, *Journal de l'Assemblée des Notables*, 107. Its *rapporteur* gave Monsieur's bureau similar information, A.N. C1, 30 April.
114. B.A. Luckner, 'The Role of the French Bishops in the Aristocratic Revolt of 1787–88', unpublished MA thesis, University of Manchester, 1969, 154.
115. Brienne, *Journal de l'Assemblée des Notables*, xxiv–xxviii.
116. Castries Diary, Journal, II, 362, 365.
117. Marmontel, *Mémoires*, ed. M. Tourneux, Paris, 1891, III, 128–9; Brienne, *Journal de l'Assemblée des Notables*, 124.
118. Castries's version runs: 'All three went to the king together and talked to him about the political crisis; and all three, fearing Necker or rather to displease the king or at least not to please the queen, demanded reinforcement from the king in the person of the archbishop of Toulouse.' Brienne then asked the king for Necker as his auxiliary and was told 'that he had only been appointed to avoid Necker'.
119. Lescure, ed., *Correspondance secrète*, II, 131.
120. Castries Diary, Journal, II, 363–6.
121. Bachaumont, *Mémoires secrètes*, XXXV, 355.
122. Brienne, *Journal de l'Assemblée des Notables*, 59, 61.
123. Brienne, *Journal de l'Assemblée des Notables*, 59.
124. Madame de Staël, *Considérations sur . . . la Révolution française*, op. posth, Paris, 1843, 99.
125. Castries Diary, Journal, II, 363, 4 May.
126. Castries Diary, Journal, II, 371.
127. Lescure, ed., *Correspondance secrète*, II, 142–3.
128. Brienne, *Journal de l'Assemblée des Notables*, 59.
129. Calonne to d'Angiviller, A.N. 297 A.P. 3.119.
130. D'Ormesson Papers, Mémoires, A.N. 144 A.P. 130, f. 102, cited in Ilovaisky, *La Disgrâce*, 120.
131. A.N. 297 A. P. 3.113, Brienne to Calonne, 22 June.
132. A.N. 297 A.P. 3. 113, Amelot to Calonne, 22 June.
133. Castries Diary, Journal, II, f. 381.
134. Bombelles, *Journal*, II, 195; Lescure, ed., *Correspondance secrète*, II, 140.
135. Louis asked Brienne to have one memorandum ready for 5 p.m. to give him time to digest it between returning from hunting and the evening committees which started at 7 p.m.
136. Letter of Madame Élisabeth to Madame de Bombelles, Madame Élisabeth, *Correspondance de Mme Élisabeth*, ed. F. Feuillet de Conches, 1868, 103–4.
137. A.N. 297 A.P. 3.114.

Chapter 9: The Road to the Estates-General

1. Bombelles, *Journal*, II, 215–16. See also T. Kaiser, 'From the Austrian Committee to the Foreign Plot: Marie-Antoinette, Austrophobia and the Terror', *French Historical Studies*

26 (2003), 579–617, and op. cit., 'Who's Afraid of Marie-Antoinette? Diplomacy, Austrophobia and the Queen', *French History* 14 (2000), 241–71.

2. Droz, *Histoire du règne de Louis XVI*, II, 14.
3. Castries Diary, Journal, II. f. 383; Mansel, *Court of France*, 4.
4. Malesherbes, *Malesherbes à Louis XVI ou les Avertissements de Cassandra: Mémoires inédits 1787–1788*, ed. V. André, Paris, 2010, 84 and 87–8.
5. Castries Diary, Journal, II, f. 392.
6. Castries Diary, Journal, II, f. 392.
7. Castries Diary, Journal, II, f. 386.
8. Castries Diary, Journal, II, ff. 374 and 398.
9. Droz, *Histoire du règne de Louis XVI*, II, 1.
10. Stone, *The Parlement of Paris*, 156.
11. Doyle, 'The Parlements', 165.
12. Malesherbes is possibly referring to the publication of Montesquieu's *De l'esprit des lois*, in 1748, exactly forty years before the composition of his memorandum.
13. Malesherbes, *Malesherbes à Louis XVI*, 78–9.
14. Hardman, *Overture to Revolution*, 127.
15. Published in Soulavie, *Mémoires historiques et politiques*, VI, 240–4.
16. Malesherbes, *Malesherbes à Louis XVI*, 147.
17. Malesherbes, *Malesherbes à Louis XVI*, 177.
18. Malesherbes, *Malesherbes à Louis XVI*, 179.
19. Malesherbes, *Malesherbes à Louis XVI*, 174.
20. Stone, *The Parlement of Paris*, 156.
21. Malesherbes, *Malesherbes à Louis XVI*, 106.
22. Letter to Joseph of 23 November.
23. G. Sallier-Chaumont de Laroche, *Annales françaises depuis le commencement du règne de Louis XVI jusqu'aux états-généraux, 1774–1789*, Paris, 1813, 128–9.
24. A.P., I, 284.
25. M. Marion, *Le garde des sceaux Lamoignon*, Paris, 1905, *passim*.
26. Malesherbes, *Malesherbes à Louis XVI*, 231–5.
27. Malesherbes, *Malesherbes à Louis XVI*, 106.
28. Sallier-Chaumont de Laroche, *Annales françaises*, 144, and J. Weber, *Mémoires concernant Marie-Antoinette*, ed. S.A. Berville and J.F. Barrière, 1822, II, 126.
29. A. Chérest, *La chute de l'Ancien régime, 1787–1789*, Paris, 1884–86, I, 475.
30. A.N. O¹354 no. 5, 6 May, 7.45.
31. He was right to be worried: when the *parlement* returned in triumph in September it issued an injunction against him to explain his conduct.
32. A.N. O¹354 no. 54.
33. Castries Diary, Journal, II, f. 387
34. A.N. O'354 no. 102.
35. Droz, *Histoire du règne de Louis XVI*, II, 97.
36. The king to Boisgelin, 15 July 1788, published in *Louis XVI, Marie-Antoinette et Mme Élisabeth*, I, 203.
37. Bombelles, *Journal*, II, 213.
38. M. Price, 'The Comte de Vergennes and the Baron de Breteuil', unpublished PhD thesis, Cambridge University, 1988, 360–70.
39. Bombelles, *Journal*, II, 209.
40. Bombelles, *Journal*, II, 215.
41. Bombelles, *Journal*, II, 207 and 227.
42. Malesherbes, *Malesherbes à Louis XVI*, 101.
43. Bombelles, *Journal*, II, 227.
44. The relevant documents have been published in *Louis XVI, Marie-Antoinette et Mme Élisabeth*, I, 204–19.
45. Bombelles, *Journal*, II, 240–1.
46. *Louis XVI, Marie-Antoinette et Mme Élisabeth*, I, 217–18.

47. E.g., when Bertrand de Molleville asked Montmorin to read out in council a memorandum on dismissing the Estates, Montmorin refused on the grounds that 'Necker would stop me and desire to have it communicated to himself before it was read, on which the king would order it to be delivered to him'. A.F. Bertrand de Molleville, *Last Year of the Reign of Louis XVI*, Boston, 1909, I, 164.

48. Sallier-Chaumont de Laroche, *Annales*, 126.

49. Price, 'The Comte de Vergennes and the Baron de Breteuil', 379–86.

50. Bombelles, *Journal*, II, 234–5.

51. Bombelles, *Journal*, II, 236.

52. Sallier-Chaumont de Laroche, *Annales*, 186, n. 1.

53. Published in Soulavie, *Mémoires historiques et politiques*, VI, 240–4.

54. Filleul, *Montmorency-Luxembourg*, 284.

55. Filleul, *Montmorency-Luxembourg*, 284.

56. Filleul, *Montmorency-Luxembourg*, 56–7.

57. Soulavie, *Mémoires historiques et politiques*, VI, 242–3.

58. C.L.F. de Barentin, *Mémoire autographe sur les derniers conseils du Roi Louis XVI*, ed. M. Champion, Paris, 1844, 48.

59. A.N. XIB 8988.

60. P.-V. Malouet, *Mémoires*, Paris, 1874, I, 220–1.

61. Article on Necker by Lally Tollendal in the *Biographie-Michaud*.

62. Chérest, *La chute de l'Ancien régime*, II, 221; the details of the discussion preceding the *Résultat* are to be found in Barentin, *Mémoire autographe*, 71–3, and J. Necker, *De la Révolution française*, Paris, 1797, 87ff.

63. Lenoir Papers, MS 1423, résidus, 122.

64. Barentin, *Memoire autographe*, 67.

65. Bombelles, *Journal*, II, 223.

66. D'Angiviller, *Mémoires*, 146.

67. C.-A. de Calonne, *Lettre au roi*, London, 1789, 54.

68. Malouet, *Mémoires*, I, 249–50.

69. Malesherbes, *Malesherbes à Louis XVI*, 155.

70. Speech in the Assembly of Notables by Le Blanc de Castillon cited in Hardman, *Overture to Revolution*, 151–2.

71. Véri, fragment of his journal, ed. Castries, 84–6.

72. The word is that of his friend Véri.

73. Soulavie, *Mémoires historiques et politiques*, III, 151–2.

74. Véri, fragment of his journal, ed. Castries, 84–6.

75. Mercy to Joseph II, 23 February 1788.

76. Bombelles, *Journal*, II, 208.

77. Bombelles, *Journal*, II, 205.

78. Bombelles, *Journal*, II, 215–16.

Chapter 10: The Silent King and the Third Estate

1. A.N. K679 no. 10.

2. This at least was the aim of Artois's best friend Vaudreuil: Bombelles, *Journal*, II, 314, entry for 13 May 1789.

3. Bombelles, *Journal*, II, 297.

4. Bombelles, *Journal*, II, 303.

5. Bombelles, *Journal*, II, 299 and 302–3.

6. Bombelles, *Journal*, II, 304.

7. Shapiro, *Traumatic Politics*, 45 and 49.

8. Bombelles, *Journal*, II, 306.

9. Bombelles, *Journal*, II, 309.

10. These have been published in *La Révolution française* LVI (1909), 193–8 and 318–29.

11. Saint-Priest, *Memoires*, I, 221; Bombelles, *Journal*, II, 310.
12. Louis XVI to Necker, *c.* 1 May 1789, J. Hardman, ed., *The French Revolution Sourcebook*, London and New York, 1999, 91.
13. Barentin, *Mémoire autographe*, 146-7.
14. Malouet, *Mémoires*, I, 250 and 259.
15. Bertrand de Molleville, *Mémoires secrets*, I, 157-9.
16. C.L.F. de Barentin, *Lettres et bulletins à Louis XVI*, ed. A. Aulard, Paris, 1915, 10, 27 and 56.
17. Bailly, *Mémoires*, ed. S.A. Berville and J.F. Barrière, Paris, 1821, I, 94.
18. Bombelles, *Journal*, II, 326-8.
19. Bombelles, *Journal*, II, 328.
20. États-Généraux: G. Lefebvre et al., eds, *Recueil de documents relatifs aux États-Généraux de 1789*, Paris, 1953-70, I(2), 55.
21. États-Généraux, *Recueil*, I(2), 171.
22. États-Généraux, *Recueil*, I(2), 48.
23. D'Angiviller, *Mémoires*, 152.
24. Bombelles, *Journal*, II, 336.
25. Comtesse d'Adhémar, *Souvenirs sur Marie-Antoinette* . . ., Paris, 1836, quoted in N. Hampson, *Prelude to Terror: The Constituent Assembly and the Failure of Consensus, 1789-1791*, Oxford, 1988, 43. I am indebted to the late Professor Hampson for drawing my attention to these memoirs.
26. Necker, *Révolution française*, I, 286; Montjoie, *Seconde partie* . . ., 44.
27. Adhémar, *Souvenirs*, III, 156-7.
28. Malouet, *Mémoires*, I, 261.
29. Necker, *Révolution française*, I, 200.
30. Barentin, *Mémoire autographe*, 99
31. Saint-Priest, *Mémoires*, I, 223.
32. États Généraux, *Recueil*, I(2), 94.
33. Mercy to Joseph II, 4 July 1789.
34. Necker, *Révolution française*, 253.
35. D'Angiviller, *Mémoires*, 154.
36. Letter transcribed in Adhémar, *Souvenirs*, III, 171-5.
37. Montmorin took a similar view; A.N. K679 nos 86 and 87-8 for their memoranda for the king.
38. D'Angiviller, *Mémoires*, 154-5.
39. As director of the king's buildings.
40. D'Angiviller, *Mémoires*, 158-60.
41. Comte de Vaudreuil, *Correspondance intime du comte de Vaudreuil et du comte d'Artois*, ed. L. Pingaud, 1889, I, xxvii-xxviii.
42. Mercy to Joseph II, 4 July 1789.
43. That, at least, is my reading of the second and third paragraphs of Barentin's letter of 27 June.
44. Bombelles, *Journal*, II, 300.
45. Duc de Castries, *L'Aube de la Révolution*, Paris, 1978, 202.
46. Shapiro, *Traumatic Politics*, 90.
47. Droz, *Histoire du règne de Louis XVI*, II, 247; Necker, *Révolution française*, I, 313.
48. États-Généraux, *Recueil*, I(2), 311.
49. Bombelles, *Journal*, II, 338.
50. Bombelles, *Journal*, II, 344.
51. *Moniteur*, 1790, no. 4 (III-33), cited in Louis XVI, *Louis XVI a la parole*, ed. P. and P. Girault de Coursac, Paris, 1989, 195.
52. These are published by P. Caron in 'La Tentative de contre-révolution de juin-juillet 1789', *Revue d'Histoire moderne* VIII (1906), 25-30; Caron draws a perverse conclusion from his own evidence.

53. Bombelles, *Journal*, II, 298, entry for 23 April.
54. Félix, *Louis XVI et Marie-Antoinette*, 476.
55. J. Godechot, *The Taking of the Bastille*, trans. J. Stewart, London, 1970, 182.
56. Bombelles, *Journal*, II, 339.
57. Bombelles, *Journal*, II, 344 and 342.
58. Bombelles, *Journal*, II, 295.
59. D'Angiviller, *Mémoires*, 166–70.
60. Bombelles, *Journal*, II, 344
61. Bombelles, *Journal*, II, 316.
62. Droz, *Histoire du règne de Louis XVI*, II, 299.
63. Bombelles, *Journal*, II, 344.
64. Bombelles, *Journal*, II, 335.
65. M. Price, 'The "Ministry of the Hundred Hours": A Reappraisal', *French History* 4:3 (1990), 339; Raigecourt-Bombelles, *Correspondance du marquis et de la marquise de Raigecourt avec le marquis et la marquise de Bombelles pendant l'émigration, 1790–1800*, ed. M. de la Rocheterie, Paris, 1892, 168.
66. A.N. C185 (123) 9.
67. Necker, *Révolution française*, II, 5.
68. Price, 'The "Ministry of the Hundred Hours"', 335.
69. Price, 'The "Ministry of the Hundred Hours"', 336–7.
70. S.F. Scott, *The Response of the Royal Army to the French Revolution: Role and Development of the Line Army, 1787–93*, Oxford, 1973, 59 and 80.
71. Paris, *Procès-Verbal de l'Assemblée Générale des électeurs de Paris*, Paris, 1790, 152–4.
72. Paris, *Procès-Verbal*, 186.
73. Paris, *Procès-Verbal*, 394. Intercepted note dated 14 July.
74. Message to the National Assembly, published idem., 403.
75. J. Peuchet, *Mémoires tirées des archives de la police de Paris*, Paris, 1828, III, 182.
76. Paris, *Procès-Verbal*, 393–4.
77. Moreau, *Mes souvenirs*, II, 439–41.
78. 'Journal de Fersen', in Comte de Fersen, *Le comte de Fersen et la cour de France*, ed. R.M. Klinckowstrom, Paris, 1878, II, 6.
79. A.N. C185 (123) 1.
80. Droz, *Histoire du règne de Louis XVI*, II, 345.
81. Comte de Paroy, *Mémoires*, Paris, 1895, 42.
82. Marquis de Lafayette, *Mémoires, correspondance et manuscripts du général Lafayette*, Paris, 1837, II, 362; comte d'Allonville, *Mémoires secrets de 1770 à 1830*, Paris, 1838–45, II, 68.
83. Montjoie, *Éloge historique et funèbre de Louis XVI*, Paris, 1796, 141.
84. Besenval, *Mémoires*, II, 367.
85. Saint-Priest, *Mémoires*, I, 240–1.
86. Malouet, *Mémoires*, I, 250.
87. Shapiro, *Traumatic Politics*, *passim*.
88. Hardman, ed., *French Revolution Sourcebook*, 108.

Chapter 11: The Invasion of a Palace

1. Published in A. Mousset, *Un témoin ignoré de la Révolution: le comte de Fernan Nunez*, Paris, 1924, 228.
2. Caiani, *Louis XVI*, 64.
3. T. Tackett, *Becoming a Revolutionary: The Deputies of the French National Assembly and the Emergence of a Revolutionary Culture*, University Park, PA, 2006, 170.
4. A.P. ix, 28–31.
5. Baron Acton, *Lectures on the French Revolution*, London, 1910, 43–50.
6. J. Hardman, *Robespierre*, London and New York, 1999, 25.

7. Cited in Petitfils, *Louis XVI*, 712.
8. The best book on the *monarchiens* is R. Griffiths, *Le Centre perdu: Malouet et les 'monar-chiens' dans la Révolution française*, Grenoble, 1988, especially 55–80.
9. Wick, 'The Court Nobility and the French Revolution', 263–84.
10. Hardman, *Robespierre*, 22.
11. See e.g., Saint-Priest, *Mémoires*, I, 229.
12. Malouet, *Mémoires*, I, 304–5.
13. Shapiro, *Traumatic Politics*, 153.
14. Cited in Tackett, *Becoming a Revolutionary*, 182.
15. A.N. C31 (263) 6.
16. Hampson, *Prelude to Terror*, 78.
17. I have based this account of the October Days on Saint-Priest, *Mémoires*, I, 8–23.
18. Necker, *Révolution française*, 77–9.
19. B.N., nouv. acq. fr. 9434 f. 209.
20. Necker, *Révolution française*, II, 73.
21. Padover, *Louis XVI*, 192.
22. See J. Adamson, *The Noble Revolt: The Overthrow of Charles I*, London, 2007.
23. J. Mallet du Pan, *Mémoires et correspondance de Mallet du Pan pour servir à l'histoire de la Révolution française*, ed. A. Sayous, Paris, 1851, I, 181, n.
24. Necker, *Sur l'administration de M. Necker par lui-même*, Paris, 1791, 328.
25. Lever, *Louis XVI*, 534.
26. Hampson, *Prelude to Terror*, 188.
27. Saint-Priest, *Mémoires*, I, 89.
28. Cited in Lever, *Louis XVI*, 538.
29. Louis-Philippe, *Memoirs*, 59.
30. Mansel, *Court of France*, 19.
31. Padover, *Louis XVI*, 193.
32. A. de Bacourt, ed., *Correspondance entre le comte de Mirabeau et le Comte de La Marck*, Paris, 1851, 2 vols, I, 57, La Marck to Mercy; Lafayette, *Mémoires*, III, 148–55.
33. Necker, *Révolution française*, II, 77–9.

Chapter 12: The Revolution Caricatures Itself

1. C.L.F. de Barentin, *Mémoire pour M. de Barentin . . . sur la plainte pour M. le procureur du roi au Châtelet*, Paris, 1790.
2. B. Shapiro, 'Revolutionary Justice in 1789–1790: The Comité des Recherches, the Châtelet, and the Fayettist Coalition', *French Historical Studies* 17:3 (Spring 1992), 656–69.
3. On the civil list see Caiani, *Louis XVI*, 56–82.
4. The following section on presentation is based on Caiani, *Louis XVI*, 133–59.
5. Caiani, *Louis XVI*, 157.
6. On the orders of chivalry see Caiani, *Louis XVI*, 160–91.
7. A.N. C184, no. 341, cited in Caiani, *Louis XVI*, 186.
8. A.N. C220 no. 38, cited in Caiani, *Louis XVI*, 189.
9. Mansel, *Court of France*, 21–3 and 29–30.
10. Caiani, *Louis XVI*, 90.
11. Élisabeth, *Correspondance*, I, 145.
12. Droz, *Histoire du règne de Louis XVI*, II, 121.
13. Caiani, *Louis XVI*, 133, n. 4.
14. Shapiro, 'Revolutionary Justice in 1789–1790', 662.
15. Caiani, *Louis XVI*, 120
16. Padover, *Louis XVI*, 197.
17. A.N. C184, no. 316, cited in Caiani, *Louis XVI*, 121.
18. Cited in Lever, *Louis XVI*, 571.

19. Élisabeth, *Correspondance*, I, 290.
20. Griffiths, *Le Centre perdu*, 89.
21. A reference to the *parlementaire théorie de classes*, that each *parlement* was a part of an original whole.
22. A.N. C184.115 nos 248–52, cited in Padover, *Louis XVI*, 205. Padover found 'numerous' such petitions in the Archives Nationales.
23. A.N. C187, La Porte to the king, 2 March 1791, quoted in Mansel, *Court of France*, 33–4.
24. Lafayette, *Mémoires*, II, 367.
25. See especially the 8th and 28th notes, Bacourt, ed., *Correspondance*, I, 355 and 424.
26. Talleyrand, *Mémoires*, 123.
27. A.P. LIV, 580.
28. Caiani, *Louis XVI*, 93–4.
29. There were some draft letters to the pope, largely inspired by Archbishop Boisgelin, found in the *armoire de fer*. These have been published in A.P. LIV, 475–78.
30. Published in Hue, *Dernières années*, 480,
31. Catalogue sale in the Hotel Druot, 6 May 1958. The date 18 January 1791 is written in the king's hand.
32. Undated but 14 April 1791, A.P. LIV 474.
33. A.P. LIV, 474, 474–5.
34. A.P. LIV, 474, 467, La Porte to the king, 20 April 1791.
35. Padover, *Louis XVI*, 214,
36. Griffiths, *Le Centre perdu*, 95.
37. Caiani, *Louis XVI*, 104.
38. Duchesse de Tourzel, *Mémoires*, ed. duc des Cars, Paris, 1904, I, 302; Bacourt, ed., *Correspondance*, I, 390 and II, 311; Marie-Antoinette, *Lettres*, 23.

Chapter 13: The Flight to Montmédy

1. Cited in Padover, *Louis XVI*, 196.
2. D'Angiviller, *Mémoires*, 182–3.
3. Marie-Antoinette to Mercy, 29 June 1790, *Marie-Antoinette Correspondance (1770–1793)*, ed. E. Lever, Paris, 2005, 512.
4. P. and P. Girault de Coursac, *Enquête sur le procès du roi Louis XVI*, Paris, 1982, 192.
5. Bacourt, ed., *Correspondance*, I, 260.
6. Extract from Mirabeau's 9th note for the court.
7. Bacourt, ed., *Correspondance*, I, 146, cited in M. Price, 'Mirabeau and the Court: Some New Evidence', *French Historical Studies* 29:1 (2006), 37–76.
8. Cited in Petitfils, *Louis XVI*, 777.
9. Bombelles, *Journal*, III, 199.
10. A.N. C222 no. 14.
11. J. Hardman and J.M. Roberts, eds, *French Revolution Documents*, Oxford, 1966–73, I, 291.
12. Fersen, *Le comte de Fersen*, II, 236.
13. Price, *Fall of the French Monarchy*, 116.
14. Cited in Girault de Coursac, *Enquête*, 302.
15. Bouillé (son of the general), *Souvenirs*, Paris, 1906, 180, my italics.
16. Bacourt, ed., *Correspondance*, I, 167.
17. The king to Bouillé, 1 September 1790, published in A.P. LIV, 513–14.
18. Marquis de Bouillé, *Mémoires*, ed. S.A. Berville and J.F. Barrière, Paris, 1821, 165–9 and 174.
19. Bouillé, *Mémoires*, 213.
20. Bacourt, ed., *Correspondance*, I, 331.
21. Bouillé, *Mémoires*, 245.
22. Bouillé, *Mémoires*, 245.

23. Price, *Fall of the French Monarchy*, 158.
24. A. Sorel, *L'Europe et la Révolution française*, II, *La Chute de la royauté*, Paris, 1908, 227.
25. Comte de Pimodan, *Le comte de Mercy-Argenteau*, Paris, 1911, 274–5, 284 and 289; Mercy to Marie-Antoinette, 27 April and 11 May 1791; Bouillé, *Mémoires*, 266.
26. E.g., Marie-Antoinette to Mercy, 14 April 1791.
27. M. Kennedy, *The Jacobin Clubs in the French Revolution: The First Years*, Princeton, NJ, 1982, 220–2.
28. Cited in *Le Trait de lumière ou le roi considéré au milieu de périls avant son départ pour Montmédy*, Paris, 1791, 10.
29. Caiani, *Louis XVI*, 41–6.
30. Duc de Choiseul, *Relation du départ de Louis XVI le 20 juin 1791*, Paris, 1822, 34–5; I. Dunlop, *Marie-Antoinette*, London, 1993, 246.
31. M. Robespierre, *Oeuvres*, ed. Société des Études Robespierristes, Paris, 1912–67, VII, 518–23 and VIII, 383.
32. *Opinion d'un publiciste*, Paris, 1791, 5.
33. Price, *Fall of the French Monarchy*, 197.
34. Bacourt, ed., *Correspondance*, I, 166.
35. Cited in P. and P. Girault de Coursac, *Sur la route de Varennes*, Paris, 1984, 228.
36. Girault de Coursac, *Sur la route*, 229–30.
37. Fersen (on behalf of Breteuil) to Marie-Antoinette, 26 July 1791, Fersen, *Le comte de Fersen*, II, 236.
38. Marie-Antoinette to Mercy, 4 June 1791; Mercy to Kaunitz, 22 June 1791, published in Pimodan, *Le comte de Mercy-Argenteau*, 289; Campan, *Mémoires*, 237–9.
39. J. Michelet, *History of the French Revolution*, trans. C. Cocks, Chicago, 1967, 580–95.
40. Mirabeau to La Marck, 4 June 1790, Bacourt, ed., *Correspondance*, I, 331.
41. Tourzel, *Mémoires*, I, 324–5; her eye-witness account forms the basis of this section.
42. M. Reinhard, *La Chute de la royauté*, Paris, 1977, 27.
43. From the minutes drawn up by the Municipality of Varennes and published as an appendix to E. Bimbenet, *La Fuite de Louis XVI à Varennes*, Paris, 1868.
44. Campan, *Mémoires*, 50.
45. Cited in Price, *Fall of the French Monarchy*, 183.
46. The king to Bouillé, 3 July 1791, *Louis XVI, Marie-Antoinette et Mme Élisabeth*, IV, 459.
47. Hampson, *Prelude to Terror*, 174.
48. Published in M. Mortimer-Ternaux, *Histoire de la Terreur*, Paris, 1862–81, I, 353–1.
49. A.N. KK375.
50. G. Rudé, *The Crowd in the French Revolution*, Oxford, 1967.
51. Marie-Antoinette, *Marie-Antoinette, Fersen et Barnave: leur correspondance*, ed. O.G. Heidenstam, Paris, 1913, 39 and 79.
52. Théodore de Lameth, *Notes et souvenirs*, ed. E. Welvert, Paris, 1913, 224–5 and 388.
53. Choiseul, *Relation*, 33–5; Hue, *Dernières années*, 220–1.
54. *Marie-Antoinette, Fersen et Barnave*, 42.
55. The view of G. Michon, *Adrien Duport et le parti Feuillant*, Paris, 1924, is the best account of the revision, despite Michon's hostility to the king and the triumvirs.
56. Marie-Antoinette to Mercy, 26 August 1791.
57. *Marie-Antoinette, Fersen et Barnave*, 86.
58. *Marie-Antoinette, Fersen et Barnave*, 78.
59. Hardman and Roberts, eds, *French Revolution Documents*, I, 347–66, for the text of the constitution and Louis's speech.
60. Griffiths, *Le Centre perdu*, 104.
61. J. Arnaud-Bouteloup, *Le Rôle politique de Marie-Antoinette*, Paris, 1924, 260; Fersen, *Le comte de Fersen*, I, 141–2; *Louis XVI, Marie-Antoinette et Mme Élisabeth*, II, 168–9; Pimodan, *Le comte de Mercy-Argenteau*, 296–7.
62. Calonne to Catherine II, 28 September 1791, P.R.O. P.C. I/127.388.
63. Archives of Austria, Frankreich 15 Hoffcorrespondenz, 7, cited in Louis XVI, *Louis XVI a la parole*, 270.

NOTES to pp. 404–21

64. Archives of Austria, Familien Acten 18 88.3 ff. 108–25, published in *Louis XVI, Marie-Antoinette et Mme Élisabeth*, II, 365–75 and in Louis XVI, *Louis XVI a la parole*, 263–8.

Chapter 14: Playing by the Book of the Constitution

1. Bertrand de Molleville, *Mémoires secrets*, I, 210.
2. Bertrand de Molleville, *Mémoires secrets*, I, 210 and II, 139; Dumouriez, *Mémoires*, 1822–23, II, 139.
3. P.L. Roederer, *Chronique de cinquante jours*, Paris, 1832, 281.
4. Roederer, *Chronique*, 282.
5. *Marie-Antoinette et Barnave: Correspondance secrète*, ed. Alma Söderjhelm, 1934, 87.
6. Louis-Philippe, *Memoirs*, 119–23.
7. Fersen, *Le comte de Fersen*, I, 199.
8. Bacourt, ed., *Correspondance*, II, 337.
9. Bertrand de Molleville, *Mémoires secrets*, I, 205.
10. A.N. C221 160 (148) pièce 19, quoted in Louis XVI, *Louis XVI a la parole*, 276.
11. Fersen, *Le comte de Fersen*, I, 269, Marie-Antoinette to Fersen, 7 December 1791.
12. J. Flammermont, *Négotiations secrètes de Louis XVI et du baron de Breteuil avec la cour de Berlin*, Paris, 1885, 17 and n.
13. Flammermont, *Négotiations secrètes*, 9–10, the text of this letter.
14. J. Chaumié, *Le Réseau d'Antraigues et la contre-Révolution*, Paris, 1965, 147.
15. A.A.E., Autriche, 363 ff. 531f. 34, cited in Girault de Coursac, *Enquête*, 373.
16. A.A.E., Trèves, Sup. 4, f. 22, cited in Girault de Coursac, *Enquête*, 338.
17. L.C. Bigot de Sainte-Croix, *Histoire de la conspiration du 10 août 1792*, London, 1793, 80, 87, 88.
18. Hardman, ed., *French Revolution Sourcebook*, 141.
19. *Louis XVI, Marie-Antoinette et Mme Élisabeth*, IV, 296–303.
20. A.P. LIV, 488.
21. Bertrand de Molleville, *Mémoires secrets*, II, 51 and 58; Bacourt, ed., *Correspondance*, II, 358.
22. A.P. LV, 539.
23. Pellenc (Mirabeau's secretary) to La Marck, 14 March 1792, published in H. Glagau, *Die Franzosiche Legislative . . . 1791–92*, Berlin, 1896, 298.
24. Madame Roland, *Mémoires*, Paris, 2004, 230.
25. B.N. 40 Lb, 10536.
26. *Louis XVI, Marie-Antoinette et Mme Élisabeth*, VI, 245–56; Bertrand de Molleville, *Mémoires secrets*, II, 145; Campan, *Mémoires*, 286–7; Staël, *Considérations*, I, 372.
27. Bigot de Sainte-Croix, *Histoire*, 80, 87, 88.
28. Soulavie argued that this had been the case throughout the reign of Louis XVI with such ministers as Turgot and Necker playing this role.
29. Betrand de Molleville, *Mémoires secrets*, II, 188.
30. Dumouriez, *Mémoires*, II, 278–9 and 294–6.
31. A.N. C185 CII no. 32.
32. A.N. C185 CII, nos 87–8; Campan, *Mémoires*, 279; Lescure, ed., *Correspondance secrète*, II, 600.
33. Hue, *Dernières années*, 282; Mallet du Pan dates this note to 3 August; Louis XVI, *Louis XVI a la parole*, 302.
34. Roederer, *Chronique*, 50–3 and 76–8; Dumouriez, *Mémoires*, II, 153.
35. A. Söderjhelm, ed., *Fersen et Marie-Antoinette: correspondance et journal intime inédits du comte Axel de Fersen*, Paris, 1930, 261.
36. Arnaud-Bouteloup, *Le rôle politique*, 338.
37. Fersen to Taube, 29 July 1792, in Fersen, *Le comte de Fersen*, II, 33.
38. Cited in Petitfils, *Louis XVI*, 860.
39. Lafayette, *Mémoires*, III, 346.

40. Lafayette, *Mémoires*, III, 357.
41. Bertrand de Molleville, *Mémoires secrets*, III, 10; Lafayette, *Mémoires*, III, 344.
42. Price, *Fall of the French Monarchy*, 290.
43. Michon, *Adrien Duport*, 421.
44. Bertrand de Molleville, *Mémoires secrets*, III, 10; Lafayette, *Mémoires*, III, 346.
45. Mercy to Marie-Antoinette, 9 July 1792.
46. Note of 10 July, Fersen, *Le comte de Fersen*, II, 323.
47. Letter to Lally-Tollendal, published by A. Thiers, *Histoire de la Révolution française*, Brussels, 1844, II, 374.
48. L. Pingaud, 'Un ministre de Louis XVI, Terrier de Monciel', *Le Correspondant*, August 1879, 590; A. Mathiez, 'Les Girondins à la veille du 10 août', *Annales historiques de la Révolution française* (1931), 194–5.
49. Lafayette, *Mémoires*, III, 348.
50. Bigot de Sainte-Croix, *Histoire*, 95–6.
51. Bertrand de Molleville, *Mémoires secrets*, III, 10–45; Malouet, *Mémoires*, II, 220–6; Bacourt, ed., *Correspondance*, II, 374, Montmorin to La Marck.
52. Padover, *Louis XVI*, 258–9 and 265.
53. *Annales historiques de la Révolution française* (1951), 198–201.
54. Roederer, *Chronique*, 299.
55. The following account of the rising is based mainly on Roederer, Madame de Tourzel, and Reinhard, *La Chute*.
56. Bertrand de Molleville, *Mémoires secrets*, III, 24
57. Bertrand de Molleville, *Mémoires secrets*, III, 38, conversation between Bertrand de Molleville and Montmorin; marquis de Beaucourt, *Captivité de Louis XVI*, Paris, 1892, I, 289.
58. Chaumié, *Le Réseau d'Antraigues*, 216.
59. Journal of John Moore, *Revue de la Révolution*, V, 149.
60. Beaucourt, *Captivité*, I, 30.
61. Tourzel, *Mémoires*, II, 228–9.

Chapter 15: The Prisoner in the Temple

1. Report of the Commune of 26 December, published in Beaucourt, *Captivité*, II, 23.
2. Beaucourt, *Captivité*, I, 240; J.-B. Cléry, *Journal de ce qui s'est passé à la tour du Temple pendant la captivité de Louis XVI, roi de France*, London, 1798, 40 and 52.
3. Beaucourt, *Captivité*, I, 214 and 240.
4. Hue, *Dernières années*, 360; Cléry, *Journal*, 97.
5. Beaucourt, *Captivité*, I, 235.
6. Cléry, *Journal*, 28–33.
7. Beaucourt, *Captivité*, I, 241.
8. A. Soboul, ed., *Le Procès de Louis XVI*, Paris, 1966, 86.
9. At least there are none in his papers either in the Archives nationales or in the Public Record Office. A.P. LIV, 449 for the letter Louis annotated 'point répondu'.
10. Hue, *Dernières années*, 370 and 399–400; Campan, *Mémoires*, 285–6.
11. The record of Louis's appearance before the Convention is given in A.P. LV, 7–15.
12. Cléry, *Journal*, 152–3.
13. Such as Théodore de Lameth, Jaurès and Walzer.
14. Cited in D. Jordan, *The King's Trial: Louis XVI vs. the French Revolution*, Berkeley, CA, and London, 1979, 115.
15. P. Lombard, *Le Procès du roi*, Paris, 1993, 189.
16. Cited in Petitfils, *Louis XVI*, 904.
17. Cléry, *Journal*, 152–3.
18. Beaucourt, *Captivité*, II, 207.
19. Beaucourt, *Captivité*, II, 181.
20. G.-J.-B. Target, *Observations sur le procès de Louis XVI*, Paris, 1793.

21. E. Seligman, *La Justice pendant la Révolution*, Paris, 1913, 420–2.
22. Miromesnil, *Correspondance politique*, I, xvi, letter of 15 December to Barère.
23. A.N. C243 dossier 305.7.
24. Beaucourt, *Captivité*, I, 290 and II, 234.
25. Beaucourt, *Captivité*, II, 231; Hue, *Dernières années*, 429, from a manuscript given by Malesherbes to Hue in prison.
26. The speeches of Sèze and the king are given in A.P. LV, 617–34.
27. Beaucourt, *Captivité*, II, 234 and I, 291.
28. Soboul, *Procès*, 200–4.
29. T. de Lameth, *Mémoires*, ed. E. Welvert, Paris, 1913, 243.
30. Hue, *Dernières années*, 430–1.
31. Cléry, *Journal*, 207, and Hue, *Dernières années*, 439.
32. Cléry, *Journal*, 211–13.
33. Beaucourt, *Captivité*, I, 291.
34. Beaucourt, *Captivité*, I, 19–20.
35. Abbé Edgeworth, *Dernières heures de Louis XVI*, Paris, 1816, 210–12 and 217.
36. Cléry, *Journal*, 220; Beaucourt, *Captivité*, I, 215–16 and 240.
37. Beaucourt, *Captivité*, I, 328 and 345; Edgeworth, *Dernières heures*, 220.
38. Edgeworth, *Dernières heures*, 225–7.
39. Beaucourt, *Captivité*, II, 172, the account of the *Semaines Parisiennes*.
40. P. de Vaissière, *La mort de Louis XVI*, Paris, 1910, 125 and 131–3; L.-B. Mercier, *Le Nouveau Paris*, III, 4; Beaucourt, *Captivité*, I, 398.
41. Beaucourt, *Captivité*, I, 337 and 348; Allonville, *Mémoires secrets*, III, 159–60; *Le Républicain*, 22 January 1793.
42. Griffiths, *Le Centre perdu*.

BIBLIOGRAPHY

MANUSCRIPT SOURCES

Louis XVI

Archives nationales (A.N.) K161, 163 and 164, 'cartons des rois'; communications to the king vastly outnumber those from him; K164, no. 3, correspondence with Vergennes, has been published together with Louis's surviving replies from the Tugny-Vergennes archive in *Louis XVI and the comte de Vergennes: Correspondence, 1774-1787*, ed. J. Hardman and M. Price, Oxford, 1998.

A.N. AEI-4, the king's diary, a microfilm copy of the original in the Musée des Archives.

A.N. C183-85, papers found in the *armoire de fer*; documents considered important by the Convention are printed in *Archives Parlementaires* (A.P.) LIV 428ff.; there is a detailed inventory of the remainder in LV 668ff.

A.N. C220-23 (Convention Nationale, Papiers des Tuileries); four boxes of letters from and to Louis XVI, mostly after 1789, captured after 10 August.

A.N. KK375, *Registre de perte et gain des parties de billard faites par le Roi contre la Reine et Madame Élisabeth à commencer du trente juillet 1791*.

Archives du Ministère des affaires étrangères (A.A.E.), especially Correspondance polititque (CP) Angleterre, CP Autriche and CP Espagne; and Mémoires et documents France (MDF).

Bibliothèque Nationale (B.N.), Rés. Geo. C4349, *Reconnaissance des environs de Versailles faites par Monseigneur le Dauphin en 1769*.

Papers of ministers and those in the ministerial milieu

D'Amécourt, *rapporteur du Roi* in the *parlement*: B.N. nouv. acq. fr. 22103-12 (of special interest is his 'Journal du règne de Louis XV', 22111, and the section 'Ministres de Louis XVI' starting at f. 1).

Brienne: A.N. 4 A.P. 188.

Calonne: A.N. 297 A.P. (especially 297 A.P. 3 ff. 1-137 relating to the 1787 Assembly of Notables). A.N. K677 nos 102-79 contain many items covered by Calonne's private papers but in a more finished state; Public Record Office P.C.1/125.

Castries: Archives de la Marine, Journal de Castries, MS 182/7964, 1-2; A.N. A.P. 306, the Castries Papers, especially 306.18-24.

Dupont-Karl Friedrichs von Baden: B. Erdmannsdorfer, ed., *Politische Correspondenz Karl Friedrichs von Baden 1783-1806*, Heidelberg, 1888, 2 vols; A.N. 144 A.P. 131 dossier 4 no. 11.

Joly de Fleury: B.N. fonds Joly de Fleury, 1432-44.

La Porte: A.N. C192.

Lenoir: Bibliothèque municipale d'Orléans, MS 1421–3 (fragmentary memoirs left by the *lieutenant de police*).

Malesherbes: A.N. 154 A.P. 11.147.

Miromesnil: A.N. K163 no. 8. A.N. 158 A.P. 3 dossier 16, seventeen letters from Miromesnil to the *parlementaire* Duval d'Eprémesnil, B.N. nouv. acq. fr. 20073.

D'Ormesson: A.N. 144 A.P. 130–3; the minister's diary is in 130 and the minutes of the *comité des finances* are at 131 dossier 5.

Vergennes: A.A.E., Mémoires et documents France (MDF) 1375–1400.

Véri: Archives Départementales de La Drôme (Valence), MS Journal (unclassified); the archives also contain de Witte's copy of this diary of which cahiers 100–2 are missing in the original.

The Assembly of Notables of 1787

Bibliothèque de l'Arsenal:

MS 3975–6: the minutes of the second bureau of the Assembly, presided over by the comte d'Artois.

MS 3978: a fuller version of the preceding containing not only the formal opinions of the members but also the debates for the first two 'divisions'.

MS 4546: a diary of the bureau kept by the duc de Montmorency-Laval, one of its members.

Gérard, *prêteur-royal* of Strasbourg: diary of the 1787 Assembly of Notables, A.A.E. MDF 1402.

PRINTED PRIMARY SOURCES

Adhémar, comtesse d', *Souvenirs sur Marie-Antoinette . . .*, Paris, 1836, 4 vols.

Allemand-Gay, M.-T. and J. Coudert, *Un magistrate lorrain au XVIIIe siècle: Le Premier Président de Coeurderoy (1738–1800) et son diaire*, Paris, 1997.

Allonville, comte d', *Mémoires secrets de 1770 à 1830*, Paris, 1838–45, 6 vols.

D'Angiviller, *Mémoires*, Copenhagen, 1933.

Arneth, A. von, ed., *Marie-Antoinette, Joseph II und Leopold II: Ihr Briefwechsel*, Vienna, 1866.

Assemblée des Notables de 1787, *Procès-verbal*, Paris, 1788.

Augeard, J.M., *Mémoires secrets*, ed. E. Bavoux, 1866.

Bachaumont, L. Petit de, *Mémoires secrètes pour servir à l'histoire de la République des Lettres*, London, 1777–89, 36 vols.

Bacourt, A. de, ed., *Correspondance entre le comte de Mirabeau et le comte de la Marck*, Paris, 1851, 3 vols.

Bailly, *Mémoires*, ed. S.A. Berville and J.F. Barrière, Paris, 1821, 3 vols.

Barentin, C.L.F. de, *Lettres et bulletins à Louis XVI*, ed. A. Aulard, Paris, 1915.

—— *Mémoire autographe sur les derniers Conseils du Roi Louis XVI*, ed. M. Champion, Paris, 1844.

—— *Mémoire pour M. de Barentin ... sur la plainte pour M. le procureur du roi au Châtelet*, Paris, 1790.

Barnave, *Introduction à la Révolution française*, ed. G. Rudé, 1960.

Beaumarchais, P.-A.C. de, *Correspondance*, ed. B.N. Morton and D.C. Spinelli, Paris, 1969–78, 4 vols.

Bertrand de Molleville, A.F., comte de, *Mémoires secrets pour servir à l'histoire de la dernière année du règne de Louis XVI, roi de France*, London, 1797, 3 vols.

Besenval, baron de, *Mémoires*, ed. S.A. Berville and J.F. Barrière, Paris, 1821, 2 vols.

Bigot de Sainte-Croix, L.C., *Histoire de la conspiration du 10 août 1792*, London, 1793.

Billaud de Varennes, J.N., *Despotisme des ministres de France*, Amsterdam, 1789.

Bombelles, marquis de, *Journal*, ed. J. Grassion, F. Durif and J. Charon-Bordas, Geneva, 1978–98, 4 vols.

Bouillé, marquis de, *Memoires*, ed. S.A. Berville and J.F. Barrière, Paris, 1821.

Bouillé (son of the general), *Souvenirs*, Paris, 1906.

Brienne, comte de and Loménie de, *Journal de l'Assemblée des Notables de 1787*, ed. P. Chevallier, Paris, 1960.

Burke, E., *Reflections on the Revolution in France*, ed. L.G. Mitchell, Oxford, 1993.

Burliabled, Prince [alias Paul Jones], *La Vie de Louis XVI jusqu'au 24 août 1774*, London, 1774.

Calonne, C.-A. de [attrib.], *Les Comments*, 1781.

— *Lettre au roi*, London, 1789.

— [attrib.], *Lettre du Marquis de Caraccioli à M. d'Alembert*, 1781.

— *Réponse de M. de Calonne à l'écrit de M. Necker, publié en avril 1787*, London, 1788.

Campan, J.L.H., *Mémoires sur la vie de Marie-Antoinette par Mme Campan*, Paris, 1849.

Campbell, P.R., 'Louis XVI King of the French', in *The Political Culture of the French Revolution*, ed. C. Lucas, Oxford, 1988.

Castries, duc de, *Papiers de famille*, Paris, 1978.

Choiseul, duc de, *Relation du départ de Louis XVI le 20 juin 1791*, Paris, 1822.

Cléry, J.-B., *Journal de ce qui s'est passé à la tour du Temple pendant la captivité de Louis XVI, roi de France*, London, 1798.

Coeurderoi, M.-J., *L'Assemblée des Notables de 1787 et l'esprit de réforme: Les réflexions de Michel-Joseph Coeurderoy*, ed. M.-T. Allemand-Gay, Paris, 2008.

Croÿ, duc de, *Journal, 1718–1784*, ed. vicomte de Grouchy and P. Coffin, Paris, 1906–07, 4 vols.

Despatches from Paris 1784–1790, ed. O. Browning, London, 1909–10.

Dumouriez, *Memoires*, 1822–23, 4 vols.

Duquesnoy, Adrien, *Journal*, 1894, 2 vols.

Edgeworth, abbé, *Dernières heures de Louis XVI*, Paris, 1816.

Élisabeth, Madame, *Correspondance de Mme Élisabeth*, ed. F. Feuillet de Conches, 1868.

États-Généraux: Lefebvre, G. et al., eds, *Recueil de documents relatifs aux États-Généraux de 1789*, Paris, 1953–70, 4 vols.

Fersen, comte de, *Le comte de Fersen et la cour de France*, ed. R.M. Klinckowstrom, Paris, 1878, 2 vols.

Flammermont, J., ed., *Rapport . . . sur les Correspondance des agents diplomatiques étrangères en France avant la Révolution*, Paris, 1896.

George III, *The Correspondence of King George III from 1760 to December 1783*, ed. Sir John Fortescue, London, 1927–28, 2 vols.

Georgel, J.-F., *Mémoires pour servir à l'histoire des événements de la fin du XVIIIe siècle*, Paris, 1820.

Glagau, H. *Reformversuche und Sturz des Absolutismus in Frankreich (1774–88)*, Munich, 1908 (an appendix contains letters between Calonne and the king on the subject of the Assembly of Notables).

Hardman, J., ed., *The French Revolution Sourcebook*, London and New York, 1999.

Hardman, J. and M. Price, eds, *Louis XVI and the comte de Vergennes: Correspondence, 1774–1787*, Oxford, 1998 (cited as *Louis XVI–Vergennes Correspondence*).

Hardman, J. and J.M. Roberts, eds, *French Revolution Documents*, Oxford, 1966–73.

Hézecques, comte de, *Page à la cour de Louis XVI, Souvenirs*, Paris, 1987.

Hue, F., *Dernières années du règne de Louis XVI*, 3rd edn, Paris, 1860.

Lafayette, marquis de, *Mémoires, correspondance et manuscrits du général Lafayette*, Paris, 1837–38, 6 vols.

Lally-Tollendal, article on Necker in the *Biographie-Michaud*.

Lameth, T. de, *Notes et souvenirs*, ed. E. Welvert, Paris, 1913.

Lescure, ed., *Correspondance secrète inédite sur Louis XVI, Marie-Antoinette, la cour et la ville de 1777 à 1792*, 1866, 2 vols.

Le Tellier, mayor of Harfleur, *Voyage de Louis XVI dans sa Province de Normandie*, Paris, 1787.

Lévis, duc de, *Souvenirs et portraits, 1780–1789*, Paris, 1813.

Louis XV, *Correspondance secrète inédite*, ed. M.E. Boutaric, 1866, 2 vols.

— *Lettres de Louis XV a son petit-fits . . .*, ed. P. Amiguet, 1938.

Louis XVI, *Journal*, ed. L. Nicolardot, Paris, 1873.

—— *Louis XVI a la parole*, ed. P. and P. Girault de Coursac, Paris, 1989.

—— *Louis XVI, Marie-Antoinette et Mme Élisabeth, lettres et documents inédits*, ed. F. Feuillet de Conches, Paris, 1864–69, 6 vols.

—— *Réflexions sur mes entretiens avec M. le duc de la Vauguyon*, ed. E. Falloux, Paris, 1851.

Louis-Auguste, dauphin, *Description de la forêt de Compiègne, comme elle étoit en 1765, avec le guide de la forêt*, Paris, 1766.

Louis-Ferdinand, dauphin, *Choix de lettres addressées à M. de Nicolaï, évêque de Nancy par le Dauphin . . . (1750–1767)*, ed. A. de Boislisle, Nogent-le-Rotrou, 1875.

Louis-Philippe, *Memoirs*, ed. and trans., J. Hardman, New York, 1977.

Luynes, duc de, *Mémoires du duc de Luynes sur la cour de Louis XV, 1735–58*, ed. L. Dussieux and E. Soulié, Paris, 1860–65, 17 vols.

Malesherbes, *Malesherbes à Louis XVI ou les Avertissements de Cassandra: Mémoires inédits 1787–1788*, ed. V. André, Paris, 2010.

—— *Nouveaux documents inédits*, ed. P. Grosclaude, Paris, 1964.

Mallet du Pan, *Mémoires et correspondance de Mallet du Pan pour servir à l'histoire de la Révolution française*, ed. A. Sayous, Paris, 1851, 2 vols.

Malouet, P.-V. *Mémoires*, Paris, 1874, 2 vols.

Marie-Antoinette, *Correspondance secrète entre Marie-Thérèse et le comte de Mercy-Argenteau*, ed. A. d'Arneth and M. Geffroy, 2nd edn, Paris, 1875, 3 vols.

—— *Lettres de Marie-Antoinette*, ed. M. de la Rocheterie et le marquis de Beaucourt, Paris, 1895–96, 92 vols.

—— *Marie-Antoinette et Barnave: Correspondance secrète*, ed. Alma Söderjhelm, 1934.

—— *Marie-Antoinette, Fersen et Barnave: Leur correspondance du comte de Mercy-Argenteau*, ed. O.G. Heidenstam, 1913.

—— *Marie-Antoinette, Joseph II und Leopold II: Ihr Briefwechsel*, ed. A von Arneth, 2nd edn, Vienna, 1866.

Marmontel, *Mémoires*, ed. J. Renwick, 1972, 2 vols.

—— *Mémoires*, ed. M. Tourneux, Paris, 1891, 3 vols.

Mercy-Argenteau, *Correspondance secrète avec l'Empereur Joseph II et le prince de Kaunitz*, ed. A. d'Arneth and J. Flammermont, Paris, 1891, 2 vols.

Miromesnil, *Correspondance politique*, ed. P. Le Verdier, 1899–, 4 vols.

Montbarey, prince de, *Mémoires du prince de Montbarey*, Paris, 1826–27, 3 vols.

Montjoie, *Éloge historique et funèbre de Louis XVI*, 1796.

Montmorency-Luxembourg, duc de, *Le duc de Montmorency-Luxembourg*, ed. Paul Filleul, 1939 (includes the duc's diary).

Montyon, Auget, baron de, *Particularités sur les ministres des finances les plus célèbres*, Paris, 1812.

Moreau, J.-N., *Les Devoirs du prince*, 1773.

—— *Mes souvenirs*, ed. C. Hermelin, Paris, 1898–1901, 2 vols.

Morellet, abbé de, *Lettres à Lord Shelburne depuis 1772 jusqu'à 1803*, ed. E. Fitzmaurice, Paris, 1898.

Necker, J., *De la Révolution française*, Paris, 1797.

—— *Mémoire*, 6 March 1787.

—— *Sur l'administration de M. Necker par lui-même*, Paris, 1791.

Paine, T., *The Rights of Man*, ed. G.J. Holyoake, London, 1950.

Papon, abbé, *Histoire du gouvernement français depuis l'Assemblée des Notables tenue le 22 février 1787, jusqu'à la fin de décembre du même année*, London, 1788.

Paris, *Procès-Verbal de l'Assemblée Générale des électeurs de Paris*, Paris, 1790.

Paroy, comte de, *Mémoires*, Paris, 1895.

Pasquier, *Souvenirs du chancelier Pasquier*, ed. R. Lacour-Gayet, Paris, 1964.

Proyart, abbé, *Oeuvres complètes*, Paris, 1819, 6 vols.

Raigecourt-Bombelles, *Correspondance du marquis et de la marquise de Raigecourt avec le marquis et la marquise de Bombelles pendant l'émigration, 1790–1800*, ed. M. de la Rocheterie, Paris, 1892.

Robespierre, M., *Oeuvres*, ed., Société des Études Robespierristes, Paris, 1912–67, 10 vols.

Roederer, P.L., *Chronique de cinquante jours*, 1832.

Roland, Madame, *Mémoires de Madame Roland*, Paris, 2004.

[Ruault], *Gazette d'un Parisien sous la Révolution . . . 1783–1796*, ed. E. Vassal, Paris, 1975.

Saint-Priest, comte de, *Memoires*, ed. baron de Barante, Paris, 1929.

Sallier-Chaumont de Laroche, G., *Annales françaises depuis le commencement du règne de Louis XVI jusqu'aux états-généraux, 1774–1789*, Paris, 1813.

Ségur, comte de, *Mémoires, ou Souvenirs et anecdotes*, 1827, 3 vols.

Sénac de Meilhan, G., *Du gouvernement, des moeurs et des conditions en France avant la Révolution, avec le caractère des principaux personnages du règne de Louis XVI*, London, 1795.

Soulavie, J.-L. *Historical and Political Memoirs of the Reign of Lewis XVI from his Marriage to his Death*, London, 1802, 6 vols.

—— *Mémoires historiques et politiques du règne de Louis XVI*, Paris, 1801, 6 vols.

Staël, Madame de, *Considérations sur . . . la Révolution française*, op. posth., Paris, 1843.

Staël-Holstein, baron de, *Correspondance diplomatique*, ed. L. Léouzon Le Duc, Paris, 1881.

Talleyrand, C.M. de, *Mémoires*, ed. duc de Broglie, Paris, 1891–92.

Target, G.-J.-B., 'Journal de Target 1787', in *Un avocat au XVIIIe siècle*, Paris 1893.

—— *Observations sur le procès de Louis XVI*, Paris, 1793.

Tourzel, duchesse de, *Mémoires*, ed. duc des Cars, Paris, 1904, 2 vols.

Le Trait de lumière ou le roi considéré au milieu de perils avant son depart pour Montmédy, Paris, 1791.

Turgot, A.J.R., *Oeuvres*, ed. G. Schelle, Paris, 1913–23, 5 vols.

—— *Oeuvres complètes*, 2nd edn, Paris, 1808, 8 vols.

Vaudreuil, comte de, *Correspondance intime du comte de Vaudreuil et du comte d'Artois*, ed. L. Pingaud, 1889, 2 vols.

Véri, abbé de, fragment of his journal, ed. duc de Castries, *Revue de Paris* (Nov. 1953).

—— *Journal, 1774–80*, ed. J. de Witte, Paris, 1928–30, 2 vols.

Walpole, H., *Règne de Richard III, ou doutes historiques sur les crimes qui lui sont imputés*, trans. Louis XVI, ed. Roussel l'Épinal, Paris, 1800.

Weber, J., *Mémoires concernant Marie-Antoinette*, ed. S.A. Berville and J.F. Barrière, Paris, 1822, 2 vols.

SECONDARY SOURCES

Acton, Baron, *Lectures on the French Revolution*, London, 1910.

Adamson, J., *The Noble Revolt: The Overthrow of Charles I*, London, 2007.

Antoine, M., 'Les comités des ministres sous Louis XV', *Revue Historique de Droit* (1951).

—— *Louis XV*, Paris, 1989.

Ardascheff, P.M., *Les Intendants de province sous Louis XVI*, Paris, 1909.

Arnaud-Bouteloup, J., *Le Rôle politique de Marie-Antoinette*, Paris, 1924.

Aston, N., *The End of an Elite: The French Bishops and the Coming of the French Revolution, 1786–1790*, Oxford, 1992.

Baker, K.M., *Inventing the French Revolution: Essays in Political Culture in the Eighteenth Century*, Cambridge, 1990.

—— 'Politics and Public Opinion', in *Press and Politics in Pre-Revolutionary France*, ed. J.R. Censer and J.D. Popkin, Berkeley, CA, 1987.

Beales, D., *Joseph II*, Cambridge, 1987.

Beaucourt, marquis de, *Captivité de Louis XVI*, Paris, 1892, 2 vols.

Bimbenet, E., *La Fuite de Louis XVI à Varennes*, Paris, 1868.

Blanc, L., *Histoire de la Révolution française*, 1847–63, 12 vols.

Blanning, T.C., *The French Revolution: Class War or Culture Clash*, 2nd edn, Basingstoke, 1998.

—— *The Origins of the French Revolutionary Wars*, London, 1986.

Bosher, J., *French Public Finances 1770–95*, Cambridge, 1970.

—— 'The Premiers Commis des Finances in the Reign of Louis XVI', *French Historical Studies* 3:4 (Autumn 1964), 475–94.

—— *The Single Duty Project: A Study of the Movement for a French Customs Union in the Eighteenth Century*, London, 1964.

Browne, R., 'The Diamond Necklace Affair Revisited', *Renaissance and Modern Studies* 33 (1989).

Burley, P., 'Louis XVI and a New Monarchy', unpublished PhD thesis, London University, 1981.

Caiani, A., *Louis XVI and the French Revolution 1789–1792*, Cambridge, 2012.

Campbell, P.R., *Power and Politics in Old Regime France 1720–1745*, London and New York, 1996.

Caron, P., 'La Tentative de contre-révolution de juin–juillet 1789', *Revue d'Histoire moderne* VIII (1906), 5–34 and 649–78.

Carré, H., *Quelques mots sur la presse clandestine*, Paris, 1893.

Castries, duc de, *L'Aube de la Révolution*, Paris, 1978.

Chaumié, J., *Le Réseau d'Antraigues et la contre-Révolution*, Paris, 1965.

Chérest, A., *La Chute de l'Ancien régime, 1787–1789*, Paris, 1884–86, 3 vols.

Cobb, R., *The Police and the People: French Popular Protest 1789–1820*, Oxford, 1970.

Cochin, A., *Les Sociétés de pensée et la Révolution en Bretagne (1788–1789)*, Paris, 1925, 2 vols.

Collins, J., *The State in Early Modern France*, Cambridge, 1995.

Corwin, E.S., 'The French Objective in the American Revolution', *American Historical Review* 21 (1915–16), 33–61.

Cubells, M., *La Provence des Lumières: Les parlementaires d'Aix au XVIIIe siècle*, Paris, 1984.

Darnton, R., 'The Brissot Dossier', *French Historical Studies* 17 (1991), 191–205.

—— *The Literary Underground of the Old Regime*, Cambridge, MA, 1982.

Doniol, H., *Histoire de la participation de la France à l'établissement des États-Unis d'Amérique*, Paris, 1886–89, 5 vols.

Doyle, W., 'The Parlements', in *The French Revolution and the Creation of Modern Political Culture*, I, *The Political Culture of the Old Regime*, ed. K.M. Baker, Oxford, 1987.

Droz, J.F.X., *Histoire du règne de Louis XVI*, Brussels, 1839, 2 vols.

Duckworth, C., 'Louis XVI and English History: A French Reaction to Walpole, Hume and Gibbon on Richard III', *Studies on Voltaire* 176 (1979), 385–401.

Duindam, J., *Vienna and Versailles: The Courts of Europe's Dynastic Rivals, 1550–1780*, Cambridge, 2003.

Dull, J., *The French Navy and Independence: A Study of Arms and Diplomacy, 1774–1787*, Princeton, 1975.

Dunlop, I., *Marie-Antoinette*, London, 1993.

Dunn, S., *The Deaths of Louis XVI: Regicide and the French Political Imagination*, Princeton, NJ, 1994.

Dussieux, L., *Le Château de Versailles*, Versailles, 1881, 2 vols.

Echeverria, D., *The Maupeou Revolution*, Baton Rouge, LA, 1985.

Egret, J., *Louis XV et l'opposition parlementaire*, Paris, 1970.

—— *Necker*, Paris, 1975.

—— *La Pré-Révolution française 1787–1788*, Paris, 1962.

—— 'La seconde Assemblée des Notables', *Annales historiques de la Révolution française* (1949), 193–228.

Faure, E., *La Disgrâce de Turgot*, Paris, 1964.

Fay, B., *Louis XVI ou la fin d'un monde*, Paris, 1955.

Félix, J., 'The Financial Origins of the French Revolution', in *The Origins of the French Revolution*, ed. P. Campbell, Basingstoke, 2005, 35–62.

—— *Louis XVI et Marie-Antoinette*, Paris, 2006.

Filleul, P., *Le duc de Montmorency Luxembourg*, Paris, 1939.

Fitzsimmons, M., 'The Committee of the Constitution and the Remaking of France, 1787–1791', *French History* 4:1 (1990), 23–47.

—— 'From the Estates-General to the National Assembly, May 5–August 4, 1789,' in P. Campbell, ed., *The Origins of the French Revolution*, Basingstoke, 2005, 268–89.

—— 'Privilege and the Polity in France, 1786–1791,' *American Historical Review* 92 (1987), 269–95.

Flammermont, J., *Le Chancelier Maupeou at les parlements*, Paris, 1883.

—— *Négotiations secrètes de Louis XVI et du baron de Breteuil avec la cour de Berlin, décembre 1791–juillet 1792*, Paris, 1885.

Fréville, H., *L'Intendance de Bretagne, 1689–1790*, Rennes, 1953, 3 vols.

Furet, F., *The French Revolution, 1770–1814*, trans. A. Neville, Oxford, 1996.

Girault de Coursac, P., *L'Éducation d'un roi, Louis XVI*, Paris, 1972.

—— 'Louis XVI et Vergennes,' *Revue d'Histoire Diplomatique* 3–4 (1987), 275–88.

Girault de Coursac, P. and P., *Enquête sur le procès du roi Louis XVI*, Paris, 1982.

—— *Guerre d'Amérique et liberté des mers 1778–83*, Paris, 1991.

—— *Louis XVI et Marie-Antoinette: Vie conjugale, vie politique*, Paris, 1990.

—— *Louis XVI, roi martyr?* Paris, 1976.

—— *Sur la route de Varennes*, Paris, 1984.

Glagau, H., *Die Franzosische Legislative . . . 1791–92*, Berlin, 1896.

—— *Reformversuche und Sturz des Absolutismus in Frankreich (1774–1788)*, Munich, 1908.

Godechot, J., *The Taking of the Bastille*, trans. J. Stewart, London, 1970.

Goldstone, G.J.A., *Revolution and Rebellion in the Early Modern World*, Berkeley, CA, 1993.

Goodwin, A., 'Calonne, the Assembly of French Notables of 1787 and the Origins of the Révolte Nobiliaire,' *English Historical Review* CCLX (May 1946), 202–34, and CCLXI (September 1946), 329–77.

Granier de Cassignac, M.A., *Histoire des causes de la Révolution française*, Paris, 1850.

Griffiths, R., *Le Centre perdu: Malouet et les 'monarchiens' dans la Révolution française*, Grenoble, 1988.

Grosclaude, P., *Malesherbes: Témoin et interprète de son temps*, Paris, 1961.

Gruder, V., 'Les Notables à la fin de l'ancien régime: L'Avertissement de 1787,' *Dix-Huitième Siècle* 14 (1982), 45–56.

—— *The Notables and the Nation: The Political Schooling of the French, 1787–1788*, Cambridge, MA, and London, 2007.

Habermas, J., *The Structural Transformation of the Public Sphere: An Enquiry into a Category of Bourgeois Society*, 1962, Cambridge, MA, 1989.

Hampson, N., *Prelude to Terror: The Constituent Assembly and the Failure of Consensus, 1789–1791*, Oxford, 1988,

Hardman, J., *French Politics 1774–1789*, London, 1995.

—— *Louis XVI*, New Haven, CT, and London, 1993.

—— *Louis XVI: The Silent King*, London and New York, 2000.

—— 'Ministerial Politics from the Accession of Louis XVI to the Assembly of Notables, 1774–87,' unpublished DPhil thesis, Oxford University, 1972.

—— *Overture to Revolution: The 1787 Assembly of Notables and the Crisis of France's Old Regime*, Oxford and New York, 2010.

—— *Robespierre*, London and New York, 1999.

Harris, R.D., *Necker in the Revolution of 1789*, London, 1986.

—— *Necker: Reform Statesman of the Ancien Régime*, Berkeley, CA, 1979.

Henshall, N., *The Myth of Absolutism: Change and Continuity in Early Modern European Monarchy*, London, 1992.

Hudson, R., *The Minister from France: Conrad-Alexandre Gérard, 1729–1790*, Euclid, OH, 1994.

Ilovaisky, O., *La Disgrâce de Calonne*, Paris, 2008.

Jarrett, D., *The Begetters of Revolution. England's Involvement with France, 1759–1789*, London, 1973.

Jones, P.M., *Reform and Revolution in France: The Politics of Transition, 1774–1791*, Cambridge, 1995.

Jordan, D., *The King's Trial: Louis XVI vs. the French Revolution*, Berkeley, CA, and London, 1979.

Kaiser, T., 'From the Austrian Committee to the Foreign Plot: Marie-Antoinette, Austrophobia and the Terror', *French Historical Studies* 26 (2003), 579–617.

—— 'From Fiscal Crisis to Revolution: The Court and French Foreign Policy, 1787–1789', in T.E. Kaiser and D.K. Van Kley, eds, *Unleashing the Deluge: Essays on the Origins of the French Revolution*, Stanford, CA, 2011.

—— 'Who's Afraid of Marie-Antoinette? Diplomacy, Austrophobia and the Queen', *French History* 14 (2000), 241–71.

Kaplan, S., *Bread, Politics and Political Economy in the Reign of Louis XV*, The Hague, 1976, 2 vols.

Kennedy, M., *The Jacobin Clubs in the French Revolution: The First Years*, Princeton, NJ, 1982.

Kwass, M.D., *Privilege and the Politics of Taxation in Eighteenth-Century France: Liberté, Egalité, Fiscalité*, Cambridge, 2000.

Labourdette, J.F., *Vergennes: ministre principal de Louis XVI*, Paris, 1990.

Labrousse, E., *La Crise de l'économie française à la fin de l'ancien régime et au début de la Révolution*, Paris, 1944.

Lacour-Gayet, R., *Calonne*, Paris, 1963.

Lacour-Gayet, R. (père), *La Marine militaire de la France sous le règne de Louis XVI*, Paris, 1905.

Lamblin, G., 'Louis XVI angliciste', *Études anglaises* 22 (1969), 118–36.

Lameth, T. de, *Mémoires*, ed. E. Welvert, Paris, 1913.

Laugier, L., *Turgot*, Paris, 1979.

——*Un ministère réformateur sous Louis XV: Le Triumvirat (1770–1774)*, Paris, 1975.

Legay, M.-L., *Les États provinciaux dans la construction de l'état moderne: au XVIIe et XVIIIe siècles*, Paris, 2001.

Lever, E., *Louis XVI*, Paris, 1985.

Lombard, P., *Le Procès du roi*, Paris, 1993.

Luçay, comte de, *Les Secrétaires d'État en France depuis les origines jusqu'à 1774*, Paris, 1881.

Luckner, B.A., 'The Role of the French Bishops in the Aristocratic Revolt of 1787–88', unpublished MA thesis, University of Manchester, 1969.

Lüthy, H., *La Banque protestante en France*, Paris, 1959–61, 2 vols.

Mansel, P., *The Court of France, 1789–1830*, Cambridge, 1988.

—— *Louis XVIII*, London, 1981.

Marion, M., *Dictionnaire des institutions de la France xviie–xviiie siècles*, Paris, 1989.

——*Le garde des sceaux Lamoignon*, Paris, 1905.

Mathews, G.T., *The Royal General Farms*, New York, 1958.

Mathiez, A., 'Les Girondins à la veille du 10 août', *Annales historiques de la Révolution française* (1931), 193–212.

Maupeou, J. de, *Le Chancelier Maupeou*, Paris, 1942.

McManners, J., *Church and Society in Eighteenth-Century France*, Oxford, 1998, 2 vols.

Melton, J. van H., *The Rise of the Public in Enlightenment Europe*, Cambridge, 2000.

Michelet, J., *Histoire de la Révolution française*, ed. G. Walter, 1952, 2 vols.

—— *History of the French Revolution*, trans. C. Cocks, Chicago, 1967.

Michon, G., *Adrien Duport et le parti Feuillant*, Paris, 1924.

Morineau, M., 'Budgets de l'état et gestion des finances royales en France au dix-huitième siècle', *Revue Historique* CCLXIV/2 (1980), 289–335.

Morris, R., *The Peacemakers: The Great Powers and American Independence*, New York, 1965.

Mortimer-Ternaux, M., *Histoire de la Terreur*, 1862–81, 8 vols.

Mousnier, R., *Les Institutions de la France sous la monarchie absolue*, vol. II, Paris, 1974.

Mousset, A., *Un témoin ignoré de la Révolution: le Comte de Fernan Nunez*, Paris, 1924.

Padover, S., *The Life and Death of Louis XVI*, London, 1965.

Parker, P.D., *Class and State in Ancien Régime France: The Road to Modernity?* London, 1996.

Patterson, A.T., *The Other Armada: The Franco-Spanish Attempt to Invade Britain in 1779*, Manchester, 1960.

Petitfils, J.-C., *Louis XVI*, Paris, 2005.

Peuchet, J., *Mémoires tirées des archives de la police de Paris*, Paris, 1828.

Pimodan, comte de, *Le comte de Mercy-Argenteau*, Paris, 1911.

Pingaud, L., 'Un ministre de Louis XVI, Terrier de Monciel', *Le Correspondant*, August 1879.

Price, M., 'The Comte de Vergennes and the Baron de Breteuil', unpublished PhD thesis, Cambridge University, 1988.

—— *The Fall of the French Monarchy: Louis XVI, Marie-Antoinette and the baron de Breteuil*, London, 2002.

—— 'The "Ministry of the Hundred Hours": A Reappraisal', *French History* 4:3 (1990), 318–39.

—— 'Mirabeau and the Court: Some New Evidence', *French Historical Studies* 29:1 (2006), 37–76.

—— *Preserving the Monarchy: The Comte de Vergennes, 1774–1787*, Cambridge, 1995.

Proyart, abbé, *Vie du Dauphin*, Paris, 1872.

Pugh, W., 'Calonne's New Deal', *Journal of Modern History* XI (Sept. 1939), 289–312.

Ranke, A. von, *Uber Die Versammlung der franzosischen Notabeln im Jahre 1787*, Berlin, 1846.

Reinhard, M., *La Chute de la royauté: 10 août 1792*, Paris, 1969.

Renouvin, P., *Les Assemblées Provinciales de 1787*, Paris, 1921.

Riley, J.C., 'French Finances 1727–1768', *Journal of Modern History* LIX (1987), 209–43.

Rogister, J., *Louis XV and the Parlement of Paris, 1737–1755*, Cambridge, 1995.

Rudé, G., *The Crowd in the French Revolution*, Oxford, 1967.

Saricks, A., *Pierre-Samuel Dupont de Nemours*, Lawrence, KS, 1965.

Schama, S., *Citizens: A Chronicle of the French Revolution*, London, 1989

Schelle, G., *Du Pont de Nemours et l'École Physiocratique*, Paris, 1888.

Scott, H., *British Foreign Policy in the Age of the American Revolution*, London, 1990.

Scott, S.F., *The Response of the Royal Army to the French Revolution: Role and Development of the Line Army, 1787–93*, Oxford, 1973.

Seligman, E., *La justice pendant la Révolution*, Paris, 1913.

Shapiro, B., *Revolutionary Justice in Paris, 1789–1790*, Cambridge, 1993.

—— 'Revolutionary Justice in 1789–1790: The Comité des Recherches, the Châtelet, and the Fayettist Coalition', *French Historical Studies* 17:3 (Spring 1992), 656–69.

—— *Traumatic Politics: The Deputies and the King in the Early French Revolution*, University Park, PA, 2009.

Skocpol, T., *States and Social Revolutions: A Comparative Analysis of France, Russia and China*, Cambridge, 1979.

Soboul, A., ed., *Le Procès de Louis XVI*, Paris, 1966.

Söderjhelm, A., ed., *Fersen et Marie-Antoinette: correspondance et journal intime inédits du comte Axel de Fersen*, Paris, 1930.

Sonenscher, M., *Sans-Culottes*, Princeton, NJ, 2008.

Sorel, A. *Europe and the French Revolution: The Political Traditions of the Old Regime*, trans. and ed. A. Cobban and J.W. Hunt, London, 1969.

—— *L'Europe et la Révolution française*, II, *La Chute de la royauté*, Paris, 1908.

Stone, B., *The Genesis of the French Revolution: A Global-Historical Interpretation*, Cambridge, 1994.

—— *The Parlement of Paris 1774–1789*, Chapel Hill, NC, 1981.

Suzanne, G., *La Tactique financière de Calonne*, Paris, 1901.

Swann, J., *Politics and the Parlement of Paris under Louis XV, 1754–1774*, Cambridge, 1995.

—— *Provincial Power and Absolute Monarchy: The Estates General of Burgundy 1661–1790*, Cambridge, 2003.

—— '"Silence, Respect, Obedience"': Political Culture in Louis XV's France', in H. Scott and

B. Simms, eds, *Cultures of Power in Europe During the Long Eighteenth Century*, Cambridge, 2007, 225–48.

Tackett, T., *Becoming a Revolutionary: The Deputies of the French National Assembly and the Emergence of a Revolutionary Culture*, University Park, PA, 2006.

Thiers, A., *Histoire de la Révolution française*, Brussels, 1844, 2 vols.

Tocqueville, A. de, *The Ancien Régime and the French Revolution*, ed. H. Brogan, London, 1966.

—— *Coup d'oeil sur le règne de Louis XVI*, Paris, 1850.

Trotsky, L., *The History of the Russian Revolution*, trans. M. Eastman, London, 1967.

Vaissière, P. de, *La Mort de Louis XVI*, Paris, 1910.

Van Kley, D., *The Damiens Affair and the Unravelling of the Ancien Régime, 1750–1770*, Princeton, NJ, 1984.

—— *The Jansenists and the Expulsion of the Jesuits from France, 1757–65*, New Haven, CT, 1975.

—— *The Religious Origins of the French Revolution: From Calvin to the Civil Constitution, 1560–1791*, New Haven, CT, and London, 1996.

Vignon, E.-J., *Études historiques sur l'administration des voies publics au dix-septième et dix-huitième siècles*, Paris, 1862.

Wahl, W.A., *Die Notabelnversammlung von 1787*, Freiburg im Breisgau, 1899.

Walzer, M., *Regicide and Revolution*, Cambridge, 1974.

Welshinger, H., *La Mission secrète de Mirabeau à Berlin (1786–1787)*, Paris, 1900.

Wick, D., *A Conspiracy of Well-Intentioned Men: The Society of Thirty and the French Revolution*, New York, 1987.

—— 'The Court Nobility and the French Revolution: The Example of the Society of Thirty', *Eighteenth-Century Studies* XIII (1980), 263–84.

INDEX